D0071482

EVIDENCE

IN A NUTSHELL

FIFTH EDITION

By

PAUL F. ROTHSTEIN
Professor of Law
Georgetown University Law Center

MYRNA S. RAEDER
Professor of Law
Southwestern Law School

DAVID CRUMP
Newell H. Blakely Professor of Law
University of Houston Law Center

THOMSON

WEST

Mat #40434768

Nutshell Series, In a Nutshell, the Nutshell Logo and West Group are trademarks registered in the U.S. Patent and Trademark Office.

COPYRIGHT © 1970, 1981 WEST PUBLISHING CO.
© West, a Thomson business, 1997, 2003
© 2007 Thomson/West
        610 Opperman Drive
        St. Paul, MN 55123
        1–800–328–9352

Printed in the United States of America

ISBN: 978–0–314–16666–1

PREFACE: USING THIS BOOK

Fifth Edition

Legions of law students have successfully used Evidence in a Nutshell (1) to study for exams, (2) as optional outside reading during the Evidence course, or (3) as a course-book assigned by the professor. The book is designed to promote understanding and remembering of any Evidence course you might be taking in any law school today. Student-friendly features include:

—copious sign-post-type headings;

—informativo black letter summaries as you go along;

—a table of contents that is actually a comprehensive course outline;

—the entire text is sequentially keyed to the Federal Rules of Evidence;

—sections and subsections are labeled conspicuously with the applicable rule number;

—each section first succinctly describes the main features of the rule, then gives pithy examples of its application, and finally explores issues like you might get on an exam;

—the important cases you studied in the course are included and easy to find;

—A CONVENIENT COPY OF THE FEDERAL RULES OF EVIDENCE IS AT THE BACK.

This new edition includes, *inter alia*, a number of recent developments: The revolution in constitutional confrontation law accomplished by the Supreme Court in *Crawford* and *Davis*; new amendments to the Federal Rules; and some late-breaking matters concerning the constitutional "right to defend" and privileges, to name a few.

Is there one key concept in this book that can unlock the Evidence course? Maybe not entirely, but here we turn to the world's leading cultural anthropologist, who, as part of his examination of legal institutions, studied an earlier edition of this Nutshell, and had this to say, quoting from it:

> [T]he rules of evidence…are motivated…by a distrust of juries as "rational triers of fact"…The judge's job in admissibility questions is to decide, as [Prof. Rothstein] finely puts it, when "the trial will be better off without the evidence."[1]

That comes close to a key.

About the Authors and the Genesis of This Book (For those who like to know these things)

This is the fifth edition of the original ROTHSTEIN'S EVIDENCE IN A NUTSHELL, which proved enormously successful. Rothstein, a law professor at Georgetown University in Washington, D.C., is nationally known for his ability to make difficult points of law clear through his writings, lectures, and media appearances.

For the most recent editions, Prof. Rothstein has been joined by an equally talented team: law professors Myrna Raeder and David Crump, prolific writers and award winners in their own right.

The aim of the book, as always, is to provide a simple text and roadmap through the Evidence thicket, with plenty of guideposts along the way. Over the course of the various editions, new subjects and developments have been added. A few have been shortened, such as "Burdens

---

[1] Clifford Geertz, Local Knowledge: Further Essays in Interpretive Anthropology, 172 (1983).

of Proof and Presumptions." A student who wants a really definitive treatment of that subject is referred to the Second Edition. A few subjects that are no longer essential have been jettisoned altogether.

The three authors first met on an American Bar Association committee. Rothstein, the chairperson, had formerly advised Congress during the drafting of the Federal Rules of Evidence. He now felt a study should be instituted by the committee, critiquing the Rules' first decade of operation in the courts. The study lasted several years, with the three present authors in active roles along with other members. At its conclusion, the committee published the results in an influential report appearing at 120 F.R.D. 299 (1987). Many of its suggestions have been enacted into law,

The present authors individually went on to other Evidence and Evidence reform efforts, like the panel amending the Uniform Rules of Evidence. The three combine experience teaching law students, lawyers, bar review courses, and judges; writing books and articles; trying both sides of civil and criminal cases; briefing and arguing cases on appeal (including to the Supreme Court); and drafting and amending evidence rules on the state and federal level. First and foremost, however, the authors are very experienced teachers of Evidence to *law students*, the people for whom this book is written, and who have contributed valuable insights over the years about how students come to understand things. These insights have helped enormously to make the book a staple at the nation's law schools.

P.F.R.
M.S.R.
D.C.

*

SUMMARY OUTLINE

―――――――

                                                              Page
PREFACE -- III
DETAILED OUTLINE AND TABLE OF CONTENTS ----------- XIII
TABLE OF CASES --- XXXV

Chapter 1. Interpreting the Rules and Other Basics: Offers, Objections, and the Judge's Function ---------------------------------- 1
   I. From Common Law to Codification: How the Rules Are Interpreted ----------------------------- 1
  II. Offers, Objections, and Instructions ------------- 9
 III. Preliminary Questions of Fact and Conditional Relevancy ----------------------------------- 17
  IV. Role of Rules Beyond Exclusion of Pieces of Evidence From Juries: Non–Jury & Administrative Trials; Appeals; Judge & Attorney Comment ----------------------------------- 28

Chapter 2. Judicial Notice, Presumptions, and Burdens: Substitutes for Evidence 40
   I. Judicial Notice ----------------------------------- 40
  II. Burdens of Proof ---------------------------------- 44
 III. Presumptions ------------------------------------- 47

Chapter 3. Relevancy, Its Counterweights, and Related Exclusionary Rules ------------- 58
   I. Relevancy --- 58
  II. Counterweights to Relevance: Prejudice, Confusion, Time Consumption, Etc. --------------- 69

Page

Chapter 3. Relevancy, Its Counterweights, and Related Exclusionary Rules—Continued

III. Exclusionary Rules for Remedial Measures, Compromise Negotiations, Withdrawn Guilty Pleas, and Insurance 85

Chapter 4. A Special Relevancy vs. Counterweights Problem Area: Similar Acts, Character, Propensity 100

I. An Overview of the Propensity–Related Rules 100

II. Permissible Uses of Character as Substantive Circumstantial Evidence.................... 109

III. Similar Incidents Offered for Non–Character Circumstantial Purposes 115

IV. Special Rules for Sexual Assaults and Related Offenses.................... 132

V. Procedural Issues Raised by Similar Acts Evidence.................... 139

VI. Character and Similar–Acts Evidence in Civil Cases.................... 144

VII. Habit and Routine Practice.................... 146

VIII. Character as an "Essential Element" and the Like.................... 149

IX. Credibility as Affected by the Witness' Character.................... 153

X. Some Recurring Themes Cutting Across This Entire Propensity Chapter.................... 169

Chapter 5. Privileges 177

I. Policies, Procedures, and General Principles Underlying Privileges.................... 177

II. Privileges Under the F.R.E.: State Rules or Federal Common Law 191

III. Attorney–Client Privilege 198

Page

Chapter 5. Privileges—Continued

  IV. Marital Privileges: Two Separate Privileges Distinguished... 213

   V. Physician–Patient and Psychotherapist–Patient Privileges.. 225

  VI. Other Claimed Privileges, Established or Not 230

 VII. Governmental Privileges 232

VIII. The Privilege Against Self–Incrimination....... 237

  IX. Exclusionary Rules Premised on Deterrence Rationales 244

   X. Rules That Prevent Invocation of Privilege From Implying Guilt or Fault 246

Chapter 6. Witnesses: Competency, Examination, and Impeachment............................. 250

   I. Incompetency (or Disqualification) of Witnesses 251

  II. Impeachment: Some General Principles.......... 257

 III. Prior Inconsistent Statements....................... 261

 IV. Impeachment by Contradiction...................... 271

   V. The "Collateral Matter" Rule: A Limit on Impeachment by Prior Inconsistent Statement and Contradiction 274

  VI. Bias... 277

 VII. Character–Related Impeachment (Treated in Chapter 4): Reputation, Opinion, Convictions and Prior Bad Acts 283

VIII. Other Kinds of Impeachment 284

  IX. Support or Rehabilitation of Credibility.......... 286

   X. Direct and Cross Examination: Procedure, Methods, Limits 292

  XI. Witness Preparation and Refreshing of Recollection 296

Page

Chapter 7. Opinions, Experts, and Scientific Evidence 303

I. Ordinary Witnesses: Opinion and Firsthand Knowledge 303

II. Expert Testimony 308

III. Impeachment of Experts 370

Chapter 8. Hearsay: The Basic Theory, Rationale, and Constitutional Considerations 372

I. Defining Hearsay 372

II. Conduct as Hearsay or Non–Hearsay 391

III. Some Common Situations Where Out–of–Court Declarations Are Not Hearsay Because Not Offered for the "Truth of the Matter" Declared 409

IV. Out–of–Court Statements or Conduct Showing the Declarant's State of Mind or Belief 418

V. Hearsay and the Constitution: The Confrontation Clause 434

VI. The Due Process and Compulsory Process Clauses 457

Chapter 9. Hearsay Rule Modifications for Admissions and Witnesses' Prior Statements 460

I. Mapping the Hearsay Escape Valves and Their Underlying Policies 460

II. The Exemption for Certain Prior Statements of Presently Testifying Witnesses 469

III. The Exemption for Admissions of a Party Opponent, Her Agent, or Her Co–Conspirator 481

Page

Chapter 10.   Exceptions to the Hearsay Rule -- 503
    I. Policies Underlying Hearsay Exceptions ------- 503
   II. Exceptions for Which Unavailability Is Not
       Required -- 503
  III. Exceptions for Which Unavailability Is Re-
       quired-- 561
   IV. The Catch–All or Residual Hearsay Exception 585
    V. Final Thoughts About Hearsay-------------------- 593

**Chapter 11.   Authentication, Exhibits, and
         the Best Evidence (Original Writing)
         Rule** --- 595
    I. Authentication of Documents and Real Evi-
       dence-- 595
   II. The Original Writing or Best Evidence Rule --- 600
  III. The Parol Evidence Rule ---------------------------- 605
   IV. The Manner of Introducing Exhibits ------------ 607

APPENDIX: THE FEDERAL RULES OF EVIDENCE -------------- 617

*

DETAILED OUTLINE
AND
TABLE OF CONTENTS

Page

PREFACE --- III
SUMMARY OUTLINE --- VII
TABLE OF CASES -- XXXV

**Chapter 1. Interpreting the Rules and Other
   Basics: Offers, Objections, and the
   Judge's Function** ----------------------------------- 1
  I. *From Common Law to Codification: How the
     Rules Are Interpreted* ----------------------------- 1
     The Sources of Evidence Law, From Common
     Law to **F.R.E. 101** ----------------------------- 1
     Evidentiary Policies in a Jury Trial System:
     The Common Law and **F.R.E 102** ------------- 2
     The Policies Favoring Admissibility and Dis-
     cretion in the F.R.E. ------------------------------ 5
     Advantages and Disadvantages of a Discre-
     tion–Based Codification ---------------------------- 7
  II. *Offers, Objections, and Instructions* -------------- 9
     The Necessity for Requesting Action by the
     Trial Judge: **F.R.E. 103** --------------------------- 9
     Curative and Cautionary Instructions to the
     Jury: Common Law and **F.R.E. 105** ---------- 13
  III. *Preliminary Questions of Fact and Condition-
      al Relevancy* ------------------------------------- 17
     Preliminary Questions of Fact and **F.R.E.
     104(a)**: The Judge's Evidentiary Findings   17

Page

Chapter 1. Interpreting the Rules and Other Basics: Offers, Objections, and the Judge's Function—Continued

"Conditional Relevancy" and **F.R.E. 104(b)**: Preserving Jury Decisionmaking When the Relevancy of One Piece of Evidence Depends on Another ------------------------------- 24

IV. *Role of Rules Beyond Exclusion of Pieces of Evidence From Juries: Non–Jury & Administrative Trials; Appeals; Judge & Attorney Comment* ------------------------------------- 28

Non–Jury Trials and Administrative Hearings 28

Harmless Error and Abuse of Discretion ------- 30

Judicial Comment on Weight of Evidence ------ 33

Argument by Attorneys to the Jury-------------- 35

Chapter 2. Judicial Notice, Presumptions, and Burdens: Substitutes for Evidence 40

I. *Judicial Notice* ----------------------------------- 40

"Adjudicative" Facts Under **F.R.E. 201** -------- 40

"Legislative" and "Evaluative" Facts ----------- 42

II. *Burdens of Proof* ------------------------------- 44

The Burdens of Pleading, Production, and Persuasion --- 44

The Burden of Production ------------------------- 45

The Burden of Persuasion ------------------------- 46

III. *Presumptions* ------------------------------------ 47

Mandatory and Permissive Presumptions ------ 47

Criminal Presumptions and Their Restriction by the Constitution----------------------------- 49

Evidence Rebutting the Presumed Fact: What Effect? -- 52

Presumptions Under the Federal Rules: **F.R.E. 301 and 302** -------------------------------- 55

Chapter 3. Relevancy, Its Counterweights, and Related Exclusionary Rules ------------- 58

I. *Relevancy* --- 58

The Definition of Relevant Evidence: **F.R.E. 401** -- 58

Page

Chapter 3. Relevancy, Its Counterweights, and Related Exclusionary Rules—Continued

Relevant Evidence Is Admissible Unless There Is an Exclusionary Rule: **F.R.E. 402**   61

Statistical Probabilities: A Particular Problem of Relevancy ------------------------------------- 63

II. *Counterweights to Relevance: Prejudice, Confusion, Time Consumption, Etc.* ---------------- 69

Prejudice: Extreme Over–Valuation or Decision on an Improper Basis ------------------------ 69

Other Counterweights in Addition to Prejudice -- 75

Individual Versus Categorical Balancing -------- 78

F.R.E. 403 Creates an Unevenly Weighted Balancing Test, Which Is Loaded in Favor of Admissibility: Unless "Substantially Outweighed," Probative Value Supports Admissibility -- 78

Illustration of the Balancing: Offering Replications: Results of Experiments That Attempt to Recreate a Litigated Event or Portion Thereof; Re-enactments; Simulations; Models; Photos; Graphic Representations --- 81

Illustration of the Balancing (Perhaps Tempered by Extrinsic Policies): Flight, Bribery, Spoliation (the Failure to Adduce Evidence) and Other Arguable Implied Admissions --- 83

III. *Exclusionary Rules for Remedial Measures, Compromise Negotiations, Withdrawn Guilty Pleas, and Insurance* --------------------- 85

Subsequent Remedial Measures: **F.R.E. 407** -- 85

Compromises, Settlement Negotiations, and Medical Payments: **F.R.E. 408–09** ------------- 90

Withdrawn Guilty Pleas and Plea Negotiations: **F.R.E. 410** -------------------------------------- 94

Liability Insurance: **F.R.E. 411** ------------------- 96

Page

Chapter 4. A Special Relevancy vs. Counter-weights Problem Area: Similar Acts, Character, Propensity 100

I. *An Overview of the Propensity–Related Rules* .. 100

The Theory of the Rules: Propensity Is "Relevant" But Sometimes Prejudicial, Misleading, Too Time Consuming, or Just Plain Not Fair 100

The Evidentiary Rules: A Road Map to **F.R.E. 404–406** and Related Rules 105

II. *Permissible Uses of Character as Substantive Circumstantial Evidence* 109

Good Character, Offered at the Criminal Defendant's Option: **F.R.E. 404(a)(1) and 405** 109

The Defendant's Option to Offer Character Evidence on a "Pertinent Trait": the "Mercy Rule" Allowing "Good Guy" Evidence 109

Impeachment of Character Witnesses by "Have You Heards" 110

The Prosecution's Rebuttal of the Defendant's Character Evidence: **F.R.E. 404(a)(1)** 112

Character of the Victim in Self–Defense and Other Cases: **F.R.E. 404(a)(2)** 113

III. *Similar Incidents Offered for Non–Character Circumstantial Purposes* 115

Intent, Identity and Other Factors as Shown by Similar Incidents: **F.R.E. 404(b)**: "M.O.I.P.P.K.I.A.", the "Other Crimes, Wrongs, or Acts" or "Uncharged Misconduct" Principle 115

Plan, as Shown by Similar Incidents: **F.R.E. 404(b)** Continued 118

Identity: **F.R.E. 404(b)** Continued 123

Intent or Knowledge: **F.R.E. 404(b)** Continued 124

Motive: **F.R.E. 404(b)** Continued 129

Opportunity: **F.R.E. 404(b)** Continued 130

Page

Chapter 4. A Special Relevancy vs. Counter-weights Problem Area: Similar Acts, Character, Propensity—Continued

Preparation: **F.R.E. 404(b)** Continued............ 131

Absence of Mistake or Accident: **F.R.E. 404(b)** Continued.............................. 131

IV. *Special Rules for Sexual Assaults and Related Offenses* 132

The "Rape Shield": The Common Law and **F.R.E. 412** 132

The Wide–Open Admissibility of Sexual Misconduct Against Sexual Offense Defendants: **F.R.E. 413 through 415**.............. 137

V. *Procedural Issues Raised by Similar Acts Evidence* 139

The Coverage of **F.R.E. 404(b)** 139

The Standard of Proof for **404(b)**: Evidence to "Support a Finding": **F.R.E. 104(b)** 140

Acquittal as Not Excluding **404(b)** Evidence .. 142

VI. *Character and Similar–Acts Evidence in Civil Cases* 144

Similar Acts Evidence in Civil Cases: **F.R.E. 404(b)** 144

Substantive Use of Character–Propensity Not Allowed in Civil Cases: **F.R.E. 404(a)(1) and (a)(2)** 145

These Civil Case Rules Applied to Negligence Cases.............................. 145

VII. *Habit and Routine Practice: **F.R.E. 406**........ 146*

VIII. *Character as an "Essential Element" and the Like: **F.R.E. 405(b)** and Related Notions* 149

IX. *Credibility as Affected by the Witness' Character* 153

Impeachment by Opinion, Reputation, Criminal Conviction, and Bad Acts: **F.R.E. 608 and 609**.............................. 153

Page

Chapter 4. A Special Relevancy vs. Counterweights Problem Area: Similar Acts, Character, Propensity—Continued

Character Impeachment by Opinion or Reputation Evidence: **F.R.E. 608(a)** ------------------ 155

Character Impeachment by Criminal Convictions: **F.R.E. 609** ---------------------------------- 156

F.R.E. 609: The Current Rule---------------- 157

The Balancing Tests: A Favorable Balance for the Criminal Defendant; Rule 403 for Other Witnesses --------------------- 160

Crimes of "Dishonesty or False Statement": The "Automatic Admit" ---------- 162

Other Issues: Time Remoteness, Pardon, and Appealability---------------------------- 164

Impeachment by Non–Convicted–For Misconduct "Probative of Untruthfulness": **F.R.E. 608(b)** -------------------------------------- 166

Character or Propensity for Incredibility of Victim and Perpetrator in Sex Cases --------- 169

X. *Some Recurring Themes Cutting Across This Entire Propensity Chapter*----------------------- 169

Balancing and Instructions -------------------------- 169

Remedies for Introduction of Impermissible Propensity Evidence: Fighting Fire With Fire--- 171

Two Helpful Questions----------------------------- 172

(1) The Generality/Specificity Question-- 172

(2) The Question Concerning Kind of Evidence ------------------------------------ 173

Reputation, Opinion, Specific Instances: The Required Foundation ----------------------------- 174

Specific Instances: Further Restrictions--------- 175

Concessions, Offers to Stipulate------------------- 176

Chapter 5. Privileges ----------------------------------- 177

I. *Policies, Procedures, and General Principles Underlying Privileges* ----------------------------- 177

Page

Chapter 5. Privileges—Continued

Privileges as Narrow Exceptions to Everyone's Duty to Give Evidence (Testimony, Documents, Etc.) _____ 177

Policies Underlying Privileges _____ 178

Common Themes Concerning Assertion and Waiver of Privilege _____ 183

The General Concept of Confidentiality: Third Persons as an Illustration _____ 185

The General Concept of "Communication" ____ 187

The Benefits of Privileges Versus Their Costs: An Unknowable Balance _____ 189

II. *Privileges Under the F.R.E.: State Rules or Federal Common Law:* **F.R.E. 501** _____ 191

State Privilege Law as Applicable in Some Federal Cases _____ 192

Evolution of a "Common Law" of Federal Privileges Under Rule 501 _____ 194

III. *Attorney–Client Privilege* _____ 198

Definition and Limits of Attorney–Client Privilege _____ 198

Attorney-Client Privilege in a Corporate Setting _____ 204

Assertion and Waiver of Attorney–Client Privilege _____ 206

Other Common Attorney–Client Privilege Issues _____ 211

Work Product Immunity as Distinguished From Attorney–Client Privilege _____ 212

Refreshing Recollection With Privileged Information: The Potential for Waiver _____ 213

IV. *Marital Privileges: Two Separate Privileges Distinguished* _____ 213

The "Confidential Communications" Privilege in the Marital Context _____ 214

The "Adverse Spousal Testimony" Privilege (as Distinct From the Communications Privilege) _____ 218

Page

Chapter 5.   Privileges—Continued

The Adverse Spousal Testimony Privilege:
Who Holds It? Is It Really Two Privileges?   221

V. *Physician–Patient and Psychotherapist–Patient Privileges* -------------------------------------   225

Definition of the Physician–Patient Privilege..   225

Exceptions and Limits-----------------------------   226

Evolution or Adoption of a Psychotherapist
Privilege and Its Limits-----------------------   228

VI. *Other Claimed Privileges, Established or Not*   230

VII. *Governmental Privileges* -----------------------   232

Policies Underlying Required Reports Privileges---   232

Coverage and Limits of Required Report Privileges ---   233

Governmental Privileges for State and Military Secrets, Informers, Intra–Agency Communications, etc. -----------------------------------   235

VIII. *The Privilege Against Self–Incrimination* ------   237

Definition of the Privilege Against Self–Incrimination---   237

Limits, Exceptions, and Waiver of the Privilege Against Self–Incrimination -----------------   240

IX. *Exclusionary Rules Premised on Deterrence
Rationales* --   244

Illegally Seized Evidence -----------------------   244

Evidence Obtained as a Result of Other Misconduct--   245

X. *Rules That Prevent Invocation of Privilege
From Implying Guilt or Fault* ------------------   246

Chapter 6.   Witnesses: Competency, Examination, and Impeachment---------------------------   250

Introduction: The Order of Presentation at Trial: Examinations, Arguments, and Charge (Jury Instructions)-----------------------   250

Page

Chapter 6. Witnesses: Competency, Examination, and Impeachment—Continued

I. *Incompetency (or Disqualification) of Witnesses* --- 251

General Rules of Witness Competency: From Common Law to **F.R.E. 601** ------------------- 251

"Dead Man's Rules" Under State Law --------- 253

The Competency of Jurors to Impeach Their Verdicts: **F.R.E. 606(b)** ---------------------------- 254

The Competency of Hypnotically Refreshed Testimony -- 256

II. *Impeachment: Some General Principles* --------- 257

Who Can Impeach Whom, and When?: Common Law and **F.R.E. 607** ----------------------------- 258

III. *Prior Inconsistent Statements* ----------------------- 261

Distinguishing Impeachment by Prior Inconsistent Statements From Their Substantive Use --- 261

Pragmatic Inconsistency Versus Absolute Irreconcilability --- 263

The Common Law Predicate for a Prior Inconsistent Statement: Queen Caroline's Rule --- 265

The Federal Predicate for Prior Inconsistent Statements: **F.R.E. 613** ----------------------------- 269

Constitutional Considerations --------------------- 270

IV. *Impeachment by Contradiction* ----------------------- 271

Constitutional Considerations --------------------- 273

V. *The "Collateral Matter" Rule: A Limit on Impeachment by Prior Inconsistent Statement and Contradiction* ----------------------------- 274

(1) The "Linchpin" Doctrine ------------------ 276

(2) Where the Inconsistency Relates to Matters That Are Themselves Impeaching, Rather Than Substantive 276

Page

Chapter 6. Witnesses: Competency, Examination, and Impeachment—Continued

VI. *Bias* 277

The Admissibility of Bias Under the Common Law and Rule 403 277

Are There Foundation Requirements for Bias Evidence? 280

    (a) Out-of-Court Conduct or Facts Indicating Bias 281

    (b) Prior Out-of-Court Statements of the Witness Evidencing Bias 282

VII. *Character–Related Impeachment (Treated in Chapter 4): Reputation, Opinion, Convictions and Prior Bad Acts* 283

VIII. *Other Kinds of Impeachment* 284

IX. *Support or Rehabilitation of Credibility* 286

General Limits on Rehabilitation of Credibility: A Counterpart Response to the Attack 286

Prior Consistent Statements 287

Other Permissible Support of Credibility 289

X. *Direct and Cross Examination: Procedure, Methods, Limits* 292

Method of Examination of Witnesses: Leading and Non–Leading Questions and Related Matters: **F.R.E. 611** 292

The Scope of Cross–Examination: Common Law and **F.R.E. 611** 294

XI. *Witness Preparation and Refreshing of Recollection* 296

Witness Preparation and Sequestration: **F.R.E. 615** 297

Refreshing Recollection by Means of Documents: **F.R.E. 612** 298

Page

Chapter 7. Opinions, Experts, and Scientific Evidence-- 303

I. *Ordinary Witnesses: Opinion and Firsthand Knowledge*-- 303

Lay Knowledge and Lay Opinion Under the Common Law ------------------------------------ 303

Lay Knowledge and Opinion Under **F.R.E. 602 and 701**: The "Perception" and "Helpfulness" Tests ------------------------------ 304

Firsthand (Personal) Knowledge, Opinion: Relationships to Preliminary Facts Rule, Hearsay Rule------------------------------------ 305

Lay Testimony: Very Broad Opinions ------------ 306

II. *Expert Testimony*-------------------------------------- 308

Introduction: Experts: Special Latitude Under Both Common Law and F.R.E. ------------------ 308

Regulation of Experts Under the Common Law: Mainly Procedural: A Necessary Step to Understanding the F.R.E. -------------------- 313

A. *Reform of Experts Under the F.R.E.: Phase One: Liberalization Regarding Procedures* 316

Liberalized Procedural Treatment of Experts Under the F.R.E.: **Rules 702–705** as Initially Enacted (and Still Largely in Place Today) -- 316

Fears Concerning the Effects of the Procedural Liberalizations in the F.R.E. in the Absence of Substantive Standards Concerning the Reliability of the Testimony Itself-------- 329

B. *Reform of Experts Under the F.R.E.: Phase Two: Changing the Substantive Standard for Scientific Experts From Frye to Daubert* 333

Introduction -- 333

What Is "Scientific Evidence"? An Amorphous Category of Expert Evidence Singled Out for Special Rigorous Treatment ---------- 337

Scientific Evidence: The Tests for Admissibility-- 338

The Common Law *Frye* Test: "General Acceptance"------------------------------------ 339

Page

Chapter 7. Opinions, Experts, and Scientific Evidence—Continued

Tests Based on the F.R.E. in the Immediately Pre–*Daubert* Era 343

The *Daubert* Test: "Reliability", "Fit", and "The Scientific Method" 344

Daubert-Style "Reliability": A Multi–Factor Inquiry 347

Scientific Evidence After *Daubert* 349

C. *Reform of Experts Under the F.R.E.: Phase Three: Daubert's Substantive Standards Extended (In Loosened Form) by Kumho to All Experts and Codified (Perhaps Augmented) in* **F.R.E. 702** 354

Kumho Tire: Applying *Daubert's* Reliability Test to All Experts 354

Open Questions in the Post-*Daubert*/*Kumho* World 356

Amended **F.R.E. 702**: Codifying *Daubert* and *Kumho* or Adding Restrictions? 357

Categories of Expert and Scientific Evidence .. 358

Standard Traffic Violation Evidence 359

Other Tests on Bodily Substances: Paternity, Rape, Assault, and Homicide: Identifying the Culprit: Blood, DNA 359

Syndrome Evidence: From Child Abuse Accommodation Syndrome to Rape Trauma Syndrome 363

Evidentiary Issues in Syndrome Evidence: **F.R.E. 404 and 702** 365

Constitutional Implications of Expert Testimony 367

III. *Impeachment of Experts* 370

Use of the Literature: Authoritative Treatises and Articles Under **F.R.E. 803(18)**; Other Attacks 370

Page

Chapter 8. Hearsay: The Basic Theory, Rationale, and Constitutional Considerations _____ 372

I. *Defining Hearsay* _____ 372
What Is This Thing Called Hearsay? The True Rationale_____ 372
Under the True Rationale, Hearsay Can Consist of Oral, Written, or Recorded Declarations _____ 377
The False Rationale _____ 378
Definitions of Hearsay Under the True Rationale: Common Law and **F.R.E. 801** _____ 379
The Hearsay Determination Involves No Balancing on the Facts of the Individual Case 382
Would it Cure the Hearsay Defect if the "Out-of-Court" Declaration Was Made in Another Court? _____ 383
Should it Cure the Hearsay Defect in an Out-of-Court Declaration if the Declarant Also Presently Testifies?: Prior Statements_____ 386
II. *Conduct as Hearsay or Non–Hearsay:* **F.R.E. 801(a)** _____ 391
Conduct, Assertive and Non–Assertive: Statements Implied From Conduct_____ 391
Conduct: Limitations Inherent in **F.R.E. 801**'s Definition of Hearsay _____ 396
Conduct: The Element of Human Voluntariness_____ 397
Conduct: Omission _____ 400
Conduct: Mistake and Insincerity _____ 403
Special Trustworthiness as Generally Irrelevant to Hearsay or Non–Hearsay_____ 405
III. *Some Common Situations Where Out–of–Court Declarations Are Not Hearsay Because Not Offered for the "Truth of the Matter" Declared:* **F.R.E. 801(c)** _____ 409

Page

Chapter 8. Hearsay: The Basic Theory, Rationale, and Constitutional Considerations—Continued

Out-of-Court Declarations Offered Merely to Show They Were Made: (1) Proving Defamation ----- 409

Out-of-Court Declarations Offered Merely to Show They Were Made: (2) Statements Constituting a Contract or Gift ----- 411

Out-of-Court Declarations Offered Merely to Show They Were Made: (3) Apparent Authority ----- 413

Out-of-Court Declarations Offered Merely to Show They Were Made: (4) Statements Offered to Show the Effect They Had Upon a Particular Listener (or Reader) at the Time ----- 415

IV. *Out–of–Court Statements or Conduct Showing the Declarant's State of Mind or Belief: F.R.E. 801(c)* ----- 418

Evidence of State of Belief for Its Own Sake ----- 418

Evidence of State of Belief for Its Own Sake: Intent, Knowledge, or Feelings ----- 423

Reputation ----- 431

V. *Hearsay and the Constitution: The Confrontation Clause* ----- 434

The Relationship Between Hearsay and the Confrontation Clause ----- 434

The First Attempt at a Comprehensive Theory of the Confrontation Clause: "Unavailability," "Reliability," and "Firmly Rooted Exceptions": The *Roberts* Reliability Framework ----- 437

Crawford: Rejecting the Roberts' Reliability Framework for a "Testimonial" Approach ----- 440

Davis: Defining Emergencies in the Context of Excited Utterances Made to Law Enforcement ----- 443

Page

Chapter 8. Hearsay: The Basic Theory, Rationale, and Constitutional Considerations—Continued

Is the *Roberts* Framework Still Applicable to "Non-testimonial" Statements?..................... 446

Some Implications of the Law After *Davis*...... 448

Beyond Hearsay: Other Implications of the Confrontation Clause............................... 450

    (1) Trial Witness Format: The *Coy* and *Craig* Cases................................ 450

    (2) The Criminal Defendant's Right to Cross Examine Without Undue Restriction of the Questions.............. 455

VI. *The Due Process and Compulsory Process Clauses* 457

Chapter 9. Hearsay Rule Modifications for Admissions and Witnesses' Prior Statements 460

I. *Mapping the Hearsay Escape Valves and Their Underlying Policies* 460

"Exemptions" and "Exceptions" From the Hearsay Rule: **F.R.E. 801–804**...................... 460

Policies Underlying Hearsay Exceptions: Necessity and Trustworthiness......................... 463

Policies Underlying the Exemptions: Fairness and Pragmatism....................................... 465

The Relationship of Exemptions and Exceptions to Other Parts of the F.R.E. 466

II. *The Exemption for Certain Prior Statements of Presently Testifying Witnesses* 469

Inconsistent Statements "Under Oath" in "Prior Proceedings": **F.R.E. 801(d)(1)(A)** 469

Prior Consistent Statements: **F.R.E. 801(d)(1)(B)** 471

Prior Statements of Identification: **F.R.E. 801(d)(1)(C)** 474

Page

Chapter 9. Hearsay Rule Modifications for Admissions and Witnesses' Prior Statements—Continued

The Results of the Prior Statement Exemptions: Constitutional and Pragmatic Aspects 476

  Constitutional Aspects 476

    (1) Method of Taking of Prior Statement: Right to Counsel and to Due Process 476

    (2) At Trial: Confrontation 477

  Pragmatic Aspects 479

III. *The Exemption for Admissions of a Party Opponent, Her Agent, or Her Co–Conspirator* 481

The Common Law: An Exemption or Exception 481

The Federal Rules: An Exemption From Hearsay for Admissions of Approximately the Common Law Dimensions—**F.R.E. 801(d)(2)** 483

Individual or Personal Party Admissions: Express and Implied (or Adoptive) Admissions: **F.R.E. 801(d)(2)(A) and (B)**—Essentially the Same as the Common Law Position 484

  (a) Express Admissions 484

  (b) Implied or Adoptive Admissions 485

Vicarious Admissions: (1) Admissions of Conventional Agents: **F.R.E. 801(d)(2)(C) and (D)**—Compared With Common Law 490

  (a) The Narrow Common Law View: Confinement to Authorized "Speaking" and "Writing" Agents 491

  (b) The Broader "Scope of Employment" View Under **F.R.E. 801(d)(2)(D)** 491

Page

Chapter 9. Hearsay Rule Modifications for Admissions and Witnesses' Prior Statements—Continued

    (c) F.R.E. Abolition of Common Law Prohibition of In–House Admissions _____ 492

    (d) Non–Inclusion of the Predecessor-in-Interest Principle in F.R.E. Admissions _____ 493

    (e) Broad Applications of F.R.E. Provisions _____ 493

    (f) Former Pleadings as Possible Admissions _____ 494

Vicarious Admissions: (2) Co–Conspirator Statements: **F.R.E. 801(d)(2)(E)**—Compared With Common Law _____ 495

Admissions and Confessions of Alleged Criminals: Constitutional Considerations _____ 499

Chapter 10. Exceptions to the Hearsay Rule __ 503

I. Policies Underlying Hearsay Exceptions (See the Preceding Chapter) _____ 503

II. Exceptions for Which Unavailability Is Not Required: **F.R.E. 803** _____ 503

Present Sense Impressions and Excited Utterances: **F.R.E. 803(1) and (2)** _____ 504

    (a) Excited Utterances—The More Traditional of the Two _____ 504

    (b) Present Sense Impressions—A More Recent Expansion of Excited Utterances _____ 508

Declarations of Declarant's Concurrent State of Mind and the Like: **F.R.E. 803(3)** _____ 510

Page

Chapter 10. Exceptions to the Hearsay Rule—Continued

Although They Are Declarations of Declarant's Current State of Mind, Declarations of Memory or Belief to Establish the Fact Remembered or Believed Are Not Permitted: Such "Backward–Looking" Inferences Are Prohibited 513

Statements of Intention Under the State of Mind Exception, Offered as Circumstantial Evidence of Declarant's Probable Subsequent Conduct: "Forward–Looking" Inferences Permitted 514

Declarant's Declaration of His Own State of Mind Used to Prove Another Person's Probable Subsequent Conduct 515

Statements for Medical Diagnosis and Treatment: **F.R.E. 803(4)** 518

Past Recollection Recorded: **F.R.E. 803(5)** 524

Business Records: **F.R.E. 803(6)** ("Records of Regularly Conducted Activity") 526

Accident Investigation Reports 529

Police Records as Business Records 532

Hospital Records 536

Computerized Records 539

The Foundation for Business Records Generally, Aside From Special Computer Problems 542

Government Records and Reports: **F.R.E. 803(8)** ("Public Records and Reports") 543

(1) Law Enforcement Records and the Like in Criminal Cases 545

Page

Chapter 10. Exceptions to the Hearsay Rule—Continued

(2) "Self–Serving" Use of Government Records in Other Contexts: Civil Cases 549

(3) The Meaning of "Factual Findings Resulting From an Investigation" 550

(4) Government Records Containing Information Obtained From Someone Outside the Office or Agency 552

(5) The Trustworthiness Proviso and Rule 403: Other Unreliability Issues 553

(6) Some General Observations About Public Records 556

Absence of an Entry in a Record: **F.R.E. 803(7) and (10)** 556

Miscellaneous Rule 803 Hearsay Exceptions ... 558

III. *Exceptions for Which Unavailability Is Required: **F.R.E. 804*** 561

The Definition of Unavailability: **F.R.E. 804(a)** 561

Former Testimony: **F.R.E. 804(b)(1)** 564

Is Former Testimony Changed Under **F.R.E. 804(b)(1)**? 567

Statements Under Belief of Impending Death (Known as "Dying Declarations"): **F.R.E. 804(b)(2)** 572

Declarations Against Interest: **F.R.E. 804(b)(3)** 574

General Parameters of the Against–Interest Hearsay Exception Both at Common Law and Today 575

Special Aspects Under the Federal Rules of Evidence 580

Focus on Declarations Against Penal Interest Offered in Criminal Cases: Third Party Confessions 581

Page

Chapter 10. Exceptions to the Hearsay Rule—Continued

          (1) Third Party Confessions Exculpatory of the Criminal Defendant on Trial ------------------------------- 581

          (2) Inculpatory Ones --------------------- 582

  Waiver by Misconduct: **F.R.E. 804(b)(6)** ------- 583

 IV. The Catch–All or Residual Hearsay Exception 585

  The Drafting of the Catch–All Exception: **F.R.E. 807** --- 587

  The Catch–All as Interpreted ---------------------- 590

  Hearsay Exceptions Outside the Current F.R.E.: Child Hearsay and Other Exceptions -- 592

 V. Final Thoughts About Hearsay --------------------- 593

  Multiple Hearsay and Impeachment: **F.R.E. 805–806** --- 593

Chapter 11. Authentication, Exhibits, and the Best Evidence (Original Writing) Rule -- 595

 I. Authentication of Documents and Real Evidence -- 595

  Authentication by Indications That the Item Is What Its Proponent Claims: **F.R.E. 901** 595

  Authentication in Special Situations: Circumstantial Evidence, Chain of Custody, Voices, and Self–Authentication -------------------------- 597

 II. The Original Writing or Best Evidence Rule --- 600

  The Basic Rule: **F.R.E. 1001–02** ----------------- 600

  Duplicates: The "Matrix" Provision—**F.R.E. 1003** --- 602

  The Narrowness of the Original Writing Rule: Only When the "Content" of the Writing Is What Is to Be Proved ------------------------------ 603

  Some Exceptions to the Best Evidence Rule --- 604

 III. The Parol Evidence Rule ----------------------------- 605

 IV. The Manner of Introducing Exhibits ------------- 607

Page

Chapter 11. Authentication, Exhibits, and the Best Evidence (Original Writing) Rule—Continued

How Exhibits Are Treated 607

The Procedure for Exhibits, From Marking, to Conveyance to the Jury 609

Examples of Foundations for Exhibits and of Objections 612

The Rule of Completeness: **F.R.E. 106** 614

APPENDIX: THE FEDERAL RULES OF EVIDENCE 617

*

TABLE OF CASES

References are to Pages

A

Abel, United States v., 469 U.S. 45, 105 S.Ct. 465, 83 L.Ed.2d 450 (1984), *63, 280*

Air Disaster at Lockerbie Scotland on Dec. 21, 1988, In re, 37 F.3d 804 (2nd Cir.1994), *553*

Ake v. Oklahoma, 470 U.S. 68, 105 S.Ct. 1087, 84 L.Ed.2d 53 (1985), *341, 370*

Alcalde, People v., 24 Cal.2d 177, 148 P.2d 627 (Cal.1944), *515*

Alzanki, United States v., 54 F.3d 994 (1st Cir.1995), *352*

Angelo v. Bacharach Instrument Co., 555 F.2d 1164 (3rd Cir.1977), *555*

Apprendi v. New Jersey, 530 U.S. 466, 120 S.Ct. 2348, 147 L.Ed.2d 435 (2000), *42, 49*

Arcoren v. United States, 929 F.2d 1235 (8th Cir.1991), *365*

Arizona v. Fulminante, 499 U.S. 279, 111 S.Ct. 1246, 113 L.Ed.2d 302 (1991), *32, 500*

Arizona v. Macumber, 112 Ariz. 569, 544 P.2d 1084 (Ariz.1976), *181*

Arizona v. Youngblood, 488 U.S. 51, 109 S.Ct. 333, 102 L.Ed.2d 281 (1988), *368*

Arthur Young & Co., United States v., 465 U.S. 805, 104 S.Ct. 1495, 79 L.Ed.2d 826 (1984), *195*

Ash, United States v., 413 U.S. 300, 93 S.Ct. 2568, 37 L.Ed.2d 619 (1973), *477*

Awkard v. United States, 352 F.2d 641, 122 U.S.App.D.C. 165 (D.C.Cir. 1965), *171*

Azure, United States v., 801 F.2d 336 (8th Cir.1986), *365*

B

Baker v. Elcona Homes Corp., 588 F.2d 551 (6th Cir.1978), *555*

Balsys, United States v., 524 U.S. 666, 118 S.Ct. 2218, 141 L.Ed.2d 575 (1998), *238*

Barefoot v. Estelle, 463 U.S. 880, 103 S.Ct. 3383, 77 L.Ed.2d 1090 (1983), *369*

Beech Aircraft Corp. v. Rainey, 488 U.S. 153, 109 S.Ct. 439, 102 L.Ed.2d 445 (1988), *551, 552, 553, 554*

Beechum, United States v., 582 F.2d 898 (5th Cir.1978), *124*

Bemis v. Edwards, 45 F.3d 1369 (9th Cir.1995), *508*

Berkey Photo, Inc. v. Eastman Kodak Co., 74 F.R.D. 613 (S.D.N.Y. 1977), *299*

Biggers v. Tennessee, 390 U.S. 404, 88 S.Ct. 979, 19 L.Ed.2d 1267 (1968), *477*

Blackburn, United States v., 992 F.2d 666 (7th Cir.1993), *540*

Bogosian v. Gulf Oil Corp., 738 F.2d 587 (3rd Cir.1984), *299*

Bonds, United States v., 12 F.3d 540 (6th Cir.1993), *349*

Bourjaily v. United States, 483 U.S. 171, 107 S.Ct. 2775, 97 L.Ed.2d 144 (1987), *2, 19, 22, 23, 63, 497, 498*

Bradley v. Brown, 42 F.3d 434 (7th Cir.1994), *351*

Brady v. Maryland, 373 U.S. 83, 83 S.Ct. 1194, 10 L.Ed.2d 215 (1963), *458*

Braswell v. United States, 487 U.S. 99, 108 S.Ct. 2284, 101 L.Ed.2d 98 (1988), *242*

Bridges v. State, 247 Wis. 350, 19 N.W.2d 529 (Wis.1945), *431*

Brigham Young University v. Lillywhite, 118 F.2d 836 (10th Cir.1941), *150*

Brown, United States v., 9 F.3d 907 (11th Cir.1993), *547*

Brown, United States v., 634 F.2d 819 (5th Cir.1981), *182*

Brown, United States v., 557 F.2d 541 (6th Cir.1977), *343*

Bruton v. United States, 391 U.S. 123, 88 S.Ct. 1620, 20 L.Ed.2d 476 (1968), *502, 578*

Buchanan v. Kentucky, 483 U.S. 402, 107 S.Ct. 2906, 97 L.Ed.2d 336 (1987), *368*

C

Caceres, United States v., 440 U.S. 741, 99 S.Ct. 1465, 59 L.Ed.2d 733 (1979), *246*

Cain, United States v., 615 F.2d 380 (5th Cir.1980), *536*

California v. Beheler, 463 U.S. 1121, 103 S.Ct. 3517, 77 L.Ed.2d 1275 (1983), *500*

California v. Green, 399 U.S. 149, 90 S.Ct. 1930, 26 L.Ed.2d 489 (1970), *389, 441, 474, 477*

Castro–Ayon, United States v., 537 F.2d 1055 (9th Cir.1976), *470*

Cepeda Penes, United States v., 577 F.2d 754 (1st Cir.1978), *557*

Chambers v. Mississippi, 410 U.S. 284, 93 S.Ct. 1038, 35 L.Ed.2d 297 (1973), *260, 457, 458, 581*

Charley, United States v., 189 F.3d 1251 (10th Cir.1999), cert. denied Charley v. United States, 528 U.S. 1098, 120 S.Ct. 842, 145 L.Ed.2d 707 (2000), *357*

Chavez v. Martinez, 538 U.S. 760, 123 S.Ct. 1994, 155 L.Ed.2d 984 (2003), *241*

Cheney v. United States Dist. Court for Dist. of Columbia, 542 U.S. 367, 124 S.Ct. 2576, 159 L.Ed.2d 459 (2004), *236*

Chestnut v. Ford Motor Co., 445 F.2d 967 (4th Cir.1971), *585*

Chischilly, United States v., 30 F.3d 1144 (9th Cir.1994), *352*

Ciccarelli v. Gichner Systems Group, Inc., 862 F.Supp. 1293 (M.D.Pa. 1994), *583*

Clark v. Stewart, 126 Ohio St. 263, 185 N.E. 71 (Ohio 1933), *150, 151, 176*

Cleveland Tankers, Inc., In re, 67 F.3d 1200 (6th Cir.1995), *552*

Coastal States Gas Corp. v. Department of Energy, 617 F.2d 854, 199 U.S.App.D.C. 272 (D.C.Cir.1980), *201*

Cohen v. Illinois Institute of Technology, 524 F.2d 818 (7th Cir.1975), *544*

Collins, People v., 68 Cal.2d 319, 66 Cal.Rptr. 497, 438 P.2d 33 (Cal.1968), *63, 65, 66, 67*

Commodity Futures Trading Com'n v. Weintraub, 471 U.S. 343, 105 S.Ct. 1986, 85 L.Ed.2d 372 (1985), *204*

Cooper v. Oklahoma, 517 U.S. 348, 116 S.Ct. 1373, 134 L.Ed.2d 498 (1996), *52*

Cotton, United States v., 535 U.S. 625, 122 S.Ct. 1781, 152 L.Ed.2d 860 (2002), *42*

County Court of Ulster County, N. Y. v. Allen, 442 U.S. 140, 99 S.Ct. 2213, 60 L.Ed.2d 777 (1979), *49, 50*

Coy v. Iowa, 487 U.S. 1012, 108 S.Ct. 2798, 101 L.Ed.2d 857 (1988), *450, 451, 452, 453*

Crawford v. Washington, 541 U.S. 36, 124 S.Ct. 1354, 158 L.Ed.2d 177 (2004), *434, 435, 436, 440, 441, 442, 443, 444, 445, 446, 447, 449, 451, 453, 454, 577, 578, 582, 583, 590*

Crowder, United States v., 87 F.3d 1405, 318 U.S.App.D.C. 396 (D.C.Cir.1996), *128*

Cruz v. New York, 481 U.S. 186, 107 S.Ct. 1714, 95 L.Ed.2d 162 (1987), *502, 578*

D

Daubert v. Merrell Dow Pharmaceuticals, Inc., 43 F.3d 1311 (9th Cir.1995), cert. denied 516 U.S. 869, 116 S.Ct. 189, 133 L.Ed.2d 126 (1995), *350*

Daubert v. Merrell Dow Pharmaceuticals, Inc., 509 U.S. 579, 113 S.Ct. 2786, 125 L.Ed.2d 469 (1993), *2, 62, 315, 316, 318, 321, 324, 328, 333, 334, 337, 339, 340, 341, 343, 344, 345, 346, 347, 349, 350, 351, 352, 353, 354, 355, 356, 357, 358, 365, 366, 369, 370, 554, 609*

Davis, State v., 111 P.3d 144 (Wash. 2005), *443*

Davis v. Alaska, 415 U.S. 308, 94 S.Ct. 1105, 39 L.Ed.2d 347 (1974), *165, 258, 455*

Davis v. Washington, ___ U.S. ___, 126 S.Ct. 2266, 165 L.Ed.2d 224 (2006), *443, 444, 445, 446, 447, 448, 449, 582, 590*

Dawsey v. Olin Corp., 782 F.2d 1254 (5th Cir.1986), *560*

Deeb, United States v., 13 F.3d 1532 (11th Cir.1994), *568*

Delaware v. Fensterer, 474 U.S. 15, 106 S.Ct. 292, 88 L.Ed.2d 15 (1985), *323*

Delaware v. Van Arsdall, 475 U.S. 673, 106 S.Ct. 1431, 89 L.Ed.2d 674 (1986), *455*

Diaz, United States v., 936 F.2d 786 (5th Cir.1991), *561*

DiCaro, United States v., 772 F.2d 1314 (7th Cir.1985), *474*

Dickerson v. United States, 530 U.S. 428, 120 S.Ct. 2326, 147 L.Ed.2d 405 (2000), *242, 477, 501*

Dionisio, United States v., 410 U.S. 1, 93 S.Ct. 764, 35 L.Ed.2d 67 (1973), *243, 368*

Distaff, Inc. v. Springfield Contracting Corp., 984 F.2d 108 (4th Cir. 1993), *550*

Doe v. United States, 487 U.S. 201, 108 S.Ct. 2341, 101 L.Ed.2d 184 (1988), *243*

Doe, United States v., 465 U.S. 605, 104 S.Ct. 1237, 79 L.Ed.2d 552 (1984), *242*

Donnelly v. United States, 228 U.S. 243, 33 S.Ct. 449, 57 L.Ed. 820 (1913), *581*

Dowling v. American Hawaii Cruises, Inc., 971 F.2d 423 (9th Cir.1992), *196*

Dowling v. United States, 493 U.S. 342, 110 S.Ct. 668, 107 L.Ed.2d 708 (1990), *31, 142, 143, 176*

Downing, United States v., 753 F.2d 1224 (3rd Cir.1985), *344, 349*

Doyle v. Ohio, 426 U.S. 610, 96 S.Ct. 2240, 49 L.Ed.2d 91 (1976), *271, 488*

Drake, People v., 748 P.2d 1237 (Colo.1988), *341*

Dukagjini, United States v., 326 F.3d 45 (2nd Cir.2003), *311*

Duncan, United States v., 42 F.3d 97 (2nd Cir.1994), *332*

Dunnigan, United States v., 507 U.S. 87, 113 S.Ct. 1111, 122 L.Ed.2d 445 (1993), *135*

Dutton v. Evans, 400 U.S. 74, 91 S.Ct. 210, 27 L.Ed.2d 213 (1970), *496*

E

Eastern Air Lines, Inc. v. McDonnell Douglas Corp., 532 F.2d 957 (5th Cir.1976), *544*

Edwards v. Arizona, 451 U.S. 477, 101 S.Ct. 1880, 68 L.Ed.2d 378 (1981), *501*

Elkins, United States v., 885 F.2d 775 (11th Cir.1989), *592*

Ellis, United States v., 935 F.2d 385 (1st Cir.1991), *591*

Erie R. Co. v. Tompkins, 304 U.S. 64, 58 S.Ct. 817, 82 L.Ed. 1188 (1938), *193*

Estelle v. McGuire, 502 U.S. 62, 112 S.Ct. 475, 116 L.Ed.2d 385 (1991), *126, 127, 143, 366, 369*

F

Farber, Matter of, 78 N.J. 259, 394 A.2d 330 (N.J.1978), cert. denied New York Times Co. v. New Jersey, 439 U.S. 007, 99 S.Ct. 598, 58 L.Ed.2d 670 (1978), *182*

Farley, United States v., 11 F.3d 1385 (7th Cir.1993), *235*

Ferguson v. Moore, 98 Tenn. 342, 39 S.W. 341 (Tenn.1897), *36*

Fernandez, United States v., 892 F.2d 976 (11th Cir.1989), *591*

Francis v. Franklin, 471 U.S. 307, 105 S.Ct. 1965, 85 L.Ed.2d 344 (1985), *49*

Frye v. United States, 293 F. 1013 (D.C.Cir.1923), *62, 315, 316, 333, 334, 335, 337, 339, 340, 341, 342, 343, 344, 345, 346, 347, 348, 349, 350, 351, 352, 353, 355, 356, 358, 365, 370*

F.T.C. v. Grolier Inc., 462 U.S. 19, 103 S.Ct. 2209, 76 L.Ed.2d 387 (1983), *213*

G

Garner v. Wolfinbarger, 430 F.2d 1093 (5th Cir.1970), *204*

General Elec. Co. v. Joiner, 522 U.S. 136, 118 S.Ct. 512, 139 L.Ed.2d 508 (1997), *346, 351*

Gichner v. Antonio Troiano Tile & Marble Co., 410 F.2d 238, 133 U.S.App.D.C. 250 (D.C.Cir.1969), *580*

Gilbert v. California, 388 U.S. 263, 87 S.Ct. 1951, 18 L.Ed.2d 1178 (1967), *477*

Gillespie, United States v., 852 F.2d 475 (9th Cir.1988), *366*

Gilliard, United States v., 133 F.3d 809 (11th Cir.1998), *335*

Gillock, United States v., 445 U.S. 360, 100 S.Ct. 1185, 63 L.Ed.2d 454 (1980), *193*

Golden, United States v., 532 F.2d 1244 (9th Cir.1976), *322, 467*

Grady, United States v., 544 F.2d 598 (2nd Cir.1976), *546*

Grand Cent. Partnership, Inc. v. Cuomo, 166 F.3d 473 (2nd Cir.1999), *236*

Grand Jury Investigation, In re, 918 F.2d 374 (3rd Cir.1990), *196*

Grand Jury Proceedings, In re, 5 F.3d 397 (9th Cir.1993), *196*

Grand Jury Subpoena Duces Tecum, In re, 112 F.3d 910 (8th Cir.1997), *201*

Gray v. Maryland, 523 U.S. 185, 118 S.Ct. 1151, 140 L.Ed.2d 294 (1998), *502, 578*

Green v. Bock Laundry Mach. Co., 490 U.S. 504, 109 S.Ct. 1981, 104 L.Ed.2d 557 (1989), *2, 160*

Griffin v. California, 380 U.S. 609, 85 S.Ct. 1229, 14 L.Ed.2d 106 (1965), *237, 247, 248*

Gulf States Utilities Co. v. Ecodyne Corp., 635 F.2d 517 (5th Cir.1981), *28*

H

Haakanson v. State, 760 P.2d 1030 (Alaska App.1988), *365, 367*

Hale, United States v., 978 F.2d 1016 (8th Cir.1992), *557*

Hale, United States v., 422 U.S. 171, 95 S.Ct. 2133, 45 L.Ed.2d 99 (1975), *488*

Hammann v. Hartford Acc. and Indem. Co., 620 F.2d 588 (6th Cir. 1980), *118, 131*

Hammon v. State, 829 N.E.2d 444 (Ind.2005), *443, 444*

Hancock v. Dodson, 958 F.2d 1367 (6th Cir.1992), *495*

Hankey, United States v., 203 F.3d 1160 (9th Cir.2000), *355*

Hansen, United States v., 583 F.2d 325 (7th Cir.1978), *545*

Harris v. New York, 401 U.S. 222, 91 S.Ct. 643, 28 L.Ed.2d 1 (1971), *271, 501*

Harris v. United States, 536 U.S. 545, 122 S.Ct. 2406, 153 L.Ed.2d 524 (2002), *42*

Havens, United States v., 446 U.S. 620, 100 S.Ct. 1912, 64 L.Ed.2d 559 (1980), *168, 244, 245, 271, 273*

Hayes, United States v., 861 F.2d 1225 (10th Cir.1988), *548*

Hembd, State v., 305 Minn. 120, 232 N.W.2d 872 (Minn.1975), *182*

Hemingway v. Ochsner Clinic, 608 F.2d 1040 (5th Cir.1979), *559*

Hiibel v. Sixth Judicial Dist. Court of Nevada, Humboldt County, 542 U.S. 177, 124 S.Ct. 2451, 159 L.Ed.2d 292 (2004), *238*

Holmes v. South Carolina, 547 U.S. 319, 126 S.Ct. 1727, 164 L.Ed.2d 503 (2006), *459*

Hoosier, United States v., 542 F.2d 687 (6th Cir.1976), *485*

Houston Oxygen Co. v. Davis, 139 Tex. 1, 161 S.W.2d 474 (Tex.Com. App.1942), *510*

Hubbell, United States v., 530 U.S. 27, 120 S.Ct. 2037, 147 L.Ed.2d 24 (2000), *242*

Huddleston v. United States, 485 U.S. 681, 108 S.Ct. 1496, 99 L.Ed.2d 771 (1988), *25, 140, 141, 142*

Hudson v. Hightower, 394 S.W.2d 46 (Tex.Civ.App.-Austin 1965), *171*

I

Iaconetti, United States v., 540 F.2d 574 (2nd Cir.1976), *586*

Iaconetti, United States v., 406 F.Supp. 554 (E.D.N.Y.1976), affirmed in part 540 F.2d 574 (2nd Cir.1976), cert. denied Iaconetti v. United States, 429 U.S. 1041, 97 S.Ct. 739, 50 L.Ed.2d 752 (1977), *493*

Idaho v. Wright, 497 U.S. 805, 110 S.Ct. 3139, 111 L.Ed.2d 638 (1990), *447, 591*

Illinois v. Perkins, 496 U.S. 292, 110 S.Ct. 2394, 110 L.Ed.2d 243 (1990), *501*

In re (see name of party)

J

Jackson v. Denno, 378 U.S. 368, 84 S.Ct. 1774, 12 L.Ed.2d 908 (1964), *22*

Jaffee v. Redmond, 518 U.S. 1, 116 S.Ct. 1923, 135 L.Ed.2d 337 (1996), *194, 195, 197, 228, 229*

James v. Illinois, 493 U.S. 307, 110 S.Ct. 648, 107 L.Ed.2d 676 (1990), *245, 274*

Japanese Electronic Products Antitrust Litigation, In re, 723 F.2d 238 (3rd Cir.1983), *591*

Jarzbek, State v., 204 Conn. 683, 529 A.2d 1245 (Conn.1987), *584*

Jenkins v. Anderson, 447 U.S. 231, 100 S.Ct. 2124, 65 L.Ed.2d 86 (1980), *271, 488*

Jeter, People v., 587 N.Y.S.2d 583, 600 N.E.2d 214 (N.Y.1992), *341*

Johnson v. Lutz, 253 N.Y. 124, 170 N.E. 517 (N.Y.1930), *533*

K

Kastigar v. United States, 406 U.S. 441, 92 S.Ct. 1653, 32 L.Ed.2d 212 (1972), *239*

Kilgus, United States v., 571 F.2d 508 (9th Cir.1978), *343*

Kirby v. Illinois, 406 U.S. 682, 92 S.Ct. 1877, 32 L.Ed.2d 411 (1972), *477*

Kuhlmann v. Wilson, 477 U.S. 436, 106 S.Ct. 2616, 91 L.Ed.2d 364 (1986), *502*

Kumho Tire Co., Ltd. v. Carmichael, 526 U.S. 137, 119 S.Ct. 1167, 143 L.Ed.2d 238 (1999), *318, 321, 324, 328, 337, 354, 355, 356, 357, 358, 366, 369*

L

Leahy, People v., 34 Cal.Rptr.2d 663, 882 P.2d 321 (Cal.1994), *353*

Lee v. Illinois, 476 U.S. 530, 106 S.Ct. 2056, 90 L.Ed.2d 514 (1986), *502*

Lewis v. State, 591 So.2d 922 (Fla.1991), *136*

Lindsey, In re, 158 F.3d 1263, 332 U.S.App.D.C. 357 (D.C.Cir.1998), *201, 236*

Lippay v. Christos, 996 F.2d 1490 (3rd Cir.1993), *494*

Llera Plaza, United States v., 188 F.Supp.2d 549 (E.D.Pa.2002), *334*

Lloyd v. American Export Lines, Inc., 580 F.2d 1179 (3rd Cir.1978), *569*

Loper v. Andrews, 404 S.W.2d 300 (Tex.1966), *538*

Luce v. United States, 469 U.S. 38, 105 S.Ct. 460, 83 L.Ed.2d 443 (1984), *166*

M

Mack, State v., 292 N.W.2d 764 (Minn.1980), *257*

Maggipinto v. Reichman, 607 F.2d 621 (3rd Cir.1979), *559*

Malloy v. Hogan, 378 U.S. 1, 84 S.Ct. 1489, 12 L.Ed.2d 653 (1964), *237*

Marenghi, United States v., 893 F.Supp. 85 (D.Me.1995), *364*

Marsee v. United States Tobacco Co., 866 F.2d 319 (10th Cir.1989), *553*

Marshall, United States v., 856 F.2d 896 (7th Cir.1988), *592*

Martin v. Ohio, 480 U.S. 228, 107 S.Ct. 1098, 94 L.Ed.2d 267 (1987), *52*

Maryland v. Craig, 497 U.S. 836, 110 S.Ct. 3157, 111 L.Ed.2d 666 (1990), *450, 452, 453, 454*

Matter of (see name of party)

McGrane, People v., 12 A.D.2d 465, 207 N.Y.S.2d 88 (N.Y.A.D. 1 Dept.1960), *36*

McKinney v. Rees, 993 F.2d 1378 (9th Cir.1993), *144*

McKune v. Lile, 536 U.S. 24, 122 S.Ct. 2017, 153 L.Ed.2d 47 (2002), *241*

Medico, United States v., 557 F.2d 309 (2nd Cir.1977), *586*

Melville v. American Home Assur. Co., 443 F.Supp. 1064 (E.D.Pa.1977), rev'd on other grounds 584 F.2d 1306 (3rd Cir.1978), *549*

Mezzanatto, United States v., 513 U.S. 196, 115 S.Ct. 797, 130 L.Ed.2d 697 (1995), *95*

Michigan v. Harvey, 494 U.S. 344, 110 S.Ct. 1176, 108 L.Ed.2d 293 (1990), *271*

Michigan v. Lucas, 500 U.S. 145, 111 S.Ct. 1743, 114 L.Ed.2d 205 (1991), *134, 328, 456*

Minnick v. Mississippi, 498 U.S. 146, 111 S.Ct. 486, 112 L.Ed.2d 489 (1990), *501*

Miranda v. Arizona, 384 U.S. 436, 86 S.Ct. 1602, 16 L.Ed.2d 694 (1966), *242, 243, 244, 270, 271, 477, 488, 500, 501*

Mitchell v. United States, 526 U.S. 314, 119 S.Ct. 1307, 143 L.Ed.2d 424 (1999), *241*

Montana v. Egelhoff, 518 U.S. 37, 116 S.Ct. 2013, 135 L.Ed.2d 361 (1996), *135, 181, 182, 458*

Montiel v. City of Los Angeles, 2 F.3d 335 (9th Cir.1993), *555*

Moore v. Duckworth, 687 F.2d 1063 (7th Cir.1982), *136*

Moore, United States v., 571 F.2d 76 (2nd Cir.1978), *516*

Moran v. Burbine, 475 U.S. 412, 106 S.Ct. 1135, 89 L.Ed.2d 410 (1986), *501*

Moss v. Ole South Real Estate, Inc., 933 F.2d 1300 (5th Cir.1991), *553*

Mullaney v. Wilbur, 421 U.S. 684, 95 S.Ct. 1881, 44 L.Ed.2d 508 (1975), *51*

Mutual Life Ins. Co. of New York v. Hillmon, 145 U.S. 285, 12 S.Ct. 909, 36 L.Ed. 706 (1892), *514, 515, 516*

N

Napier, United States v., 518 F.2d 316 (9th Cir.1975), *506*

Neder v. United States, 527 U.S. 1, 119 S.Ct. 1827, 144 L.Ed.2d 35 (1999), *32*

Nelson v. O'Neil, 402 U.S. 622, 91 S.Ct. 1723, 29 L.Ed.2d 222 (1971), *389, 478*

New York v. Quarles, 467 U.S. 649, 104 S.Ct. 2626, 81 L.Ed.2d 550 (1984), *501*

Nivica, United States v., 887 F.2d 1110 (1st Cir.1989), *592*

Nixon, United States v., 418 U.S. 683, 94 S.Ct. 3090, 41 L.Ed.2d 1039 (1974), *236, 498*

North, United States v., 920 F.2d 940, 287 U.S.App.D.C. 146 (D.C.Cir. 1990), *239*

O

Oates, United States v., 560 F.2d 45 (2nd Cir.1977), *536*

Obayagbona, United States v., 627 F.Supp. 329 (E.D.N.Y.1985), *592*

O'Conner v. Commonwealth Edison Co., 13 F.3d 1090 (7th Cir.1994), *351*

Ohio v. Reiner, 532 U.S. 17, 121 S.Ct. 1252, 149 L.Ed.2d 158 (2001), *238*

Ohio v. Roberts, 448 U.S. 56, 100 S.Ct. 2531, 65 L.Ed.2d 597 (1980), *434, 437, 438, 439, 440, 446, 447, 448, 453, 570, 571*

Ohler v. United States, 529 U.S. 753, 120 S.Ct. 1851, 146 L.Ed.2d 826 (2000), *159*

Oil Spill by Amoco Cadiz Off Coast of France on March 16, 1978, Matter of, 954 F.2d 1279 (7th Cir.1992), *544, 553*

Old Chief v. United States, 519 U.S. 172, 117 S.Ct. 644, 136 L.Ed.2d 574 (1997), *73, 127, 128, 129, 152, 164, 176, 426*

Olden v. Kentucky, 488 U.S. 227, 109 S.Ct. 480, 102 L.Ed.2d 513 (1988), *135, 456*

Olivarez v. McKinney, 510 U.S. 1020, 114 S.Ct. 622, 126 L.Ed.2d 586 (1993), *144*

Oregon v. Elstad, 470 U.S. 298, 105 S.Ct. 1285, 84 L.Ed.2d 222 (1985), *501*

Orozco, United States v., 590 F.2d 789 (9th Cir.1979), *547*

Owens, United States v., 484 U.S. 554, 108 S.Ct. 838, 98 L.Ed.2d 951 (1988), *389, 441, 478, 479, 548*

P

Palmer v. Hoffman, 318 U.S. 109, 63 S.Ct. 477, 87 L.Ed. 645 (1943), *529, 532*

Paoli R.R. Yard PCB Litigation, In re, 35 F.3d 717 (3rd Cir.1994), *349*

Parke v. Raley, 506 U.S. 20, 113 S.Ct. 517, 121 L.Ed.2d 391 (1992), *157*

Parker v. Randolph, 442 U.S. 62, 99 S.Ct. 2132, 60 L.Ed.2d 713 (1979), *502*

Patterson v. New York, 432 U.S. 197, 97 S.Ct. 2319, 53 L.Ed.2d 281 (1977), *51*

Payner, United States v., 447 U.S. 727, 100 S.Ct. 2439, 65 L.Ed.2d 468 (1980), *246*

Pelullo, United States v., 964 F.2d 193 (3rd Cir.1992), *586*

Pennsylvania v. Muniz, 496 U.S. 582, 110 S.Ct. 2638, 110 L.Ed.2d 528 (1990), *243*

Pennsylvania v. Ritchie, 480 U.S. 39, 107 S.Ct. 989, 94 L.Ed.2d 40 (1987), *455*

People v. _____ (see opposing party)

Peoples, United States v., 250 F.3d 630 (8th Cir.2001), *307*

Peseti, State v., 65 P.3d 119 (Hawai'i 2003), *182*

Pheaster, United States v., 544 F.2d 353 (9th Cir.1976), *516*

Picciandra, United States v., 788 F.2d 39 (1st Cir.1986), *548*

Pierce County, Wash. v. Guillen, 537 U.S. 129, 123 S.Ct. 720, 154 L.Ed.2d 610 (2003), *234*

Portuondo v. Agard, 529 U.S. 61, 120 S.Ct. 1119, 146 L.Ed.2d 47 (2000), *248*

Posado, United States v., 57 F.3d 428 (5th Cir.1995), *335, 352*

Powell v. Texas, 492 U.S. 680, 109 S.Ct. 3146, 106 L.Ed.2d 551 (1989), *368*

Q

Qike, People v., 182 Misc.2d 737, 700 N.Y.S.2d 640 (N.Y.Sup.1999), *182*

Quezada, United States v., 754 F.2d 1190 (5th Cir.1985), *547*

Quong, United States v., 303 F.2d 499 (6th Cir.1962), *543*

R

Rawlings v. Kentucky, 448 U.S. 98, 100 S.Ct. 2556, 65 L.Ed.2d 633 (1980), *246*

Redland Soccer Club, Inc. v. Department of Army of United States, 55 F.3d 827 (3rd Cir.1995), *235*

Rex v. _____ (see opposing party)

Reynolds, United States v., 345 U.S. 1, 73 S.Ct. 528, 97 L.Ed. 727 (1953), *235*

Rhode Island v. Innis, 446 U.S. 291, 100 S.Ct. 1682, 64 L.Ed.2d 297 (1980), *501*

Ricciardi v. Children's Hosp. Medical Center, 811 F.2d 18 (1st Cir. 1987), *538*

Richardson v. Marsh, 481 U.S. 200, 107 S.Ct. 1702, 95 L.Ed.2d 176 (1987), *502, 578*

Ring v. Arizona, 536 U.S. 584, 122 S.Ct. 2428, 153 L.Ed.2d 556 (2002), *42*

Roberts, United States v., 844 F.2d 537 (8th Cir.1988), *592*

Rochin v. California, 342 U.S. 165, 72 S.Ct. 205, 96 L.Ed. 183 (1952), *243, 245, 368*

Rock v. Arkansas, 483 U.S. 44, 107 S.Ct. 2704, 97 L.Ed.2d 37 (1987), *135, 256, 369, 458*

Rouco, United States v., 765 F.2d 983 (11th Cir.1985), *584*

Ruffin, United States v., 575 F.2d 346 (2nd Cir.1978), *544, 586*

S

Salazar v. State, 559 P.2d 66 (Alaska 1976), *182*

Salerno, United States v., 505 U.S. 317, 112 S.Ct. 2503, 120 L.Ed.2d 255 (1992), *569, 570*

Sanders, United States v., 749 F.2d 195 (5th Cir.1984), *540*

Sandstrom v. Montana, 442 U.S. 510, 99 S.Ct. 2450, 61 L.Ed.2d 39 (1979), *49*

Sawyer, United States v., 607 F.2d 1190 (7th Cir.1979), *548*

Scheffer, United States v., 523 U.S. 303, 118 S.Ct. 1261, 140 L.Ed.2d 413 (1998), *335, 352*

Scheffer, United States v., 520 U.S. 1227, 117 S.Ct. 1817, 137 L.Ed.2d 1026 (1997), *458*

Schmerber v. California, 384 U.S. 757, 86 S.Ct. 1826, 16 L.Ed.2d 908 (1966), *243, 368*

Scholle, United States v., 553 F.2d 1109 (8th Cir.1977), *547, 548*

School Dist. of Ferndale, Mich., United States v., 577 F.2d 1339 (6th Cir.1978), *555*

Scop, United States v., 846 F.2d 135 (2nd Cir.1988), *332*

Sealed Case, In re, 148 F.3d 1073, 331 U.S.App.D.C. 219 (D.C.Cir.1998), *237*

Sealed Case, In re, 121 F.3d 729, 326 U.S.App.D.C. 276 (D.C.Cir.1997), *236, 237*

Securities and Exchange Commission v. General Refractories Co., 400 F.Supp. 1248 (D.D.C.1975), *530, 550*

Shepard v. United States, 290 U.S. 96, 54 S.Ct. 22, 78 L.Ed. 196 (1933), *517*

Skipper, State v., 228 Conn. 610, 637 A.2d 1101 (Conn.1994), *68, 361*

Smith v. State of Illinois, 390 U.S. 129, 88 S.Ct. 748, 19 L.Ed.2d 956 (1968), *235, 456*

Smith, Rex v., 114 L.T.R. 239 (Crim.App.1915), *118*

Smith, United States v., 869 F.2d 348 (7th Cir.1989), *323*

Smith, United States v., 521 F.2d 957, 172 U.S.App.D.C. 297 (D.C.Cir. 1975), *546, 553*

Sokolow, United States v., 81 F.3d 397 (3rd Cir.1996), *548*

Sporck v. Peil, 759 F.2d 312 (3rd Cir.1985), *299*

Starzecpyzel, United States v., 880 F.Supp. 1027 (S.D.N.Y.1995), *334*

State v. _____ (see opposing party)

State Farm Mut. Auto. Ins. Co. v. Campbell, 538 U.S. 408, 123 S.Ct. 1513, 155 L.Ed.2d 585 (2003), *99*

Stephens v. Miller, 13 F.3d 998 (7th Cir.1994), *136*

Steward v. State, 652 N.E.2d 490 (Ind.1995), *353, 365*

Stovall v. Denno, 388 U.S. 293, 87 S.Ct. 1967, 18 L.Ed.2d 1199 (1967), *477*

Sullivan v. Detroit & Windsor Ferry Co., 255 Mich. 575, 238 N.W. 221 (Mich.1931), *150*

Swallow, State v., 350 N.W.2d 606 (S.D.1984), *367*

Swidler & Berlin v. United States, 524 U.S. 399, 118 S.Ct. 2081, 141 L.Ed.2d 379 (1998), *184*

T

Tampa Bay Shipbuilding & Repair Co. v. Cedar Shipping Co., Ltd., 320 F.3d 1213 (11th Cir.2003), *307*

Tanner v. United States, 483 U.S. 107, 107 S.Ct. 2739, 97 L.Ed.2d 90 (1987), *255*

Tenet v. Doe, 544 U.S. 1, 125 S.Ct. 1230, 161 L.Ed.2d 82 (2005), *235*

Tennenbaum v. Deloitte & Touche, 77 F.3d 337 (9th Cir.1996), *197*

Tome v. United States, 513 U.S. 150, 115 S.Ct. 696, 130 L.Ed.2d 574 (1995), *287, 288, 472, 473, 474*

Trammel v. United States, 445 U.S. 40, 100 S.Ct. 906, 63 L.Ed.2d 186 (1980), *194, 222, 223, 224*

Tran Trong Cuong, United States v., 18 F.3d 1132 (4th Cir.1994), *323*

U

United Air Lines, Inc. v. Austin Travel Corp., 867 F.2d 737 (2nd Cir.1989), *555*

United States v. _____ (see opposing party)

University of Pennsylvania v. E.E.O.C., 493 U.S. 182, 110 S.Ct. 577, 107 L.Ed.2d 571 (1990), *196*

Upjohn Co. v. United States, 449 U.S. 383, 101 S.Ct. 677, 66 L.Ed.2d 584 (1981), *194, 205, 213*

W

Wade, United States v., 388 U.S. 218, 87 S.Ct. 1926, 18 L.Ed.2d 1149 (1967), *477*

Walder v. United States, 347 U.S. 62, 74 S.Ct. 354, 98 L.Ed. 503 (1954), *245, 273*

Washington v. Texas, 388 U.S. 14, 87 S.Ct. 1920, 18 L.Ed.2d 1019 (1967), *458*

Watson, United States v., 260 F.3d 301 (3rd Cir.2001), *329*

Watts v. Delaware Coach Co., 44 Del. 283, 58 A.2d 689 (Del.Super.1948), *538, 539*

Watts v. Smith, 226 A.2d 160 (D.C.App.1967), *522*

White v. Illinois, 502 U.S. 346, 112 S.Ct. 736, 116 L.Ed.2d 848 (1992), *438, 439, 507*

Whorton v. Bockting, 127 S.Ct. 1173, 167 L.Ed.2d 1 (2007), *447*

Wicker, State v., 66 Wash.App. 409, 832 P.2d 127 (Wash.App. Div. 1 1992), *311*

Williams, State v., 388 A.2d 500 (Me.1978), *344*

Williams, United States v., 583 F.2d 1194 (2nd Cir.1978), *344*

Williamson v. United States, 512 U.S. 594, 114 S.Ct. 2431, 129 L.Ed.2d 476 (1994), *502, 578, 583*

Willis, United States v., 38 F.3d 170 (5th Cir.1994), *364*

Winship, In re, 397 U.S. 358, 90 S.Ct. 1068, 25 L.Ed.2d 368 (1970), *49*

Workman v. Cleveland–Cliffs Iron Co., 68 F.R.D. 562 (N.D.Ohio 1975), *586*

Wright v. Tatham, 7 Ad. & El. 313 (Ex.Ch.1837), *397*

Wyatt v. United States, 362 U.S. 525, 80 S.Ct. 901, 4 L.Ed.2d 931 (1960), *223*

Y

Yakobov, United States v., 712 F.2d 20 (2nd Cir.1983), *557*

Young Bros., Inc., United States v., 728 F.2d 682 (5th Cir.1984), *541*

Z

Zenith Radio Corp. v. Matsushita Elec. Indus. Co., Ltd., 505 F.Supp. 1190 (E.D.Pa.1980), *591*

Zolin, United States v., 491 U.S. 554, 109 S.Ct. 2619, 105 L.Ed.2d 469 (1989), *23, 202, 203*

EVIDENCE

IN A NUTSHELL

FIFTH EDITION

*

CHAPTER 1

INTERPRETING THE RULES AND OTHER BASICS: OFFERS, OBJECTIONS, AND THE JUDGE'S FUNCTION

I. FROM COMMON LAW TO CODIFICATION: HOW THE RULES ARE INTERPRETED

The Sources of Evidence Law, From Common Law to F.R.E. 101

The study of Evidence is the study of the legal regulation of proof of facts and the inferences and arguments that arise from such proof, in the trial of a civil or criminal lawsuit. While evidence law was originally almost entirely decisional law, it is now mainly codified in statutes and rules of court. The most influential codification of evidence law has been the Federal Rules of Evidence ("F.R.E."), 28 U.S.C.A. (Rules Appendix). This code was adopted by Congress to govern proceedings in federal courts, effective July 1, 1975. See F.R.E. 101. The enacted rules were based largely on a draft prepared by the Rules Advisory Committee, a distinguished panel of lawyers, judges, and evidence scholars. The draft was approved and transmitted to Congress by the Supreme Court. However, since several rules were significantly changed by Congress, care must be taken when reading the Advisory Committee's Notes. On the Rules generally, see Rothstein, FEDERAL RULES OF EVIDENCE (3d ed. 2007, updated annually).

The Federal Rules draw heavily on the earlier California Evidence Code and on the Uniform Rules of Evidence of the National Conference of Commissioners on Uniform State Laws, promulgated in 1953 as a model for state adoption. Although influential, the Uniform Rules were not widely adopted. In 1974 they were amended to conform substantially to the Federal Rules of Evidence. The majority of states by now have codified their evidence law along the lines of the Federal or Uniform Rules. But some populous states are still largely in the common-law mode.

The Federal Rules did not depart greatly from what was regarded as the better reasoned rulings found previously under the common law system.

Due to the guideline nature of the rules, many splits of authority have developed in applying them. In interpreting the rules, the Supreme Court has declared it generally looks to their "plain meaning," *Bourjaily v. United States* (S.Ct.1987), unless that result would be absurd, *Green v. Bock Laundry Mach. Co.* (S.Ct.1989). In other cases, the Court has used common law, legislative history, or the Advisory Committee's Notes as guides to interpretation; or has taken greater flights of judicial creativity. See *Daubert v. Merrell Dow Pharmaceuticals, Inc.* (S.Ct.1993).

In addition to strictly evidentiary sources, state and federal constitutions exert some constraint on evidence rules and rulings, particularly in criminal cases. It should be noted, however, that in most matters, evidence law makes no distinction between civil and criminal lawsuits.

Evidentiary Policies in a Jury Trial System: The Common Law and F.R.E 102

Since jurors are the primary factfinders in our system, evidentiary rules often reflect our comfort level, or lack thereof, with lay juries. The common law sprang from roots that included a marked distrust of jurors. There were numerous restrictions on what the jurors could hear, because they were considered incapable of sorting out bad evidence from good. This eroded slightly in the more recent common law.

The philosophy of the Federal Rules is that jurors should be more trusted with evidence and should have broader accessibility to the relevant facts. Still, the distrust is there in considerable measure; and the recent common law, although in liberalized interpretation, largely persists under the Federal Rules. The drafters did tend to codify those decisions that favored admissibility where they had a choice.

Evidence rules' interaction with jurors begins with what we call *voir dire* examination, or the questioning of a panel as a part of jury selection. Evidence rules define and limit the questions that may be asked, to avoid tainting the subsequent trial.

The attention of some Evidence scholars has been directed towards how jurors process information during trial. Some commentators posit that jurors reason "deductively" rather than "inductively." That is, instead of considering each new item of information separately and adding it to a growing structure, as is normally assumed, these commentators argue that jurors at some early point create already-completed possible stories and alternative stories, in their minds, deciding whether the subsequent evidence better fits one or the other, c.g., murder or self defense. Either way they are determining probabilities.

Some mathematically-inclined scholars believe that jurors do not understand how probabilities really work, and that more rigorous attention should be paid to how jurors evaluate the probativity of evidence—a concern which Evidence law extensively addresses but without scientific precision.

The importance of jurors concerning evaluation of evidence is underlined by the rules that make it extremely difficult to overturn a jury verdict based on alleged juror improprieties or misconduct.

The study of Evidence law is primarily the study of rules of exclusion. It should yield insights, however, into other matters as well, such as tactical arguments to triers of fact. For example, in a jury trial, when evidence is objected to, arguments may be made to the judge by the two lawyers in an effort to show that the legitimate probativeness or reliability of an objected-to piece of evidence is or is not below the point where it is desirable to admit it. If the argument for exclusion fails, the same arguments often may be resurrected in the lawyers' final summation to the jurors at the end of the trial, to induce jurors to discount or increase the weight they ascribe to the piece of evidence. There is not, however, always an overlap of factors relating to admissibility and those related to weight. For example, the existence or not of a confidential marital or professional relationship may determine whether a piece of evidence is admissible or privileged, but may have no logical bearing on the weight of the evidence (although on particular facts it may). This is because this particular evidence rule (privilege), like a number of others, is concerned with matters other than the force or reliability of the evidence.

By the same token, arguments on both sides of the admissibility question can be arguments for and against peremptory judicial rulings such as motions to dismiss, directed verdicts, judgments notwithstanding the verdict, new trials, etc., since these rulings can hinge on whether evidence is admissible and probative enough to be "jury-worthy". Thus, for example, evidentiary rules and arguments can be determinative in motions for summary judgment, which try to foreshadow, at the beginning of a case, whether there would be sufficient admissible evidence during a trial forceful enough to create a genuine issue of fact before the jury.

Pretrial discovery proceedings are also influenced directly by evidence rules. Discovery not likely to lead to admissible evidence may be forbidden. And certain evidentiary objections relating to deposition material may have to be made during the deposition or they will be considered waived when the deposition is offered at trial.

Thus, most of the rules of evidence have their origins in conditions thought to be conducive to sound jury trials. They are based on concerns about relevancy, prejudice, misleadingness, surprise, confusion, or protraction; with the accuracy, economy, or speed of the dispute-resolving mechanism; with the reliability of particular pieces of evidence; and with standards of fairness or evenhandedness between adversary parties. F.R.E. 102 states some of these policies. Others are in other rules, such as 403. But it must be added immediately that there also are evidence rules that have little to do with the effectiveness of jury trials, but that arise from extrinsic policies. For example, some evidentiary privileges are designed to stimulate socially desirable communications (e.g., between doctor and patient), even if the process of truth-determination is impaired as a result. These rules are concerned primarily with conduct outside the courthouse. They may also, however, have become part of our concept of adjudicatory fairness.

The Policies Favoring Admissibility and Discretion in the F.R.E.

Two themes found in the F.R.E. are *admissibility* and *discretion*. Throughout their entire length and breadth, the F.R.E. favor admissibility and grant strong doses of judicial discretion. The discretion is encouraged to be exercised toward admissibility.

The policy of favoring admissibility is manifest in the fundamental, easily satisfied definition of relevance (Rule 401) and in the way the balancing of the counterweights to relevancy is tilted against exclusion (Rule 403). The F.R.E. limit witness incompetencies (Article VI), and they allow a party freely to impeach that party's own witnesses (Rule 607), all contrary to some former law. Article VII expanded the nature and scope of admissible expert testimony and codified the more liberal of existing decisions to such an extent that the Supreme Court ultimately found it necessary to superimpose a reliability requirement that has been further defined and codified in amended Rule 702. The exclusion of hearsay is relaxed (Article VIII). The authentication-of-documents requirement is whittled down (Article IX), and there is an expanded list of self-authenticating documents, i.e., documents that on their face are authenticated (Rule 902). The best evidence rule for documents is also altered so that xeroxes and photocopies are freely admitted on a par with originals in most cases (Article X). All of these doctrines illustrate the pro-admissibility theme of the F.R.E.

What about the theme of discretion? The "great override," Rule 403, grants the judge wide discretion to exclude evidence by a balancing of relatively subjective factors but tilts the factors toward admission. In addition, the judge is given discretion over the order and manner of presentation of evidence and the examination of witnesses (Rule 611). This Rule permits discretion concerning the form of questions-and-answers (e.g., "yes-no" or narrative responses), the scope of cross-examination, the scope and permissibility of rebuttal and surre-buttal, the number of witnesses, and lawyer questioning that may harass witnesses. The judge also has discretion over whether and when to allow leading questions.

Discretion and breadth of phrasing engendering discretion appear at every turn, not merely in the sections referred to here. Nevertheless, discretion is not unlimited. There are standards that must be learned. Failure to master them can spell disaster in the trial of cases—all the more so where there is discretion, because counsel who is familiar with the standards guiding discretion can motivate that discretion.

Advantages and Disadvantages of a Discretion–Based Codification

These twin themes of admissibility and discretion have certain implications in addition to those already mentioned. Some of the effects may be perceived as disadvantageous. Broad discretion means that even under the codification there will still be considerable diversity from circuit to circuit, district to district, and judge to judge—sometimes, the very kind of disparities that rules and codes are meant to eliminate. Discretion and broad phrases engender differences of opinion as to meaning and as to how discretion should be exercised.

Discretion also means that all of evidence law will not appear between the two covers of the codification. Old cases and new cases will still play a tremendous role, despite some exaggerated promises for a code. It is misleading to say that the common law, or at least the common law process, is abolished; it cannot be entirely abolished where there are broad provisions and open grants of discretion. In addition, discretion means that dissatisfied litigants will be able to focus some of their dissatisfaction on the judge personally. The judge cannot say that the result was entirely compelled by law. Discretion also gives some new license to appellate judges, who can reverse distasteful decisions for nothing more precise than abuse of discretion.

Another disadvantage of discretion is that it means uncertainty, which leads to wasteful and inaccurate decisions about settlement or litigation. The ability of lawyers to plan, predict and advise—to apportion expenses to a case in advance, to give a reading of what it will cost and of the probabilities of outcomes—is impaired under a code that gives broad discretion. Can lawyers precisely plan a case or give intelligent predictions of the outcome when they cannot know what evidence is going to be admissible because admissibility hinges on the discretion of the judge? Lawyers and their clients may feel they cannot make informed decisions.

Finally, discretion breeds appeals. Lawyers must get appellate courts to define the limits of the discretion—to say what the broad phrases mean.

Many of these disadvantages may be perceived as advantages, providing a "flexibility" that is necessary because the drafters could not foresee and codify the desirable solution for all problems in advance.

The rules may not accomplish the goals of codification 100 per cent; they may only accomplish them 50 or 70 per cent. They have been amended and will need further amending as problems are revealed.

Nevertheless, codified rules of evidence are desirable. At the very least, they cause all the judges to shoot toward the same target, something they had not been doing under uncodified common law, even within a given jurisdiction. Authority can be gathered together in convenient annotations to rules. Law students can conveniently study a code. It is uniform law they learn and subsequently spread. A code is an appealing focus for the continuing education of practitioners. A system of rules thus tends toward simplification, uniformity, professionalism and expedition, even though these goals will never be accomplished perfectly.

By the same token, adoption of an evidence code does not mean that lawyers should give up arguing the fine points of interpretation for their clients and engaging in the sophisticated use and distinguishing of case decisions. There is no other way to give content to generalized words like "helpful," "of assistance" and other broad formulations that recur throughout the code. This function of lawyers means that the courts may ultimately choose intelligently what is the best interpretation of each provision in the code, and drafters may make amendments when needed.

It is also worth noting that not all evidence subjects are covered by the F.R.E. There are large gaps. For example, the Rules authorize many different kinds of attacks on witness credibility, but they do not even mention the possibility of impeachment based on the alleged biases or prejudices of witnesses. The courts have been left to infer the permissibility and limits of this type of impeachment. It would seem that many of the gaps are intentional. The drafters appear to have decided, out of humility respecting their own foresight, to provide only a skeleton, with details to be worked out over time. Unregulated subjects often fall within Rule 403, the rule that balances relevance against prejudice and other counterweights, which can be seen as authority for continuing, or developing, the common law, insofar as it responds to the almost all-encompassing factors in the rule.

II. OFFERS, OBJECTIONS, AND INSTRUCTIONS

The Necessity for Requesting Action by the Trial Judge: F.R.E. 103

As a general rule, no action by the trial judge is error in the absence of an offer, request or objection. Thus, improper admittance of evidence will be waived

without timely objection, improper exclusion will be waived without an offer of proof that places the substance of the proposed evidence on the record, and the right to a limiting instruction will be waived without a request.

Notwithstanding the above black-letter rule, it is usually not error for the trial judge to issue a correct ruling or instruction when it is not requested, *if she chooses to do so*. But it is generally not required. Occasionally a trial judge will be required to act of her own motion: so-called "plain error" committed by the judge at trial is not waived and may be rectified even if it is noticed for the first time on appeal. "Plain error" exists where the error is so fundamental that justice would be egregiously denied were it considered waived or so palpable that it should have come to the judge's attention without solicitation. See F.R.E. 103(d). In other instances, however, Rule 103 provides that there is no error even upon improper reception or exclusion of evidence, in the absence of a proper objection, request, or offer of proof.

Objections to evidence must specify their grounds in a particular enough way to identify the issue, unless the grounds are self-evident. F.R.E. 103(a)(1). Otherwise the trial court will be sustained whatever it does, provided there is some conceivable rationale. In jurisdictions with enacted evidence codes or rules, it sometimes is wise to add rule numbers and subdivisions to one's objections.

To preserve the right to appeal an improper exclusion of evidence by the judge, a formal offer of proof (or "proffer" as it is sometimes called) stating the proposed purpose and expected substance of an offered piece of evidence must be made by the offering attorney to the trial judge unless the purpose and substance of the evidence is self-evident. Otherwise the appellate court will ordinarily sustain even an erroneous exclusion. See F.R.E. 103(a)(2). This requirement sometimes seems counterintuitive, because it means that once the trial judge excludes a piece of evidence, the proponent still must get the substance of it into the record, usually outside the jury's presence, to preserve the right to appeal the alleged error. But there are reasons for this rule: the appellate court cannot determine such issues as relevance, cumulativeness, or harmfulness of exclusion, unless it knows what the evidence is. And there is some hope that if the trial judge hears what the evidence will be, she may correct the ruling without need for appeal.

The requirement of making the substance of the evidence known may be difficult where it is cross examination that is being blocked by the objection. The witness often is adverse and the precise answer unknown. Sometimes the best that can be done is to explain what is hoped to be developed. In direct examination situations, there are several ways to make a proffer, that is, make the substance of the evidence known: first, by questions and answers of the witness before the judge; second, by oral summary by counsel; or third, by written submission. Probably the most common method is for counsel simply to state on the record what is expected to be proved, but the actual choice depends on the discretion of the judge, or on the power of opposing counsel to insist on an offer by question and answer in some circumstances. The jury generally is not privy to any of these types of offers, but both counsel should be.

In most jurisdictions there are procedures for making objections in advance of trial (or in advance of the offer) to sensitive evidence that a lawyer expects the opponent will seek to introduce. This device is sometimes called a "motion in limine." "In limine" is Latin for "at the threshold." The motion seeks to nip in the bud, "at the threshold," i.e., before trial begins, or at least before the offer, any attempt to introduce the evidence at trial. A motion in limine may request, for example, that the trial court preliminarily exclude any mention of insurance, or of offers of settlement. The attorney may be concerned that the mere mentioning or asking of a question on these subjects at trial, even if an immediate objection at that time is sustained, will be incurably inflammatory. Or, the attorney may need to know in advance what the ruling would be, for planning purposes. For example, she may wish to know if her client can be impeached by certain evidence (e.g., a conviction) in order to plan whether to put the client on the stand or instead to use alternative witnesses. In some jurisdictions, certain objections may be ineffective or may even be waived if anticipatable and not made through this procedure.

An attorney may sometimes be under an obligation to (or just may find it desirable to) notify in advance of the intention to offer certain sensitive evidence which may be objectionable, so it can be objected to in limine; or himself to secure an advance ruling of admissibility. This would also be called a motion in limine.

A number of jurisdictions hold that a court's ruling on a motion in limine cannot be asserted as error on appeal unless the issue was raised again at the appropriate time at trial, by the attorney ruled against. F.R.E. Rule 103(a)(2) was amended to clarify that a party need not renew an objection or offer of proof once the court "makes a definitive ruling on the record admitting or excluding evidence." In other words, a pretrial ruling need not be challenged at trial, as long as the previous ruling was "definitive." Just what is "definitive" will no doubt be subject to litigation, particularly since trial judges do not like to constrain their flexibility at trial. Therefore, it is likely that when counsel asks if the in limine ruling is definitive, the answer may be "to the extent that the factual basis on which the ruling is grounded is not contradicted by the testimony at trial."

In such case, it may still be prudent to renew the objection or offer of proof at trial.

Curative and Cautionary Instructions to the Jury: Common Law and F.R.E. 105

The judge may order the jurors to disregard evidence that has erroneously been placed before them. The judge also may instruct them to limit their consideration of admitted evidence to stated, proper purposes. Mistrials, as an alternative remedy for erroneously heard evidence, are seldom granted and occur only where an instruction to disregard is deemed insufficient to cure the prejudice. Mistrials in criminal cases may, on certain occasions, present double jeopardy problems.

Imagine that a witness answers a question before the judge has time to sustain an objection to it. Or imagine that a piece of evidence, earlier admitted, is shown to be inadmissible by later events. In such circumstances, the judge has power to strike the answer or evidence, and to instruct the jury to disregard it. ("I move to strike" is the proper form of objection in these situations where the evidence has already come in, rather than "I object" or "objection". The lawyer should also ask that the instruction be given immediately, and should ask again for another similar one at the end of the trial before submission of the case to the jury. The timing on the instruction and whether to give it once or both times will be discretionary with the judge.)

Where jurors are ordered to disregard a piece of evidence they think is probative, however, they may be influenced by that piece of evidence anyway. For example, persuasive evidence may be inadmissible because of the doctor-patient privilege, designed to encourage persons to make full disclosure to their doctors. Or suppose the jurors are instructed to disregard a confession because it was preceded by incomplete warnings. Suppose in addition they know the gun has been found where the confession relates that the confessor buried it. There is some likelihood, often disregarded by the law, that the jurors will not be able to obey the instruction.

There are other examples. To what extent can a jury really heed an instruction that defendant's insurance should not be considered in a personal injury case, or that prior crimes of the criminal accused should be disregarded?

Indeed, instructions to disregard seemingly important, damaging evidence may be like telling someone to ignore the elephant that is in the room with them. Not only is the instruction futile, but some studies confirm that we are contrarians in this regard, focusing on what we are told to ignore. Consequently, counsel may want to think twice before asking for such an instruction, which may simply reinforce the improper evidence. Indeed, even the mere raising of an objection (motion to strike) signals to the jury that there is something significant about the evidence. Thus, lawyers may be placed in the difficult position of deciding whether an objection or request for an instruction will bring unwanted attention to the evidence, knowing that their failure to do so may result in a waiver for purposes of appellate review. When counsel believes that an instruction will not cure the prejudice, a motion for mistrial often will be made. This too has potentially adverse consequences for the party making the request if it is denied.

It would be a mistake, however, to become unduly cynical about the jury's efforts to follow instructions. Jurors usually try hard to uphold their oaths and follow the law. An instruction may completely cure the problem when the evidence is not devastating or has obvious defects in reliability. And sometimes the instruction has the side effect of tarnishing the proponent of the improper evidence.

An instruction to disregard may in some instances alert the jurors that the law regards the evidence as suspect and may cause them to devalue its force even if they don't obey and disregard the evidence entirely—in short, they may be induced by the instruction to utilize the evidence with caution.

"Limiting instructions" are used because sometimes evidence is admissible for only one of several possible purposes or against one of several possible persons. The jury, by means of a limiting instruction, is ordered to consider the evidence for that use only.

The following instructions are typical of instructions that are given in this connection.

(a) "John's confession can be considered only against John, but not against George, his co-defendant." Imagine that the confession states that "George and I did it together," and it details George's participation in the crime. (Note: A confession of this kind, unless redacted, could not properly be used in a joint trial absent special conditions. The law recognizes that an instruction might be ineffective in this situation.)

(b) "The defendant's testimony that he is qualified to give an opinion of what is a safe speed on a certain road may be impeached by evidence of his prior collisions, but those collisions may not be considered with respect to the likelihood he was responsible for the present collision."

(c) "Similar injuries on the same premises are not evidence of negligence or the happening of the injury in controversy, but they may be considered on the issues of the existence of, and notice of, a dangerous condition."

These kinds of limiting instructions may be given when the evidence is introduced, or at the close of all the evidence and argument, or both. Their effectiveness depends both on the type of evidence and on the clarity of the instruction. Perhaps a jury would be better able to give the evidence appropriate weight if they were told more about why the evidence is suspect for certain inferences.

One area in which jurors frequently are requested to "compartmentalize" their minds in this fashion is the area of hearsay evidence, because often a piece of evidence is excludable hearsay if used for one purpose, but permissible if used for another purpose. As in most cases of "multiple admissibility" (i.e., cases where there is a permitted and a prohibited potential use of the evidence), the evidence is usually admitted for the permitted purpose, with cautionary instructions, notwithstanding the danger of an improper use. Only in an aggravated case is this not so.

Two classic examples will suffice to illustrate this point.

First, in a suit for alienation of his wife's affections, plaintiff had to prove (1) a change in the wife's state of mind toward him (2) induced by the defendant. Evidence was offered that the wife had recently said to the husband that she had received various attentions (gifts, favors, dinners) from the defendant which she would continue to welcome, and that the husband was distasteful to her. This was admissible on issue (1) under an exception to the hearsay rule for state of mind, but inadmissible hearsay on issue (2). The court admitted the evidence under proper limiting instructions. (Would a better solution have been to redact the statement, i.e., sever it into parts and admit only part?)

Second, in a suit for defamation, plaintiff offered testimony of his foreman that workers had stated, as a reason for quitting, that defendant had said plaintiff's materials, with which they had to work, were unsafe. This statement of defendant was the defamation alleged, and the exodus of the workers constituted the claimed damages. The court held that the foreman's report of what the workers said could be offered to prove that the damage was attributable to the defamation, but not to prove the defamation had been uttered by the defendant. The former purpose came within an exception to the hearsay rule for state of mind, said the court, but the latter did not. Since there was other evidence of the utterance of the defamation by defendant, the exclusion of the evidence was reversible error. It should have been admitted with a limiting instruction. (Why do you suppose the court found the fact of other evidence to be significant in this ruling?)

When a court must decide whether to admit or exclude evidence capable of permissible and impermissible uses, Rule 403 requires it to apply a balancing test that favors admissibility but allows exclusion if the improper tendency is excessive. Limiting instructions are to be considered in this balance. That is to say, the lessening of prejudice that may be accomplished by a limiting instruction can sometimes tip the balance in favor of admissibility. In practice the evidence usually is admitted with a cautionary instruction given at the option of the objecting party. The authority for a limiting instruction is Rule 105.

III. PRELIMINARY QUESTIONS OF FACT AND CONDITIONAL RELEVANCY

Preliminary Questions of Fact and F.R.E. 104(a): The Judge's Evidentiary Findings

Evidence rules (other than rules of relevance) may call for determinations of fact in order to decide whether evidence is admissible. These are called "preliminary facts." Different jurisdictions follow different rules as to how this function is allocated between judge and jury. Under the most widely prevailing view, however, the judge makes the determination of

such a preliminary question of fact and F.R.E. 104(a) codifies this practice. (When *relevance* of evidence hinges on the existence of another fact, the F.R.E. have a different method of determination, treated in the next section infra.)

In many instances, admissibility of relevant evidence is made, by a rule of evidence, contingent on the finding of a certain fact. This is called a preliminary fact. For example, the husband-wife privilege applies to bar the evidencing of a relevant interspousal communication only if the putative spouses were married. Their marriage, then, is a preliminary issue of fact.

Sometimes there is a coincidence of a preliminary issue and an ultimate substantive issue in the same case. Thus, for example, in a suit for non-support, the issue of marriage between plaintiff and defendant may govern not only the admissibility of a piece of evidence but also the plaintiff's right to support. The determination for each purpose in the case would be done independently, and inconsistency between them would be permitted. Usually the judge would determine the question for evidentiary purposes, and the jury would for purposes of the case at large.

In the federal courts, Rule 104(a) governs the preliminary issue. It provides that the judge alone decides the preliminary facts that determine admissibility of relevant evidence. Thus, the judge decides whether a particular piece of hearsay is sufficiently "excited" to qualify for the hearsay exception for excited utterances, just as the judge decides the marriage issue referred to above for privilege purposes. If some fact must be determined to decide the *relevance* of a piece of evidence, the F.R.E. provide a different regimen—Rule 104(b), discussed in the next section below.

One problem of preliminary fact that is particularly acute concerns the co-conspirator exemption from the hearsay rule, under which relevant out-of-court statements of a co-conspirator are admissible against a fellow conspirator. The rule operates to admit the evidence if there was a conspiracy between the party the evidence is offered against and the alleged co-conspirator (who made the statement), but only if the statement was made in the course of and in furtherance of the conspiracy. The existence of the conspiracy between these parties, and whether the statement was in the course of and in furtherance of the conspiracy, are the preliminary facts. Courts sometimes have become confused as to (a) who is to make the determination of these preliminary facts, which may be in dispute; (b) what is the burden of proof; (c) what evidence is needed; (d) what is to be the role of the statement itself; and (e) how is the issue to be kept separate from the substantive issue of conspiracy in the case at large, if it is a criminal conspiracy case.

The Supreme Court, in *Bourjaily v. United States* (S.Ct.1987), finally settled some of these issues for federal courts by holding that the judge decides these preliminary questions concerning the co-conspirator exemption, pursuant to Rule 104(a), by a preponderance-of-probabilities standard, separate from the jury, who decides similar issues for the criminal conspiracy case at large by a beyond-a-reasonable-doubt standard; and that, on the preliminary issue, inadmissible evidence, including the statement itself, may be considered. The question was reserved as to whether it would be sufficient if the statement itself were the *sole* evidence of a preliminary fact. (In some states, like California, these co-conspirator preliminary facts are still considered to be matters of conditional relevance treated under a Rule like 104(b), rather than 104(a), and thus are to be determined instead mainly by the jury. See section immediately infra.)

In 1997, F.R.E. 801(d)(2) was amended to codify *Bourjaily* concerning proof of the preliminary facts under the

co-conspirator (and other agent-statement) rule but clarified that the disputed statement itself may not be the
sole evidence.

There are many other examples of preliminary type
facts that may be disputed in a particular case: The
privilege against self-incrimination hinges upon the possible incriminating nature of the information sought.
The admissibility of copies may depend upon whether the
original document is available. A witness may give testimony only if she has first-hand knowledge. An expert
opinion is admissible only if the witness is qualified to
give it. Some of these facts control the admissibility of
undisputedly relevant evidence and are thus governed by
104(a). But some may determine the relevance itself of
the evidence, and those are governed by the different
scheme of 104(b), treated in the next section below. It is
not always easy to determine which is which. Concerning
some of the specific facts posed in this paragraph, Rule
602 expressly subjects the first-hand knowledge matter
to the 104(b) regimen. Rule 1008 has a special provision
concerning original documents.

Where there is a genuine dispute over the existence of
a preliminary fact or condition, under Rule 104(a), the
court normally makes the finding it is required to make,
before the evidence is admissible. That is the end of the
matter, except insofar as the jury is permitted to consider
showings like those made to the judge, in assessing
weight if the judge admits the evidence. (The jury theoretically does not know the judge already judged similar
showings.) But notice that not all such preliminary showings will have relevance to weight. Consider, for example,
the preliminary facts that determine marital privileges.

Where the preliminary facts are pertinent to weight as
well as to admissibility, judges may find it economical to
have the showings made at the same time for both judge
and jury, rather than made out of the jury's hearing for

purposes of the preliminary fact and then made again before the jury for purposes of weight. So too where there is a co-incidence of preliminary fact and some issue in the case at large as in the marital support and criminal conspiracy cases above. (This all presupposes that the evidence offered on the preliminary issue in the particular case happens to be of an admissible variety, so the jury could hear it, which is not always the case under Rule 104(a), as indicated above.)

Wherever evidence is offered and is dependent on preliminary facts which might also come before the jury at a later time, the judge may take the economic course and conditionally admit or conditionally exclude until he hears the evidence at such later time. The attorneys would have to ask for revisiting the issue then. Care should be taken to be sure the jury does not hear inadmissible material which only the judge is entitled to hear on the preliminary issue.

Under a very different approach from 104(a), used in some jurisdictions, at least as to some preliminary questions, once the judge finds the prerequisite to admissibility to exist, the jurors are given the evidence, are requested to make the determination again on their own, and are told to disregard the evidence if they do not find the preliminary fact to exist. It should be noted that this double preliminary fact finding (judge first, then jury) may lead a judge to be less than scrupulous in his finding, and to favor admissibility, in reliance on the jury to do the job of exclusion. This may offset the advantage the double fact finding method would give to an objector even though that method theoretically accords him two chances at exclusion. An example might be where a criminal confession is alleged to be inadmissible because involuntarily given. At first blush, the criminal defendant might like to have a double fact-finding method applied, but it may not really be "two bites at the apple" if the judge does not rigorously perform his function because he figures the jury will.

Under some rulings in some jurisdictions, contrary to 104(a), the jury alone is allowed to make the determination whether a prerequisite fact or condition exists (perhaps with an initial screening for "some evidence" thereof—but not a finding—by the judge), and is instructed to disregard the evidence if the fact or condition does not exist. This mode of preliminary fact determination—akin to that set up only for questions of conditional relevance by F.R.E. 104(b) below—is clearly impermissible in the constitutional area, at least in cases concerning involuntary confessions. See *Jackson v. Denno* (S.Ct.1964).

In the last two methods mentioned, where the jury is asked to disregard evidence it finds inadmissible, it may be unrealistic to expect the jury to disregard in cases where the legal reason that compelled them to find the evidence inadmissible would not to the ordinary lay mind deprive the evidence of all weight. For example, while a totally coerced confession might have no weight to a lay mind, a confession that is "involuntary" under the legal standard often does not rise to a degree of involuntariness that a lay person would think deprives it of all weight, especially if the confession relates facts only the perpetrator of the crime could possibly have known.

Theoretically, one might suppose that a preliminary issue of fact should have its own law of burdens, proof, and pleading, like any issue in the case, but courts often leave the matter in great obscurity. F.R.E. 104(a) provides no express statement. Practice varies, although *Bourjaily* has indicated that preliminary facts under 104(a) are probably usually governed by the preponderance standard in federal court. Theoretically, preliminary facts may be assumed to exist, or not exist, unless and until evidence to the contrary appears. Either the proponent or the opponent of the evidence may have the burden, depending on the situation. For example, in the marital privilege illustration, the opponent of the evidence may have the burden to show marriage and privilege. In the hearsay exemption or exception situation, the proponent of the hearsay may have the burden to show that the conditions for the exemption or exception are fulfilled. But again, the matter is left in great obscurity by the courts.

Rule 104(a) does not require judges to limit what they hear in determining preliminary issues, to admissible evidence, except that privileged material is expressly forbidden. Courts frequently, however, examine in camera, allegedly privileged material to decide if the privilege bars that selfsame material itself from the jury. For example, in order to decide if the "crime-fraud exception" to attorney client privilege applies to an attorney letter offered to be put in evidence before the jury, the judge may examine the letter itself. This takes some stretched "interpreting" of the rule's prohibition of looking at privileged material. Perhaps the argument is that the material is not yet privileged. It is not privileged until the judge decides that it is, after the preliminary inquiry. See *United States v. Zolin* (S.Ct.1989).

At any rate, it is clear that the judge can consider information from a very wide range of sources that may not themselves be admissible. In deciding admissibility of hearsay under a hearsay exception or exemption, for example, it is now clear the judge can consider the content of the hearsay statement itself, even though this is not necessarily what was meant by the provision freeing the hearing from the ordinary rules of evidence. In *Bourjaily*, the Court allowed consideration of an alleged co-conspirator's statement in order to decide whether it qualified as a co-conspirator's statement. Such an approach has been criticized as "bootstrapping"—i.e., evidence pulling itself in by its own bootstraps. But supporters argue that more rigor is not required where the issue is only whether the jury can hear admittedly relevant evidence.

"Conditional Relevancy" and F.R.E. 104(b): Preserving Jury Decisionmaking When the Relevancy of One Piece of Evidence Depends on Another

Sometimes the *relevancy* of one piece of evidence depends on the establishment of a related fact. This is a preliminary fact, of sorts, too, but arguably it deserves different treatment. The F.R.E. call this "relevancy conditioned on fact." It is the subject of Rule 104(b). Under Rule 104(b), unlike Rule 104(a), the existence of the fact here is to be decided by the jury. The judge's only function is to decide whether there is minimally sufficient evidence to support a jury finding of it.

The distinction between "preliminary facts" under Rule 104(a) and "relevancy conditioned on fact" under Rule 104(b) is not always easy to draw. The difference has to do with whether the F.R.E. define the finding as a prerequisite to non-relevance-based admissibility, governed by subsection (a), or whether the one fact determines the relevancy of the other, which situation is governed by subsection (b).

For example, imagine a defendant accused of one crime, against whom the prosecution wishes to offer evidence of a similar, "signature" crime to prove the defendant's intent or identity. The Rules require that this evidence must actually pertain to intent or identity and that its prejudicial tendencies must not overwhelm this proper use. The judge must decide these issues as matters of "preliminary fact" under Rule 104(a).

But there is another condition to admissibility here, because the "signature" offense is relevant only if it is established that this defendant committed it. The relevance of the similar offense, in other words, is conditioned on the fact that the defendant now on trial was the perpetrator. In *Huddleston v. United States* (S.Ct. 1988), the Supreme Court held that this question is governed by Rule 104(b), not 104(a), and thus it is the jury who decides whether the defendant committed the other offense—and then decides how much weight to give it in deciding defendant's guilt of the primary offense. The judge's only function, under Rule 104(b), is to decide whether there is some evidence that defendant was the perpetrator of the similar offense—enough, at least, to support a jury finding to this effect, whatever the judge may think.

A skeptic might object to this resolution on the ground that there is no particular reason to define the findings concerning identity, intent, and prejudice as "preliminary facts" while the defendant-as-perpetrator problem is defined as a problem of "relevancy conditioned on fact." The skeptic has a point. There is little in these definitions to sharply distinguish the two applications. There is, however, something important that underlies the distinction. It preserves a wide role for the jury in the kinds of things citizens look to the jury for while deferring to the judge for things juries are not particularly good at. The jury is traditionally thought of as able to decide the who-was-the-perpetrator issue, while the judge more appropriately decides whether potential prejudice so overbalances probativity that the jury should not hear the evidence at all. In the final analysis, though, the perpetrator issue became one of relevancy conditioned on fact, primarily because the Supreme Court so characterized it.

In fact, scholars have debated the question whether "conditional" relevancy under Rule 104(b) is a useful concept at all, as distinguished from "relevancy" generally. Some suggest conditional relevancy is a myth. The classic case of conditional relevancy is a knife found in the possession of the knife-murder defendant. It is often said that finding a knife on defendant is irrelevant unless it was the knife used in the murder, if we put aside the argument that it may show familiarity-with-knives. But that is plainly false. It is *relevant* if it *might* be the knife used in the murder, no matter how small the possibility. The fact that a knife that *might be* the murder weapon was found on defendant advances slightly the possibility he possesses the murder weapon as compared with not finding any knife on him. This is true even without any proof this knife *was* the murder knife. For until proved otherwise, there is a possibility (no matter how tiny) that it was, and connecting him with it adds this tiny increment to the possibility he committed the murder. This tiny increment is enough, under the definition of relevancy in Rule 401 ("...any tendency to make the existence of any fact ... more probable..."). It might, however, be desirable to hold this evidence inadmissible on other grounds, such as its slim worth, its misleading nature to the jury, the likelihood of juror exaggeration or prejudice, and undue time consumption. But it is *relevant*. Indeed, the knife evidence would be relevant on this theory even if we don't know whether a gun or a knife or some other weapon was used in the murder, because it is possible it was a knife and possibly this one—possibilities that are not there if the evidence is not offered. See Rothstein, *Intellectual Coherence in an Evidence Code*, 28 Loyola (L.A.) L. Rev. 1259, 1265 (1995). Arguably relevancy always assumes unanswered fact questions upon which the actual connection to the case is conditioned. Every question of relevancy may be really a question of relevancy conditioned on fact and vice versa.

Relevancy conditioned on fact under Rule 104(b) need not be established by any *finding* on anyone's part. Rather the evidence will be admissible upon *some minimally sufficient showing* to the judge that a reasonable juror could find that the fact or condition exists, even if the judge doesn't believe it does. If this minimum showing is made and not wiped out, the jury receives the evidence and considers counter-showings in assessing weight. Probably there should be no instruction that the jury must actually find the fact establishing relevancy in some separate cerebration, although this is not entirely clear. The judge's role is intended to insure at least some possibility that the evidence has some worth before it is received. However, the judge can only rely on admissible evidence.

The F.R.E.'s requirements of authentication/identification of documents and items, and first-hand knowledge of witnesses, are in this category. Once the minimal prima facie showing is made, attempts to defeat it are normally matters of weight for the jury. F.R.E. 602 (first-hand knowledge), 901(a) (authentication) and 1008 (the best evidence rule) expressly provide that certain fact questions determining the operation of these admissibility rules will be handled pursuant to the scheme of 104(b)— i.e., with the jury making the real determination, after the judge has performed only a screening function. Most rules, however, do not specify whether 104(a) or 104(b) applies to their factual requirements, and the matter is left to analysis and decisions.

In conclusion, the differences between Rule 104(a) and (b) that are likely to be overlooked can be summarized as follows. First, the preponderance standard before the judge, of Rule 104(a), is a heavier one to meet than the 104(b) standard, which only requires the judge to find that a reasonable juror could support the determination. Second, Rule 104(a) permits the judge to consult inadmissible evidence while Rule 104(b) requires admissible evidence because it is the jury making the ultimate valuation.

IV. ROLE OF RULES BEYOND EXCLUSION OF PIECES OF EVIDENCE FROM JURIES: NON–JURY & ADMINISTRATIVE TRIALS; APPEALS; JUDGE & ATTORNEY COMMENT

Non–Jury Trials and Administrative Hearings

Evidence is less likely to be inadmissible in non-jury trials because judges are not as susceptible to misleading and prejudice as juries. Judges also may be more able to disregard certain improper evidence or inferences. Thus also mistrials as a remedy for prejudicial material that has "snuck" in are less likely; and evidence is more frequently believed confinable to proper uses where proper and improper ones are possible.

To what extent should evidence law that has evolved mainly for jury trials be modified where the judge is the trier of fact? Some decisions have suggested that exclusion for prejudice, misleadingness, or confusion, is inappropriate in non-jury cases except perhaps in rare instances where judges are deemed to be susceptible to the same sort of undue influence as juries. See, e.g., *Gulf States Utilities Co. v. Ecodyne Corp.* (5th Cir.1981) (prejudice factor in F.R.E. 403 "has no ... application in bench trials").

The argument is this. Exclusion based on these negative factors in jury cases presupposes that judges can spot and quantify the negative influences, decide what the evidence is really worth without them, and compare that with what the jury will think the evidence is worth. In sum, the judge decides if the trial will be better off (or more accurate) with or without the evidence. See Rule 403. Obviously then, judges can evaluate such evidence properly, uninfluenced by the negative factors. Exclusion in a judge trial would require the judge to first hear the evidence anyway. So it would be futile to then declare the evidence "excluded". Only in exceptional cases—for example where a confession is legally involuntary but may recount something only the criminal perpetrator would know—should the evidence be excluded on grounds that the judge is as susceptible to it as a jury, and that the judge need not hear it to exclude it, since facts of involuntariness can be considered by the judge without hearing the confession.

Generally, however, courts adhere to the rubric that the same rules of evidence apply to jury and non-jury cases alike. The F.R.E. make no express distinction. Still, the concepts of prejudice, misleadingness, confusion, and protraction will produce some results that are different in jury and non-jury cases. This is so because, as indicated above, what is likely to be misconstrued or exaggerated when a jury applies law to fact will not necessarily be misconstrued or exaggerated by a judge, nor will as much time be needed to put facts in perspective.

Of perhaps more impact, however, is the informal appellate practice of giving trial judges in bench trials a greater benefit of the doubt. Appellate courts treat erroneous exclusion of evidence in the same manner as they do for jury trials. But with respect to evidence alleged to have been erroneously *admitted,* they indulge a presumption that, if there was sufficient competent evidence to support the findings, the trial judge, being knowledgeable of the law, relied on competent evidence only, whatever else may also have been heard at trial. This presumption sometimes prevails even in the face of an expression by the trial judge of an erroneous view of which evidence was admissible. The presumption would thus be overcome only when there is a clear indication or expression that the judge actually *relied* on inadmissible evidence.

In consequence of all this, trial judges in non-jury cases tend to admit freely ("I'll admit this piece of evidence for whatever it is worth"), sidestepping or reserving ruling on admissibility questions that may be raised about the evidence. They then hold ruling unnecessary on the grounds that their final verdict is reached on the basis of the *unquestioned* evidence. If they have ruled to admit, they find the verdict facts expressly on the basis of evidence that has not been questioned.

As a result of these several factors, rules of evidence have a somewhat muffled impact in judge trials. Privileges, however, are generally fully enforced.

Rules of evidence may or may not be enforced in administrative proceedings, depending upon the administrative tribunal's particular adjective law. Privilege, however, is usually recognized. The law or regulations of a number of federal agencies have incorporated the Federal Rules of Evidence, at least to some extent, either expressly or by reference to "the rules that govern evidence in non-jury trials in Federal District Courts" or similar language, often with certain exceptions. Section 556(d) of the Administrative Procedure Act does not require the F.R.E. to be applied and appears more receptive to evidence. As a practical matter, a large number of agencies find the Federal Rules of Evidence influential in carrying out the general mandate that reliable evidence be used. Some authority has developed in various jurisdictions that administrative agency rulings on evidence may not be more restrictive, or more prone to exclude, than the rules applicable in courts.

Harmless Error and Abuse of Discretion

Errors committed by the trial court may be regarded by the appellate court as "harmless."

The standard for determining what constitutes "prejudicial" (reversible) as opposed to "harmless" (non-reversible) error varies from jurisdiction to jurisdiction, and may also vary according to whether a criminal, civil, or criminal-constitutional issue is involved. The variance will be in the degree of probability with which it must appear that the error affected the verdict, from "may have" through "probably did." One articulation regards error (in the admission of evidence) as harmless if there was sufficient other evidence upon which a reasonable juror could have based the verdict that was handed down, even if the erroneously admitted piece of evidence probably was the decisive one in the jury's mind.

F.R.E. 103(a) provides, somewhat vaguely, that errors are not cognizable unless they affect a "substantial right" of a party. The Federal Rules of Civil and Criminal Procedure have similarly vague provisions.

The United States Supreme Court has restricted state and federal courts' freedom to choose among these tests in cases of errors affecting certain constitutional rights of the accused in criminal proceedings, indicating that some can never be harmless, and requiring with respect to others that the error be "harmless beyond a reasonable doubt." Other views may apply to yet other constitutional errors. We are not speaking of the standard for determining error in the first place, but only for constitutional harmlessness. A different standard may be used to test the constitutionality of the underlying evidence rule or ruling. For example, the Supreme Court has stated that due process only bars evidence that is "so extremely unfair that its admission violates 'fundamental conceptions of justice.' " *Dowling v. United States* (S.Ct.1990).

Curative jury instructions often can render harmless, an error in the admission of evidence (or admission for too broad a purpose). But this principle, too, has its limits, particularly in criminal cases of constitutional error against the defendant.

For example, the United States Supreme Court has held, at least on particular facts, and sometimes more generally, that, e.g., an instruction to the jury to disregard an involuntary confession will not cure the harmfulness of error in its admission; that a co-defendant's confession implicating the defendant, even if subjected to a limiting instruction, ordinarily cannot be introduced in a joint trial without opportunity of the latter to effectively cross examine the confessor and in most situations such introduction, even with limiting instructions would be prejudicial error; and that a jury instruction to disregard evidence of former convictions that were obtained without counsel did not render introduction of the evidence harmless.

In *Arizona v. Fulminante* (S.Ct.1991), the United States Supreme Court discussed the constitutional-harmless-error doctrine in detail, holding that even trial errors of constitutional dimension against a criminal defendant (here admission of an involuntary confession) can be found harmless at least if the harmlessness can be inferred beyond a reasonable doubt. Only as to "structural" defects (which this was not) will the question whether they were "harmless" not be asked. Only in such "structural" cases will reversal be automatic if constitutional error is found. A structural error is one that not only undermines confidence in the result, but destroys the very structure of the trial process as a reliable method for determining results at all. Examples of structural error are the failure to appoint counsel or the absence of an impartial judge. Thus, evidentiary rulings almost always are subject to a harmless error analysis. *Neder v. United States* (S.Ct.1999), the Court's most recent harmless error decision, held that the doctrine applies even to a jury instruction that omits an element of an offense.

Thus, harmless error analysis often makes it difficult to obtain a reversal on appeal based on evidentiary rulings. This difficulty is compounded because most evidentiary decisions are routinely reviewed on an abuse of discretion standard. In other words, an appellate court will not substitute its own judgment (de novo) even though it disagrees with the trial judge. This also results in seeming inconsistencies in case law, since an appellate court can affirm two decisions, one admitting and the other excluding the same type of evidence in substantially the same circumstances, because deference is given to reasonable rulings by trial judges.

Judicial Comment on Weight of Evidence

Many jurisdictions have rules against the judge commenting to the jury on the weight of the evidence. In others, the judge may make balanced comment, so long as the jurors are given to understand that they are free to decide for themselves.

In federal courts, trial judges are allowed to give jurors their views as to weight of the evidence. This power of the judge was codified in an original draft of the Federal Rules of Evidence as a power to "fairly and impartially sum up the evidence and comment to the jury upon the weight of the evidence and the credibility of the witnesses" at the close of all the evidence and argument of counsel, so long as the judge also "instructs the jury that they are to determine for themselves the weight of the evidence and the credit to be given to the witnesses and that they are not bound by the judge's summation and comment."

The deletion of these provisions from the Federal Rules of Evidence as finally enacted was not intended to abridge the power. Rather, the subject was deemed to be a matter of "procedure," not "evidence." The thought also seems to have been, however, that codifying the power would over-encourage its use. Dubbed "controversial," the power was finally implicitly but not explicitly left with the judge, who often declines to use it.

Sometimes the power to comment is expressed more cautiously as merely a power to "marshal" or "summarize" the evidence.

Other jurisdictions may expressly prohibit summarization or direct comment by the judge on weight or credibility. The prohibition is normally put in terms of a ban on direct individualized comment only, because the judge in all jurisdictions is allowed to give instructions to disregard, limiting instructions, instructions concerning presumptions, or similar statements concerning generalized types of evidence, given when evidence is received or in the court's general "charge" to the jury at the end of the trial before jury deliberations.

Even in "no comment" jurisdictions judges may instruct on permissible and impermissible inferences from generalized categories or kinds of evidence, such as evidence of flight, attempted suicide, types of impeachment, etc. The instructions may refer to various factual conditions under which such inferences may be drawn, perhaps covering only those involved in the actual case. They may also refer to various considerations the jury should make with regard to evaluating various kinds of witness testimony, such as eyewitness testimony or expert testimony, again perhaps referring only to factors or considerations that may be raised by the evidence in the particular case.

"Pattern" jury instructions (substantive, procedural, and evidentiary), perhaps drafted by bar or bench groups and based on cases, exist in many jurisdictions, and they frequently achieve official or quasi-official status. Lawyers may still fight tooth and nail over which of the "standardized" instructions should and should not be given, with what alterations for the particular case, and what other evidentiary instructions should or should not be given, and the exact wording of both kinds. Usually there is a procedure for attorneys on both sides to submit proposed sets of instructions to the judge for consideration and a hearing on pros and cons of each instruction. This usually takes place toward the end of the trial before the case is submitted to the jury for decision, but can take place earlier.

Since the jury is likely to look to the judge for guidance, instructions can be very important. Lawyers' final jury arguments are likely to be in terms of the instructions, in part. Even when the judge opts to give the instructions after closing arguments rather than before, he will have let the parties know before final argument what the instructions will be.

Although lawmakers and courts have not often realized it, liberalization of the law of evidence, to increase admissibility and judicial discretion, may be more acceptable where a broad judicial power to comment or at least warn against pitfalls is also incorporated. For example, the liberalized reception of hearsay evidence and of expert testimony on ultimate issues found under the Federal Rules of Evidence makes more sense if the jury can be judicially cautioned about the weight of such evidence.

A judge also has the prerogative in most jurisdictions to examine, and even call to the stand, witnesses. Exercise of this power can imply a view regarding the weight of evidence. A trial judge oversteps the appropriate boundaries when he or she can be characterized as having become an advocate for a party.

Argument by Attorneys to the Jury

Jury argument is subject to limits growing out of the rules of admissibility of evidence, the rules of professional ethical conduct, and local decisions and practice.

The lawyer is allowed to directly address or argue to the jury only at the opening and closing of the trial.

Most limitations on argument to the jury concerning evidence are implicit in the evidence rules and rulings themselves. The rules governing professional ethics in the particular jurisdiction and judicial and other interpretations thereof also impose limits. Other judicial decisions do so as well; as may local custom and practice.

Just a few examples will suffice to illustrate the range of things found:

The attorney's own personal knowledge or personal belief in the truth or falsity of the evidence is ordinarily not proper argument. See, e.g., American Bar Association ("A.B.A.") Code of Professional Responsibility, DR 7–106; A.B.A. Model Rule of Professional Conduct 3.4; A.B.A. Defense Function Standard 7.7; A.B.A. Prosecution Function Standard 5.8; all setting out this and some other restrictions on argument. A lawyer should not weep. See, e.g., *Ferguson v. Moore* (Tenn.1897); *People v. McGrane* (N.Y.App.Div.1960). Constitutional law prohibits any direct or indirect adverse comment on the criminal defendant's invocation of the fifth amendment privilege not to testify. The judge is similarly prohibited and may have to give a jury instruction against drawing any adverse inference, at least if requested by the defense.

Where failure to produce a witness is sought to be pointed out by one side against the other, it is usually held improper if the witness was equally available to both, although the argument may be allowed if the witness is associated with the opponent. Similar restrictions attend the frequently found "missing witness" jury instruction. Most courts ban the so-called "per diem" argument whereby counsel for a personal injury plaintiff, in closing argument addressed to compensatory damages, asks the jurors to imagine what pay they themselves would want in order for them to voluntarily undergo for one day, hour, minute, or second, pain or disability like the plaintiff's, and asks them to multiply that figure by the expected duration of the plaintiff's condition. Some courts ban likening parties or witnesses to famous villains or heroes of history.

Opening statements or closing arguments are improper if they draw inferences the evidence in the case cannot reasonably be construed to support, or if they distort the applicable law. See DR 7–106; Model Rule 3.4; Defense Function Standards 7.4, 7.7, 7.8; Prosecution Function Standards 5.5, 5.8, 5.9. Thus, it is sound practice to learn what the judge will instruct on the law before closing argument.

Along these lines, juries are frequently instructed that statements of the attorneys are not evidence; that their own recollection of the evidence governs; and that the law is to be taken from the judge, not the attorneys.

The attorneys may, however, draw (or more properly, urge the drawing of) inferences liberally from the evidence, even if there are opposing inferences. The main limit is that the inference must be a reasonable one. Likewise it is proper to suggest reasonable conclusions about credibility. Attorneys must strive not to couch any of this in terms of their own personal beliefs, but this rule is leniently applied so long as attorneys do not suggest they know something the jury does not.

Thus, it is not uncommon for one attorney to argue that a particular witness's hesitating testimony, varying statements, or relation to a party make the witness unworthy of belief, while the opposing attorney may use the same factors to argue instead that the witness is credible.

The attorneys can state correct law and use simple examples or analogies to explain such concepts as negligence, breach of contract, or burden of proof. The limit is reached when the argument distorts the law or urges the jury to disregard it. Thus, a "golden rule" argument, urging jurors to find for the plaintiff as a means of fulfilling their duty to "do unto others as you would have them do unto you," has been held improper because it is inconsistent with the jurors' duty, instead, to base their verdict on the preponderance of evidence and the law.

Argumentation includes both the opening statement, before the evidence, and the final argument, after it is closed. Lawyers' addressing the jury at any other time during the trial phase is improper.

The purpose of an opening statement is supposed to be simply to tell what that side in good faith expects the evidence will be and will show (see, e.g., Prosecution Function Standard 5.5, Defense Function Standard 7.4). Thus it is frequently said not to be "argument" at all, although factual inferences are often allowed within the limits indicated. Arguing that there is a reasonable doubt about guilt, has been held improper in opening statement in a number of localities.

Closing arguments perform a similar but broader function, looking back at the trial retrospectively. They urge on the jury what that particular side feels they have proved and what can be fairly inferred from it. There is considerably more latitude here. Lots of argumentation is allowed but still within limits of reasonableness. Closing arguments combine factual inferences with application of the law all in the light most favorable to the arguer's side. See Prosecution Function Standard 5.8; Defense Function Standard 7.7; cf. DR 7–106.

Attorneys sometimes, improperly, use evidentiary objections and responsive statements to communicate certain matters to the witness or to the jury (rather than waiting for final argument), or to fluster or break the dramatic impact of the opponent. Courts take a dim view of verbose "speaking objections" made before the jury for ulterior purposes. Legitimate evidentiary matters that are likely to influence the jury should, ideally, be taken up at the bench ("may we approach the bench, your honor"), or in chambers, or before the trial. On the other hand, brief objections before the jury may be regarded by the trial judge as more economical and expeditious in many instances. The attorney must always balance many conflicting factors: pleasing the judge; the risk of creating adverse reaction in the jury by objecting (e.g., a smell of "cover-up," obstructionism, distrust of the jury, technicalism, or delaying tactics), particularly if ruled against by the judge; the need to protect the record, i.e., preserve errors for appeal; the need to keep out truly damaging evidence; the need to avoid the jury hearing arguments they shouldn't hear; etc. Sometimes asking to approach the bench will be appropriate, sometimes not. Objections before the jury may sometimes need to be short, sometimes longer. Sometimes forsaking even valid objections can be wise if the evidence is not particularly important.

Obtaining in limine evidentiary rulings outside the presence of the jury should be considered by counsel if she anticipates that there will be prejudicial references to inadmissible evidence in opponent's opening statement (as well as in the more standard situations where she anticipates she or her opponent may offer evidence at trial whose admissibility may be questioned). The remedy when opposing counsel does mention inadmissible evidence in opening is to request an immediate curative instruction or mistrial if tactically advisable.

Alleged misconduct in closing arguments rarely results in reversals because great latitude of argument is allowed and "it's understood it's just argument." Alleged misstatements are often regarded as harmless in the totality of the whole trial.

Many lawyers believe objections during their opponent's opening or closing statements are likely to be counterproductive because of juror disapproval.

CHAPTER 2

JUDICIAL NOTICE, PRESUMP-
TIONS, AND BURDENS: SUB-
STITUTES FOR EVIDENCE

I. JUDICIAL NOTICE

Judicial notice is a shortcut that dispenses with proof, on the ground that there are some propositions that are so self-evident or capable of verification that they do not need to be proven.

Do we really need a witness to tell us what time the sun set on a particular day or that Independence Day is July 4th? Judicial notice has long been a way to permit litigants to shortcut proving the obvious. An analogous shortcut can be accomplished by the special civil discovery mechanism known as requests for admissions. Stipulations can accomplish a similar result. So can partial directed verdicts of particular factual findings. In short, there are ways to supply facts to the jury other than through evidence. Judicial notice is prominent among them.

"Adjudicative" Facts Under F.R.E. 201

F.R.E. 201 provides for judicial notice of "adjudicative" facts if they are indisputable enough. Adjudicative facts are what we would generally call the "who, what, why, when and where" of the particular lawsuit. Under this Rule, adjudicative facts not subject to reasonable dispute may be judicially noticed (and then read out to the jury) if they are (1) "generally known within the territorial jurisdiction of the trial court" or (2) capable of accurate and ready determination from "reliable sources whose accuracy cannot reasonably be questioned." A party is entitled to an opportunity to be heard on the propriety of taking judicial notice, but this opportunity may occur even after the decision to take judicial notice has been made. Judicial notice is mandatory under Rule 201 if a party requests it and supplies the judge with "the necessary information." The necessary information is not defined. Presumably it encompasses a source "whose accuracy cannot reasonably be questioned" as referred to in the rule, such as a calendar if one seeks to prove the date of a holiday or an almanac to prove the time of sunset. Even in the absence of a request, a court still may take judicial notice of a properly noticeable fact in its discretion.

The Rule states that judicial notice can be taken at any time, or any stage of proceedings, including the pleading phase, or even on appeal. For example, Rule 201 supplies the only way to contradict factual statements in pleadings challenged for failure to state a claim. If, for example, a pleading were to state that Christmas Day occurred in July, the court would be free to disregard this allegation, even though it must accept all other kinds of factual assertions as true for purposes of a motion to dismiss.

In civil cases, the jury is instructed to accept the judicially noticed fact as true. In criminal cases, Rule 201(g) mandates that the jury be told it is not required to accept any judicially noticed fact as conclusive. Arguably this provision means that in a criminal jury trial, the court cannot take judicial notice of a true adjudicative fact at any time after it instructs the jury. Thus, in federal court, if a prosecutor forgot to introduce evidence or obtain judicial notice that a bank was federally insured, or that a park, prison or military base was federal in nature, there would technically be no evidence on a jurisdictionally required element, and the omission arguably could not be cured after, e.g., a guilty verdict. The result would be an acquittal. This principle would create some anomalous acquittals (with retrial perhaps impossible owing to the constitutional prohibition of double jeopardy which operates when there was insufficient evidence to establish guilt at the first trial). Courts have sought to avoid this effect (not always successfully) by deciding that the indisputable facts at issue are really legislative rather than adjudicative or by some other sleight-of-hand.

This problem does not arise in states that follow Uniform Rule 201(g), which requires juries to accept judicially noticed facts as conclusive in all cases. In this regard, F.R.E. 201's requirement of a nonbinding jury instruction in criminal cases arguably is illogical. It operates when the fact allows no reasonable dispute, yet expressly invites the jury to dispute it anyway. This consideration supports the Uniform Rule. The F.R.E. requirement, however, can be defended in spite of its apparent anomaly, by reference to the policy in favor of requiring each factual element of a crime to be found by the jury. This may even be a constitutional requirement. See *Apprendi v. New Jersey* (S.Ct.2000); *Ring v. Arizona* (S.Ct.2002). Cf. *Harris v. United States* (S.Ct.2002); *United States v. Cotton* (S.Ct.2002).

"Legislative" and "Evaluative" Facts

Rule 201 does not cover any type of fact that is not "adjudicative." This limit of coverage means that when judicial notice is taken of facts that are not adjudicative, the determination is not bound by any of the restrictions in the rule regarding sources, indisputability, or the level of or kind of demonstration needed before taking judicial notice; or regarding advance notice, hearing, jury instructions, or indeed any other provisions of the rule.

These non-adjudicative facts, not governed by Rule 201, are typically classified as "evaluative" or "legislative."

Evaluative facts are those which are so basic that they inform how we think about the world or about particular evidence. For example, if someone testifies that it was raining at the time an accident occurred, no one need say that rain makes roads slippery or hampers visibility. And although jurors evaluating evidence about a falling body cannot do so without knowing that there is such a thing as gravity, the law imposes no requirement that this well-known fact be conveyed to the jurors by documents or witnesses. These are evaluative facts rather than adjudicative ones. Evaluative facts, then, are common-sense notions, which we allow jurors to use in evaluating the evidence without being told. Indeed, different jurors may disagree about them (theoretically so long as each is reasonable). For example they may disagree about how much more stopping distance is necessitated by a certain degree of rain.

"Legislative" facts are more difficult to categorize, since they are not necessarily facts at all, let alone indisputable. Legislative facts include any reasonable proposition utilized by judges in their creation or interpretation of law. Legislative history, articles not in evidence, or even informal discussions with experts to better determine policy issues may be the sources. Or just the judge's experience. Actually, a fact need not even concern legislation to be "legislative". Evolution of common law is based on judges' views of societal propositions, which properly are considered as legislative facts. For example, just in the field of Evidence, the judicial creation, maintenance, and contouring, of husband-wife privilege, has depended upon disputable judicial notions that husbands and wives will communicate more with a privilege, would resent adverse spousal testimony, and that therefore strengthened, communicative marriages result from privilege, which in consequence produce certain specific benefits to society in a measure that outweighs the degree of loss of truth in the litigation.

Judicial notice of law is also not subject to Rule 201. Federal Rule of Criminal Procedure 26.1 and Federal Rule of Civil Procedure 44.1 govern proof of foreign law. In many jurisdictions, like California, a separate evidentiary rule exists for noticing law, whether local, within the United States, or foreign.

II. BURDENS OF PROOF

The Burdens of Pleading, Production, and Persuasion

In every case, for every issue, there is a burden of production of evidence (or burden of going forward with the evidence), and a persuasion burden. Discharging, or preventing the discharge of, these burdens is the goal of introducing evidence. There also is a burden of pleading, which defines which party must raise the issue in the pleadings.

The allocation of the burdens of pleading, production and persuasion differs on an issue-by-issue basis. For any particular question, the allocation and weight of the burden may have evolved from considerations of convenience, of relative accessibility of proof, of who is disturbing the status quo, of what is likely to be the truth in the absence of evidence, of the unusualness of the claim, of whether the matter raises an exception to a general rule, or of public policies such as deterrence. A particular burden may be on one party as to some issues, and on the other party as to other issues in the same case. Even as to one particular issue, all three burdens may not be on the same party.

Furthermore, the production burden may "shift" from one party to the other during the course of the trial. What this means is that as evidence is introduced, first one party, then the other, may run the risk of a directed verdict or equivalent ruling if he allows the state of the evidence to remain as it is. The party on whom this risk rests is said to have the burden of "going forward with the evidence," i.e., of producing evidence.

The Burden of Production

A party has the burden of *production* when, if he allows the evidence to stay as it is, the issue will be concluded against him as a matter of law. For example, at the close of the prosecution's evidence in a murder case, and again at the end of all of the evidence, the judge can direct an acquittal unless some reasonable juror could find beyond a reasonable doubt that the defendant killed the victim. In the absence of evidence meeting this standard, the prosecutor has failed to carry the burden of production. Thus, the state will suffer an adverse judicial ruling establishing that fact without the aid of the jury.

In a civil wrongful death case, all the judge need be able to say is that some reasonable juror could find the fact by a preponderance of the evidence. In other words, the standard for the persuasion burden influences the production burden. The failure to meet the production burden, and hence the resulting court order (called generically a "peremptory" ruling or order), may pertain to only one issue, foreclosing only it from further debate; or, if that issue is determinative, the ruling will determine the entire case. Owing to the criminal defendant's right to trial by jury, however, the prosecutor in a criminal case cannot obtain a peremptory ruling on the elements of the offense.

Putting aside any presumption or special criminal dispensation, the standard for a peremptory judicial ruling on a matter of fact (e.g., summary judgment, directed verdict, or judgment notwithstanding the verdict) is whether a reasonable person could find in favor of the non-moving party on the issue (regardless of what the judge thinks personally). If some reasonable person could, the motion must be denied. The jury must be allowed the chance to find for the non-moving party. If no reasonable person could, the motion should be granted, to prevent an irrational finding by the jury. The losing party is said to have failed to carry the burden of production.

The Burden of Persuasion

In effect, the fact-finders in a case are instructed by the law that they are to resolve each issue in a stated way, unless convinced to a certain degree (i.e., by a preponderance, or by clear and convincing evidence, or beyond a reasonable doubt) that it is the other way. This process may be compared to the effect of an electric switch, which starts out in one of its two positions, and rests there with some degree of stickiness unless and until sufficient force is mustered to dislodge it to the other position. The party who loses the issue if it is not dislodged has the "burden of persuasion," and the degree of force needed is defined by the standard (preponderance, clear and convincing, or beyond reasonable doubt) for that burden. In other words, the switch starts out lodged in the position that is against the position of the party with the burden.

Let us return to our example of a murder prosecution. Assume that the prosecution has discharged its production burden and the case "gets to the jury" on the issue. Still, the prosecution will suffer an adverse verdict if the jury is not persuaded beyond a reasonable doubt that the defendant killed the victim. Thus, as respects this issue, the risk of non-persuasion, or the so-called burden of persuasion, is on the prosecution, as was the production burden.

To what degree must the prosecution convince the minds of the jurors? The jurors must be convinced "beyond a reasonable doubt," and they must be so instructed. Belief that it is slightly more probable than not that defendant killed the victim would be insufficient to convict. While proof corresponding to a 51% probability would be insufficient in a criminal case, it might be sufficient for a plaintiff's verdict in an analogous civil wrongful death action, because for most civil issues, the persuasion burden is by a preponderance of the evidence—which refers to quality not quantity and means more likely than not. Thus, for example, O.J. Simpson's criminal acquittal of the much publicized killing, was not necessarily inconsistent with the civil jury's subsequent verdict holding him civilly liable for the same killing. (Nor is it technically double jeopardy although many are troubled by such multiple proceedings.)

III. PRESUMPTIONS

Mandatory and Permissive Presumptions

A presumption is a legal mechanism that helps a party meet, or prevent another party from meeting, or on occasion shifts, a burden or burdens of proof.

A "presumption" is a direction of law to a judge indicating what satisfies the production burden on the presumed fact. Alternatively, or in addition, it may provide a legal instruction to the jury, to be heeded in considering whether the persuasion burden is overcome. In the case of a true or "mandatory" presumption, the mandate is that if fact A is established then fact B *must be* taken as similarly established, where there is no evidence directed either way at fact B itself. A "permissive" presumption is similar, except that a reasonable person *may*, rather than must, find fact B. Whether, to what extent, and how, the permissive presumption should "tilt" the finding toward B is controversial.

The initial fact, from which the presumption follows, is called the "basic" fact. The target fact that is inferred from the basic fact is called the "presumed" fact. For example, there is a presumption that a properly mailed letter was received. Proper mailing is the basic fact; receipt the presumed fact. For a true or mandatory presumption, the presumed fact (receipt) is conclusively established by establishment of the basic fact (mailing) even if there is no other evidence supporting the presumed fact, so long as none opposes it (even circumstantially).

Thus far we have assumed that there is no evidence in the case directed at the presumed fact, B, itself. If there is such evidence and it tends to rebut presumed fact B, what should be the role of the presumption? When there is reasonably acceptable evidence of non-B, the presumption, whether permissive or mandatory, cannot command that B follows, no matter how conclusively established A is. (We assume that the presumption is not of the narrow class called "irrebuttable" or "conclusive" presumptions, which actually are equivalent to a legal definition that fact A equals fact B. Such presumptions are, then, rules of substantive law, not evidence or procedure.)

What remaining role the presumption is to have, if any, upon introduction of evidence of non-B, and what the jury is to be told about the presumption, if anything, is highly controversial and varies widely from, e.g., "no effect" through "evidence of B" to imposing a burden to persuade of non-B.

Criminal Presumptions and Their Restriction by the Constitution

In criminal cases, a constitutional right-to-jury-trial problem and other constitutional problems can arise if jurors are told, for example because of a presumption, that they *must* find a critical fact against the defendant. It may also be unconstitutional to have presumptions against the criminal defendant that too strongly *tilt* jurors toward establishing factual elements of the crime. The instructions to jurors will be examined closely to see if they could be construed in these impermissible ways by the jurors. Thus, In *Sandstrom v. Montana* (S.Ct.1979), the Supreme Court held that instructing a jury that a person intends the ordinary consequences of his acts was unconstitutional because it may have been interpreted by the jury to constrain them too much on the issue of intent or even to shift the burden of persuasion to the defendant to prove non-intent. It risked lessening the prosecution's constitutional burden to prove to the jury each element of the crime beyond a reasonable doubt as required by due process as articulated in *In re Winship* (S.Ct.1970). Accord, *Francis v. Franklin* (S.Ct.1985). See also *Apprendi* and the cases cited with it under Judicial Notice, above.

Criminal presumptions (of elements against the accused) that clearly are said in instructions to have weaker effect stand on a better footing than the *Sandstrom* presumption. The test of the constitutional validity under the federal due process clause of *very* weak presumptions was established by the Supreme Court in *Ulster County Court of New York v. Allen* (S.Ct.1979). It is a relatively easy-to-pass test: There must be merely a "rational connection" (or common-sense connection) between the basic and presumed facts, or between fact A and fact B, as these facts exist in the context of the case.

Thus, the *facts of the particular case* are to be taken into account in deciding whether this test is met.

Slightly stronger presumptions may need to meet a slightly more rigorous "rational connection" test: Fact A must be sufficient to justify a rational conclusion of fact B beyond a reasonable doubt, and the connection must be found apart from the particular facts of the case; although apparently it may be based on facts found by Congress and not otherwise apparent.

In *Ulster County* itself, the defendants were passengers in a car where a gun was found. The applicable New York law created a presumption that, from their presence in the car, possession of the weapon on the part of each passenger could be inferred if the jury so desired. It was clear in the jury instructions that the prosecution still had to prove possession beyond a reasonable doubt, but the presumption could be considered by the jury or not, as they in their complete discretion saw fit, in deciding whether that burden was met. It was not stated that the presumption alone could be sufficient. The jury was totally free to consider all the relevant facts.

The Court applied the weaker rational connection test, as described above, and found the test met. The Court admitted that, in general, it may not always follow that guns found on premises or in cars are possessed by all who are present, when one considers hitch-hikers, or guns hidden in trunks or glove compartments, or otherwise concealed. Nevertheless, in this case, the gun was large, within the reach of all, and sticking out of the bag of the only minor passenger, a 16–year-old girl. The gun readily could have been stashed there at the last minute by any of the passengers. It was reasonable to assume possession on the part of the other adult passengers in the absence of contrary facts, and with this simple conclusion, the presumption was constitutional.

The relationship between burdens and presumptions in criminal cases is illustrated by the Supreme Court cases of *Mullaney v. Wilbur* (S.Ct.1975) and *Patterson v. New York* (S.Ct.1977). In *Mullaney*, a presumption, rendered in an instruction to the jury as shifting the burden of persuasion to the murder defendant (to prove by a preponderance) on the issue of "malice aforethought" (meaning not done in the heat of passion on sudden adequate provocation, which would reduce the homicide to manslaughter), was held unconstitutional. This holding followed because, as is indicated above, due process requires that each element of the crime be proved by the prosecution to the jury beyond a reasonable doubt—and malice aforethought was an element of the crime.

In contrast, *Patterson,* in a factually similar case, permitted similar burden shifting on the issue of "extreme emotional disturbance", which, like the malice aforethought issue in *Mullaney*, would reduce murder to manslaughter. It was permitted so long as the issue was drafted, in the statute defining the crime, as an affirmative defense, as in *Patterson*, not as an element of the offense, which the prosecution must prove, as in *Mullaney*. This seems to place form over substance. But perhaps the Court began to see, after *Mullaney,* that if this could not be done, legislatures might forgo giving defendants any escape along these lines at all.

As a result of *Patterson*, when one considers the constitutionality of placing the burden on the defendant, the focus is on the legislature's drafting of the particular criminal statutory offense under which the defendant is charged. Therefore, burden-shifting for many issues thought of as elements defining the crime may still withstand constitutional scrutiny, if they simply are designated as affirmative defenses in that statute rather than part of the crime's definition. The Supreme Court has upheld burden shifting on the issue of self-defense, for example, on the theory that this was an affirmative defense. *Martin v. Ohio* (S.Ct.1987). Burden shifting on insanity has also been allowed. However, it may still be unconstitutional, for example, to shift the burden to the defendant to prove his alibi, because the prosecution has the obligation to prove the defendant committed the crime beyond a reasonable doubt. "The crime" may have certain irreducible elements (perhaps as determined by history or importance) that must be proved by the prosecution, however designated in the statute. The state should not be able to in effect largely evade its burden to prove the essence of the crime, by simply designating a rebuttal of central factual matter an affirmative defense called alibi. The *degree* of the burden shifted to defendant may also matter. Cf. the Supreme Court decision in *Cooper v. Oklahoma* (S.Ct.1996), holding that although it is constitutional for a state to presume a defendant competent, requiring the defendant to demonstrate incompetency by any standard greater than a preponderance of the evidence violates due process.

Evidence Rebutting the Presumed Fact: What Effect?

We will consider the question in this heading in the context of civil cases, to avoid the special complications of criminal cases.

The effect to be given a presumption if there is evidence of non-B (i.e., any direct or circumstantial evidence rebutting the presumed fact, B) usually is left to be treated by judicial decision. Such questions sometimes have been treated obscurely and inconsistently even within the same jurisdiction, concerning the same presumption. Occasionally attempts have been made to codify particular answers.

In order to examine some of the possible answers, let us again consider the common presumption that delivery of a letter (fact B, or the presumed fact) is presumed from proper mailing (fact A, or the basic fact). Let us assume that the plaintiff, who normally has the burden on such things, relies solely on the presumption to prove delivery. If it is a mandatory presumption, then once proper mailing is established, delivery *must be* taken as established by the judge and jury if there is no evidence of non-delivery. The plaintiff would be entitled to an instruction requiring the jury to do so. If the presumption were only *permissive*, we would merely have a jury issue as to delivery. Should jurors be told to give any special weight to the fact of proper mailing in this determination? Answers have varied.

The harder question, however, concerns evidence that rebuts the presumed fact. Suppose that the defendant has introduced some somewhat creditable evidence of non-delivery (non-B)—for example, the defendant's mail-room clerk testifies that he does not remember receiving the letter, and the circumstances are such that one could feel that he would remember if he had received it. In this situation courts have used a wealth of picturesque rationales, to reach a dizzying array of results concerning what, if any, is to be the remaining effect of the presumption. Here are just a few.

View (1): The "Bursting Bubble" Theory, or Presumptions as "Bats of the Night". One view is that the presumption, and, under one version, even the common-sense notion underlying the presumption, disappears from the case completely. Thus, the presumption plays no role after the introduction of the defendant's evidence of non-B, and the case is to be determined exactly as if it and perhaps the common-sense notion never existed. A party who depended upon the presumption could lose as a matter of law unless the other evidence, unaided by the presumption or its common-sense equivalent, furnishes sufficient proof. This treatment of presumptions, in one or other of its variants, has sometimes been called the "bursting bubble" theory. Presumptions have been likened to "bats of the night," called out only when the issue is obscured by darkness. They "take flight" in the "light of real proof." In our hypothetical case, defendant's evidence that the mail clerk does not remember delivery is weak—but it is some evidence rebutting the presumed fact. In the absence of other evidence, plaintiff may lose under the fullest version of the bursting bubble theory, because the presumption and its underlying common sense notion may both be gone.

View (2): The Inference No Longer Is Compelled, but the Presumption Satisfies the Proponent's Burden of Production and Will Support a (Permissive) Finding by the Jury. In this view, despite the rebuttal evidence, the presumption suffices (even if the common sense notion alone ordinarily would not) to carry the proponent's (plaintiff's) burden of production and gets him to the jury; and may be considered by the jury in discharging his persuasion burden. The jury is still told the plaintiff has the burden of proving delivery by a preponderance. How much weight the presumption is to be given by the jury, over and above any common-sense weight, and how it is to be articulated to them, is subject to great variation. Under this view, then, the presumption continues with some force, embodied in some kind of jury instruction, but is not mandatory any longer, even if it was originally. The presumption continues in the case (for both the trier-of-law and trier-of-fact) and thus creates or lends strength to a connection of A and B (or to the analogous common-sense inference, if any). Just how much strength is lent is undetermined, and courts vary concerning what to tell the jury.

In connection with the first two views, it is also possible to hold that the presumption abates for purposes of the jury's deliberations if or only if the jury believes the mailroom clerk.

View (3): Burden Shifting. In this view, the presumption continues in the case even if there is contrary evidence, by shifting the burden of persuasion. This theory would shift to our defendant the burden of persuading the jury by defendant's evidence of non-delivery. Under some versions of this view, this might happen only if the base fact of proper mailing is believed by the jury or is otherwise necessarily established. In other words, assuming the evidence of the basic fact (proper mailing) satisfies the jury, the defendant would have the burden of disproving the presumed fact (i.e., proving non-delivery) by a preponderance of the evidence. In our hypothetical case, defendant's evidence that the mail clerk "doesn't remember" delivery probably would raise a jury issue, even though it is not terribly strong. Under the instruction that would be given, that the burden is on defendant to prove non-delivery if the jury finds proper mailing, the jury might well legitimately decline to find in defendant's favor, but if it did find in defendant's favor, its verdict probably also would be legitimate.

This last theory, View (3) above, was the one adopted by the Uniform Rules of Evidence. Several states have adopted this provision. It automatically answers, in what is possibly the only feasible way (as unsatisfactory as it might be), many of the important questions relating to the weight of presumptions, raised above, which the other views seem necessarily to leave in limbo. The Uniform Rule also avoids the Draconian, all-or-nothing approach of the bursting bubble theory, which gives the presumption binding effect if unrebutted but pulls the rug from beneath it if there is any contrary evidence.

Presumptions Under the Federal Rules: F.R.E. 301 and 302

The Federal Rules of Evidence do not address criminal presumptions at all, leaving that matter to case law.

Concerning civil proceedings, the Federal Rules of Evidence do not codify particular presumptions. They deal only with the *effect* of a presumption, once it is found in other sources of law. Thus, the question whether there is a presumption is left to other decisional and statutory law and other rules.

Actually, the effect of presumptions is only partly prescribed in the governing Rule, F.R.E. 301, and even then, confusingly.

The Rule merely provides that "a presumption imposes on the party against whom it is directed the burden of going forward with evidence to rebut or meet the presumption, but does not shift to such party the burden of proof in the sense of the risk of nonpersuasion." Thus, where there is no evidence of non-B (i.e., the party against whom the presumption is directed fails to "go forward" and produce "evidence to rebut the presumption"), Rule 301 provides for all presumptions the effect described above for mandatory presumptions—the production burden not being met, the presumed fact (fact B) is established against that party. Where the party against whom the presumption is directed *does* meet the "burden of going forward with evidence to rebut the presumption" (i.e., adduces evidence of non-B, thereby satisfying the production burden and getting the issue of B-or-non-B before the jury), the Rule's language, quoted above, merely provides that our View (3) above (shifting the persuasion burden) shall *not* apply. *It does not say which of the other views, or variations on them, shall apply.* All of them remain consistent with what is said. Thus, Rule 301 leaves many unanswered questions.

Another lurking question is whether Rule 301, in prescribing basically the mandatory effect for "presumptions" found elsewhere in the law, means to include presumptions that were formerly "permissive presumptions", since they were sometimes called "inferences"

rather than "presumptions". Formerly mandato[r]
sumptions are clearly included, since they are univer[s]
called "presumptions".

Criminal cases are excepted from Rule 301. So are
presumptions for which some different effect has been
provided by a rule or statute. It is unclear whether such
different effect must be expressly provided, or whether
interpretation is enough. Furthermore, Rule 302 mandates applying not 301 but rather the *state* law of effect
of any presumptions that presume *ultimate elements* of
claims or defenses governed by state substantive law,
when such claims or defenses are litigated in federal
courts (e.g., in cases based on diversity jurisdiction). The
state law of effect of presumptions often will be different
from F.R.E. 301, since, for example, the Uniform Rule is
different. Where the state law of the effect of presumptions is to govern, the state law probably also must be
the source for the existence of the presumption. What
this means is that state presumption law normally governs in diversity cases, at least on important ultimate
issues ("elements"), consistently with the *Erie* doctrine,
and the federal presumption law set forth in Rule 301
governs in federal question cases.

CHAPTER 3

NCY, ITS COUNTER-
WEIGHTS, AND RELATED
EXCLUSIONARY RULES

I. RELEVANCY

The Definition of Relevant Evidence: Rule 401

The first requisite for evidence to be admissible is that it must be relevant. But this threshold is extraordinarily low. Evidence is relevant if it has "any tendency" to render some fact that is "of consequence" to the outcome under the applicable substantive law and pleadings, "more probable or less probable" in any degree than it appeared before the introduction of the evidence. F.R.E. 401.

Relevancy does not require that the fact be made to appear more probable *than not*. We are not, under the relevancy standard, testing the sufficiency of the party's total proof in the case as a whole, but rather only a particular brick used in building the edifice. See F.R.E. 401.

Notice that the standard of relevancy implies that the judge and jury must have resort (to a limited extent) to other propositions not in the record in order to determine whether a piece of evidence renders an offered proposition more probable than before. Thus, love letters between the accused and the victim's wife would be relevant in a homicide prosecution, without any formal proof of the notion that a person writing such letters is more likely to have committed the crime than one who did not. Similarly, an accused thief's pecuniary position before and after the alleged theft, prior efforts to borrow, and the outcome of those efforts, may be relevant. The state of intoxication of one of a group of companions at a given time will often be indicative of the state of one of the others at the same time. In each case the evidence relies on an assumption concerning human behavior that is not required to be proved.

Often it is easy to overlook the fact that relevance is in this sense a societally relative concept. Judges, jurors, witnesses and defendants all may share certain societal assumptions that determine the relevance and force of evidence. But even within that shared framework, there will be differences of experience and therefore of assumptions. In a multicultural society like ours, there may be wide differences. The only guide implicit in the definition of relevance, seems to be that the assumptions must be reasonable. But to whom? Does an African–American inner city jury have experiences that affect their perceptions of the likelihood that a White policeman who has used racial slurs against African–Americans, would plant evidence against an African–American criminal defendant?

Should we allow (or even require) evidence on some of these matters? Should the prosecution be allowed to call an expert to explain reasons why a complainant's delay in reporting a crime does not necessarily mean that the complainant fabricated the event? See generally Raeder, *Irrelevancy: It's All in the Eyes of the Beholder,* 34 Houston L. Rev. 103 (1997).

"Immateriality" is the term used by some common-law authorities to indicate that a particular piece of evidence is relevant to a proposition of fact, but that the proposition itself is not an issue under the substantive law, the pleadings, or other mechanisms that set the issues. For example, there may be evidence very relevant to establishing contributory negligence, but contributory negligence may not be a defense or limiter on liability under the law governing a workers' compensation action (where the injury and its job-relatedness is all that need be found). The evidence of contributory negligence would be "immaterial" and therefore "irrelevant". The same might be true of evidence of contributory negligence in a tort negligence case in a jurisdiction where contributory negligence *is* a legal defense but has not been properly pled by the defendant or where it has been conceded away by her or her lawyer in some binding fashion during pretrial stages.

Instead of requiring evidence to be "material," the Federal Rules of Evidence require that the fact to which the evidence is addressed be a proposition that is "of consequence to the determination of the action," which amounts to the same thing. F.R.E. 401.

"Relevancy" as used in this book and in common legal parlance subsumes "materiality" or, in federal court, the "of consequence" nature of the evidence. Thus, we will say that evidence is relevant if, and only if, both the following are satisfied: (1) the evidence has probative value for the fact proposition it is meant to conduce to and (2) that fact proposition itself is "material" or "of consequence."

Sometimes evidence is relevant only if certain other facts are also put in evidence. If those facts are not yet in evidence, a conditional ruling of admissibility may result, based upon the offering counsel's representations that the evidence will be "connected up" by what will be introduced in evidence later. If counsel defaults on the promise, and the proper motion is made, the evidence may be stricken or a mistrial declared, depending on the degree and remediable nature of the prejudice.

The Rule 401 definition of relevance actually is breathtaking in its inclusiveness when read literally. By finding relevance whenever there is "any" tendency to advance or decrease the apparent probability of a fact at issue, the F.R.E. encompass all items with even the slightest probative value or that a reasonable person could think advances or decreases probability in any degree no matter how tiny. Even infinitesimal probative value will do if the Rule is taken literally, and thus, it can be said that anything even remotely arguable is relevant—that the Rule is indiscriminate, universally making anything that is possible, relevant. See Crump, *On the Uses of Irrelevant Evidence*, 34 Houston L.Rev. 1 (1997).

Courts do not usually engage in this literal reading of the Rule, however. Instead, they tend to label evidence that lacks substantial probative value as "irrelevant," even though this reading may be inconsistent with the precise words of Rule 401.

Because of its breadth, Rule 401 is not very useful as a basis for exclusions of evidence that depend on close questions. There are other exclusionary rules, and they are adequate to limit what relevance unchecked would let in.

Relevant Evidence Is Admissible Unless There Is an Exclusionary Rule: Rule 402

Relevance is universally required for admissibility, but is not itself alone sufficient to produce admissibility. The evidence must pass other tests or hurdles as well (which are the subject of much of the remainder of this book and most of the rules of evidence). The Federal Rules suggest that at least there is a kind of rebuttable presumption of admissibility that attaches to evidence found to be relevant. Specifically, F.R.E. 402 provides that relevant evidence is admissible unless rendered inadmissible by some other source of law: these or other Congressionally authorized rules; statutes; or the Constitution.

This "presumption" of admissibility attaching to relevant evidence is confirmed by F.R.E. 403, which codifies the ad hoc, largely discretionary common law power of the judge to exclude relevant evidence in a particular case, but only if the judge finds that *"unfair"* prejudice or another similar factor *"substantially outweighs"* the probative value. The italicized words seem to confirm that relevant evidence is ordinarily admissible unless substantial reason can be found to keep it out. Thus relevant evidence should be assumed to overcome the other tests or hurdles until it is shown otherwise. Some commentators refer to F.R.E. Rule 401 as "logical relevancy" and to F.R.E. Rule 403 as "legal relevancy."

Common-law standards which are more restrictive than relevancy do not apply to the Federal Rules, unless authorized by Congress, a statute, other rules, or the Constitution.

Rule 402, as is stated above, provides that relevant evidence is admissible unless there is an exclusionary principle that excludes it. The Rule expressly provides that the exclusionary principles must be found in the F.R.E., other rules authorized by Congress, a statute, or the Constitution. The Supreme Court has interpreted Rule 402 to prohibit the application of any common-law doctrine which is more restrictive than the relevancy standard if it is not found in these sources. For example, in *Daubert v. Merrell Dow Pharmaceuticals, Inc.* (S.Ct. 1993), the Court rejected the former common-law *Frye* standard, which had restricted the admission of scientific experts to those espousing generally scientifically accepted principles, because it was not provided for in the F.R.E. or other cognizable source. The former common-law requirement that the foundation for co-conspirator statements had to be established by independent evidence was rejected in *Bourjaily v. United States* (S.Ct. 1987), on similar grounds. Whether strict preclusion of common law in this fashion is being, will be, and can be adhered to unflinchingly, is not free from doubt.[1]

In contrast, so long as evidence *admissible* under a common-law doctrine is relevant, it is admissible unless it is excluded by some provision, even if the common-law doctrine is not mentioned in the rules. For example, it is proper to impeach a witness based on bias, because although bias is nowhere mentioned in the Rules, it is relevant. *United States v. Abel* (S.Ct.1984).

Certain rules expressly authorize limited common law development to admit or exclude in certain narrow areas. For example, Rule 501 authorizes development and interpretation of an evolving common law of privileges. The residual hearsay exception (F.R.E. Rule 807) was designed to permit some flexibility in the hearsay rules.

Statistical Probabilities: A Particular Problem of Relevancy

Statistical probability evidence may provide information about likelihoods that are fundamental to the basic cerebrations of a jury about the probative force, or weight, of other evidence, and the ultimate determination of the case, that otherwise might be left to covert individual experience-based assumptions. The court may be especially leery of displacing what passes as the "common sense" of the jurors, however imperfect, with influential expert testimony in such a fundamental area unless highly satisfied that it is correct and not misleading.

The most famous statistical probability case is *People v. Collins* (Cal.1968), involving an interracial couple accused of robbery, in which the prosecutor created esti-

1. However, it is clear that the common law is influencing *interpretation of the meaning* of most of the rules.

mates for the frequency of occurrence in the population, of each individual characteristic of the couple, which estimates were not empirically based, and then, with the aid of an expert, multiplied them together to get a total probability of occurrence. The odds of another couple matching the description of a blond woman with a pony-tail and an African–American man with a mustache and a beard driving a yellow convertible car with a white top were thereby posited as one in twelve million.

The California Supreme Court reversed the conviction because of a series of defects, most of them unlikely to be recognized by the jury: (1) the lack of empirical basis for the statistical frequency of the individual features (variables), (2) the multiplying together of variables not shown to be independent (like the beard and mustache), contrary to good statistical theory, (3) the misleading bottom line figure of one-in-twelve-million (said by the prosecution to the jury to be a "conservative estimate"), which was not only overwhelming to the jurors, but also almost inevitably appeared to them to represent the chances of guilt whereas at best it only represented the likelihood that the couple was near the scene, (4) the failure to crank in a figure for the uncertainty or inaccuracy or lack of credibility of the reports describing the features of the couple allegedly seen near the scene of the crime and those describing the allegedly matching features of the couple on trial (the beard, mustache, blond hair, pony tail, and car, for example, being gone at trial), and (5) the fact that the one-in-twelve-million figure means that there may have been two couples with these same features in the metropolitan area of approximately twenty-four million people surrounding the neighborhood of the crime. The court felt that, far from indicating guilt, such a figure, even if properly arrived at, suggested there was at least one other couple than defendants in the relevant population, who could fit the description, and thus the possibility of innocence arguably was not one in twelve million, but more like one in two, which the court seemed to think would per se furnish a reasonable doubt concerning the defendants' guilt.

The *Collins* case has been cited to support complete mistrust of mathematical statistical probability evidence. *Collins* did suggest rather broadly at some points that such evidence was always unfair because the jury would be overwhelmed by the numbers and not understand their limited helpfulness. But California and most other states now shy away from that broad reading of *Collins*, indeed appearing even to embrace the introduction of infinitestimal probabilities, such as the very small chances of other matches of blood DNA found at the scene, heard in the widely publicized *O.J. Simpson* case, amounting to one chance in a number that exceeded the population of the earth. Such testimony, not always with such high figures, is now common in courts throughout the United States.

It would seem that the objection to the evidence in *Collins* as overwhelming the jury can be cured in an appropriate case by a well qualified expert using accurate information and precise but understandable language that includes proper limitations of the evidence. There must be no problems which the jury cannot intelligently allow for or that take more time to illuminate than the evidence is worth. In other words, the evidence must not be prejudicial, misleading, or unduly time consuming, general principles or counterweights to relevancy appearing in rules such as F.R.E. 403 and the rules relating to expert testimony, F.R.E. Article VII, treated infra.

Very special scrutiny in this regard is often given to this sensitive variety of evidence. Some judges retain a decided skepticism, requiring an exceptionally thorough foundation for admissibility.

Statistical evidence is used widely and successfully in civil discrimination cases to establish disparate treatment of racial or gender groups. Estimates based on sophisticated mathematical economic models are standard in predicting economic losses in damage awards of all kinds, and in showing market effect in antitrust cases. These uses are perhaps distinguishable from *Collins*, but they make the point that evidence that is statistical or mathematical in nature does not necessarily derail a trial.

In criminal cases, DNA evidence (genetically "matching" biological traces from the crime scene to the defendant) is usually presented by an expert who computes the probability of a coincidental match, i.e., the probability that someone picked at random would match the DNA characteristics at issue. Essentially, this is the same process that was attempted to be done in *Collins*, although badly. Care must be taken to assure precision in language, because it is easy for jurors to infer wrong information from DNA statistics. The pro-prosecution fallacy confuses the probability of a coincidental match with the probability of guilt, while the pro-defense fallacy bases the probability of guilt on the number of individuals who possess the given trait. For example, if 5% of the population had a particular set of traits, the pro-prosecution fallacy would state a 95% chance of guilt, while the pro-defense fallacy would simply compute 5% of the population, thereby finding a 1 in 50,000 chance of guilt in a city of 1,000,000 people. In fact, the actual probability of guilt also depends on things like access, motive, etc., applied to the raw figures.

Laboratory error rate in testing samples may also affect the weight such evidence should be given by the jury. Thus, some commentators argue that it is highly misleading to tell the jury that there is a one in a million chance of a coincidental match, if the laboratory's error rate produces a mistake one time out of every two hundred tests.

Like *Collins*, DNA tests basically measure a series of individual features of the DNA and calculate the chances of them all occurring together. As in *Collins*, the problem of dependant variables must be safeguarded against.

Some scholars have advocated a statistical equation called Bayes' Theorem which if allowed would tell a jury how each new piece of evidence should affect their estimate of the probability that an event occurred. Bayes' Theorem provides a formula to combine the prior probability estimate with the information provided by the new evidence to obtain a new probability. Either the prior probability, or the new probability that is to be combined with the prior probability to arrive at a "final" probability, might come from frequency-based statistics, such as the percentage of the population which possesses a given blood or DNA type, or from subjective estimates of the defendant's probable guilt. However, to the extent that any of the numbers are subjective, the new probability will also be subjective.

An example of Bayesian analysis is found in likelihood ratios, which are sometimes offered in paternity cases involving, e.g., DNA genetic testing. But because Bayes' Theorem cannot operate without an existing probability, established beforehand, experts often follow the convention of assuming that there is a 50% antecedent probability of the defendant's paternity. In other words, the expert assumes that the chance of the defendant being the father, based on all of the non-DNA evidence in the case, is at least equal to the chance of any other male having fathered the child. This kind of Bayesian logic is controversial and seldom allowed in criminal cases because prior probabilities are created without taking into account the presumption of innocence. See *State v. Skipper* (Conn.1994) (reversing conviction on constitutional grounds because Bayesian paternity statistics were introduced).

Some forms of probability evidence or argument are questioned by some "antiprobabilists" on the ground that they indicate what "might have" happened, not what actually happened in the case at hand. See generally, McCord, *A Primer for the Non-mathematically Inclined on Mathematical Evidence in Criminal Cases: People v. Collins and Beyond*, 47 Wash. & Lee L. Rev. 741 (1990); Tribe, *Trial By Mathematics: Precision and Ritual in the Legal Process*, 84 Harv. L. Rev. 1329 (1971). In one familiar hypothetical, 501 out of 1,000 spectators are gate-crashers at a rodeo. That's all we know. There is no evidence of which spectators are and are not gate-crashers. A committed probabilist might view the fact that 501 out of 1000 are gate-crashers not only as admissible, but as sufficient alone to survive directed verdict motions and uphold a civil finding that each of the 1,000 individuals (tried individually) is liable for gate-crashing, without any other evidence. This is because, as to each, the chances are slightly greater (501 out of 1000) that he/she belonged to the larger group (gate-crashers as opposed to the non-gate-crashers). Thus such probabilists might be characterized as utilitarians who believe in maximizing the number of correct verdicts. These verdicts of liable for all 1000 people would be correct 501 times and incorrect 499 times. In contrast, the contrary (and maybe "prevailing") view is that each of the 1,000 spectators is entitled to a favorable directed verdict, although this result would be wrong in 501 cases.

II. COUNTERWEIGHTS TO RELEVANCE: PREJUDICE, CONFUSION, TIME CONSUMPTION, ETC.

Prejudice: Extreme Over–Valuation or Decision on an Improper Basis

At common law and under the Rules, relevant evidence may be excluded pursuant to a very specific rule; to a less specific guideline type rule; or to a very broad rule allowing balancing by relatively untrammeled wide judicial discretion. Very often the policy concern behind excluding evidence is avoidance of "prejudice," i.e., a tendency of the evidence to influence the fact-finder unduly or to induce decision on an improper basis. Thus, evidence is excluded because the law or the judge distrusts the jury's ability to properly evaluate evidence.

Many exclusionary rules and rulings exclude relevant evidence on the rationale that juries would be inclined to give the particular piece or class of evidence an effect different (usually greater) than they ought. That is, the evidence is "prejudicial," and by that is meant that juries could not be trusted to give it its logical, rational weight, or to perceive that it had none, but instead would, perhaps because of the emotional impact of the evidence, or a logical fallacy, allow it to be persuasive to an extent or on a basis that the law deems improper. This can happen where the evidence has some warranted weight as well as where it has none, so long as there is the danger that the jury will not evaluate it properly, but will be overly or incorrectly influenced by it, to an extent that renders the trial more accurate (or fairer) without the evidence.

Two kinds of "prejudice" sometimes are described: (1) exaggeration and (2) decision on an improper basis.

The first category of prejudice ("exaggeration") embraces cases where evidence is excluded because of concern with its over-persuasiveness before the jury on the issue for which the evidence is offered. Such evidence is sometimes called "misleading". If judges or rule-makers were scrupulously to make the computation called for, they would be required to estimate what probability the jury would ascribe (a) having the benefit of the piece of evidence and (b) without it. They would then have to decide what probability a wholly rational trier-of-fact would ascribe if given the piece of evidence. In general, only when exclusion rather than admission would cause the real jury to come closer to the probability ascribed by the wholly rational trier in receipt of the evidence, should the evidence be excluded.[2] Our concept of the role of the jury would seem to require that there be a rather large disparity before exclusion.

Of course, precise numbers cannot be affixed nor exact probabilities estimated in this fashion; nor do judges or rule-makers engage in such a strictly mathematical computation. Nevertheless, this is the general *sort* of judgment the "exaggeration" model of prejudice calls for. The judge or law-maker is supposed to be able to (a) estimate probability better than the jury (to arrive at the probability a wholly rational trier would ascribe), and (b) predict what the jury will do with and without the evidence. It is done routinely in a practical, less-than-precise, necessarily somewhat subjective, way.

It is apparent that the "numbers" in the computation become vastly different depending upon what other proof for and against the fact there is in the particular case. Yet if we are to have specific rules, sometimes the law

2. Remember, since it is relevant evidence possessed of some probative value that we are considering excluding because of this counterweight, there will be some distortion of the chances of total accuracy of the ultimate finding whichever way we go: admission or exclusion, and these two distortions must be compared.

will need to make the judgment for a class of evidence as a whole, irrespective of its combination with other particular items in a particular case. Also, some consideration must be given to the fact that exclusion of evidence may cause the offering party to produce other evidence that might not otherwise be offered, changing the probabilities. So availability of other more accurate or less prejudicial evidence must also be considered.

Prejudice of the second type in the heading is the tendency of the evidence to distract the jury from proper issues, rather than its tendency to induce exaggeration. The Advisory Committee's Notes to Rule 403 speak of an "undue tendency to suggest decision on an improper basis, commonly, though not necessarily, an emotional one." As a matter of terminology, such evidence might also be called "misleading" in certain settings or, in some instances, may be said to induce a kind of "confusion of the issues," although there may be other meanings of these terms, too.

This type of prejudice, too, must be weighed against the legitimate probative value of the evidence which would be sacrificed if the evidence is excluded, as described above.

In a theft case, imagine that the prosecutor offers evidence that the defendant started a barroom brawl six months after the theft incident. The relevance or probative value of this evidence is low: it is based on the inference that law-breaking brawlers are more likely than other people to break the law by committing theft (all other things being equal). But even making the (perhaps unrealistic) assumptions that (a) jurors will recognize that this strand of relevance or probative value is low, and (b) they will therefore not indulge in the first kind of prejudice (i.e., will not exaggerate the degree to which one kind of law-breaking indicates the other), there is still the second kind of prejudice: jurors may decide that a person who starts fights in bars is less worthy of the law's protection, or that he should be punished for other or general badness, regardless of whether he committed the presently charged crime. To use the words of the Advisory Committee Note, the evidence "suggests" to the jurors, albeit indirectly, that they should make their decision on an "improper basis."

The usual ban on introducing other crimes of a criminal defendant is in part based on this distraction or "improper basis" rationale, as well as the exaggeration rationale. So is the usual exclusion of liability insurance. We exclude liability insurance in negligence cases not merely because the jury may exaggerate its logical force (i.e., exaggerate the extent to which such insurance tends to make one careless since he feels his insurance makes him immune from the financial consequences of his negligence), but also because it suggests decision on an improper basis by inviting jurors to decide that the defendant won't have to pay, and so a plaintiff's verdict won't do anybody any substantial harm. Only the deep pocket of the insurance company will be affected. The cost will be distributed or spread widely in a painless way or in small unnoticeable increments on a large group, rather than concentrated devastatingly on the victim. These would be improper bases for decision.

Sometimes evidence may be considered "unfairly" prejudicial only if other less prejudicial means are reasonably available to prove the matter sought to be proved. For example, although courts may be hostile to the introduction of grisly autopsy photographs due to their prejudice (tendency to inflame the jury into convicting *someone*), their admissibility may depend on whether they have peculiar probative value on the particular facts of the case, which cannot equally well be offered by other means such as oral descriptions or lab reports. In the highly publicized prosecution of sports figure and actor

O.J. Simpson for killing his ex-wife and her friend, numerous (but not all) autopsy photographs of the victims bodies were admitted on the theory that the manner of infliction and placement of the wounds were not otherwise precisely communicable in the way necessary to determine such things as whether the state of mind for first degree murder was present, who perished first, the time needed to commit the crimes, why there may have been little blood on the defendant, whether the killings were professional, etc. California, where the trial took place, is more indulgent of autopsy photo evidence than many other jurisdictions.

One corollary of this general principle is that lawyers should always be mindful that an offer to concede (stipulate) to a fact may preclude the other side from introducing possibly more damning evidence of the fact. In effect, the court may require that the offer be accepted. The stipulation or concession is then read to the jury. (They may even be instructed they must accept the fact as true.) See, for example, the Supreme Court decision in *Old Chief v. United States* (S.Ct.1997), in which the defendant was convicted of the crime of "being a convicted felon in possession of a firearm, using or carrying a firearm during the commission of a violent crime, and assault with a dangerous weapon". The Court held that in view of defendant's offer to concede his status as being a convicted felon, and to contest only possession, the prosecution was not allowed to introduce evidence of his prior conviction for assault causing serious bodily injury, since such evidence, though necessary if there were no such concession, would now only serve to unfairly prejudice defendant on the other charges.

Old Chief was not a case where the prosecution would be deprived of something adding some legitimate value to the case such as painting a more vivid picture. A number of courts are extremely reluctant to preclude a piece of evidence through this procedure, at least if there is any legitimate additional value to the evidence over and above what would be supplied by the stipulation. For example, when the prosecution offers evidence of other crimes to show intent (a narrow permitted use of other crimes evidence), even though the defendant is willing to concede that whoever committed the crime had the requisite intent, many trial judges will not permit the stipulation. Judicial philosophy varies greatly on this issue, with other judges quite ready to do so wherever the Rule 403 balance appears to makes it a fair bargain.

Returning to the general subject of prejudice, prejudice to the *prosecution* can also occur. For example, in the same *Simpson* case, evidence of a White police detective's anti-Black racist comments was deemed potentially prejudicial in both our senses because (1) the evidence might (in the judge's view) cause the predominantly Black inner-city jury to leap too readily to the conclusion the detective might plant evidence, or lie on the stand, against the Black defendant (although some argue that the jurors' readiness to do this was indeed the experienced and accurate level of response and the White or affluent community's view the myth) and (2) the evidence supported a suggestion of acquittal based not necessarily on doubt of guilt but on the "improper basis" of disapproving of police conduct. Thus only a limited amount of this evidence was admitted. As the calculus calls for, the judge attempted to let in only enough of this evidence to achieve what the judge felt was the accurate amount of effect on the jury in view of the judge's notion of the predilection of this jury to exaggerate or give improper scope to this kind of evidence. In other words, it was a Rule 403–type balancing, which is often (perhaps necessarily) somewhat subjective.

When relevant evidence is excluded on the basis of either or both of the two kinds of distrust of jurors discussed in this section, it is usually said to be excluded because it is "prejudicial." "Misleading", or "confusion of the issues" are terms also used. In a sense all evidence is "prejudicial" insofar as it helps one side and hinders the other, no matter how legitimately and logically. But the term "prejudicial" is normally used to mean "unduly" or "unwarrantedly" or "unfairly" prejudicial. It is meant to connote evoking an emotional, non-analytical, or over-reactive response.

"Prejudice" as used in this discussion (and in rules like F.R.E. 403) is generally considered to be concerned with distortions of the fact-finding function of the trial. Prejudice to other interests, for example embarrassment or invasion of privacy of a party or witness, or infringement of other societal goals, is not part of this particular weighing and balancing. But see Rules 412 (protecting privacy of sex victims and encouraging reporting of offenses), 501 (various privileges intended to secure societal benefits), and 611(a)(3) (judicial power to protect witnesses from harassment or undue embarrassment).

Other Counterweights in Addition to Prejudice

Evidence rules often call for the judge to balance, or they themselves already have balanced, probativity against prejudice and other factors including protraction, unfair surprise, confusion of issues, misleadingness, and cumulativeness.

Prejudice is but one of the factors or counterweights that must be balanced against probativity. Others may include time consumption, unfair surprise, confusion of the issues, and the others in the heading. Many are at least partly redundant or overlapping. Cumulativeness is related to time consumption and a low increment of probative value. Misleadingness is probably encompassed by the notion of prejudice. Confusion of the issues refers to either a tendency to decide based on the wrong issue (a form of prejudice) or the protraction entailed by pursuing marginally probative side issues. A rule like F.R.E. 403 lists redundant factors just to be sure to cover the waterfront.

All of these counterweights except surprise are listed in F.R.E. 403, the general balancing rule. "Surprise" is purposely omitted as a counterweight in F.R.E. 403. Formerly, this counterweight permitted exclusion of evidence if the judge felt the evidence was "sprung" on the opposing attorney with insufficient advance warning to effectively prepare to combat it. The theory of the omission in 403 is that modern discovery, coupled with the possibility of a continuance (temporary recess or brief postponement) of the trial, minimizes the chance of an attorney having to combat new undisclosed evidence on the spur of the moment.

This kind of "ambush" however, still often occurs, contrary to 403's assumption. Discovery is limited; and judges hate continuances. In criminal cases, little discovery is available by law at the federal level and in most states. Even in civil cases, where a number of discovery mechanisms are available, there may be economic or other reasons for a lawyer seeking or getting less than adequate discovery. Indeed, the discovery rules penalize what a judge decides is costly or excessive discovery, so that what a lawyer may feel he or she needs, can be sought only at some risk. The evidence rules and the discovery rules provide opposing incentives here.

Perhaps evidence suddenly sprung on one can still be excluded because it risks "prejudicing" or "misleading" the jury, words that are included in Rule 403. Potential weaknesses in the evidence cannot be adequately revealed to the jury if the opponent of the evidence has not had time to prepare to reveal them. Certainly, if the offeror was under obligation to disclose the evidence in discovery, but did not, there are clear grounds for exclusion at trial under the Federal Rules of Civil Procedure and state analogues and under some criminal procedure discovery rules where they exist. Similarly, a few evidentiary rules such as F.R.E. 404(b), 413 through 415, and 807, also have notice provisions, and non-compliance can result in exclusion, basically because of the surprise. Several states make greater use of notice provisions in their evidence rules than do the F.R.E., requiring, for example, notice of the basis of expert testimony (covered in federal court by the Federal Rules of Civil Procedure) and notice of expected use of a variety of hearsay exceptions. The latest version of the Uniform Rules also added several notice provisions.

With respect to the counterweight known as "time consumption," often evidence is offered whose legitimate persuasive power is so minor that it is not worth the time to receive it, even if the fact-finder can be counted on to give it only the weight and effect it deserves. Indeed, "time" seems to be the only reason for excluding evidence of no or very slight relevance where the jury can be counted on to spot its lack of value and will not indulge in giving it prejudicial effect. Including "time" as a consideration implies that we are willing to compromise a small increment of accuracy in the interest of handling more cases more quickly.

"Time consumption" is related to the other counterweights as well. Remember, a piece of evidence may be considered "misleading" or "prejudicial" in the exaggeration sense if it appears to have probative force that in fact it does not have. This appearance of great probative force however can often be reduced by spending time on the evidence. Some sensitive scientific techniques, whose limited reliability is difficult for lay jurors to understand without great expenditures of time on explanations, provide examples. For instance, polygraph results are usually relevant, but they are excluded anyway because it is difficult to confine accurately their proper application by lay jurors. To do so would require a trial within a trial, perhaps longer than the trial itself, about the intricacies of the polygraph, and this effort would likely end in confusion (perhaps as to the real issue), residual tendencies to mislead, and probably, after all the explanations, something that adds little.

Individual Versus Categorical Balancing

In certain areas the balance between probative value and the counterweights is struck as a matter of law for a class of evidence as a whole. In this situation, the law evolves a more-or-less categorical rule, rather than relying on an ad hoc balancing as under F.R.E. 403. For example, Rule 411 prohibits proof of liability insurance offered to show fault. F.R.E. 404 contains a blanket exclusion for evidence of character used to prove an act in conformity with the character subject to certain exceptions. The exclusion cannot be overridden by Rule 403. But evidence coming within the exceptions still must pass muster under 403 to be admissible because the exceptions are exceptions only to the ban of Rule 404.

In other areas (those of a less recurrent nature), the law permits the judge to perform an *ad hoc* balancing of these factors on the facts of the particular case. In the F.R.E., this principle is contained in Rule 403. Thus, F.R.E. 403 allows the judge to exclude evidence in a particular case, even though there is no specific rule of exclusion, based on a conclusion that the probative value (relevance) of the evidence is "substantially outweighed" by the listed counterweights.

F.R.E. 403 Creates an Unevenly Weighted Balancing Test, Which Is Loaded in Favor of Admissibility: Unless "Substantially Outweighed," Probative Value Supports Admissibility

Many items of evidence will incorporate both some probative value and some prejudice (or other counterweights). For example, in a theft case, a similar theft committed earlier by the same defendant may be legitimately probative, but it also tends to introduce prejudice in terms of both an exaggeration of the legitimate inference and an inducement to punish for past or general "badness". Most evidence combines some probative value with some counterweights.

Rule 403 creates a balancing test for evidence of this kind to which it applies, but it is an unevenly weighted test. The balance is deliberately weighted in favor of admissibility. Specifically, the Rule directs the judge to admit an item of evidence that has probative value unless that value is "substantially outweighed"—not just outweighed, but "substantially" so—by the contrary factors. Thus a small amount of prejudice, or even a significant amount, is not enough to exclude if the probative value is high. Even prejudice that equals the probative value is not enough to exclude. Indeed, so strong is the pro-admissibility policy of Rule 403, that the language does not authorize exclusion even when the prejudice *exceeds* the probative value! It must "substantially" exceed it.

This balance cannot be done by precise mathematics. It requires evaluation of all aspects of the evidence, in context. The trial judge is in a better position to gauge the matter than an appellate court, which sees only the written record. The Rule states that evidence "may" be excluded under its authority. This implies a broad grant of discretion to the trial judge. Reversal by an appellate court is confined to abuses of the trial judge's broad discretion. A considerable range of decision is therefore allowed the trial judge. Thus, Rule 403 is not a rule in the categorical sense, but a guideline of the most general kind. Rule 403 is often referred to as the "great override—one way". This is because not only does it cover (and allow admission or exclusion of) evidence unprovided for in other rules; but it also, as a general matter, can override *permissions* to introduce evidence given in other rules, although not *exclusions*. Hence, it can override other rules but only in one direction. This is because permissions (as opposed to exclusions) in other rules, are generally not absolute and are stated only as exceptions to the bans of the very rules in which they appear (and thus not to exclusion under Rule 403). Thus, exceptions to, for example, the hearsay rule, are still subject to exclusion under Rule 403. Only a very few permissions of evidence in the F.R.E. are absolute (mandatory) and thus not subject to 403 exclusion.

Rules subsequent to 403 in Article IV of the F.R.E. purport to strike the balance between probative value and its counterweights for particular categories of evidence. This is not *entirely* true, however, for two reasons: (1) They resolve the balance definitively only for evidence they exclude. As to this evidence, the ban is stated as categorical. No balancing can render the evidence admissible on the facts of any case. But as to evidence they permit, most of them expressly or impliedly subject it to the balancing of Rule 403 on the facts of the particular case. (2) The exclusions are not based merely on the counterweights, but also on certain other extrinsic policies in some instances.

It should additionally be noted here that F.R.E. Articles VI (Witnesses), VII (Opinions and Experts), IX (Authentication), and X (Original Documents), as well as the state and common-law analogs of these articles, also owe much to the probativity-versus-counterweights balancing.

Much of this book concerns various manifestations of the balancing spoken of here, as well as some other themes of Evidence Law. But two broad areas showing the balancing are specifically noted immediately below merely for general orientation to the ways it may manifest itself.

Illustration of the Balancing: Offering Replications: Results of Experiments That Attempt to Recreate a Litigated Event or Portion Thereof; Re-enactments; Simulations; Models; Photos; Graphic Representations

Although other rules may also apply to these disparate kinds of evidence, the ad hoc probativity-and-its-counterweights balance (F.R.E. 403) imposes a kind of "rule of thumb" requirement that when evidence purports to replicate a litigated event or portion thereof for the jury, the replication must be substantially similar to the thing replicated. This is because otherwise the degree of replication might be exaggerated and misunderstood (the evidence would be "prejudicial" or "misleading"), undue time consumed in explanation of the differences, or dangerous confusion engendered, between the replication and the real event. There is "wiggle room" in the word "substantially", and it responds to the balancing: Can the jury properly evaluate any differences without undue time consumption in view of what the evidence at the end is likely to be worth in terms of additional value to the case?

The inquiry the court makes here is into whether there is any dissimilarity from the actual conditions, of a kind that is likely to make a significant difference, that would be difficult for the jury to detect or assess, at least without undue time being spent on explanations. The question is whether the evidence exhibits substantial similarity to the event. A prima facie case of acceptability on this must be shown, or appear from the other evidence or the thing itself, before the opponent has the burden to show anything in order to bar the evidence. This substantial similarity, then, is the foundation that must be laid. Some courts have said that if this prima facie case is made, the evidence is admissible and contrary showings are merely matters of weight unless they reveal a very severe deficiency. It probably depends on what is shown.

The more technical the area, the more the court suspects there may be differences of some consequence, and will need to be convinced otherwise. In a non-technical area, the court may be willing to assume, without much of a showing, that there are no significant differences that will go unnoticed by the jury.

Computerized animations and simulations and video-taped demonstrations play an ever growing courtroom role, and they often require a rigorous foundation in this regard. Separate questions may exist concerning the validity of the underlying technique involved. This issue is discussed in the chapter concerning experts and scientific evidence.

Opportunity for the other side to participate in an experiment or other re-enactment or re-creation is usually considered only a matter of weight, as is the question whether it was conducted by an impartial (court-appointed or agreed upon) expert.

With much of the evidence dealt with here, particularly explanatory aids such as charts, and computer simulations, the court considers, in addition, the need for this kind of explanation, and the effect of giving the jury double information on one selected aspect of the case (if, e.g., the evidence summarizes or is based on other evidence).[3]

3. Similar selective re-emphasis can occur whenever any item of evidence already shown during the trial goes to the jury room. Theoretically, the decision of what goes to the jury room should be made separately from what is received as evidence and shown during the course of the trial. Obviously we are talking about a kind of prejudice or misleadingness, as well as time consumption.

Visual aids are now common in the court. Enlargements of documents and photographs, posters, anatomical models, pieces of equipment, etc., are all used by litigators to explain concepts to jurors and focus them on important evidence. Sophisticated electronic and mechanical aids are increasingly used in these endeavors.

The F.R.E. drafters apparently felt the fact situations that come up in all the areas treated in this section are so diverse that no specific rule expressing the probativity-versus-counterweights balance could be fashioned. They largely left the matter to the general ad hoc balancing process described herein in earlier sections and codified in Rule 403.[4] Under that balancing, "significant" difference ("substantial" similarity) and other factors described in this section continue to affect admissibility, although they may be expressed and interpreted in terms of probative value, prejudice, confusion, misleadingness, time and the other elements of Rule 403.

The admissibility of other product or premises failures in personal injury litigation concerning a current product or premises failure is subject to a comparable test of "substantial similarity" pursuant to Rule 403.

Illustration of the Balancing (Perhaps Tempered by Extrinsic Policies): Flight, Bribery, Spoliation (the Failure to Adduce Evidence) and Other Arguable Implied Admissions

There are many kinds of conduct that may in certain circumstances indicate a consciousness of guilt or adverse facts: intimidation or bribery of a witness, destroying or hiding evidence, failure to produce evidence, attempting suicide while awaiting trial, offering to pay medical costs for a personal injury, attempting to settle a claim, safety or remedial

4. Some additional mechanical rules may, however, apply concerning other aspects of the same evidence.

measures taken after an injury, fleeing, refusal to submit to a physical examination, silence in the face of accusation, or invocation of a privilege. Despite their relevance, the counterweights perhaps boosted by extrinsic policies may dictate exclusion of some of these types of evidence in certain cases, and both categorical rules and ad hoc balancing have roles in different situations. Some of these are more fully dealt with in subsequent sections.

The reader should consider the facts one would like to know more about in these examples before deciding in a particular case how probative (logically forceful) the evidence is, and should call to mind factors he or she feels should bear on admissibility, which may be quite different. Should the law confine itself to the balancing of relevancy (probative force) and its counterweights? Or are there other germane social policies? For example, a policy to encourage settlement of disputes (in connection with offers to pay after an injury) or a policy to encourage safety measures (in connection with the admissibility of such measures)? In fact, there is a categorical ban on both these lines of proof, with exceptions, which will be discussed below.

Where there is no categorical exclusion, the admissibility of these kinds of evidence is controlled by Rule 403. (See Ch. 9, infra for an easily surmounted hearsay objection.)

A common example is the defendant's act of absenting himself from the jurisdiction after a crime. Such evidence may be relevant and probative in some degree, because it may have some legitimate tendency to suggest flight perhaps because of consciousness of guilt or of adverse facts, which in turn suggests that the facts may be in accord with that consciousness. The evidence also may be misleading, however. For example there may be other possible reasons for leaving. Or the person may not have known of the accusation. Or it may be prejudicial in other ways, e.g., if it is intertwined with acts of falsification of identity or violence in connection with the absenting.

Nevertheless, the tendency both of the common law, and of the F.R.E. pursuant to Rule 403, is to admit evidence of flight, even if it is indirect and speculative and even when it contains some prejudice or other counterweights. Exclusion, under the unevenly weighted balancing test of Rule 403, is likely to follow only if the inference of consciousness of guilt is particularly weak, and the prejudice or other counterweights are particularly strong. This determination is heavily fact-specific. When is a weakness in the inference merely a matter of weight, and when does it rise to the level of impeding admissibility? Is this just a matter of degree, basically subjective with the judge, influenced by the skill of the arguments of the lawyers? Frequently "yes", not only in this area, but in almost every area under Rule 403.

Thus, a lawyer unsuccessfully resisting admissibility before the judge under Rule 403 should retain her notes, to argue many of the same factors to the jury as matters decreasing the weight or force jurors should give to the evidence. The other lawyer should do the same in the opposite direction. This is a lesson applicable well beyond this particular type of evidence.

III.   EXCLUSIONARY RULES FOR REMEDIAL MEASURES, COMPROMISE NEGOTIATIONS, WITHDRAWN GUILTY PLEAS, AND INSURANCE

Subsequent Remedial Measures: F.R.E. 407

Subsequent safety or remedial measures are a type of possible implied admission which is subject to a general exclusion, with certain exceptions.

F.R.E. 407 expresses the traditional doctrine about subsequent remedial measures, and it reasonably reflects the common law:

"When, after an injury or harm allegedly caused by an event, measures are taken that, if taken previously, would have made the injury or harm less likely to occur, evidence of the subsequent measures is not admissible to prove negligence, culpable conduct [, a defect in a product, a defect in a product's design, or a need for a warning or instruction.] [The bracketed language was added in 1997.] This rule does not require the exclusion of evidence of subsequent measures when offered for another purpose, such as proving ownership, control, or feasibility of precautionary measures, if controverted, or impeachment."

The rule is set out here because its drafting—dividing purposes into the permissible and the impermissible—is typical of many of the rules in F.R.E. Article IV we treat subsequently.

The policy of this rule is not confined to the balancing of relevance and prejudice and the other counterweights. Extrinsic social policy is also involved. For, in addition to embodying a concern about the jury exaggerating the extent to which evidence of corrective measures indicates fault, the rule seeks to encourage potential parties to lawsuits to take corrective measures, by not penalizing them for changes that might otherwise be regarded by a jury as implied admissions. There may also be a policy of avoiding disparate treatment that rewards recalcitrant defendants while punishing those who act socially responsibly. The rule is willing to sacrifice (on the altar of these extrinsic social policies) mildly probative evidence, that is, evidence which *might* be an admission of liability or fault but on the other hand might merely express a humanitarian willingness to do more than the law requires, or a willingness to do what the law only now, because of the mishap, requires, or a desire to avoid future even baseless claims or innocently inflicted or accidental injuries even though the person or entity taking the precautionary measure believes there would be no liability for them.

The rule is not confined to fixing or altering things, conditions, or practices that produced personal injury, such as premises, products, or methods of inspection. It also includes, for example, the instituting by a company of new rules, the discharge of employees, the addition of warnings, the changing of trade practices, and any other measures that would make less likely to recur, an asserted violation of any tangible or intangible legal interest (including, e.g., discrimination or employment or anti-trust violation) that might be regarded as an injury for purposes of a lawsuit. The rule expands the ban beyond "safety measures" to the broader concept of "remedial measures," sometimes called "corrective" measures. The rule might, for example, exclude (in a case brought against a bank for embezzlement committed by one of its employees) evidence of a subsequent investigation by auditors seeking to reduce the likelihood of future em-bezzlements, even though the issue is business security rather than safety. At least this would be included if it resulted in changes.

The "exceptions" expressed by the last sentence of the rule represent a compromise between the encourage-ment-of-change rationale and the need for particularized kinds of information on issues separate from fault. The evidence expressed by the exceptions is likely to be so probative that it ought not to be sacrificed on the altar of extrinsic policy. And the evidence is not so likely to be exaggerated or misunderstood. If these favorable assump-tions cannot be made on the facts of a particular case, Rule 403 can still keep the evidence out.

An example of the "exceptions" might be this. If a defendant denies that he owns the vehicle whose brakes allegedly failed, but the defendant has paid for subsequent repairs of them, the latter may be offered not to show admission of fault but to prove ownership or control. Rule 403 might prevent this if ownership is a peripheral issue or can be proved easily some other way. Notice that the permissible purposes listed in the Rule are not exhaustive (see the "such as" language). Any purpose other than a prohibited purpose is a permissible purpose.

The better reasoned cases reject the view that evidence offered for the permissible purposes under the rule is automatically admissible. They conclude, instead, that such evidence is still subject to Rule 403 balancing. This is because the relief accorded by the exceptions is only from the ban of *this* rule, 407. In other words, in the example, if the prejudicial tendency of the brake-repair evidence to show fault "substantially outweighs" its probative value in proving ownership, it is excludable.

Another, related issue concerns whether Rule 403 can be used to *admit* into evidence matters *banned* by the first sentence of Rule 407. For example, a remedial measure particularly probative of negligence might be claimed admissible on this ground. But given the categorical nature of the exclusion and its basis in encouragement of improvements, this argument is unpersuasive, and has been widely rejected.

Prior to the amendment, and in the many jurisdictions without the amendment, are remedial or safety measures admissible in a strict products liability action? The answer depends in part on the issue to which they would be relevant. It can be argued that "culpability" or "negligence"—fault—is not in issue in such an action, because liability attaches irrespective of negligence and, indeed, attaches even if the manufacturer exercises all possible care. All that is banned by the express words of the unamended rule is evidence offered to show "negligence or culpable conduct", i.e., fault. This no-fault reasoning supports admissibility, assuming there is something other than fault the evidence is relevant to and that such relevance outweighs the tendency to induce decision on the erroneous issue of fault. Because fault is not in issue, presumably the tendency of the jury to use the evidence on that issue is more easily controlled.

On the other hand, it might be argued that sale of a defective product is indeed "culpable conduct." This reasoning could bring the evidence within the Rule, thus barring the evidence, unless the evidence is offered on another issue (such as, for example, feasibility of an alternative design, which is an issue in products liability cases alleging a design defect) and that use outweighs. Perhaps a distinction can be drawn on this basis amongst different kinds of strict liability. In some jurisdictions, manufacturing defect cases seem truly no-fault, but design defect and warnings defect cases come very close to negligence cases.

Some courts have engaged in sophisticated economic analyses to supposedly demonstrate that the policy favoring exclusion also applies (or does not apply) to strict liability actions. One such argument is that producers of mass distribution products will make product improvements after an injury even without the stimulus of this rule because they would not want to risk massive liability. Some say this proves too much: that the rule is not needed in mass-product *negligence* cases either. Alternatively, it has been argued that manufacturers do not always fear massive liability. They may believe the mishap was caused not by problems with the product but rather by a stupid and peculiar misuse by one customer. The rule, it is argued, might stimulate such a manufacturer to improve the product to prevent such misuse, a socially desirable result.

Frequently a count in negligence is joined with the strict liability claim. Can the evidence practicably be admitted only on one count?

Before the 1997 revision, courts split on all these issues related to strict liability. F.R.E. 407 now adopts the view that the exclusion applies alike to strict product liability and negligence. There has been some complaint that this rule interferes with substantive tort policy in diversity cases. For example, California and a number of states permit evidence of subsequent remedial measures concerning product liability.

Compromises, Settlement Negotiations, and Medical Payments: F.R.E. 408–09

Offers to pay, compromise, or settle a disputed claim, and related negotiations and statements, are a type of possible implied or actual admission which is subject to a general exclusion, but there are a number of exceptions. F.R.E. 408. Payment of medical or similar expenses is also typically not admissible to prove liability. F.R.E. 409.

The driving force that motivates these prohibitions is the extrinsic policy in favor of encouraging settlements. The court system would break down from overload if all cases were tried. Or we would have to sink huge resources into the courts. Encouragement of humanitarian acts is also at work here.

The prohibitions are also based on the likelihood that something other than consciousness of guilt or adverse facts stimulated the offer (e.g., a motive to buy peace, or a charitable motive), which may be overlooked by the jury. This supports exclusion on the probativity-versus-counterweights balancing.

F.R.E. 408 does, however, require that the claim be "disputed" and that the effort be to "compromise" (settle). The negotiations must be "compromise negotiations". If one party demands payment under a contract and the other party flatly offers to pay without disputing liability, or negotiating, Rule 408 does not exclude evidence of the offer (in a lawsuit, say, for subsequently failing to make the payment).

Under the common law, statements of fact or opinion made during settlement discussions usually were considered to be outside the exclusion, which extended only to the fact that discussions were undertaken and to any actual offers made. There was an exception, in some jurisdictions, if the statements of fact or opinion were expressly said to be either hypothetical ("what if I were to say . . . ") or "without prejudice"—magic phrases that were a trap for clients with unwary lawyers who did not know the magic words were needed. The requirement gave rise to endless disputes as to whether the magic words were in fact uttered.

Instead, a policy to encourage settlement arguably should include full immunity for statements of fact and opinion, because they are essential to parties forming a realistic picture of relative strengths and weaknesses, properly evaluating their cases, and thus to reaching settlement. F.R.E. 408 gives statements during negotiations full immunity, on a par with the other matters immunized, by categorically excluding "conduct or statements made during compromise negotiations." Some controversy has arisen over whether civil settlements and statements made in civil settlement discussions, the focus of the rule, are banned from admission in subsequent related criminal litigation. Most courts take the position that the language of the rule precludes later use of the evidence in either kind of case. A very recent amendment to the Rule codifies this result except as to a

limited category of such evidence, i.e., "conduct or statements" made in the course of a civil settlement negotia-
tion with a government agency. The amendment makes
these admissible in a criminal case (subject to Rule 403)
on grounds of fairness: a party ought not to be able to
make factual assertions or implications in one case with
the government and disavow them in another. But in
order not to deter unduly civil settlements with the
government, the settlement, offer, or attempt to settle
itself (as distinct from any "conduct or statements"
made in the course thereof) is still inadmissible. Such
evidence is seen as more ambiguous than specific statements or conduct.

A separate question concerns settlements the defendant has concluded with or offered to third parties injured in the same occurrence. Generally, the courts have
held that these, too, are embraced by the ban, in accordance with its policy of encouraging settlement. This
result has been reached in spite of the apparently unin-
tentional use of the phrase "*the* claim" in F.R.E. 408.
Uniform Rule 408, and a number of states, add "or any
other claim."

Original F.R.E. 408 (like current Rule 408 in a number
of states) prohibited evidence only when offered to prove
"liability for or invalidity of the claim or its amount" and
said nothing about using it for impeachment of a witness' credibility by inconsistency or contradiction (added
as a banned purpose to F.R.E. 408 only very recently).
Since the original rule also said, as it currently does, that
uses other than the prohibited use are permitted, it was
often argued that a defendant's offer to settle could be
introduced not substantively as an admission of liability,
but as prior conduct (or an implied statement) inconsistent with—and therefore impeaching—his current testimony that he is not liable. Most courts, however, felt
that this impeachment-of-credibility use was so close to

the prohibited use that the policies behind the Rule would be offended if it were admissible. As indicated above, F.R.E. 408 was amended very recently to codify this result.

For similar reasons, the old rule invited arguments that a specific *statement of fact or opinion* made in compromise negotiations, that is directly opposite to the same party's specific testimony at trial, could be used for impeachment. The same amendment language referred to just above, banning use of evidence under the rule when offered for impeachment by inconsistency or contradiction, also covers (and therefore bans) this use, as well.

Settlements and settlement negotiations between the defendant and third persons injured in the same occurrence are often admitted *if the third person testifies* for the defendant. This is normally viewed not as *impeachment by inconsistency or contradiction* (now banned by the rule pursuant to the amendment), but as *impeachment by potential bias*. Rule 408 has an express list of examples of permissible purposes for Rule 408 evidence, and "proving a witness' bias or prejudice" is one of them.[5] Permissible purposes may be regarded as "exceptions" to the ban expressed by the Rule.

But cases within the "exceptions" are merely excepted from the ban embodied by this particular rule, 408. They are still subject to possible exclusion on particular facts under the balancing of Rule 403. (The reverse is not true: evidence banned by 408 cannot be made admissible by 403, since the ban is absolute.)

Under Rule 409, evidence of paying or offering to pay medical expenses upon injury to another is also excluded.

5. The others are "negating a contention of undue delay" and "proving an effort to obstruct a criminal investigation or prosecution." Any other purpose that is not one of the two prohibited purposes (described above) is also not prohibited by the Rule.

The rule rests on the assumption, first, that the offer stems from humane impulses rather than consciousness of guilt or adverse facts, and second, that to admit evidence of medical payments would be to discourage people from offering them. However, contrary to Rule 408, Rule 409 does not protect conduct or statements that are not part of the offer to pay expenses. Also, the Rule only excludes evidence about medical "and similar" payments; it does not expressly cover payments of lost wages or financial damages generally. But 409 does not require a "dispute".

Withdrawn Guilty Pleas and Plea Negotiations: F.R.E. 410

The use, as admissions, of certain criminal pleas and related statements is usually restricted.

Former criminal and civil pleas or pleadings—that is, pleas or pleadings in other cases, whether withdrawn or not; amended, superseded, or withdrawn pleas or pleadings in the present case; etc.—and statements made in connection with them, are obvious candidates for attempts to find and use damaging admissions and impeaching statements inconsistent with the pleader's present position. As with all the express and implied admissions under consideration here and above, they survive the hearsay rule: If they are hearsay, the F.R.E. exempt them from hearsay, while states following traditional hearsay definitions like California treat admissions as a hearsay exception.

Nevertheless, under common law rules in some jurisdictions, certain prior judicial submissions of this kind can be used only under certain conditions, owing to various policy considerations and concern over probativity and misleading the jury. The extrinsic policy at work here is similar to that underlying Rule 408, the encouragement of settlements, in that sheltering these prior submissions may encourage admissions by protecting the option of withdrawal or limiting the consequences of the admission.

The law varies widely from jurisdiction to jurisdiction and situation to situation, and in many jurisdictions, the use of civil pleadings as admissions is unrestricted.

As always, admissibility does not mean these ostensible admissions cannot be explained away to the jury as a matter of weight.

F.R.E. 410 generally prohibits the introduction (whether in the same case or in subsequent civil or criminal proceedings) of certain criminal-case filings and statements: a withdrawn guilty plea, a plea of nolo contendere ("I do not plead guilty, but I will not contest the charges, so you may enter a conviction against me"), statements made in court at hearings concerning the acceptance of the plea, and statements made to prosecuting attorneys in plea discussions. Whether the rule should be re-drafted to reach the latter statements if made to non-attorneys, principally investigating officers and police, has been controversial. Under Rule 410 as written, a factual admission made to an FBI agent or police officer in negotiations is not excludable from evidence; it is a confession, much like any other confession. Rule 410 appears to reflect a policy of allowing into evidence such confessions to police officers and avoiding factual controversies about whether they were part of plea negotiations. Perhaps there are situations in which the police should be considered agents of the prosecutor for these purposes.

In *United States v. Mezzanatto* (S.Ct.1995), the Supreme Court held that the defendant's advance agreement to waive the protections of Rule 410 was enforceable absent a showing that it was unknowingly or involuntarily made. Though the waiver upheld in the

case was only for impeachment use if defendant testified inconsistently, the rationale of the decision does
not seem so limited. Some prosecutors now routinely
request such agreements as a condition of engaging in
plea bargaining. A dissenting justice argued that the
decision had the potential to eviscerate the operation
of Rule 410. The majority, however, pointed out that
almost all evidentiary rules are subject to voluntary
and knowing waiver, including the most important
constitutional rules, and that prosecuting attorneys
could be expected to adapt their insistence upon waivers to obtain valid and useful plea agreements.

Liability Insurance: F.R.E. 411

**In most jurisdictions evidence revealing the pres-
ence or absence of liability insurance is inadmissible
in fault-related cases, save in exceptional situations
(F.R.E. 411). Similar authority exists with respect to
showing financial strength or weakness of the parties.**

Suggestion that the defendant is insured against the
liability at issue is prejudicial because (a) the jury may
overemphasize the tendency of insurance to encourage
carelessness (does insurance really suggest carelessness,
or rather, foresight and prudence?) and (b) the jury is
believed prone to "pin the bill on the deepest pocket."
Thus, this evidence generally is excludable when offered
to prove fault. See, e.g., F.R.E. 411. The balance may
swing in favor of admissibility where there are circumstances rendering a particularized inference of carelessness extremely reliable (e.g., defendant driver says immediately prior to the collision, "I have insurance, so I don't
care if I hit anything"). But cf. F.R.E. 411 (maybe still
the prohibited purpose: to prove negligence).

Insurance evidence *may* be admissible if offered for a
purpose other than proof of fault or lack of fault. It is felt
that the probativity-versus-counterweights balance is
more likely to come out positive—for admissibility—in

such a situation. This may be the case where, for example, (1) the evidence has direct impeachment value (e.g., plaintiff attempts to reveal possible bias by showing that a defense witness is an employee of defendant's insurer); (2) there is a specific admission or other very probative evidence that cannot be severed from the evidence of defendant's insurance (some authorities feel this is still offered on the forbidden issue, negligence); (3) ownership of a vehicle, or its control, or some similar issue, is at stake, and it can best be resolved by reference to the insurance policy covering the item; (4) the defendant has falsely (and improperly) denied being insured or plaintiff has falsely (and improperly) suggested defendant is insured (so that contradiction shows untruthfulness or removes the false inference); or (5) during jury selection, potential jurors are sought to be identified for challenge on the ground of bias because of their or their families' insurance affiliations.[6]

Before any of these enumerated "exceptions" will be applied and the evidence admitted, however, the judge will need to consider whether, on the particular facts, probativity is substantially outweighed by prejudice or other counterweights. In other words, as with the rules regarding remedial measures and offers of compromise, the exceptions in Rule 411 do not make the evidence automatically admissible. They merely remove the evidence from Rule 411's general prohibition, leaving other exclusionary rules still potentially applicable. Thus, the requirement of balancing under Rule 403 still must be fulfilled. Limiting instructions to the jury, e.g., that the insurance may not be considered as evidence of negli-

---

6. To minimize prejudice in this last situation, many jurisdictions routinely inquire into insurance affiliation on a form or in a general session, directed at an entire array of prospective jurors, perhaps before any jurors are associated with any particular case. There may be further particularized inquiries thereafter, directed at those who have indicated something of concern, taken up outside the presence of other jurors.

gence or ability to bear the burden, may help, and should
be given if the evidence is admitted and the instruction
requested.

As with Rules 407 and 408, the potentially permissible
exceptional purposes listed in 411 ("proof of agency,
ownership, or control, or bias or prejudice of a witness")
are not exhaustive. Any purpose other than the forbidden
offer ("offered upon the issue of whether the [insured]
acted negligently or otherwise wrongfully") would be
included. And, as in 407 and 408, if evidence is offered
for the forbidden purpose, neither Rule 403 nor any
other rule can get the evidence admitted.

Most jurisdictions take the view that liability insurance
may be inquired into upon discovery. The reason is the
policy in favor of settlement. Knowledge of funds available for payment often stimulates settlement. Notice that
discovery of insurance may be outside the usual discovery limits because it may not be "reasonably calculated"
to lead to admissible evidence. Nevertheless, insurance is
normally made discoverable by a separate, specific rule.
See Fed. R. Civ. P. 26(a)(1)(D). Note also that discovera-
bility does not affect whether the fact of insurance is
excludable from evidence.

Evidence of defendant's ability to pay may be admissible in some jurisdictions where punitive damages are at
issue. This is because punitive damages are supposed to
be assessed by the jury in an amount to hurt but not
wipe the defendant out. Liability insurance may be part
of the assets available to pay all or part of the judgment
and so must be part of the calculations. But if the
presence of a claim for punitive damages increases the
likelihood that insurance will be discoverable and/or admissible, litigants may be tempted to add unsupportable
claims for punitive damages. Screening by the law and by
the judge to be sure the case is the type that would
support punitive damages can minimize this danger.
Bifurcation of trials can help eliminate improper use on

liability, of insurance or financial evidence admissible only on the issue of amount of punitive damages. Under bifurcation, used by many courts in this situation, the hearing on punitive damages comes only after the jury has decided liability. The Supreme Court has raised some doubts about the extent to which punitive damages may be based on ability to pay, but the effects this will have on traditional practices is yet to be determined. See *State Farm Mut. Automobile Ins. Co. v. Campbell* (S.Ct.2003).

Evidence of defendant's *lack* of insurance is subject to similar restrictions as evidence he is insured. Evidence concerning plaintiff's insurance status is similarly restricted. This includes (though it is not covered by the Rule), plaintiff's health insurance, since, in most jurisdictions, under the "collateral source rule", the jury is not supposed to reduce plaintiff's recovery for personal injury medical damages based on payments from plaintiff's health insurer because plaintiff paid for them and thus defendant should not benefit from them (and also because there is some notion that damages do not entirely make the plaintiff whole). To safeguard enforcement of the collateral source rule, normally the jury should not hear evidence of plaintiff's health insurance.

Evidence of a plaintiff's or defendant's wealth or poverty bears a resemblance to insurance evidence, but has not been sufficiently manifest in recurring situations to result in a codified rule. Such evidence frequently is excluded for reasons similar to those operable in the insurance area, except where roughly similar exceptional circumstances swing the balancing factors toward admissibility. For example, if there is a dispute as to whether *A* bought an expensive item for her own account, or as agent for *B*, the relative strengths and weaknesses of their wealth might be received to illuminate this issue. Similarly, a legitimate claim for punitive damages might justify reception of otherwise forbidden financial evidence.

CHAPTER 4

A SPECIAL RELEVANCY VS. COUNTERWEIGHTS PROBLEM AREA: SIMILAR ACTS, CHARACTER, PROPENSITY

I. AN OVERVIEW OF THE PROPENSITY–RELATED RULES

The Theory of the Rules: Propensity Is "Relevant" But Sometimes Prejudicial, Misleading, Too Time Consuming, or Just Plain Not Fair

In determining whether a person acted in a certain way on a particular occasion—for example, whether a witness has reported correctly or lied or made a mistake, or whether a particular person did or did not commit a rape, or was or was not careful, or turned a corner in an automobile in a particular way—it is logical to reason that one who has exhibited a pattern of behavior of the kind in question or a propensity for it is more likely to have acted in accord with that pattern or propensity on the occasion in issue, than someone who has not exhibited the pattern or propensity or has exhibited a contrary one, all other things being equal.

At least as a matter of logic, a pattern or propensity can be proved, with varying persuasiveness, by showing specific instances of like conduct on the part of the person; by showing the person's reputation in the relevant respect; or by introducing the personal opinion of those who know him, as to the relevant characteristic. Further, logically speaking, the persuasiveness of the evidence will vary according to how precisely like the conduct in issue the other instances of conduct, or the quality reputed or opined, are. Instances of, or a reputation for, parking violations may not be particularly persuasive on the issue of credibility or the issue of whether the defendant committed the rape charged. Instances of, or a reputation for, lying or sex crimes, might be.

We see, therefore, that it is always *relevant* to prove a pattern of, or propensity for, the kind of conduct in issue, on the part of the person whose conduct is in issue (although there will be varying degrees of relevance or probativity). If this mode of proof, argument, or reasoning is objectionable, it must be for some other reason than that it is irrelevant. The dangers in it may be that the jury will over-emphasize its logical force, become unduly emotionally disposed in favor of or against one side or the other, punish or exact payment for past sins regardless of findings concerning the present one, or (where a witness is involved) hold a party responsible to an undue extent for the sins of his witnesses. It may unduly harass, annoy, humiliate, discourage from coming forward, or invade the privacy of, the party or witness. And there is the danger that what is at most a subsidiary inquiry will become too time consuming or central or will protract, distract, and confuse, with respect to the main issue. It may engender its own rebuttals and explanations, carrying the inquiry even farther afield, yet into areas that will be difficult to keep distinct from the main inquiry. To allow the evidence without the rebuttals and explanations may produce its own distortions, dissatisfactions, and unfairness. It tends to become a "trial within a trial".

Part of these considerations is that introduction of particular instances selected from a person's entire life can catch opposing counsel (or the witness or party) unawares, and place upon him a tremendous burden to anticipate which instances will be selected, and to prepare for them, without which preparation the evidence could be very misleading. (For this reason F.R.E. 404(b) was amended to require advance notice when such evidence is offered against a criminal defendant under one of the exceptional gateways permitting such evidence.)

There is also the desirability of encouraging reform and rehabilitation by letting people know that it is not futile to change their ways—that they can live down past derelictions and that they will not be unnecessarily dogged by them the rest of their lives.

All these factors must be weighed in the particular context. In the calculus it should be recognized that the evidence may have only an attenuated logical tendency to establish the proposition for which it is offered, again depending upon the context. Finally, the efficacy of cautionary instructions in reducing the dangers is a factor to be considered in the balance.

Other considerations may be: (1) In a criminal case "it is better that many guilty go free than that an innocent be punished." Might this mean that a kind of evidence barred to the prosecution might be acceptable when introduced in defense? (2) Is a jury especially prone to overemphasize propensity evidence introduced by the prosecution? (3) Is a propensity to abstain from certain acts probative or persuasive in the same degree as a propensity to commit certain acts? (4) Of the three forms of propensity evidence (reputation, personal opinion, specific instances), which is the most probative? Which is the least probative? Which is most likely to unduly prejudice the jury? The least? Which is the most time consuming? The most likely to distract the inquiry into collateral incidents likely to be confused with the main inquiry? Which the least? Which is most likely to lead to a side "trial within a trial"? There might be a reluctance to permit the most probative evidence if at the same time it is the most unduly prejudicial, time consuming, and confusing.

Fig. 1

F.R.E. 404: The General Prohibition: The "Char→Act" Chain

The chart below shows the chain of inference prohibited in general under the F.R.E. because of the considerations outlined above.

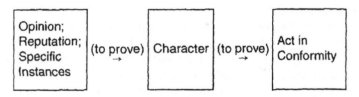

Description for Fig. 1:

The above chain is the generally prohibited chain under the F.R.E. (Rule 404). The principal question is "What is meant by 'character'?" Is it *any* propensity, whether general or specific? Whether considered good, bad, or morally neutral? Does the answer depend upon what danger the rule is meant to guard against: the inspiring of moral approval-disapproval; or a deceptive appearance of strength on the part of a weak inference; or both?

As we stated, the pictured chain (char→act chain) is the generally prohibited chain under the F.R.E. However, F.R.E. 404(a)(1) through (3) list some special exceptions allowing (when read together with F.R.E. 405(a)) *opinion* and *reputation* for the purpose expressed by the chain, *in certain circumstances* (character of accused, of victim, etc., as defined and regulated there). *Specific instances* offered for the purpose expressed by the chain are inadmissible (except for the impeachment allowed by F.R.E. 608 and 609 dealing with convictions and with misconduct bespeaking falsity that has not resulted in conviction; and the prior or subsequent sexual misconduct of an alleged sexual offender allowed by Rules 413 through 415).

All uses of specific instances allowed by F.R.E. 404–405 (other crimes, wrongs, acts, for certain permitted purposes; specific instances used to challenge or test a character witness; and situations where character or a trait are "elements") are *not* for the purpose expressed by the char→act chain depicted above. Specific instances, opinion, and reputation, not offered for the purpose expressed by the depicted char→act chain, are not subject to any per se ban and thus are governed by the ad hoc balancing of the general provisions of Rule 403. Such evidence, then, need not be recognized expressly by any provision or exception in Rules 404–405, but for tidiness the drafters did mention in 404 and 405 a few types of such evidence as not being within the per se ban of 404–405. Be aware that evidence allowed by 404–405 (whether expressly or by implication) is still not automatically admissible, but rather is subject to the balancing of Rule 403.

If "habit" is substituted for "character" in the above char→act chart, the chain is then usually permitted (F.R.E. 406). Is there a propensity that is neither "habit" nor "character", that might appear as the middle term in the chart, at least conceptually speaking? (For example, a psychological compulsion, illness, or personality trait?)

End of Description for Fig. 1.

The Evidentiary Rules: A Road Map to F.R.E. 404–406 and Related Rules

Rules (including "exceptions") have evolved in response to the various considerations discussed in the text preceding Figure 1, which considerations are in major part the considerations discussed under the "balancing" process in Chapter Three, supra. These complex "rules" (and their "exceptions") as they exist in most jurisdictions including under the F.R.E., may be summarized by the following black letters (which restate more expansively Figure 1):

The term "propensity" means a "tendency" or "penchant." "Character" is a propensity that is general (i.e. propensity for "honesty" or "dishonesty," "violence" or "non-violence") as opposed to specific (i.e., propensity for executing certain kinds of violent or dishonest acts, or for executing them in a certain manner) and is possessed of good or bad moral connotations. "Habit" is a very strong and very specific propensity in which acts occur somewhat invariably and automatically and which take some deliberation to vary, qualities which we may take "character" not to have. ("Routine practice" is "habit" of an organization.) Propensities of each of these types, at least conceptually if not under the law, could be established by proof of specific instances of conduct, by proof of reputation for the propensity, or by someone's personal opinion about whether the propensity is possessed or not.

There is a general legal ban on establishing propensity in any fashion, UNLESS

(1) the propensity is not offered to show an act in conformity with the propensity, or if so offered,

(2) it is not a character type of propensity, e.g., it fits *any* one or more of the following three criteria:

(a) it is not a general propensity, but rather a specific propensity (as in many of the cases where other crimes, wrongs, or acts specifically like the incident to be proved are allowed under the rubric that they establish identity, motive, knowledge, intent, plan, absence of mistake, etc.),

(b) it does not have good or bad moral connotations,

(c) it is a habit;

(3) or, if it is a character-type propensity offered to show an act in conformity with it, it fits the special rules for exceptions generally known as

(a) character of the accused (substantive evidence),

(b) character of the victim (substantive evidence),

(c) credibility-character of witnesses (credibility evidence), or,

(d) under recently added provisions 413 through 415 of the F.R.E., not yet widely adopted among the states, character of a sexual offender (substantive and possibly also credibility evidence).

In such cases (i.e., categories (1) through (3)) there is no automatic ban and admissibility is determined on an individualized, fact-specific, case-by-case basis upon consideration of the general factors and policies (relevancy and its counterweights) listed in Chapter Three, supra, and in F.R.E. 403, perhaps in some jurisdictions more specifically codified by particular rules or rulings.

The form of the evidence used to establish the propensity in category (3) (exclusive of the credibility-character and the new sex-offender evidence) was historically limited to reputation evidence but more recently has been expanded to embrace both reputation and personal opinion evidence but still excludes specific instance evidence. The habit rule, the credibility-character rule, and the sex-offender rule admit specific instances (and only specific instances in the last).

A few jurisdictions place special limits on the habit or routine practice evidence, requiring corroboration of or lack of eyewitnesses to the occurrence.

Showings concerning the victim in rape and similar cases are often the subject of separate, special, more restrictive regulation to protect the victim from what has been considered unfair, unnecessary, privacy-infringing character attacks that discourage complainants from reporting rapes.

Generally speaking, F.R.E. 404 through 406 (substantive use of character and habit), 412 (showings concerning victim in rape and the like), 413 through 415 (showings concerning sex offenders) and 608 through 609 (witness's credibility-character), and similar provisions of the codes modeled on the F.R.E., codify all this law. Significant changes in the F.R.E. and its progeny from traditional law include licensing both reputation and personal opinion testimony where previous law permitted only reputation; an attempt to disapprove the qualifications on habit that relate to eyewitnesses and corroboration; and a broadening of the form of question permitted to challenge a character-witness's knowledge or standards, allowing "did you know" of certain contrary instances, as well as the traditional "have you heard." The evidence discussed concerning rape victims and similar sex victims is also restricted. The other sex provisions, i.e., those concerning sex *offenders*, were added by the F.R.E. They are not yet widely adopted even by F.R.E.-pattern states. They broaden traditional law, under which similar evidence was frequently squeezed into

evidence, though with difficulty, through existing admissibility gateways.

Let us elaborate. There is a general ban on proof of propensity adduced for purposes of soliciting the sort of reasoning we have been discussing—that is, establishing a propensity in order to show an act in conformity with it—but the exceptions are many. First of all, a question can be raised, at least in many jurisdictions, as to whether the ban applies at all to propensity that cannot be called "character." Although there is not universal agreement, "character" may be defined as a propensity that has a "good" or "bad" moral connotation; and is general rather than specific, i.e., a propensity for dishonesty rather than for using a particular modus operandi in conducting a particular type of fraudulent scheme. "Character" appears also to be distinct from the propensity known as "habit," which, in addition to being specific, is not necessarily morally tinged, and is in some degree automatic. "Character" and "character trait" are probably alternative ways to say nearly the same thing. "Character" seems to refer to an extremely broad or general propensity such as "he is a good person" made up of a sum of "character traits" such as propensity for nonviolence, honesty, law abidingness, etc., also general and also tinged with moral approbation, but slightly less general than character. In any event, both are characterized by their generality and moral tinge, as compared with propensities we would not put in the realm of character, and neither has the automaticity and specificity of habit.

A number of other exceptions are commonly found, also reflected in the above black-letter summary. The remainder of the chapter will illuminate the main ones.

II. PERMISSIBLE USES OF CHARACTER AS SUBSTANTIVE CIRCUMSTANTIAL EVIDENCE

Good Character, Offered at the Criminal Defendant's Option: F.R.E. 404(a)(1) and 405

The Defendant's Option to Offer Character Evidence on a "Pertinent Trait": the "Mercy Rule" Allowing "Good Guy" Evidence

In a criminal case, the defendant (D) may reduce the likelihood that D committed the crime by showing his good character (character-type propensity for not committing the crime—known as "good guy" evidence). This principle is called the "character of the accused" or "mercy" rule, the latter because the principle is a special dispensation to the criminal defendant. The showing is usually confined to testimony as to the defendant's reputation for the particular trait in issue, that is, the "pertinent" trait (e.g., reputation for peaceableness or nonviolence in an assault or homicide case; reputation for trustworthiness with property in an embezzlement case), given by a witness who must be shown to be familiar with D's reputation in D's community reasonably near the time of the crime. Personal opinion testimony is also permitted in most (but not all) jurisdictions, but again only if the witness opines on the particular character trait in issue and is familiar enough with D to give such an opinion. E.g. F.R.E. 404(a)(1) as delimited by 405(a). (Although lay opinion is what is contemplated by this provision, do you think expert opinion may also be embraced?)

Can such good character evidence alone raise a reasonable doubt in favor of a criminal defendant? As a practical matter, it can and does, occasionally producing an otherwise unlikely acquittal, which cannot be challenged on appeal. While a number of highly respectable courts have in the past differed, most courts today refuse to expressly instruct the jury that good character alone can raise a reasonable doubt, telling the jury only that character is a factor to be considered in their evaluation of the total evidence in the case.

Impeachment of Character Witnesses by "Have You Heards"

The evidence of D's good character will usually be given by someone other than the D himself; thus he is not opened up to character assassination under the guise of impeachment. However, D's character witnesses may be subjected not only to the more customary varieties of impeachment, but also to a kind of cross-examination for impeachment that is potentially exceptionally damaging to the defendant: defendant's prior derelictions are inquired into ostensibly not to reflect on the defendant, but to show that the good character witnesses are not actually familiar with that whereof they speak or if they are they have suspect judgment. See, e.g., F.R.E. 405(a), second sentence. This in theory does not involve the kind of propensity reasoning under discussion although in practice, despite cautionary instructions, it tends to tarnish the defendant along propensity lines. If challenged, the prosecution may be required to show the judge that the prosecutor has a good faith basis for believing there possibly might be such wrongdoing, in order for the questions to be proper.

On this theory of impeachment, the reasoning is that the crime or other misconduct of D did occur, but the basis for the impeachment is not an inference about D, but rather that D's witness (or the community) was unaware of wrongdoing or improperly analyzed it in evaluating the defendant's character. (It is, however, usually not permitted to ask good character witnesses whether their opinions would be different if the defendant committed the very crime charged, although this kind of question has been upheld when the character witness was an expert, and sometimes in other circumstances as well, depending on the jurisdiction.)

Under traditional common-law, the prosecution, in performing this kind of impeachment that inquires into other derelictions of the defendant, was ordinarily confined to asking the witness, on cross examination, "Have you *heard* that the defendant did X [a wrong, not necessarily a conviction or crime, directly relevant to the character trait testified to by the witness]?" The Advisory Committee Note to F.R.E. 405(a) also allows the question to be put in the form "Did you *know* that ..." This reflects the modern trend which permits the good character witness's direct examination to be in terms of opinion as well as reputation (although the advisory committee draws no distinction in allowing the "know" question), and reflects that there is really a minuscule difference to the witness and the jury between the two forms of the question, although in logic, the "have you heard" form would seem to make it easier to confine the evidence to its proper role, impeachment. The prosecution will not be permitted to introduce extrinsic evidence concerning the incident in any event. In other words, this particular line of attack on the credibility of the good character witness stops with cross-examination of him or her.

This approved procedure presents a very serious danger of unsubstantiated imputation of wrong-doing, for which the good faith requirement is only an imperfect answer. Courts do not always impose the requirement, and when they do, they frequently find it is satisfied by the most cursory showing, probably because it is somewhat justified for the cross examiner to say to the judge

"I don't know if there is any wrongdoing; that's why I'm asking" at least when the question the prosecutor asks the witness does not refer to specifics that imply that there was a particular instance.

This license to impeach good character witnesses should be distinguished from the other license given the prosecutor upon the introduction by defendant of good character evidence: the right to show bad character (character-type propensity) substantively—i.e., to directly and frankly demonstrate that the defendant *is* the sort of person who will have committed the crime—discussed immediately infra. It is also to be distinguished from the license given the prosecutor if the defendant takes the stand to testify to any matter in the case: the license to impeach the defendant's veracity to the same extent as any witness' veracity may be impeached, including a showing of a propensity for falsehood, except in rare circumstances where an instruction is deemed insufficient to guard against undue prejudice because the witness is the defendant.

The Prosecution's Rebuttal of the Defendant's Character Evidence: F.R.E. 404(a)(1)

Although the prosecution normally may not *initiate* substantive bad character showings about the defendant in order to suggest defendant acted in conformity with his character and thus to increase the likelihood he committed the crime, nevertheless the prosecutor may *respond* to defendant's substantive good character evidence (described above) with such substantive bad character evidence for just such a purpose. The prosecution may thus show D's bad character in order to rebut D's good character evidence, that is, frankly to establish that the defendant is indeed the "kind of person" who would commit the crime. In addition, Rule 404(a)(1) has been amended to permit the prosecution to prove the defendant's bad character to respond to defense evidence showing the same trait of the victim's character (permitted through an exception discussed below). Thus, if the defendant claims the victim had a violent character, the prosecutor now can show that the defendant also had this trait.

This rule, allowing the prosecutor's rebuttal of either kind of defense showing, also goes under the name "character of the accused" (see, e.g., F.R.E. 404(a)(1)), like defendant's good character evidence above; and the evidence is similarly limited to well grounded, closely pertinent reputation (and opinion, in most jurisdictions) as opposed to specific instances. See F.R.E. 405(a). Such "bad character" witnesses can be impeached in the same way as indicated above for "good character" witnesses.

Character of the Victim in Self–Defense and Other Cases: F.R.E. 404(a)(2)

In a criminal case where self-defense is put in issue by the defendant, the question whether the victim was the aggressor can be illuminated with showings concerning the victim's character-propensity for violence, but in most jurisdictions only if such showings are initiated by the defendant. (Only then may the prosecution respond with similar opposite showings concerning the victim.)

In certain jurisdictions the entire permission to do any of this concerning the victim would be confined to homicide cases (where, of course, the deceased victim is unavailable). In others, like the F.R.E., it might encompass prosecutions for the various kinds of assault and battery as well. In some jurisdictions, unlike the F.R.E., the analogy would extend to permitting such a showing in civil assault, battery, and/or wrongful death cases involving an issue of self-defense.

F.R.E. 404(a)(2) permits "evidence of a pertinent trait of character of the victim of the crime offered by an accused, or by the prosecution to rebut the same; or evidence of a character trait of peacefulness of the victim offered by the prosecution in a homicide case to rebut evidence [for example, non-character factual evidence given by a witness who saw the victim attacking the defendant] that the victim was the first aggressor." Notice that the "door opener" by the defendant that licenses the prosecution to show character of the homicide victim may or may not itself be a character showing. For other crime victims, it must be a character showing. For crime victims other than homicide, the issue is not confined to self-defense and first aggressor. Note that the whole rule is confined to criminal cases. Although some jurisdictions allow specific instance evidence, F.R.E. 405(a) limits evidence admissible under 404(a)(2) to opinion and reputation evidence. Some jurisdictions confine it to reputation evidence. As in the case of good and bad character showings concerning the defendant (see above), the reputation or opinion witness would have to have sufficient knowledge to so testify; the trait testified about would have to be "pertinent"; and the witness could be impeached by all the methods indicated there for character witnesses.

The quoted language of 404(a)(2) looks like it would encompass showings about the alleged victim in rape or other sex cases, but that is covered by a special rule, Rule 412. Showings of that nature are discussed infra.

Evidence of violent acts, reputation, character, etc., of an assault, battery, or homicide victim, that were known to the defendant, offered to render self-defensive measures of the defendant reasonable in the light of this knowledge, looks as though it would be covered here. But in fact the rules and rulings we are discussing are exceptions to the ban on a certain chain of propensity reasoning (that a person acted in conformity with his character-propensity—the "char→act" inference). This evidence in no way involves that prohibited chain of reasoning, and so needs no special exception. It would be governed by an ad hoc consideration of the factors enumerated in Rule 403, and is usually found to be admissible.

III. SIMILAR INCIDENTS OFFERED FOR NON–CHARACTER CIRCUM-STANTIAL PURPOSES

Intent, Identity and Other Factors as Shown by Similar Incidents: F.R.E. 404(b): "M.O.I.P.P.K.I.A.", the "Other Crimes, Wrongs, or Acts" or "Uncharged Misconduct" Principle

In certain circumstances, the prosecution may initiate a substantive showing against the defendant *something* like those above, except that it will consist of specific instances and, if it involves propensity reasoning at all, it will be too specific a propensity to be considered "character" although it may suggest character.

This will be pursuant to a rule like F.R.E. 404(b) or its traditional common-law analogue. Under such a rule, specific instances of conduct ("other crimes, wrongs, acts"), although they may suggest character, are allowed if the character chain of reasoning (depicted in the "char→act" chart above) is not the avowed purpose, assuming the avowed purpose is a substantially relevant one and the danger of character use by the jury is considered low enough in comparison (under a rule like F.R.E. 403) that it can be sufficiently guarded against by a jury instruction.

Such evidence is usually allowed if there is sufficient reason to believe defendant committed the other conduct and the conduct is considered necessary to show such important intermediate or ultimate factors as "motive, opportunity, intent, preparation, plan, knowledge, identity, or absence of mistake or accident" (known by their acronym "MOIPPKIA" and ordinarily listed as non-exhaustive examples in the rule or decisional law), or to show any other similar factor that, like the listed factors, does not involve the prohibited character inference (the chain depicted in the "char→act" chart, above). The listed factors are meant to connote situations where the evidence would be highly probative in advancing the argument of defendant's guilt.

Admissibility is confined to specific instances, and may be confined further by decision to conduct very like that charged, at least in certain situations.

This gateway to admissibility is often referred to as the "other crimes, wrongs, or acts" or "uncharged misconduct" gateway, "uncharged" referring to the fact that the misconduct is not part of the formal charges in the case in which it is offered. Civil libertarians have suggested that in some cases the offered misconduct is purposely withheld by the prosecutor from formal charges in order to get around the requirement of proof beyond a reasonable doubt.

F.R.E. 404(b) embodies the traditional admissibility gateway under discussion here, expressly listing the mentioned string of non-exhaustive permissible purposes ("motive, opportunity, [etc.]"—MOIPPKIA) in precisely the language quoted just above where we listed the MOIPPKIA purposes. You will note the extreme brevity, abstraction, and cryptic nature of the entries on the list. This is exactly how they appear in the rule and in decisional law. Each stands for a line of cases or type of case that should be mastered.

Rule 404(b) is generally considered an "inclusionary" rule in the sense that the list of proper purposes is merely illustrative and not exclusive, and this is supported by the entire grammatical structure of the rule and the words "such as" that introduce the list, much the same as is described above in connection with Rule 407 (subsequent remedial measures). Specific acts ("other crimes, wrongs, or acts") are authorized (unless barred by another rule, e.g., Rule 403) for *any* relevant or material purpose other than the purpose specifically and expressly prohibited by the rule.

That expressly prohibited purpose is: "to prove the character of a person in order to show action in conformity therewith"—that is, our "char→act" purpose, as shown on the chart. Evidence offered solely for that purpose cannot be made admissible by use of Rule 403.

Remember; that purpose, the impermissible purpose (as made clear by the chart and the rule) has two elements, both of which must be present for it to be an impermissible purpose: (1) that the propensity be a *character* type propensity, meaning a very *general,* morally bad or good tendency; and (2) that the propensity be used to prove an act in conformity with it. MOIPPKIA purposes, i.e., permissible purposes, differ on one or other of these elements, or both. Thus Rule 404(b), the MOIPPKIA rule, on its face authorizes acts offered on a non-character, specific propensity theory as well as those offered on non-propensity theories. It authorizes acts offered for *any* purpose other than the prohibited character purpose as long as the evidence survives relevancy-and-its-counterweights concerns under F.R.E. 401 and 403, and all other applicable rules (for example, the acts may not be proved up through inadmissible hearsay or by privileged material).

Rule 404(b) is not exclusively confined to criminal cases, nor to conduct of parties, nor to bad conduct, nor does it require that convictions be the form of the evidence where bad conduct is offered.

Let us examine some of the permitted purposes (catchwords in the MOIPPKIA rule). We will not necessarily take them in order of the acronym.

Plan, as Shown by Similar Incidents: F.R.E. 404(b) Continued

This is perhaps the quintessential permissible purpose under the rule. The primordial English common law case giving rise to it was a prosecution for the bathtub drowning of the defendant's wife. The fact that several other wives of his had also been found drowned in the bathtub was admitted against him. *Rex v. Smith* (Crim. App. 1915) (historically referred to as the "Brides of the Bath" case). It was noted in the case that he inherited property from each of his dead wives.

No conviction for the earlier deaths is necessary in a situation like "Brides of the Bath." Any current admissible evidence (for example, witness testimony) of the other bathtub deaths will do. The evidence thereof need only convince the jury that they happened, not beyond a reasonable doubt. No formal proof of defendant's connection with them is needed, since a jury could infer that from the occurrences themselves.

"Design" was the admissible purpose. This is the equivalent of "plan" in the modern Rule, 404(b). Other of the catchwords or permissible purposes in the Rule that might apply to the "Brides of the Bath" facts are "intent", "knowledge", "motive", or "absence of mistake or accident". "Pattern", though not in the Rule, is sometimes used. There is considerable overlap among all these concepts.

A comparable case under the F.R.E. involved an allegation of intentional burning by a Mr. Hammann of his own barn, to collect insurance. Earlier fires destroying other insured farm buildings of Hammann were allowed to be shown. *Hammann v. Hartford Accident & Indemni-*

ty Co. (6th Cir.1980). This case also shows that F.R.E. 404(b) applies in civil cases, too, for the evidence was offered by the insurance company in defending against a suit by Hammann to collect the insurance on the property.

Rule 404(b) applies to conduct of any party *or any relevant non-party person* in both criminal and civil cases. The common law was probably in accord but that is not entirely clear.

Notice that "plan", in common with some of the other catchwords, allows the evidence, in appropriate circumstances, to show "actus reus" (the commission of the act) as well as "mens rea" (the accompanying required intent). The specific propensity shown can be to do the act, or to do it intentionally or knowingly.

In "Brides of the Bath", one other wife drowning may have done the trick almost as well as the many in the actual case but it is difficult to say. It could tip the scales against admissibility pursuant to the Rule 403-type balancing by the judge that must take place as a second step in the analysis if the evidence passes through one of the listed gateways expressed by the MOIPPKIA catchwords. Especially could it tip the balance if the balance seems close. Something depends upon the liberality of the jurisdiction, even under similarly worded rules. As a matter of weight in the eyes of the jury the number of other deaths may make a difference.

It normally would not matter in a case like this whether the "other" incidents happened before or after the charged event. In "Brides of the Bath" they happened *after*. *Before* is more usual.

It helps but perhaps was not indispensable on the powerful facts of this case, that a common theme in the incidents was that the wives left him their property. It is helpful though not essential to making a case of "motive" or "plan." It might matter to the weight of the evidence, however. Or to admissibility in a closer case or in some strict jurisdictions. Is it indispensable that the other deaths were also in the bathtub? That they were drownings? Courts vary even under the same rule as to how similar the events must be—i.e., as to when dissimilarity will be left to the jury as a matter of weight and when it will affect admissibility. Differences in facts may explain *some* of the variation in the decisions, but not all. For example, if the plan is to kill off all relatives that stand in the way of the defendant's inheriting a fortune, their manner of death need not be similar to advance the plan.

On the other hand, if the charge is robbing a small convenience store, is it enough to show that the defendant committed prior robberies of similar stores? How similar? What, if any, *other* similarities must be demonstrated? This is a greatly debated area. Just when does "character" cross over into "pattern"? Where exactly is the line between character-type (general) propensity and specific propensity? If facts showing some dissimilarity of the events, are held not to impede admissibility under the other acts rule itself, they might still do so under the 403–type balancing, especially in an otherwise close balance, or at least they may affect weight.

"Brides of the Bath" is frequently cited for the proposition that crimes bearing earmarks (or a distinctive set of traits or a modus operandi) in common with the formally charged crime are admissible even regardless of whether there was a common plan or scheme in the lay sense of all the crimes falling within a single master plan formulated at one time for them all. The definition of a common plan is extended, on this interpretation of the case, to include wrongs having a separate but similar plan (blueprint) underlying each even if they were not planned together. The notion of a plan in common thus covers them even if each was planned and executed spontaneously without thought of the next or the last— even if the idea for each successive one arose only after and not because of the last. The permissible purpose may be described as showing a "plan" (a word in Rule 404(b)), common "design" (a word not expressly used by 404(b)), "pattern" (again, not expressly in the Rule), or even "identity" (in the Rule). Some decisions say the common features must be so distinctive as to constitute a kind of signature (peculiar handiwork) of the defendant. Others seem to require less.

Thus, other assaults by the defendant against the same person (or sometimes same class of person) he is charged with assaulting in the present case, are frequently permitted. How similar the persons must be when assaults against the same class of person are permitted is in dispute. See Raeder, *The Admissibility of Prior Acts of Domestic Violence: Simpson and Beyond,* 69 S. Cal. L. Rev. 1463 (1996).

Evidence of other offenses committed by the criminal defendant is allowed on a quite broad basis where both the charged and the other offense are sex offenses. Few courts require that the victims be the same. There may be no requirement that they even be of the same kind. Many courts do not feel that both offenses must be sex offenses of the same type or that the circumstances or methods be similar. And even those that do, disagree about how narrowly or broadly to define the type or the requisite similarity. Most are beginning to say "extend the circle; draw it broadly; do not require rigid similarity". Thus, in sex cases, prior (or subsequent) sex offenses that would not seem to qualify based on the similarity standards the particular jurisdiction applies to non-sex cases, nevertheless frequently are admitted because the court believes sex offenders are more prone to continually and indiscriminately sexually offending than other offenders, owing to a "lustful disposition" or "sickness." Statistics may be marshaled either way on this point. Under the F.R.E. sex offenders are dealt with specially under Rules 413–15, infra.

Of course a single plan to commit a series of interdependent crimes embracing the one charged may often be shown by proving up the other crimes. The "plan" catchword clearly covers this. Consider, for example, a bank robbery used to get money to obtain explosives for a terrorist attack. Either of the crimes may be admissible on the issue of the commission of, or on the issue of intent for, the other crime that may be formally charged. Sometimes the same result is achieved by declaring that both incidents are part of the same crime: that the "other" crime is not really an "other" crime, but part of the same crime that is charged. For example, this theory has been used where a car is stolen to use as the getaway vehicle immediately prior to or after a charged bank robbery. But the car theft could also be viewed as another crime that is part of the "plan" embracing the bank robbery. "Motive" could additionally be added to the list of catchwords usable here, if the charged and the evidentiary crime were reversed.

Notice that conceptually there is a fundamentally different theory underlying the evidence offer in the "Brides of the Bath" case as compared with the offer in the bankrobbery-terrorism case (or the car-theft-bankrobbery case):

The "Brides of the Bath" offer involves specific-propensity reasoning: that because he did it (or did it intentionally) the other times, he more likely did it (or did it intentionally) this time. In other words, he had a specific propensity to drown his wives in the bathtub, perhaps to get their property, and acted in accord with that propensity this time. This requires a degree of similarity between the wrongs. Because the propensity is so specific, it is not character-type propensity, although exactly where the line is drawn between specific and general, i.e., between character propensity and specific propensity, is uncertain. See generally Rothstein, *Intellectual Coherence in an Evidence Code*, 28 LOY. L.A. L.REV. 1259 (1995).

On the other hand, in the bankrobbery-terrorism case, no propensity reasoning is involved in the offer at all (although the jury may indulge in such). No similarity of the crimes is needed.

Yet the same catchwords may be used in the two cases. Most of the catchwords have this dual potential, and the rule is used to admit evidence in both kinds of cases. Conceptually, it might be said the rule (or even a single catchword) mixes apples and oranges, but this has been traditional and is continued.

Identity: F.R.E. 404(b) Continued

X was a supermarket customer on a day when the supermarket received from a customer a check signed with a fictitious name. The check was discovered in the cash register at the end of the day when the daily "take" is totalled. No one remembers who gave the store the check. The fact that X had passed similar bogus checks in similar circumstances in the past, was admitted to help show that he was the one (from among the many customers of the supermarket that day) who had passed this bogus check. "Identity" was the catchword, although others might have been used as well. There is the same question here as discussed above, about how similar the crimes must be regarding the circumstances and manner of commission, and how numerous. Jurisdictions differ. But any previous check incident involving a fictitious name (not necessarily the same one) or forgery, committed by the defendant, would probably have an easy time getting in. However, a number of courts require a much higher degree of similarity for identity than for plan or intent, reasoning that the modus operandi must be distinctive. Thus, the mere fact that a witness can identify the defendant charged with robbery as having committed a prior robbery might not be sufficient unless the manner of the robbery indicates that the two crimes were perpetrated by the same individual. Even so, courts vary on just how distinctive the "signature" must be. Is it enough to rob mom and pop stores in the same vicinity, or must the defendant wear the same outfit or utter the same words when doing so?

Intent or Knowledge: F.R.E. 404(b) Continued

If instead of a check with a fictitious name, the supermarket case had involved a check with insufficient funds, other similar insufficient funds checks passed by the same person could be offered to show it was intentional (done with knowledge there were insufficient funds, rather than a case of accidental overdrawing or mistaken estimate of the amount in the bank) pursuant to the catchwords "intent," "knowledge," or "absence of mistake or accident."

In *United States v. Beechum* (5th Cir.1978), defendant post office employee was found with a rare coin that was missing from the mails. He was charged with stealing it. He defended that it fell from the mail and he was returning it. It was allowed to be shown by the prosecution that defendant also had in his possession at the time, credit cards that belonged to others. He was not authorized by the cards' owners. There was little or no proof he stole them from the mail. The court said such proof was not necessary anyway, and allowed this "other crime" evidence under the catchword "intent". It was more likely, the court said, that he did not intend to return the coin, because he had not returned the cards.

In so ruling, the court held that mere *relevance* to a permitted purpose ("intent") is all that is required under F.R.E. 404(b). The crimes did not need to have similar elements. Since *any* increment in possibility satisfies the relevance standard (see Chapter 3, supra), it would seem that *any* other crime, no matter how dissimilar, would have done the trick. A person who had *any* criminal intent before (even to assault someone or commit a parking violation) is *slightly* more likely than someone who did not, to have criminal intent with respect to the coin, all other things being equal. The court (at least if read logically) leaves the degree of required similarity to be determined by the judge under F.R.E. 403 (which must always be applied as a second step after evidence is fitted through the portal of one of the catchwords of 404(b)) and, if it survives that scrutiny, to the jury as a matter of weight. Although questioned by some, the treatment of similarity in this case is exerting an influence on the law under 404(b).

To say that the judge must determine the similarity requirement under F.R.E. 403 essentially begs the question of what degree of similarity is required, and provides little guidance. Rule 403 is usually considered to accord the trial judge much leeway (discretion).

This approach provides the defendant little solid protection against the very real danger of prejudice along character lines, while potentially admitting evidence which, because of the dissimilarity of the crimes, has only slight legitimate probative value. While the court by fiat states that the other crime must at least be one involving a dispossessive intent, that pronouncement seems rather arbitrary since it follows from nothing the court says, and says nothing beyond the facts of this case.

One recurring issue is whether demonstrating the "intent" of the defendant is a legitimate 404(b) purpose when defendant claims not to have committed the crime, i.e., the only controverted issue is whether the act was committed or who committed it, it being conceded that if it was committed, whoever committed it must have had the criminal intention to do it.

In that regard consider *Estelle v. McGuire* (S.Ct.1991), a murder prosecution for the death of an infant in which "battered child syndrome" testimony relating to prior injury of the child (which could be inferred to be at the hands of the accused) was introduced in the prosecution's main case. The defense had not made (and did not make) any express claim that defendant or anyone had inflicted the death accidentally (non-intentionally). Instead the defense seemed to suggest that others who had access to the child may intentionally have killed the child.

The U.S. Supreme Court held it was not a constitutional due process violation for the prosecution to introduce this evidence, because the prosecution retained its burden to prove all of the essential elements beyond a reasonable doubt, including intention, whatever the defense raised or didn't raise or suggested. We might add that this is especially so because, at the time the prosecution puts on its main case, there is no commitment by the defense as to what it is or is not disputing. Even if there has been some informal indication, the defense is entitled to change its mind at any time before it puts on its case, or even during its case. Of course, the law could require (and some jurisdictions do require) the prosecution to wait and see, and introduce this evidence in rebuttal if needed. But the Court was disinclined to follow this course, or at least disinclined to impose it on jurisdictions as a matter of constitutional law, saying instead, "The evidence of battered child syndrome was relevant to show intent, and nothing in the Due Process Clause of the Fourteenth Amendment requires the State to refrain from introducing relevant evidence simply because the defense chooses not to contest the point."

Would it matter if the defendant is willing to actually bindingly stipulate (concede) in advance that whoever committed the crime had to have had the requisite intent (perhaps because of the nature of the wounds), rather than simply not contesting the issue? The Court, in the quotation, seems to say that, at least insofar as a constitutional mandate would be concerned, this would make no difference, although we might add that it might make a difference under a jurisdiction's own trial rules.

On the question of an actual concession by defendant of the only fact the "other crime" is admissible to prove, see, subsequent to *McGuire*, the case of *Old Chief v. United States* (S.Ct.1997). The Supreme Court held, in a prosecution for the statutory crime of being a "convicted felon in possession of a firearm", that defendant's willingness to concede bindingly that he was a convicted felon of the type that could not legally possess a firearm (disputing only possession), precluded prosecution proof of defendant's prior felony conviction, including its name and nature, under Rule 403, since the concession was better and less prejudicial proof fairly conclusively establishing the only point (status as convicted felon) the prior felony conviction was admissible for. (For this permissible use, see infra under non-character, non-circumstantial uses; Rule 405(b) permits it when necessary to prove an essential element of a charge). There was thus no legitimate need for the prosecution's proof of the prior felony conviction, which proof would only prejudice defendant along prohibited character lines especially because he was charged with other crimes similar to the one for which he was previously convicted. Rule 403. The Court thus seemed to suggest a general proposition that a concession or alternative evidence can in appropriate circumstances preclude prosecution proof that entails some prejudice along with its probative value. An exception mentioned by the court would be where the prosecution's proof would add something legitimate to the picture (or add persuasive power) that would be lacking if only the concession (or alternative evidence) were accepted, such as telling the full story better. But the Court saw no such function for the prosecution's proof in *Old Chief*, where that proof was directed only at establishing a particular status, which could equally well be proved (and less prejudicially) by accepting the stipulation (which is then read to the jury who is told it establishes the fact). The present authors would add that the additional "something" added by the prosecution's evidence would have to be not only legitimate, but also, under Rule 403, sufficient to outweigh the risk of prejudice introduced by the prosecution's evidence.

In a case immediately after *Old Chief*, the Supreme Court remanded for re-consideration in the light of *Old Chief*, a case under F.R.E. 404(b) where defendant was prosecuted for possession of narcotics with intent to distribute. Defendant had challenged only possession, conceding that anyone possessing that large amount of the narcotic necessarily had intent to distribute. The lower court held that such concession precluded prosecution proof of prior crimes of distributing narcotics. The prior crimes were admissible under 404(b) only to show intent. As intent was conceded, there was no legitimate reason for the evidence, with its accompanying character prejudice. The Supreme Court remanded for re-consideration in the light of *Old Chief*. See *United States v. Crowder* (D.C.Cir.1996). On remand, the D.C. Circuit held that *Old Chief* precluded any per se rule against introducing such prosecution evidence. While many defense counsel originally viewed *Old Chief* as a favorable decision, courts have mostly limited its application to cases in which a former conviction is an element of the offense. *Old Chief* in practice mainly benefits the prosecution whose "choice will generally survive a Rule 403 analysis when a defendant seeks to force the substitution of an admission for evidence creating a coherent narrative of his thoughts and actions in perpetrating the offense for which he is being tried," to quote a passage from the decision itself. Nevertheless, *Old Chief* confirms a theoretical framework that is of some value in evidence questions generally.

The question of the extent to which a permissible catchword issue must be disputed can come up under all of the catchwords, as can the question of the effect of a concession. Different decisions reach different conclusions as an evidentiary matter.

The position a court takes concerning whether dispute makes a difference can determine whether the judge allows the other wrongs to be introduced in the prosecution's case-in-chief, or only after it becomes clear from the defense case what is disputed (which would mean that the wrong can come in, if at all, only in the prosecution's rebuttal case, not its case-in-chief).

Motive: F.R.E. 404(b) Continued

For an example of "motive," see "Brides of the Bath", *supra*, particularly where it may be inferred from the pattern and the facts that the defendant may have been motivated in each instance to get the property of the dead wife. See also the robbery-terrorism case, *supra*, where the current prosecution is for the bank robbery. Another example might be where the killing of a police officer is charged, and it is alleged that the killing was committed by the defendant because the officer was pursuing the defendant for another serious crime. The other crime may be allowed to be shown as part of the story of the motive for the present crime. A similar case would be where defendant is charged with killing a former cohort in crime because the cohort refused to divide the proceeds of a previous theft the two committed. The previous theft may be admissible.

Notice that "motive" used in "Brides of the Bath" licenses the evidence on a specific-propensity theory, but in the other examples mentioned in the last paragraph above, "motive" licenses the evidence on a non-propensity theory, further illustrating the duality of the catchwords, as indicated earlier. Notice that in "Brides of the Bath", as distinguished from our other examples of motive, some similarity between the crimes would be required. It very much depends upon the situation and the theory of the offer under 404(b), and what use of which catchwords is being made.

Opportunity: F.R.E. 404(b) Continued

This catchword encompasses opportunity both in the sense of having the skills, tools, intelligence, knowledge, or other wherewithal to commit the charged crime; and in the sense of being at or having access to the location of the charged crime. Thus the catchword "opportunity" would encompass (among other things) showing previous illegal access to a secure place in a prosecution for taking something from the secure place; previous experience with illegally de-activating burglar alarms in a prosecution for theft from a place protected by a burglar alarm; and defendant's commission of an "unrelated" crime in a certain city on a certain date, where defendant contends in the current prosecution for another crime in that city on that date, that he was not in that city on that date.

With respect to a number of the examples here as well as many of those above, there is disagreement over whether and when (1) the catchword the evidence is offered to prove, must actually be in dispute; and (2) it would be sufficient to introduce merely the fact that *some* other wrong was committed, without naming it. These are probably F.R.E. 403–type matters, with some leeway given the trial judge, depending on the particular facts. Notice also that varying degrees of similarity (between the charged and the offered act) would be required under the varying examples in the last paragraph above. No similarity other than location would be required in the last of the examples. Whatever similarity is required may go to only one feature (i.e., committed in the same city; or involving a similar burglar alarm). It all depends upon the particular situation, not necessarily the particular catchword.

Some of the situations discussed in our current section here relating to "opportunity" may also come under the catchword "knowledge" or "preparation."

Preparation: F.R.E. 404(b) Continued

This would cover the terrorism prosecution, supra, in which an earlier bank robbery to gather the financial means, is sought to be admitted. It would also cover stealing burglary tools to commit a later, charged, burglary; and any crimes committed in practicing to execute a later, charged, crime. Some of these same cases may also fit under "opportunity". Notice that similarity of crimes would not be required in some of the particular examples mentioned in this paragraph; and, although this is not *always inevitably* so under this catchword, no propensity theory (specific propensity) is involved.

Absence of Mistake or Accident: F.R.E. 404(b) Continued

See the "Brides of the Bath", *Hammann*, and insufficient funds cases, supra, for examples of this heading.

Having now studied each of the catchwords, and the distinction between the impermissible and permissible purposes, how would you justify the common reception of evidence of other similar crimes to show "predisposition" to commit the present crime, where police entrapment is raised as a defense? Under the law of entrapment such "predisposition" negates the defense. Cf. F.R.E. 404(b), 405(b).

IV. SPECIAL RULES FOR SEXUAL ASSAULTS AND RELATED OFFENSES

A series of special rules, F.R.E. 412 and F.R.E. 413 through 415, apply to sexual assaults and related offenses. These rules set up special protection for the alleged victim, creating a "shield" against use of the victim's sexual propensities, character, or conduct on other occasions, if any. At the same time, the rules provide for wide-open use against the defendant of defendant's prior sexual misconduct, if any.

The "Rape Shield": The Common Law and F.R.E. 412

The common law allowed evidence of the propensity of an alleged victim of a sexual assault in ways that seem unfamiliar to us today. Prior sexual conduct of the alleged victim was liberally admissible as relevant to such issues as consent. Many courts also allowed evidence of the alleged victim's reputation for "unchastity." These kinds of evidence not only invaded the privacy of the alleged victim but also often were of little relevance or probative value, yet were presented as though they were very meaningful. Conduct with another than the defendant, for example, might be offered on but shed little real light on the question whether there was consent in the particular case on trial. Any probative value would be especially slim in modern times. The law tended to perpetuate outmoded stereotypes of women, and fostered using the trial to punish women deemed to be immoral, regardless of the merits of the prosecution.

In addition to the obvious risk of prejudice, misleading the jury, confusion of the issues, and undue time consumption, unrestrained admissibility discouraged victims from coming forward and frequently subjected them, when they did come forward, to what some have called a "second rape", this time psychologically, at the hands of defense counsel.

F.R.E. 412 and somewhat similar state laws dramatically changed the common law in these respects. Rule 412 creates a so-called "rape shield" protecting against use of "other sexual behavior" or sexual "predisposition" of a "victim" (male or female) in any case involving "sexual misconduct." Under this provision, other consensual or non-consensual sexual behavior and sexual propensity evidence is not admissible to prove consent or other substantive issues, nor to impeach the alleged victim as witness, in such cases. The federal rule is also written broadly enough to encompass homosexual acts of complainants.

There are several exceptions in subsection (b) of the Rule. Specific instance evidence may be admissible if offered to prove that the source of semen, injury or similar physical evidence is not the defendant. In this situation, we might note incidentally, the evidence is not offered on a propensity theory. In addition, there is an exception for prior specific instances of behavior with the same defendant (which often will be more clearly relevant to consent than when the behavior is with another, even though both involve a propensity theory); an exception for any evidence required by the Constitution to be admitted; and an exception for civil cases (which admits the evidence if its probative value substantially outweighs any "harm to any victim" or "unfair prejudice to any party"—a kind of reverse and expanded Rule 403 test—but reputation evidence is admissible only if placed in controversy by the alleged victim).

While the prohibitions of 412 override all other permissions to introduce evidence found elsewhere in the F.R.E. that might seem to be applicable to the same evidence, evidence admissible pursuant to the exceptions (permissions) in 412 is expressly required to comply with all other rules of evidence (e.g., the hearsay rule, privilege, opinion and expert rules, etc.). Thus, other rules could exclude evidence seemingly admissible under the rape shield. Presumably this includes Rules 404 and 405 (character and conduct and forms of proof thereof, in general), to the extent applicable; but the exact relationship is obscure. Obviously 404(a)(2) (character of victim) is of modified applicability. Rule 403 would generally be available to exclude evidence within the exceptions to 412, except in civil cases, where Rule 403 is probably preempted by 412's specific civil balancing provision. The constitutional exception conceivably might have to be unconstrained by other rules at least in some instances.

Rule 412 also requires 14 days advance, pretrial, specific notice and description of evidence proposed to be offered under the Rule, given to all parties and the alleged victim, who also have a right to attend and be heard at the mandatory, private admissibility hearing. The record of and submissions to the hearing are sealed unless and until the court orders otherwise. The judge may eliminate or reduce the notice time for good cause. On the constitutionality of depriving a defendant of otherwise good and probably constitutionally necessarily admissible evidence (defendant's own past sexual conduct with complainant) because of failure to comply with a rape-shield 10–day advance notice provision, see the U.S. Supreme Court decision in *Michigan v. Lucas* (S.Ct. 1991), which held that it was constitutional to exclude such defense evidence for failure to give notice, at least on the facts.

Even aside from notice provisions, "rape shields", by making certain defense evidence inadmissible, can sometimes operate to deprive a defendant of evidence that legitimately contributes to his defense and raises a logical reasonable doubt as to his guilt. Whether this handicap to defendants outweighs the benefits to society from a rape shield law is the subject of some continuing debate. At some point restrictions on defense evidence can run afoul of constitutional mandates such as due process, compulsory process, or confrontation. When these constitutional mandates kick in to command the reception of evidence for the defense, they would override a contrary evidentiary exclusion contained in, for example, a rape shield, even if the evidentiary exclusion made no express exception, as Rule 412 does, for constitutionally mandated evidence.

On the question of a constitutional right to defend versus exclusionary rules and rulings like rape-shields, privileges, etc., that are concerned in part with other than accuracy of the trial (thus making the claim of unconstitutionality of exclusion more persuasive), see Chapter 5 under "Policies Underlying Privileges" (particularly *Egelhoff* which somewhat cuts against the theory that legitimate evidentiary exclusions can be unconstitutional); Chapter 8 under "The Criminal Defendant's Right to Cross Examine Without Undue Restriction" dealing with the confrontation clause, particularly the discussion of the Supreme Court decision in *Olden*, which reversed a conviction because defendant was prohibited from cross-examining a rape complainant about another important sexual relationship; Chapter 8 under "The Due Process and Compulsory Process Clauses"; *Rock v. Arkansas* (S.Ct.1987) (a criminal defendant has right to testify for self even in violation of evidence rule—here, a rule automatically barring hypnotically enhanced testimony); *United States v. Dunnigan* (S.Ct.

1993) (right to testify in own behalf); but see *Stephens v. Miller* (7th Cir.1994) (affirming exclusion of specific graphic sexual language that defendant alleged had angered attempted-rape complainant and stimulated her to fabricate the charge). See generally, Rothstein, *New Federal Evidence Rule 412 on Sex Victim's Character,* 15 Crim. L. Bull. 353 (1979).

A number of courts have upheld specific rape shields generally. See, e.g., *Moore v. Duckworth* (7th Cir.1982) (upholding facial validity of Indiana rape shield). However, particular applications of state rape shields have been found to be unconstitutional. For example, *Lewis v. State* (Fla.1991), reversed the exclusion of evidence that the complainant, who was the defendant's stepdaughter, had a sexual relationship with her boyfriend, where the defense was that she fabricated the claim of rape because she believed that a scheduled gynecological exam would reveal her sexual activity to her mother who was discouraging the relationship.

The constitutional guarantees most in issue under a rape shield would be the emerging but very uncertain due process and compulsory process rights to introduce significant sound defensive evidence from any source; the evolving but as yet uncertainly defined due process right to testify in your own defense; and the right to confront witnesses against you, which may invalidate undue restrictions on cross examination and impeachment. None of these rights is absolute.

Issues that remain controversial both under rape shields and the constitution include the introduction of evidence that the complainant was a prostitute, that she previously engaged in a similar pattern of promiscuity, that she previously reported 'false' claims of rape, and evidence of sexual activity with others supporting the defendant's claim that he believed the complainant consented. Even when such evidence violates a particular rule or statute, depending on the specific facts in question, it may be constitutionally required.

The Wide–Open Admissibility of Sexual Misconduct Against Sexual Offense Defendants: F.R.E. 413 through 415

Approximately 20 years after the effective date of the F.R.E., a number of highly publicized sexual assault and child molestation cases resulted in the adoption of F.R.E. 413 through 415 broadening the reception, in such civil and criminal cases, of other specific incidents of sexual assault and child molestation by the defendant. There is no express requirement that the victim, nature of the conduct, circumstances, or modus operandi be at all similar, except *possibly* (and even this is not clear) the offered offense and the charged offense must be in the same one of the two categories described by the rules ("sexual assault" and "child molestation") assuming these two categories are mutually exclusive. Substantial advance notice must be given of evidence to be offered under Rules 413–415.

By allowing the incidents to be "considered for [their] bearing on any matter to which [they are] relevant", these new Rules permit the evidence to be used for the character-propensity reasoning, not merely the specific-propensity reasoning, discussed earlier. This suggests, among other things, a relaxation of how specifically like the charged conduct the offered conduct must be.

In the absence of 413–415, at least some cases in the sex crime and child molestation area have been more restrictive, insisting that the prosecutor clearly articulate a theory of offer that strongly pinpoints one of the permitted MOIPPKIA purposes under Rule 404(b) or its state analogue—for example allowing the evidence only where the commission of a highly ambiguous act is admitted and the prior conduct is truly necessary to show motive, intent, or lack of mistake or accident.

While it is fairly clear that the intention behind Rules 413 through 415 was to pre-empt applicability of Rules 404 and 405 to exclude evidence encompassed by 413–15, it is not entirely clear from the text whether Rule 403 can still be used to limit admissibility. There are things in the text that could be used to justify either conclusion. Yet judges will still have to be mindful of the Congressional intention to expand reception of the evidence.

It can be argued that the best reading of Rules 413 through 415 is that Rule 403 does apply, for otherwise the provisions appear rather Draconian, are in conflict with historical views of the role of other crimes evidence, and may even run afoul of the constitution.

By-and-large, the courts that have reached this issue have generally felt Rule 403 applies, some suggesting that otherwise, in criminal cases, the rules might be unconstitutional when used against the criminal defendant.

Given the Congressional intent to broadly permit evidence of the defendant's past sexual misconduct, it is arguable that Congress considered factors like those in Rule 403, deeming the evidence not unduly prejudicial or the like (at least in most cases); and that therefore Rule 403 (if applicable at all) should be saved for the rare case where the nature of the previous act is particularly graphic compared to the crime charged, or massively prejudicial in some other way, rather than deeming, as has been traditional, that any character-propensity reasoning is prejudicial.

Cf. Cal. Evid. Code 1108 (sexual misconduct permitted subject to state equivalent of Rule 403). The 1999 revision to the Uniform Rules explicitly rejected as bad policy, Rules 413 through 415 and a lustful disposition exception to the character ban.

V. PROCEDURAL ISSUES RAISED BY SIMILAR ACTS EVIDENCE

The Coverage of F.R.E. 404(b)

Assuming we want to offer a bad act under MOIPP-KIA, should the evidence be limited to evidence of other *crimes*? Normally it is not. To convictions—at least if there is one? Normally not. Must such acts have been the subject of an inculpatory judgment of some kind? Normally not. The testimony of witnesses, e.g., the other alleged victims, that the other acts occurred, and that they occurred at the hands of this person, would normally suffice. In the discussion of the "Brides of the Bath" case, supra, we suggested that it may not even be necessary to actually introduce separate evidence that the defendant was the person responsible for the former deaths if a jury could draw that inference from the circumstances. Of course the prior bad act must be proven by admissible evidence. Thus, the previous alleged victim or an eyewitness may be required to testify in person.

How many "other instances" are needed? Would one other suffice in some circumstances? At least in "Brides of the Bath" we suggested that *maybe* one might be all that was needed. Can the other wrongdoing occur after rather than before the charged crime? Again, in "Brides", we said yes.

The F.R.E. and most codifications have no specification on any of these matters, which are therefore left to the general, nonspecific policies of a rule like F.R.E. 403 (relevance and its counterweights), to be computed on the facts of the particular case, as part of the "second step" in the analysis as referred to above, frequently with somewhat wide leeway allowed to the trial judge. Thus, unless decisions require a different result, all of the factors raised in the last paragraph will be merely factors to be considered with other factors and circumstances, but not automatically conclusive, in the admissibility determination. They may affect weight if the evidence is admitted.

The Supreme Court has spoken concerning F.R.E. interpretation of two of the underlying issues suggested by the paragraphs above: (1) With what degree of certitude must unconvicted wrongs be proved (a) to the judge to be admissible, and (b) to the jury to be usable? (2) Suppose the other acts have been the subject of an *exculpatory* judgment? We will now examine these in order.

The Standard of Proof for 404(b): Evidence to "Support a Finding": F.R.E. 104(b)

In *Huddleston v. United States* (S.Ct.1988), the trial judge admitted evidence of Huddleston's prior sales of stolen televisions and appliances in his trial for selling and possessing stolen video tapes. The only controverted issue under the present charges was the defendant's knowledge that the tapes were stolen. Huddleston claimed that his sale of the televisions was only admissible if they were stolen (and if, presumably, he knew they were stolen). Since the government had failed to prove such to the judge by a preponderance, defendant argued, the evidence was inadmissible.

The Supreme Court rejected the argument, holding the prior acts were properly admitted, because the jury could have reasonably inferred these preliminary facts from the televisions' low price, the large quantity of them offered for sale, the defendant's inability to produce a bill of sale, and evidence of his involvement in other sales of stolen merchandise obtained from the same source, including, apparently, the present charges.

The Supreme Court held, broadly, that a trial judge is not required to make a preliminary finding that the government has proved by a preponderance of evidence that defendant committed earlier offenses, before submitting them to the jury under Rule 404(b). Instead, the evidence is admissible if there is, in the trial judge's view, merely sufficient evidence to support a jury finding (by a preponderance) thereof. The Court did not say whether the jurors should be *instructed* that they must find this in order to use the evidence.

In other words, the judge was to apply the Rule 104(b) standard, not the Rule 104(a) standard, to the preliminary facts, in determining admissibility. *Huddleston* affects all conditional relevancy questions raised under Rule 404(b). Therefore, any doubt whether the defendant committed the prior act will be decided by a 104(b) analysis.

Some states still adhere to some variety of a "clear and convincing evidence" standard under their 404(b)-type rulings, as a threshold for judge and/or jury, based on the rationale that the risk of prejudice from admitting or using such acts is so great that it should not be allowed unless the evidence is compelling that the prior act occurred, was criminal (not accidental), and that the defendant committed it. After *Huddleston*, the American Bar Association urged an amendment to Rule 404(b) to similar effect, attempting to change *Huddleston*. At present the rule has not been so amended.

In *Huddleston*, the Court does express concern that its low standard for the preliminary fact determination makes admissibility likely in doubtful cases, with consequent risk of jury prejudice. Nevertheless, the Court reasons that the F.R.E. intended to freely admit such acts and that sufficient protection against prejudice is afforded by the trial judge's determination that the evidence is submitted for a proper purpose, by relevancy requirements, by the Rule 403 balancing test, and by jury instructions limiting the evidence to its proper purpose. However, the Court agrees that the strength of the evidence establishing the similar act and the defendant's involvement in it is a factor which may be considered, among others, in the Rule 403 analysis.

A few scholars have consistently argued against a "clear and convincing evidence" standard, or even a "preponderance of evidence" standard, believing these standards to be too high to impose on the judge (as a precondition to admissibility) or on the jury (as a precondition to use of the evidence) via an instruction.

Some base this on a broader theory found in some of the literature in the area: that evidence such as we have in "Brides of the Bath" and *Huddleston* relies not at all on propensity, but on the "doctrine of chances"—that guilt (of both the "other" and the "charged" wrongs) is likely because of the odds against an innocent person being repeatedly involved in similar suspicious circumstances. Thus, the fact that no *one* incident can meet the clear and convincing or preponderance standard should not be determinative. Cf. Edward Imwinkelried, Uncharged Misconduct Evidence, Sec. 4.01 (2d ed. 1999).

A good case can be made that the doctrine of chances (with its pivotal and undeniable tenet that innocent people are less likely involved in multiple nefarious happenings) is really disguised propensity reasoning that begs all the important questions in the area and can present all the same evils as character evidence. See Rothstein, *Intellectual Coherence in an Evidence Code*, 28 Loy. L.A. L. Rev. 1259 (1995).

Acquittal as Not Excluding 404(b) Evidence

The Supreme Court addressed the legitimacy of introducing prior acts which were the subject of acquittals in *Dowling v. United States* (S.Ct.1990). *Dowling* held that an incident for which the defendant had previously been acquitted could be introduced pursuant to Rule 404(b) without violating double jeopardy or due process, federal evidence law, res judicata, or collateral estoppel. An acquittal can be based on a technical element, even though the jury believes the defendant committed the act beyond a reasonable doubt. Or an acquittal can be based on the fact that the jury believed defendant *probably* committed the act, but not beyond a reasonable doubt. An acquittal is thus not necessarily a finding that the act did not occur. May defendant respond with the acquittal?

It should be remembered that *Dowling* does not *require* a judge to admit prior conduct that resulted in an acquittal. It only permits it. It establishes that there is no per se exclusion of such evidence. In specific cases, the introduction of such evidence is dependent on surviving the Rule 403 balancing test on the particular facts, a matter on which trial judges are given great leeway.

Could a jurisdiction have a rule that freely permits other wrongs of a criminal defendant to be admissible to prove defendant's character in order to show he likely committed the charged crime? Or is traditional Rule 404(b), generally prohibiting such, compelled by the constitution? Are F.R.E. Rules 413–415, permitting such evidence in the sex-crime area, constitutional? As indicated above in our discussion of Rules 413–415, a number of courts have felt that such evidence is constitutional so long as the judge scrutinizes it pursuant to Rule 403. The Supreme Court has not ruled. Might sex crimes stand on a different constitutional basis than other "other crimes" evidence?

In *Estelle v. McGuire*, mentioned earlier in this chapter, the U.S. Supreme Court apparently meant to leave the general constitutional "other crimes" question open. The Court said somewhat hypothetically that it expressed no opinion on whether a state law would violate due process if it permitted the use of prior crimes to show character to commit a charged crime.

However, the Ninth Circuit, in *McKinney v. Rees* (9th Cir.1993), held that the particular other acts evidence in *McKinney* deprived defendant of a fair trial and violated his right to due process. In this murder case the court said "[t]he jury was offered the image of a man with a knife collection, who sat in his dormitory room sharpening knives, scratching morbid inscriptions on the wall, and occasionally venturing forth in camouflage with a knife strapped to his body." Although the victim had been killed with a knife, it was not one which was linked to any knife known to be possessed by the defendant.

The F.R.E., like some previous cases, do not limit showings permitted under the principle of 404(b) to the prosecution. Thus, the defense could invoke it to show that someone else committed the crime. But as a practical matter such cases are rare.

VI. CHARACTER AND SIMILAR–ACTS EVIDENCE IN CIVIL CASES

Similar Acts Evidence in Civil Cases: F.R.E. 404(b)

The use of similar-acts evidence in civil cases is analogous to that in criminal cases. There is a general prohibition of character-propensity use, with the same allowance of use for other purposes.

The MOIPPKIA categories have their analogies in civil cases (whether or not involving crimes), although the categories in some jurisdictions may go under slightly different appellations. F.R.E. 404(b), however, applies the same MOIPPKIA catchwords to civil and criminal cases alike, without distinction.

For example, prior false claims brought by the plaintiff, of the same sort as the present claim, are frequently admitted to show the falsity of the present claim.

By way of further example, prior frauds perpetrated by the defendant may be admissible to increase the likelihood that she/he committed the fraud charged, or did so with intent, if they are regarded as of a proper number and quite similar to the present charge, or are part of a common plan or scheme with the present one. In civil cases, similar acts can also show knowledge or notice, where that is relevant.

Substantive Use of Character–Propensity Not Allowed in Civil Cases: F.R.E. 404(a)(1) and (a)(2)

Under the F.R.E. there is no express analogy in any kind of civil case to the admissibility provisions of Rule 404(a)(1) (criminal defendant's good character showing and responsive showing by prosecution) or Rule 404(a)(2) (character of victim in criminal case). In federal courts, therefore, F.R.E. 404(a)(1) and (a)(2) do not license these uses of character in civil cases, only criminal cases. Thus the general prohibition of character to prove an act in conformity (to which prohibition (a)(1) and (a)(2) are exceptions) would apply.

However, in a few jurisdictions, where the commission of a crime is in issue in a civil case, as where the complaint charges defendant with a tort that is also a crime or where life insurance depends (pursuant to the terms of the policy) upon whether the insured deceased met his demise through his own criminal act, courts may permit evidence of the alleged wrongdoer's good and bad traits to the same extent as if he were being tried criminally. Thus 404(a)(1) would have a civil analogue in those jurisdictions. Some jurisdictions have a civil analogue to 404(a)(2) (victim's character) as well.

These Civil Case Rules Applied to Negligence Cases

Attempts to show the general negligent disposition, or even general disposition to drunkenness, of plaintiff or defendant often come up in civil cases, frequently concerning driving.

As in criminal cases, and pursuant to the rules above, *opinion and reputation* evidence to establish general traits of negligence or intoxication, or even driving negligently or while intoxicated, or even driving negligently or while intoxicated in identical situations, to establish negligent or drunken driving on a particular occasion, is generally excluded.

Similarly, pursuant to these rules, as in criminal cases, other *incidents* of negligence, or of intoxication, not related to driving, offered to establish negligent or drunken driving on a particular occasion, are also excluded as impermissible character evidence, unless some special nexus can be shown. There are also many decisions excluding insufficiently related drunken driving incidents. Similarity of circumstances can help admissibility.

Evidence in these last two paragraphs may be admissible if it can qualify for the rigorous requirements of habit evidence, immediately below.

VII. HABIT AND ROUTINE PRACTICE: F.R.E. 406

A strong, specific, consistent, somewhat involuntary or automatic habit, shown by sufficiently numerous instances or by the opinion of someone who is in a position to know, is usually admissible to establish an act, whether it is inculpatory or exculpatory or merely circumstantially relevant in some way. The same is true of a routine practice of an organization.

The habit or routine practice must consist of nearly automatic repetition of a very particular act nearly identical to that in issue whenever (or almost whenever) a nearly identical set of circumstances is presented.

Perhaps because it was not "automatic" enough, or could be contrived, one case held that defendant's regular attendance every week at religious services at the time of the crime was not admissible to help establish that he was probably at those services rather than at the scene of the crime. Similarly, a plaintiff's sexual history was not discoverable despite a claim of "habit" of living with men to derive economic benefit from them. Is "always" putting on a seat belt before driving, a habit? Obviously, simply claiming someone is a "good driver" or "accident prone" is not.

There would seem to be little basis for a distinction between civil and criminal cases, except perhaps when the habit or routine practice is a bad one of the defendant. F.R.E. Rule 406 dealing with habit and routine practice draws no distinction between civil and criminal cases.

However, Rule 406 does not say habit/routine/practice to show an act in conformity is "admissible," but only "relevant," something that was always known. The problem with the evidence, from the standpoint of both civil and criminal cases, if problem there was, stemmed from the countervailing factors of prejudice, misleadingness, time consumption, etc.—not relevance. Thus, under 406, admissibility is still controlled to some extent by ad hoc consideration of those factors, pursuant to Rule 403. Previous law applying the same factors received habit and routine practice much more favorably than character, and this has continued. On occasion 403 may allow some distinction between a civil and a criminal case.

The "relevance" is expressly declared by 406 to exist "regardless" of whether there are "eyewitnesses" or "corroboration." Previously, some jurisdictions had admitted routine practice (and perhaps habit) evidence only if there were no eyewitnesses to the act sought to be established by the pattern; some only if there was corroboration of that act; and some only if there was corroboration of the pattern. The "relevance regardless" language of 406 does not insure that these requirements may not be re-imposed by a judge. For no one ever doubted what the rule declares: that the evidence is "relevant" regardless of these requirements. The requirements were imposed pursuant to the countervailing factors now listed in Rule 403, which may still be considered.

Presumably, however, the language of the rule is meant to do more than declare relevance. It is meant to tilt in favor of admissibility. A judge would have to have some special reason on the facts of a particular case to exclude a proven habit or routine practice, or to reimpose the disapproved requirements.

Routine business practice amounting to the "habit" of an organization—for example, that letters put in a certain place are regularly mailed, proved by the testimony of someone in a position to know, for the purpose of establishing that a particular letter was mailed—is ordinarily admissible if sufficient regularity is adequately proved. F.R.E. 406 treats habit and routine practice identically in all respects.

As under previous law, there is no specification in the F.R.E. as to how to establish the habit or practice—by reputation, opinion, or specific instances—and the matter seems to vary from case to case, controlled by the general language of Rule 403, which probably serves, among other things, to require enough evidence to establish relative invariability of the habit or practice without redundancy. Reputation may not be permissible, as there is no hearsay exception for establishing habit (or routine practice) by reputation, as there is for establishing character. See F.R.E. 803(21).

VIII. CHARACTER AS AN "ESSENTIAL ELEMENT" AND THE LIKE: F.R.E. 405(b) AND RELATED NOTIONS

To be distinguished from evidence offered for purposes of the propensity reasoning under discussion in this chapter, is evidence of propensity, character, reputation, or particular instances of conduct, offered to prove the truth or falsity of an alleged libel or slander representing the propensity, character, reputation, or conduct to be such-and-such. This is a much more direct, non-circumstantial, use of the evidence, and the case could hardly be proved without it. This is normally admissible pursuant to the general rules relating to relevancy and relevancy's counterweights, e.g., F.R.E. 403. Its admissibility vel non is not usually the subject of a specific rule. Cf. F.R.E. 405(b) (where character itself is an "essential element" of a charge, claim or defense, rather than merely circumstantial evidence, the character may be proved by reputation, opinion, or specific instances).

Similarly beyond the scope of the discussion are cases where the issue of damages for defamation engenders a comparison of the plaintiffs reputation before and after the defamation. Again, this is generally not the subject of any specific rule and its admissibility would normally depend upon how the relevancy-and-its-counterweights factors and other rules not specifically addressed to the problem (hearsay, privilege, etc.) may happen to line up on the facts of a particular case. (Because this is a more direct and less circumstantial use of the evidence, and proof of the issue would be difficult without it, it is generally admissible.)

Also distinguishable as not involving our "propensity reasoning," and as therefore handled like the other matters in the last paragraph, and often admissible, are the

following: (1) Previous dangerous conduct (or a reputation therefor) on the part of some person, offered to
establish that the defendant was negligent in entrusting
a dangerous instrumentality (or position) to that person
when defendant knew or should have known of the
conduct or reputation. See *Clark v. Stewart* (Ohio 1933)
(bad driving record in non-similar circumstances; entrustment of a car). (2) Other accidents on the premises
introduced either to show that the defendant should have
been on notice of the dangerous condition and was therefore negligent in failing to repair, or to show that there
was a dangerous condition. See *Sullivan v. Detroit &
Windsor Ferry Co.* (Mich.1931). (But safe condition generally may not be shown by absence of accident. Why
not?) (3) Practices of others introduced to show what
reasonable people in the circumstances do, for purposes
of establishing a standard of care. See *Brigham Young
Univ. v. Lillywhite* (10th Cir.1941).

It may happen that evidence permissible under one of
the theories will also be susceptible of an impermissible
use along the lines of another of the theories. This can
occur, for example, where a principal (e.g., an employer)
is being sued for some catastrophe committed by his
agent with a firearm or automobile. A theory of negligent
entrustment of the instrumentality (firearm, car) by the
principal to the agent (whom the principal allegedly
should have known was reckless) may be used against
the principal (in a claim asserting the principal's own
negligence). That claim may be joined with a claim of
negligence of the agent, both against the agent; and
against the principal on a vicarious liability, respondeat
superior theory whereby the principal, even if found
personally innocent, may be held responsible for negligence of the agent committed within the scope of the
employment. The negligent entrustment theory may require introducing prior instances of or reputation for

reckless conduct on the part of the agent with other firearms or automobiles (even though not very similar to the charged conduct) which were or should have been known to the principal, that may not otherwise be admissible since other uses would involve forbidden character-propensity reasoning. See *Clark*, immediately supra, for just such a multiple claim case.

The negligent entrustment use is not a propensity use and is not prohibited. Indeed, it might be hard to prove negligent entrustment without it. In such a multiple claim case, the court, upon request, will normally instruct that this evidence can be used to help establish that the principal knew or should have known of prior careless acts or reputation and therefore was negligent in entrusting the agent; but it cannot be used against either the principal or the agent on a theory that it renders it likely that the agent was guilty of the particular instance of misfeasance charged.[1] This latter would be a forbidden character-propensity use, for we are assuming there is not enough similarity, etc., to qualify in this jurisdiction for admissibility on this latter theory. It is questionable whether such instruction will be followed.

Where law enforcement personnel have been alleged to use excessive force this same problem can arise, if the municipality is also charged.

Only occasionally will the risk of misuse be considered great enough and incurable enough to bar the evidence entirely or require separate trials. Basically, this is a Rule 403 computation: does the potential for prejudicial (impermissible) use substantially outweigh the permissible use despite the cautionary instruction? Normally it is

---

1. Ironically, this instruction means that it is O.K. to find that the defendant should have made the very inference the jury is forbidden to make: that one who was reckless before is likely to do it again.

held that it does not: negligent entrustment is difficult to establish without such evidence.

If you were the principal's or municipality's lawyer, is there a stipulation that you might consider offering which might totally prevent the evidence coming in for any purpose?

Another kind of evidence that must be carefully distinguished that does not involve propensity reasoning is prior convictions of a criminal defendant introduced in enhancement of the penalty, under a statute so providing (as in so-called three-strikes laws), or introduced as an element of the charged crime (as in the federal law under which it is a crime for a previously convicted felon to possess a firearm). Admissibility is probably assured where the penalty hinges on other crimes or the crime charged consists of several component crimes, each of which must be proved. Such evidence is necessary and direct, rather than merely circumstantial. Cf. F.R.E. 405(b). But see the possibility of stipulation or concession to avoid proof, presented by *Old Chief* discussed earlier in this Chapter and Chapter 3.

Must such evidence introduced for penalty purposes be barred from presentation to the jury before verdict? If not, is a limiting instruction required? Desirable? How would you phrase such an instruction? Is it likely to be efficacious? Can the exact nature of the conviction be suppressed to reduce prejudice? Would it necessarily reduce prejudice? Cf. *Old Chief*, supra.

In some jurisdictions, otherwise inadmissible prior misconduct or convictions may be admissible if punitive damages are a bona-fide issue. How do you account for this? Is there a criminal analogy? Should this be allowed only after a finding of liability has been returned?

IX. CREDIBILITY AS AFFECTED BY THE WITNESS' CHARACTER

Impeachment by Opinion, Reputation, Criminal Conviction, and Bad Acts: F.R.E. 608 and 609

The subject here is showings concerning a *witness'* general character of or propensity for *credibility and accuracy,* or the opposite.

This subsection will deal mainly with *impeachment* of a witness' character of or propensity for credibility and accuracy. *Support* thereof, which is generally allowed only after it has been attacked (impeached), is also logically part of the subject of this heading but will not be treated here because its principles are somewhat analogous to impeachment and the general subject of support of credibility is treated in the general chapter on credibility of witnesses.

In the area of impeachment of witnesses, testimony in the form of *reputation* for a character or propensity for non-veracity (lying or innocent inaccuracy) is permitted to be shown. *Personal opinion* on the witness' character or propensity for non-veracity was originally not allowed, but F.R.E. 608 and codes based thereon allow it. *Specific instances* of conduct bespeaking character or propensity for non-veracity must be divided in two (each admissible according to its own peculiar rules, to be discussed later): (1) *misconduct not resulting in a conviction;*[2] and (2)

---

2. At least conceptually the fact that the misconduct did not result in a conviction could come about for many different reasons: the person was never caught; the misconduct never came to the attention of authorities; it was not a legal wrong; it was civilly but not criminally wrong; it never became the subject of judicial proceedings; there was an acquittal; it became the subject only of a civil adjudication either of "guilt" or "innocence"; no charges were brought, regardless of whether an arrest was or was not made; charges were dropped; etc.

convictions.[3]

The *reputation* must be for telling falsehoods or untruths (lies or honest mistakes); the *personal opinion* has to be of the witness' veracity (lying, mistake); and the *specific conduct* must be of a sort that evidences a propensity for non-veracity (lying, mistake). Thus, we would expect that instances of fraud or misrepresentation could be shown, as opposed to rape, although some jurisdictions take such an expansive view regarding what reliably and unprejudicially evidences non-veracity, that virtually any serious wrong is encompassed. How broadly or narrowly the circle of permissibility is drawn must be ascertained from the statutes, rules, and cases in the particular jurisdiction. The kinds of convictions permitted may be defined broadly ("crimes", "felonies or misdemeanors") or in such vague terms as "infamous crimes," "crimes of moral turpitude," "felonies," "crimes of dishonesty or false statement"; or they may be more specifically defined or enumerated. One of the more petty disputes engendered by the language has been whether traffic offenses are included. The kinds of wrongdoing allowed may be described differently for convictions and non-convictions.

While all the forms of propensity impeachment evidence (reputation, opinion, specific instances of conduct) present considerable danger of undue prejudice where a party-witness is being impeached, the danger seems greatest where specific instances are alleged, particularly where they are convictions, and most particularly where that witness is the defendant in a criminal case. Nevertheless, the probative value is generally considered to outweigh this consideration, if the evidence otherwise complies with the rules applicable to that category of

3. At least conceptually this would include, in addition to regular convictions, non-final convictions, appealable convictions, convictions being appealed, collaterally attackable convictions, and convictions being collaterally attacked, etc.

impeachment, although cautionary instructions are required if requested and the judge frequently has discretion to disallow the evidence in an aggravated case, and a duty to do so in some particularly aggravated cases. The law, however, varies on this from jurisdiction to jurisdiction, and many gradations and variations are found. The F.R.E. in many instances require a careful balancing of probative value against prejudice on the particular facts, particularly where the criminal defendant is the witness being impeached by convictions not directly related to lying. See F.R.E. 609(a).

Let us examine more specifically each of the permissible forms of propensity impeachment evidence.

Character Impeachment by Opinion or Reputation Evidence: F.R.E. 608(a)

At this juncture, it is well to recall a point made earlier: reputation as to propensity for non-veracity is an allowable form of impeachment in most jurisdictions, including those adopting the F.R.E. or its progeny. F.R.E.-type jurisdictions also allow witnesses to give a personal opinion as to the propensity of another witness in this regard. (Lay opinions of persons knowing the witness are what seems to be contemplated. Does the provision also, however, open the door to expert opinion by a psychiatrist or psychologist? Cases permitting this are rare.)

In general, the rules as to both types of impeachment (reputation and personal opinion) are the same. No foundation need be laid on cross examination of the witness-to-be-impeached, in the sense used in connection with impeachment by prior inconsistent statements (see general impeachment chapter). In other words, extrinsic evidence may be introduced when the time comes, without any preparation of or forewarning to of the witness-to-be-impeached. However, a foundation must be laid in the sense that the reputation (or opinion) witness must be shown to be familiar with the reputation (or with the person the witness is opining about).

If the matter of the reputation is approached on cross-examination of the witness being impeached, the cross-examiner may be estopped from introducing the extrinsic evidence, since it may be redundant, depending upon what happens on that cross examination.

F.R.E. 608 codifies the matter of impeachment by opinion and reputation evidence as follows:

> "The credibility of a witness may be attacked . . . by evidence in the form of opinion or reputation, but . . . the evidence may refer only to character for . . . untruthfulness. . . . Specific instances of . . . conduct . . . may, . . . in the discretion of the court, if probative of truthfulness . . . be inquired into on cross-examination of the witness . . . concerning the [veracity-] character . . . of another witness as to which character the witness being cross-examined has testified."

The last quoted sentence is not directly concerned with how to impeach by opinion or reputation for non-veracity, but rather with how to attack, by testing his familiarity with the subject of his testimony, the credibility of a witness *who has attempted such impeachment*. Thus, it refers to *good* rather than *bad* specific instances. The specific instances are not conduct of the witness being cross-examined, but of the person being testified about. The language is included to complete the picture and indicate what an attorney opens the door to by attempting impeachment by opinion or reputation for non-veracity. Just what specific acts are probative of truthfulness is not self-evident.

Character Impeachment by Criminal Convictions: F.R.E. 609

As noted above, use of a witness' former convictions that comply with the particular jurisdiction's parameters for this kind of impeachment, is a common form of attack on the witness' credibility. Under this form of impeachment, no foundation need be laid in the sense used in connection with prior inconsistent statements (see general impeachment chapter). In other words, the matter need not be approached first on cross-examination. If the cross-examiner does inquire into the conviction on cross-examination of the witness-to-be-impeached and the witness admits the conviction, the impeacher can go no further and cannot introduce extrinsic evidence. Absent extraordinary circumstances, the only extrinsic evidence permitted in any event is just the record of or the fact of conviction (with no aggravating details). Sometimes even the name of the crime may be suppressed if it is regarded as unnecessary and prejudicial. Mitigating details are more freely admitted, more so if the matter comes up on cross-examination and the witness at that time wishes to state them. But this may open the door to contradictory evidence and the trial judge must be given considerable leeway about whether and how far to go down this road at all.

The trial judge may be given discretion to exclude convictions on the basis that the misconduct is too remote in time. There may be a detailed rule concerning the matter of staleness. E.g., F.R.E. 609(b).

Can the validity of the prior conviction be challenged in the current proceeding? Cf. *Parke v. Raley* (S.Ct.1992), allowing states to presume validity for sentencing enhancement purposes.

F.R.E. 609: The Current Rule

Where impeachment of a non-party witness is involved, traditionally the trial judge had little discretion respecting exclusion on the basis of prejudice, need for the evidence, or relevance of the kind of crime to truth-telling ability. The statute or rule frequently was deemed to preclude such discretion by enumerating kinds of crimes that may be used. But a change to F.R.E. 609 makes such evidence subject to Rule 403 balancing if the conviction does not relate directly to dishonesty or false statement.

Where a party-witness is being impeached, particularly a criminal defendant, discretion of some kind is often accorded by rule, legislation, or judicial fiat. F.R.E. 609 has an enhanced balancing provision for the situation of the criminal accused, tilted more against admissibility than Rule 403; but again, there is no balancing if the conviction directly relates to lying.

Below is the current version of F.R.E. 609(a) (not identical to what is found in the states, even in those with F.R.E.-based codes, because of Congressional changes, and also because of greater policy disagreement here than in some other evidence areas):

Rule 609.   Impeachment by Evidence of Conviction of Crime

(a) General Rule.—For the purpose of attacking the character for truthfulness of a witness,

(1) evidence that a witness other than an accused has been convicted of a crime shall be admitted, subject to Rule 403, if the crime was punishable by death or imprisonment in excess of one year under the law under which the witness was convicted, and evidence that an accused has been convicted of such a crime shall be admitted if the court determines that the probative value of admitting this evidence outweighs its prejudicial effect to the accused; and

(2) evidence that any witness has been convicted of a crime shall be admitted regardless of the punishment, if it readily can be determined that establishing the elements of the crime required proof or admission

of an act of dishonesty or false statement by the witness.

In 1990, Rule 609(a) was changed in several ways (included in the provision above), not necessarily reflected in state codifications based on the previous F.R.E.:

First, a limitation that the conviction must be elicited during cross-examination was eliminated. This deletion reflected practice in the circuits which had ignored the limitation, at least insofar as deemed necessary to allow witnesses to "remove the sting" of impeachment by testifying to the conviction on direct (see Advisory Committee Note to 1990 Amendment; it is doubtful the provision ever meant to prevent that). However, *Ohler v. United States* (S.Ct.2000), hold that criminal defendants who are witnesses on their own behalf, and pre-emptively introduce evidence of their own prior conviction on their direct examination, may not claim on appeal that a ruling of admissibility of the evidence was error, even if the pre-emptive introduction on direct exam was done only to remove the sting of the prosecution introducing the evidence (the trial judge having ruled, when an advance request was made, that the evidence would be admissible by the prosecution). In this situation, it cannot be asserted on appeal that this ruling of the trial judge, motivating the pre-emptive move, was error, even if it indeed was.

Second, the previous version of Rule 609 allowed the conviction to be established by public record during cross, as an alternative to the witness confessing there to the conviction. This public record provision was also eliminated. Does the elimination of this language mean that no extrinsic evidence can contradict a denial? The Advisory Committee Note assumes (rightly) exactly the opposite: that, since there is now no specification of how or when the conviction can be proved, the conviction can be proved through any form and at any time that is necessary and complies with the other rules of evidence, in the judge's discretion: cross-examination; or record or independent testimony, during cross-exam or later. The Note recognizes the power of the judge to regulate details of proof under Rules 403 and 611(a) to avoid undue delay, needless consumption of time, etc.

The Balancing Tests: A Favorable Balance for the Criminal Defendant; Rule 403 for Other Witnesses

Finally, another revision to Rule 609(a)(1) affected what appeared to be an uneven-handed balancing provision. The earlier rule at least on its face seemed to prohibit any balancing-type exclusion of convictions of any witness other than a criminal (and perhaps civil) defendant (and perhaps other defense witnesses), since it permitted exclusion only for prejudice to a "defendant". This exclusion for prejudice only applied to non-falsity crimes. Then, as now, the intention seemed to be that no balancing at all could be done regarding crimes of falsity.

This lopsided result between plaintiff and defendant in civil cases was eventually prohibited, despite the face of the rule, by *Green v. Bock Laundry Machine Co.* (S.Ct. 1989). *Green* concluded that the rule could not have meant what it seemed to say, because establishing vastly different standards for impeaching civil plaintiffs as compared with civil defendants would violate due process.

As a result the Rule was amended (as shown above) to make clear that Rule 403 balancing could operate to exclude non-falsity convictions of all witnesses other than the criminal defendant (who was given even more protection from impeachment as a witness, by a new especially protective balancing provision). However, this also altered the earlier explicit policy decision which prohibited the exclusion on balancing grounds of otherwise qualifying convictions of prosecution witnesses.

Originally, the inclusion of a balancing test favoring the defendant (by which was probably meant the criminal defendant who testified in his own behalf) resulted from a compromise between significantly disparate philosophies about the probity versus prejudice of prior convictions used solely for impeachment and their effect on a criminal defendant. One view rejects all but convictions for crimes involving falsity like embezzlement or perjury because of the potential that other types of crimes, for example assault, even if or especially if they are serious felonies, will be misused as substantive evidence proving that the defendant was more likely to have committed the crime in question, with little or no offsetting benefit in terms of tendency to prove lying.

In contrast, the other view was that all felonies (crimes punishable by more than one year in prison) have considerable predictive value for truthfulness. This theory stems from the "moral turpitude" view of some jurisdictions, like California and Texas, which hold that a person who has committed a serious crime indicates a "readiness to do evil" and a willingness to violate societal norms in any context, including the perjury laws.

The current Rule 609 balancing test, while providing a balancing for all witnesses attacked with non-falsity felonies, still preserves more favorable balancing treatment for criminal defendant-witnesses: A special balancing provision presumptively excludes *his* conviction unless the prosecution (the offeror of the impeaching conviction) demonstrates that its probative value outweighs its prejudice to the accused. The burden is the reverse of the burden under Rule 403 (which applies respecting other witnesses under Rule 609 and admits the evidence unless the *objector* shows that its prejudice outweighs *substantially* its probative value). Notice that the 403 burden is not only the reverse (presumptively *admitting* the conviction) but is heavier, because of the word "substantially".

The typical factors considered in these balancings include similarity, temporal remoteness, need for the defendant's testimony, and centrality of credibility to the case. Students often find it difficult to understand that unlike Rule 404(b) where evidence of similarity is a factor favoring admission, similarity often makes it less likely a conviction will be admitted under Rule 609. Similarity can be prejudicial because jurors will be tempted to use the evidence substantively (the defendant committed this crime, because he committed the previous crime), rather than to show the defendant is lying, and this may not be a permitted use unless the evidence also satisfies one of the MOIPPKIA catchwords under Rule 404(b).

Crimes of "Dishonesty or False Statement": The "Automatic Admit"

Because of their high probative value on credibility, Rule 609(a)(2) makes convictions for crimes of "dishonesty or false statement" admissible without any reference to balancing, regardless of whether they are felonies or misdemeanors. This "no balancing" approach to crimes having to do with dishonesty or false statement remains unchanged from the older version.

Presumably this category of crimes means crimes that involve some form of deceit or falsification.

It is theoretically arguable that convictions of crimes of dishonesty or false statement (Rule 609(a)(2)) are still subject to Rule 403 balancing, despite Congress' failure to subject them to express balancing language as in 609(a)(1) (felonies not of dishonesty or false statement). But most courts reject this argument, because of Congress' care in addressing the balancing problem. And the Rule says that this evidence "shall be admitted" rather than "is admissible". The latter is the phrase usually used when it is intended that 403 can impliedly apply. However, Rule 403 (or its equivalent) is available in some states even for these crimes.

The convictions subject to automatic admission under (a)(2) have typically been confined to "crimen falsi," i.e., crimes in which falsity is an element, such as perjury, embezzlement or mail fraud. But because "dishonesty" can be interpreted broadly, a minority of courts include theft crimes, which can include petit theft (a misdemeanor), because (a)(2) crimes are not limited to felonies. This result has been disapproved in the Advisory Committee Note, but the language of the rule was not modified to forbid such impeachment. The 1999 Uniform Rules revision to Rule 609 substituted "a crime of untruthfulness or falsification" for "dishonesty or false statement," and explicitly requires the "statutory elements of the conviction" to "necessarily involve untruthfulness or falsification."

This last provision of the Uniform Rules regarding "statutory elements" responds to a problem that had surfaced under original F.R.E. 609(a)(2), which merely described the type of crime covered as a "crime involving dishonesty or false statement". Could a crime qualify if it was committed under circumstances involving dishonesty or false statement, even if the statutory elements of the crime charged did not on their face nor inevitably involve dishonesty or false statement? For example, could criminal trespass be considered a crime of dishonesty or false statement if it were perpetrated by pretending to be a meter reader? A very recent amendment to F.R.E. 609(a)(2) handles this problem in a different way. See the language of F.R.E. 609(a)(2) set forth several pages above where we reproduce the rule as currently amended. Do you think this language is clear?[4]

4. The Uniform and Federal rules revisions concerning the definition and determination of 609(a)(2) crimes responded to issues raised

Does the court have any discretion to sanitize such convictions, permitting the jury to hear only the fact that the defendant was convicted of "a crime", "a felony", or "a misdemeanor" without naming it (assuming, which is not always the case, that the witness or party hurt by the evidence would prefer the sanitized version)? While this is permitted in dealing with convictions under (a)(1) (general felonies not relating to falsity), it does not appear to be an option for (a)(2) convictions (conviction relating to falsity) because that provision seems impliedly to contemplate that the jury should know at least that the crime related to falsity or deception (although the exact crime need not necessarily be named). In some states, sanitizing is prohibited because jury speculation about the nature of the crime is considered a greater problem than prejudice from the name. In contrast, other states sanitize all convictions. The Supreme Court case of *Old Chief*, supra, under Rule 404(b) (see "intent"), may have some implications for how a defendant may prevent details.

Other Issues: Time Remoteness, Pardon, and Appealability

Both under the F.R.E. and most state practice, remoteness in time is an important factor weighing for exclusion of convictions offered for impeachment. For example, Rule 609(b) makes evidence of a conviction inadmissible if a period of more than ten years has elapsed since the date of the conviction or of the release of the witness from the confinement imposed for that conviction, whichever is later, "unless the court determines, in the interests of justice, that the probative value of the conviction supported by specific facts and circumstances substantially outweighs its prejudicial effect." Advance somewhat detailed written notice must

by the A.B.A. report chaired by Prof. Rothstein mentioned earlier herein.

be given of intent to attempt to utilize the quoted exception. Rule 609(b) applies to all convictions under Rule 609(a). Some states apply an absolute ban for convictions more than 5 or 10 years old.

Under the F.R.E., and in many states, even if the conviction clears these specific "staleness" provisions, time can be a factor in the general balancing, where permitted.

The effect of a pardon, annulment, or certificate of rehabilitation varies greatly by jurisdiction. At least in F.R.E.-type jurisdictions, the pendency of an appeal does not render evidence of a conviction inadmissible, but evidence that the appeal is pending is admissible. While juvenile adjudications are generally not admissible in most jurisdictions, in criminal cases evidence of a juvenile adjudication of a witness other than the accused may be permitted by rule or required by constitutional decision. *Davis v. Alaska* (S.Ct.1974), held that the confrontation clause required that a criminal defendant be allowed to show by cross-examination that the government witness was on probation from a juvenile adjudication. The witness was important and may have been under suspicion himself in the present case, and was perhaps beholden to the authorities or motivated to divert suspicion away from himself. *Davis* has implications beyond the impeachment covered by this section. The case is perhaps more aptly described as involving impeachment by bias than general propensity to lie. The implications possibly extend to other forms of impeachment, and even beyond impeachment. The Court so far, however, has not given *Davis* an expansive reading.

Determining whether a defendant will be impeached by prior convictions is a key decision in any criminal trial. For strategic reasons the defense will want to bring an in limine motion (i.e., an advance motion, usually in advance of trial), preferably before voir dire (i.e., before

screening and selection of the jurors) and at the latest
before opening statements, to ascertain whether the pri-
or convictions are going to be ruled admissible for impeachment, especially in jurisdictions where the categories of usable convictions are not clearly spelled out or
there is wide judicial discretion. If the answer is yes,
defendants will often elect to exercise their fifth amendment right not to testify. Empirical data appears to
support this choice: if all other factors are equal, juries
are more prone to convict a defendant who has a prior
criminal history. However, this choice is not cost free. In
Luce v. United States (S.Ct.1984), the Supreme Court
held that a defendant must take the stand and be impeached in order to preserve a claim for appeal that the
trial judge ruled erroneously that the conviction can be
used. If the defendant does not testify, the question of
whether the impeachment ruling was proper is waived.
So defendant may have made a critical choice (to not
testify) based on an erroneous ruling by the trial judge,
and yet cannot challenge the ruling on appeal.

Impeachment by Non–Convicted–For Misconduct "Probative of Untruthfulness"

Some jurisdictions do not permit this line of impeachment at all because it is so marginal. Those that do,
confine the inquiry to cross-examination (of the witness-
to-be-impeached). No extrinsic evidence[5] establishing the
misconduct is permitted. The witness' answer concerning
whether he committed the misconduct or not must be
accepted (although not necessarily his first answer: some
"badgering" seems to be permitted so long as it is
confined to the cross-examination). The trial judge is
given enormous discretion to permit or disallow the
inquiry based upon (a) the relevance of the kind of
misconduct to truth-telling, (b) proximity or remoteness

5.   Extrinsic evidence means other witnesses, documents, recordings,
etc.

of the misconduct in time, and (c) all of the other factors we have discussed that influence the exercise of a judge's discretion in matters of evidence, including prejudice, misleadingness, need, time, confusion, etc. The ruling will seldom be reversed, particularly if the judge opts to exclude.

A very few jurisdictions are more liberal than this and permit this evidence on a basis similar to that under convictions (immediately above) or require the trial judge to permit very wide inquiry into all kinds of misconduct not resulting in conviction upon cross-examination (while at the same time still forbidding extrinsic evidence).

F.R.E. 608(b) codifies the matter as follows:

"Specific instances of the conduct of a witness, for the purpose of attacking ... [credibility] *character for truthfulness*, other than conviction of crime ... may not be proved by extrinsic evidence. They may, however, in the discretion of the court, if probative of ... untruthfulness, be inquired into on cross-examination of the witness ... concerning the witness' character for ... untruthfulness...."[6]

The F.R.E. has retained the traditional rule banning extrinsic evidence (i.e., evidence other than adduced through cross examining the witness being impeached) of these specific acts. Extrinsic proof of such acts, for which there has been no conviction, would be time consuming, distracting, prejudicial, not directly related to the issues being proven in the case, and not particularly probative. They are worth, perhaps, a little time and effort, but not

6. The brackets indicate a word recently deleted and the italics a phrase substituted for it to clarify that the rule reaches misconduct directed at general character for credibility, not, for example, misconduct that shows a particular bias (as for example assaulting the party testified against). Bias showings are controlled only by Rule 403 and are free of the categorical restrictions concerning extrinsic evidence and nature of the wrongdoing.

highlighting. Hence, cross-exam concerning them is enough. The law wishes to avoid a trial within a trial on a basically collateral issue, and to avoid the ensuing confusion as to just what is the important issue in the case.

Care should be taken not to treat Rule 608(b) as applicable to or banning evidence which is admissible on some other theory than impeachment by general propensity for non-veracity, such as impeachment by showing possible bias, interest, or motive, which is constrained only by Rule 403 and liberally permitted. For example, suppose it is sought to be shown that a prosecution witness had committed another crime for which he is not being prosecuted. This would be meant to suggest a possible motive to please the prosecution, or a possible "deal" for the testimony, which could color the testimony. Cf. *United States v. Havens* (S.Ct.1980).

A witness (whether a party or not) being impeached (in a civil or criminal case) by misconduct treated in this section under a rule like 608(b) may have a legitimate claim of constitutional privilege to refuse to answer the impeachment questions, if her answers may open her up to criminal prosecution for a transaction being inquired into in the impeachment. The Fifth Amendment to the Federal Constitution provides a privilege against self-incrimination. It would not apply to impeachment by convictions, above, because conviction ordinarily removes the possibility of further incrimination.

The criminal defendant as a witness in her own behalf, by choosing to take the stand (which she cannot be compelled to do, owing to the Fifth Amendment privilege), will ordinarily be deemed to have waived the right to refuse to answer questions substantively related to the charges, but it has been held that she retains the privilege to the extent other crimes (for which there has not yet been a conviction) are inquired into.

Character or Propensity for Incredibility of Victim and Perpetrator in Sex Cases

In the whole discussion above concerning impeachment of witnesses by opinion, reputation, criminal conviction, and other bad acts, it should be remembered that F.R.E. 412 ("rape shield") protecting sex victims, and F.R.E. 413–15 expanding evidence against sex offenders, may constrict, or expand, respectively, the kinds of propensity or character impeachment attack on credibility that may be brought to bear against such victims and offenders when they appear as witnesses in cases involving themselves. The same is true of the state analogues of these rules. Such rules usually apply to credibility evidence as well as substantive evidence and are discussed supra in this propensity chapter under substantive evidence, which is their most obvious focus.

X.   SOME RECURRING THEMES CUTTING ACROSS THIS ENTIRE PROPENSITY CHAPTER

Balancing and Instructions

Where evidence is offered on and meets the requirements of one of the permissible theories, but there is a danger of one of the impermissible uses being made by the jury, if the evidence is admitted the opponent of the evidence is entitled to an instruction attempting to forbid the jury from making the impermissible use, and, as always, to a parallel limitation on argument. (A frank explanation to the jury of the dangers and probative shortcomings of the evidence would serve much better than such an instruction.) If, however, the legitimate value of the evidence is considered to be outweighed by the risk of misuse and a cautionary instruction is deemed insufficiently efficacious, the evidence will be excluded.

This problem is most acutely presented where a criminal defendant takes the stand as a defense witness, and the prosecution seeks to impeach him by showing his character-propensity for falsehood, for example by prior convictions, which may be permitted; but which could easily be taken by the jury as evidence of character-propensity to commit crimes including the present one, or could cause the jury to convict for past badness, which normally are not permitted purposes. While such danger could be sufficient to result in exclusion under the judge's balancing power (frequently but not always given the judge for this situation), if the evidence is admitted, the defendant is entitled to an instruction cautioning the jury against the improper use, at least if the defendant wants one. The judge in making a balancing power admissibility determination may consider such fact-specific matters as how similar to the present crime the conviction is; how old it is (although it is not beyond the limit of the rule); its relationship to truth-telling; other evidence on the permissible and impermissible issue; the feasibility of limiting the details; the efficacy of limiting instructions; the effect on defendant's willingness to testify and the need for and importance of his testimony; the cruciality of his credibility on the facts; the closeness of the entire case; his record between the conviction and the trial (did his "propensity for falsehood" continue?); etc. Some authority requires the judge's considerations to be put on the record.

An analogous problem is presented where the accused's good character witnesses are sought to be impeached by inquiry into their knowledge of former derelictions of the accused. This is generally permitted in the form and for the purpose stated earlier in this chapter (i.e., to impeach the knowledge and standards of the good character witness), with cautionary instructions against any other use of the evidence (e.g., to make it likely the accused committed the crime currently charged), but on occasion the evidence may be excluded because, on the facts, the danger of the impermissible use outweighs the permissible use. For example in *Awkard v. United States* (D.C.Cir.1965) the impeaching value was slight because the good character witness being impeached did not testify in direct examination as to familiarity with defendant in the locale of or at the time of the purported wrongdoing of defendant, but rather that he knew him at another place and another period of time.

Even where there is only one possible use of the evidence, and that a permissible one, the opponent may be able to ask for an instruction cautioning against the danger of overemphasis, and for some regulation of argument.

Remedies for Introduction of Impermissible Propensity Evidence: Fighting Fire With Fire

As in the case of other impermissible evidence, where a propensity has been impermissibly introduced by one side, without the fault of the other (i.e., the other could not have been expected to object sooner before it was introduced), an argument can be made that a contrary propensity (or proof that tends to dispel the effect of the impermissible evidence) should now be allowed to be shown even though it would not otherwise be admissible. The court will consider, however, the comparative adequacy and desirability of other remedies, such as a motion to strike (which results in an instruction to the jury to disregard) or a mistrial.

See for an example of this problem, *Hudson v. Hightower* (Tex.Civ.App.1965). Defendant in an auto collision case testifies seemingly somewhat accidentally and unexpectedly that he normally entered the relevant intersection slowly. Plaintiff then produces a witness who states that defendant normally went through that intersection "too fast—50 or 60 m.p.h." The judge instructs the jury that the sole purpose of the latter testimony is to "rebut [defendant's] testimony as to how he customarily entered the intersection ... and it is no evidence of the speed or the manner in which [defendant] entered the intersection on the date of the collision in question."

Two Helpful Questions

When evidence of propensity is not per se forbidden, there are two questions that can be helpful to the offering attorney to make sure it is in proper form: (1) "Is the propensity I am seeking to prove, of the legally requisite specificity (e.g., traits legally considered pertinent to the issue rather than unrelated or broader traits)?" and (2) "Am I proving it with the legally proper kind of evidence (i.e., opinion, reputation, or specific instances)?"

(1) The Generality/Specificity Question

In an assault-and-battery or murder prosecution, where the accused wishes to exercise his special dispensation to show his good character, may the accused show general good character for morality and law abidingness, or his character for honesty with property; or is the accused confined to a showing of character for non-violence and peaceableness? If in response in the same case the prosecution wishes to increase the apparent probability of guilt by showing the defendant's character for committing such acts, will a propensity for criminality in general suffice, or for theft, or must it be a propensity for violent crime? Notice that none of the alternatives in our examples is so specific as to take the matter out of the realm of character. But within the realm of character, the most specific character trait, concerning the very kind of crime in issue, is required, in our examples here, as we have learned in this chapter. It is true that "generally lawless" persons may be somewhat more disposed to murder or assault than others.

But not significantly enough to outweigh the dangers, the law feels.

We have also seen that the MOIPPKIA rule allows *non-character* propensity, i.e., propensity so specific, it is not considered character-propensity. Thus, here too, the generality/specificity question must be asked.

In the area of impeachment, how does the generality/specificity question play out? If a witness is sought to be impeached, can a propensity for immorality or illegality in general, or for violence, be shown? There may be some slight tendency for dissolute persons to be more mendacious than others, everything else being equal. Or must it be a propensity for telling falsehoods, more specifically? We have seen in this chapter that frequently (although not always) the witness' propensity specifically for non-veracity (honest error as well as dishonest deception) is all that may be shown. For example, under the F.R.E., Rule 608 (opinion, reputation, and non-convictions, all for impeachment purposes) requires considerable specific relationship to veracity. Rule 609 (convictions) does for non-felonies, but not for felonies (crimes punishable by more than a year). For a more precise answer, see the rules earlier in this chapter.

(2) The Question Concerning Kind of Evidence

Once the generality or specificity that is required by the law is ascertained and the attorney proposes to prove (for substantive or impeachment purposes) a propensity that meets the requirement, the attorney is confronted with the second question: What kind of evidence may be used to establish that propensity? As we have seen, conceptually there are at least three feasible varieties: Testimony by someone as to that someone's perception of the subject person's reputation for the propensity; testimony by someone as to that someone's own personal opinion of the subject person in the relevant respect (that is, with respect to the propensity); and testimony or other proof of specific instances of conduct evidencing the propensity.

Generally speaking, the rules discussed above in this chapter reveal that the common law traditionally has been more receptive to reputation evidence (for which a tacit or express exception to the hearsay rule must be made) than to either opinion or specific instance evidence, to prove character-propensity where permitted. Can you say why? But see F.R.E. 405 and 608 generally allowing reputation and opinion evidence (is this only lay opinion?), but still generally barring specific instance evidence.

We have seen above in this chapter, however, that there are occasions under traditional law and the F.R.E., where specific instances are allowed, perhaps exclusively in some instances. See, e.g., F.R.E. 404(b) (other crimes, wrongs, and acts, for MOIPPKIA), 405(a) final sentence (to impeach character witness), 405(b) ("essential element"), 406 (habit), 608(b) (impeachment by non-convictions), and 609 (impeachment by convictions). See also F.R.E. 413 through 415 (other sexual acts of sex offenders). Remember, in some of these, the inquiry into specific instances is confined to cross-examination. See discussion of the particular rules above in this chapter.

Reputation, Opinion, Specific Instances: The Required Foundation

Under all three of the forms of evidence—reputation, opinion, and specific instances—there is a requirement that the person testifying thereto must be familiar with that whereof he or she speaks. Thus, in the case of reputation testimony, courts normally require that the witness and the subject have lived or done business in reasonable proximity to each other for a substantial period in the fairly recent past, and that the reputation reported be the reputation in that community and be relatively current. A prerequisite

**for personal opinion testimony would be that the wit-
ness and the subject person have had some substantial
recent contact, relationship, or the like, that would
furnish a reasonable basis for a current opinion. Recent or current means near the act to be established
by the propensity. Specific instances, if provable, also
may only be established by competent evidence thereof.**

If this foundation appears, weaknesses in the evidence
in terms of degree of the witness's exposure to what he
or she is testifying about would be matters of weight and
not admissibility.

Specific Instances: Further Restrictions

**Respecting specific instances of conduct, while
there is little uniformity, courts may restrict the
adduction of details (perhaps favoring mitigating
details). In addition, in some jurisdictions in some
instances there may be a preference for the most
economical and trustworthy form of proof available:
a record of the conviction, etc. There is also frequently a requirement of temporal proximity between the conduct sought to be put into evidence
and the conduct in issue. Additionally, there may
be authority relating to the effect of formal legal
dispositions that may have occurred with respect to
the specific instance.**

With respect to the last point in the heading, while
there is little uniformity, some authority in some jurisdictions suggests that mere charges that have been
dropped and arrests that have not resulted in charges,
are barred as evidence of misconduct, and may even
prevent the underlying misconduct from being evidenced
even if it is evidenced by some other means, such as a
witness. At the very least, the favorable (or at least not
unfavorable) legal disposition of the incident ought to be
allowed to be shown to curtail or destroy the force of the
evidence. Instructions to the jury cautioning about what
can be deduced from a mere charge or arrest are found.

We would expect a similar result where the alleged misconduct was the subject of an exculpatory civil or criminal adjudication, or, perhaps, a pardon, or, on a proper occasion, where an appeal, say of a conviction, is pending. Would you say the presence of a ground for collateral attack (e.g., habeas corpus) of a conviction should have a similar effect? Some of these matters are dealt with, as respects convictions used for impeachment, in F.R.E. 609(c)-(e). But in general they are not subject to rule and are handled on a more ad hoc basis. See, concerning the effect of acquittal, the Supreme Court decision in *Dowling*, supra, under procedural aspects of 404(b).

Even if some of these matters do not affect admissibility, they are certainly fertile ground for arguments to the fact-finder respecting weight.

On the possibility of limiting adduction of details of a previous wrong, see the Supreme Court decision in *Old Chief*, supra, under 404(b) (where intent is discussed).

Concessions, Offers to Stipulate

In many instances in this chapter, the evidence is admissible to prove only one of two or more things it could be taken as indicating by a jury. Sometimes the evidence might be quite damaging to a party, if received. Yet the judge may feel the danger of impermissible use is not great enough to exclude the evidence altogether, feeling that a cautionary instruction limiting the evidence to the permissible use is sufficient. The attorney resisting the evidence may then wish to consider the possibility of offering to stipulate to or concede the fact the evidence is admissible to prove, in the hope that this will eliminate the only theory of admissibility of the evidence. See, e.g., the Supreme Court decision in *Old Chief*, supra, under 404(b), where "intent" is discussed. See also *Clark v. Stewart*, supra, under VIII.

CHAPTER 5

PRIVILEGES

I. POLICIES, PROCEDURES, AND GENERAL PRINCIPLES UNDER-LYING PRIVILEGES

Privileges as Narrow Exceptions to Everyone's Duty to Give Evidence (Testimony, Documents, Etc.)

The term privilege means a freedom from compulsion to give evidence, or a right to prevent or bar evidence from other sources, usually on grounds unrelated to the goals of litigation.

In the absence of privilege, parties, witnesses, and others, can be compelled by a court to give testimony or other material they may have, that is needed for court proceedings, even if it is damaging to themselves or others. The usual principle is that the law is entitled to every person's evidence. Similarly, a person normally cannot prevent another person from disclosing confidences or other matters under legal compulsion or voluntarily, for use in judicial proceedings. Privileges are a narrow exception to these general rules. As such, they sometimes interfere with the truth-seeking function of the law. It always should be borne in mind that privileges operate to exclude good proof, in the name of some other social objective. For this reason, courts often say privileges should be narrowly construed.

Determinations of coverage for most true privileges, however, are not made on an *ad hoc* balancing of the competing considerations on the facts of each case, as would be done in the case of a "qualified" privilege. Instead, the definitions and limits of most true privileges are fixed by law. The reason is that most true privileges are designed to promote certain kinds of relationships, and particularly to promote confidential communications within these socially desirable relationships. Uncertainty of coverage at the time of the communication reduces the encouragement to communicate. On privileges generally, see Rothstein and S. Crump, FEDERAL TESTIMONIAL PRIVILEGES (2d ed. 2007, updated annually).

Policies Underlying Privileges

As just indicated, a common policy underlying privileges is *to encourage desirable communications* within certain kinds of special relationships, for purposes that society particularly wishes to foster. The privileges for confidential communications in the attorney-client, physician-patient, psychotherapist-patient, and husband-wife contexts are examples. It is frequently asserted that these relationships would not accomplish their purposes, or would accomplish them far less effectively, without legal protection of confidences through rules of privilege. Although this conclusion is controversial, it is the foundation of several of our most important privileges.

A second, and distinct, policy is *to protect the desired relationship itself*, even to the extent that it is not dependent upon confidential communications. Thus, to foster the marital relationship, many jurisdictions recognize a privilege of one spouse to refuse to testify against the other. This privilege usually extends to adverse testimony on any subject, whether it concerns confidential communications or not.

Other policies may be *to uphold the integrity* of a profession; *to avoid futile efforts to coerce testimony* against principled resistance; *to avoid likely perjury* if so coerced; or *to subserve commonly shared principles of privacy, fairness, or morality*. These are often given as reasons for the clergy-penitent privilege (although some of the other policies also support it); and they are sometimes mentioned as secondary reasons for the attorney-client, physician-patient, psychotherapist-patient, or spousal privileges.

Other privileges operate *to advance economic policies*, such as those protecting trade secrets, or *to encourage voluntary compliance with law*, as in the case of privileges for certain required reports to government agencies, which may also incorporate *"housekeeping" concerns* about disruptive requests for documents and document loss. Still other privileges serve *to limit governmental invasion of the security of individuals*. The privilege against self-incrimination is an example. Some privileges against evidence are intended *to discourage bad behavior*, e.g. on the part of law enforcement. The constitutional and statutory prohibitions against evidence obtained from an illegal search and seizure, "unmirandized" or counsel-less interrogations or line-ups, unconscionable obtaining of confessions, or improper electronic surveillance, are in part based on this notion.

The limits of these policies, together with the need for particular types of information, define the boundaries and exceptions to privileges. For example, communications intended to facilitate further commission of crime or fraud are not protected by the attorney-client privilege. The discovery of this information is particularly necessary, and a rule of nondisclosure is inappropriate because none of the purposes of the attorney-client relationship can support the privilege when the object is crime or fraud. This is one example of how the law limits privileges narrowly to their legitimate policy because of their tendency to frustrate the truth-seeking function.

Most rules of evidence, including privilege, on occasion may render inadmissible, relevant evidence offered on behalf of a criminal defendant, that could help raise a genuine reasonable doubt concerning defendant's guilt. At some point, such exclusion may trench on the defendant's constitutional right to present information in defense, under the confrontation, compulsory process, or due process clauses of the Constitution.[1]

The Supreme Court has held, for example, that a confidentiality privilege covering juvenile records potentially strongly impeaching a principal government witness, violates confrontation rights; that the government's shielding with informer privilege the identity of an important prosecution witness (or key potential witness or source for the defense even if not proffered by the prosecution) may similarly offend; that cloaking potential defensive information with state or military secrets privilege may be inconsistent with prosecution; that a peculiar and unfounded statute barring co-criminals from testifying for defendants was unconstitutional; and that outmoded limits on a hearsay exception and on cross-examining one's own witness that in combination prevented a defendant from offering powerful reliable exculpatory evidence (the witness' multiple confessions to the crime), must give way. The Court has also ruled that a jurisdiction's rule against hypnotically refreshed testimony could not be applied so as to automatically exclude testimony of a criminal defendant who had herself undergone hypnosis (but did not rule the same way concerning a jurisdiction's automatic exclusion of polygraph

1. This matter is largely beyond our scope, but is addressed briefly in chapters dealing with other subjects such as Hearsay, Rape Shield, and Impeachment. See Chapter 4 under rape shield; Chapter 6 in the introduction to "II. Impeachment: Some General Principles"; and Chapter 8, under "The Criminal Defendant's Right to Cross Examine Without Undue Restriction" which deals with the confrontation clause, and, also in that chapter, under "The Due Process and Compulsory Process Clauses".

evidence which evidence in this case favored the defendant).[2]

The Court has not recognized a broad right to introduce all relevant defensive evidence that could contribute to a reasonable doubt. Instead the Court prefers a piecemeal approach embracing only aggravated cases that clearly offend a particular constitutional provision in a major way. In *Montana v. Egelhoff* (S.Ct.1996), the Supreme Court seemed to give the green light generally to most traditional exclusionary rules (for example, F.R.E. 403 and the Hearsay Rule) even when they interfere with the criminal defense by excluding relevant evidence offered on behalf of the defendant. The Court even includes "privilege" in its list of traditional exclusionary rules that permissibly curtail defense's right to introduce relevant evidence; and specifically approves, partly on social policy grounds, the state restriction involved in the case itself: exclusion of evidence of intoxication at least insofar as it bears on the mental state for deliberate homicide.

In a number of cases the Supreme Court has permitted reasonable restrictions on, for example, relevant cross-

2. The general issue also surfaces in lower state and federal courts. For example, various forms of journalist privilege have been asserted to prevent criminal defendants from obtaining potentially useful information, as have a variety of government official information privileges. Even attorney-client, priest-penitent, and husband-wife privileges have been asserted to prevent a criminal defendant from obtaining what might be a confession to the crime by another person to the latter's lawyer, priest, or spouse. See, e.g., *Arizona v. Macumber* (Ariz.1976) (attorney-client; client had allegedly confessed but died; his family inherits, and asserts, the privilege). The court in this case held that privilege does not give way, but the family of the deceased client subsequently waived the privilege. However, at that point the judge examined the allegedly privileged statements and found them to be unreliable hearsay. While results have been mixed concerning most privileges, it is usually held that the government cannot both prosecute and at the same time assert governmental privilege to deprive the defendant of potentially useful information.

examination by the defense; or permitted exclusion of other relevant defense evidence for procedural defaults such as failure to give timely notice or discovery where a jurisdiction requires such.

Contentions that defendant's rights are being infringed are most likely to be raised and sustained in areas like privilege or rape shield where, arguably, exclusion of relevant evidence is based at least in part on furthering extrinsic social policies rather than furthering, as under Rule 403, the accuracy or functioning of the fact-finding process. But cf. *Egelhoff*, supra, suggesting that even fostering social policies may sometimes be an acceptable basis for curtailing defense evidence. See generally on the right to introduce defensive evidence and its limits in today's law, Imwinkelried & Garland, Exculpatory Evidence: The Accused's Constitutional Right to Introduce Favorable Evidence (3d ed. 2004).

For cases indicating that various confidentiality privileges of witnesses can impermissibly deny defendants' constitutional rights, see, e.g., *State v. Peseti* (Hawaii 2003); *Salazar v. State* (Alaska 1976); and *State v. Hembd* (Minn.1975). A journalist privilege was held subject to a defendant's constitutional compulsory-process right to obtain defensive evidence in *Matter of Farber* (N.J.1978). But see *United States v. Brown* (5th Cir. 1981) (spousal privilege sustained though it impeded defendant's ability to obtain material to impeach [confront] a government witness). *People v. Qike* (N.Y.Sup. 1999) suppressed a tape recording obtained by a criminal defendant through illegal eavesdropping, where the statute prohibited its use at trial, even though the criminal defendant claimed its exclusion violated due process. However, the court indicated the evidence could be admissible for impeachment. See generally Comment, *Defendant vs. Witness, Measuring Confrontation and*

Compulsory Process Rights Against Statutory Communications Privileges, 30 Stan. L. Rev. 935 (1978).

Common Themes Concerning Assertion and Waiver of Privilege

There may be two types of "holders" of a privilege of the kind that is intended to encourage accurate communication of confidential information. The primary holder is the one whose immediate interests are harmed if disclosure occurs. This individual is the communicator whom the law seeks to encourage. Thus, normally, the primary holder's express assertion or express waiver of the privilege should prevail over anyone else's wishes, including those of a secondary holder. A secondary holder is one who is allowed to assert the privilege in certain instances where the primary holder is unable to personally assert the privilege. Consider, for example, litigation to which the primary holder is not a party, or a proceeding of which the primary holder is unaware, where someone is called to give evidence which breaches the privileged statement. The encouragement-of-communications policy would be furthered if primary holders (communicators) knew that someone (e.g., the witness, or one of the litigants in the action, or the government, or the judge) would be likely to assert the privilege for them.

Thus, the assertion of a confidential communications privilege by a secondary holder is most clearly justified when it can be assumed that the primary holder would not wish disclosure. If the primary holder knows that privileged material is being sought for disclosure, and is able to but has not asserted the privilege, this condition may not be met. Additional problems arise upon events such as the death of the primary holder, when the need or desire for nondisclosure may be somewhat diminished. In such a situation, courts may decide no longer to recognize certain kinds of privileges. Most of the communications privileges, however, endure, in most jurisdictions, even after death, on the theory that a communicator may worry about embarrassment or damage to his or her family, heirs, or memory. See, e.g., *Swidler & Berlin v. United States* (S.Ct.1998) (attorney-client privilege normally survives the client's death; the client's family takes over the right to exercise the privilege). Excepted may be certain defined situations such as a contest between two competing beneficiaries under a will where the deceased client's will-drafting communications with his attorney may be considered necessary to reveal in order to effectuate the wishes of the client.

A primary holder can waive a confidential communications privilege by voluntarily bringing into issue a matter which can best be proved by information contained in the communication. Concerning the attorney-client privilege, some examples may be where the client sues the attorney concerning the services to which the communication is related; claims ineffective assistance of counsel; resists paying legal fees; presses a disciplinary proceeding against the lawyer; or claims advice of counsel as a defense to some kind of proceeding. (In some of these, lawyers may be allowed to disclose to defend themselves whether or not the client has initiated the action.) Another might be where the client voluntarily embarks on a discussion of part of the communication and subsequently seeks to keep another part secret. The same principle, however, suggests that a person does not lose a privilege by being compelled to do some act which if done voluntarily would result in a loss of the privilege. Thus, assuming that copies of income tax returns are within a certain privilege, if a taxpayer is erroneously compelled by a court over objection to produce such copies for discovery purposes, there are decisions holding that the privilege to prevent later introduction of such copies into evidence will not be lost.

If the holder voluntarily allows disclosure in one action, the question arises whether the privilege should be deemed waived in subsequent litigation. If disclosure in the subsequent action would be harmful, it is arguable that a prior waiver, in a situation where the disclosure was not so harmful, should not bind the holder. A rule of once-and-for-all waiver arguably would inhibit the earlier disclosure. In the attorney-client context distinctions are sometimes drawn concerning whether the right to claim privilege later was expressly reserved and if measures were attempted to limit dissemination from the first proceeding.

The General Concept of Confidentiality: Third Persons as an Illustration

The communications privileges, such as the husband-wife, attorney-client, and physician-patient privileges, usually depend by definition upon the communication being intended as confidential or secret. Normally, under these privileges, a reasonably avoidable third person, unnecessary to the communication or the work of the relationship, who is present at or otherwise gains access to the communication, can render unavailable a confidential communications privilege. According to a number of decisions, *negligence* of the communicator, as respects access by the third party, allows only the third party to testify; but the communicator's voluntarily *intentionally* or *knowingly* giving or allowing access can destroy confidentiality and hence the entire privilege, even as to testimony by the direct parties to the communication, including the person the privilege was designed to protect. If, however, the third party obtained access solely through actions of a party to the communication who could not waive the privilege for the communicator, the privilege usually remains intact. For example, the client may not be bound by the disclosures that a loose-lipped attorney makes without authorization. However, some courts require the client to object when the confidential information becomes public in order to avoid acquiescence in the disclosure.

Third persons may be viewed by the law as "necessary" to or desirably facilitative of the lawyer-client or doctor-patient communication or relationship. (This is less frequently so in the husband-wife situation.) Thus, other lawyers working on the matter, clerks, secretaries, and co-clients will often be tolerated under the lawyer-client privilege, and nurses, family of the patient, etc., may be allowed under the doctor-patient privilege. The presence of minor children has been a matter of some dispute under the husband-wife privilege. If a third person is deemed necessary or facilitative, her access will have no effect on the privilege and the evidence will remain fully suppressible when sought from any source otherwise covered by the privilege, even if the access was intended and known by the parties to the communication.

The approach may be different under rules of privilege that are supported by other policies, such as privileges protecting disclosures in certain kinds of governmentally required reports. Here, the policy is to encourage voluntary compliance with the law, not to protect confidential relationships. While the decisions are by no means uniform, some have held that a particular required report privilege will not ordinarily be waived or lost by the fact that an unnecessary third person has been privy to the report, even if the access was intentional on the reporter's part. Of course, persons within the government who necessarily have access are not considered third persons.

Thus, if a polluter tells or shows a friend what he reported in a written report to an environmental agency, the privilege, which extends to the written report, may not be destroyed and may be assertable later, e.g. in court. However, courts here may disagree, and the issue is complex. For example, it is possible that the third person may be allowed to testify to her recollection of the disclosure.

Of course, as in all communications privileges, the reporter and others can be asked what they themselves know about the acts reported,[3] independently of what the report says. It is the privileged *communication*, not the subject matter, that may not be evidenced. What was done (not what was said in the report) is a proper inquiry, as long as knowledge of what was done does not come from the report. This principle would also allow asking the third person what the reporter told her about the pollution if the polluter is not referring to what he said in the report but merely the facts, even if they are also reported in the report.

The General Concept of "Communication"

The privileges covering confidential communications privilege only "communications." But they may be express or implied communications. A nod or shake of the head, or a pointing of a finger, are clearly implied communications. They are meant as communicative acts. Some jurisdictions may extend the concept of implied communications further, to acts not as clearly mere substitutes for words, but still intentionally communicative in confidence and in reliance on the relationship, as for example placing an incriminating item in a drawer privately, but intentionally in front of one's lawyer or spouse.

Jurisdictions vary concerning the treatment of back-and-forth dialogue. Are the attorney's questions or replies or advice to the client privileged, or is it only the client's confidential communications that are covered? There seem to be three views about whether the lawyer's statements are covered: (1) yes, the communications are

3. This is obviously a different matter.

protected both ways; (2) no, it is only the client's communications that are privileged, not the attorney's; or (3) it depends upon whether the attorney's communications are reflective of (evidence of) those of the client, so that the attorney's communications are privileged to the extent needed to protect the client's.

The federal cases appear to adopt the third view. However, given the purposes of the privilege, it seems the protection should extend unconditionally both ways. Any other approach may create uncertainty and therefore deter communications, and it may lead the attorney to censor advice that otherwise would result in compliance with the law. A similar question arises under, e.g., doctor-patient and husband-wife privilege. The policy considerations may not be identical under husband-wife privilege where both may be primary holders respecting their own communications. Moreover, an attorney's replies or advice would typically be protected by work product, even if not privileged.

A somewhat similar question arises concerning a variety of matters that may not technically be communications between the parties but seem close thereto. For example, uncommunicated matters in the file of an attorney, physician, or psychotherapist concerning the client or patient. Here a sensible view might be to protect insofar as privileged communications are inferentially revealed, if the material is not otherwise protected as attorney work-product. To some extent the treatment of these matters depends upon which of the policies, above, is considered operative; and if encouragement is the goal, what exactly are we trying to encourage. Some decisions suggest we want to encourage more than communication: that we want to encourage the seeking of professional help and the work of the relationship more generally. The answers may vary from privilege to privilege. For example, the seeking of psychiatric help may be attempted to be specially encouraged because of the frequent "skittishness" of patients who need it.

The Benefits of Privileges Versus Their Costs: An Unknowable Balance

Citizens may or may not be aware, at the time they are making a privileged communication, that it is privileged. It is doubtful that most citizens have a precise notion of the extent of coverage of a privilege, even if they know about its existence. Do people know or think about whether husband-wife, physician-patient, or attorney-client privilege covers them when they are communicating? Are they aware of required report privileges? At least where there is no printed report form or professional advisor alerting people to privilege, removal of the privilege, or making exceptions to coverage, might have little effect on future communications. On the other hand, constriction or abolition of a privilege may be more likely to be publicized and come to the attention of citizens than the existence of a privilege in the first place. Further, a feeling of unfair deception and consequent over-caution might ultimately be engendered by exceptions and gaps. This all could discourage socially desirable communication. But whether and how much this would occur is an open question.

Some believe that criminal, civil, and professional disciplinary sanctions for unauthorized disclosure could render communications privilege unnecessary. Communicators would know unauthorized disclosure would be punished and would still feel secure and encouraged to communicate. Such sanctions and prohibitions do exist, along with privilege, in many instances, in, for example, the physician, psychiatrist, lawyer, and clergy contexts. While these non-privilege constraints on unauthorized disclosure might put the communicator's mind at rest concerning public disclosure, they do nothing about disclosure as evidence in court. Is this of significant dimension?

It also has been argued that the standard rules of evidence (e.g., the hearsay rule) or the general privilege against self-incrimination would adequately prevent disclosure in most cases, without other rules of privilege. Out-of-court communications covered by confidential communications privileges are usually hearsay. They often may qualify, however, for exceptions to or exemptions from the hearsay rule. The privilege against self-incrimination similarly does not cover the waterfront. The panoply of privileges we have today provides much more protection than either of these. Whether the additional protection is worth the price is another question.

The existence and shape of communications privileges are premised upon certain *assumed* answers to the questions raised in the last several paragraphs, which are basically effect and cost-benefit questions. The assumed answers have never really been satisfactorily tested. The assumption is made that privileges do make a difference in fostering the desired kinds of communications, that the communications foster the work of the particular relationship, that the work is socially beneficial, and that this all occurs in an amount that outweighs the costs to litigation. Any privilege must, theoretically, satisfy these criteria.

The truth, however, is that we do not and perhaps cannot know many of these things very reliably. The assumed benefits of a privilege inevitably clash at some point with the goal of ascertaining facts truthfully. How much accuracy of fact-finding is sacrificed is a guess. This is the policy battleground upon which the creation, abolition, definitions, exceptions, and limits of privileges are determined. All with little empirical knowledge.

If there is a basis for determining these things, it is not at all clear that the list of privileges the law recognizes is the best list to have. Can't we think of other privileges equally or more compelling under these criteria than at least some on the list? Should some privileges be added, some dropped?

The list and the definitions and shape of privileges on the list theoretically are an attempt to craft protection where it is thought to be most needed and to pay the most social dividends. Omissions of privileges from the list, and limits and exceptions to privileges on the list, are theoretically crafted to avoid extension of protection to areas where it pays fewer dividends or where evidence is most needed by the court.

But history may have more to do with it than rationality. There is a tendency to stick with what history gives us even if we could now do a better job. Because of the cost to truth, the law tends to hold the line against extending privilege further than accepted tradition. Conversely, the law is reluctant to contract traditional privilege, owing to a respect for, expectations concerning, and reliance on, precedent. Nevertheless, we shall see that there is some room for evolution pursuant to the more rational considerations expressed above. Particularly is this so under the privilege standard of the F.R.E. Further, state and federal statutory privileges do to some extent wax and wane.

II. PRIVILEGES UNDER THE F.R.E.: STATE RULES OR FEDERAL COMMON LAW

Article V of the F.R.E. deals with privileges. It consists of one rule: Rule 501. Instead of providing specific rules of evidentiary privilege, Rule 501 provides that the matter is to be governed by "the principles of

the common law as they may be interpreted by the
courts of the United States in the light of reason and
experience," except in certain state law cases, where
state privilege law is to apply even though the case is
in federal court. An earlier draft had expressly formulated specific privilege rules, including lawyer-client,
psychotherapist-patient, adverse spousal testimony,
and other privileges, plus some general provisions on
such matters as waiver and invocation. These all were
to govern in every kind of case in federal court. However, this draft (sometimes called the "Supreme
Court" draft because technically its method of transmission to Congress was by the Court) was rejected by
Congress. Because the rejection was not principally on
the merits of the privileges in the draft, but rather
mainly to provide flexibility and some deference to
state law, the draft still exerts influence under current Rule 501.

State Privilege Law as Applicable in Some Federal Cases

In all but three places there is no deference to state
evidence law in federal court in the Federal Rules of
Evidence. Deference to state evidence law is found in
similar form in the three places: Article III (presumptions), Article V (privileges), and Article VI (competency
of witnesses). In Articles III (presumptions) and VI (competency of witnesses), when federal evidence law is to
govern, the federal evidence law is specifically prescribed.
For privileges, however, it is left to common law development. Article V. In these areas of express deference to
state evidence law, the state evidence law governs only in
a civil case and even then only when the matter sought
to be proved is an "element" of a "claim or defense" as
to which state law supplies the "rule of decision."

Diversity cases are the usual cases in which state law
comes into play, as opposed to, for example, federal
prosecutions, or civil actions under such federal laws as

the federal securities, tax, and antitrust laws. Thus, a state privilege cannot compel an analogous federal privilege in criminal cases. *United States v. Gillock* (S.Ct. 1980). However, in diversity cases the law to be applied will typically be that of the state in which the federal court is sitting, including its applicable choice-of-law rules. Interestingly, work product "privilege" requires the application of federal law even in state-law cases because it is found in the Federal Rules of Civil Procedure. These procedural rules apply to all civil actions, except in those rare instances when such application violates the dictates of *Erie R. Co. v. Tompkins* (S.Ct. 1938), and its progeny. Thus, ordinarily, in diversity cases in federal court, state attorney-client privilege will control, but federal law, not state, will control the work product issues.

What of cases with joined federal and state issues— that is, issues of both types mixed? Might not the same piece of evidence have a dual capacity? Instead of a difficult-to-execute jury instruction to use the evidence on one issue but not the other, perhaps the judge could use Rule 403 to exclude the evidence altogether, or apply the law favoring admissibility, or try to determine the predominant character (state or federal) of the action, or refuse to join certain state and federal claims. Most cases of apparent conflict, however, appear to favor federal law. Some of these solutions may be difficult to justify under the text of the rule, although they may be supported by some language in the drafting history, particularly the Senate report on an earlier draft.[4] Applicability of privilege in such a mixed case, during depositions and discovery, before state and federal issues are separated, is especially difficult.

    4. Prof. Rothstein was a Congressional Advisor on the Rules and contributed that language to the draft, which has become influential even under the current provision.

It is not entirely clear what is encompassed by the term "privilege" as used in Rule 501, but the term is interpreted narrowly. It does not include rules banning remedial measures, compromise or settlement efforts, insurance, character, and the like, because they are in Article IV (Relevancy and Its Limits); and it also does not apply to matters usually classed as incompetencies of witnesses, dealt with in Article VI (Witnesses). Instead, the privilege rule, Rule 501, covers such questions as the existence and scope of marital, medical, and psychiatric privileges, privileges related to attorneys, accountants, journalists, and informants, and privileges covering governmental matters and required reports, among others.

Evolution of a "Common Law" of Federal Privileges Under Rule 501

The creation or evolution of federal privilege law by reference to "principles of ... common law ... interpreted ... in the light of reason and experience" (as F.R.E. 501 provides for non-state-law cases) can be seen in Supreme Court decisions such as *Upjohn Co. v. United States* (S.Ct.1981) (definition of attorney-client privilege in corporate setting); *Trammel v. United States* (S.Ct. 1980) (testifying spouse is the only holder of spousal testimonial privilege); and *Jaffee v. Redmond* (S.Ct.1996) (recognizing a psychotherapist-patient privilege, encompassing social workers). *Jaffee* definitively answers the broad question: Does Rule 501 use the term "common law" strictly to require direct federal authority or common-law precedent recognizing a particular privilege (which would preclude new, previously unrecognized privileges); or does it use the term in the looser sense of a common law process permitting recognition of new privileges based on *general policies* found in the common law? *Jaffee* allows the latter, i.e. evolution, including the recognition of new privileges. The psychotherapist-patient privilege recognized in or created by *Jaffee* did not exist at common law, and its existence even today is overwhelmingly a creature of the state legislatures rather than judiciaries, yet the Court had no hesitancy adopting the privilege for federal courts and extending it to cover statements made to social workers.

Although *Jaffee* clearly adopts the "looser view," the question remains, whether it is confined to privileges that have substantial precedent in modern cases, statutes, or rules in lower courts and in other jurisdictions. *Jaffee* expressly relied on such widespread adoption. It is on this basis that a claim of psychotherapist-patient privilege, for example, can be distinguished from a claim of parent-child or researcher-source privilege, all three privileges being unknown at common law. For although general policies of confidentiality and encouragement of communications and relationships (not specifically addressed to these three particular kinds of communications/relationships) can be found in the common law (under other privileges) to support in a general way all three of these newer claims, modern state statutes and decisions around the country in state and federal jurisdictions tend to support the psychotherapist-patient privilege but not the other two privileges. At the same time, the dissent in *Jaffee* points out that the dimensions of the psychotherapist-patient privilege vary immensely, and its extension to social workers is far from unanimous. Thus, the result depends on how broadly one reads the "common law" standard of Rule 501.

Under the same federal-law branch of Rule 501, the Supreme Court has rejected arguments for an accountant-client privilege, which did not exist at common law or under federal decisions (although some states have it). *United States v. Arthur Young & Co.* (S.Ct.1984). While Congress has now enacted a narrow privilege for tax advisers who represent clients in federal tax courts in civil cases, this has not been interpreted as a general accountant-client privilege.

For recognition of a clergy-penitent privilege, which is followed in most states and, unlike the accountant-client privilege, recognized in the rejected Supreme Court draft of the F.R.E. and the common law, see *In re Grand Jury Investigation* (3d Cir.1990). The federal courts have rejected privileges under certain circumstances for peer review materials concerning university tenure decisions, *University of Pennsylvania v. EEOC* (S.Ct.1990), and a scholar's privilege akin to that of a news reporter, *In re Grand Jury Proceedings* (9th Cir.1993). A qualified privilege for self-critical analysis by corporations, on the other hand, has met with mixed success. To the extent that it is permitted there must be a strong interest in preserving the free flow of the type of information sought and proof that such information would otherwise be curtailed. See, e.g., *Dowling v. American Hawaii Cruises, Inc.* (9th Cir.1992). A proposed parent-child privilege has never garnered more than token support in the federal courts.

Rule 501 refers not to the "common law," but rather to "*principles* of the common law" as they "may be *interpreted* ... in the light of *reason and experience*." These words suggest a flexible reading. In addition, it is significant that "*may be* interpreted" is the phrase used, rather than "*have been* interpreted." This use of the future tense indicates a future-looking orientation: that it is an evolving common law that we are after, or an interpretation done in the light of modern reason and experience. The language taken as a whole, then, would seem to license at least some new privileges, not previously recognized, in cases where they share common policies with existing privileges. The same reasoning would apply to new limits or exceptions to established privileges, so that some privileges may shrink under Rule

501 even as some may grow. Whole privileges could be totally eliminated pursuant to this power, too.

Also, the phrase is "as they may be interpreted by the courts *of the United States*," not merely "federal courts." This wording seems to encourage, as per *Jaffee*, consideration of state as well as federal decisions (although it is not clear if the phrase is used in its technical sense to mean federal courts). For example, *Tennenbaum v. Deloitte & Touche* (9th Cir.1996), explicitly recognizes that in determining federal common law, courts may also look to state privilege law, "if enlightening," as well as the privilege draft rejected by Congress. Of course, state privilege law is advisory only, since it is *federal* law that the courts are fashioning under this branch of the rule. The more widespread a view is, however, the more influential in this respect it will be, as *Jaffee* indicates.

In many instances, Congressional disapproval of the earlier F.R.E. draft that codified particular privileges seems to have had little to do with the merits of its provisions (although there are some exceptions) but rather with a decision to allow for evolution and an inability to finalize the list of accepted privileges. The privilege rules also had bad timing in that they were debated during the fallout from Watergate, when executive privilege was generally being questioned, leading to the possibility that arguments over the details of privileges could derail the adoption of the entire set of federal evidence rules. The draft including specific privileges was drawn up by leading scholars, lawyers, and judges, and it was approved (albeit cursorily) by the Supreme Court. Ultimately, it has proved influential in fashioning a modern "common law" of privileges under Rule 501 especially to the extent that it was adopted by the Uniform Rules of Evidence, which have been used as a model in many states. Both sets of proposed rules were relied upon as part of the reasoning in *Jaffee*.

III. ATTORNEY–CLIENT PRIVILEGE

Definition and Limits of Attorney–Client Privilege

To facilitate informed legal services, there is in all jurisdictions a privilege covering private communications between client and attorney made pursuant to professional consultation.

The attorney-client privilege is the oldest of the common law privileges. Its purpose is similar to that of other privileges fostering confidentiality. Because of the policy to foster legitimate legal services, advice about how to commit crimes or frauds would not be privileged, nor would statements by a client seeking such advice. Similarly, attorneys involved in activities for a corporation of a "business" as opposed to "professional legal" nature, frequently find that the communications made pursuant thereto are held not privileged.

The following is a good statement of the lawyer-client privilege. It appears in the Uniform Rules, adopted in a number of states.

Rule 502. Lawyer–Client Privilege

(a) *Definitions.* In this rule:

(1) "Client" means a person, including a public officer, corporation, association, or other organization or entity, either public or private, for whom a lawyer renders professional legal services or who consults a lawyer with a view to obtaining professional legal services from the lawyer.

(2) A communication is "confidential" if not intended to be disclosed to third persons other than those to whom disclosure is made in furtherance of the rendition of professional legal services to the client or those reasonably necessary for the transmission of the communication.

(3) "Lawyer" means a person authorized, or reasonably believed by the client to be authorized, to engage in the practice of law in any State or country.

(4) "Representative of the client" means a person having authority to obtain professional legal services, or to act on legal advice rendered, on behalf of the client or a person who, for the purpose of effectuating legal representation for the client, makes or receives a confidential communication while acting in the scope of employment for the client.

(5) "Representative of the lawyer" means a person employed by the lawyer to assist the lawyer in rendering professional legal services.

(b) *General rule of privilege.* A client has a privilege to refuse to disclose and to prevent any other person from disclosing confidential communications, made for the purpose of facilitating the rendition of professional legal services to the client,

(1) between the client or a representative of the client and the client's lawyer or a representative of the lawyer,

(2) between the lawyer and a representative of the lawyer,

(3) by the client or a representative of the client or the client's lawyer or a representative of the lawyer to a lawyer or a representative of a lawyer representing another party in a pending action and concerning a matter of common interest therein,

(4) between representatives of the client or between the client and a representative of the client, or

(5) among lawyers and their representatives representing the same client.

(c) *Who may claim privilege.* The privilege under this rule may be claimed by the client, the client's guardian or conservator, the personal representative of a deceased client, or the successor, trustee, or similar representative of a corporation, association, or other organization, whether or not in existence. A person who was the lawyer or the lawyer's representative at the time of the communication is presumed to have authority to claim the privilege, but only on behalf of the client.

(d) *Exceptions.* There is no privilege under this rule:

(1) if the services of the lawyer were sought or obtained to enable or aid anyone to commit or plan to commit what the client knew or reasonably should have known was a crime or fraud;

(2) as to a communication relevant to an issue between parties who claim through the same deceased client, regardless of whether the claims are by testate or intestate succession or by transaction inter vivos;

(3) as to a communication relevant to an issue of breach of duty by a lawyer to the client or by a client to the lawyer;

(4) as to a communication necessary for a lawyer to defend in a legal proceeding an accusation that the lawyer assisted the client in criminal or fraudulent conduct (added in 1999 revision);

(5) as to a communication relevant to an issue concerning an attested document to which the lawyer is an attesting witness;

(6) as to a communication relevant to a matter of common interest between or among two or more clients if the communication was made by any of them to a lawyer retained or consulted in common, when offered in an action between or among any of the clients; or

(7) as to a communication between a public officer or agency and its lawyers unless the communication concerns a pending investigation, claim, or action and the court determines that disclosure will seriously impair the ability of the public officer or agency to act upon the claim or conduct a pending investigation, litigation, or proceeding in the public interest.[5]

A number of important questions that have troubled courts over the years are not completely addressed by this draft, or by the earlier Supreme Court draft of the F.R.E. upon which it is based. See Rothstein, *The Proposed Amendments to the F.R.E.*, 62 Geo. L.J. 125, 133–34 (1973) (which also discusses the other privileges in that draft).

For example, courts are divided as to whether and when the *mere fact* of consultation of a lawyer, and the identity of a lawyer's client, may be privileged. Similar questions arise about other generalized information, such as the broad kind of work rendered (family law, criminal, tax, etc.) and the amount of fees charged or time put in. Some courts feel none of these matters can qualify. But

5. See also provision (a)(1) above, which this (d)(7) provision may be regarded as qualifying. The analogous rule, 503, in the Supreme Court Draft F.R.E. had only the (a)(1) provision, suggesting a fuller attorney-client privilege for the government. There has been some disagreement in the cases on the existence of an attorney-client privilege for public officers or agencies in the grand jury or criminal trial context. See e.g. *In re Grand Jury Subpoena Duces Tecum* (8th Cir.1997) (no government attorney-client privilege for notes of a meeting between U.S. President's wife, her attorney, and White House counsel regarding her and the President's alleged participation in a land development scheme; so held in part because White House has no privilege concerning criminal proceedings, there being a public interest in ferreting out official wrongdoing—perhaps hinting that the citizens of the U.S. are in reality the client). See also, to somewhat similar effect, *In re Lindsey* (D.C.Cir.1998). The privilege appears to apply more broadly and less controversially in civil proceedings. See generally *Coastal States Gas Corp. v. Department of Energy* (D.C.Cir.1980).

other courts disagree, particularly when the matter is intertwined with other sensitive issues. Most often protection is denied unless the information furnishes the last link in a chain incriminating the client, specifically reveals other confidences, or involves some similar exceptional circumstance.

There is also no mention in the original Uniform Rule or Supreme Court draft, of how the privilege is to be determined. In *United States v. Zolin* (S.Ct.1989), the U.S. Supreme Court decided in the context of applying the crime-fraud exception that the allegedly privileged communication itself can be considered by the court to determine whether the privilege applies. This decision resolved a question raised by the application of F.R.E. 104(a) to privilege issues. Rule 104(a) grants great latitude to the judge in deciding questions of admissibility, prescribing that the only evidence rules that apply in the process of making such a decision are those with respect to privilege. The Court found that this apparent exclusion of privileged material only applies to an admissibility determination *if the material is indeed privileged*, which is not established in a case like this until after the ruling is made. By permitting the judge to consider the statement, *Zolin* parted ways with those states, like California, that forbid review of any allegedly confidential communication. *Zolin* permits judicial inspection whenever there is evidence that could justify a good-faith belief by a reasonable person that the opponent of privilege can establish its claim that future crime or fraud is involved in the communication.

This is a fairly loose standard. It means that the judge will review the statement in camera whenever he or she considers it significant, particularly since it does not appear that the judge must consider countervailing evidence in determining whether to review the statement. Perhaps a standard virtually prohibiting in camera review would make it impossible to demonstrate the absence of a privilege or the existence of waiver. On the other hand, the judge's virtually automatic inspection arguably runs counter to privilege policy by making the information less confidential. *Zolin* also clarified that parts of the allegedly privileged material that accidentally had been revealed could be used to trigger in camera review as well as to decide the privilege issue. "Independent" evidence was not needed.

The 1999 revision to Uniform Rule 104 condensed several procedural suggestions made by the American Bar Association evidence project headed by Professor Rothstein. Uniform Rule 104(b) now provides that both the person claiming a privilege, and the person claiming an exception to a privilege, must satisfy a burden of persuasion, rather than simply a burden of production on the relevant issue. In addition, like *Zolin*, it permits the court to review the allegedly privileged material if there is a factual basis to support a good faith belief that a review is necessary.

Note that the crime or fraud in the crime-fraud exception, is a *future* crime or fraud. Thus, a client's statement, "I want your advice on how to commit a crime I am planning," is not privileged, but "I've just committed a crime and I want your advice on how to defend myself," is squarely privileged. Defending a past crime or fraud is just the sort of thing the privilege is designed to cover. Harder examples occur between the two extremes represented by the quotes. For example, the client may say "I want to know how to accomplish business result X" in a complicated regulatory environment where it may not be clear whether X is illegal or where there may be a legal way to accomplish X although X would normally be illegal. How would the Uniform Rule, above, handle this? Suppose the attorney in this situation, advises an illegal method? Would this strip the client of privilege?

Does anything depend upon whether a client realizes illegal advice has been given? Follows the advice? Is privilege lost covering only communications *after* a certain point in this example?

The Uniform Rule provision above makes significant the *client's* culpability (know or should have known was illegal), rather than the attorney's. In addition, the test is whether the advice was sought *or obtained* by the client to commit an illegality.

A few jurisdictions abrogate the privilege not only for crime or fraud but for other torts as well.

The language of (d)(3), creating an exception for claims of breach of duty, is ambiguous. It clearly appears to cover a malpractice claim, but given the underlying policy, it is more difficult to determine whether it extends to a claim of ineffective assistance of counsel made in order to get a criminal conviction reversed, or a suit by a lawyer for fees, or a disciplinary proceeding, or a case where the client raises a defense of reliance on advice of counsel.

Attorney-Client Privilege in a Corporate Setting

Corporations may avail themselves of attorney-client privilege. But questions have arisen as to who is in the shoes of the client for purposes of claiming or waiving the corporation's privilege—the stockholders? Or the management? Which group of shareholders?—especially when these various corporate constituents are at odds with one another. See *Garner v. Wolfinbarger* (5th Cir. 1970) (setting up a multi-factor test). *Commodity Futures Trading Commission v. Weintraub* (S.Ct.1985), held that the trustee of a bankrupt corporation has the power to waive the privilege for earlier communications.

One area of considerable controversy is the extent to which the corporation's agents' or employees' reports to the corporation or its lawyer are privileged. At least two views (with permutations) exist:

The "control group" test confines the privilege to communications from those persons authorized to seek and/or act on legal advice. This approach limits the privilege to a high group of officials or at least ones with authority as respects that particular operation. Under the "control group" test, it is possible to take the view that there is one control group in a corporation, or that different transactions or different geographic areas have different control groups.[6]

In contrast to the control group test, the other view in its commonest form expands the corporate privilege to encompass, additionally, any employee communication of a legal nature expressly or impliedly directed to be made by the company if related to the employee's work and legal representation of the company.[7]

In *Upjohn Co. v. United States* (S.Ct.1981), for purposes of the federal privilege, the Supreme Court rejected the control group test in favor of a broader approach. See generally Rothstein, *The Story of Upjohn Co. v. United States: One Man's Journey to Extend Lawyer-Client Confidentiality and the Social Forces That Affected It*, in EVIDENCE STORIES (2006). The case upheld the availability of the privilege to resist a subpoena in a federal tax investigation where corporate counsel had communicated with employees outside the control group, but with corporate authority and concerning those employees' duties, in order to determine the extent of past wrongdoing in

6. Perhaps one can get around the strictures of a control group test by having the attorney represent the employees, too, so that they are also clients, but this approach would create other dangers and disadvantages and a possible conflict-of-interest, although it is not always out of the question.

7. One common formulation of a view along these lines appears in the definition of "representative of the client" in the Uniform Rule reproduced above. It replaced an earlier draft codifying only the control group test, which many states adopted and still have. The Supreme Court Draft of the F.R.E. finessed the question.

the corporation and its legal effect respecting the corporation. While *Upjohn* did not exhaustively articulate a "test" or specific criteria triggering the privilege, it is arguable from the case that the employee's confidential communication must be made at the request of a superior to secure legal advice on behalf of the corporation concerning a matter within the scope of the employee's duties. The privilege applies to communications made to in-house as well as outside counsel.

A related problem arises in the context of insurance agents' reports about automobile collisions. The agent will have interviewed the insured and included the information in the report. The agent will also have personally generated information. Is such an agent an agent of the insured, of the attorney, or of the insurance company? Who is the client? Answers have varied, but there is a marked tendency toward privileging these kinds of reports if other requirements governing the privilege are met, and if the report contemplates ultimate use by an attorney.

Assertion and Waiver of Attorney–Client Privilege

Attorney-client privilege once was justified on the ground that it was thought to protect the lawyer's honor, but this policy rarely applies any longer. Instead, the rule more often is based on the policy that it encourages clients to lay the facts fully before their counsel. As a result, the privilege is the client's alone. The client may assert the privilege even when not a party to the cause in which the privileged testimony is sought. If the client is present at the hearing, he must assert the privilege personally or by attorney, or it will be waived. If the client is not present and is not a party to the proceedings, the privilege may be called to the court's attention by anyone present, such as the attorney for the absent client, or for a party in the case; or the court of its own motion may protect the privilege. The old "eavesdropper" rule, which allowed third parties to testify to the communication in circumstances where the lawyer and client themselves need not, is abolished by the modern view prevailing in most courts.[8] However, privilege only applies to conversations that take place in situations where it is reasonable to believe that the conversation will not be overheard. Cell phones are a particular problem, since depending on the technology involved, some cell-phone conversations can be overheard accidentally.

In some circumstances, more than one party has been regarded as "the client" for purposes of assertion or waiver of the privilege. This can arise, for example, where different persons claim under the original client making the communication (as successors, heirs, grantees, etc.), or where multiple clients in a matter of common interest consulted the attorney together. Sometimes the problem arises where these parties are now on opposite sides of the litigation or are otherwise not in agreement on the exercise of the privilege. The trend has been to regard the joint-client material as generally confidential but "not confidential as between these parties." Thus the material should not be disclosed, except where the two "clients" agree to waiver or are litigating against each other, in which case the material is generally held unprivileged.

The privilege also may be waived by disclosure. Disclosure of part of a communication or series of communications may waive as to all that is related to it. Compelled disclosure or disclosure in contexts that are themselves privileged by another privilege does not result in waiver. Waiver by inadvertent disclosure during civil discovery is a hotly contested issue. This problem can arise when a small number of privileged documents are accidentally surrendered to opposing counsel as a mistake during a transfer of a massive number of legitimately discoverable

8. The eavesdropper rule persists as to other privileges in some jurisdictions.

documents. Courts vary significantly in their approach to waiver in this context.

In December 2006, Federal Rule of Civil Procedure 26(b)(5) was amended to provide a uniform procedure to govern such claims of inadvertent disclosure of information that is alleged to be privileged (or alleged to be protected as work-product or trial-preparation material). After notification, the party to whom the material was accidentally disclosed, must promptly return, sequester, or destroy the specified information and any copies, and may not use or disclose the information until the claim of privilege is resolved either by agreement or by the court.[9] However, the Rule does not adopt any standard to be applied for determining the claim. In other words, it does not say what effect on privilege the inadvertent disclosure has. The matter is left to existing case-law: Some courts hold that privilege is automatically lost; some hold that privilege persists (either because waiver/disclosure was not intentional or because the disclosing lawyer is not deemed authorized by the client, the privilege holder, to disclose in this fashion); and some hold that it depends upon the diligence utilized by the party claiming privilege, to attempt to screen out the protected material in the first place and the diligence and rapidity with which the accidental disclosure was detected and notified to the other party.

But a newly *proposed* Federal Rule of Evidence, Rule 502 (which can only be enacted by an affirmative act of Congress) would mandate the last position—that is, there is no waiver if reasonable steps had been taken to prevent the disclosure, and retrieval of the information was promptly demanded. In addition, a waiver, if found pursuant to this formula, would not result in waiver with respect to other documents or information related to it—

9. This is commonly referred to as a "claw-back."

that is, other material concerning the same subject matter.[10]

The proposed rule also provides that the court may enter an order preserving confidentiality, and that all parties, future parties, and non-parties (whether in the present or any future litigation in any federal or state court) would be bound by it.[11]

10. Courts currently differ on whether, when, and the extent to which such "subject matter" waiver (construed with varying degrees of breadth) occurs when there has been waiver (whether inadvertent or intentional) as to a particular document or piece of information. But most courts have adopted a "fairness" test in both situations, perhaps with more reluctance to find subject-matter waiver in the inadvertent situation. "Fairness" also looks at whether the disclosing party obtains any unjust advantage by revealing part but not all of the subject matter, and whether the need for context requires the additional disclosure.

11. This provision would cover not only the situations just discussed where there would still be confidentiality that could be preserved, but also could be used if a court recognizes "selective waiver", whereby a party intentionally waives privilege in order to disclose a document to one party, but wishes to preserve the confidentiality of the document (and related matter) as against any future litigant. For example, it might facilitate the investigation and law enforcement function of the Securities and Exchange Commission (S.E.C.) if a company being investigated for securities fraud, could provide privileged documents to the S.E.C. without fear of waiver should private investors later sue the company. A number of agencies offer reduced penalties for such co-operation, but fear of waiver as to third parties is a disincentive to such co-operation. The proposal as yet takes no position on selective waiver and only a few courts allow it.

There is a constitutional question as to whether a federal rule could authorize an order binding on state courts in the fashion provided in this proposed Rule.

The proposed court-order provision would also facilitate so-called "quick peek" agreements, whereby a party makes no (or little) attempt to screen for privilege the often massive amounts of documents requested of it in discovery, but hands them all over, on the understanding that the receiving party may look ("peek") at them all in order to make a decision as to which they want to use in trial. Once this narrowing down takes place, the agreement provides that privilege may be claimed (at least as against the party who has received the documents for a

The advent of the fax machine and e-mail and internet communications has created even more issues, because of the potential for exposure to unauthorized persons. It is common to attach a notice claiming confidentiality and demanding immediate return if they reach someone other than the designated recipient. Is this sufficient, or does the mere use of such a device waive the privilege, especially if the document by chance winds up in the wrong hands?

Regarding some of the examples of inadvertent disclosure in these last several paragraphs, can the cat ever be stuffed back into the bag once opposing counsel learns the secret, even if the judge holds that the document itself has not lost its privileged status? What is the ethical responsibility of counsel who has mistakenly received the information? Some courts sanction attorneys if the material appears privileged on its face or is obviously misdirected, and the attorney does not notify the discloser or reveals or makes unauthorized use of the information.

If an asserted privilege is erroneously sustained, the aggrieved party may complain on appeal of the exclusion of relevant evidence. The erroneous denial of the privilege, however, is more problematic. Relevant evidence has been admitted. The party who as a result loses the lawsuit arguably has suffered no legally cognizable harm (if she is not also the privilege holder). Relevant evidence has come in against her. If she *is* the privilege holder (client) she would be able to appeal. What is the duty of the witness (say, the lawyer or the client) in this situation? Since the client has a remedy (appeal), some courts hold the witness has a duty to testify in response to the

"peek") if there are any privileged documents in the narrowed group. It is argued that this procedure is very economic, but most courts currently do not permit it, or at least do not permit it to bar access of third parties who are not party to the agreement. One of the main purposes of the court-order provision of the proposed Rule, is to change this. The order would be binding on the receiving party and any third parties.

trial judge's erroneous order and is correctly held in contempt for refusal to do so. But if the client is not a party, the situation is otherwise.

Other Common Attorney–Client Privilege Issues

It is likely that a communication from lawyer to client will inferentially reveal a communication from client to lawyer, with the result that communications both ways should be covered as a general matter. Some states and some federal decisions so provide. Even if a lawyer's communication does not reveal that of the client and is unprivileged, the communication may still be treated as opinion work product.

Privileged lawyer-client communications may be made in writing or orally. One rule dictated by practical considerations, however, is that documents existing *before* (that is, not arising out of nor created for) the lawyer-client relationship, that in the hands of the client were susceptible to discovery (that is, were not then privileged under any privilege), cannot be brought within this privilege or the work product privilege by delivery to the lawyer. However, responding to a subpoena or other request for such documents may require or reveal a *selection* made among the documents, by lawyer or client. The selection itself may be information that *is* privileged, and the court may take steps to protect it. A similar principle covering the act of production may operate under other privileges as well, particularly the privilege against self-incrimination which ordinarily does not cover existing documents.

In some kinds of cases, notably those involving wills or intestate succession to property, the lawyer-client privilege has on occasion been held to die with the client. The effect of ethical rules requiring attorneys to keep the confidences of their clients must be considered separately from the question of privilege.

Work Product Immunity as Distinguished From Attorney–Client Privilege

This immunity prevents access to material prepared for or in anticipation of litigation. It is a qualified immunity, giving way for "good cause," which means there must be a showing of "substantial need" for the information and that it cannot otherwise be obtained without "undue hardship." Although opinion work product, which is the creative product of the "mental processes" of an attorney, is sometimes referred to as "absolute," the boundaries of work product are murky.

The theory is that better law results where lawyers do not fear to work up their cases thoroughly and to memorialize their thoughts on paper. Work product protects the attorney's labors, not the client's confidences. Usually, courts refer to work product as an immunity, rather than a privilege. This term reflects its origins as a creature of discovery, rather than trial practice, although it has now spread; and refers to its abrogation for good cause.

Work product immunity also differs from true privileges in that the Federal Rules of Civil Procedure codify this doctrine separately for discovery (Fed. R. Civ. P. 26(b)(3)), rather than relying on the general provisions making trial privileges applicable during discovery. An analogous doctrine, however, applies at trial.

Unlike attorney-client privilege, a showing of "substantial need" and inability to obtain the substantial equivalent of the material without "undue hardship" defeats the work product immunity, even though the holder has done nothing which would cause a waiver. Additional protection is given to so-called "core" work product, that is, the "mental impressions, conclusions, opinions, or legal theories of an attorney . . . ." The court in this instance is directed by the Federal Rules of Civil

Procedure that it "shall" protect this so-called opinion work product. However, the *Upjohn* case, cited above, rather explicitly left as an open question, what, if any, showing could defeat this so-called "core" work product.

F.T.C. v. Grolier (S.Ct.1983) rejected the view that work product protection terminates at the end of present litigation in federal court. A number of courts hold that, unlike the attorney-client privilege, the work product protection belongs to the lawyer rather than or in addition to the client.

Refreshing Recollection With Privileged Information: The Potential for Waiver

What would be the opponent's right to discovery under F.R.E. 612 where a witness uses a report, privileged for some reason (such as work product or attorney-client privilege) to refresh his or her recollection for trial? A similar question arises if a party or her attorney gives an expert witness work product (or otherwise privileged material) for the witness to review in reaching an expert opinion. Rule 612 provides that documents used to refresh recollection can be subject to discovery. But Rule 612 is silent as to what the result is when the underlying information is privileged. Does the privilege endure? Is it waived? Courts vary in their approaches. In civil cases, this issue commonly, although not exclusively, arises when the witness is being deposed.

IV. MARITAL PRIVILEGES: TWO SEPARATE PRIVILEGES DISTINGUISHED

The ancient common law incompetency of one spouse to testify for or against the other in legal proceedings (based on a fictional unity of husband and wife) eventually eroded into two broad privilege

principles: first, the confidential marital communications privilege, and second, the privilege not to testify against one's spouse, which may be treated as including a third, the privilege to prevent adverse spousal testimony against one's self.

Variations of these (or some of these) privileges are now widely accorded by statute (essentially codifying the common law development described in the black letters) except in a few states and in federal courts, where they are still a matter of common law.

First, the confidential communications privilege protects confidential communications made during the marital relationship (theoretically regardless of whether the form of the evidence thereof is spousal testimony or not), so as to foster such communications.

Second, an unwilling spouse called to testify against the other spouse may have a privilege to refuse to do so (whether or not the testimony involves a confidential communication), so as to avoid rupture of the relationship.

Third, co-extensive with the second, some jurisdictions permit a spouse to prevent the other spouse from testifying against him/her, even if the testifying spouse is willing. The second and third are usually confined to criminal cases, and are jointly referred to as the adverse spousal testimony privilege.

As with most privileges, the statutes and the judicial interpretations must be examined closely, but certain generalizations can be made.

The "Confidential Communications" Privilege in the Marital Context

The *confidential marital communications* privilege permits the suppression in any civil or criminal case of so much of a spouse's testimony as may reveal confidences passed between the spouses in the marital relationship.

The privilege thus only applies to a "confidential communication".

A cluster of problems arises surrounding the requirements both of "confidentiality" and of "communication." Can the act of placing money in a bank account, observed by a spouse, be an implied "communication?" Although there are different rulings on this, usually, the spouse's observation of an act done for reasons independent of the observation is not considered a communication. Under this view, the observed act would not be privileged, but a later statement of it, say to a spouse not present during the act, might be.

If this kind of act can be a communication, is it "confidential," where others could perceive it, but only the spouse knew its significance in a course of criminal dealings?

Is the act of putting something in a drawer at home (such as a gun) privileged insofar as viewed by the opposite spouse? Does it matter whether the spouse placing it in the drawer would not have done so openly but for the marital relation? Does it matter if he meant to hide it from the spouse? Courts have varied in their answers to these kinds of questions, but it is easy to see that under the concepts of "confidential" or "communication", these facts could make a difference. Were the acts *intended* to be both confidential and communications? We may also be concerned here with yet another concept. The matter must be a "marital" communication.

Concerning "confidentiality" in more orthodox contexts, which is usually said to be a matter of intention or inferred intention, a third person overhearing or obtaining access to the contents of an interspousal communication may be held to destroy confidentiality, a key requirement of the privilege. This will be so where this occurs with the knowledge, recklessness, consent or complicity of the relevant spouse. Sometimes, with lesser orders of spousal fault for the disclosure, the privilege of the spouse to remain silent or keep the other spouse silent may still prevail, but not to keep the third party silent (assuming third party testimony can ever be covered—a matter on which jurisdictions vary). These outcomes may also depend upon which spouse, communicator or communicatee, was responsible for the disclosure to the third party,[12] upon who the third party was,[13] and upon the law of the particular jurisdiction. The communicator's and communicatee's privileges may be affected differently according to their relative responsibility for the disclosure to the third party.

There also are questions concerning who may normally assert the privilege. As to each statement, should the communicatee thereof be a secondary holder only, able to raise it only on behalf of the communicator and not able to override his or her wishes? But a previous communication of the communicatee spouse may be revealed in a communication by the communicator. Should they both, therefore, have the privilege over both sides of the conversation? Always? Or only when the one reflects the other?

There is also dispute about whether positive waiver (or affirmative consent to disclosure in court), is required for waiver in court. In other words, does the privilege have to be affirmatively raised, or is it raised unless affirmatively waived?

In the following statutes, consider what it is that seems to be included in the category that can be excluded

12. Should a communicatee spouse, assuming he or she cannot waive the privilege for the communicator, be able to breach the privilege by unauthorizedly giving access to the third party?

13. A minor child of the family being present, for example, conceivably might have no effect on the full applicability of the privilege, by analogy to the presence of necessary parties under the lawyer-client privilege. There is some dispute about this.

from evidence. I.e., what person's or persons' testimony? Only spousal testimony? Both spouses? Third parties? Exhibits such as a purloined interspousal letter or clandestine recording? And who, in the following statutes, communicator or communicatee, witness or non-witness spouse, would seem to hold the privilege?:

(1) "Neither spouse shall be compelled to testify as to a confidential communication made to him or her by his or her spouse." This gives control to the spouse who is on the stand to testify, but not over his or her own communication, only communications made by the other. Furthermore, the communicator is at the mercy of the witness, whether the communicator wants to reveal (say the communication was favorable) or doesn't want to reveal the communication. Both these features seem to defeat the communication-encouraging policy of the privilege. Further, no evidence of a spousal communication other than spousal testimony is suppressible.

(2) An identical statute except "be compelled to" is omitted. This formula would appear to allow prevention by either spouse. It even could authorize exclusion against the wishes of both.

(3) An identical statute to (1) except "made to him or her by his or her spouse" is omitted and "marital" is inserted before "communication." This allows the witness-spouse control over disclosure of both sides of the conversation, including her own (this last thing is an improvement), but still leaves the non-witness spouse with no control over disclosure his own communications, should he want to reveal them or keep them secret. Thus this provision still allows a spouse to keep out a statement by the other spouse that this other wishes to have in, or to reveal it against his wishes. On a separate point, this statute seems to more clearly recognize the possibility of privileged communications "relayed" by an intermediary.

(4) "Neither spouse shall testify to confidential marital communications without the consent of the other." This formula appears to give control to the non-testifying spouse. It would allow that spouse (say the husband) to stop the witness spouse (say the wife) from testifying to her own statement which she wishes to testify to, perhaps to clear herself of criminal wrongdoing. It also allows him to have her compelled (say in a civil case) to testify against herself (that is, to disclose a communication she made that hurts her case) if he wants. Does any of this square with the privilege's policy? This formula also appears to mean the privilege is automatically asserted unless affirmatively waived by positive consent. Like the other examples, this statute, by addressing only testimony by a spouse, does not seem to allow suppression of other forms of testimony as to spousal conversations: e.g., third party testimony (where, e.g., both spouses justifiably thought they were speaking secretly, or the communicator did, but it was overheard by or access to it was obtained by the third party anyway), a letter written by one spouse to the other that was subsequently stolen without fault of the spouses (or a copy unauthorizedly given to a third party by the communicatee), or a surreptitious (or communicatee arranged) tape recording.

Perhaps because these differences in wording do not reflect reasoned legislative intent, courts do not always feel bound by statutory language in marital privilege cases. The privilege's purpose or shape at common law has often provided justification for interpreting away variant language. On the other hand, some courts are strict adherents to statutory language.

The "Adverse Spousal Testimony" Privilege (as Distinct From the Communications Privilege)

The other marital privilege, for *adverse spousal testimony* (sometimes called the "anti-marital facts" privilege), permits the suppression of all testimony of one spouse against the other, usually only in the latter's criminal prosecution. The distinctions between the privileges, where the privileges remain "pure," may be generalized in the following fashion:

The *communications* privilege applies only to prevent disclosure of confidential marital communications; the *adverse spousal testimony* privilege can entirely prevent the spouse from taking the stand as a witness adverse to the other connubial partner, regardless of the subject matter of the expected testimony, i.e., whether or not it involves a communication. The communications privilege applies in civil and criminal litigation unless subject to an exception; the testimonial privilege is usually confined to criminal cases. The communications privilege applies regardless of whether the testimony is for or against the spouse; the adverse testimonial privilege can prevent only testimony adverse to the spouse. The communications privilege applies whether or not a spouse is party to the litigation; the testimonial privilege requires a spouse as a party. Indeed, the communications privilege can apply even where neither of the spouses is a party nor a witness. Only the adverse spousal testimony privilege applies when the testimony does not relate to a matter transpiring during the marriage; the communication under the communications privilege must have transpired during the marriage.[14] In addition, the communications privilege may cover evidence other than spousal testimony; the testimonial privilege cannot. Such "other evi-

14. This follows from the respective policies: the communications privilege is intended to encourage marital communications in the population generally, hence the communicators must have been married when communicating but not necessarily at the time of the testimony; whereas the adverse testimony privilege is meant to prevent the strain testimony puts on the marriage, and hence the parties must be married at the time of the testimony, regardless of whether they were married at the time the events testified to transpired.

dence" might be the letter that constitutes the communication, testimony of third persons having knowledge of the communication's contents, a tape recording, etc. Finally, only the adverse spousal testimony privilege is destroyed by divorce. This is because the marital communications privilege is said to be intended to encourage spouses in the population generally, to confide in each other; whereas the aim of the privilege against adverse spousal testimony is said to be to preserve and promote harmony in the particular marriage before the court.[15]

Both marital privileges are often subject to a number of exceptions, limiting them, for example, to criminal cases only, or conversely refusing to apply them at all in certain criminal cases, usually those involving crimes against the spouse or a child of either of the spouses. Their application in civil cases is equally inconsistent, with the most common exceptions being for cases in which the spouses are adverse parties or for tort actions based on criminal activity that would be subject to an exception. The adverse spousal privilege is typically limited to cases in which the spouse is a party rather than injured indirectly by the testimony, and federal courts generally restrict its invocation to criminal cases. Some

15. Would it really harm marital harmony for one spouse to testify under compulsion of law against the other? One suggestion has been that the real reason for the privilege is something else: either that adverse spousal testimony deeply offends our "sense of justice;" or that the privilege is intended to prevent the temptation to perjury.

Perhaps, given its purpose, the adverse spousal testimony privilege should end at separation or a showing of irreconcilability. Conversely, perhaps the argument can be made that it should be extended to those who cohabitate, and even to same-sex couples. But such modifications of the law have generally been felt by courts and legislators to open up greater problems, and have not been made. A few cases have found that either a particular marriage was so weak that it was futile to hope for marital harmony, or so strong that it was fatuous to suppose compelled testimony would weaken it. But by and large, these kinds of computations are eschewed.

statutes relating to both spousal privileges prohibit their invocation in cases involving separation and divorce. The application of a crime-fraud or "spousal co-conspirators" exception to the marital communications privilege, like that in the attorney-client area but perhaps of slightly different scope, is gaining adherence, but courts differ over its application to the adverse spousal testimony privilege.

The Adverse Spousal Testimony Privilege: Who Holds It? Is It Really Two Privileges?

The traditional approach was to consider both spouses (witness and defendant) as primary holders, with the consequence that each could assert it regardless of the wishes of the other. Some courts, however, have abandoned this rule for one more responsive to the "marital harmony" rationale of the privilege. This approach normally means that the witness spouse's wishes should control. The witness-spouse's willingness to testify signifies there is little marital harmony in the marriage to preserve, unless the willingness is secured by extrinsic pressures (e.g. threats of charges against the witness by the prosecution). Unwillingness signifies marital harmony, unless produced, e.g., by threats from the defendant. Perhaps the law should also consider not only harmony in the particular marriage, but whether the marriage is the *kind* that ought to be preserved. On the other hand, that is a difficult computation, and our natural abhorrence at the spectacle of marital betrayal may argue for allowing both spouses the privilege and allowing it irrespective of the kind of marriage involved. This natural abhorrence theory supports considering adverse spousal testimony as affected by not just one privilege, but two separate ones, held by the two spouses respectively. This was, in essence, the traditional view. See generally, exploring the ins and outs of these various rationales, Rothstein, *A Re–Evaluation of the Privilege Against Adverse Spousal Testimony in Light of Its Purpose*, 12 Int'l & Compar.L.Q. 1189 (1963) (cited by the Supreme Court in *Trammel*, infra, as support for its decision).

Traditionally, at common-law, and still in some states, the defendant-spouse lost the privilege where the charge being tried was one of physical violence against the other spouse (witness-spouse). But the witness-spouse still retained the privilege, i.e., retained an unqualified right to admit or exclude. The reason for the abrogation of the defendant's privilege was said to be "special necessity" for the testimony of the victim, who might be the only witness (although nothing hinged on whether or not there were in fact other witnesses). But one can think of an abundance of fact situations where there is more "necessity" for the spousal testimony, both from the standpoint of availability of other evidence and the standpoint of need for conviction, than in some of the cases comprehended by this so-called "necessity exception" to the privilege. For example, a murder by defendant against a third party where the defendant's wife is the only witness (not embraced by the necessity exception), compared with a minor assault by defendant against his wife where there are many other witnesses (included within the exception). Further, it must be remembered that the witness-spouse, in these necessity exception cases, retained the option not to testify. If the testimony is necessary, is it not equally so even if the witness desired not to testify? The entire "necessity exception" seems really to be the product of some rough sense of justice that says the victim-witness-spouse ought to have the power to forgive or not. As such, it may reflect the notion that, if there has been a crime of violence against the wife, there may be no marital harmony to preserve unless she forgives. But then it should make no difference whether the crime of violence is actually the one charged in the case, as long as it can be shown there was a crime of violence committed by defendant against his wife. That, however, may be hard to administer.

In *Wyatt v. United States* (S.Ct.1960), a Mann Act prosecution against a husband for prostituting his wife interstate (which the court equated with a crime of violence against her), the wife was compelled to testify, because her raising of privilege was presumed to be the product of coercion on his part and thus an indirect exercise of his lost privilege. Under this doctrine, both spouses may lose the privilege if the refusal to testify is felt by the court to stem from intimidation by the defendant spouse perhaps owing to the nature of the crime.

Finally, in *Trammel v. United States* (S.Ct.1980), an importing heroin prosecution, the Supreme Court adopted the overall position that the witness-spouse alone has the privilege (i.e., has sole control over whether she testifies) in federal prosecutions, whether or not the charges fit the crime-of-violence-against-spouse category. Presumably this is subject to a *Wyatt*-like principle that the witness's raising of the privilege may in some cases be rejected as the product of intimidation from the defendant. By the time of *Trammel*, approximately half the states had also modified the traditional rule in a similar direction.

This approach limits the privilege to those cases in which the policy of preserving marriage is meaningful. In other words, it is based on the assumption that the marriage already is undermined if one spouse is willing to testify voluntarily against the other as she was in *Trammel*.

The Supreme Court decision in *Trammel* arguably overlooked the fact that the witness-spouse's (wife's) willingness to testify in *Trammel*, which willingness was taken as an indicator of little marital harmony, may instead merely have indicated that, despite a harmonious marriage, she felt pressured by the promise of leniency or threat of prosecution that apparently was dangled (rightly or wrongly) before her by the prosecution. Especially if there are children involved, this can be a powerful incentive to waive one's privilege even if the marriage is strong. The court did not note the "Hobson's choice" thus given her; the strain on a harmonious marriage this choice could produce; or the arguable incentive to prosecutors to place in this dilemma future witness-spouses whom perhaps they might not otherwise have thought of charging. Possibly in some future case with aggravated facts in this regard, the way is still open to argue that willingness to testify is more the product of pressure or coercion than lack of marital harmony.

Conversely, the Court did not specifically note that if the witness had been *unwilling* to testify, the unwillingness, assumed under the new rule to indicate marital harmony that could be saved with privilege, may in fact not indicate marital harmony at all. The witness-spouse could have been subjected to blackmail, intimidation or actual violence by the other spouse in an effort to prevent her testimony.

Notwithstanding this failure of the Court in *Trammel* to *explicitly* recognize the possibility of such intimidation by the defendant, the *Wyatt* implications along these lines may continue: the witness's unwillingness to testify (i.e., her raising of privilege) may be vitiated as actually or irrebuttably presumed coerced by defendant in certain circumstances.

V. PHYSICIAN–PATIENT AND PSYCHOTHERAPIST–PATIENT PRIVILEGES

Definition of the Physician–Patient Privilege

In a majority of states there is a privilege covering private communications from a patient to a physician if the information is germane to the purposes of a consultation for treatment, prescription, or cure, as opposed to preparation for litigation, application for insurance or employment, or other non-treatment purposes.

The aim of the law with respect to the physician-patient privilege is to facilitate informed medical care and promote the free exchange of information necessary thereto. Because of the broader implications of this policy, the privilege is sometimes, although not universally, extended to cover matters in the doctor's files that were not communicated by or to the patient, such as information obtained by the doctor concerning the patient from other doctors and hospitals, physicians' uncommunicated opinions about the patient, facts observed by the doctor concerning the patient, communications by the doctor with other doctors about the patient, and communications passing from the doctor to the patient (as well as the reverse). In some jurisdictions these matters are covered only to the extent that they may inferentially reflect communications from the patient. In each instance, of course, the information must relate to the patient's care.

There is a diversity of authority concerning these extensions, as well as the related matters of whether the privilege should cover the simple facts that a doctor was visited (or retained) or that a communication was made. Perhaps there is a policy not only to encourage information, but also to encourage the seeking of professional help, that would justify privileging much of this information.

In view of the fact that the primary purpose of the privilege is to encourage the patient to communicate, perhaps the test of whether communicated information is germane to treatment should be whether the patient thought (or reasonably thought) it was germane.

Would alcohol smelled by the doctor on the patient's breath be privileged? Should it be ruled out because it is not a communication? We know that some jurisdictions extend the privilege beyond verbal communications. Is this something the patient may be able to hide if he thinks it is not privileged? Is it good for society and for health care for the doctor to find out this information?

Since a purpose of the privilege is to improve treatment, the presence of a nurse at the consultation would not ordinarily destroy the privilege. Perhaps this principle could be extended to third persons generally if they facilitate treatment. What about physicians' assistants who help collect billing information? Or a friend brought by the patient for moral support? There is disagreement. Family members usually qualify. Should the privilege terminate upon the patient's death? Assurances that secrecy will endure even if the patient should die may significantly encourage some kinds of patient-to-doctor disclosure.

Exceptions and Limits

The bringing of a personal injury action by the patient will generally accomplish a waiver at least as respects the physical condition he puts in issue and probably as respects all doctors and medical conditions in the patient's past and present life that may be relevant, which is usually a very broad waiver indeed. In fact, the physician-patient privilege is subject to so many exceptions in various jurisdictions that it is narrow in practice. It is arguable that patients have health incentives to be full, complete, and above-board with their doctors (as assumed, for example, by the declarations-to-physicians exception to the hearsay rule) and thus privilege is not really compellingly necessary where there is any strong countervailing need for the evidence.

If the communication to the doctor is for purposes of preparing litigation or preparing the doctor as a witness, or to obtain insurance or employment, the information may be held to be outside the scope of this privilege, because it then is not conveyed for purposes of treatment. The litigation communication may be within the attorney-client or attorney-work-product privileges if the doctor can be viewed as an agent of either the attorney or client for purposes of facilitating the work or communications between attorney and client.

Doctors, like lawyers and members of the clergy, have an ethical duty of non-disclosure. They may also have a similar tort-law and implied contractual duty. The duties under these various concepts are roughly analogous to the privilege and have somewhat comparable exceptions. There may be criminal or other laws requiring disclosure by the doctor of, e.g., suspected child abuse, and her various confidentiality duties, and the privilege, would be adjusted accordingly. Presumably there would be a similar adjustment to allow for the fact that tort law in some jurisdictions requires psychiatrists to reveal specific physical threats voiced by the patient concerning specific identifiable people. The situation of the lawyer may be the same in some places. Some jurisdictions' versions of the legal ethics confidentiality obligation and attorney-client privilege expressly except situations of potential physical injury. As respects confidentiality, a jurisdiction's privilege law, criminal law, tort law, and ethical rules should but do not always exactly track each other.

Evolution or Adoption of a Psychotherapist Privilege and Its Limits

Because of the special skittishness of mental health patients in seeking help and making disclosures related to their condition, a number of jurisdictions recognize only a psychotherapist-patient privilege, rather than a general physician-patient privilege. This was the position of unenacted but influential Supreme Court Draft F.R.E. Rule 504. The definition of psychotherapist there, however, might have been broad enough to include, e.g., an ordinary doctor treating even merely a broken bone if the doctor was sufficiently attentive to the emotional or mental state of the patient.[16]

It has been suggested that the accelerating recognition of psychotherapist privilege in our increasingly secular society reflects that for a growing number of people the psychiatrist is replacing the cleric.[17] Society has long recognized a priest-penitent privilege.

Unlike the husband-wife and lawyer-client privileges, the doctor-patient privilege (including any psychotherapist-patient privilege), did not exist at common law, and is generally deemed to require special enactment. This left its status in doubt under the current federal-law branch of F.R.E. 501, which refers privilege questions to an evolving common law process. However, in *Jaffe,* supra, the Supreme Court did not confine itself to common-law sources, and decided that not only does a psy-

16. "A 'psychotherapist' is (A) a person authorized to practice medicine in any state or nation, or reasonably believed by the patient so to be, while engaged in the diagnosis or treatment of a mental or emotional condition, including drug addiction, or (B) a person licensed or certified as a psychologist under the laws of any state or nation, while similarly engaged."

17. *Jaffee,* supra, made a somewhat similar argument for extending the psychotherapist privilege to cover social workers conducting therapeutic counseling: that many people today cannot afford but need psychiatrists.

chotherapist-patient privilege apply, but it extends to statements made to social workers, at least when they are acting analogously to psychotherapeutic counselors. The Court eschewed making it a qualified privilege, subject to weighing and balancing, because sufficient encouragement of patients required advance certainty of applicability. But the Court expressly left it to future decisions to prescribe what categorical exceptions there would be, for example an exception to prevent potential physical harm.

The Supreme Court has not expressly recognized a more general physician-patient privilege under the federal branch of Rule 501. That privilege has had mixed reception in the lower federal courts. The rejected but influential Supreme Court draft of the F.R.E. had no general physician-patient privilege, but did have a psychotherapist-patient privilege. The drafters had deemed privilege necessary to encourage timorous patients in the one area, but not the other. Medical patients were deemed less timorous and physical health incentives more effective. It may also have been thought that physical medical diagnosis is not as dependant on patient disclosures, relying more on physical examinations and tests, something mentioned in passing in *Jaffee*. The drafters noted that although widespread, the state physician-patient privileges were riddled with so many exceptions that not much privilege was left, corroborating the judgment that such privilege is not really necessary.

Arguably, the psychotherapist privilege in *Jaffee* may be viewed as a part of, and supporting by inference, a general physician-patient privilege. On the other hand, as noted, *Jaffee* makes the point that a psychotherapist's work depends more heavily on voluntary self-critical disclosures than does the general physician's work. This statement may bode ill for a general physician-patient privilege.

Under state law, psychotherapist privileges vary enormously in definition and are subject to widely differing exceptions. Psychotherapist-patient or physician-patient privileges may not be available in workers' compensation cases; criminal cases generally, or some kinds of criminal cases, such as homicide or some kinds of homicide; cases involving the validity of wills; medical malpractice cases; cases involving mental illness; child abuse cases; certain family law, juvenile, custody, or neglect proceedings; and a host of other situations.

In civil cases, the psychotherapist privilege is typically waived if the holder puts his or her mental or (sometimes) physical state into issue. In other words, privilege cannot act in aid of a sword if damages are being claimed for mental or physical injury.[18] A difficult issue arises if an adversary first raises the mental state of the opponent as an issue in the case, the opponent responds, and the adversary then argues that these circumstances defeat the privilege. For example, in a child custody contest (assuming the privilege is not expressly per se inapplicable there) one spouse may claim that the other is mentally unfit to raise the child and thereby attempt to defeat the privilege concerning the latter parent's previous psychotherapist communications.

VI. OTHER CLAIMED PRIVILEGES, ESTABLISHED OR NOT

Are there other socially desirable relationships or professions whose work or solidarity ought to be facilitated in a fashion similar to that extended to doctors, lawyers, and spouses? To name just a few possibilities, should there be a journalist-informant, or accountant-client

18. A personal injury suit can place in issue the plaintiff's mental health because there is usually a mental element to the damages, such as pain and suffering.

privilege? Why isn't it considered as desirable to foster, with privilege, communications between other family members such as a parent and child, or siblings, as it is between husband and wife? Perhaps it also would be desirable to foster the world's various forms of desirable work by means of a boss-secretary privilege; or a researcher-subject privilege. Why not a "friend" privilege that would result in nondisclosure of confidences among close friends? Shouldn't we be seeking to prevent the strain, temptation to perjury, or violation of privacy, that ensues from compelling adverse testimony in all these relationships? Don't friends and family members counsel each other and contribute to society's mental health and sense of well-being?

The policy of limiting the extent to which privileges defeat the truth-seeking function, as well as the difficulty of defining them, have led most jurisdictions to reject many of these privileges.

A number of states have some form of journalist, and/or accountant privileges. A very few jurisdictions seem to recognize some kind of parent-child privilege. A clergy privilege exists in most states, but is uncertain in federal privilege law. Friends, siblings, and other family members have not been recognized. A researcher privilege is not unknown. A number of jurisdictions have codified qualified privileges for statements made to rape or substance-abuse counselors, or for peer review in hospitals. This sort of privilege has been suggested for domestic violence counselors as well. A generalized self-evaluation privilege is supported by some authority. A few other privileges are found in various states and in some federal courts. There are also a number of statutory privileges peculiar to certain regulatory areas, such as a federal privilege covering information related to airplane accident investigations, and declaring that the information cannot be used in certain court proceedings.

Remember, the door is not closed on the evolution of federal privilege law. And privileges wax and wane in states, too, as the result of both statutory and judicial flux.

VII. GOVERNMENTAL PRIVILEGES

Policies Underlying Required Reports Privileges

Certain records required by the government to be kept or submitted may be attended by a "required report privilege."

Statutory or regulatory provisions found in many jurisdictions require a motorist involved in a collision to report that an accident has occurred, and later to report the facts; require the investigating officer to report the facts (from observation and/or interviewed persons); and may require persons (perhaps the motorist) to give information to the officer for the report. An accompanying statutory privilege sometimes renders confidential one, some, or all of these required reports. This privilege is an example of a class of statutory privileges providing for nondisclosure of required reports, which individual citizens, companies, or government employees are obligated by law (either absolutely or as a condition of receiving government benefits) to submit to state and federal governmental agencies.

Required report privilege statutes differ widely in form, substance, and judicial interpretation. They are normally individually tailored to a particular regulatory area: income tax returns; census reports; claims for veteran's benefits; patent applications; filing of corporate trade, securities, financial, product, work-conditions, or environmental information with various agencies; unemployment compensation claims; public assistance records; selective service records; social security records; information obtained from citizens in conjunction with health services; public health records; and adoption records, to name a few.

The privileges generally seem to be founded upon *either one or both* of two distinct policies:

(1) *Encouragement of Voluntary Compliance.* The intent here is to encourage citizens (or companies) to accurately and fully report potentially self-damaging information which they would otherwise hesitate to furnish for fear of the consequences resulting from later uses of such information. It is this kind of statute that will principally concern us.

(2) *Governmental Concerns.* The concern here is with the government's internal processes, i.e., (a) preventing disclosure of government officers' and investigators' notations or opinions; (b) preserving documents from loss, destruction, alteration or wear; (c) avoiding the general inconvenience resulting from frequent demands for disclosure; or (d) preventing direct exertion of judicial power on executive personnel, a policy with "separation of powers" overtones.

Coverage and Limits of Required Report Privileges

Access to privileged information under a required report privilege may be denied to the judicial tribunal, or to parties, the general public, administrative agencies, or any one or combination of these. Disclosure for purposes of litigation is what most concerns most lawyers and is generally what we mean when we speak of privilege. Some statutes provide very generally that the government shall not publicly disclose the required report. Courts have often held that such a statute will not prevent use of the report in litigation. Other statutes specifically provide that the record shall be kept confidential except when ordered produced by a court of law. On the other hand, a number of statutes provide that the record shall not be produced for use in any court proceeding, shall not be referred to in court, shall not be used in civil cases, or shall not be used in any litigation except that involving the governmental department to which the report is required to be made.

Some statutes provide that the report may be released to specified government agencies, used for specific regulatory purposes, or used in court by a specified agency. Still another approach has been to prohibit disclosure if the report will be used to the reporter's prejudice or to prohibit "use against" the reporter. A few statutes provide that they apply in "actions arising out of the facts on which the report is based."

The Supreme Court recently addressed and carefully delineated the scope of the evidentiary and discovery privilege provided by a federal statute that protected reports and data collected by state agencies to identify potential accident sites in order for the state to obtain federal funding for highway safety improvements. *Pierce Co. v. Guillen* (S.Ct.2003).

Some decisions suggest that a report that could not be used in a substantive capacity may be used to refresh the memory of a witness or to impeach the reporter by a prior inconsistent statement, on a theory that "the door has been opened."

No existing required report privilege prevents disclosure of the facts of the reported occurrence by sources that can supply them regardless of any privileged report. For example, consider the testimony of first-hand witnesses to the occurrence, whom a party calls to testify. It is no objection to such evidence that the same facts happen to be mentioned in the required report. Thus, even the reporter herself could be asked for her first-hand observations of the occurrence, though she has previously put them in a privileged report.

Governmental Privileges for State and Military Secrets, Informers, Intra–Agency Communications, Etc.

The required report privileges may be analytically distinguished from five other privileges or non-disclosure principles applicable to information in the hands of the government. Two of them have their origin at common law: the governmental privileges not to disclose *military or diplomatic secrets of state* (and, perhaps, certain other official information) and not to reveal the *identity of an informer*. *United States v. Reynolds* (S.Ct.1953) is one of the few Supreme Court cases to discuss the privileges concerning "secrets of state" and "military secrets." *Tenet v. Doe* (S.Ct.2005) discussed *Reynolds* in holding that claims by alleged spies were barred by the long-standing rule prohibiting suits against the government based on covert espionage agreements. See also *Smith v. Illinois* (S.Ct.1968) (right to confrontation infringed by informer identity privilege in case where informer was put on as a government witness).

A third principle is the federal statutory permission given to government agency heads to make rules prohibiting subordinates from disclosing *intra-departmental communications, agency files, and information obtained by agency investigation*. Originally in 5 U.S.C.A. 301 the statute's reach was subsequently considerably contracted principally by the Federal Freedom of Information Act ("F.O.I.A."), 5 U.S.C.A. 552, providing broad public access to administrative documents with certain exceptions. Evolving from these provisions, which primarily regulate public access, has been a set of ill-defined principles, more properly regarded as "privilege," controlling disclosure in court. The privilege principles are not exactly co-extensive with the provisions. See, e.g., *Redland Soccer Club, Inc. v. Department of Army of United States* (3d Cir.1995), and *United States v. Farley* (7th Cir.1993), for discussion of a "deliberative process" privilege, one of the privileges in this area. Not only is the "deliberative process" of officials, offices or agencies likely to be protected (in a qualified way), but so, too, is law enforcement information, particularly concerning a pending investigation, and certain private personnel matters. The Second Circuit has refused to apply the "deliberative process" protection to state agencies in the F.O.I.A. context. See *Grand Cent. Partnership, Inc. v. Cuomo* (2d Cir.1999).

A fourth privilege encompasses some of the fundamental principles of the above mentioned privileges and is embodied in state statutes which provide that "a public officer cannot be examined as to communications made in official confidence, when the *public interest would suffer* by the disclosure." A somewhat analogous judge-made rule exists in some jurisdictions.

These four nondisclosure principles are extensively qualified.

Finally, there is a fifth type of privilege or group of privileges loosely called *executive privilege*, exercisable by the President or by certain of his officers.[19] This privilege rests on several policies, including the constitutional separation of powers.[20] In *United States v. Nixon* (S.Ct. 1974) the Supreme Court indicated this is not an absolute but a qualified privilege. See also *In re Sealed Case* (D.C.Cir.1997) (presidential communications privilege extends to communications between aides in preparing advice to give to the President). See also *In re Grand Jury Testimony of Bruce Lindsey* (D.C.Cir.1998) (does

19. State executives may also possess executive privilege.

20. But the President (or Vice President) may not always have to claim executive privilege as to particular documents, in order to raise a claim that separation of powers principles enable them to resist an oppressive or excessive discovery request that may interfere with their duties. See *Cheney v. U.S. Dist. Court for Dist. of Columbia* (S.Ct.2004).

Sealed Case apply to discussions within White House concerning Presidential scandal?). See also a second case with a similar name, *In re Sealed Case* (D.C.Cir.1998) (refusing to recognize a "protective function privilege" that would cover information about the President and his meetings obtained by the Secret Service while guarding the President, because the Secret Service failed to convince the court one was necessary). The "deliberative process" privilege, above, is sometimes said to be part of the executive or executive branch privilege.

VIII. THE PRIVILEGE AGAINST SELF–INCRIMINATION

Definition of the Privilege Against Self–Incrimination

The privilege against self-incrimination guaranteed by the federal Constitution is actually two privileges: (1) The privilege of the criminally accused, which includes both (a) a right not to take the witness stand and, if he or she does take the stand, (b) a right to turn away impeachment questions that might open up evidence of *other* crimes (any fear of incrimination in the *present* case being waived by taking the stand). (2) The privilege of other civil or criminal witnesses to turn away particular questions that might open up crimes of theirs. "Open up" in both instances means increase the likelihood of criminal prosecution or criminal liability.

The Supreme Court decisions in *Malloy v. Hogan* (S.Ct.1964) and *Griffin v. California* (S.Ct.1965) established that both of these privileges embodied in the Fifth Amendment, which regulates the federal government, apply not only in federal but also in state proceedings through the Fourteenth Amendment, which regulates state governments. State constitutions also have similar privileges which on occasion are interpreted to afford greater protection to the privilege claimant (lesser protection, of course, being impermissible). But by-and-large, the federal interpretations of the federal privilege have tended to sweep the field.

Unless waived, the witness' privilege can be invoked by any civil or criminal witness to resist giving testimony in court, whenever it can be made to appear to the judge that there is some appreciable likelihood that information disclosed by the invoker might be used either investigatively or as evidence, in a way that would increase the chances of the invoker's prosecution for or conviction of some crime under any state or federal law anywhere in the United States.[21] The standard is the same for the criminal accused's right to turn away particular questions.

In *Ohio v. Reiner* (S.Ct.2001), the Supreme Court made clear that full privilege is available to a criminal defendant despite her claim of innocence, so long as it is reasonable to apprehend danger from the answers at trial. However, *Hiibel v. Sixth Judicial Dist. Court of Nevada, Humboldt County* (S.Ct.2004) held that a suspect's conviction for refusal, when properly stopped and questioned, to identify himself, in violation of Nevada's "stop and identify" law, did not violate his Fifth Amendment right against self-incrimination, absent a showing that disclosure of his name presented any reasonable danger of incrimination.

Determination (without breaching the privilege) of whether there *is* a valid fear of incrimination can occasionally be problematic. One help is that the standard is low: any appreciable possibility of increased exposure does the trick. Sometimes a look at the circumstances and the face of the question will be sufficient. Sometimes at least some of the allegedly privileged information may

---

21. Fear of foreign prosecution is beyond the scope of the privilege. See *United States v. Balsys* (S.Ct.1998).

have to be revealed to the judge *in camera*. Courts must tread the fine line between allowing a mere claim of privilege to be sufficient in every case and prying so deeply into allegedly privileged matter that the privilege is effectively defeated in the effort to determine its applicability.

If the possibility of prosecution is removed, for example by the expiration of the statute of limitations or by the fact that conviction or acquittal has already taken place, there is no privilege, at least insofar as the privilege would be based on fear of *that* crime. Similarly, the grant of "use" immunity (guaranteeing that this particular testimony will not be used against the witness) removes the chance the testimony will incriminate. *United States v. Oliver North* (D.C.Cir.1990). Broader immunity, from prosecution for the crime altogether, even on other evidence than the testimony, is not required. *Kastigar v. United States* (S.Ct.1972). Violation of the privilege (or giving an immunity grant and then compelling the testimony) by one jurisdiction probably means an automatic immunity from use by another jurisdiction, even though no jurisdiction (except the federal) has the power to grant directly an immunity from use in other jurisdictions.

While a criminal defendant's privilege includes the right not to take the stand, which is exercised out of the jury's hearing and, under the decisions, should not ordinarily be brought to the attention of the jury, other witnesses must normally come forward, take the oath and assert their privilege to refuse to answer particular questions. Courts differ on the propriety of a party calling a witness who it knows or should know may "take the Fifth" as to projected questions, and asking the questions anyway, forcing the witness to assert the privilege in front of the jury.

Limits, Exceptions, and Waiver of the Privilege Against Self–Incrimination

The privilege against self-incrimination may be lost insofar as it is based on a crime whose facts have been voluntarily discussed, wholly or partially, earlier in the same testimony, provided that at that earlier point the witness could properly have refused to do so and could reasonably have known that he or she could have so refused. The extent of this waiver by a criminal defendant who takes the witness stand in his own behalf is discussed infra, in Chapter Six, under the subject of the scope of cross-examination of witnesses generally, with which it gets confused.

Unlike some other privileges, express and implied waivers of the privilege against self-incrimination are usually effective for and only for the duration of the immediate proceedings. Waiver in one case thus may not mean waiver in another case, even though the matter testified to would be exactly the same. The witness may assert the privilege and refuse to testify in the later case, although, if other rules of evidence are complied with, the transcript of the earlier testimony might be received in the second case.

If the privilege is waived during the hearing of some preliminary matter, the question arises whether it is waived for the trial proper. Federal courts usually permit the witness to "take the Fifth" despite earlier testimony in other proceedings in the current case. See F.R.E. 104(d). This, however, is not necessarily part-and-parcel of the constitutional right, but rather merely a matter of administering it, about which state courts may differ.

Similarly, a defendant retains the privilege at sentencing, even if the conviction resulted from a guilty plea, or the defendant made statements to establish the factual basis for the pleas. See *Mitchell v. United States* (S.Ct. 1999).

The privilege applies to testimonial silence other than in court in such settings as administrative hearings, police interrogations, Congressional hearings, and other situations where the government requires information.[22] A second violation of the privilege may take place where information wrongfully obtained by violating the privilege at one time is later sought to be used, as where an improperly police-obtained confession is sought to be introduced against the confessor in court. This, the due process clause, and the right to counsel under the Sixth Amendment, are the genesis of the rule barring the admissibility of involuntary confessions or those obtained by police in violation of the famous "Miranda" rights (the right of a suspect to be advised she may remain silent, that anything she says may be used against her, that she has a right to her own counsel, or to state

22. However, the Fifth Amendment self-incrimination violation is not complete unless or until there is something that can be called a "criminal case" against the person whose rights are allegedly violated and the information is sought to be used there. This is because the self-incrimination right as specified in the Fifth Amendment is a right not to be a "witness" against oneself "in a criminal case". See *Chavez v. Martinez* (S.Ct.2003). However, governmental coercion may be a violation of another constitutional right—the right to Due Process—even in the absence of any possibility of use in a criminal case.

Also, again in the words of the Fifth Amendment's self-incrimination clause itself, in order for there to be a violation of that clause, the information must be considered "compelled." *McKune v. Lile* (S.Ct. 2002) held that adverse consequences faced by a state prisoner for refusing to make admissions concerning his offense that were required for participation in a sexual abuse treatment program were not so severe as to amount to compelled self-incrimination. The consequences were basically denial of entrance into and benefits of participating in the program, including certain prison privileges. In deciding what can be considered "compelled", however, the Court took into account the prison setting and the reasonableness of the requirement for entrance into a legitimate and societally beneficial program.

supplied counsel if she cannot afford one—advice deemed needed for, among other things, effective exercise of the privilege). The Court has now clarified that *Miranda* is constitutionally based. See *Dickerson v. United States* (S.Ct.2000).

Ordinarily business records are not protected by the privilege. Reports which the government requires to be kept are not within this privilege (but see Required Reports Privilege, supra). Even very personal and private records, such as diaries, may not be protected, although this is not crystal clear at the present time. One may generalize that already-existing documents of any kind are probably not within the privilege and may be compelled to be produced unless the government's method of obtaining them is improper under some other principle.

On occasion, the act of requiring an individual to produce such an unprivileged document may itself be protected by the Fifth Amendment privilege because it compels essentially an admission that the document exists, is in the possession of the witness, and is authentic. See *United States v. Doe* (S.Ct.1984). As a corollary, *United States v. Hubbell* (S.Ct.2000) held that a grant of use immunity precluded prosecution in a subsequent unrelated case where the defendant's act of producing the documents was used by the government to discover the evidence used to obtain the later indictment. However, since the Fifth Amendment is an individual privilege, this act of production doctrine does not reach documents subpoenaed from a corporate custodian. *Braswell v. United States* (S.Ct.1988).

Requiring *non-testimonial* evidence from an individual in or out of court is not within the privilege. Examples include taking fingerprint, DNA, blood, breath, urine, or writing samples (simply to analyze or compare with other samples); and the requiring of such things as bodily displays, trying on clothing, uttering voice samples (for comparison or to see if speech is slurred), appearing at lineups, posing for photos, standing up, assuming a certain stance, walking, gesturing, or performing tasks to check physical dexterity or balance. These things are often required of suspects for various tests, drug or intoxication gauging, or identification procedures.

Of course, there may be something else wrong (other than this privilege) with the way they were obtained in the particular case. For example there may be a violation of the Fourth Amendment prohibition of unreasonable searches and seizures (including arrest) or a violation of the due process clause which prohibits barbaric or extreme practices such as stomach pumping or certain risky medical procedures or bodily intrusions not properly medically performed. See generally the Supreme Court decisions in *Schmerber v. California* (S.Ct.1966) (taking blood required for intoxication test was not covered by the privilege, because privilege applies only to testimonial evidence; other constitutional provisions also discussed); *United States v. Dionisio* (S.Ct.1973) (requiring voice exemplar for comparison does not violate the privilege; other constitutional provisions also discussed); *Doe v. United States* (S.Ct.1988) (general discussion of "testimonial"); *Rochin v. California* (S.Ct.1952) (stomach pumping).

In *Pennsylvania v. Muniz* (S.Ct.1990), a drunk driving suspect was asked routine police booking questions such as name, age, height, and weight, which he answered vaguely. He was also asked a question calling for a simple computation, to test his sobriety: when was his sixth birthday. He responded he could not figure it. The Supreme Court suggested all these responses were possibly "testimonial" and "incriminatory" in nature under the privilege. But only the "sixth birthday" response was in fact held inadmissible (for lack of *Miranda* warnings). Routine booking questions are given a special exemption from the *Miranda* warnings requirement. Thus, the responses to the routine booking questions, while perhaps testimonial and self-incriminatory in nature, and therefore forbidden if improperly compelled, were not considered improperly compelled in this case. So the court did not need to decide definitely whether they were indeed "testimonial". Certain other questions (e.g., a request to count, which was performed satisfactorily) were answered in a way that did not incriminate, so no definite decision was made concerning whether the answers were testimonial.

IX. EXCLUSIONARY RULES PREMISED ON DETERRENCE RATIONALES

Illegally Seized Evidence

Evidence obtained as a result of violation of the federal constitutional prohibition against unreasonable searches and seizures (contained in the Fourth and incorporated in the Fourteenth Amendment) cannot be admitted as substantive evidence in the prosecution's case-in-chief in a federal or state criminal case against the person whose rights were invaded. Thus, there will be not only whatever ordinary civil, criminal, administrative, and equitable sanctions are provided for violation of constitutional rights, but also a quasi-privilege to exclude evidence.

There is an exception to this quasi-privilege (as there is to many privileges to exclude evidence, constitutional or otherwise, particularly as respects illegally obtained evidence) for *impeachment* use of the evidence, where the defendant, who has been the victim of the illegal search or seizure, takes the stand and denies possession of the seized materials or testifies contrary to the statement obtained as a result of the illegal search or seizure. See the Supreme Court decisions in *United States v. Havens*

(S.Ct.1980) and *Walder v. United States* (S.Ct.1954). However, *Havens* has not been extended to permit impeachment of defense *witnesses* with illegally obtained evidence. See *James v. Illinois* (S.Ct.1990). In addition, exceptions to the privilege are provided by such doctrines as good faith reliance, inevitable discovery, lack of standing, and attenuation.

Evidence Obtained as a Result of Other Misconduct

Electronic and mechanical eavesdropping is subject to comprehensive federal prohibitory legislation, including a broad exclusionary evidence rule, covering federal and state proceedings and officials (as well as private persons), but with a warrant exception.[23] These matters may also be covered by the constitutional search and seizure provisions, which the statute is meant to satisfy. States may also prohibit (on a broader but not narrower basis) such conduct and refuse to admit evidence obtained in violation.

Rochin v. California (S.Ct.1952), should also be regarded as establishing an analogue to privilege of the sort we are discussing. It holds that evidence obtained as a result of violation of a criminal accused's due process right to be free of abusive treatment at the hands of the state would itself be a violation of his right to due process if introduced against him in the case. There the accused was made to vomit incriminating evidence that he had swallowed, in a manner that "shocked the conscience," according to the Supreme Court.

Federal courts have generally refused to create exclusionary rules for official misconduct that is not the

23. The circumstances under which a warrant can be obtained and certain procedural safeguards are not as rigorous as they were before the recent legislative response to the bombing of the World Trade Center known as 9–11.

subject of some specific statutory, constitutional, or court-rule provision. E.g., *United States v. Caceres* (S.Ct. 1979) (no exclusion merely because I.R.S. failed to follow its own regulations in investigation). And even though the policy in most cases of exclusion seems to be to increase the inducement to public officials to act properly in carrying out investigations by providing a remedy in addition to other remedies available to deter the misconduct, generally only those whose rights were invaded may invoke the privilege, and only to suppress evidence used against them. See *Rawlings v. Kentucky* (S.Ct.1980) (defendant has no standing to challenge search of third party's purse that contained narcotic of defendant); *United States v. Payner* (S.Ct.1980) (defendant cannot complain of search of another's briefcase; the Court refused to create a privilege under its supervisory power either). Private misconduct may be regarded as official misconduct if public officials were complicitous in it.

Numerous questions, in state and federal courts, exist concerning such matters as what other kinds of illegality (than discussed above) may result in exclusion, when may private conduct (as opposed to governmental conduct) result in exclusion, is the evidence excluded in civil cases, and how conflicts-of-laws are to be handled where the rules of different jurisdictions are different concerning what is illegal or whether to exclude, and the police, the conduct, and the court are spread among them.

X. RULES THAT PREVENT INVOCATION OF PRIVILEGE FROM IMPLYING GUILT OR FAULT

This area is beset by uncertainty, except as respects some applications of the federal constitutional privilege against self-incrimination. There the implication is forbidden, at least if the claim of privilege is proper. The trend seems to be, however, toward banning the

drawing of adverse inferences from privilege claims, and taking precautions to help assure the ban is obeyed.

In considering the permissibility of inferring admission or consciousness of adverse fact from invocation of privilege, two issues are presented: whether the invocation means what the offeror contends, and whether the purposes of the privilege may be thwarted by allowing the inference. If we allow the inference, use of the privilege may in practical terms be penalized or discouraged; furthermore, use of the privilege might then itself produce the effect privileged against.

Suppose we forbid attorney and judge to tell the jury that the invocation of a privilege can furnish an inference against the party so invoking. Suppose further we permit or even require an instruction that the inference is *not* to be drawn. Under what circumstances would you permit argument against the privileged party to direct attention to a general dearth of evidence on her side on some issue, when that dearth is contributed to or produced by her use of the privilege? This argument may invite the jury to make the prohibited inference.

In *Griffin v. California* (S.Ct.1965), the U.S. Supreme Court held that the federal Constitution forbids, in a state or federal criminal case, a prosecutor or judge to comment adversely on a criminal defendant's exercise of the self-incrimination privilege to stay off the stand. *Griffin* applies directly only to *criminal* cases, only to the *privilege against self-incrimination*, only to the *defendant's* self-incrimination privilege, and only to *one branch* of it (the right to stay off the stand as opposed to refusing certain questions). Comment in the multitude of other situations is left to other law, which is mixed, except that the adverse inference is usually allowable only where it would make some factual sense, which may lead to distinctions based on whether the invoker is a party or not.

Even in a situation directly covered by *Griffin*, it may still be permissible for a prosecutor to refer to proof offered by the government as "uncontradicted," despite indirect possibilities that this comment may lead to inferences from the accused's silence, so long as such an inference is not so strong as to be the natural and necessary result.[24]

The former, unenacted, still influential Supreme Court draft of the F.R.E. (Rule 513), and identical Rule 511 of the Uniform Rules of Evidence (adopted in a number of states), provide as a general matter for all situations and privileges that judge and counsel may not comment on the fact that a privilege (self-incrimination or any other) has been claimed (whether on the present or any prior occasion). In addition, the rule prefers procedures that prevent privilege claims from coming to the attention of the jury. For example, an opportunity to claim privilege outside the jury's hearing should be provided. The rule also entitles a party, upon request, to a jury instruction that no inference may be drawn. Note that the party may not want such an instruction, feeling that he has more to lose than gain by attention being called to the matter. The rule is not entirely clear as to whether or when a judge may give it anyway.

Occasionally, these "no comment or inference" principles and corollaries clash with other considerations, such as where hiding the fact there has been a privilege assertion would be misleading or the assertion is inter-

---

24. Cf. *Portuondo v. Agard* (S.Ct.2000), holding that a prosecutor's comments during summation, calling the jury's attention to the fact that the defendant had an opportunity to hear other witnesses testify and to tailor his testimony, did not unlawfully burden his right to testify on his own behalf.

twined with important admissible evidence. The responses of the courts to this situation have varied.

Some jurisdictions quite liberally permit adverse inference and comment, wherever constitutionally free to do so and the facts warrant.

A distinguishable situation arises when a party or witness persists in an unlawful claim of privilege after the court has overruled it and ordered the party to testify. In this situation, it is common for courts to require the privilege to be asserted in front of the jury and to permit, or even authorize by instruction, an adverse inference.

CHAPTER 6

WITNESSES: COMPETENCY, EXAMINATION, AND IMPEACHMENT

Introduction: The Order of Presentation at Trial: Examinations, Arguments, and Charge (Jury Instructions)

The basic pattern of trial is that each party puts its case on in turn, subjecting each witness to cross examination by the other side immediately after the party's own direct examination of the witness.

The usual order of presentation of evidence at a civil trial, after jury selection and opening statements of counsel, is (1) plaintiff's case-in-chief (witnesses, documents, and other evidence); (2) defendant's case-in-chief-case (not only denying facts asserted in plaintiffs case, but also establishing affirmative defenses); (3) plaintiff's rebuttal case, possibly some of the same witnesses, but confined to rebutting defendant's case, absent an exercise of the judge's discretion; and (4) defendant's rejoinder evidence, in theory confined to the matter newly introduced by plaintiff in the previous stage. Further rebuttals and rejoinders may be allowed to new matters, in the judge's discretion. Each successive stage will be omitted if there is no new matter, but normally this occurs only after stage (2) or (3). Then follows argument of counsel ("summation"), usually opened and closed by plaintiff, and the judge's charge (instructions) to the jury. Some courts give the charge *before* closing argument so that the arguments can be presented in the light of the instructions.

A witness presented at any given stage will normally be, in uninterrupted sequence, (1) examined directly by counsel presenting the witness; (2) cross-examined by opposing counsel; (3) subjected to re-direct examination by the proponent, to repair the damage of cross-examination; and (4) subjected to a re-cross examination by opposing counsel, to repair the damage of the re-direct. In the absence of an exercise of the judge's discretion, repair is the only acceptable purpose of (3) and (4). Furthermore, they may be severely limited or even disallowed completely by the judge where the contribution of additional examination would be minimal. Further re-directs and re-crosses are possible if necessary.

The order of presentation in a criminal trial is basically the same. The most significant difference is that the Fifth Amendment's privilege against self-incrimination prohibits the prosecution from calling the criminal defendant to the stand as a witness. In civil cases, plaintiffs' lawyers often call the defendant during plaintiff's case-in-chief as an adverse witness, frequently the very first witness.

I. INCOMPETENCY (OR DISQUALIFICATION) OF WITNESSES

General Rules of Witness Competency: From Common Law to F.R.E. 601

The common law recognized various kinds of witness incompetencies, which meant automatic disqualification of a witness. At times, for example, witnesses were ruled incompetent for interest in the case, commission of felony, mental incapacity, youth, drug or alcohol intoxication or addiction, marital relationship to a party, and other causes. These incompetencies have largely become things of the past, and such matters now are mainly deemed factors to consider for whatever they are worth on particular facts under the probative-prejudice balance or in the realm of impeachment and weight.

F.R.E. 601 which applies in federal court generally adopts local state incompetencies in civil diversity and other state-law civil cases tried in federal court. The language commanding this deference to state law for incompetencies is precisely the same as for presumptions and privileges, supra, Chapter 2, Section III, and Chapter 5, Section II, including the limitation to "elements" referred to there. In all other instances, i.e., in criminal cases and civil cases governed by federal law, the Rule abolishes incompetencies except for the few mentioned specifically in Article VI, which are lack of personal knowledge (F.R.E. 602), failure to take the oath or affirmation (F.R.E. 603), and disqualification of judges and jurors as witnesses (F.R.E. 605 and 606). F.R.E. 610 states that beliefs on matters of religion can no longer be shown as affecting competency or credibility.

The question of child competency is the competency which has generated the most debate. Unlike the law in many states, the federal rules (where federal law governs) generally treat children, at least in principle, no differently than other witnesses. 18 U.S.C.A. 3509 includes a presumption that children are competent and allows exclusion of otherwise admissible child witnesses only for "compelling reason," which must be something other than mere age.

But even though children are to be treated according to the same legal principles as adults, factual differences between children and adults can make a difference to the application of even uniformly applied legal principles, such as F.R.E. 403 (balancing) and F.R.E. 603 (witness should take and presumably understand oath to tell the truth). And of course, a jury is free to consider whether a child's and an adult's testimony are to be given equal weight.

Children and mentally infirm people who are to be offered as witnesses are often subjected to a special series of questions in the opening of their direct examination, in voir dire (questioning by opponent to ascertain foundational facts before direct examination can progress), or in a hearing outside the presence of the jury. Indeed, independent foundational evidence may occasionally be taken concerning the prospective witness, from other sources. The effort is to determine whether the prospective witness (1) understands the duty to tell the truth, (2) can distinguish fact from fantasy, and (3) has the ability to communicate meaningfully with the jury. Often, for example, a child will be asked about parental admonishment for fibs and how he or she understands them. These items may be necessary to establish competency under state law. Where federal evidence law applies, they may be necessary to satisfy F.R.E. 603 (which requires administration of and presumably understanding of an oath to tell the truth); to whether the testimony will survive F.R.E. 403 (the probative-prejudice-time balance); or to weight before the jury.

While children over six years old are rarely found to be incompetent or inadmissible on these grounds, extremely young children are more problematic. Some judges have permitted testimony of children younger than three years old. A few states have enacted statutes which permit the unsworn testimony of young children in child abuse cases without any demonstration of competency.

"Dead Man's Rules" Under State Law

Some jurisdictions have statutes or rules prohibiting certain parties to certain civil transactions from

testifying concerning these transactions if the other party to the transaction is deceased and therefore cannot give his or her version of what happened.

The scope of this prohibition or witness incompetency varies widely from jurisdiction to jurisdiction and must be studied locally. Indeed, in some jurisdictions, it is not a prohibition or incompetency at all, but merely a provision that the survivor's testimony must be corroborated or that hearsay statements of the deceased are admissible to rebut it. The purpose of the rule is said to be to prevent falsification for gain where the surviving party knows that the person who could say nay to the lie, and at whose expense the gain will be gotten, is deceased. It seems to be overkill, in that many legitimate claims are sacrificed by applying the rule, when we have court processes that are fairly good at ferreting out falsehood

As is indicated above, F.R.E. 601 abolishes this and most other witness incompetencies in federal-law cases, but state rules of competency apply in certain civil cases where state law provides the rule of decision. Thus, in most diversity cases, the state's dead man's rule, if any, will apply, notwithstanding that we are in federal court.

The Competency of Jurors to Impeach Their Verdicts: F.R.E. 606(b)

Testimony of a juror showing impropriety during jury deliberations will not be received to overturn a verdict the juror participated in rendering, with certain exceptions in various jurisdictions.

The exclusionary principle here is usually termed an incompetency. See F.R.E. 606(b). The policy is to promote finality of verdicts, prevent approaches made to jurors, avoid juror harassment or intimidation, and forestall a chilling effect on jurors' freedom to deliberate and willingness to serve. Usually other methods of proof than juror testimony or affidavits will not be barred, e.g., testimony of a bailiff as to some verdict-spoiling illegal conduct he saw on the part of jurors in the jury room. These other methods of proof will be received to show whatever would constitute legal grounds for overturning a verdict under the substantive (non-evidence) law of the jurisdiction. These grounds are often severely restricted under the substantive law, in the interests of finality of judgments. Frequently there will also be some showing required, of prejudicial effect on the verdict. Since juror testimony normally cannot be received, this showing is difficult to make. The prohibition on evidence usually does not apply to proof of jury impropriety offered before a verdict is rendered (so that some remedy at that point may be taken if the law so provides). Also, there is doubt as to whether the prohibition applies to evidence of jury improprieties committed during the trial (as opposed to during deliberations) even if surfacing after the verdict and offered to overturn the verdict. But see *Tanner*, infra.

F.R.E. 606(b) has a typical, general prohibition of juror testimony or affidavit directed at invalidating or upholding the verdict. Forbidden are reports concerning (1) anything said or transpiring during deliberations, (2) any juror's mental processes, or (3) the effect of anything on any juror's vote. This largely covers the waterfront. But an exception allows showing that "extraneous prejudicial information was improperly brought to the jury's attention" (such as facts coming from forbidden media reports, third parties, or a juror's independent efforts or knowledge) or "outside influence was improperly brought to bear upon any juror" (such as threats, intimidation, violence, or bribes, from other sources than fellow jurors). In *Tanner v. United States* (S.Ct.1987), the Supreme Court held that alcohol and drug abuse by jurors during the trial, affecting jurors' attention, ability to stay awake, or judgment, would not be an extraneous influence permitting verdict impeachment under the federal rule, apparently regardless of how extreme, and whether occurring on or off the court premises, on lunch breaks, or during the proceedings themselves. Nor did the federal Constitution require a different result, though the challenged verdict was a serious criminal conviction. Presumably the same result would have obtained had it the conviction entailed the death penalty. Some states, like California, permit evidence as to statements, conduct or events in the jury room that were likely to have improperly influenced the verdict, but no evidence concerning the effect of such statements on the jurors (Cal. Evid. Code 1150).

The Competency of Hypnotically Refreshed Testimony

The use of hypnosis to refresh recollection is controversial because of debate over whether the memories so engendered are genuine, fabricated, or suggested, and then believed by the hypnotic subject and incorporated by him as "genuine", in such a confident way that a jury cannot distinguish genuine from non-genuine. The controversy usually concerns witnesses who have once been hypnotized in an attempt to retrieve lost facts into their memories, who later testify to facts remembered as a result of (or at least after) the hypnosis, presenting them as valid memories; rather than witnesses who are in a hypnotic state on the stand, which is generally not permitted. *Rock v. Arkansas* (S.Ct.1987), held that a state's per se rule excluding all post hypnotic testimony that went beyond what was remembered before the hypnosis, without scrutiny of the particular case for reliability, and without promulgating guidelines concerning when such testimony is and is not reliable, infringed on the constitutional right to testify on her own behalf, of a criminal defendant who had been subjected to such hypnosis. She had been hypnotized and later remembered exculpatory facts that the trial judge prevented her testifying to. This, the Court held, violated her rights. With this exception for criminal defendant-witnesses, some states bar witnesses from testifying to information remembered through or after hypnosis. Others regulate who can perform the hypnosis and the manner of conducting the sessions (compliance with the regulations resulting in admissibility). See, e.g., Cal. Evid. Code 795; *State v. Mack* (Minn.1980). Still others rather freely admit the evidence but allow the fact of hypnosis to be shown and argued to affect the weight. Conceptually, the matter can be viewed as one of the admissibility of purportedly scientific evidence, treated infra, Chapter 7.

II. IMPEACHMENT: SOME GENERAL PRINCIPLES

"Impeachment" encompasses attempts to show lying, mistake, poor memory, inept reporting, obstructions of perception, bias, or any other factor, innocent or not, increasing the likelihood that the facts vary from the witness's story. Impeachment is often distinguished from the more affirmative, principal kind of evidence in a case, called "substantive" evidence.

The constitutional requirement that a criminal defendant be allowed to confront witnesses against him exerts some constraints on a jurisdiction's rules and rulings limiting cross-examination or impeachment by a criminal defendant of prosecution witnesses although reasonable limits are allowed. Thus a defendant had to be allowed to cross-examine an important prosecution witness about the witness' juvenile record (he was on probation) despite a state confidentiality law surrounding such records, where the witness may have been motivated to please authorities and may have been under suspicion in the crime himself. See *Davis v. Alaska* (S.Ct.1974).[1]

Who Can Impeach Whom, and When?: Common Law and F.R.E. 607

The same rules govern your impeachment of your opponent's witnesses, whether that witness is the opposing party herself, or a non-party witness, with a few exceptions.

Usually, there is no difference between rules for impeaching a party who testifies and those for impeaching other witnesses. There are some exceptions, however, particularly concerning the protection of criminal defendants. The fact that a witness is also a party, even in a civil case, may tip the discretionary balance against admissibility, since prejudice against a party weighs heavier.

Impeachment of your opponent's witness may take place through cross-examination of the witness, or (subject to a few exceptions) through the introduction of extrinsic evidence (i.e., through other witnesses, documents, recordings, and the like). Extrinsic evidence may have to wait until it is your turn next to put on your own evidence, although the judge has some discretion.

Extrinsic impeachment is evidence elicited not by cross-examination of the witness-to-be-impeached, but rather through the testimony of independent witnesses (or perhaps tangible evidence such as documents), attacking the credibility of the witness being impeached. There are a few, but only a few, instances in which impeachment is limited to cross-examination of the same witness. The examiner in these situations must "take the

---

1. For further on this, see the constitutional discussion in Chapter 4 under rape shield, Chapter 5 under "Policies Underlying Privileges", and Chapter 8, under "The Criminal Defendant's Right to Cross Examine Without Undue Restriction" and, in that same chapter, "The Due Process and Compulsory Process Clauses".

answer" that the witness gives on cross-examination into the incident. Extrinsic evidence in such cases is prohibited even if the witness denies the wrongdoing and there is extrinsic evidence to the contrary. But "take the answer" does not necessarily mean the first answer: some "badgering" may take place, but the effort must stop with examining the witness.

Under the common law, a party could not impeach a witness he himself called to the stand unless the witness was "adverse" or the testimony both surprised and damaged the party. These restrictions do not apply under the F.R.E. or Uniform Rules, which allow a party to impeach his own witness.

The common law "voucher rule" prevented a party from impeaching its own witness, on the theory that the party was deemed to vouch for the witness' testimony. This rule never reflected reality, because lawyers often had no choice but to call fact witnesses necessary to prove their cases. For example, in criminal cases, prosecutors might have to call friends or family of the defendant if they are the best sources of information about the crime. In civil cases, a plaintiff might have to demonstrate the status of a defendant's employee to hold the employer responsible.

The common law rule was subject to several exceptions. One was where the witness called was the opposite party (or a high officer of a corporate opposite party). Another applied in certain cases of surprise. "Surprise" generally meant that the witness maintained one story before trial, changed it at trial, and gave no advance notice of the change. There also was a requirement of some positive or affirmative damage by the change in testimony. If the witness now disclaimed knowledge of the occurrence in controversy, this change was regarded as failing to give helpful testimony, but not as providing affirmatively damaging testimony. In other words, the surprise rule only applied if the witness still reported the occurrence but now stated what transpired differently, and harmfully to the party.

While the party ordinarily could not impeach its own witness at common law, *contradiction* of the witness was permitted. Thus, a party was permitted to introduce evidence facts relevant to the legal issues in the case that were at variance with the substantive facts reported by another of its own witnesses, but it could not more directly attack the perception, memory, or honesty of the witness. For example, if the witness says the light was green, another eyewitness (or other evidence) could be called to say it was red.

Also, the rule against impeaching one's own witness did not preclude reasonable efforts on direct examination to "refresh the witness's memory" or "awaken the witness's conscience" by reference to former statements.

The F.R.E., the Uniform Rules, and rules patterned after them, allow impeachment of one's own witness as freely as any other witness. See Rule 607. Thus, imagine that the only available bystander witness, having been called by plaintiff, testifies that defendant was speeding, but that plaintiff also was speeding. Plaintiff's counsel may elicit evidence, for example, of the witness's bias, e.g., that the witness is a close friend of defendant's, even though that counsel called the witness as his own to prove the favorable facts that only this witness knows. To the extent that a jurisdiction currently applies any form of the voucher rule to a criminal defendant, it runs the risk of violating a criminal defendant's constitutional rights, including due process, confrontation, and the right to present a defense. See *Chambers v. Mississippi* (S.Ct.1973).

On occasion, F.R.E. 403 may impose on F.R.E. 607 something resembling the former requirements of surprise and affirmative damage, for example where a party calls a witness knowing the witness will be harmful or unhelpful, solely to impeach her with a prior inconsistent statement the party desires to get in substantively (but cannot because of the hearsay rule).

Let us now examine a few common specific kinds of impeachment.

III. PRIOR INCONSISTENT STATEMENTS

Distinguishing Impeachment by Prior Inconsistent Statements From Their Substantive Use

A prior statement of a witness that is inconsistent with the witness' present on-the-stand testimony, usually is proved by testimony of someone who overheard it, by documentary proof, by a recording, or by the witness admitting, upon cross-examination, to having made it. The legitimate purpose is to show inconsistency—that neither the present nor the former statement can be trusted, since the witness "blows hot and cold"—not to prove the fact asserted in the former statement. If offered as evidence that they are true (i.e., as substantive evidence), prior inconsistent statements would in most cases under the traditional system be inadmissible as hearsay. But see F.R.E. 801(d)(1)(A), which makes a limited inroad on this exclusion, allowing *some* of these prior inconsistent statements in substantively; and the Uniform Rules also do so. Even under these codes, *most* prior inconsistent statements are still inadmissible substantively. (Some states, such as California, admit all prior inconsistent statements substantively).

When offered as impeachment, however, prior inconsistent statements are admissible, even under the traditional system, despite some danger of misuse by the jury for the impermissible substantive purpose. Impeachment use is outside the definition of hearsay, because it does not rely on and argue the "truth of the matter asserted" in the prior statement. The theory of the impeachment is that the mere fact that a witness said two different things is relevant, without regard to which statement is true. In other words, you can't trust either statement, because the witness "blows hot and cold".

What if calling the witness is a subterfuge, done only so the jury can hear the impeaching statement, and hopefully use it substantively, though it is not substantively admissible? The purpose is not really to impeach (neutralize) the on-the-stand testimony, because a more effective way to do that would be to refrain from calling the witness, assuming the party knew for sure how the witness would testify beforehand. The danger the jury will make substantive use of the former statement (even though muted by an instruction not to) likely outweighs, in the F.R.E. 403 calculus, any probative value that comes from impeaching some testimony that provides zero information.

Other than this situation, and perhaps a very few others, it is normally considered a sufficient safeguard, that when the prior statement is admitted, the trial judge, if requested, must instruct the jury that the only permissible usage is for impeachment (assuming that the prior statement is not within any exception to or exemption from the hearsay rule). The attorney offering the prior statement will not be permitted to argue its substantive merit to the jury. The jury is instructed that the statement can cast doubt on a witness who tells inconsistent stories, but it cannot be credited or taken as evidence of the facts related in it.[2]

2. Nor can the judge consider it as contributing any affirmative substantive weight in motions for dismissal or directed verdicts and similar peremptory rulings.

Pragmatic Inconsistency Versus Absolute Irreconcilability

To be admissible as impeachment, the prior statement need not be perfectly or absolutely inconsistent (that is, irreconcilable) with the present testimony. It need only *seem or tend* to be somewhat contrary. The real test is whether a reasonable juror might find that it tends somewhat to impeach (unless the danger of unwarranted prejudice, misleading impression, time consumption, or confusion is deemed too great, which is rare). It is thus normally for the jury to decide whether and to what extent the statement is inconsistent, that is, what impeachment weight it has.

Suppose, for example, a collision has taken place between a car and a truck. At trial, a witness testifies for the trucker, stating "The truck was proceeding at 20 m.p.h. [within the speed limit] on the correct side of the road." Suppose, however, that the same witness has made a prior statement: "The truck driver was to blame." This statement is not actually logically inconsistent with the present testimony; the two are reconcilable.[3] Nevertheless, the statement should be admitted as a prior inconsistent statement, because a reasonable juror could find that it was somewhat inconsistent as a practical matter, and thus it has impeachment value.

The example also illustrates another principle: an impeaching statement may be valuable as impeachment evidence despite a violation of the traditional opinion rule, and even though it may be an opinion by a lay

3. For example, maybe the witness thinks the truck driver, being a professional, should have taken extraordinary measures to avoid the other's negligence; or was to blame in other respects than speed or the side of the road he was on; or to blame because, in the circumstances, he should have been going less than the allowed speed or should have swerved to the wrong side of the road temporarily to avoid a hazard. The witness will be given an opportunity to explain the apparent inconsistency.

witness based more on legal conclusions than perceptions. The opinion concern is lifted for prior inconsistent statements offered for impeachment, presumably because the opinion is not offered for its reliability but to show inconsistency. Furthermore, exclusion of the statement would work a total destruction of the evidence rather than the rephrasing that would normally result from banning an opinion of a witness.

Suppose an eye-witness for the defense testifies selectively to one detail of his observation, which detail favors the defendant, then says, "I don't remember anything else." Suppose further that he had given a much more complete and detailed pretrial statement describing his observation of the defendant committing the wrongful act at issue. Though it includes the defendant-favoring detail, this more complete picture would not tend to favor the defendant. Yet the trial statement and the former statement are not logically inconsistent. Nevertheless, it may make sense to allow use of the prior statement to impeach the witness. It may suggest that the claimed forgetfulness is not credible and is motivated by coordination with the defendant.

In federal criminal trials, Rule 26.2 of the Federal Rules of Criminal Procedure provides that each side is entitled to have access to written statements, and reports of statements, of witnesses for the other side that are in the possession of that other side, and that relate to the witness' testimony. This right to access is accorded at the time that the witness testifies (not in advance), that is, after the direct examination. What constitutes a statement or report thereof is defined so as to get at substantially verbatim renditions of what the witness said rather than judgmental notes of the interviewers giving their opinion of what the witness said or work product. The judge is to make a determination whether a prior statement relates to the testimony and may excise certain privileged matter. The primary purpose of this rule is to uncover prior inconsistent statements for impeachment. In civil cases, such information may be discoverable under the Federal Rules of Civil Procedure applicable to discovery.

The Common Law Predicate for a Prior Inconsistent Statement: Queen Caroline's Rule

In traditional jurisdictions, there are elaborate foundational requirements for impeachment by prior inconsistent statements. These are sometimes referred to as the "Rule of the Queen's Case," or "Queen Caroline's Rule," since they were originally imposed during the trial of Queen Caroline in England, which has since abandoned them.

In traditional jurisdictions, as respects a prior oral inconsistent statement, the impeaching attorney must first ask the witness whether (1) the witness made a particular statement (2) to a particular person (3) at a particular time and (4) at a particular place.

Under the common law, this highly specific foundation is a prerequisite to use of a prior oral inconsistent statement. The purpose of the foundation is to furnish the witness with enough information about the former statement so that the witness can recall it. If the witness admits having made the statement, the traditional rule holds that the impeaching attorney cannot press the matter further: no extrinsic evidence of the prior inconsistent statement can be adduced.

These rules create many complexities. For example, if the witness admits having made the statement but offers an explanation for the apparent inconsistency (for example, that the former statement was a joke or was merely repeated as having been stated by another), the explanation will be permitted, for what the jury thinks it is worth. The impeaching attorney may even be prevented from offering any rebuttal of the explanation, at least with extrinsic evidence, although considerable leeway is given the trial judge on this. Similarly, under the common law, the explanation ordinarily must be made *by the witness* during *cross-examination,* if it is to be made at all; but again there is some leeway given the judge to allow extrinsic explanation. So, too, is there judicial discretion concerning the allowability of extrinsic rebuttal of an allowed extrinsic explanation.

If the witness denies having made the statement, or claims not to remember, the attorney may, but need not ever, prove up the statement and its making with extrinsic evidence such as a witness who overheard it. Normally, to so prove the statement, the attorney must wait until it is his or her turn to put on witnesses and evidence, although there is some judicial discretion about this. The attorney will not be allowed to prove the statement unless the witness has first been given the opportunity just described, the required foundation, during cross-examination.[4]

There is opportunity here for dishonest practice by unscrupulous attorneys. On cross-examination the impeaching attorney could ask about a prior inconsistent statement knowing it was never made, and having planted the seed of doubt in the jury's mind, can fail to follow up the witness' denial with any extrinsic proof. There is very little remedy for this, other than the jury's sophistication (or evaluation of counsel's behavior during trial).

Occasionally attorneys have been judicially requested on motion and out of the hearing of the jury, to show that they had at least some reason to believe there may have been a prior inconsistent statement. Occasionally the question put to the witness has been ordered strick-

---

4. Sometimes it will be given during some other examination of the witness the attorney is conducting, so long as it is before any attempt to introduce the statement.

en, or, more effectively, the jury has been instructed that there is no basis for the inference. Even more rarely some action has been taken against the attorney personally, a mistrial declared, or a case dismissed or judgment entered. Bad faith may have to be shown in order to obtain a remedy. When there is no good faith basis, a question by counsel to the witness being impeached, asking if a statement of a very specific tenor was made at a precisely specified time and place, is more dishonorable than a more general inquiry as to whether any contrary statements have been made. As to the latter, the attorney may somewhat justifiably say "I am not suggesting there was such a statement; I was just asking."

The common law procedures for introduction described in this section, anomalous though they may be, are in imprecise ways the product of policies we see at work in other areas of evidence law. It is fair and efficient to allow a witness to confront an inconsistency in advance. The foundation on cross-examination, combined with the regulation of extrinsic proof, eliminates surprise, economically provides witnesses a chance to defend themselves, conveniently supplies the jury with information for evaluating the impeachment, and minimizes the time spent on the matter, the misleading quality of the evidence, and juror confusion and distraction into collateral issues. Everything is handled before a mountain is made of a molehill. On the other hand, maybe it is indeed a mountain and it should not be allowed to look like a molehill. It depends upon whether the witness is truly mendacious or innocently mistaken.

Suppose the prior inconsistent statement was written rather than oral? It would seem that it should make no difference to the application of the foregoing rules. In general this is so, with only the following modification.

It is usually held, in traditional jurisdictions, that the foundation requirement can be satisfied in the

case of a prior written statement only by permitting the witness to examine the writing before any reference can be made to it.

The impeaching attorney, by giving the witness the statement, will obviously have warned the witness sufficiently to enable the witness to possibly recall. The cross-examiner thus need not put the specific questions reminding of time, place, and substance, required in the case of a prior oral statement. By way of foundation, then, the attorney merely presents the document (or the pertinent portion of it) to the witness, and asks whether the witness made the statement.

If the witness admits making the statement, the attorney will read or have the witness read the statement to the jury. Procedurally, the document will have been marked for identification (before presented to the witness) and perhaps moved into evidence (after it is acknowledged by the witness) before reading aloud. The attorney will be required to show the document to opposing counsel, but not significantly before the point at which it is to be shown to the witness (usually it will be nearly simultaneous).

Sometimes reading aloud, physically circulating the exhibit, and taking it into deliberations are deemed redundant, and some of these steps may be disallowed. In some courts, exhibits such as documents may not be admitted during cross-examination, and the physical introduction (if allowed) must wait until the proponent's turn to put on his or her case. In civil cases, pretrial rules may require marking in advance, perhaps before trial, although many courts exclude documents being introduced solely for impeachment or rebuttal from their scope.

In some courts the requirement that the writing must be shown to the witness is applied in such a fashion as to require that it be shown before any line of questioning leading to the inconsistent statement can be undertaken, rather than merely as a precondition to admittance of the writing itself. Thus, one very effective cross-examination technique is foreclosed: getting an unsuspecting witness to repeat on cross, in detail, the story told on direct, and to deny any possibility of error, before the attorney springs the writing. This "misconstruction" of the foundation requirement is also sometimes found where the prior statement is oral.

Another usually permitted use than impeachment or substantive use, of a witness's prior inconsistent statement, should be mentioned. The attorney on cross-examination might refer to the former statement ostensibly only to "refresh the witness's memory" or "awaken the witness's conscience," to get the witness to change the present story.

The Federal Predicate for Prior Inconsistent Statements: F.R.E. 613

The F.R.E. radically alter the foundation required for prior statements by abolishing any requirement of confronting the witness with the oral or written statement in advance. F.R.E. 613 instead requires only that, at some point during trial, the witness must be afforded an opportunity to explain or deny the statement, whether before or after introduction of the statement. The attorney supporting the witness must be able at some point to examine the witness about the statement and is entitled to see or hear it before doing so.

This is F.R.E. 613. An important aspect of the rule is that the witness's chance to deny or explain may come *after* the extrinsic evidence, for example by re-calling the witness back to the stand later. The reasons for the change are several. While the traditional rule was said to prevent attorneys from exaggerating an inconsistency that has an innocent explanation, it also sometimes warned untruthful witnesses early enough to prevent the true dimension of their mendacity from being effectively demonstrated. In addition, the new rule allows several witnesses co-operating in a falsehood to be examined before alerting them (perhaps in the cross-examination of the first of them) to a prior inconsistent statement exploding their story.

Several questions arise, however, under the new rule. What if the witness testifies, cross-examination is waived, and the witness then leaves the jurisdiction, or dies, and the attorney impeaching the witness then wishes to introduce a prior inconsistent statement? The rule says it cannot be done if the witness is not afforded an opportunity either before or after, to explain or deny it, or if the opposing party is unable to examine the witness about it. But the judge is expressly given discretion to waive this requirement if the interests of justice demand.

Presumably the rule's requirement that the opposing counsel be given the prior statement applies only at the point where the impeaching attorney actually begins inquiry into the statement itself, or attempts to introduce the statement, not, for example, when the cross-examination first gets into a line of questioning that appears to be leading to the statement. The entitlement of an opposing attorney to disclosure of the statement seems also to apply to prior statements used substantively, as well.

Constitutional Considerations

Prior inconsistent statements of criminal defendants obtained through unconstitutional means (such as illegal searches or seizures, violation of *Miranda* rights or the Sixth Amendment, etc.), while constitutionally inadmissible substantively, and therefore inadmissible in the prosecution's case-in-chief, may be admissible as im-

peachment after the defendant testifies factually inconsistently, on the grounds that the constitutional protection should not enable perjury. See the U.S. Supreme
Court decisions in *Harris v. New York* (S.Ct.1971), *Michigan v. Harvey* (S.Ct.1990), and *United States v. Havens*
(S.Ct.1980). Also constitutionally permitted is impeachment by pre-arrest silence (a kind of prior inconsistent
conduct, also embraced by the present subject) which
occurred in non-custodial situations, most typically the
defendant's failure to come forward with a defense later
asserted at trial (might this kind of evidence be allowed
even if defendant does not testify?). See *Jenkins v.
Anderson* (S.Ct.1980). However, the defendant's silence
cannot be introduced if it follows a *Miranda* warning.
See *Doyle v. Ohio* (S.Ct.1976). After receiving warnings
telling him he has the constitutional right to remain
silent, a suspect may take the advice, and thus the
silence shows nothing and serves only to undermine the
constitutional protection. For these reasons admissibility
would violate due process.

IV. IMPEACHMENT BY
CONTRADICTION

This is the second of the most frequent lines of attack
on credibility that we will take up (the first being prior
inconsistent statements). "Contradiction" as a term
should not be used to cover impeachment by prior inconsistent statements, discussed above. Instead, it consists
of independent evidence that contradicts the facts reported in the testimony of the witness. For example, if the
witness, being an eyewitness, says the northbound light
was green in an auto intersection collision, and a later
witness, also being an eyewitness, says it was red, the
latter contradicts the former. Technically, it is not really
impeachment, but substantive evidence, at least in most

cases; but it incidentally also impeaches the witness who has testified to the contrary, and thus is treated here.

Contradiction occurs wherever there is a difference in different witnesses' testimony to substantive facts (or between a witness and some piece of tangible evidence). Contradiction of one's opponent's version of operative facts not only proves one's own version, but also constitutes impeachment by contradiction.

Contradiction refers to the use of evidence of a *fact incompatible with or in conflict with* a fact reported by another witness. As in the case of prior inconsistent statements, absolute irreconcilability is not required, and the conflict may be in the circumstantial inferences to be drawn. The attempt under this line of attack is to show that some *fact* is different than reported by the witness. It is *not* to show that conflicting *statements* about some underlying fact have been made by the witness. That is within the topic of prior inconsistent statements, just completed.

If the attempt is to show that, although the witness states the killer was wearing a red sweater, the killer was in fact wearing a blue sweater, and the latter fact is proven by the testimony of other witnesses who also saw the killing, we are dealing with contradiction. If the attempt is to show that although the witness now says the killer was wearing a red sweater, the same witness earlier said the killer was wearing a blue sweater, we are dealing with impeachment by prior inconsistent statement.

Evidence contradicting the witness is admissible only if it would have been independently admissible for a substantive purpose, regardless of the contradiction. There are a few exceptions to this, as where a witness testifies to a fact important to his or another's credibility. (See Collateral Matter Rule, immediately infra.) If the evidence overcomes this hurdle, its proponent will then be permitted to argue both its impeachment and its substantive value to the jury. The impeachment aspect of the evidence may permit its introduction during rebuttal where otherwise it might be confined to the case-in-chief.

Constitutional Considerations

On occasion in a criminal case, an item of evidence specifically contradicting an exculpatory fact testified to by the criminal defendant, may be subject to some constitutional rule that prohibits its introduction by the prosecution as substantive evidence and thus prohibits it in the prosecution's case-in-chief before the defendant testifies. For example, a witness or piece of tangible evidence may have been obtained pursuant to a violation of defendant's constitutional search and seizure rights (Fourth Amendment). Can it come in as impeachment after the defendant testifies?

In a number of cases the Supreme Court has answered this question "Yes: the illegal evidence may come in to impeach; the constitutional protection should not provide a license for defendant to commit perjury." See, e.g., *Walder v. United States* (S.Ct.1954).

But if the prosecution *invites* the defendant (say by clever cross-examination) to make the impeachable statement, in order to use this principle that constitutionally impermissible evidence may be used to impeach, the prosecution will be deemed to be trying to make an end-run around the constitutional prohibition, and the impeaching evidence will not be permitted. But see *United States v. Havens* (S.Ct.1980), where the Supreme Court permitted the prosecution to introduce evidence (seized in violation of the Fourth Amendment) that was contrary to a statement the government prodded the defendant to make in cross examination, but only because the prodding question was reasonably suggested by the witness' direct examination testimony.

But *James v. Illinois* (S.Ct.1990), shows there are limits. It prohibits contradiction of a defense *witness* by evidence illegally seized from the *defendant*.

V. THE "COLLATERAL MATTER" RULE: A LIMIT ON IMPEACHMENT BY PRIOR INCONSISTENT STATEMENT AND CONTRADICTION

The inconsistency sought to be demonstrated by prior inconsistent statement or contradiction must not be on a "collateral matter." A "collateral matter" is something that is not of real importance to the litigation.

If a witness to the speed of a car in which he was a passenger, in an automobile collision case, irrelevantly relates that he happened to be wearing a red sweater on the day before the accident, he cannot be impeached by proof that he had formerly said he was wearing a blue sweater. While in some slight way this kind of impeachment indicates something about the witness's credibility as to matters of detail, the additional light it sheds is not worth the investment of time and energy and the distraction into collateral issues. This is called the "collateral matter" rule. It also sometimes is called the "nitpick" doctrine, because it prohibits impeachment on inconsequential matters. It applies not only to prohibit impeachment by prior inconsistent statement, but also to prohibit contradiction, i.e., direct evidence other than the witness' prior statement, that the fact, e.g., the sweater color, is to the contrary.

The rule is more rigorously applied to bar extrinsic evidence than to bar cross-examination of the witness, because of the greater investment of time and resources, and greater sidetracking, that extrinsic evidence entails. Nevertheless, the rule applies to both.

The red-sweater example above is, of course, an easy case. Other fact situations present closer questions. For example, if the witness had identified the car or light by color, his possible mistake concerning the color of his own sweater would be more important and the question of whether it was "collateral" would be closer. His mistake might suggest some inability to spot or remember colors. Nor would his possible mistake concerning the color of his sweater likely be deemed collateral if he had testified he remembers an important date in the litigation because it was the day he bought and wore home his new red sweater. Similarly, if it were the color of the *driver's* sweater rather than his own that he was testifying to (where identity of the driver is disputed), an inconsistency or contradiction on the color of the driver's sweater would not be on a collateral matter because the driver's sweater color is independently significant to the substantive case, not merely because of the inconsistency or contradiction.

The collateral matter rule may be more stringently administered where the fact to be attacked was elicited by the impeaching party herself upon cross-examination.

If a statement by the witness is damaging, though irrelevant, and the damaged party has not solicited the statement, fairness may dictate that refutation by specific contradiction or prior inconsistent statement be allowed (because "the door has been opened"), even though one could argue that objection to the original statement (or a motion to strike it, if it came in before time to object) should be the exclusive remedy. It may make a difference whether the statement was made on direct or cross-examination.

The collateral matter rule set forth in this section is not codified in the F.R.E. However, it arises out of general principles like those expressed in F.R.E. 403 (relevance and its counterweights).

The reasons for the rule against showing inconsistencies or contradictions regarding a collateral fact concern the relative importance of the fact and the need to avoid protraction and misleading the fact-finder. These policies suggest certain exceptions to the rule, such as the following.[5]

(1) The "Linchpin" Doctrine

Where a witness purports to have been an eyewitness in a position to accurately report the occurrence, the opponent may attempt to show the witness is mistaken about some fact concerning which he should not be mistaken were he an eyewitness. Thus, if the witness has testified to witnessing an assault and states there was an enormous crowd at the scene, the opponent will be allowed to produce witnesses to the fact that the place was virtually deserted, though their testimony might be irrelevant but for the contradiction. A prior inconsistent statement on this matter also should be allowed. This principle is sometimes called the "linchpin" doctrine: collateral impeachment is not improper if the fact is so important that it "pulls out the linchpin" from the witness's story.

(2) Where the Inconsistency Relates to Matters That Are Themselves Impeaching, Rather Than Substantive

Where the witness to be impeached testifies to a fact that, while not relevant on any substantive issue, is relevant to the credibility of this or another witness, the opponent may rebut that fact (if sufficiently important) even though his evidence would not be relevant on any substantive issue. Thus, if the witness, W, expressly denies having made a former inconsistent statement, or

5. Perhaps technically these are not exceptions, but situations where the matter is not truly "collateral" or unimportant.

denies a certain bias or connection with the case (e.g., that W is related to the party for whom W is testifying), the opponent may try to show the facts to be otherwise— by, for example, adducing extrinsic witnesses or documents (or eliciting admissions in cross-examination) to prove that W *is* related to the party for whom W is testifying, or *has* made the inconsistent statement denied. In such a case the impeachment is not only by specific contradiction, but by prior inconsistent statement or bias as well. Prior statements on these matters might also be allowed.

VI. BIAS

The Admissibility of Bias Under the Common Law and Rule 403

Evidence of conscious or unconscious bias for or against a side, witness, party, or counsel, reflects on credibility. Bias includes, among other things, financial or other interest, improper or even proper influence, relationship, friendship, or indeed anything that might affect motive. The admissibility of impeaching evidence possibly evincing bias is broad.

Permissible impeachment under this heading, generally speaking, encompasses anything which raises a suspicion that there could be a motive to fabricate or, consciously or unconsciously, to "slant" matters. Nothing as marked as bribery is required. Included are showings of family relationship; past or present employment; litigation involving the witness and a relevant person or a similar issue; common or antagonistic political or religious or social affiliation; quarrels; prior settlement of a claim between the witness and the party for whom the witness is testifying; feelings for or against the victim of the crime in issue or a party or a class or category of person or organization; prior testimony for the same or similar party or of the same kind; pending, possible, or dismissed charges against a witness for the prosecution or a plea bargain between the witness and the prosecution, whether specifically referencing an obligation to testify or co-operate in the present case or not; psychological or ideological predilections; beliefs; and many, many more indications of possible bias or interest.

F.R.E. 610 states that beliefs on matters of religion can no longer be shown as affecting credibility. Would this Rule prevent showing that a witness against a party was a member of a religious group that believed what the party stood for was evil? The question is difficult to answer. Arguably, it is bias, rather than mere belief, that is shown by such evidence. In some criminal cases, the Constitution might require allowance of such impeachment, if offered by the accused. What about showing that a witness is a member of a religious group that is a party to the litigation, for whom the witness is testifying? Does Rule 610 only prohibit a type of character inference?

Bias can be shown by compensation or monetary expectation directly or indirectly connected to the testimony or to the particular outcome testified for. One form of expected compensation may be the fame, media exposure, book and movie deals, and the like, that would ensue if a witness varnishes a high profile story well. Witnesses who seem to be magnifying the sensationalism of the facts or injecting big names into the story, in high profile cases, are often accused of this.

As to direct monetary payments, lay witness fees are generally prescribed by law. They usually include an allowance for travel and a daily or hourly wage or fee. They may or may not be linked to what the witness actually normally earns. Usually they are not. The party calling the witness pays. Amounts paid in excess of those prescribed may or may not be illegal. It may not be effective to show for impeachment that an ordinary witness is receiving only the prescribed fee, but if payment beyond the minimum is made, the fact should be admissible even if the payment is lawful. A witness who volunteers to testify may be suspect as having some ulterior motive, such as fame, a belief in a particular cause, a vendetta against one party, or a friendship or kinship with the other

An expert witness, testifying in the capacity of an expert, is entitled to additional compensation, but sometimes this is the case only if the expert must prepare specially. Expert fees may be unregulated (i.e., the subject of private bargaining) or they may be regulated in that they must be "normal" or "reasonable" charges, or regulated in some other way. Expert fees generally may be shown to the jury by way of impeachment. A counter-explanation that the fees are comparable to the expert's normal fee rates in the field for non-court work, and explaining the hours spent preparing, and what the law allows, may also be permitted. Paradoxically, an expert witness's failure to take compensation may indicate a bias, because it supports an inference of favoritism toward the championed party or cause. Perhaps, for example, she is the family doctor, hoping to get some money for the poor family impoverished by the personal injuries he is testifying about. Family doctors testify in lots of cases, and showing that the person is the family doctor can be a double edged sword. Even if the jury finds it impeaching, of course the testimony is still permissible. This is the usual rule concerning impeachment generally.

A fee contingent on the outcome of the litigation is typically not legally or ethically permissible. And the potential for impeachment where such an arrangement exists is obvious.

Bias is governed by no specific rule in the F.R.E. and its progeny. The traditional law as outlined above is continued by virtue of the general provisions of Rule 403 (relevance and its counterweights), which contain the policies that originally gave rise to this body of law. The

Supreme Court explored this issue under the F.R.E. in *United States v. Abel* (S.Ct.1984), which holds that bias evidence is relevant evidence because it affects the probability of a fact that is of consequence to the litigation: the fact of credibility of a witness, and thus the fact to which the witness addressed himself. The jury has historically been able to assess most evidence which might bear on the accuracy and truth of a witness' testimony. Therefore, evidence of bias of a witness is generally admissible under the F.R.E., just as it generally was at common law, unless it runs afoul of some specific rule like Rule 403 (the balancing of relevancy and its counterweights such as prejudice).

In *Abel* the prosecution was allowed to show that the defendant and a defense witness were members of a prison gang whose tenets required its members to lie, cheat, steal and kill to protect each other. The Court found that the attributes of the gang bore directly not only on the fact of bias, but also on its source and strength. For this reason, the Court upheld the trial judge's ruling that the evidence withstood a Rule 403 challenge. In an attempt to reduce any undue prejudice, the trial court had ordered that the jury not be told that the gang's name was the Aryan Brotherhood, and the court also offered to give a limiting instruction against general character assassination of the witness and defendant. Nevertheless, there would still, of course, be considerable residual danger of prejudice. But not enough it was ruled, to require exclusion of the evidence. Defense attorneys must consider carefully whether to call witnesses whose impeachment for bias can implicate bad acts of the defendant.

Are There Foundation Requirements for Bias Evidence?

Some courts require a foundation, of the type described above as traditional in the case of prior inconsistent statements, for the introduction of two forms of bias impeachment: conduct (or facts) evincing bias, and prior statements of the witness evincing bias. Others do so only for the latter form, and some do so for neither.

(a) Out-of-Court Conduct or Facts Indicating Bias

Suppose as impeaching attorney you wish to show via your own witnesses or documents (i.e., extrinsic evidence) that a witness for the other side is the brother of the party for whom he is testifying, or has had a quarrel with your client. Under one view you need give the witness no warning on cross-examination: You need not ask if the matters you wish to prove are true, or even refer to them. In short, you need lay no *foundation* in the sense used in connection with impeachment by prior inconsistent statement at common law, above. You may prove directly by the extrinsic evidence (when it is next your turn to put on your own evidence), without any prelude on cross-examination, the quarrel or the kinship. If you do ask about the matter on cross-examination and the witness denies it, your extrinsic evidence will tend to show the witness to be not only biased, but to have testified falsely as well. That is, you will have impeached both by bias and by specific contradiction. If you do ask on cross-examination, and the witness admits it, principles of redundancy may prevent your extrinsic evidence, depending on what exactly he admits.

On the other hand, some courts impose a foundation requirement that the witness must be confronted with the fact on cross-examination, and if the witness admits the fact (whether or not conceding bias) the extrinsic evidence may not be introduced. This approach reduces the impeacher's options, and it may reduce the impeaching effect. It is similar, in other words, to the common law predicate for prior inconsistent statements under

Queen Caroline's rule. It is probably by confusion with that rule that this rule got started, although the policy reasons recommending for and against it are quite similar.

Thus, in these jurisdictions, the witness may act strategically to admit the bias-suggesting fact in response to your question on cross-examination. This admission may reduce the effect. Worse, the witness may admit but explain it away or claim to be impartial anyway. Worse still (from your viewpoint), these courts, to avoid unnecessary protraction and distraction, may bind you by an answer admitting the essence, i.e., they may prevent your introducing your extrinsic evidence.

(b) Prior Out-of-Court Statements of the Witness Evidencing Bias

Not all courts draw a distinction between this and the other extrinsic evidence of bias described in (a) immediately above. They either do or do not impose the foundation requirement on both alike, without distinction. Those that do draw a distinction do so in order to impose on prior biased statements, but not on biased fact or conduct, the foundation requirement and the ban on extrinsic evidence if the witness admits the bias. A prior statement showing bias, falling under this subsection (b), might be, "I hate the defendant," or, "I had a quarrel with the defendant," or, "I am employed by X [the party for whom the witness is testifying]," with the declaration in each case having been made by the witness before the present testimony.

If the witness, having made this statement, makes or is induced to make a conflicting statement on the stand, and then the earlier statement is revealed, we would have impeachment by prior inconsistent statement as well as by a showing of bias. A court that would not otherwise require a foundation might apply the rules for prior inconsistent statements in such a case. The impeaching attorney, by characterizing the evidence more in terms of bias than in terms of inconsistent statement, may minimize the chance of this happening. But, as noted, many courts apply the foundation requirement to prior biased statements, regardless. The fact that a foundation requirement is much more frequently found for prior biased statement than for biased fact or conduct, is attributable to the similarity of prior biased statement to prior inconsistent statement.

The status of a foundation requirement for bias impeachment is uncertain under the F.R.E. In theory, perhaps the foundation could be imposed by virtue of Rule 403 on either or both forms of bias impeachment, since the foundation supposedly was designed to satisfy factors like those listed in that rule. Rule 613 addresses the foundation in the case of prior inconsistent statements, but it makes no specific mention of foundation for bias, although some language of 613(a) seems possibly to apply to it. The foundation requirement in the case of bias originated first in connection with biased statements and probably is a confusion with prior inconsistent statements. This factor supports the argument that it should be abandoned under the F.R.E.

VII.   CHARACTER–RELATED IMPEACHMENT (TREATED IN CHAPTER 4): REPUTATION, OPINION, CONVICTIONS AND PRIOR BAD ACTS

This line of attack—attacking the witness' propensity or character for credibility—is covered in Chapter 4, Section IX, dealing with the subject of character or propensity evidence generally. In summary, and within certain limitations, such an attack may consist of show-ing (1) opinion about, or reputation for, the witness's general character for non-veracity; (2) specific instances of un-convicted-for conduct evincing a general character for non-veracity; and (3) certain criminal convictions to like effect.

VIII. OTHER KINDS OF IMPEACHMENT

There are other forms of impeachment. For most of them, there are no special rules. Imagination and the judge's discretion under F.R.E. 403 or its state analogue, are often the only limit on what can be done in a particular case by way of attacking a witness' credibility, provided that the attacking evidence does not transgress the normal rules of evidence such as the hearsay rule or privileges.

Thus, any showing of normal or abnormal mental, perceptual, memory, or reportorial limitations of the witness, is a candidate. Obstructions of the witness' view of the matter she allegedly saw—such as intervening structures, rain, nightfall, lack of corrective lenses, lack of proper positioning or location to observe, distance, etc.—are also usually fair game.

Qualifications of expert witnesses may also be ques-tioned. At some point this kind of attack may be so strong as to amount to more than just impeachment of credibility (impeachment and credibility being merely matters of weight for the jury). It may go further and disqualify the witness from testifying as an expert on the matter. Chapter 7, infra, discusses qualifications re-quired of experts in more detail, and also discusses a special form of impeachment of experts: attacks based on treatises or articles that vary from what the expert witness has testified to. This form of impeachment has some special rules.

For most forms of impeachment of a witness' credibility, the impeachment probably cannot rise to the level of rendering a witness inadmissible (or retroactively stricken). This is subject to some possible exceptions: attacks on qualifications of experts under the circumstances noted above; showings totally negating that the witness understood the obligation to tell the truth imposed by the oath or affirmation (F.R.E. 603); showings totally and unequivocally negating that the witness had personal firsthand knowledge (required by F.R.E. 602); in some jurisdictions, impeachment of any kind that is so strong, unequivocal, and credible, that no juror could reasonably believe the witness; and, in some jurisdictions, impeachment which weakens the witness' testimony enough to cause the Rule 403 balance to tip to exclude the witness. Notice the last two say "in some jurisdictions." Many other courts believe that credibility is always subject to reasonable dispute and thus always for the jury to decide. They may extend this logic to say the Rule 403 calculus should always be done based on the assumption the witness is truthful. The 403 calculus would then only gauge the *inferences* from the fact testified to.

As a very rough rule of thumb, a court usually will permit a witness to testify, upon either no showing, or a *prima facie* showing, by the offeror, of acceptability on the matters discussed in this section, depending on the situation—frequently regardless of what is shown in opposition, at the time or later, by the opponent. These showings in opposition will most often (although not always) be regarded as merely something for the jury to consider with the prima *facie* showing, in assessing the weight of the witness' testimony.

As a general principle, witnesses are usually assumed to be telling the truth, with no showing required or even allowed, that they are, until attacked.

IX. SUPPORT OR REHABILITATION
OF CREDIBILITY

General Limits on Rehabilitation of Credibility: A Counterpart Response to the Attack

The reverse of each of the main impeachment lines of attack on credibility can be conceived of. These would be called "support," "enhancement," "bolstering," or "rehabilitation" of credibility. As a very rough rule of thumb, no showings specifically to increase a witness's personal individual credibility (as opposed to corroborating the facts the witness reports) are allowed unless there has been an attack on it first.

Painting with a broad brush, we can generalize and say that normally these lines of support will be allowed, if at all, only to the extent that a *precisely opposite counterpart* has been advanced in an impeachment attack against the witness's credibility, although the trial judge is accorded considerable leeway. Thus, prior inconsistent statements will not license the use of evidence of good general character for veracity. They may, however, at least in some jurisdictions, permit proof of prior consistent statements, the counterpart type of rehabilitation, corresponding to the type of attack.

This principle may not go so far as to hold that impeachment by a showing of poor general character for veracity can *only* be met by an opposing showing *proved in the same manner* (i.e., instances of conduct met by instances of conduct, rather than reputation). While it could be argued that any allegation that the witness has not reported the facts correctly is an attack on general propensity for truthfulness, suggesting bad general character for veracity, and thus should allow a showing supporting good general character for veracity, this ordinarily is not the case.

General notions of courtroom economy and efficiency (as codified, for example, in F.R.E. 403) are responsible for all these restrictions.

Prior Consistent Statements

In some jurisdictions, the use of prior inconsistent statements licenses the use of prior consistent statements for the purpose of repairing credibility. However, in most jurisdictions, the counterpart rule expressed above is departed from, and prior consistent statements are allowed if and only if they tend to rebut an express or implied allegation (however proved, demonstrated or insinuated) of recent fabrication, motive to fabricate, or other improper influence or motive. At common law, this meant that the consistent statement must have been uttered before the motive to falsify allegedly arose.

This is the approach taken by the Supreme Court in *Tome v. United States* (S.Ct.1995), interpreting *substantive* use of prior consistent statements under F.R.E. 801(d)(1)(B). Substantive use was not permitted under the common law, but the Court imports the common law requirements for credibility rehabilitation into the new substantive use. In other words, *Tome,* interpreting language in the rule requiring that the prior consistent statement be "offered to rebut an express or implied charge ... of recent fabrication or improper influence or motive", holds that only pre-motive statements can be used.

Under the substantive-use rule (construed in *Tome*), which establishes a new hearsay exemption for prior consistent statements of a witness not recognized at common law, the statements, of course, would be used as proof of the matters they assert, rather than rehabilitation of credibility. The credibility use, however, would also persist under the F.R.E., from the common law.

Although there is no specific provision preserving this credibility use in the F.R.E., Rules 401 through 403 make all relevant evidence (including relevant to credibility) admissible unless outweighed by other factors. Do the majority common law restrictions on use to rebuild credibility, confining us to pre-motive statements, persist under the F.R.E., when the evidence is offered on credibility? Probably so, since they were imported by the F.R.E. into the substantive use. But the only governing rules on the credibility use are Rules 401 through 403, which are very general and do not refer specifically to this matter. Conceivably the common law restriction is an interpretation of the 403 factors (also part of the common law) of judicial economy and efficiency, but not all common law courts agreed on this interpretation.

Tome does not address the question whether a post-motive consistent statement can be offered solely to repair credibility, rather than as substantive evidence. On the one hand, the most relevant consistent statements for credibility purposes are those that pre-date the alleged motive to falsify, since their use is to rebut fabrication. This argument supports limiting rehabilitation to pre-motive statements. On the other hand, vehement and repeated statements consistent with the present testimony may have at least some relevance to repairing credibility, even when they first were uttered after the alleged motive to falsify. Some states do not limit admission to pre-motive statements. For example, in California, a consistent statement can also be offered if it was made earlier than an inconsistent statement admitted to impeach the witness' credibility.

Another question concerns what precisely will be interpreted as a charge of recent fabrication or improper influence or motive. Does the mere fact that a witness has an interest in the litigation (or may even be a party), or has been cross-examined, or has been impeached under any of the forms of impeachment, mean that there is an implied allegation of fabrication or improper motive of the kind we have just mentioned? Or must the attack be a specific one, of actual fabrication, influence, or motive, arising on a certain date? It is clear that an attack may be an implied one, but how precisely implied is subject to conflicting decisions. The governing principle, here, seems to be Rule 403, but it is not much help.

Other Permissible Support of Credibility

We have implied in this section that the only support of a witness that is allowed is "rehabilitation" after attack. This concept may be relaxed, however, to permit a cursory showing of *lack of bias* (impartiality) when a witness is first introduced. In addition, showings of a witness's background, profession, residence, positioning, access to the facts, etc., are customarily allowed, though they may reflect well on credibility. As for specific contradiction, it cannot be literally subject to the rule described in this section, because each refutation of a fact by specific contradiction also supports credibility. Similarly, although a party cannot generally impeach its own witness on direct examination simply as an excuse for rehabilitation, prosecutors are often allowed to bolster witnesses who are testifying subject to a plea bargain or immunity agreement, by bringing out in advance of any attack, the fact of the agreement, which may include a showing that it requires "truthful testimony." The rationale for this exception is sometimes said to be that if the jurors hear nothing on direct about there being a quid pro quo for the testimony, they might think, unfairly, that the government was playing fast-and-loose with them by hiding bad facts, if they were to hear it first on cross-examination. Similar reasoning allows advance "pulling of the fangs" of other kinds of impeachment, as well.

Complainants in rape cases are also permitted to testify in direct testimony that they protested, reported, or complained shortly after the attack, despite the absence of any impeachment. This doctrine, called "fresh complaint", is based on the premise that if a woman had actually been assaulted, she would immediately raise a hue and cry. Because the absence of an immediate complaint might be seen as damaging her credibility, she is entitled to head off the jurors' skepticism by informing them that she had acted as a "real" victim would. This doctrine can be criticized as reinforcing the myth that genuine victims are never silent nor do they ever delay in revealing such attacks. However, even societal attitudes which may be misinformed can affect whether complaints are believed. In some jurisdictions, "fresh complaint" resembles a hearsay exception which includes the details of the accusation. In others it is treated as a type of prior consistent statement which is not dependent on the expected impeachment.

One entirely distinguishable notion concerns support of credibility, after attack, by means of direct refutation of the specific facts alleged by way of attack. Within realistic limits of time and similar practical considerations under Rule 403, refutation of the truth of *specific impeaching facts or testimony* is usually permitted. Thus, it may be shown that the particular conviction was not in fact had, the particular prior inconsistent statement not made, or a particular familial relation evidencing bias does not in fact exist.

The F.R.E. have very little to say on the matters dealt with in this section, except for the following provisions of Rule 608. Thus these matters are left largely to the broad policies of Rule 403 (relevancy and its counterweights) that may be expected to continue the general outline of existing decisional law. The relevant provisions of Rule 608 (which essentially bear out the main principles of this section to the extent they are addressed) are:

Rule 608(a)(2): "[Opinion or reputation] evidence of truthful character is admissible only after the character of the witness for truthfulness has been attacked by opinion or reputation evidence or otherwise."

Rule 608(b): "Specific instances of the conduct of a witness, for the purpose of ... supporting the witness' character for truthfulness ... may not be proved by extrinsic evidence [but] may, ... in the discretion of the court, if probative of truthfulness ... be inquired into on cross-examination of the witness ... concerning the witness' character for truthfulness...."

Note that the term "*cross*-examination," as used in this last excerpt (608(b)), makes little sense and is probably just bad drafting.

Unlike the provision quoted from 608(a) above, this provision from 608(b) does not expressly continue traditional law to the effect that ordinarily there must first be an attack on credibility before a counterpart effort to support it is undertaken. Probably the requirement continues pursuant to Rule 403 and notions of judicial economy and efficiency.

Does the quoted language from either provision permit bringing out the fact that a witness "passed" a polygraph test? Presumably this is not the type of opinion or conduct directed at character-propensity that is the province of Rule 608, and the matter would be governed by other rules such as Rule 403 and Article VII.

X. DIRECT AND CROSS EXAM-
INATION: PROCEDURE,
METHODS, LIMITS

Method of Examination of Witnesses: Leading and Non–Leading Questions and Related Matters: F.R.E. 611

Attorneys' questions to witnesses normally must call for yes-no type or short answers. More extended narrative answers are permitted to the extent that they help develop the testimony. Leading questions, which are questions that suggest the answers (1) are ordinarily improper on direct examination, with exceptions for background, hostile or adverse witnesses, or where necessary to develop testimony, and (2) are ordinarily proper on cross-examination except in the relatively rare case where the witness is friendly to the examiner.

Many jurisdictions give the judge discretion to permit an extended narrative, on the theory that getting the witness' own story may sometimes be more important than giving the examining attorney exact control of the presentation or giving the opposing attorney precise warning when objectionable material is about to be elicited, the rationales for requiring short specific questioning.

The law recognizes that leading questions can sometimes serve a valid function, even on direct examination, in refreshing memory or directing the witness' attention. For example, forgetful, aged, and child witnesses may be questioned in a leading manner, within limits. In the case of witnesses hostile or adverse to the examiner (which occasionally happens on direct examination and normally but not inevitably happens on cross-examination), the danger that leading questions present—that the witness will consciously or unconsciously acquiesce—is diminished, the need for forcing an evasive witness to answer the examiner's questions greater, and leading questions are thus allowed.

When a party calls to the stand the opposite party as a witness, though the examination may in name be direct examination, in spirit it is cross-examination, and leading will be allowed. Conversely, when that same witness is handed over by that "direct" examiner to the other side for "cross" examination, leading normally will not be permitted.

This law concerning leading questions is codified largely from the common law by F.R.E. 611(c), except that witnesses associated with adverse parties may automatically be regarded as hostile without demonstrating actual hostility.

It should be noted that there are common-law restrictions not only on leading questions, but upon those deemed "argumentative," "misleading," or "compound" (multi-faceted), as well. The F.R.E. treat these matters by reposing power in the judge to supervise witness examination, and judges are indeed restricting these kinds of questions.

F.R.E. 611(a) gives the judge immense discretion to control the mode and order of interrogating witnesses and presenting evidence in addition to the judge's power under Rule 403. Rule 611(a) specifically exhorts the judge to take reasonable measures to promote effectiveness and efficiency in ascertaining the truth and to protect witnesses from harassment or undue embarrassment.

Among other things, this provision is often relied upon by prosecutors when their witness is a child; or an adult complainant in a case involving a sexual crime. Some judges exhibit flexibility in dealing with child witnesses, changing physical arrangements, dress or speech patterns. In criminal cases, a federal statute and some state practice permit young children to be accompanied by adult companions. In some instances the child may sit on the companion's lap or hold her hand while testifying, although the judge must be careful not to appear to lend credit to the child's veracity or allow the child to be influenced. Some special arrangements may violate constitutional protections of the defendant. See discussion of screens and video hook-ups for children testifying in, e.g., child molestation cases, infra, Chapter 8, Section V.

The Scope of Cross–Examination: Common Law and F.R.E. 611

There are two views as to the permissible scope of cross-examination: (1) the "restrictive" rule, which confines the cross-examiner to matters within the scope of the direct examination, and (2) the "wide open" rule, which allows any material issue in the case to be explored (consonant with the other rules of evidence).

The two rules ("restrictive" and "wide open") express a difference of view as to the time at which a party ought to be able to present new substantive points favoring its own case out of the mouth of a witness who has been put on originally against it. The wide open rule allows new points at the time of cross-examination, while the restrictive rule is based on the view that new points should be raised by calling that witness when it is the party's own turn to call witnesses.

Actually, the two views ("restrictive" and "wide open") may be more similar in practice than in statement. For one thing, there is great flexibility about how generally or precisely a judge defines the "subjects" that were dealt with on direct, under the restrictive rule. Does a direct examination of defendant driver about the color of the light facing him confine the cross examiner to questions about the light, or did the direct exam about the light really open the general subject of negligence/care of the driver, which would license cross-exam questions about speed, inspection of tires, etc., assuming they are otherwise relevant?

Another factor making the restrictive rule sometimes not so restrictive in practice is the uncertainty a judge may feel as to what may develop from a line of cross-examination. This makes *some* judges reluctant to limit cross-examination, even in restrictive-view jurisdictions. These judges often feel that something related to the direct examination may ultimately develop from an initially seemingly unrelated cross-examination. The cross-examiner should not have to blunt the force of his or her cross-examination by revealing in advance where it is going even if they know. (Experienced trial lawyers often counsel younger lawyers to desist from cross-examining in an unpredictable situation. But this does not often represent what is in fact done.)

Buttressing these judges' reluctance to limit cross-examination is the thought that cross-examination is an important guarantee.

F.R.E. 611(b) adopts the restrictive rule, but allows the judge to make exceptions, in which event the witness during that time is treated as the cross-examiner's own witness in that, apparently, leading questions will only be allowed if necessary. Convenience of witnesses and trial efficiencies often dictate that the judge exercise discretion to permit the testimony without re-calling the witness.

Cross-examination directed at impeachment is not limited by these rules relating to the scope of cross-examination.

Most cases hold that, upon cross-examination of a criminal-accused who has voluntarily taken the stand in his or her own behalf, the privilege against self-

incrimination permits inquiry into any substantive matter, regardless of whether it was opened up on direct. The waiver of privilege accomplished by taking the stand is that broad. If inquiry is barred concerning matters not opened up by the direct-exam, it will be because of a jurisdiction's general restrictive rule regarding the proper scope of any witness's cross-examination, not because of the privilege.

Under the prevalent view, by taking the stand, an accused waives the privilege to turn away any substantive questions, but not to turn away impeachment questions that might incriminate him in other crimes for which there is still a danger of conviction. Cf. F.R.E. 608(b), final paragraph. Nor does the accused waive the right to refuse to take the stand again later.

In combination with the privilege, however, restrictive rules about scope of cross may impose an unforeseen limit. In jurisdictions having the restrictive cross-examination rule, a prosecutor may be forever foreclosed from bringing out matters which could be brought out in wide-open jurisdictions. For, where the accused takes the stand, the restrictive rule prevents the prosecutor from cross-examining him regarding substantive matters not previously opened up on direct, and the privilege against self-incrimination prevents the prosecutor from later calling him to the stand where he could testify to those same matters. So, unlike the case of the ordinary witness, the restrictive rule does not merely displace the question from cross-examination to a later point in trial.

XI. WITNESS PREPARATION AND REFRESHING OF RECOLLECTION

There are almost no formal limits on bona fide efforts to refresh a prospective witness' recollection before the witness takes the witness stand, short of coaching to tell an untruth. A document used to re-

**fresh on the witness stand, however, must be neces-
sary for recollection and disclosed to the other side. A
number of jurisdictions extend required disclosure to
documents that were used before trial, notwithstanding work-product and other privileges, in some. Access
of a witness to other testimony in the case (which can
also affect recollection) may also be regulated by sequestration.**

Witness Preparation and Sequestration: F.R.E. 615

In most jurisdictions there is a procedure called "sequestration," often informally termed "being under The
Rule," whereby witnesses may be ordered not to attend
and listen to the other testimony in the case. See F.R.E.
615 requiring the judge to enter a sequestration order
upon request and permitting it on the judge's own motion. Questions have arisen regarding whether this bars
trial witnesses from reading trial transcripts, attending
or reading depositions, listening to oral reports of testimony, discussing testimony, or watching televised portions of the trial. The judge's order pursuant to the
sequestration rule may clarify the scope of the witness
sequestration in the particular case.

The rule exempts from sequestration witnesses who
are (1) parties, (2) the designated representative of an
organization that is a party, which in criminal cases is
usually the lead investigator, or (3) essential persons,
such as an expert needed at counsel table to aid the
attorney. Questions have arisen concerning whether
there are limits on the number of witnesses a party may
get in under one or more of these exemptions in a given
case.

A fourth exemption was added for persons authorized
by statute to be present. This resulted from the Oklahoma City bombing trial. The families of the deceased
victims wanted to view the trial, and give "victim impact" statements at the death-penalty sentencing phase

to be held subsequently before the same jury if guilt were found. The trial judge, upheld by the Court of Appeals, held they could not do both, because of sequestration. Congress then legislated specifically, with retroactive effect, that such witnesses in such cases, could view the trial without being disabled from testifying.

Refreshing Recollection by Means of Documents: F.R.E. 612

What may a witness consult *on the stand* to refresh recollection? If a document is truly going to be confined to the purpose of stimulating memory—that is, the attorney putting on the witness does not intend to present the document (or have it read out loud) as evidence of facts, but rather intends that the witness's testimony giving current recollection will be the evidence—then the matter is governed by the rules for refreshing memory, rather than the stricter rules for the hearsay exception for recorded recollection, to be discussed below. The doctrine of refreshing memory is referred to as "Present Memory Refreshed", as opposed to the hearsay exception, which is referred to as "Past Recollection Recorded".

Under Present Memory Refreshed, opposing counsel will ordinarily be granted the right to examine a document used or proposed to be used to refresh memory though in some jurisdictions this right does not extend to a document presented to the witness only before taking the stand. For documents used on the stand to refresh, most jurisdictions accord an absolute right to disclosure, and the otherwise privileged or protected status of the document, if any, is normally no impediment, by the most prevalent view in federal and state courts. See F.R.E. 612 (absolute right if used on the stand; privilege not expressly mentioned) The F.R.E. have not codified the doctrine of Present Memory Refreshed as such, but have codified disclosure requirements for the doctrine in Rule 612; the doctrine itself is thus continued from the common law by implication of this Rule and Rule 611(a).

F.R.E. 612 entrusts the disclosure of a document so used *before* taking the stand, to the discretion of the judge, thereby taking a position between the two extremes that are found (no disclosure and disclosure of right). Federal cases are not entirely agreed as to the extent of waiver of privilege or similar protection (for example, attorney-client privilege or work product protection) that may surround some such documents. The use of the document to prepare the witness has most frequently been found to constitute waiver of privilege, but sometimes not. Factual distinctions concerning whose privilege it is to waive may play a role. Perhaps the best rule is that of cases that take an in-between position: that privilege (or the like) is one of the factors for the judge to consider in exercising discretion concerning disclosure under the rule.

Some decisions display considerable reluctance to order production or to find waiver, with respect to documents used before taking the stand. *Bogosian v. Gulf Oil Corp.* (3d Cir.1984) indicates that simply showing work product to a witness does not trigger disclosure or operate as a waiver. This attitude may require counsel to isolate and identify (perhaps through detailed questioning of the witness) the particular document he feels was used to prompt recollection, rather than ask for all documents the witness might have seen. Cf. *Sporck v. Peil* (3d Cir.1985).

At the other extreme, a number of decisions seem eager to order production and find waiver. *Berkey Photo, Inc. v. Eastman Kodak Co.* (S.D.N.Y.1977) warns all attorneys that (1) work product and other privileges (e.g. attorney-client privilege) surrounding a document so used will probably be held waived; (2) any documents used to prepare expert or lay witnesses, not just those employed to refresh memory, are likely to be subjected to disclosure; and (3) preparation of witnesses for depositions is within the rule. The Federal Rules of Civil Procedure probably trump the Rules of Evidence when, for example, an expert witness is "prepped" with an allegedly work-product-protected document either for deposition or trial and such document is sought by the other side in pre-trial discovery. Relatively recent reformulations of the applicable procedure rules have made it harder, but not impossible, to claim such documents are work-product-protected, and the cases are still somewhat divided.

Rule 612 is subject to the "Jencks Act", 18 U.S.C.A. 3500, which may prevent disclosure of a very narrow range of documents: certain non-verbatim reports of previous statements of government witnesses, in criminal cases. Verbatim ones may only be revealed at the time of the testimony.

For documents used purely to refresh memory, authenticating, entering into evidence, and compliance with the best evidence or original document rule will not be required. Reading of the document aloud, circulating it to the jury, and sending it into the jury room during deliberations, at the proponent's behest, is normally forbidden, at least if the document has not been challenged in some way. The opponent may be allowed to read the document aloud, introduce it into evidence, circulate it to the jury, and/or send it to the jury room during deliberations, if necessary to call attention to something important about the relationship of the document to the testimony, such as a disparity between the document and the supposedly memory-refreshed testimony. This is to cast doubt on credibility and is not an offer of the document as proof of the facts stated. Typically, at its first appearance, the item will be marked for identification in order to be able to refer to it for the record.

If the document is not used as a memory refresher, but instead is put forth or read *as evidence of the facts it relates,* that is, used substantively, it will usually be hearsay and must come within an exception to the hearsay rule. One exception to the hearsay rule that frequently becomes confused with refreshing present memory is the exception for *Past Recollection Recorded.* See F.R.E. 803(5). When used substantively in this fashion, the writing must also be authenticated and is typically subject to the best evidence or original documents rule.

The requirements to use the document as Past Recollection Recorded are as follows (though the order in which they are stated varies):

(1) The witness must have had firsthand perception of the fact the document recounts and is offered to prove;

(2) The document must have been made or adopted by the witness at a time very near the perception, or, under the F.R.E. and its progeny, at any time while it was fresh in his memory;

(3) The witness must express present confidence that the document correctly recorded the fact; and

(4) The recorded fact must no longer be remembered (or, under the F.R.E. and its progeny, fully remembered) by the witness even after consulting the document.[6]

See F.R.E. 803(5). In most jurisdictions, as in federal courts, these enumerated requirements apply only where the document is used as Past Recollection Recorded.

---

6. This requirement in effect means that usually the document must be attempted to be used to *refresh the recollection* of the witness first. If it fails to do so, then it will be attempted to be qualified as *past recollection recorded.*

In contrast, *the refreshing of memory* on or off the stand is left largely unregulated, except for the obligation to disclose, and, if the document is used on the stand, the witness must testify before he so uses it, to the fact that he can't remember without first looking at it—that is, that the document is needed to, will, and then does, refresh his memory. But a document used solely to refresh memory does not have to be written by the witness nor meet any of the above enumerated requirements, as long as the judge believes from the witness that it has the capacity to and does refresh the witness' recollection. The law feels that, memory being a peculiar and contingent thing, it may be renewed by all sorts of strange things: as one commentator put it, a piece of string or sealing wax may do it.

CHAPTER 7

OPINIONS, EXPERTS, AND SCIENTIFIC EVIDENCE

I. ORDINARY WITNESSES: OPINION AND FIRSTHAND KNOWLEDGE

Lay Knowledge and Lay Opinion Under the Common Law

The common law required that lay witnesses (1) must speak only of what they know firsthand, and (2) may testify only as to facts (i.e. they may not give opinions, inferences, or conclusions).

The first rule, requiring personal knowledge, was designed to minimize error and keep sources, relevant to evaluation, clear. The second, the rule against "opinions" (also known as "inferences" or "conclusions"), was designed to put the tribunal as close to the witness's primary component perceptions as practicable in order to minimize error and maximize the jury's role in fact-finding. The meaning of the key terms, "fact" and "opinion," often was unclear.

Even at common law, the rule against opinions was flexible. It was relaxed where articulation of more primary perceptions would be difficult for the witness, protracted, or otherwise impractical, or where insistence on strict compliance would result in more loss than gain of valuable evidence, or where the danger was small or obvious. Furthermore, at least the more modern courts recognized that what is fact and what is opinion or conclusion is relative and determined by practicality.

Thus, for example, speed was commonly allowed to be estimated, even sometimes in such terms as "fast" or "slow." Witnesses were allowed to say that a person was (or appeared to be) "angry," "kidding," "dying," "strong," "sober," or "drunk." Other examples included things like "it was a sturdy fence" or "the produce was rotten."

The theory behind these holdings, however, was that it must somehow be *necessary* to admit the conclusion. If there was no way individual component primary facts could be practicably articulated separate from their collective integration into a conclusion, the witness was allowed to give the conclusion, which was viewed as a necessary "shorthand rendition of the facts". This was sometimes called the "collective facts" exception to the rule against opinions.

Once primary perceptions were recounted, articulation of less primary ones ("conclusions," "inferences," or "opinions," by comparison) was considered superfluous, time consuming, and possibly even misleading or dangerous. In theory it was forbidden, although courts strayed from this restrictive approach where little prejudice ensued.

Lay Knowledge and Opinion Under F.R.E. 602 and 701: The "Perception" and "Helpfulness" Tests

The rule requiring firsthand (personal) knowledge in the case of lay witness testimony has been preserved by F.R.E. 602.

However, F.R.E. 701 has liberalized the introduction of lay opinions. Lay opinions are now allowed whenever they would be (1) "helpful," provided that they are also (2) "rationally based" on (3) the witness's "perception." The last requirement means that the witness must have firsthand (personal) knowledge of the matter being spoken about, a requirement that applies whether the lay witness is giving opinions or facts, as Rule 602 makes clear. The "rationally based" criterion means the opinion must not be too great a leap from what the witness personally observed or perceived.

The "helpfulness" test effectively abolishes at least the more restrictive versions of the common-law "collective facts rule." It substitutes, instead, a broader, more flexible, more receptive approach, favoring admissibility.

Firsthand (Personal) Knowledge, Opinion: Relationships to Preliminary Facts Rule, Hearsay Rule

Firsthand (personal) knowledge as a pre-requisite to admissibility, is decided by the standard of Rule 104(b) (how preliminary facts related to relevancy are determined), which admits the evidence if a rational juror could make a finding that the witness has personal knowledge. The testimony of the witness herself is usually sufficient to establish this.

The requirement of firsthand (personal) knowledge should not be confused with the hearsay rule. If a witness states "Jack shot Mary" but knows this only from others, she violates the firsthand (personal) knowledge rule. If the same witness in the same circumstances testifies instead that "Joe told me Jack shot Mary," the firsthand knowledge rule is not violated (assuming the witness has firsthand knowledge of Joe's statement), but the hearsay rule may be violated.

There is considerable dispute over whether the firsthand knowledge and the opinion rules should apply not only to restrict on-the-stand witnesses, but also to restrict declarants whose out-of-court statements may be recounted in court pursuant to an exception to the hearsay rule. Sometimes the answer depends upon which exception or exemption is involved, with out-of-court admissions of a party often being excused from compliance on the grounds that, unlike the case of in-court testimony, this valuable evidence cannot be rephrased and would be lost if the rules were applied; and anyway how can parties say that their own adverse statements were not founded on thorough, careful grounds? (Should this apply to admissions by a party's agent or co-conspirator? Admissions that are not known to be adverse when made?) Similar reasoning is on occasion applied to other exceptions or exemptions. Of course, lack of firsthand knowledge, and presence of opinion, could affect the weight of such evidence in the eyes of the jury, if the evidence is received.

Lay Testimony: Very Broad Opinions

The common law, as we have seen, relaxed the ban on lay opinions in cases of necessity; but even then, it refused to receive very broad opinions which the court felt sounded too much in terminology like an ultimate issue the fact-finder must decide, e.g. "the driver of the Ford was negligent". With one minor exception not relevant here, this so-called rule against "ultimate opinions" (a slippery concept to define) was abolished by F.R.E. 704 for both lay witnesses and expert witnesses (the latter normally given more latitude to express opinions under both the common law and the F.R.E.). Rule 704 is discussed infra in more detail under expert testimony. The thought behind abolishing the ban on ultimate opinions was that any broad opinions that truly are useless or harmful on the facts of a particular case could still be excluded by application of the requirement, appearing in both the lay and the expert rules, that the testimony must be "helpful" or "of assistance" to the fact finder, and by Rule 403.

Despite the common-law's professed stringent standards (as discussed in several of the above sections), there were special areas where these standards were administered with great "flexibility". Thus, lay testimony in terms of "sanity" or "mental competence," and, less often, "insanity" or "lack of mental competence," was occasionally permitted although this took some bending of the standards. Sometimes it was allowed even without supporting data being given by the witness. This could occur even where an ultimate issue for the factfinder in the case was phrased in closely similar terms. In this vein, California lets "intimate acquaintances" testify about sanity. See Cal. Evid. Code 870.

Rule 701 was recently amended to prohibit litigants from evading requirements applied only to experts, such as establishing their qualifications and special reliability and disclosing their identity and the substance of their testimony prior to trial. Frequently, lawyers offering individuals testifying about specialized matters would claim that they were lay witnesses who merely had lots of experience in the matter, not experts. The Rule now clarifies that those who testify to "scientific, technical or other specialized knowledge" must meet the criteria of Rule 702 relating to experts. Still, courts seem to permit evasions: *Tampa Bay Shipbuilding & Repair Co. v. Cedar Shipping Co., Ltd.* (11th Cir.2003) held that testimony offered by the plaintiff's employees as to whether charges were fair and reasonable was admissible under the amended lay opinion rule. This issue also arises concerning police officers and employees of agencies like the Drug Enforcement Administration who may have factual knowledge of the particular criminal case investigation, but interpret it in light of their experience. See, e.g., *United States v. Peoples* (8th Cir.2001), where the admission of an FBI agent's testimony about the hidden meaning of words uttered in a taped recorded conversation was reversible error because the agent, who had not been involved in the conversation, had not been qualified as an expert witness.

II. EXPERT TESTIMONY

Today's increasingly complex technical issues are often beyond the ability of ordinary jurors to resolve on the facts merely as reported by lay witnesses. Consequently, scarcely a trial goes by without some kind of expert testimony—sociologists, economists, safety experts, human factors engineers, employment discrimination experts, psychologists, and more—some good and some bad.

Can "junk science" and other unwarranted opinions of "experts," heavily relied upon by jurors, be prevented without at the same time unduly restricting "good" expert testimony genuinely needed to guide the jurors? Errors either way can have costly consequences not only for the litigants, but for society at large in cases such as modern mass liability litigation.

When should a problem with the evidence be a matter of admissibility and when merely a matter of weight? When can the jury be counted on to be sophisticated enough to handle it? When can we count on the tools of the adversary system such as cross-examination, argument, counter-evidence, and judicial instructions, to get the jury into a position to do a satisfactory job? While these are central questions in all of evidence law, they are exacerbated in the expert testimony area, where we have subjects unfamiliar to jurors—particularly (but not only) when the expert gets into matters of science.

Over time, the law has experimented with various different answers, as the following sections demonstrate.

Introduction: Experts: Special Latitude Under Both Common Law and F.R.E.

Both at common law and under the F.R.E., where the court feels that expert opinions involving special expertise will aid (or sufficiently aid) the fact-finder, a

qualified "expert witness" may be allowed to testify to them, even without having the kind of firsthand knowledge required of lay witnesses.

Thus, an expert is given a special dispensation from both the rule requiring firsthand knowledge and the rule against opinions. To the extent an expert testifies only to facts within his personal knowledge, he is, in legal effect, testifying as a lay witness.

Kinds of Experts. It might be useful at the outset to mention a few miscellaneous examples of expert testimony, to get our bearings. Who is an "expert", and what matters are appropriate for or even require expert testimony, are areas in which the law accords the trial judge broad discretion, although some law has developed in particular jurisdictions for recurring situations.

Experts are allowed on a wide range of issues at trial, and we won't attempt to do more than scratch the surface here. A police officer may be an expert in examining automobile tracks and deducing speed, force, or angle of impact. A ranch hand may be expert on the adequacy of a fence for containing cattle. Physicians are among the most frequent experts, although disputes may develop about whether the doctor must be qualified in a particular specialty to be qualified to testify.

Regarding experts generally, if the minimum qualifications to be regarded as "expert" by the court are met, shortcomings in qualifications are matters of weight and not admissibility. The minimum level is highly discretionary with the trial judge.

Common kinds of expert testimony include medical testimony on the cause, extensiveness, and duration of physical impairment in personal injury cases; professional testimony on the standard of care and its application in professional malpractice cases involving a wide variety of professions; economists' testimony on issues in antitrust cases or projecting future economic damages in a variety of tort, contract, or fraud cases; actuarial testimony on life expectancy and projected income to assess damages in wrongful death cases; testimony of experienced business-people or accountants on the behavior, operation, or value of businesses or the causes for or facts of rises or declines in stock value; real estate appraisers' evaluations of property in cases involving compensated governmental "takings" of private property; psychiatric or psychological diagnoses of mental condition in various civil and criminal cases; engineering or trade testimony concerning manufacturing defects or the adequacy of safety measures, warnings, or product designs; epidemiological and toxicological testimony concerning the causes of cancer or birth defects in toxic exposure or pharmaceutical cases; ballistics, blood, and other forensic identification testimony (relating to, e.g., fingerprints, hair, handwriting, etc.); and statistical testimony about the likelihood of a random match between a criminal defendant's DNA and DNA obtained from the crime scene (sometimes as low as one in a billion).

More controversial opinions being debated in courts today include those of, e.g., psychologists about the unreliability of eyewitness testimony; psychiatrists about the truthfulness of particular witnesses; polygraph operators about lying (unquestionably inadmissible in the past, and still normally excluded); "voiceprint" experts on voice matches; DNA experts concerning the results of new varieties of DNA tests; and various experts concerning drug courier profiles or psychological syndromes relating to abused children, victims suffering rape-trauma, and other forms of post-traumatic stress.

General Sources of Experts' Information. An expert witness's testimony giving the basis of her opinion will often involve hearsay: facts that the expert has read or heard in her education, in her experience, and from consultation with others. A doctor (and in particular, a psychiatrist) will in addition rely on much the patient has told her (and will rely in a way which frequently will involve giving credence to what was said). A hearsay objection might be raised to the giving of the opinion itself, or to recounting the basis. To suppress the opinion on hearsay grounds in every case where the opinion involved some hearsay would put an end to the whole institution of expert testimony. To suppress the recounting of hearsay constituents of the basis could deprive the jury of a valuable means to evaluate the testimony. A decision has to be made as to whether the hearsay aspects of the testimony are too prevalent or render the evidence too unreliable. How the law does this and on what standard is the subject of discussion later herein.

It is possible that expert testimony utilizing hearsay could run afoul of the constitutional confrontation clause when offered against the criminal accused. This is because hearsay involves un-cross-examinable sources to the expert. See, e.g., *State v. Wicker* (Wash.App. Div. 1, 1992), which held that the confrontation clause required that unavailability be shown prior to admitting evidence that a non-testifying technician had verified the testifying fingerprint expert's analysis. *United States v. Dukagjini* (2d Cir.2003) recently noted that an expert witness may utilize hearsay evidence while reliably applying expertise to that hearsay evidence, but may not utilize hearsay in any other aspect of his testimony. Constitutional confrontation is discussed infra, in Chapter 8, Section V.

Who May Introduce Experts? Both sides of a case will be accorded equal opportunity to produce experts if there is an issue for experts, but the court has discretion to limit the number and duration. It also has power at common law, and under some formalized provisions adopted in many jurisdictions (e.g., F.R.E. 706), to appoint, in an individual case, its own expert or experts, who can be expected to carry great weight with juries that are told, as they may be, of the special judicial appointment (in addition to the usual indication by the judge to the jury of a witness' expert status). Normally judges' experts will not impact on the parties' right to also adduce experts of their own choosing, except perhaps where there would be unnecessary redundancy.

Compensation, Etc. Expert consultants and witnesses normally are paid by the party using them. The expert's time in a deposition may be paid for by the party taking the deposition. Experts are normally paid the going rate in their field for their time, or indeed, any other amount that is negotiated. There may be some regulation of the rate in particular jurisdictions, and of course the subject of charges can be brought up before the jury as a matter affecting weight.

The extent to which an *unwilling* expert can be *compelled* to give testimony by subpoena for the trial is hotly contested. Facts within the expert's firsthand knowledge can be compelled more readily than matters requiring extra work or opinions on facts or on hypotheticals. As to facts already personally known, the expert is generally entitled only to the extraordinarily meager witness fee provided under law for ordinary witnesses. Some extra reasonable compensation would be required in the other cases, if compulsion is allowed at all.

It may be necessary for a party to examine an unretained expert, even one who technically is a stranger to the litigation, when the unretained expert's opinions form the basis for the opposing expert's testimony at trial. Because a testifying expert can (at least under the modern view) form an opinion relying on the work of others, an examination of the research or conclusions of the "stranger" expert could be critical at trial. It may be unfair to allow the stranger to remain silent in such circumstances. On the other hand, the need for the stranger expert's information is not really his doing. He may even have refused lucrative offers to become involved in the litigation.

Although experts generally have no privilege that prohibits compelling their testimony, judges are sensitive to the time and money demands imposed by such requests. The party serving the subpoena may be required to pay for the witness's time at an expert rate. Yet, the research may have been undertaken with a promise of confidentiality made to sources. Only occasionally does a jurisdiction have a privilege covering research sources. Judges of course can quash subpoenas as well as place conditions on their enforcement where special hardship is shown, or the information sought is marginal. See Federal Rule of Civil Procedure 45(3)(B)(ii).

Added complexities arise where the expert sought to be compelled to testify was employed by the other side as an expert consultant in the very case at hand.

Regulation of Experts Under the Common Law: Mainly Procedural: A Necessary Step to Understanding the F.R.E.

Expert opinion testimony at common law could be elicited in the form of (a) an opinion expressly based on examination and observation of the person or matter in controversy, or experiment conducted; or (b) an opinion on a "hypothetical" state of facts presented to the expert witness by counsel in open court, if the hypothetical was based on facts the jury could reasonably find on the evidence presented in the case (or pledged to be subsequently presented).

Subject to the trial judge's discretion, counsel examining the expert would choose one or the other format, or a mixture. This choice of formats is preserved, and augmented with more choices, under the F.R.E., as will be discussed later.

Where the expert testifies in the latter fashion (i.e., choice (b), the hypothetical format), no firsthand observation is necessary. Theoretically the jury is competent to decide ultimately how far the real facts differ from the hypothetical and what effect this should have on the value of the opinion. Experts, other evidence, and arguments of counsel, from the side opposing the opinion, help the jury in this regard.

Some later common law jurisdictions afforded an additional choice of format: the hypothetical could be in terms of evidence in the case, e.g., "Doctor, do you have an opinion based on the evidence of plaintiff in this case [or the testimony of W, X, etc., or certain documents]?", assuming that it is first established that the expert has heard or has access to the evidence referred to. The Federal Rules preserve this choice, too, with further augmentation.

Because of the latitude accorded experts in comparison to lay witnesses—a latitude often employed with mesmerizing effect on the jury—the common law tended to require a high degree of formal qualifications to be an expert; to restrict expert testimony to areas totally beyond lay knowledge; and to be stingy about the materials or information (both the facts associated with the case and the sources of expert knowledge) upon which expert witnesses relied in giving their opinion testimony—frequently disapproving of reliance on material or information that was not otherwise admitted or admissible.

It can easily be seen, however, that these are *procedural* requirements: regulations of the expert's *qualifications*, the *facial topics* of his testimony, the *general type* of material upon which he relied, and the *format* of his presentation. The common law felt that judges had inadequate understanding of the expert's specialty area to independently police the *reliability* of the basis and reasoning process by which experts reached their conclusions. Consequently, more substantive requirements were eschewed. It was believed that if the procedural requirements were met, the adversary system (cross-examination, counter-experts, opening and closing argument, etc.) would result in appropriate juror evaluation of the testimony.

Exception: Scientific Expert Testimony: The Frye Test. In one class of expert testimony, however, the common law had a heightened concern about reliability and the jury's tendency to get "snowed": expert testimony that presented novel science such as the results of lie detectors and voiceprints in criminal cases. (In some courts the special concern extended to science beyond novel science and to cases beyond criminal cases.)

Courts accordingly felt that more than procedural requirements were needed here. But even so there was still judicial humility, perhaps even heightened, about a judge's competence to independently police for good science. So, although an additional non-procedural, substantive requirement was imposed—the so-called *Frye* test— it was a requirement that deferred to prevailing thinking and practices in the scientific field, and did not impose an independent judicial reliability assessment.

This test, still followed in a number of states today but not the federal courts, was articulated in *Frye v. United States* (D.C.Cir.1923), a case which rejected an early form of lie detector evidence offered on behalf of a criminal defendant. The test requires that "the [principle or discovery] from which the deduction is made must be sufficiently established to have gained *general acceptance* in the field in which it belongs." Although *Frye* was recently supplanted in Federal Courts by the *Daubert* test (infra), general acceptance is still a factor (although no longer the only factor) under the *Daubert* test.

Frye and *Daubert* are more extensively discussed infra.

A. REFORM OF EXPERTS UNDER THE F.R.E.: PHASE ONE: LIBERALIZATION REGARDING PROCEDURES

It gradually came to be felt that the procedural safe-guards of the common law, described above, while per-haps helping to insure the integrity of expert evidence, also kept out much expert testimony that could be help-ful—particularly in an increasingly complex modern world where new areas of expertise were constantly being developed to cope with the complexity. So the Federal Rules of Evidence stepped in, in 1975, and lib-eralized the procedural rules, leaving in place for the moment (under the majority view) the substantive *Frye* test for scientific evidence but generally continuing to eschew any substantive standards or guidelines for non-scientific expert evidence.

Liberalized Procedural Treatment of Experts Un-der the F.R.E.: Rules 702–705 as Initially Enact-ed (and Still Largely in Place Today)

The F.R.E. liberalized the common-law expert testi-mony procedural rules in a number of ways in order to increase or facilitate admissibility. These liberali-zations were: (1) expansion of the class of experts (lowering required qualifications); (2) expansion of subjects or topics appropriate for expert testimony (beyond those of which the jury would be entirely ig-norant); (3) reform of the hypothetical question for-mat; (4) licensing of certain types of inadmissible evi-dence in the basis for an expert's opinion; (5) optional omission of the opinion's basis from the direct exami-

nation; and (6) abolition of the rule against ultimate opinions.

As always, there had been a number of decisions in the late common law that had foreshadowed the F.R.E. positions.

Let us focus more closely on each of the F.R.E.'s procedural liberalizations:

Procedural Liberalization #(1): The F.R.E. expanded who will be considered experts: the issue of "qualifications". Under F.R.E. 702 the category of qualified experts includes not just professionals, scientists, and people with specialized university degrees, but also expressly includes "skilled" witnesses, such as bankers, farmers, police officers, business people, and home owners, testifying in their particular area of experience. All that is required is "specialized knowledge" of a kind that will "assist" the fact-finder, acquired in any fashion: by "knowledge, skill, experience, training, or education." In other words, the expertise can be acquired not just at universities, but also in the "school of hard knocks."

As a result, for example, Drug Enforcement Administration agents have frequently testified about narcotics jargon and the typical modus operandi of drug conspiracies. Other law enforcement specialists have been allowed to describe features of and behavior of gangs and crime families, assuming other rules of evidence have been complied with. Such practical-skilled witnesses abound not just in law enforcement areas.

The trial judge under this liberalization is given wide latitude to decide if the expert is qualified. The focus is on whether the expert has the background to give the particular opinion. Thus, a burglar can be an expert on whether an item is used as a burglar tool, as can a police officer who investigates burglaries.

By-and-large, judges have not set the qualifications bar very high. It is not clear yet whether the relatively new substantive provisions treated under "Phase Three" in-fra, known as the *Daubert/Kumho* amendments, will eventually indirectly elevate in practice the qualifications required of expert witnesses. Technically, those amend-ments are directed to the substance of the expert's testimony itself, rather than her qualifications.

How an expert is qualified. Typically, on qualifications, all that is required is that the expert run through her credentials at the beginning of her direct examination, or introduce a list of written credentials. Frequently a mix of both is done. Credentials are relevant to both weight and admissibility and thus are before judge and jury. Qualification to testify as an expert in a matter may be contested, which is signaled by an objection. The objec-tion may be to the whole testimony; or a particular topic within it that seems to outstrip the qualifications the expert has presented. The opponent of the expert may object when it becomes clear what exactly the testimony proposes to address.[1] If it is known in advance, the objection can be made when the witness is called to the stand, or even before trial. The question will be thrashed out before the judge.

A judge may or may not reveal to the jury that she has found the witness to be admissible as an expert. A judge's determination that a witness is an expert is of significance solely upon the question of admissibility. So,

1. This opponent may be permitted to interrupt the direct examina-tion of the expert to ask the witness a few questions in aid of a potential qualifications objection; but it is confined to that purpose. The questions may attempt to clarify the witness' qualifications or deter-mine expected areas of testimony to see if the witness is qualified in them, qualifications being relative to testimony. This procedure may take place out of the hearing of the jury, and is known as "voir dire", a phrase having other meanings in trials as well, such as the questioning of prospective jurors.

in strict logic, the jurors ought not to be told of the determination. After hearing the witness' credentials for themselves, they should make up their own mind as to how qualified they think the witness is, for purposes of determining how much weight the expert's testimony deserves, without a boost from the judge. The practice of most judges, however, is to declare before the jury that a witness is being received as an expert on such-and-such subject.

Procedural Liberalization #(2): The F.R.E. expanded the subjects or topics that are proper for expert testimony. Under one strict common law view, an area is proper for expert testimony only if it is "totally beyond lay ken." If lay people (jurors) could be expected to know anything about it, the expert is forbidden to testify: she would be "invading the province of the jury." Thus, under a strict application, a fire chief might be prevented from testifying as to likely causes of a house or grass fire on the theory that lay people have at least some knowledge of this subject.

The test under F.R.E. 702, instead, is that an expert may testify in any area where her specialized knowledge would "assist" the trier-of-fact—a very broad, liberal, highly discretionary test. Presumably the fire chief has at least something to add to what the jury knows about likely causes of house or grass fires.

The "assist" language is widely viewed as procedural, that is, as addressing the facial logical connection of what the expert is saying or concluding, to the issues in the lawsuit that the jury or judge must decide. In other words, it is not addressed to whether what the expert is saying or concluding is reliably founded. It thus appears unaffected by the recently added provisions policing such reliability (see "Phase Three" infra).

Procedural Liberalization #(3): The F.R.E. expanded the examiner's options about the way in which experts testify: format. F.R.E. 703 and 705 make it clear that expert testimony need not be presented in the stilted format of the in-court hypothetical question, although that format is still permitted. The in-court hypothetical question normally takes something like the following form: "Now, assuming, doctor, that a patient comes to you with such-and-such and so-and-so, and has a history of such-and-such and so-and-so, and has such-and-such complaints, limitations of movement, and pain, and exhibits X, Y, and Z, and examination or tests reveal this-and-that, do you have an opinion, doctor, as to the cause [or permanence, etc.] of the condition?" "Yes, I do." "What is that opinion?" These hypothetical questions can run for a half-hour or more. Sometimes they have lasted a full afternoon. Lawyers are fond of building into their hypotheticals every conceivable favorable fact, using the opportunity to make early argument and to propagandize the jury, rather than waiting for summation at the end of the case, which is the only time such argument can properly be made. Often the expert has already formed an opinion and the recitation of the hypothetical is mere formalism.

Under F.R.E. 703 and 705 there are several alternative formats to the traditional, open-court hypothetical question (which is not prohibited), although they are not all expressly enumerated: (a) a set of facts given to the expert before trial, say in the privacy of the lawyer's office, with the expert then testifying on the stand based thereon (sometimes called an "out-of-court hypothetical"); (b) the familiar "personal observation" method, i.e., testimony based upon personal knowledge (for example, testimony by a physician who has made a personal examination of the patient); (c) testimony based upon reading the transcript in the case; (d) testimony based on the expert's attendance at the trial and listening to the facts of the case reported by other witnesses; (e) testimony based on studies or experiments undertaken or relied upon by the expert; and (f) testimony based upon a mixture of any of the above (including the in-court hypothetical).

This matter of format is unaffected by the subsequent addition to the Rules of substantive provisions codifying *Daubert* and *Kumho* (see "Phase Three" infra) intended to insure the reliability of the testimony.

Procedural Liberalization #(4): The F.R.E. expanded the permissible basis for the expert's opinion. The expert may rely on unadmitted or even inadmissible materials and information in giving an opinion, if they are of the kind that are "reasonably relied upon by experts in the particular field in forming inferences or opinions on the subject." F.R.E. 703.

Thus the opinion may be based on oral or written hearsay, textbooks or articles the expert has read in his life, statements of his teachers in his education, documents related to the case that are not in evidence, documents that violate the best evidence or the authentication rules, items that may qualify for admissibility but have not in fact been qualified or offered, reports of tests or of signs and symptoms, experiments he has run, statements to him by the patient or others about the case—indeed any kind of inadmissible or not admitted evidence—provided only that the judge find it is of a kind that is reasonably relied upon by experts in the particular field in forming inferences or opinions on the subject.

This "reasonably relied upon" requirement, by its own terms, does not apply beyond *inadmissible* or *unadmitted* material the expert relied on.

Where it applies, the requirement obviously calls for a judgment to be made by the judge that the reliance was "reasonable"—a term usually held synonymous with "customary in the field" despite good arguments that it calls for more judicial independence.

This liberalization number (4) has been frequently employed as an end run around the hearsay rule. If an attorney had a piece of hearsay and had trouble getting it into evidence under some exception to the hearsay rule, she might endeavor to find an expert who would base his opinion on it and convince the judge it was routine in his field. Judges generally demanded little factual foundation to find "reasonable reliance", although they theoretically had the power to hold a hearing and receive other experts on the question.

The expert would then usually be allowed to testify not only to his opinion but perhaps also to the actual contents of the hearsay basis of the opinion, although there was some diversity of authority on this latter.

The liberalization we are discussing here (number (4)) was often a direct or indirect gateway for hearsay items such as government, university, or industry studies; polls; surveys; second-hand statements, say, by patients; consultations with other doctors; books; articles; and other evidence that otherwise might be excluded. Or at least counsel need not take the time, trouble, and expense, to offer them and qualify them as an exception to the hearsay rule, or as permissible under the authentication and original documents rules. If the grounds of inadmissibility of the basis was privilege, some courts were more circumspect.

As a simple example of the principle of liberalization number (4) in operation, a police officer from the Drug Enforcement Administration was allowed to testify to the selling price of heroin in various cities of the world, which he had learned from other agents. *United States v. Golden* (9th Cir.1976).

This liberalization could have constitutional confrontation clause implications. But the Supreme Court held in *Delaware v. Fensterer* (S.Ct.1985) (per curiam), that the confrontation clause was not violated when the government's expert was subject to cross-examination concerning his conclusions regarding hair analysis, even though he could not remember which method of evaluation he used. This suggests to some that the Court does not care about inability to explore an expert's basis (an inability that also occurs when an expert relies on hearsay, that is, on the word or documents of others, who cannot be explored by cross examination). But the Court's new "testimonial" approach to the Confrontation Clause may affect this. See infra, Chapter 8, Section V. An expert witness connected with the government, whose testimony is offered against the criminal accused, might not be permitted to recount statements from absent persons that contributed to the formation of his opinion, if potential prosecution was in mind. Would an instruction to the jury that such statements are not offered for their truth, but rather to illustrate the basis of the opinion, prevent such a holding? Again, see Chapter 8, Section V. Before the new "testimonial" approach, Confrontation Clause objections to expert witnesses have not fared well.

However, in extreme cases, like an expert who merely summarizes out-of-court statements of others, the evidence has been rejected either on constitutional or evidentiary grounds. See *United States v. Smith* (7th Cir. 1989). Similarly, it was error for an expert to testify that a well respected doctor agreed with him. *United States v. Tran Trong Cuong* (4th Cir.1994).

Effect of subsequent amendments on this procedural liberalization #(4). Subsequent amendments to the F.R.E. (in the year 2000) have affected the specific liberalization we are discussing here (liberalization number (4)) in two ways.

First, Rule 703 was amended to make clear that the inadmissible basis itself (as opposed to the opinion based thereon), even though it survives the "reasonable reliance" calculus, may not be admitted unless the judge finds that its "probative value in assisting the jury to evaluate" the opinion "substantially outweighs its prejudicial effect". The accompanying Advisory Committee Note refers to this as a "presumption against disclosure." If the presumption is overcome and the information *is* disclosed to the jury, the intention is that ordinarily the jury will be instructed that it may only be used to evaluate the opinion. An amendment along these lines had been called for by a Report of the American Bar Association, Committee on Rules of Criminal Procedure and Evidence, "The Federal Rules of Evidence: A Fresh Review and Evaluation", 120 F.R.D. 299, at 369–70 (1987) (Rothstein, P., chair).

Second, and more importantly, substantive amendments directed at insuring reliability of the substance of the expert testimony (see the *Daubert/Kumho* amendments to Rule 702 under "Phase Three" infra), although not directed specifically at Rule 703 and this procedural liberalization number (4), have the effect of extending the "reasonable reliance" criterion to the expert's basis regardless of whether or not the basis is admissible or admitted. It also has the effect of requiring more independent scrutiny and judgment by the judge as to whether the reliance was reasonable, and provides a number of factors to look at. The inquiry is broadened beyond "kind" to "quantity" as well.

Procedural Liberalization #(5): The F.R.E. loosened practice regarding at-trial disclosure of the facts and material upon which the expert witness bases an opinion. At common law, the direct examination of the expert had to reveal her opinion's basis (including the hypothetical or other facts, and any textbooks, articles, studies, conversations, consultations, lab reports, etc., upon which she relied) for the benefit of the jury, and also so that the cross-examiner would have some advance warning with which to decide whether to cross-examine and what approach to take.

But F.R.E. 705, perhaps assuming there will have been adequate discovery beforehand (a faulty assumption in many cases, for legal and practical reasons beyond our scope here), states that this predicate is no longer required. The direct examination does not need to include the basis of the expert's opinion. The expert can give a bare opinion with the scantiest glimpse of the underlying reasons.

Admittedly, in many cases the direct examiner will not proceed this way because such a bare opinion may not be very persuasive. But on occasion, perhaps for tactical reasons, a basis will not be put in during the direct examination. For example, there may in fact be no very good basis to put in. Or there may be a substantial basis but the direct examiner, for maximum tactical effect, would like the cross-examiner to trigger it. The cross-examiner will not know which is the case and rather than be ambushed, may forgo cross examination, perhaps allowing a weakly-based expert to pull the wool over the eyes of the jury.

Specifically, F.R.E. 705 states in relevant part that "the expert may testify in terms of opinion or inference and give reasons therefor without first testifying to the underlying facts or data." Thus, after eliciting the physician-witness' credentials, a personal-injury plaintiff's lawyer could go directly into the following direct examination without establishing where or how the expert learned the facts about the plaintiff's injury and condition, what facts were assumed to be present or absent, and what, if any, materials, conversations (with the patient or others), consultations, books, articles, studies, lab reports, x-rays, hospital records, personal examinations, tests, things from his education, etc., were relied on (a potentially broader range of shakier more disguised materials because of liberalizations (4) and (5) above):

Q. Doctor, are you familiar with the facts of this case?

A. Yes.

Q. Do you have an opinion as to the cause of plaintiff's pain and disability?

A. Yes. They are caused by the automobile collision he suffered on Jan. 24.

Q. What will be their duration?

A. His condition will remain unchanged for his whole life.

Q. Doctor, will you tell the jury why you conclude as you do?

A. My reasons are that plaintiff's symptoms are typical of cases of this kind of injury and can be expected to follow the normal course.

Q. Thank you, Doctor. No further questions.

Rule 705 goes on (after the quotation from the Rule given just prior to the Q. and A. above) to provide "unless the court requires otherwise." Insufficient discovery (if not the moving party's fault) could perhaps be argued to be a reason for a court "requiring otherwise." Also an argument might be made (probably with little success) that in the Q. and A. above, the doctor's reasons given are too scanty to satisfy the Rule's reference to giving "reasons" (see same Rule quotation above). It is not clear, however, that the Rule means to *mandate* rather than merely *permit* the giving of reasons.

The rule further continues: "The expert may in any event be required to disclose the underlying facts or data on cross-examination." But this is the very trap the cross-examiner does not wish to walk into blindly.

The problem may be exacerbated where an expert used complicated statistical, mathematical, or economic models or computer programs, to arrive at her opinion.

In complex cases, more than disclosure in the direct exam would be required to satisfactorily prepare the lawyer for cross-examination. Discovery should be liberally allowed or the evidence barred.

Some of the state codes patterned on the F.R.E. require the parties to exchange in advance written summaries of expert testimony and its grounds, to make up for the possible absence of basis appearing in the direct. A similar provision for exchange of written summaries in Federal Rule of Civil Procedure 26 has sometimes met with no more than perfunctory compliance. Only time will tell whether the expert disclosure requirements now mandated in all federal districts pursuant to Rule 26 will be more rigorously enforced.

Limited expert discovery now is also provided in criminal cases by Federal Rule of Criminal Procedure 16, but the request for a prosecution expert's report triggers a reciprocal duty on the part of the defense to supply like information about its own experts. The defense is also required to provide information about any insanity defense. The amount of information actually mandated by these provisions is not great. And, as in civil cases, courts vary significantly in how seriously they treat violations of expert discovery rules. Sanctions short of exclusion may include delay of the expert testimony to give the opponent a chance to meet the evidence or an instruction to the effect that the absence of notice may be considered in evaluating the witness's testimony. Some attorneys' fees may be awarded. Exclusion of criminal defense evidence for a discovery violation was upheld by the Supreme Court in *Michigan v. Lucas* (S.Ct.1991).

The impact of this procedural liberalization number (5) may be slightly muted in at least some cases because of the subsequent substantive amendments described infra under the heading "Phase Three". These are the *Daubert/Kumho* amendments, designed to allow a party to challenge an expert's opinion as substantively unreliable on a computation of a variety of factors involved in the opinion's basis. When raised, this challenge can trigger a hearing to determine the matter, which will normally require advance disclosure of the basis in some detail.

Procedural Liberalization #(6): The F.R.E. liberalized admissibility under the so-called ultimate issue rule. This common-law rule provided that an opinion, be it an expert opinion or a lay opinion, could not be given in terms that sounded like an ultimate issue to be decided by the fact-finder in the case. Such testimony was said to "invade the province of the jury." The rule is still the law in a few states. It is abolished by F.R.E. 704, and there is no longer in federal courts a general ban on expert or lay opinions that are expressed in terms of the ultimate issue in the case. If there is any objection to such opinions, it will have to be placed on the more general ground that the opinion is not "helpful" or does not "assist" as is required by F.R.E. 701 and 702 (see supra), or violates F.R.E. 403 (the probative-prejudice-time-misleadingness balancing provision) or some other provision of the Rules.

The one exception to this principle is set out in Rule 704(b), which provides that in criminal cases an expert (apparently not only mental or medical experts but also any other expert, like an experienced policeman) cannot opine in conclusory terms directly stating whether the defendant had the mental state or condition (e.g., legal insanity, or intention to kill) constituting an element of the crime or defense. This exception has generated litigation concerning the extent to which a defense expert can characterize the defendant's mental status not only in insanity-defense cases, but also in cases where the defendant claims diminished capacity, or more generally, the absence of specific or general intent. Rule 704(b) was a reaction to a number of then-current high-profile insanity acquittals, most notably the one involving the attempted assassination of President Ronald Reagan.

This principle has been criticized as unworkable since psychiatric or psychologic experts still are (and must be) free to testify to their diagnoses, which often are expressed in terms that fall just short of but essentially amount to or add up to a statement of legal insanity or lack thereof. The trick is in how you phrase your testimony.

A number of decisions extend 704(b)'s rule against ultimate opinions to cover law enforcement officers testifying to the defendant's intent to distribute drugs. See e.g., *United States v. Watson* (3d Cir.2001), reversing because an officer testified that the defendant possessed the drugs for distribution rather than personal use. However, such courts often permit testimony that a particular amount of drugs indicated intended distribution so long as the witness does not utter the magic words that the defendant intended to distribute the drug.

Fears Concerning the Effects of the Procedural Liberalizations in the F.R.E. in the Absence of Substantive Standards Concerning the Reliability of the Testimony Itself

Fears began to be expressed that perhaps the Federal Rules of Evidence, by removing some of the procedural protections of the common law regarding experts, and by failing to provide any substantive guidance on the quality of expert conclusions, were erring in the opposite direction of the common law: opening the door too widely.[2]

For example, consider an automobile accident reconstruction expert or "accidentologist." Accident reconstruction experts are found recently in many different areas, including industrial mishaps and automobile collisions. Some may be qualified and their testimony well-based; some not. Let us suppose that such an expert, E, proposes to testify about the cause of an automobile accident. E wishes to say, "The van driver was at fault and wasn't keeping a proper lookout." This opinion is based not upon any personal observation of the accident, or traces left afterward, but rather principally upon information that comes from bystanders' statements E obtained in interviews.

Would there be any impediments to this sort of testimony under the provisions discussed? After all, the testimony seems to rely heavily on hearsay, there is no illumination of the expert's derivation process, and the expert may have slim qualifications.

Nevertheless, with an appropriate judge, all the hurdles might be overcome. The judge could be convinced that E possesses "specialized knowledge" and has something "of assistance" to offer the jury (Rule 702). And Rule 703 has been employed to allow experts to base their testimony on hearsay assuming the judge is convinced by the expert that experts in this field "reasonably" ("customarily") rely upon this kind of bystander hearsay.

Moreover, even if the judge were inclined to feel the basis was faulty, the opponent must know enough to even raise the question. Remember, under Rule 705 as outlined above, the direct examination may not have

2. Prof. Rothstein noted the danger early. Later, decisions increasingly adverted to it. Some of his writings in this regard are cited under Article VII in the A.B.A. report mentioned above.

alerted the opponent that there is a possibly faulty basis. There may have been other ways to find out, but they were not assured either.

The next impediment in our example would seem to be that E is expressing the conclusion in terms of the ultimate issue in the case ("The van driver was at fault ... didn't keep a proper lookout"). But we saw that there is no longer a ban on ultimate issue testimony (Rule 704).

Rule 403 states that, notwithstanding other Rules, the court can bar evidence in a particular case if probativity is substantially outweighed by prejudice, confusion, or misleadingness, or if the evidence will take more time than it is probably worth. Could this prevent E from testifying? It would seem unlikely, since Rule 403 is highly discretionary and the judge probably feels he already made similar calculations under Rules 702 through 704 as recounted just above.

In summary, it can easily be seen that, with the easing of the procedural requirements, and no mandatory substantive scrutiny of reliability in place, there was considerable risk that a judge would admit doubtful evidence.

Let us take another case. Suppose a financial investigator from the Internal Revenue Service takes the stand to testify that the defendant "is guilty of tax fraud," or "owns" certain taxable funds ostensibly held in the name of an independent corporation, which the government contends is a dummy or front for the defendant. The investigator's conclusion, let us further assume, is based upon his examination of bank records. Assume these documents are not at trial, have not been admitted, may not even be admissible, are not authenticated, and do not comply with the best evidence rule. They may be hearsay and may not meet the requirements of any exception. And the expert works for the government—a party in interest. Nevertheless, the rules we have been discussing seem broad enough to permit this testimony. Indeed, it is possible that the expert would never be required to specify any facts underlying these conclusions. Cf. *United States v. Duncan* (2d Cir.1994) (upholding IRS agent's testimony, based on agent's own investigation, that defendant's "false" tax returns "obstructed and defeated" the tax reporting process and included "money laundering").

This is not to say that good judges could *not* safeguard against these kinds of decisions, either at trial or on appeal, if they were so minded. See, e.g., *United States v. Scop* (2d Cir.1988), where the expert repeatedly tracked exact language of statutes and regulations and used judicially defined terms while testifying based on his assessment of the credibility of other witnesses. But the Rules did not *mandate* careful scrutiny of reliability and so trial judge discretion was very wide and appeals courts were not encouraged to reverse—largely because judges do not feel competent in areas beyond their own expertise and therefore tend to defer—some say abdicate—to the adversary process. However that may be, no concrete guidance was given by the rules in distinguishing the charlatans from the savants.

F.R.E. Article VII (Rules 702–706) laudably opened the door to many sorts of valuable modern expertise that courts earlier had barred by applying 19th Century precedents to today's vastly more complex problems. But in opening the door wider to expertise, the Rules also allowed more charlatans. Was the trade-off worth it in terms of numbers of each? Could it be fine-tuned? Questions began to be asked: Do these provisions draw the right balance between too much rigid specificity and uncontrolled discretion? Are they being administered in a way that strikes the right balance? Are the traditions and quality of the judiciary at bottom the only guarantee? Is the judiciary up to it? Or can we do better? But voices of caution were also heard: while the rules seemed to give judges too much flexibility, the opposite extreme—a rigid specification—could unduly hem him in.

In one area, there *was* a substantive standard, addressed to similar problems. That was the area of purported scientific evidence. The standard was the *Frye* standard. Was it working? And could it or something like it be adapted to apply to expert evidence more generally?

B. REFORM OF EXPERTS UNDER THE F.R.E.: PHASE TWO: CHANGING THE SUBSTANTIVE STANDARD FOR SCIENTIFIC EXPERTS FROM *FRYE* TO *DAUBERT*

Introduction

The central conceptual problem of scientific evidence is how to do the kind of balancing described in our discussion in Chapter 3 above.[3] In addition to considerations of time and expense, which are important in this area, the task is basically to insure that the real reliability of the evidence approaches that with which lay jurors are likely to endow it, considering their susceptibility to being "snowed" by science. Thus the principal questions are whether (1) the theory (including all its sub-steps), (2) any empirical studies informing the process, (3) any apparatus used, (4) the manner of conducting the operation(s), (5) the operator(s) or researcher(s), (6) the report(s), and (7) the witnesses, are reliable, (a) in general and (b) in this particular instance; and whether the extent of unreliability is readily assessable by a lay jury.

3. The problem is just an exaggerated version of the problem that inheres in all expert evidence.

The various approaches to admissibility of scientific evidence, *Frye* and *Daubert*, treated below in this section, are, conceptually speaking, ways to enable the judge to determine one or more of these questions. They concentrate, however, on the "(a)" in our analysis, that is the question of reliability of the process in general, leaving (b), its application in the particular case, to more ad hoc determinations by the trial judge using normal courtroom procedures.

Frye, in widespread use throughout the country, including most state and federal courts, from its inception in 1923 right through the advent of the F.R.E. in 1975 and up until 1993 (and through the present in some state courts), requires "general acceptance" of the science in the pertinent scientific community.

Daubert, replacing *Frye* in 1993 in federal courts and subsequently in some state courts, mandates the judge to make an independent reliability determination, examining a variety of factors including but not limited to testing, empirical studies, peer review, publication, error rate, professional standards, and *Frye*–like acceptance, to see if the evidence comports with "the scientific method".

Daubert, usually the more lenient of the two tests, may be the stricter concerning evidence that appears scientific but may not be despite being generally accepted by experts. As jurisdictions shift from the *Frye* test to the *Daubert* test, previously widely accepted techniques such as ballistics or handwriting analysis may be re-evaluated to be sure they are not being blindly accepted but are also well-based scientifically. See, e.g., *United States v. Starzecpyzel* (S.D.N.Y.1995) (handwriting); *United States v. Llera Plaza* (E.D.Pa.2002) (fingerprinting; judge reverses his earlier decision of inadmissibility; both under *Daubert*).

The opposite is also occurring: as the transition is made, evidence rejected under *Frye* because not generally accepted is being re-examined to see if it none-the-less may embody good science. This is happening with regard to polygraph evidence, although decisions rejecting it still preponderate, owing to the subjectivity of interpretation of the technique's results. See, e.g., *United States v. Posado* (5th Cir.1995), holding the former per se ban does not apply. Cf. *United States v. Gilliard* (11th Cir. 1998) (similar). However, the U.S. Supreme Court has held that a jurisdiction is constitutionally free to categorically ban polygraph evidence as to both the defense and the prosecution, as most jurisdictions still do. See *United States v. Scheffer* (S.Ct.1998).

Levels of Legal Acceptability Under Both Tests: Laying a Foundation for Admissibility. Under the various tests for admissibility of scientific evidence, a particular kind of evidence may progress over time through three distinct levels of legal acceptability. The three levels, like the tests themselves, are addressed to the acceptability of the theoretical underpinnings of the evidence, that is, to the science employed:

(1) Unacceptable as a matter of law. Sometimes a judgment of unacceptability under the particular test will have been made by the decisional (or occasionally statutory) law of the jurisdiction, for a class of evidence as a whole.

(2) The middle position. Under this, the reliability of the scientific theory employed (including, of course, the general type of machinery or apparatus used, if any) must be established as a preliminary matter to the satisfaction of the judge by evidence as part of the foundation in each particular case. Under this position, different judges may reach different results on the same matter of science, even within the same state or jurisdiction. Indeed, even the same judge may vary from case to

case, depending upon what is put into each case's record concerning the science. It is sometimes disputed whether foundation going to the scientific theory should be before the jury as well as the judge. It certainly seems that at least some of that material would be relevant to weight.

(3) Acceptable as a matter of law. Sometimes the legal acceptability of the scientific theory (including general type of machinery or apparatus) will have been accepted as a matter of established law (usually decisional, occasionally statutory, law). In other words, judicial notice is taken of the acceptability of the science involved. Thus no showing on this score will be required (although some may be indulged as a matter of weight).

Under positions (2) and (3), of course, upon offering the evidence counsel must also make a prima facie showing that, as respects any administration of the scientific technique in the particular case (as for example where a polygraph, voiceprint, DNA, or intoxication test is administered), all proper protocols or instructions were followed; that any machinery used was properly calibrated, tested, and in working order; that any operator was properly trained; and that the mode of conducting was otherwise proper. And of course the witness must be qualified. On all of these, only some minimum threshold may be required, deficiencies being left to weight.

The foundation, both as to the science and its particular administration, will often be furnished by the testifying expert herself, who may also have been the administering expert. The foundation, at least as to administration if not the science itself, frequently is laid before both judge and jury at the same time, since it can affect both admissibility and weight.

To determine the level of legal acceptance of particular scientific evidence in a particular jurisdiction, legal research should be directed not merely at the generic category (e.g., radar speed detection or DNA identification) but at the particular sub-variety (the specific kind of speed radar or DNA technique) employed in the particular case. New variations of previously accepted techniques appear on the scene rapidly and may not yet have the same legal status. For example, the RFLP form of DNA testing is now accepted but some of the newer PCR methods or analysis involving mitochondrial DNA may not be considered as reliable or acceptable.

What Is "Scientific Evidence"? An Amorphous Category of Expert Evidence Singled Out for Special Rigorous Treatment

For nearly one hundred years, at least before 1999's *Kumho* decision, infra, courts singled out scientific evidence for more rigorous treatment than expert evidence generally. The more rigorous treatment consisted of higher barriers to entry into evidence. The predominant guidelines erecting the barriers became known as the *Frye,* and later the *Daubert,* tests. These standards were viewed either as especially rigorous applications of the general standards applicable to all experts, or as special standards that apply in addition. Under a code like the F.R.E. special standards conceptually had to be linked to *something* in the code, if only some very general item of language such as the "of assistance" or "scientific knowledge" language of Rule 702, the "reasonable reliance" language of Rule 703, or the "misleadingness" language of Rule 403. This is because Rule 402 commands that *all* relevant evidence (which this usually is) is admissible unless otherwise provided by rule, statute, or constitution.

Just what was included in the special category of expert evidence called scientific evidence deserving special additional scrutiny was never very clear. It seemed to include (a) evidence which may have a scientific aura of infallibility to a jury (the so-called "black box" mystique as in drug and alcohol intoxication tests and radar speed clocking); (b) evidence it is difficult for a judge or jury to evaluate; (c) evidence with which the judiciary has little historical experience (such as animal studies, or epidemiological, toxicological, or pharmacological evidence, used to show the potential of substances to cause cancer or birth defects in humans); (d) evidence that is novel (such as DNA identification or new forms of blood serology); (e) evidence that was invented for the particular case (e.g. uniquely designed tests or a tailored re-analysis of older scientific findings); or (f) evidence deemed to usurp something in the peculiar "heartland" province of the fact-finder (like lie detection through the polygraph or voice-stress indicator, voice identification through voiceprints, and certain probabilistic, statistical, and mathematical evidence). Evidence regarded as "scientific" and in need of special treatment frequently had more than one of these features. For example, voiceprint, polygraph, and DNA evidence obviously fall into several of the categories. Medicine, economics, psychiatry, and the like, tended to be treated according to only the general expert testimony standards, as did expert evidence relying mainly on skill or practical experience, and ballistics, fingerprint, and handwriting evidence. Social science evidence was unclear.

A number of courts seemed to believe the special scrutiny accorded scientific evidence applied only in criminal cases.

Scientific Evidence: The Tests for Admissibility

Depending upon the jurisdiction, the admissibility of scientific evidence is determined by either (1) the common-law test (the *"Frye"* test), requiring general acceptance by the relevant scientific community; or (2) the new test (*"Daubert"* test), requiring that the evidence derive from application of "the scientific method". The most populous states still apply *Frye*. Federal courts and a majority of states apply *Daubert*. Both tests are directed essentially at the acceptability of the theory (the science). They apply *in addition to* all other applicable evidentiary standards affecting any aspect of the evidence, including those that would apply to expert evidence generally.

The Common Law Frye Test: "General Acceptance"

The traditional test was articulated in *Frye v. United States* (D.C.Cir.1923), which rejected an early form of lie detector evidence offered on behalf of a criminal defendant:

> Just when a scientific principle or discovery crosses the line between the experimental and demonstrable stages is difficult to define. Somewhere in this twilight zone the evidential force of the principle must be recognized, and while courts will go a long way in admitting expert testimony deduced from a well-recognized scientific principle or discovery, the thing from which the deduction is made must be sufficiently established to have gained general acceptance in the particular field in which it belongs.

Until recently this was the dominant test, and even now it is followed by a number of states.

With contested scientific techniques, *Frye* could engender an admissibility hearing—a *"Frye* hearing"—before the judge about whether or not there was the requisite general acceptance. At the hearing, sometimes other experts would be called to inform the court on the question of general acceptance. It was always uncertain as to whether and to what extent the hearing or at least similar information could also be before the jury to aid them in assessing the weight of the evidence if it were ultimately admitted. The *Daubert* standard, below, which replaces *Frye* under the Federal Rules of Evidence and in a number of states, engenders similar hearings, with similar uncertainty.

Frye raises difficult questions about what is the relevant "field." For example, in the case of DNA, is it forensic technicians? Molecular biologists? Physical scientists? Population geneticists? Others? All of these? Some of these? The answer could make a great deal of difference. Similarly, what does "general acceptance" mean? How large a slice of the "field" must accept? What must they accept? That it has X% [or Y%, or Z%] reliability? Or that the percent reliability is sufficient for certain purposes? The court's purposes? Or the scientist's purposes?

Questions also are raised about what level of abstraction or generality to focus the test on. Some accepted principle at some level is involved in practically every piece of purported scientific evidence ever offered. What about accepted principles combined or deployed or applied in an unusual way? Some courts even seemed to require general agreement on the particular *result* or *conclusion* obtained from application of a scientific technique. *Frye* was infinitely manipulable. The *Daubert* test under the F.R.E. below raises many of the same questions.

Despite its open questions and manipulability, however, *Frye* tended to be applied in a restrictive, conservative way, keeping out evidence that might be reliable and scientifically sound, but was so new that it had no established "track record". The thought was that judges and jurors are not capable of understanding and sorting wheat from chaff in scientific areas and must therefore defer to the collective judgment of "establishment" or "mainstream" scientists. While this may cost us the evidence of the occasional Galileo (who was out-of-step with the establishment, but happened to be correct), more often it will spare us the charlatans, courts believed.

Frye is considered a conservative test, in that it delays valid science getting into the courtroom. Age by itself, however, does not assure general acceptance under *Frye*. Voiceprint technology, which has been around for half a century still receives mixed reviews under *Frye*. Compare *People v. Jeter* (N.Y.1992) (voiceprint still subject to *Frye* hearing; any error in admission was harmless) with *People v. Drake* (Colo.1988) (rejecting voiceprint). Periodic scientific reports on a scientific technique can influence its *Frye* acceptability. See, e.g., National Academy of Sciences, National Research Council, Report of Committee on Sound Spectrography: "On the Theory and Practice of Voice Identification" (National Academy of Sciences Press, 1979). This report, to which Prof. Rothstein was consultant, raised sufficient questions about real-world forensic applications as opposed to lab applications, that somewhat widespread judicial acceptance of voiceprint evidence declined subsequently. General acceptance and peer review by the scientific community are also factors (among others) under the *Daubert* test of the F.R.E., infra.

Policy considerations cited in favor of *Frye* include the difficulty faced by the opponent in mounting a challenge to new science. Although *Ake v. Oklahoma* (S.Ct.1985), held that an expert must be provided for an indigent criminal defendant in a capital case when his defense is insanity, obtaining funding for sophisticated challenges to novel scientific theories may be difficult in many civil and criminal cases.

Ironically, the *Frye* test may act in exactly the opposite way once the evidence has been generally accepted. It would seem that the more accepted a technique, the fewer experts there are to point out the shortcomings of the evidence to the jury. Additionally, the relevant "field," if construed narrowly, may consist of the very people who have an interest in the use of the technique in litigation.

On a more fundamental level, why should the "field," and not the courts, determine acceptable levels of reliability? This concern seems especially valid if the "field's" primary occupation is law enforcement or litigation (as with polygraphs, voiceprints and forensic use of DNA) as opposed to a field that has other incentives to accuracy (e.g., medicine).

Courts generally state in applying the *Frye* test, that if the test is failed, the evidence is inadmissible regardless of showings of reliability that may be made. Some have suggested, instead, that the test should merely control whether judicial notice of reliability of the theory will be taken without evidence thereof.

A few courts, becoming dissatisfied with *Frye* over time, attempted a naked balancing of factors, without a "test," an approach which in practice often focused on reliability, particularly the scientific basis for the opinion. Other factors were looked at, too. Thus instead of holding that voiceprint or polygraph evidence or other particular variety of scientific evidence is admissible or inadmissible as a general matter, some of these courts might satisfy themselves that the science was at least somewhat reliable. Then perhaps in some situations they might look at whether the case was civil or criminal; which party was offering the evidence; what issue it was offered upon (e.g. a substantive or a credibility issue); whether trial was before a judge or jury; the availability of scientific rebuttal testimony; what other evidence there was in the case; how necessary or determinative the scientific evidence would be; whether it was corroborated; whether the result was positive or negative; whether the expert moderated his claims to certainty; whether the process, components, and result would be clearly and precisely conveyed to the jury in a way they could visualize or understand; whether the expert was appointed by the court; whether the scientific test was agreed to by the parties; what safeguards were taken when the technique was administered; etc. The courts, of course, also always sought to be assured that the procedure was properly conducted, with proper equipment in proper repair, whatever approach was taken, *Frye* or otherwise.

The special standards of *Frye* and *Daubert* are addressed only to the soundness of the science, that is, the theoretical underpinnings of the evidence and its appropriateness to the case at hand. Thus, they do not preempt other evidence issues.

Tests Based on the F.R.E. in the Immediately Pre–Daubert Era

Immediately prior to *Daubert v. Merrell Dow Pharmaceuticals, Inc.* (S.Ct.1993), the federal courts were not entirely unified in their approach to scientific evidence. Surprisingly, the specific language of neither the Federal Rules of Evidence nor their Advisory Committee Notes directly addressed the problem, nor mentioned *Frye,* which had been the predominant test in both state and federal courts.

Mirroring the states, the most prevalent view was that the *Frye* test controlled even after adoption of the Federal Rules of Evidence. See, e.g., *United States v. Kilgus* (9th Cir.1978), rejecting evidence of a "forward looking infrared system" for distinguishing among night flying planes of the same model; and *United States v. Brown* (6th Cir.1977), rejecting "ion microprobic analysis" for comparison and identification of hair samples.

On the other hand, the drafters' comments to F.R.E. 702 through 706 evinced an intent to increase receptivity of expert testimony and to widen the kinds of information experts may rely on and report. A few courts considered these comments to broaden admissibility of scientific evidence. See, e.g., *United States v. Williams* (2d Cir.1978) holding that the F.R.E. were meant to overturn the *Frye* test, and admitting voiceprint evidence pursuant to an "of assistance" standard. Cf. *State v. Williams* (Me.1978) (similar ruling under Maine Rules, modeled on the F.R.E.).

United States v. Downing (3d Cir.1985), was one of the most influential of the immediately pre-*Daubert* decisions that rejected *Frye*. *Downing* concerned the admissibility of expert testimony about the reliability of eyewitness identifications. The opinion requires judges to focus on (1) the soundness of the scientific technique or process, (2) the possibility that its admission would confuse the jury, and (3) the proffered connection between the result presented and the disputed factual issue in the case. *Downing* suggested multiple factors to be considered beyond scientific acceptance, including novelty, specialized literature concerning the technique, qualifications and stature of the experts, non-judicial uses of the technique, error rate, types of errors and acceptance in other litigated cases. This reasoning came close to anticipating the reasoning of the Supreme Court in *Daubert*.

The Daubert Test: "Reliability", "Fit", and "The Scientific Method"

In *Daubert v. Merrell Dow Pharmaceuticals, Inc.* (S.Ct. 1993), the Supreme Court finally spoke concerning the standard for regulating scientific experts pursuant to the F.R.E. It rejected the *Frye* test, and made the trial judge responsible for making his or her own determination, largely without concrete guidance, of the "reliability" (or "scientific validity") of the testimony, and its "fit" to the issues in the case, to use the Court's own words.

Daubert did not address the merits of the *Frye* test, but was based on a "plain meaning" analysis of the Rules. The Court concluded that *Frye* (a creature of purely decisional law) had been superseded by the Federal Rules, primarily because F.R.E. 402 provides that all relevant evidence is admissible unless excluded pursuant to other Rules, the Constitution or a statute. The only applicable criteria were those found within Rule 702 and other provisions of the F.R.E. While recognizing there might be arguments tying *Frye* to language of the Rules, the Court found such arguments unconvincing.

The Court buttressed its conclusion that *Frye* cannot be found in the Rules by referring to the general liberal thrust of the F.R.E., particularly Article VII's philosophy to relax traditional barriers to expert and opinion evidence. However, the court notes that *some* standards related to reliability are needed because experts are given wide latitude in their testimony by the rules. It would thus not be sufficient to say that once an expert is shown to have credentials and to be qualified, he or she can testify to anything, and that the adversary process applied to it is a sufficient safeguard.

The trial judge is charged by the decision with being a "gatekeeper". He or she must decide whether the things the scientific expert will say will express "scientific knowledge", the phrase used by Rule 702 to describe the kind of information such an expert supplies to the fact-finder. The Court says that, to be called "scientific knowledge", information must be attended not necessarily by certainty, but by a substantial degree of "reliability" ("scientific validity"), which is to be achieved by complying with "The Scientific Method."

The judge must also find, the Court says, that the testimony will "assist the trier of fact to understand the evidence or to determine a fact in issue," as Rule 702 requires. The Court calls this an issue of relevance, which it alternatively characterizes as an issue of "fit" between the testimony and some question to be resolved by the trier. At points in the opinion the court seems to regard this as merely a matter of the logical connection between the facial verbal statements made by the expert (regardless of whether they are well or ill founded) and the issues in the case. Construed this way, this "fit" requirement is rather obvious and adds little to the analysis. The example the court gives, however, seems to point in another direction. The example is that scientific testimony about how the phases of the moon progress would "fit" a case where the issue was whether a particular night was moonlit or not, but not one where the issue was whether someone behaved like a lunatic (or werewolf) on a particular night (presumably because there is nothing scientific to the old legends that the moon produces lunacy or lupine changes in some humans). This version of "fit" seems more related to the Court's other requirement, scientific reliability or validity measured by the scientific method. Thus, in later cases, "fit" appears to relate to whether the expert has unjustifiably extrapolated from an accepted premise to an unfounded conclusion. See the Advisory Committee Note to subsequently amended Rule 702 (infra) quoting *General Electric Co. v. Joiner* (S.Ct.1997), for the proposition that sometimes a trial court "may conclude that there is simply too great an analytical gap between the data and the opinion proffered."

The Court mentions that in appropriate circumstances a judge may appoint an expert or experts under Rule 706, not only on the main matter in question, but perhaps to aid in determining whether a party's proferred expert complies with the scientific method and is scientifically reliable or valid (not whether it is correct).

Unlike *Frye*, which places responsibility for determining scientific validity on the scientific community, *Dau-*

bert makes the judge the gatekeeper, although, as indicated in the next subsection immediately below, he or she may still look to the scientific community for guidance. Many judges, not being scientists, do not feel competent to perform this function, and preferred *Frye*.

While courts sometimes were unsure under *Frye* whether the emphasis was on scientific acceptance of the underlying methodology or the result, the Court in *Daubert* expressly says the focus is on assuring the scientific nature of the methodology, reasoning, principles, procedure, and process, rather than on the results or conclusions they generate. The evidence must derive from application of a methodology which students of science (and the *Daubert* decision itself) call "The Scientific Method," some of the earmarks of which the Court gives us in terms of suggested rough considerations to be applied to offered evidence. These are listed in the subsection immediately below.

Daubert-Style "Reliability": A Multi–Factor Inquiry

In order to give guidance to lower courts in applying the new reading of Rule 702—the "reliability" or "scientific method" or "scientific knowledge" requirement— the Supreme Court in *Daubert* provided the following flexible guidelines, which some commentators have dubbed *"Frye plus"* because general acceptance is one of the factors:

(1) "Falsifiability," or testability of the theory to determine whether the results can be falsified. The inquiry here is (a) are the basic assumptions in their nature *testable*; (b) have they in fact been tested; and (c) has the testing verified them? To what extent? In cases involving causation of injury by allegedly toxic substances (as in *Daubert* itself), this comes down to whether there have been epidemiological studies show-

ing a relationship between exposure to the substance and the particular injury, in a population or group.

(2) "Peer review and publication." Has there been appropriate exposure to review by colleagues through such things as publication and/or presentation at meetings? Have the reviews been favorable? To what degree?

(3) "The known or potential rate of error." Is the rate of error appropriately low?

(4) Standards and controls. Are there professional-organization standards that are maintained and applied for controlling the technique's operation?

(5) "Acceptance in the scientific community." Has there been some substantial or widespread degree of acceptance, even if not universal? What degree of acceptance and rejection has there been?

None of these factors are indispensible or dispositive. The list is not exhaustive. They are merely considerations to be weighed, concerning the offered evidence.

Notice that general acceptance (key under *Frye*) and peer review and publication (often felt necessary to satisfy general acceptance under *Frye)* still have a role, though no longer a determinative one. The court expressly eschews the rigid defining of a relevant field or requiring some particular degree of acceptance, or even specifying what exactly should be accepted, preferring to say only that if there is widespread scientific disapproval affecting the evidence at any level, this is a negative factor to be considered in computing scientific validity or reliability.

Of the listed factors, it appears that the Court most heavily emphasized testability.

Because these are not meant to be exclusive, other factors discussed earlier hereinabove or in cases such as

Downing may also provide guidance. Since the *Daubert* decision, Judge Becker, the author of *Downing*, has elaborated on these criteria in *In re Paoli Railroad Yard PCB Litigation* (3d Cir.1994). See also the useful augmentation and explication of the list of *Daubert* factors in *United States v. Bonds* (6th Cir.1993) (forensic DNA). The Advisory note to subsequently amended Rule 702 (infra) also contains principles gleaned from cases arising after *Daubert*, including whether the research was independent or created for the litigation; whether the expert has made an unwarranted extrapolation from the facts; whether alternative explanations have been eliminated; whether the opinion is as careful as if made in regular professional work; and whether the type of expertise is itself considered reliable (not astrology).

Soundly scientifically based evidence that is so new it has no track record may fare better under *Daubert* than *Frye*; whereas unsoundly based evidence that nevertheless has substantial support in its particular field may fare better under *Frye*. Traditionally acceptable expert evidence based more on "feel" and intangible experience of the expert than on scientific studies may also fare better under *Frye*, unless the application of the tests is different for such evidence.

Scientific Evidence After Daubert

The trial court in *Daubert* had granted summary judgment against the plaintiff because the plaintiff's experts based their opinion that the morning sickness drug Bendectin caused birth defects on a methodology that diverged significantly from that which was generally accepted. The Ninth Circuit affirmed. Absence of peer review was a major factor. Both the trial court and the Court of Appeals applied *Frye*. The Supreme Court took the case, articulated the new test, and remanded the case to be decided by reference to its new multifactor guidelines, a result which at the time was hailed as a victory both by the plaintiffs and defendants and their respective bars.[4] The *Daubert* remand resulted in the Ninth Circuit's reaffirming its earlier ruling that the expert evidence was inadmissible, thereby making summary judgment appropriate, as it was nearly the only evidence of plaintiff on causation. This time the Supreme Court avoided the substantive question of scientific validity and denied certiorari.

4. This was in part because it was not clear how the somewhat general standards spawned by the Supreme Court in *Daubert* would be interpreted on remand to the lower court (or by lower courts generally in the future, a matter which is still not very clear); and in part because the decision both elevated and lowered the standard, depending upon the class of former cases it was compared too. The plaintiffs argued (in addition to arguing that *Frye* was complied with) that *Frye* did not apply and therefore *no substantive standard applied at all*, but rather only requirements of qualifications of the expert applied. *Frye* did not apply, they claimed, because either (1) *Daubert* was not a kind of case *Frye* applied to, being (a) a civil case or (b) a kind of science not subject to *Frye*; or (2) *Frye* should be overruled. The defendants argued a rigorous application of *Frye* was in order. As you can see, the Court split the baby—a substantive standard was imposed but not rigid *Frye*. So, compared to what might-have-been (i.e., the two extremes—no substantive standards, or rigorous application of *Frye)*, the Court came out in the middle. Prof. Rothstein participated in the case and urged that scrutiny of qualifications was not enough because of the broad latitude given by the law to expert witnesses and the vast sway they have with the jury; and that consequently there should be an additional "gatekeeper" role for the judge.

The plaintiffs' and defendants' bar as a whole also both claimed victory, for the same reasons. The *Daubert* case represented a continuing kind of case for them: traditional scientists testifying for defendant companies that there was no causal connection between plaintiffs' disease and an allegedly toxic product, exposure, medicine, or substance; but certain non-traditional approaches testified to by plaintiffs' more "outlyer"-type (but not necessarily incorrect) experts indicating a causal connection. Frequently the proposed expert testimony of plaintiff would be the only or a critical piece of testimony for the plaintiff on causation, and if it was inadmissible, plaintiff's case would be dismissed as a matter of law.

Thus, while the vagueness of the new standard permits argument in favor of testimony which would be barred by *Frye*, it also permits the court to bar evidence which would be admitted by *Frye*, or come to the same result as a *Frye* court. Strict and liberal interpretations can be made of both *Frye* and *Daubert* and it is over-simplistic to say the one test is stricter than the other.

Many post-*Daubert* civil cases have been similarly cautious about admitting scientific evidence.[5] Expertise not surviving a *Daubert* analysis includes clinical ecology testimony concerning multiple chemical sensitivity disorder, *Bradley v. Brown* (7th Cir.1994), and testimony that radiation caused the plaintiff's cataracts, *O'Conner v. Commonwealth Edison Co.* (7th Cir.1994).

In fact, post-*Daubert* summary judgment or judgment as a matter of law in civil cases has become common in federal court because judges can exclude an expert who provides an essential element such as causation when their affidavits lack reliability. In such situations, a dispute arose about the proper standard of review. Is it de novo (the typical summary judgment review standard) or abuse of discretion (the expert review standard)? This issue reached the Supreme Court in *General Electric Co. v. Joiner* (S.Ct.1997), which affirmed a summary judgment, and applied an abuse of discretion standard, despite the fact that the expert's exclusion was the sole cause of the summary judgment. Thus, as in *Daubert*, the Court appeared to encourage judges to use their discretion as gatekeepers to keep out questionable expertise.[6]

5. The Rand Civil Justice Institute has rigorously reported on the effect of *Daubert* on civil cases in a statistical study to which Prof. Rothstein was an advisor. See Changes in the Standards for Admitting Expert Evidence in Federal Civil Cases Since the Daubert Decision (Pub. No. MR–1439–ICJ, Rand Institute for Civil Justice, Santa Monica, California, 2001).

6. Summary judgment or the like is to be granted against the plaintiff if admissible evidence supporting a critical proposition of

Post-*Daubert* criminal cases have been much less critical of new science, treating criticisms as going to weight, rather than admissibility. See, e.g., *United States v. Chischilly* (9th Cir.1994) (permitting on behalf of the prosecution testimony and statistics concerning the RFLP method of DNA analysis, despite a challenge based on population substructure where the defendant was a Native American). A "victimologist" called by the prosecution to explain the reactions of abuse victims towards their abusers also survived a *Daubert* challenge. See *United States v. Alzanki* (1st Cir.1995). It has even been held that polygraphs are no longer subject to a per se ban. *United States v. Posado* (5th Cir.1995). However, in *United States v. Scheffer* (S.Ct.1998), the Supreme Court upheld a military rule of evidence prohibiting all polygraphs, despite a constitutional challenge by a defendant who wanted to introduce exculpatory polygraph evidence. Because a 2003 study of the polygraph and lie detection by the National Research Council was highly skeptical, it is unlikely that polygraphs will gain widespread admission. National Research Council, *The Polygraph and Lie Detection*, National Academic Press (2003).

Although *Daubert* has already become influential among the states which have adopted variants of the Federal Rules, a number of states still adhere to *Frye*,

plaintiff's falls below a minimum. The minimum is usually articulated as "evidence sufficient to support the proposition in the mind of a reasonable fact-finder" notwithstanding that the judge or other reasonable fact-finders would not so find. Can expert testimony to causation that is admissible under *Daubert* ever fall below that minimum? This is a debated proposition. It is clear that if the expert only testifies to general capacity to cause (e.g. that epidemiological studies show a statistical rise in the malady when the alleged causative agent is introduced into a studied population and it clearly appears to be a causal relationship; but the malady also occurs in the absence of the that causative agent), this may not be sufficient to show actual cause in the specific case (perhaps unless the statistics show a rise greater than double).

see, e.g. *People v. Leahy* (Cal.1994) (horizontal gaze nystagmus test (HGN) subject to *Frye* hearing), or to some state standard of reliability which may be informed by *Daubert*, e.g., *Steward v. State* (Ind.1995) (child sexual abuse accommodation syndrome).

In 1999, the Uniform Rules of Evidence (a recommended set of rules for states generally conforming to the Federal Rules) departed from F.R.E. 702, and created a rule that uses the *Frye* standard to initially determine admissibility, but permits the losing side to challenge the decision based on reliability. In other words, if the testimony is generally accepted, it will not be admitted if the opponent shows it is unreliable. Conversely, if it is not generally accepted, it will be admitted if the opponent shows it is reliable. Prof. Raeder advised on the revision.

Regardless of which test a jurisdiction adopts, some of the most difficult scientific issues include determining causation in toxic tort and medicinal drug cases, horizontal gaze nystagmus tests (HGN) in drunk driving cases, repressed memory in criminal and civil cases based on child abuse, new types of DNA analysis, and whether (or when) compliance with DNA protocols is a matter of admissibility or weight or both.

In order to aid judges making *Daubert* decisions, the Federal Judicial Center created a Reference Manual on Scientific Evidence (1994). This volume, a compendium of materials composed by various scientists, lawyers, judges, and professors, is mainly a series of chapters called "Reference Guides", each on an individual field of science. Drafted by leading scientists in each particular field, in simple, legally reviewed language, they are offered as guides for judges handling cases involving scientific evidence, to aid them in determining what "The Scientific Method" required by *Daubert*, consists of in that particular field. The reference guides also have extensive legal materials and case citations illustrating the legal application of the scientific methodologies set forth. E.g., the opening reference guide on Epidemiology has legal materials by Prof. Rothstein, who also was a peer-reviewer of the whole volume. A second edition of the Manual was published in 2000.

In class actions and other complex civil litigation, judges now appear to be making more use of court appointed experts (see F.R.E. 706) to help decide scientific validity issues under *Daubert*.

C. REFORM OF EXPERTS UNDER THE F.R.E.: PHASE THREE: *DAUBERT'S* SUBSTANTIVE STANDARDS EXTENDED (IN LOOSENED FORM) BY *KUMHO* TO ALL EXPERTS AND CODIFIED (PERHAPS AUGMENTED) IN RULE 702

Kumho Tire: Applying *Daubert's* Reliability Test to All Experts

Rule 702 allows the testimony not only of experts who are presenting "scientific knowledge" but also experts presenting "technical or other specialized knowledge" gained through "skill, experience, training, or education" that may be less than formal. In other words, it allows both scientific and non-scientific experts. *Daubert* did not settle whether the *Daubert* test applies beyond scientific experts. Six years after the *Daubert* decision, however, *Kumho Tire Co., Ltd. v. Carmichael* (S.Ct.1999) answered that question by applying *Daubert's* general reliability or "gatekeeper" requirement to all expert testimony.

But *Kumho* was not very edifying about how judges should adapt the more specific *Daubert* factors to non-scientific experts. Obviously the *Daubert* factors are tailored to the scientific context and do not quite seem to fit non-scientific expertise. Many forms of non-scientific expert evidence cannot be expected to live up to the "scientific method" in terms of testability, replicable studies, calculated formalized error rates, etc. For example, an expert in art testifying that a Van Gogh painting is a fake. Yet such experts may well have something of value and relatively reliable to offer, provided they comply with some kind of criteria special to their field.

Kumho said this much: that trial courts *may* consider one or more of the specific factors that *Daubert* mentioned when doing so will help determine that testimony's reliability. The Court emphasized what it had said in *Daubert* in connection with scientific experts: that reliability is a "flexible" inquiry and that the list of specific factors neither necessarily nor exclusively applies in every case.

The two examples of applying *Daubert* properly to non-scientific technical or experience based witnesses given in *Kumho* both include references to general acceptance. For example, *Kumho* suggested that a perfume tester's ability to distinguish among 140 odors at a sniff, could be tested by asking whether his *preparation is of a kind that others in the field would recognize as acceptable.* Thus, after *Kumho,* it is fair to ask whether *Frye*, rather than being dead in federal courts, has now spread even beyond its original target, scientific experts. In a large number of *Daubert* and *Kumho* rulings, judges seem to prefer and are emphasizing the "acceptance" factor, which they feel competent to handle.

United States v. Hankey (9th Cir.2000), illustrates the difficulty of testing experience-based non-scientific experts. In *Hankey,* a police officer's testimony regarding a gang's code of silence was admitted post-*Kumho* where its reliability was based on years of experience and personal knowledge. But does simple experience mean reliability?

What *Kumho* at least *tries* to do is what *Daubert* tried to do, and that is impose a gatekeeper task on trial judges to scrutinize for a threshold level of reliability. *Kumho* shows the nature of the task in this revealing quote: the admissibility question to be decided was whether the testimony "fell outside the range where experts might reasonably differ, and where the jury must decide among the conflicting views of different experts, even though the evidence is 'shaky' ". Just what the range of reasonable difference is, and when evidence is just *too* shaky to be within it, is the continuing point of controversy and will get fleshed out by decisions over time. *Kumho* itself is not too enlightening on the end points of the range, because the particular testimony was so bad (at least as portrayed by the Court) as to be outside the range on any measure. There was little outside support for the vague criteria the mechanical engineering expert professed to having used to determine whether the tire failure in the case was due to abuse or a defect in the tire, and his conclusion on that controverted issue, the central one in the case, seemed to contradict the very criteria he professed to have adopted, so that his testimony appeared to have very little objective or articulable basis at all.

Nevertheless, it is clear that it is now harder to introduce expert evidence of the non-scientific variety than was the case previous to *Daubert/Kumho,* because non-scientific expert testimony was not previously subject to any substantive scrutiny for reliability or acceptance. Remember, *Frye* did not apply to it.

It remains to be seen what the total effect of *Daubert* and *Kumho* will be on the overall receptivity of courts to expert evidence in general.

Open Questions in the Post-*Daubert/Kumho* World

Defining the *Daubert/Kumho* boundaries has become a cottage industry. Open issues include the extent of pretrial discovery which should be permitted in criminal cases to challenge new science; whether criminal indigents are entitled to funding to mount such attacks; and whether Rule 403 adds barriers to expert testimony other than those inherent in *Daubert/Kumho*. Courts have discretion as to whether to hold a hearing at all. What considerations should govern? It was held to be error (albeit harmless) to permit an unconditional opinion of sexual abuse without a reliability determination in *United States v. Charley* (10th Cir.1999). What should be the nature of any Rule 104(a) in limine hearing conducted by the judge? When and to what extent, if ever, should/can it be referred to a magistrate for fact-finding? How often and under what conditions will the court appoint independent experts to aid such hearings?

Amended Rule 702: Codifying *Daubert* and *Kumho* or Adding Restrictions?

In December, 2000, Rule 702 was amended "in response" to *Daubert* and *Kumho*. The rule now requires, in addition to its other provisions, a showing that:

(1) the expert's testimony is based upon sufficient facts or data,

(2) the expert's testimony is the product of reliable principles and methods, and

(3) the witness has applied the principles and methods reliably to the facts of the case.

Some have questioned whether amended Rule 702 is more restrictive than the Supreme Court's "flexible" *Daubert/Kumho* test. For example, is the mention of sufficient facts or data an additional requirement? What are its implications for summary judgment and directed verdicts? Does the third criteria mean that proper performance of protocols goes to admissibility, not simply the weight of the evidence as in a number of previous cases? These issues will undoubtedly create new fodder for litigation.

Categories of Expert and Scientific Evidence

Cases have always tended to be decided according to categories of what kind of expertise is involved, and this continues to be the case. From repeated applications of *Frye, Daubert, Kumho,* the expert testimony rules, and other of the rules of evidence (such as Rule 403), a series of much more specific rules will emerge expressing the admissibility result for each particular category of expert or scientific and other specialized evidence—for example, that evidence of such-and-such type [e.g., animal studies to show something "causes" cancer in humans], displaying such-and-such characteristics [e.g., meets certain statistical parameters], in such-and-such kind of case [e.g., a toxic tort case], is admissible only where there is not such-and-such other kind of evidence available [e.g., epidemiological studies], assuming a foundation is laid showing acceptable procedures were followed.

Indeed, it is possible to draw some limited generalizations about the admissibility of particular kinds of expert evidence at this point. In the next bold face sections below we present some of these. We will not purport to be exhaustive, but will mention only some common and interesting areas. But preliminarily to that, a few general words of caution are in order, lest the reader be under a misconception about the durability of the categories we will sketch. First, the *Daubert/Kumho* principles have introduced some flux into the law. Categories are being re-examined. And second, advancement of knowledge tends to change things. Science and other areas of specialty are fast changing. Techniques mature. New ones or new variations are invented. Legal research on admissibility of kinds of expert evidence in your jurisdiction should be directed not at, for example, "radar speed detection" or "blood typing," but rather at the *specific variety* involved in your case, since there are many competing methods of each, some more accepted than others. Newer techniques tend to be less accepted than established ones, but as time passes they often achieve more acceptability. For example, there is standing radar, moving radar, and more than a dozen varieties of each, at the present time.

Now let's get to our categories:

Standard Traffic Violation Evidence

The more standard varieties of blood, breath, or urine tests for intoxication by alcohol or drugs have met with favor—as have established varieties of radar and "vascar" speed tests—provided acceptable procedures and machinery were used, the operators trained, the equipment properly calibrated, and no special confounding factors are present, at least to a threshold degree. Frequently a jurisdiction will have a statute prescribing conditions under which such intoxication or speed evidence will be received and its legal effect under various circumstances.

Other Standard Tests on Bodily Substances: Paternity, Rape, Assault, and Homicide Cases: Identifying the Culprit

The traditionally established forms of blood type comparisons (A, B, O, etc. blood-typing and some of the more well-established refinements thereof) are generally admissible upon a foundation showing acceptable procedures.

For example, using traditional serology in a paternity case, a blood typing expert may testify that fathers having certain blood types, when mated with mothers having certain blood types, can produce children of only certain blood types and not others. Thus, while the

expert may be able to say this man could not be the
father by this mother of this child, the expert could never
say this man *is definitely* the father, but at most only
that a man of *the same blood-type as this man* is definitely the father. Nevertheless, this latter testimony would
seem to be at least relevant, and it would be probative in
an amount inversely proportional to the size of the class
having this man's blood-type (which in turn depends
upon how many different "markers" were examined in
the blood and what the frequency of each is, in the
relevant population—theoretically, enough distinctive
markers could narrow the class to only the defendant).

The situation is quite similar where the blood typing
comparison (or other similar standard bodily trace comparison) is offered to help establish or exclude a connection between a criminal defendant and a crime, where
traces of what is alleged to be his blood (or semen or the
like) are found on either the scene, the victim, or a
weapon; or traces of what is alleged to be the victim's
blood (or the like) are found on the defendant, his
belongings, his premises, or his weapon. It is possible to
be definitive only if there is no match. A match will be
only a likelihood, varying with the number of markers
isolated.

Some courts were originally reluctant to admit this
kind of evidence concerning paternity or criminal identification when the evidence has been offered to show
connection, as opposed to lack of connection, fearing that
jurors might not realize how inconclusive it is when
offered to show connection.

Because there are many new markers in blood discovered almost every year or so, up-to-the-minute research
in a particular jurisdiction will be needed to reveal the
state of acceptability of anything other than the commonest variety of these tests. Of course there is always a
first case.

In recent years, standard serology has been eclipsed in popular consciousness by DNA analysis, although traditional serology still plays a role in backing up DNA tests or where available financial resources or samples are insufficient to conduct DNA testing. In essence, forensic DNA identification is a process quite similar to that just described for more traditional serology—a toting up and matching of a series of markers or features of the DNA.

DNA experts can, as in the case of more traditional serology, testify to characteristics and population statistics that exclude some people absolutely. Indeed, DNA exonerations of more than 125 individuals who were convicted of serious crime, many of them positively identified by victims and other eye-witnesses and implicated by seemingly unequivocal expert testimony of various kinds, have raised questions about the criminal justice system generally.

Besides exclusion, DNA inclusions seem to pinpoint the "donor" with nearly absolute precision by narrowing the group of potential people having the particular DNA characteristics to an extremely tiny fraction of the population. The reasoning is the same as in traditional serology, but so many "markers" or features are involved that the class of "donors" becomes amazingly tiny, at least in cases of optimal conditions.

However, even here probability figures which appear to pinpoint the defendant as an extremely likely father or assailant may be misleading on several grounds. For example, estimating the likelihood that a random man fathered the child compared with the defendant requires an assumption about access to the mother. The paternity calculations often start with the arbitrary assumption that the defendant is as likely to be the father as any other randomly selected male. In *State v. Skipper* (Conn. 1994), an attempt to convert the paternity index into a probability of paternity by assuming the odds were 50%

that the defendant was the father, was found to run afoul of the presumption of innocence. Moreover, the evidence frequently ignores the fact that relatives have more similarity in their DNA patterns than strangers. Thus, if a brother, uncle or cousin could also be the child's father, the general population-frequency statistics may be highly misleading.

Most of these same strengths and fallacies apply not only to paternity cases, but also to the forensic use of DNA to identify an unknown assailant through traces left in ordinary assault, murder, or rape. In the latter, seminal fluid may contain the DNA. In any of them, blood, hair (particularly if there is a follicle), saliva, skin tissue, etc., may supply DNA.

There are other problems, as well. For example, the error rate of a lab, or particular errors in this case, may change the probabilities. There may be doubt about the population studies and mathematics going into assessing how many people have a particular DNA structure. Other problems also arise.

One major problem is that a jury may have difficulty understanding, for example, that the enormous probability figure at best only shows who the donor of a studied sample was, not the circumstances under which the sample was deposited, which may have been quite innocent.

Of course, Rule 403 may provide a tool to safeguard against all these problems, if the judge can inform himself or herself of what to look for. Is opposing counsel equipped to alert the jury?

A central extremely difficult question, across the board, is, When should problems with the evidence be deemed to rise beyond ad hoc determination under 403 and be deemed to invalidate the entire technique? Conversely, when should they be deemed less than 403 problems, and merely matters of weight? There is no systematic answer as yet.

Courts have split on the question in paternity cases, of when a jury must find in accord with the obvious conclusions from traditional serology (blood-type) comparisons offered in their conclusive aspect (that this individual could not be the father), where there is only lay evidence pointing to a contrary conclusion, no contrary blood evidence, and no evidence directed at impugning the reliability of the procedure in the particular case. Some courts have allowed the jury almost complete freedom in this regard. On what theory might a jury disregard such apparently conclusive evidence? What about assault or rape cases? With respect to paternity, this area is becoming increasingly controlled by statutes.

Syndrome Evidence: From Child Abuse Accommodation Syndrome to Rape Trauma Syndrome

Syndrome evidence has become increasingly important in the prosecution of sexual offenders, child abuse cases, and certain other kinds of cases. Some uses of this evidence, such as testimony explaining rape trauma syndrome, seem relatively well established, but others, such as profiles of child molesters, have met with less success. Many claimed psychological syndromes explaining behaviors of abused persons are applications or variations upon the diagnosis of Post Traumatic Stress Disorder, which is recognized in the Mental Health Professionals' Diagnostic Manual DSM–IV. Some such applications are controversial both legally and among mental health professionals, while others are widely accepted.

Syndromes of victims often are used to explain how individuals react to events in ways which may not be obvious or familiar. This evidence provides a social science framework for jurors to better interpret the actions of the person suffering from the syndrome, which actions may look to a lay person to be inconsistent with being a victim. In addition to its use for evaluating credibility, victim syndrome evidence also may be offered as direct evidence of a crime or defense. Some courts permit an expert to testify that the person suffers from the syndrome. Others allow only an opinion that the behavior is consistent with the syndrome. Still others allow only a generalized description of the syndrome, its causes and effects, prohibiting any type of opinion concerning the individual in question. Finally, depending upon the syndrome, there are courts that tend to exclude such evidence altogether.

Rape Trauma Syndrome (RTS) is used by prosecutors on rebuttal to explain why such behavior as delay in reporting is common among rape victims and does not by itself signify that the complainant was not raped. More controversially, when the defense is consent, prosecutors may attempt to establish RTS as a direct rebuttal. In contrast, the defense may attempt to argue that if a complainant does not demonstrate RTS symptoms, she was not raped. This latter inference is also controversial, because not every person who is raped suffers from RTS. See generally Frazier & Borgida, *Rape Trauma Syndrome: A Review of Case Law and Psychological Research*, 16 Law & Hum. Behav. 293 (1992).

Battered Woman Syndrome (BWS) has been offered in defense in murder cases to demonstrate why a woman honestly believed her life was in danger when she killed her batterer, to describe the cycle of violence associated with much domestic violence, and to explain why women do not leave their assailants. BWS has also been argued as a way of demonstrating duress as an excuse for the battered woman committing a crime. Compare *United States v. Willis* (5th Cir.1994) (not relevant to duress) with *United States v. Marenghi* (D.Me.1995) (not per se irrelevant). Prosecutors have also attempted to introduce

BWS, primarily in rebuttal, to show why a complainant may recant her previous claim that the defendant battered her. See, e.g., *Arcoren v. United States* (8th Cir. 1991). See generally Raeder, *The Double Edged Sword: The Admissibility of Battered Woman Syndrome Evidence By and Against Batterers in Domestic Violence Related Cases*, 67 Colo. L. Rev. 789 (1996). Cf. Raeder, *The Better Way: The Role of Batterers' Profiles and Expert "Social Framework" Background in Cases Implicating Domestic Violence*, 68 U. Colo. L. Rev. 147 (1997).

Child Sexual Abuse Accommodation Syndrome (CSAAS) also has a number of uses in prosecuting child abuse cases. Its least problematic use is in rebuttal, to explain why a child might delay reporting abuse, act lovingly towards the assailant, or recant allegations of actual abuse. But the use of CSAAS is highly controversial to demonstrate that child abuse occurred or that the child was telling the truth about the abuse. Decisions concerning its admissibility vary significantly. See, e.g., *United States v. Azure* (8th Cir.1986), finding reversible error where the expert testified that the victim was telling the truth about her sexual abuse; *Steward v. State* (Ind.1995), which surveyed the case law and held the syndrome was not admissible to show that child abuse occurred, but the court had discretion to admit the syndrome testimony to the extent it was relevant to rebuttal.

Evidentiary Issues in Syndrome Evidence: F.R.E. 404 and 702

The issues raised by expert testimony, particularly Rule 702, *Daubert* and *Frye* issues, can be impediments to syndrome evidence. *Haakanson v. Alaska* (Alaska App. 1988) applied the *Frye* standard to conclude that a child sexual abuser profile was inadmissible for lack of general acceptance. Few decisions have had the occasion to apply

Daubert or *Kumho* to such problems as yet. Can the theory be tested in the fashion *Daubert* suggests? This kind of evidence may become a battleground for development of the rules governing experts.

Several syndromes have met with little opposition on scientific grounds. Vietnam Veterans's Syndrome, in which the person suffers a flashback to a war experience and reacts as if in combat, has been introduced by the defense in a number of cases to mitigate guilt as well as to lower the potential sentence.

The Battered Baby (or Shaken Baby) Syndrome has been favorably received as a medical diagnosis that demonstrates that a small child's physical injuries were not accidental. See *Estelle v. McGuire* (S.Ct.1991). This syndrome is not really a psychological syndrome like the other syndromes considered. Perhaps illogically, this seems to help it with courts.

More controversial psychological evidence includes batterer's or child molester's profiles. This, of course, is not a victim's syndrome. Besides the lack of agreement about the definition of such profiles, which hinders their admissibility as expert testimony, they often are barred as inadmissible character evidence when offered by the prosecution. See, e.g., *United States v. Gillespie* (9th Cir.1988), holding that the admission of common characteristics of child molesters was error.

The latter concern, that certain profile or syndrome evidence is improper character or propensity evidence, is based not upon issues of expert testimony per se, but upon Rule 404, which prohibits evidence of character to prove action in conformity. Thus, if an expert—even a qualified expert with a scientifically sound basis—considers traits or actions of an individual to match a profile or syndrome from which to draw the conclusion that the individual has a propensity toward the conduct at issue, the objection is that the syndrome is character evidence, which under Rule 404 is used improperly if it is employed to prove action in conformity. See *Haakanson, supra,* which rejected use of child sexual abuser profile on both Rule 404 grounds and grounds relating to expert testimony.

On the contrary, perhaps it can be argued that the evidence is not "character" evidence but rather another kind of more documentable, psychological propensity, or that it is offered not to show character-propensity but another issue such as motive, intent or identity of the perpetrator. See Rule 404(b). Cf. *State v. Swallow* (S.D. 1984), which allowed limited use of pedophilia evidence.

For federal courts, how does the adoption of Rules 413 through 415, basically allowing offender sexual propensity evidence, affect the character concern respecting sex offender profiles? Those rules, discussed in Chapter 4, Section IV, provide that evidence of other sexual offenses of the defendant are admissible for any matter to which it is relevant. Is this limited to direct evidence of prior acts, or does it extend to expert opinion of the kind we are addressing here?

Of course, when the evidence is used to explain known behavior of a victim, as in rape trauma or child abuse accommodation syndromes, it is not being used to show action in conformity. Thus, victim-behavior evidence may not be as likely to violate Rule 404.

Constitutional Implications of Expert Testimony

It must be noted that in the absence of proper consent to certain of the scientific or medical procedures discussed in this chapter, conducted on certain parties or witnesses, a problem of compelled self-incrimination conceivably could arise. The most common way in which such a question arises, is when a defendant submits psychiatric testimony supporting an insanity defense, and the prosecution counters it with psychiatric testimony based on court-ordered interviews with the defendant. *Buchanan v. Kentucky* (S.Ct.1987), found no bar to rebuttal by reports of an examination requested by the defendant. Where the self-incriminating evidence is derived from *non-testimonial* sources, the constitutional privilege does not apply because the Fifth Amendment protects only against *testimonial* self-incrimination. *Schmerber v. California* (S.Ct.1966) (extraction of blood did not violate privilege); *United States v. Dionisio* (S.Ct. 1973) (requiring voice exemplars for comparison and identification did not violate privilege). Barbaric or offensive practices (for example stomach pumping to obtain evidence as in *Rochin v. California* (S.Ct.1952)), may violate general due process.

Consider also the constitutional right to counsel and right to be free of unreasonable searches and seizures. For example, *Powell v. Texas* (S.Ct.1989) (per curiam), held that psychiatric testimony offered by the prosecution which was based on an examination taken without notice to counsel violated both the guarantee against compelled self-incrimination and the right to counsel. *Schmerber* and *Dionisio* also discuss a number of constitutional rights in addition to the privilege against self-incrimination, finding no violation on the facts.

Arizona v. Youngblood (S.Ct.1988), held that in a child molestation case the failure of police to preserve clothing with semen samples defendant subsequently wanted to test for evidence of innocence was not a denial of due process in the absence of bad faith by the police. Thus, negligent or even intentional destruction of evidence or samples which a criminal defendant desires to submit to expert analysis does not violate the Constitution as long as it is not done to deprive the defendant of evidence, or perhaps with knowledge that the particular evidence is sought by the defendant. Policies to destroy samples automatically after a certain time, say to save space, will probably normally pass muster. Ironically, more than ten years after Youngblood was convicted, a small semen stain was located that had been incapable of DNA analysis at the time of trial. Newer DNA technology confirmed that the DNA was not Youngblood's. In other words, the very case that refused to require law enforcement to retain potentially exculpatory evidence probably involved an innocent man.

Other constitutional aspects of expert or scientific evidence have also come before the Supreme Court. In *Barefoot v. Estelle* (S.Ct.1983) the Court permitted a psychiatric opinion on the defendant's future dangerousness for sentencing purposes (the death penalty) despite a brief by the American Psychiatric Association arguing that two out of three predictions of future violence made by psychiatrists are wrong. *Estelle v. McGuire* (S.Ct. 1991) upheld the introduction of battered child syndrome to show the intentional nature of the physical child abuse in question. *Rock v. Arkansas* (S.Ct.1987) rejected a per se rule which excluded all hypnotically refreshed testimony as infringing in that case on accused's right to testify in her own behalf. Although this last is not "expert" evidence, some courts have treated it by the standards of "scientific" evidence. This pro-admissibility stance has echoes in *Daubert*, which concluded that "[v]igorous cross-examination, presentation of contrary evidence, and careful instruction on the burden of proof are the traditional and appropriate means of attacking shaky but admissible evidence," although there are things in *Daubert* looking in the opposite direction, as well, which is what causes uncertainty as to the exact admissibility threshold *Daubert* and *Kumho* actually impose in individual cases.

For another constitutional question relating to experts, see our earlier discussion that expert testimony can incorporate hearsay and in extreme situations therefore can possibly violate the confrontation clause when used against a criminal defendant. The Supreme Court, however, has not yet endorsed this notion.

Finally on constitutional matters concerning expert testimony, the extent of an indigent defendant's right to have experts at state expense is still in flux. See, e.g., *Ake v. Oklahoma* (S.Ct.1985), holding that an indigent had a right in a capital case to have an expert at state expense on the issue of insanity.

III. IMPEACHMENT OF EXPERTS

Use of the Literature: Authoritative Treatises and Articles Under F.R.E. 803(18); Other Attacks

Statements from treatises, articles, and other reference works traditionally are hearsay if offered for their truth. Some jurisdictions have a special exception to the hearsay rule to cover certain classes of source materials. F.R.E. 803(18) is a hearsay exception allowing the reading to the jury (but not introduction as an exhibit) of "statements in published treatises, periodicals or pamphlets [in] history, medicine, or other science or art . . . to the extent called to the attention of an expert upon cross-examination or relied upon by the expert witness in direct examination . . . [if] established as reliable authority by . . . testimony or judicial notice." The tendency of the rules to defer to the judgments of trades or professions is manifest here, as well as in Rule 703, which allows experts to base opinions on the kind of materials used in the profession. See also Rule 803(6) (business records). Cf. *Frye* and *Daubert*.

Under the common law, the use of treatises and articles was restricted to impeachment of experts who testified contrary to them. The theory was not that the publication is true, but that there is an inconsistency.

But F.R.E. 803(18) extends admissibility to substantive use. Now the publication may be used for its truth.

In jurisdictions that do not recognize a hearsay exception, statements in articles and treatises are generally admissible, if at all, only as *impeachment* of a witness who purports to be an expert in the field, and not for their truth. See, e.g., Cal. Evid. Code 721. See end of Chapter 10, infra, for more on the use of treatises and articles in these capacities.

In addition to this form of impeachment, any form of impeachment permitted against ordinary witnesses is also permitted against experts. Furthermore, anything that detracts from an expert witness's expertise may also be fair game as impeachment of him. Lawyers opposing an expert frequently ask leave for a "voir dire" after the portion of the direct examination devoted to the expert's qualifications, before any opinion is rendered. Voir dire is, essentially, early cross-examination, in theory confined to attempting to show that the expert is not at all qualified to testify on the subject he will testify on. But if unsuccessful in excluding the testimony, the questioning still stands, for whatever impeachment value it has.

CHAPTER 8

HEARSAY: THE BASIC THEORY, RATIONALE, AND CONSTITUTIONAL CONSIDERATIONS

I. DEFINING HEARSAY

What Is This Thing Called Hearsay? The True Rationale

W (witness) reports on the stand that she heard D (declarant who made the statement, not defendant) state out of court that he (D) saw X shoot Y. Perhaps W relates D's story in relevant detail, but D does not testify. W's testimony as to what D said is hearsay if offered to establish that the shooting took place, that X did it, or that it was in any other respect as stated by D.

What is wrong with W's testimony above, which is the basic hearsay situation? Let's briefly consider the matter for a moment, without reaching a conclusion until a few paragraphs hence.

W (witness) may be lying, mistaken, joking, misremembering, or reporting ineptly. She may be speaking loosely, carelessly, incompletely, or misleadingly. She may not be entirely credible, accurate, or sincere. There may be some consciously or unconsciously produced disparity between the picture she gives the fact-finder of what was said and what was actually said. Her veracity is in issue.

But don't these dangers accompany all testimony given in court? Normally we rely on certain courtroom features to incline a witness toward faithful reporting and to alert the fact-finder to some of the otherwise hidden pitfalls involved in accepting the testimony. We rely on court-room confrontation, the threat or actuality of cross-examination, the open display of the witness, the oath, the possibility of penalties for perjury and contempt, the solemnity and seriousness of the situation, and the wit-ness' contemplation of the stakes involved in the litiga-tion. Our apprehensions concerning W (the witness) in our hypothetical case seem to be taken care of at least as well as in any other case. W is on the stand. These potential problems with W (witness) are *not* the reason this evidence is hearsay.

But what about D (the out-of-court declarant)? *He* may have been lying or mistaken (or any of the other things we said of W). There may be a variance between the picture D gives of what happened and what actually happened. His veracity, like W's, is in issue. But D has not been subjected to the courtroom. *Therefore, W's testimony as to what D said outside of the courtroom is hearsay.*

On the facts of the case as we have given them, D is, albeit indirectly, acting as a witness to legally relevant facts (although we do not call D a witness), and ought to be subjected to the courtroom processes designed for such witnesses. He is, in effect, an absent, invisible witness. The dangers associated with any witness' report of facts—the risk of misperception, inaccurate memory, ambiguous or misread narration, insincerity—that is, the possibility of mistake, lying, or joking—are present and are especially significant when D cannot be cross-exam-ined, does not risk a perjury penalty, and is not subject to the other courtroom features designed to help insure that reports of fact are accurately given and received. In addition to the obviously missing safeguards, the benefit to the fact-finder of seeing a witness testify and face those he implicates, watching his demeanor, knowing he is under oath, are typically missing when D is absent.

Even if D's statement were videotaped, watching it is not the same as witnessing live testimony. And, of course, the other courtroom safeguards would be missing, too.

The question, "Is the declarant acting as an absent witness to legally relevant facts," as opposed to acting as a verbally contracting party or acting in some other capacity (in which roles the dangers of misperception, memory, and reporting, of fact, are not as significant nor as akin to those involved in ordinary witness testimony), is a good shorthand test of whether the declarant's words are being offered in a hearsay capacity.

The determination of whether we are dealing with hearsay involves a two-step analysis: (1) Is an out-of-court statement being evidenced? If "No", we cannot have hearsay. If "Yes," then we may or may not have hearsay, depending on the answer to the second question. (2) *Why* is this out-of-court statement being put in evidence? It is hearsay only if it is being put in as reliable evidence of the facts it states, rather than being put in, for example, because it (the statement) itself constitutes a slander or an acceptance of a contract or the crime of making threats.

The evidence (in the example opening this chapter) of what D (declarant) said, is hearsay, because D was untestable by the courtroom processes. In justification of this rule, consider the following parade of potential horribles, which are by no means exhaustive. D may have been suffering from myopia or some other defect of physical perceptual capacity. D may have been under the influence of a drug or intoxicant; or deficient in mind, memory, or linguistic ability either to a normal or abnormal extent. D may be a careless person, or may have been careless on that occasion. Weather conditions may have interfered with D's observation. D may not have been wearing needed corrective lenses. There may have been characteristics about the shooter, perhaps noticed but not understood by D, which would mean the shooter could not have been X as D reported. D may have been unfamiliar with X. D may have made contradictory statements about who killed Y, either then or on other occasions. D may harbor a long-standing grudge against X. D may have said on some occasion, "I'd lie to see X burn." The prosecutor may have made a "deal" with D. D might be the real killer or related to the real killer (i.e., someone other than X). D may have been repeating a rumor, or deducing that X shot Y from clues rather than first-hand eye-witness observation. D may have been speaking of a different X. The gun may have been filled with blanks or not loaded. The whole scene may have been done for a film. Or D may have been making an accusation scarcely believing it, to discover, by X's response, whether there was any truth to it. Or D may have been joking. While a similar parade of horribles could be made concerning the reliability of W's (witness's) perception and report (of what D, declarant, said), it is not W's, but D's we are concerned with.

The things itemized in the last paragraph would affect the weight, and perhaps the admissibility, of the evidence. There are many ways they might be revealed in court with D on the stand, including close scrutiny of and pressure on his demeanor and manner, deeper inquiry into the facts, etc.

One should consider that there may be other ways to protect the opponent of the evidence with respect to some of these "horribles" than requiring the proponent to put D on the stand as the price of using his statement. For example, it has been suggested that we allow the hearsay in and leave it up to X (i.e., the opponent of the evidence, whom we assume is X, the guy D's statement essentially accuses) to produce D if X wants to test the hearsay. Some have said that this might be sound when D is sitting in the visitors' gallery or is testifying in some capacity in the cause, or is a party, but otherwise the burden of producing D would be unfairly great. Others have pointed to common-law restrictions on cross-examining and impeaching one's own witness, as an argument against putting any such burden on X. Similarly, still others have felt that if D, whose out-of-court statement implicates X, cannot be found, is dead, is beyond the subpoena reach of the court, or is otherwise unavailable, by the time of trial, then the risk of that unavailability should fall on the proponent of D's statement, not the opponent. In other words, the prosecutor in our case should be disadvantaged by that unavailability (that is, D's accusatory statement should not come in), rather than the statement coming in against X and X being hamstrung in attempting to show its unreliability. An astute observer might ask why in theory there should be such a preference for the opponent of the evidence, which in law there is.

Another suggestion has been that X can bring out at least some of the potential "horribles" mentioned concerning D's (declarant's) report, through independent evidence or by examining W (the witness reporting D's statement), without examining D himself. It should be realized, however, that W may not be familiar with D, D's capacities and vantage point, the weather conditions at the shooting, etc. W did not necessarily hear D's declaration at the same time and place as the shooting. Go back through the facts on the list of potential "horribles". There are quite a few that W may not necessarily know about.

As to some of the potential horribles, it might be sufficient to call to the jury's attention the possibility they exist, by argumentation of counsel and/or instruction from the judge. The jury often weighs evidence in the light of possibilities or likelihoods that are not specifically evidenced in the case at bar. Conceivably the jury might even take account of the possibilities without any mention of them by judge or counsel. The jury often weighs and perhaps discounts hearsay in daily life. They have experience with it.

But all these alternative suggestions to the hearsay rule by and large are ill-received by courts.

Under the True Rationale, Hearsay Can Consist of Oral, Written, or Recorded Declarations

In the original hypothetical opening this chapter, if D's out-of-court oral declaration had instead been made by him in writing, or recorded on tape, and the writing or tape were attempted to be introduced into evidence, rather than W's testimony, we still have hearsay.

Had we deemed the evidence hearsay in our hypothetical because we worried that courtroom safeguards would be inadequate against the possibility of W's (witness's) inaccuracy (in recounting D's out-of-court statement), then the writing we are speaking of in the heading here would not be hearsay. This is because the writing (which was made by D and *is* the out-of-court statement we are talking about) eliminates W as a reporter of the contents of the statement, and substitutes the writing. We do not have analogous worries concerning the writing as "reporter". Inauthenticity or alteration of the writing are possibilities, but as to those possibilities, the writing is no different than any writing customarily offered in court, for which we rely on the courtroom machinery. The same analysis applies for audio or video recordings, offered at trial, of the out-of-court declaration.

But it was not W's inaccuracy that worried us. It was D's. And that remains the same, whether the evidence is oral, written, or recorded. An argument could be made that this worry is attenuated, at least in the case of some writings or recordings that people make with great seriousness. But even a sworn affidavit, which bears a penalty if falsely sworn, is not considered to have safeguards sufficient to substitute for the courtroom. Nevertheless, the argument plays a role when we come to consider specific exceptions to the hearsay rule embracing certain textbooks, transcripts, and written records.

The False Rationale

The hearsay rule is often thought by novices to be based on the notion that there are peculiar dangers involved in perceiving, remembering, and recounting a statement (perhaps mainly an oral statement), as opposed to perceiving, remembering, and recounting some other fact. This is demonstrably not the rationale for the hearsay rule, but is worth remembering for other reasons.

In the familiar childhood party game of "telephone," a secret message is whispered from one person to the next person, on down a long line of people. The message usually comes out remarkably distorted at the end. There is some loss of fidelity at each transfer point. As this proves, it is indeed difficult to hear, remember and report oral statements with exactitude. But this is not the real reason for the hearsay rule.

Under this false hearsay rationale, it is W's (witness's) inaccuracy, rather than D's (declarant's), with which we are concerned. Under the true rationale, as we have seen, it is just the opposite.

Under the false hearsay rationale, since oral statements are difficult to hear, remember, and report, testimony as to the terms of oral contracts, slanders, and other oral statements would be hearsay whatever the purpose of their offer, which, as we shall see, is not the law. Furthermore, conduct could not be hearsay even in the clearest case of an implied declaration; and written or recorded statements of declarants could not be hearsay. Again, such is not the law. Finally, the hearsay exceptions are based on special trustworthiness of the *declarant*, not the ease with which his words may be accurately transferred. All of this demonstrates that the special difficulty of transferring oral (or even written) information is not the operative concept behind the hearsay rule.

Nevertheless, the difficulty of perceiving, remembering, and reporting statements forms a good basis for arguments as to weight, or exclusion under rules like F.R.E. 403 or the rule requiring the original document treated in Chapter 11, in the many cases where statements, oral or written, are reported on the stand for purposes which do not involve inadmissible hearsay. For example, oral or written contracts or defamations; impeachment by prior oral or written statements; and hearsay statements coming in through exemptions or exceptions to the hearsay rule, particularly "chain" hearsay using multiple exceptions resembling the "telephone" game.

Definitions of Hearsay Under the True Rationale: Common Law and F.R.E. 801

It may be helpful to approach hearsay analysis by asking the following three questions: (1) Is the evidence hearsay? (2) If so, does it fall within a hearsay exception or exemption? (3) In a criminal case, does the admission or exclusion of the particular hearsay violate the constitution? For now we are concerned with the first question.

Consider the following definitions of hearsay. They all have been used in the cases or rules. All courts, jurisdictions, and commentators, adopt one or other of them, or sometimes shift back and forth among them. On occasion, these different definitions can produce different results. They are all, however, based on the theory explicated above in this chapter.

1. Hearsay evidence is testimony in court, or written evidence, of a statement made out of court, which statement is offered to show the truth of the matter stated therein.

   a. A "statement" as used above may be either express or implied. Words or conduct from which a statement is implied need not necessarily have been intended by the declarant as a substitute for the statement.

   b. [Alternative to "a," yielding a different result in certain cases.] A "statement" is a verbal or written assertion, and may not be implied except from something intended by declarant at the time as a substitute for the statement.

2. Hearsay evidence is testimony in court, or written evidence, of a statement made out of court, which statement depends for its value upon the credibility, veracity, accuracy, or [and?] sincerity of its out-of-court maker.

3. Hearsay evidence is testimony in court, or written evidence, of a statement made out of court, where cross-examination, the oath, the possibility of perjury penalties, and the solemnity and importance of the courtroom proceedings would have been substantially helpful (as respects reliability) had the statement been subject to them when made.

4. Hearsay evidence is evidence offered to show that a belief was held by someone [while?] not presently testifying, which belief is offered to show the truth of the matter believed.

Note that the F.R.E. has adopted the approach suggested in 1b, with the additional wrinkle of specially defining out of the category certain narrow types of witness and party statements that would otherwise seem to be within it. Since this special "defining out" appears in the general definition rule, we call the evidence that is defined out, "exemptions" rather than "exceptions." The exceptions appear in different rules.[1]

Putting aside these special situations, in determining whether a statement is hearsay under the F.R.E. or other codes which focus on whether the statement is being offered for its truth, you should ask yourself, "must the statement be true in order for it to be relevant?" This question is important in focusing your analysis because first impressions of whether the statement is hearsay can prove false. For example, what of the statement "I can speak," offered for the proposition that the declarant can speak? On first glance, one might think that these are the very words used to prove the identical proposition, which normally is the key to whether a statement is offered for its truth, that is, offered in a hearsay capacity. However, when you ask the question "do the words have to be true in order to be relevant," the answer is no. The declarant could have said "I am a tuna-fish sandwich" and the statement would still demonstrate that the declarant could speak.

It is always important to remember that statements are not hearsay for all purposes, only for those that depend on their truth. Thus, relevance is a key issue in determining whether a statement is hearsay. Is it relevant only for its truth? If so, it is hearsay. If it is relevant for some other purpose, it will not be hearsay insofar as offered for that purpose. Of course, it cannot be offered for any purpose that is not relevant. See Garland, *An Overview of Relevance and Hearsay: A Nine Step Analytical Guide*, 22 Sw. L. Rev. 1039 (1993).

1. This chapter of the book will not deal with exemptions and exceptions, which appear in later chapters.

It is only *out-of-court* statements that we are talking about. While the out-of-court nature of the statement is indispensable, it is not alone sufficient, to make the statement hearsay. While the fact that a statement is an out-of-court statement should alert you that you *may* be dealing with hearsay, it is not enough. Only if that statement is offered for its truth, as opposed to other purposes, would it be hearsay. And even then you have not answered the admissibility question, because it may be within an exception to or exemption from the hearsay rule. After determining that, you are still not done in determining admissibility, because, even though it may survive the hearsay rule, other rules of evidence may apply to keep it out, e.g., Rule 403 (the probativity versus prejudice, etc. rule), privilege, the character rule, relevancy, etc. The rules of evidence are individual filters, or hurdles, *all* of which a piece of evidence must survive, that is, pass through or overcome, in order to be admissible.

But for now, we are only concerned with whether evidence is hearsay in the first place.

The Hearsay Determination Involves No Balancing on the Facts of the Individual Case

In the initial determination of hearsay, doctrine takes no account of the reliability and necessities in the particular case.

Suppose D (declarant) in the original hypothetical opening this chapter was the only eyewitness and he is now dead; and there is no other evidence either way on the issue. Assume further that there appears to be nothing suggesting that D is lying or unreliable. It would seem that the jury is more likely to reach a correct result if the evidence is admitted than if it is excluded. This becomes highlighted if we further suppose that his statement is the only thing that can clear Q of a charge of murder. Remember that all that is needed to acquit is a reasonable doubt. And yet, the evidence is hearsay (with no apparent exemption or exception).

But considerations such as these have no part in the traditional hearsay determination, except to the formalistic extent that need and reliability are recognized in the exemptions and exceptions to the hearsay rule, infra. If it is hearsay (which this is), and it does not come within one of the recognized exemptions or exceptions (which this probably would not), it is inadmissible. And yet, the average citizen, in making important decisions in his or her daily life, commonly relies on his or her ability to correctly evaluate hearsay. Even attempts under some of the newer codes to add a broad new exception, sometimes dubbed the "catch-all" exception, to the traditional exceptions, do not go all the way toward embracing such evidence. As we shall see when we come to the "catch-all" provision, it does not indeed catch *all*, nor even *most*. At any rate, even in those jurisdictions, although trustworthiness and necessity may be appraised in the particular case under the catch-all exceptions, the initial determination of hearsay-or-not is made without such appraisal.

It should also be noted that there are times when an out-of-court declaration, nearer the time of the occurrence, might be more accurate than the declarant's present testimony would be, and should be preferred. But again, this seldom plays an official role, except as mentioned hereinafter in connection with specific exceptions or exemptions.

Would it Cure the Hearsay Defect if the "Out-of-Court" Declaration Was Made in Another Court?

If D's (declarant's) declaration in our prototype hypothetical opening this chapter, though reported by W (witness) at the present trial, was made not on the

street as assumed in the hypothetical, but rather at another trial in D's capacity as a witness there, we may have a candidate for special treatment as an exemption or exception in certain narrow circumstances, but the declaration is still hearsay.

The dangers of hearsay may be somewhat diminished in this situation. Although there still will be no present cross-examination of and no present judicial safeguards applied to the statement, it will have been subjected to them at the earlier trial. Certainly if the direct-examination from the earlier trial comes in at the second trial, so would the earlier cross-examination. One problem is, however, that the declarant's demeanor would not be before the fact-finder for appraisal in the second trial (unless there were a videotape of the earlier statement, which is still not quite the same as live demeanor).

In general theory, most authority agrees that if this evidence is to stand on a better footing than the evidence in the original hypothetical, it should be taken care of as an exemption or exception only.

Although exemptions or exceptions are not the subject of this chapter, we may foreshadow later chapters by noting that, in some narrow circumstances, an exemption or exception is indeed made for some of this kind of evidence. There may be a requirement that the stimuli to accuracy and the incentives to test D's statement be substantially the same at the two trials. To help insure this safeguard there might be a requirement of similarity between the two trials as to issues and stakes, and sometimes parties, insofar as deemed necessary to allay concerns on this front.[2]

2. Obviously there won't be any additional cross-examination of the statement beyond what was done at the first trial if the statement from the first trial is admitted at the second. If the second trial involves different facts, issues, matters, stakes, or law, there may be some new things one would wish to explore on cross-examination. Or old things one would wish to explore more thoroughly or intensely. Perhaps only

The commonest example of the situation in the black-letter is where D's statement is in the form of testimony he gave at an earlier trial or deposition in the same case. Unavailability of the declarant at the current proceeding may be a requirement for current admission of his prior testimony because the law suspects information originally gathered specifically for testimonial purposes. The usual manner of evidencing the earlier statement in the present trial, is through a recording or a transcript. Analytically this is the same as an oral report of the earlier statement, by the same witness or another who heard it.

If the declarant appears as a witness at the present trial, but it is his statement at the earlier trial that is sought to be admitted at the present trial[3], there might

if that is not so, should the former testimony be let in. The need for additional cross-examination in the second trial is reduced if we are sure the attention, care, efforts, and incentives of the witness and the cross-examiner (and his client), in the earlier trial, were focused, with at least the same intensity and willingness to spend time and money, on the same facts, and on those facts as having the same significance, consequences, importance, and stakes, as would be the case in the present trial. This is sometimes summarized as a requirement of identity or similarity of interest or motive; or identity or similarity of issues or stakes or both.

Similarity of opportunity to and motive to cross-examine are regarded as more important than what the party actually did with that opportunity in the earlier case, since strategic concerns often dictate the latter. If the motives and interests are the same, presumably the strategic judgments would be the same.

Would you require that the identical party opposes the evidence in both cases, or is it enough that someone with a similar motive and interest opposed it in the earlier case? Is someone else's opportunity to cross-examine, a good reason to take away yours? If they represented similar interests? Even so, might you yourself have exercised the opportunity differently than they did? Should this matter?

3. One reason a lawyer might wish to do this is to have an additional piece of evidence of the same facts that the witness' present testimony reports, so there would be two pieces of evidence of the same

be good reason to dispense with any requirement that there have been an opportunity at the earlier proceeding to cross-examine, and that the parties, issues or motives there have been similar to those here. For now there is an additional chance to cross-examine.

The next section below explores whether the fact the declarant currently testifies should cure the hearsay defect regardless of whether the former statement was made at an earlier proceeding.

Should it Cure the Hearsay Defect in an Out-of-Court Declaration if the Declarant Also Presently Testifies?: Prior Statements

In the example opening this chapter, would it cure the defect if D, rather than W, reported on the stand D's prior statement (without disavowing its truth)?

There are several reasons why D might recount his statement when testifying. D might remember only that he said so-and-so, and not remember the facts any longer; or the earlier statement might be offered as a piece of evidence, additional to his present testimony, attesting to the same facts. It would be a forceful piece, being closer to the facts in point of time. The commonest example is the station-house line-up identification recounted on the stand by the person who made the identification.

The controversy amongst scholars on how to treat this situation centers around whether it is the lack of courtroom safeguards, or the lack of courtroom safeguards at the time of making the statement, that is significant. The argument is made that the statement is good evidence of the facts because, although the declarant/witness could

thing (even though both uttered by the same person). It is generally better to have two pieces of evidence of something than one, assuming the judge does not find it unnecessarily redundant. Here it might not be unnecessarily redundant, because the former statement is closer in time to the events.

not be cross-examined then, he is cross-examinable now. We use the phrase "cross-examination" as a surrogate for all the courtroom safeguards mentioned earlier. The counter-argument is that by now it is too late, the story has hardened. Do you think there is any reason to make a distinction between statements of identification on the street or at the station-house and other out-of-court statements? Some jurisdictions do, as we shall see in coming chapters. For now we are dealing with theory.

If the present opportunity to cross-examine is considered to cure the hearsay defect concerning the prior statement, then it may be argued that it should not matter how and through whom the earlier statement is reported—e.g., via a document or another witness who overheard it—so long as the original witness/declarant is present in court (testifying?) and can be cross-examined on it.

There would be no hearsay problem at all if the earlier statement is now to be used merely to refresh the witness/declarant's memory for an on-the-stand present-memory statement, assuming it can be satisfactorily confined to that.

What about using the earlier statement merely to bolster the credibility of the witness and his present testimony to the same effect? Prior statements of a witness (consistent or inconsistent with his present testimony) offered only on the issue of credibility are not considered offered for their truth and are thus not considered hearsay. This is explained more fully below. But even though the evidence may not be hearsay, courtroom economies usually forbid prior consistent statements to support credibility, even when consistency is attacked, except in certain narrow situations. In contrast, inconsistent statements to attack credibility are freely allowed. The different treatment is due to the conceptual difficulty of distinguishing credibility use from substantive use in the consistent-statement context. It also arises out of a fear that witnesses will prepare and make self-serving, bolstering out-of-court statements. Also, inconsistent statements are more probative on credibility than consistent ones.

Some feel that if a witness's prior statement would come in on credibility, it is silly and frequently impossible to refuse it substantive effect. Does it make sense to distinguish between prior consistent and inconsistent ones in this regard? Some jurisdictions do.

In deciding the hearsay or non-hearsay status of a former statement of a witness, distinctions could theoretically be made, concerning the adequacy of the present opportunity to cross-examine, among the following cases, in some of which the present opportunity seems more adequate than others: (1) where the witness remembers the facts stated in the former statement and vouches that they are true;[4] (2) where the witness remembers making the statement and that it was true, but doesn't remember the facts now; (3) where the witness remembers making the statement and feels it "must have been true;" (4) where the witness says "if I said it, it was true;" (5) where the witness says "I said it; it wasn't true;" (6) where the witness says "I didn't say it, and it wasn't true;" (7) where the witness doesn't remember whether or not he made the statement, and (a) denies, (b) affirms, (c) doesn't remember the underlying facts

---

4. The example we are after here is not one where the former statement is referred to merely to refresh the witness' recollection and the witness then incorporates the facts from the earlier statement into his present testimony as his current recollection, with the earlier statement not being used itself as evidence of the facts. We mean here that the former statement is itself offered as evidence of the facts, perhaps additional to the current testimony. If the former statement is written, in our example, it may, under certain circumstances qualify as the hearsay exception for past recollection recorded, treated infra in this book. Here we are concerned with the theory of whether it is hearsay in the first place.

reported in it, or (d) tells a different story now. The statement might be evidenced by another witness, a document, or a recording, where the witness won't say he made it. Although theoretically distinctions may be made amongst these enumerated examples as to the adequacy of current cross-examination, as yet the courts do not seem to be making a distinction. This is so despite the fact that it would seem exceedingly difficult to elicit in cross-exam anything meaningful about the prior statement or the underlying facts it reports in some of the enumerated examples. See, on the adequacy of cross-examination of a witness in various of these postures, the *Green, O'Neil,* and *Owens* cases and annexed discussion, infra, Chapter 9, under "The Results of the Prior Statement Exemptions: Constitutional and Pragmatic Aspects."

There are special considerations where a witness tells one story on the stand, and the opposing attorney wishes to adduce that the witness told a contrary story on some previous occasion, out of court.

Suppose D (declarant), after saying on some earlier out-of-court occasion, that the Ford went through the red light, turns coat and now comes as a live witness to the stand and says the Ford went through on green.

First, it is clear the reference by the attorney to the prior story to stimulate the witness' memory or to secure present assent to its accuracy based on current memory of the facts presents no hearsay problem so long as it is satisfactorily confined to that. The attorney's reference is not evidence, and if the attempt to get the witness to adopt the story succeeds, the former statement would become current testimony. Similarly, if the witness will say the statement was probably true although he doesn't remember the facts, we may have no problem (if the previous statement is written), for it will usually comply with the requirements for the exception to the hearsay rule for "past recollection recorded."

But suppose it is regarded as futile to attempt to use the previous statement in these ways. Assume, however, that the witness will admit, or the attorney is prepared to prove another way, that the witness at least *made* the previous statement. Assume also that the attorney is prepared to prove the contents of the previous statement, either through the witness' admission that he made the statement as quoted by the attorney, or via another witness or document or audio or video recording. Can the previous statement be offered on the theory that it is evidence of the fact that the Ford did go through the red light, which is what it states? D (declarant) is on the stand and available for questioning about the prior statement.

However, unlike the situation mentioned earlier where D testifies to (without repudiating) his own prior out-of-court statement, here the witness does not stand behind his earlier statement at all. This might render it difficult for the opponent of the earlier statement to conduct a searching, cross-examining type of examination concerning the earlier statement.

On the other hand, can this opponent really complain? The witness has already fulfilled the dream of anyone conducting such a cross-examination or challenge to any statement: the witness has repudiated the statement.

The evidence offered for these purposes is usually regarded as hearsay (there is a narrow exception to this in F.R.E.-type codes, treated in the next chapter).

Suppose the theory of the attorney offering the prior inconsistent statement is confined to *impeachment*, i.e., to demonstrating that this is the sort of witness who cannot be trusted on either occasion because he "blows hot and cold." Today he says the Ford had a green.

Previously he said the Ford went through the red light. He can't be believed on either occasion. Neither statement can be trusted.

It is usually held in these circumstances that the earlier statement is offered not as true, but to cast doubt on both statements; that the offeror does not depend upon the veracity or testimonial qualities of the witness on the earlier occasion, and that the out-of-court statement is not being offered as an accurate reflection of the facts it reports, i.e., that the Ford went through the red light. It is said not to detract from the aim of the evidence, that on the former occasion the witness may have been mistaken, lying, etc. The offeror is supposedly attempting to bring out just such possibilities with respect to both occasions.

Courts therefore conclude that the lack of courtroom safeguards respecting the earlier statement is not important, and there is no hearsay, when the statement is offered for and confined to this purpose. The declaration is not offered for the truth of the matter declared.

II.   CONDUCT AS HEARSAY OR NON–HEARSAY: F.R.E. 801(a)

Conduct, Assertive and Non–Assertive: Statements Implied From Conduct

So-called "assertive" behavior of declarants, such as pointing or nodding, is frequently considered to be hearsay. So-called "non-assertive" behavior is more controversial, as are declarant's words offered as meaning something other than they purport to say.

Let us return to the original hypothetical involving an oral declaration by D (declarant) that X shot Y, reported on the stand by W (witness) as substantive evidence of X's guilt. D does not testify. Suppose instead of making a declaration, D, after being in the position of an eye-witness, behaved in some non-verbal fashion as though he believed X shot Y, and this out-of court behavior is reported on the stand by W (who observed D's behavior) for the same purposes as the declaration was. Clearly, if the behavior were intended by D to be a substitute for the declaration, as for example where D points to X in response to an inquiry as to who was the shooter, it should be treated no differently from the declaration, for the policy considerations are the same. Where behavior is intended by D in this fashion to be a substitute for words, we call it "assertive." D intends it to be a communication. A similar example would be a nod of D's head in affirmation if asked if X shot Y.

Suppose the behavior by D (declarant) that is supposed to indicate X's guilt, is non-assertive—not intended by D as a substitute for words. More concretely, let us suppose that it is conclusively established that the victim was the beloved brother of D and D directly observed the shooting that killed him. W testifies that immediately after the victim fell, W observed D chasing X. (Perhaps W herself was not positioned so as to be able to see the actual killing, but only the aftermath.) Of course, such evidence is offered at the trial as a kind of implied statement of or implied assertion of the chased person's (X's) guilt—as evidence that D believed in X's guilt, which makes X's guilt more likely—but probably not as something intended by D at the time as a communication to the watchers or a substitute for the words "X did it." This non-intention of D at the time is what is responsible for the short-hand term, "non-assertive," used to characterize this kind of behavior. The judge decides if behavior is assertive or non-assertive, but these examples are clear. Let's examine this chasing behavior, which is non-assertive.

You will note that the evidence of chasing is offered on the theory that D's apparent belief in X's guilt was translated into action rather than words. The chain of reasoning urged here by the offeror (the prosecutor in the prosecution of X for the murder of Y) is that because D behaved in this way, D probably believed X shot Y; the belief was probably well founded in direct observation of facts corresponding to and giving rise to the belief; therefore, X probably did shoot Y. The chain of reasoning in the original hypothetical involving an express declaration, "X shot Y," was identical except that the word "declared" should be substituted for the word "behaved," so the inference chain would read: because D declared this, D probably believed it; the belief was probably well founded; therefore X probably did shoot Y. A similar chain is present in the case of "pointing" just above, too, and "nodding". In each case a belief is sought to be inferred from an outward manifestation (words or conduct); and a fact is sought to be inferred from the belief in it. It would seem that there are many of the same possibilities of unreliability (mistake, dishonesty, attempt to divert suspicion, etc.) in each case. The reader should try to ascribe each type of possible unreliability to a link in the reasoning chain just set out.

In some ways, however, the evidence is more reliable in the case involving chasing than in the case of the express declaration, pointing, or nodding. Persons generally require more certainty before taking action such as chasing than before speaking, pointing, or nodding. Talk is cheap. It is less likely that a person will act out (to the extent of chasing) a lie or joke than speak one (or point or nod one). And the jury is more "on guard" in drawing the offered inference from the chasing than they are in believing a direct verbal declaration (or specific pointing or nodding). For these reasons, there is perhaps less need to insist on the courtroom safeguards in the chasing example than in the case of the express declaration or pointing or nodding. Also, chasing "looks" less like traditional testimony.

On the other hand, the chasing of X by D may have been due to something like, say, a desire to secure a scared X as a witness to the slaying committed by someone else, or an unkind word by X about the just deceased brother, or, less likely, an old money debt owed by X to D of which D happened to be reminded at the moment, which possibilities (major ambiguities) have no analogue in the case of the express declaration (or, perhaps, the pointing or nodding). In this sense, the "chasing" evidence is *less* reliable than the declaration or pointing/nodding, and there may be *more* need for safeguards.

But perhaps these new dangers are not comparable to those involved in accepting statements as true, and are therefore not in the peculiar province of the courtroom processes (cross-exam, etc.) discussed. Perhaps they are provable other ways than by having D on the stand. Perhaps the jury will make allowance for them regardless of whether they are shown, at least if prodded.

The problem would be much the same if D, rather than declaring X's guilt or manifesting it by pointing, nodding, or chasing, called X a "filthy swine," and this were later reported in court to indicate that D saw X shoot Y. In this case, we are implying one statement from another, rather than from conduct, but the problem is much the same: conduct or statement offered as meaning something else—i.e., as amounting to a belief in or implied statement of another fact, to help prove the fact. It is not clear whether this "filthy swine" evidence would be regarded as assertive or non-assertive of the proposition that X is guilty. Based on our discussion of intention and relative reliability in the last few paragraphs, it seems more like non-assertive.

These problems are all usually characterized as part of a debate about whether and when action is considered an "implied declaration" under the hearsay rule.

Prior to the F.R.E., the authorities were in considerable disagreement over whether to regard as "declarations" for purposes of the hearsay rule, such non-assertive actions like the chasing and perhaps the "filthy swine" example, where the implied statement offered for its truth is not *intended* to be made by the actor or declarant. The majority common-law and the English position held that even though "non-assertive," such conduct can be hearsay. The F.R.E. position is to the contrary.

The non-F.R.E. authority that regards such conduct offered for such purposes as declarations and hence hearsay, of course limits itself to cases like those described above (chasing, nodding, pointing, i.e., both the assertive and non-assertive category) where the actor's conduct (like declarant's words in the ordinary hearsay case) are offered as a reflection of his belief which is in turn offered as an accurate reflection of some other fact that is the fact of legal significance in the lawsuit (or leads thereto). For only then are there weaknesses in the inference the offeror seeks to draw which are analogous to the weaknesses inherent in ordinary witness testimony and ordinary hearsay and which the courtroom processes discussed are deemed peculiarly adept at minimizing or exposing. Only then are the credibility, accuracy, or sincerity of the actor drawn into issue. In other words, the person whose words or conduct is being testified to (the out-of-court person, the "declarant") must be being offered as in effect an absent witness to something. W's testimony in a murder case that she had seen the conduct of the defendant in killing the victim, would not present a hearsay problem (even though it is a report of out-of-court conduct) because it does not meet this criterion. The conduct itself is of legal significance. This example has its analogue where an out-of-court express declaration is offered for itself and not as a representation of any further fact; as, for example, where a slander or oral contract which is the subject of suit is proven by one who overheard it. In each case the out-of-court person is not in effect acting as an absent witness.

Conduct: Limitations Inherent in F.R.E. 801's Definition of Hearsay

An "exclusion" from the hearsay rule is inherent in the F.R.E.'s basic definition of hearsay in Rule 801 (a)-(c): "Hearsay" is an out-of-court "statement" offered for its truth; "statement" is either an "express assertion" or "nonverbal conduct intended by the actor as an assertion." Thus, only assertive, as opposed to non-assertive, physical acts or omissions can be hearsay. Non-assertive acts or omissions, therefore, are excluded from the F.R.E.'s hearsay rule. Note that no provision is made for words (verbal conduct) offered as amounting to another (implied) statement that is offered for its truth. For example, the "filthy swine" case, immediately supra. The result of this omission is uncertain.

F.R.E. Rule 104(a) assigns the judge the task of deciding if the act was intended as an assertion (communication). This can be difficult and may involve deciding the motivation and even the honesty of the declarant in many instances. See generally Park, *"I Didn't Tell Them Anything About You": Implied Assertions as Hearsay Under the Federal Rules of Evidence*, 74 Minn. L. Rev. 783 (1990). Cf. Tribe, *Triangulating Hearsay*, 87 Harv. L. Rev. 957 (1974) (propounding a theory under which, unlike the F.R.E., both assertive and non-assertive conduct should be hearsay because of the credibility issues involved in both, a view like that involved in the majority

common-law and English precedent, see *Wright v. Tatham* (Exchequer Chamber, 1837)).

Notice that under all definitions of hearsay, there must be something that can be considered an out-of-court express or implied *statement* of or *assertion* of some fact whose truth is important to the litigation. Questions or orders may not have this quality of stating or asserting a fact, unless an implied statement of or assertion of a fact (whose truth is important to the litigation) can be found in the particular circumstances of the case.

Conduct: The Element of Human Voluntariness

Non-human effects or behavior (such as those of machines or animals) normally are not considered hearsay because they are not "statements," even though they may seem analogous to statements. Involuntary human conduct, as well as conduct not intended as assertion, also is not hearsay under the F.R.E., although the common law sometimes so characterized it.

Consider the following pieces of evidence. In each case, you are to assume that the effort is to prove the direction of the wind, and whether or not it was raining, at the time of the occurrence in controversy.

(1) Testimony as to the behavior of weather vanes, sails on the lake, and rain detection equipment at the time.

(2) Testimony as to the behavior of cows in a nearby field. Assume it is proven that it is the habit of cows to lie down in the rain, and face into the wind. In one case it was sought to be proved that certain chickens held by X belonged to Y, by showing they flocked to Y's premises and bedded down there upon being released by X.

(3) Testimony by a witness who was not herself in a position to tell whether it was raining or to sense the wind (being, say, at a sheltered window, covered by an

over-hang, high up in a tall building), that the passersby had their umbrellas up and were hunched as though walking into the wind when proceeding in one direction.

(4) The witness in (3) reports that, rather than seeing umbrellas, she shouted down "is it raining?" and the passersby replied that it was.

(5) The same cases as (3) and (4) except that only one passerby is involved, rather than many.

Consider also the following:

(6) An observation that people turned up their collars and wrapped their coats around themselves, offered to prove it was cold on that occasion, (a) where the evidence shows this action was done to express to another (say someone in a window) that it was cold, or (b) where there is no evidence it was done for such purpose.

(7) Police use of tear gas is sought to be proved by showing that people staggered from the building coughing and wiping their eyes (a) where tears were also seen, (b) where tears were not seen but would not have been susceptible of being seen if present, or (c) where there is disputed evidence that a person making a delivery dropped and broke a keg of chemical nearby that would have a similar effect.

Of course there are differences in weight among these pieces of evidence, and the differences would manifest themselves not only in the jury's evaluation of the evidence, but probably also in the balancing process affecting admissibility, i.e., the balancing of probative value against its counterweights as epitomized by F.R.E. 403. But what about the hearsay rule?

Most courts would agree that (1) and (2) are not hearsay. Inaccuracies that might inhere in machinery or in an animal's perception and reaction are not regarded as peculiar subjects of the courtroom safeguards we have been speaking about. However, in some cases an expert foundation might be required to explain how a dog was trained or how equipment works. The F.R.E. eliminates nonhumans from hearsay consideration by defining a declarant as a "person" who makes a statement.

Does this exclusion reach signs stamped out by an assembly line process, or output created by computer programs, or is the fact of some human activity directing the effort sufficient to identify a human declarant? If these are offered for the truth of their recitals, the latter is the correct answer. Would testimony about what time was on a clock rely on the credibility of the one who set the clock? Yes. It probably should be deemed hearsay.

Most would agree that (4) is hearsay; and most would decide that the application of the hearsay rule, like the requirement of cross examination in court in ordinary cases, cannot turn upon how many people say the same thing (see (5)), although where a witness has become unavoidably unavailable for cross examination after giving direct testimony—e.g., has become sick or has died—this factor may influence the decision as to what is to be done. Most courts would also agree that 6(a) is hearsay.

As to the others, there is bound to be substantial disagreement. Several of them, however, are pretty clearly not intended as statements under the F.R.E. What can be said about them is that courts agree in principle that the application of the hearsay rule should not hinge on distinctions regarding the probativity of the evidence; and yet it is difficult to escape the conclusion that a degree of voluntariness of the declaration or conduct, and at least some opportunity for premeditation, mistake, or fabrication, is needed for the hearsay rule to be applicable. Only then is the evidence within the traditional province of the courtroom safeguards and perhaps outside the jury's competence to evaluate without them. Only then is the jury likely to be unduly gullible. Thus, a startled physical flinching, offered to prove an explosion, would generally be admissible and might even be likened to evidence that a person was seen hurtling through the air, offered for the same purpose. It should be noted in this connection, that there is a specific exception to the hearsay rule, discussed infra, for certain kinds of spontaneous utterances, stimulated by excitement over a shocking occurrence, or, if not so excited, made immediately upon the perception. It is to be wondered whether it is true that such reports are likely to be superior to other forms of hearsay, or whether, on the other hand, persons are less careful in such circumstances. Perhaps the feeling is that the jury is equipped to evaluate that kind of possibility of inaccuracy as opposed to conscious deception, relatively unlikely in such spontaneous reactions.

Conduct: Omission

A number of cases involving the *absence* of statements or conduct by "declarants" have presented a problem which has split authorities.

Seller delivers corn to Buyer, pursuant to a purchase contract between them calling for Grade One corn. Grades of corn are clearly ascertainable. Buyer complains that Grade Two corn was delivered, which is inferior. Buyer therefore sues Seller for breach of contract. It is stipulated that the corn delivered came from a certain bulk lot; and that all corn in a bulk lot is of uniform grade (fungible). Seller introduces in defense evidence that Seller had sold to others, as Grade One corn, corn from precisely the same bulk lot as that from which the corn delivered to Buyer was drawn; and that none of these other customers ever complained. An agent of Seller's company having personal knowledge of this testifies. The other customers do not. The inference Seller hopes will be drawn from this evidence is that the corn was Grade One. Is this hearsay?

The problem is essentially the same as that involved in the hypothetical about D (putative "declarant") chasing X (the putative shooter), above, except that some might find it more difficult to imply a statement from silence than from affirmative conduct. The customers whose non-complaints (conduct) are offered play essentially the same out-of-court role as D. W (witness) is the testifying agent of Seller's company. The evidence is offered on the theory that the non-complaining customers believed they received Grade One corn, or at least did not believe otherwise, as manifest by their out-of-court silence, and this state of belief was probably founded on the corresponding fact in the real world that it was Grade One corn they received. As in the case of the express declaration, the pointing, the nodding, and the chasing, the chain of inference sought to be drawn involves two distinct links or deductions: (1) that the persons held the belief (or lacked a contrary one), and (2) that they did so because the facts were in accord therewith. These same two are also involved in accepting as true any statement made on or off the stand. Both links are fallible.

Some possible unreliabilities in the first link or inference (that the person or persons had the belief it was Grade One corn and/or did not have a contrary belief) are, of course, that the customers may have believed it was Grade Two, but may have forgone complaint because complaint was too much trouble, or because of a bribe, a wish not to jeopardize good and generally advantageous business relations, a selling price such that it was not worth complaining, a minor disparity between the value of Grade One and Grade Two corn, a contemplated usage for which the two grades were equally adequate (such as feeding pigs), or some other factor giving rise to a reluctance to complain. Of course, the likelihood of these varies with the facts, e.g., the number of non-complaining customers, the prices paid, and the difference in value between the two grades.

Coming to weaknesses in the second link or inference (that the facts were in accord with the belief), even if the customers believed the corn they received was Grade One, their belief may have been incorrect. They may have failed to inspect or to inspect properly, their inspection facilities may have been poor, someone may have been careless, information as to the criteria for determining grades may have been deficient, etc. Again, the particular facts, such as the number of customers, would be important to the strength of the inference.

Requiring the customers to be subjected to courtroom processes would certainly help to some extent, but not entirely in the customary manner. Clearly there are certain other ways for the buyer who is opposing the evidence, to at least somewhat help herself. For example, other evidence could be brought illuminating these possibilities. Or, indeed, the buyer herself might be able to call the customers and subject them to courtroom processes if they are known and available. Or, to some extent, the buyer could rely on the sophistication of the jury, at least with instruction and argument. Courts are in disagreement over what the result should be. Sometimes, a court will ignore the hearsay question, and focus only on the probativity-and-its-counterweights balancing, simply admitting evidence of omission when it finds that a reasonable person in the same circumstances would have felt compelled to act (complain, respond). Under the F.R.E. this is probably appropriate because the silence was probably not meant to be an assertion (communication) by the silent customers, even though it may indicate the belief the product was the higher grade. Thus, the only question would be the balancing under Rule 403.

A similar case is presented where an out-of-court silence in the face of an accusation is offered as implied acquiescence—an admission of the guilt or fact charged by the accuser—or where lack of response to a letter or bill is offered as an implied admission of the correctness of the facts stated therein. Notice that the accusation, letter, or bill itself is not offered in a hearsay capacity (i.e., not itself offered as evidence of the truth of its recitals), but as a predicate for the lack of response, which lack would itself on one theory, be hearsay (but perhaps within the exception or exemption for admissions discussed infra). Other considerations, however, might dictate exclusion of this line of proof. E.g., particular facts might render it slimly probative of acquiescence and inadmissible under the probativity-and-its-counterweights balancing in Rule 403. In the criminal context, constitutional concerns may also be implicated if, for example, police were present or making the accusation in certain circumstances. Under the F.R.E., any hearsay challenge would probably be headed off because the silence or lack of reply is probably not intended by the non-responder to be an assertion (communication) even though it may indicate the belief it is offered to show.

Conduct: Mistake and Insincerity

The possibility of mistake (innocent inaccuracy) and insincerity (lying, joking) on the part of the person who is not presented seems to be the touchstone of hearsay.

In the foregoing examples involving committive and omittive non-assertive conduct, the weaknesses in what we have called the second link or inference (i.e., that the belief and the objective fact correspond) seem to be analogous to those that infect the same link or inference wherever a statement is propounded as true; except that perhaps some kinds of conduct suggest that greater care was taken in fashioning the generating belief than do some kinds of statements. Without exactitude, we may summarize weaknesses in this link (the link between belief and fact) as "the possibility of mistake."

Weaknesses in the first link (the link or inference that the words or conduct evidence the propounded state of belief) may be summarized without exactitude as "the possibility of insincerity" (lying, joking), when we are dealing with any express statement (made on or off the stand) offered as true; and as "the possibility of insincerity or other explanation for the conduct" in the case of conduct offered in the fashion described in preceding sections. An example of "other explanation" would be the money debt, unkind word, or desire to secure a witness which we said might have motivated D (putative "declarant") to chase X (putative shooter), rather than any belief in X's having done the shooting.

While the possibility of insincerity may be attenuated in the case of certain conduct as compared with certain declarations, owing to the fact that more energy is expended or more "put on the line" by D in the case of certain conduct, there is usually the addition of the possibility of "other explanation" for the conduct. But questions may be raised as to (1) whether the possibility of "other explanation" is something peculiarly within the province of the pertinent courtroom safeguards, since it generally does not arise in connection with statements; and (2) whether the jury will ignore or significantly misevaluate the possibility of other explanation without the specific courtroom safeguards that are the concern of the hearsay rule.

We will come to cases involving out-of-court declarations in which one or more of the possible unreliabilities in one or other of these links is of no concern. This may come about because the link is not involved in the theory upon which the evidence is offered. E.g., in a suit for misrepresentation by defendant to plaintiff that the land the defendant was selling to plaintiff was 500 acres (admittedly said by defendant), statements of plaintiff about the "250 acre tract" made just before completion of the sale, offered to establish plaintiff's knowledge of the true 250–acre size (proved true by other evidence that the land was 250 acres) and thus to prove plaintiff's lack of reliance on defendant's misrepresentation, would not involve the second link, i.e., the link between belief and objective fact. This may not be hearsay because not offered for the truth of the statement, or may be within the special exception or principle for state-of-mind, infra.

Alternatively, the unreliability in one or other, or both, of the links might be reduced, or practically eliminated, as where a person knowingly makes a declaration of a self-damaging fact. It is relatively likely here that the person held the belief in the fact (he is *probably* not speaking insincerely, that is, lying or joking); and it is relatively likely that he was careful before forming the belief, so the the belief likely corresponds to the objective fact. Thus, both links are relatively well assured. This may constitute the hearsay exception for declarations against interest. The fact that the possibility of unreliability is only present to minor degree ordinarily will not mean the evidence is not hearsay; if it has any effect, it will normally be by way of playing a role in the shape of an exception to the hearsay rule.

The question in these kinds of cases is, will the remaining possibilities of unreliability necessitate subjection to the courtroom safeguards and render the evidence inadmissible hearsay?

Special Trustworthiness as Generally Irrelevant to Hearsay or Non–Hearsay

In the original determination of hearsay, as opposed to the creation of the exceptions and exemptions,

**special trustworthiness of the evidence has tradition-
ally played little role.**

In drawing a possible distinction between the case
where D declares X's guilt and the case where D acts as
though X is guilty by chasing X, we said that because
talk is cheaper than action, the conduct evidence was the
more trustworthy in certain respects, namely D's sincerity and his care in ascertaining the facts. Different kinds
of action can be distinguished along the same lines. It
would seem that in the corn hypothetical mentioned
above, the customers might have more to lose from being
wrong or deceptive than D would in the hypothetical
about chasing X, at least if the chasing followed some
minor crime rather than murder. This of course would
depend upon particular undisclosed facts in the two
cases, such as the price paid for the corn, the disparity in
value between the two grades, the contemplated usage of
the corn, the vigor, length, and difficulty of the chase,
etc.

Cases of extraordinary reliability can be imagined, in
the conduct area. A sea captain inspects a ship and then
embarks on it with his wife and children. This is offered
as evidence of the seaworthiness of the ship. He has
staked quite a lot on the correctness of his judgment of
seaworthiness, which speaks loudly for his care, sincerity, and accuracy, and for the trustworthiness and reliability of the offered inference. Of course, there is some
chance that he was mistaken or planning a suicide and
multiple killing. Suppose instead of a captain we have
just an ordinary sailor of lower competence and qualifications. This reduces the likelihood of accuracy and increases the need for safeguards.

Suppose someone bets a large sum of money that a fact
is true, and pays off, out of court. Would the person have
paid off if the fact were true? The pay-off would seem to

be some evidence that the fact is untrue, its reliability in some measure depending on the amount bet or perhaps on how that amount compares with his wealth or with the courtroom stakes in the case in which it is offered as evidence. The same situation is presented where payment by an indemnitor or insurer is attempted to be offered as evidence of the happening of the event indemnified or insured against. Or suppose someone entrusts important business to a testator around the time the testator is executing her will. This would seem to be somewhat reliable evidence of the soundness of mind with which the testator executed the will, although there are other explanations for the entruster's conduct than that he carefully determined the testator was of sound mind. Perhaps he *had* to deal with the testator, or was mistaken in his assessment of the testator.

Are we saying anything peculiar about conduct as hearsay? Express declarations similarly differ among themselves respecting reliability. In their case, the merest presence, in however minor a degree, of a risk of untrustworthiness of the sort traditionally in the province of the courtroom safeguards, will normally mean the evidence is hearsay. Special circumstances reducing that risk may play a role in the creation of exceptions to the hearsay rule, and of course affect weight and the probative-prejudice balancing outlined in an earlier chapter, but at common-law and under the F.R.E. they do not normally affect the determination of hearsay-or-not. Some deviations from this will be noted, infra.

Conduct should not be, and usually is not, treated any differently. The conduct either is or is not hearsay, and differences in its strength are matters of weight, or of the balancing mentioned. However, a supposed general greater trustworthiness of non-assertive conduct indicating a fact than express statements indicating a fact, is one reason why the F.R.E., as opposed to many common-law decisions, holds that non-assertive conduct (conduct not intended by the "declarant" to be an assertion/communication) cannot be hearsay.

While special circumstances reducing the risk of untrustworthiness would not obviate the necessity for the oath and for the opportunity to cross-examine in the case of ordinary in-court non-hearsay testimony, the analogy is not entirely apposite. For in hearsay cases we are often faced with the choice of either having the evidence without oath and cross-examination, or not having it (or not having it conveniently). The analogy would be better if we consider as our non-hearsay situation a case where the witness has become unavailable after direct but before cross-examination. Then, in certain circumstances, cross-examination might be dispensed with. But, of course, as to the witness, at least some of the courtroom safeguards, such as the oath, demeanor, etc. have been complied with.

Our examples above of especially highly reliable out-of-court conduct (embarking on a ship; paying off bets or insurance; entrusting business; etc.) would probably be considered non-assertive conduct and thus not hearsay under the F.R.E. (as opposed to the majority common-law and English view), even though the conduct, like the equivalent words, is offered as evidence of a belief, which belief in turn is offered to help establish the truth of the fact believed. Part of the rationale of the F.R.E. is that non-assertive conduct is more reliable than words. And this would apply under the F.R.E. to non-assertive conduct even when it is less reliable than in our examples concerning the ship, bet, insurance, and business entrustment.

III. SOME COMMON SITUATIONS WHERE OUT–OF–COURT DECLARATIONS ARE NOT HEARSAY BECAUSE NOT OFFERED FOR THE "TRUTH OF THE MATTER" DECLARED: F.R.E. 801(c)

Out-of-Court Declarations Offered Merely to Show They Were Made: (1) Proving Defamation

In a slander or libel action, evidence of the out-of-court slander (oral defamatory statement) or libel (printed defamatory statement) is not hearsay.

X (plaintiff) charges Y (defendant) with slander. The slander allegedly uttered by Y is "X stole a watch." X (plaintiff) introduces witnesses (Ws) who testify that they heard Y (defendant) say this, in order to prove the utterance of the slander. While this is evidence of an out-of-court statement, it is not offered to prove the truth of the matter stated by defendant—that plaintiff stole a watch—but rather merely to show that defendant said it. Indeed, plaintiff must avoid establishing its truth, or the defendant will have a valid substantive defense (the defense of truth). The evidence is offered to show that the statement was made, not that it was true. The veracity, credibility, accuracy, sincerity, etc., of the defendant in reporting plaintiff's thievery is not at all relied upon by the plaintiff in offering this evidence. Indeed, plaintiff would like to show just the reverse of these, and to make Y and Y's statement look as untrustworthy, unfounded, and malicious as possible. Nor is the evidence offered to show that defendant believed in its truth, like in the Orange–O case, infra, Part IV of this chapter. Once again, it might be in plaintiff's interests to show the opposite, to avoid jury sympathy for defendant.

The only person's credibility as a reporter of fact that is relied upon by plaintiff in this offer is W's (the witness who reports on the stand that he heard the defendant make the defamatory statement and recounts it). W *is* making *W's* statement in court and subject to cross-examination. Since the issue (at this point) is not the truth of what defendant said, but whether he said it, W's but not defendant's veracity is in issue.

Such evidence would not be considered hearsay. The out-of-court utterer (Y, the defendant) is not being used as a kind of absent witness to an objective fact which itself has the legal significance.

But it is instructive to note that something could perhaps be illuminated by having Y, the defendant, on the stand. Suppose it had been apparent at the time of the utterance, that Y was joking. Or lying. Or mistaken. Would that not affect plaintiff's case? Yes, assuming it was apparent. In that case it would not be believed by anyone listening at the time of the slander, and thus the "slander" might not be defamatory, indeed might not be slander at all; or at least the damages would be slim. This is not a question of whether defendant actually was reporting the truth about plaintiff, but of appearances.

But are there other ways to bring these appearances out? Is defendant likely to be accurate on them? Can Ws (the witnesses who recount hearing defendant Y's statement) enlighten just as well or better? This still would not be deemed hearsay.

Note that the defendant is actually present at trial and able to be called if needed or wished, so maybe the hearsay concern about lack of cross-examination is somewhat alleviated. This makes no difference to the hearsay analysis here; but cf. the exception or exemption for party admissions.

Out-of-Court Declarations Offered Merely to Show They Were Made: (2) Statements Constituting a Contract or Gift

Out-of-court statements offered as themselves creating contract or property rights are not hearsay.

A Professor places a book in front of her on a table, stating to student Jones, "This is your book, Jones." Student W overhears this and testifies to it later in court. If the purpose is to establish a gift or transfer of the property in the book from the Professor to student Jones, under a body of substantive law that holds that such a statement constitutes a gift or transfer, then the evidence is not hearsay. The out-of-court utterer (Professor) is not being used as an absent witness to some objective fact that has legal significance. Her words themselves are the operative legal event.

However, if the purpose is to establish that the book was student Jones' all along (e.g., in a lost or stolen book case), then the statement of the Professor is hearsay. For in that case the Professor is being used as an absent witness to an independent, objective fact (whose book it was prior to that moment)—that objective fact being the legally significant fact. Rather than the Professor's out-of-court statement itself being the legally significant fact, that statement is being offered as an accurate reflection of something else that is: an external, objective fact pre-existing the statement and existing independently of it, about which fact the Professor (and her words) may have been mistaken, lying, joking, etc.

In contrast, in the former case (gift case) the Professor's words themselves create the rights whereof they speak, and the Professor's credibility and accuracy as a reporter of outside fact is irrelevant. All that matters is that she said them. As to this, only the credibility and accuracy of the witness on the stand, student W, as a reporter of fact (the fact of having heard the Professor's statement), is in issue, and student W is testifying and subject to cross-examination. The issue is not whether the Professor spoke truly, but whether she (the Professor) spoke this at all. Her credibility thus is not in issue. Only W's is—in saying he heard the Professor say this.

Suppose that, under the substantive law in the non-hearsay example (the gift case), a gift or transfer is not made merely by utterance of the statement, but there must also be intent to make a gift or transfer; and/or the circumstances must be such that a reasonable or ordinary person in the situation would regard the statement as appearing to be an intentional transfer. Would it then be useful to have the Professor on the stand? Necessary? Useful in the traditional way? This probably would not be regarded as hearsay, either.

In the above examples, it makes no difference whether the statement was oral or written. And, just as the Professor's statement may be proved to show a gift or transfer, so too may the terms of an oral or written contract be proved in a suit upon the contract, by introducing the contract or by the testimony of a person who overheard it, even though it is an out-of-court statement. The same would be true for oral or written utterances constituting contract offers or acceptances. Out-of-court statements that are offered on the theory that they themselves have legal effect in this fashion, and not because they reflect the truth, are known as "verbal acts" or "operative facts." This appellation also covers the slander example in the last section, and might also be applied to the apparent agency example in the next section. Similarly, it can be used in criminal cases, when the offered words are offered because they themselves *are* the charged criminal act, as in cases of threats, solicitation, extortion, or bribery.

In the gift case, it may be that neither the words alone nor the handing over of the book alone, would constitute a gift or transfer of title to the book, but that both are needed. Still, in the context of the handing over, the words have operational legal significance that does not depend upon their truth or the existence of some other fact they report. Thus, the reasoning above establishing the non-hearsay status of the words in the gift case, still holds. To the extent that words complete an act that would otherwise be of insufficient legal effect, in this fashion, they are sometimes called verbal *parts* of acts by some courts or commentators. Still, they are not hearsay.

Out-of-Court Declarations Offered Merely to Show They Were Made: (3) Apparent Authority

Out-of-court statements offered on a theory that they contribute to establishing apparent authority are not hearsay.

X presents himself to Y at the latter's gasoline station where Y has reported leakage to the Gasco gasoline company that supplies him and maintains his premises. X drives a company car, wears a company uniform, and says to Y, the station owner, "I am the agent of the Gasco gasoline company, and am authorized to investigate your leak. Show it to me." Y, the station owner, does so, whereupon X lights a match to get a closer look, blowing the place up. Injured, Y (the station owner) sues the Gasco gasoline company on a theory of respondeat superior (vicarious responsibility) for the putative agent's (X's) negligence. The company disputes only that X was the company's agent for purposes of investigating leakage. They assert that X's investigation of the leak was outside the scope of X's employment; that X was authorized only to take orders for gasoline; and that X was expressly forbidden to investigate leaks. Thus, they maintain, X's actions were wholly unauthorized by the company. Therefore they would not be liable for his negligence.

If liability depended upon express authorization of X by the company, to investigate leaks or the leak, the only bearing X's statement to Y would have on the issue would be as evidence that the company did in fact expressly so authorize X. The offeror would hope the jury would ask themselves, "Why would X claim to be authorized to investigate the leak if it weren't true, that is, if X weren't expressly so authorized?" X would be being used as an absent witness to an objective fact: the fact of actual conferral of authorization done by the company back at the shop, which X had perceived. As such, the evidence would be hearsay. For the credibility of both the on-the-stand witness (presumably Y) who reports hearing X's statement, and X, who reports an actual act of authorization, are of concern. Yet only the former (Y, the witness on the stand) is making his statement on the stand subject to cross-examination. Because X's credibility in making his out-of-court report (when he presented himself at Y's door and spoke to him) of an actual act of authorization, is an un-taken-care-of concern, we have hearsay here.

But suppose the liability of the company can be maintained on a theory of *apparent* (as opposed to *actual*) authority to investigate the leak—that is, there would be liability not only if there were express authority, but also if it reasonably appeared to Y that X had such authority and the company was in part responsible for those appearances, regardless of actual authority. The reasonableness of Y's belief that X had such authority, i.e., the reasonableness of the appearance of authority, would be in issue. The facts that X (1) drove a company car, (2) wore a company uniform, (3) was the person with whom Y customarily dealt in Y's relations with the company, and (4) said "I have authority to investigate the leak," are all relevant to a determination of whether it reasonably appeared that X had the authority, i.e., to a determination of whether it was reasonable and justified to suppose that X was authorized to investigate the leak.

Offered on this theory, the evidence would not be hearsay. The actual credibility (truth) of X's out-of-court statement of authority to plaintiff would not be in issue. X would not be being used as an absent witness to objective fact.

Understanding might be facilitated if you suppose that as a matter of law the presence or absence of factor (4) [the statement] is determinative on these facts, i.e., where the other three are also present. Then it becomes apparent that the case is analogous to the verbal act or operative fact cases.

Can the jury be effectively confined to using the statement along these lines? The law usually assumes they can.

In this apparent authority example, we do not have hearsay because we are only concerned with whether X made the statement, not with its objective truth. Only the witness on the stand who reports hearing the statement needs to be telling the truth, not X. And we have that witness on the stand subject to cross-examination, etc., while he is making his report.

The facts listed with numbers several paragraphs above, are also relevant to the issue of whether Y (plaintiff) actually believed X was Gasco's agent for examining the leak, which issue, too, is raised by a theory of apparent authority. Offered in this capacity, the evidence would come within the principle of the next section infra.

Out-of-Court Declarations Offered Merely to Show They Were Made: (4) Statements Offered to Show the Effect They Had Upon a Particular Listener (or Reader) at the Time

Evidence of these out-of-court statements is generally not considered to be hearsay.

Suppose in the hypothetical in the last section concerning the gasoline leak, the company pleads that Y (plaintiff) was contributorily negligent in allowing X to approach and light a match near the leak. Y offers X's statement, "I am the agent of Gasco gasoline company and am authorized to investigate your leak; show it to me," as a circumstance tending to render reasonable, Y's reliance on X's knowing the right thing to do. The actual credibility (truth) of the statement of X is not in issue. His statement is as much the basis for a claim of justified reliance if it was false as it is if it was true—so long as nothing "fishy" about it appeared to one in Y's shoes (a question of appearances, not truth). On this theory of the offer of the evidence, X (the putative "agent") is not being used as an absent witness to objective fact. All that matters is that X said it, not that it was true. Therefore, only the on-the-stand witness's credibility (in reporting on the stand he heard X say it), not X's, is in issue. The evidence is not hearsay. Can the jury be effectively confined to this usage? The law normally presumes they can.

Mrs. Smith slips and falls on a wet patch on the floor of a grocery store. W testifies for her that he (or someone he overheard) had told the manager about the wet spot earlier that same day. This out-of-court statement to the manager is offered to show that the store management had notice of the wet spot (the existence of which wet spot is established by other evidence), and therefore the management, having such notice, acted unreasonably in failing to clean it up. The actual credibility (truth) of the out-of-court statement to the manager is not in issue under this theory. The fact that the statement was made, and not its truth, is important. It would be otherwise if the evidence were offered to substantiate the fact that there was a wet spot there. Can the two uses be effectively separated? The law normally assumes they can, although a contrary argument can be made. But courts usually allow hearsay evidence in with a limiting instruction if a legitimate purpose can be articulated, notwithstanding illegitimate uses that might be made. In extreme cases this may not be so. This is probably not an extreme case.

What about a label which contains the word "Poison," introduced on the issue of whether the plaintiff in a personal injury action had notice that it was dangerous to drink the contents of the bottle? This is the same problem. Is there a difference, if the label is used to show that the substance in the bottle is poison? Yes.

Mrs. Jones sues a doctor who gave her X-ray treatments, which she alleges resulted in an inflamed and ulcerated condition of the area X-rayed. She offers the out-of-court statement of another doctor, who told her the inflamed and ulcerated condition would develop into cancer.

If offered on the issue of damages to help prove that the inflamed and ulcerated condition may develop into cancer, the evidence would plainly be hearsay. The actual credibility (truth) of the statement would be in issue.

It is otherwise if she offers the evidence to help show her own mental anguish and suffering (which is also on the issue of damages)—i.e., she offers it to show that because of the statement, be it actually true or false, she had grounds to feel considerable anxiety over the X-ray treatments given her by the first doctor.

A court *might* be a little hesitant to allow this, however, in a case where damages are sought for both actual prospective cancer, and the mental anxiety or distress, because the primary use the fact-finder will make of the evidence, regardless of limiting instructions, will probably be the hearsay use.

As indicated in this section, individuals sometimes act on the basis of statements they hear, regardless of whether the statements are true. For example, assume that the mother of a young child shoots X because Q told her that he (Q) saw X molest her child. The statement of Q would be relevant on the issue of whether the mother had a culpable state of mind even if Q was lying or mistaken. It would thus not be hearsay offered for this purpose. What if the statement was that Q heard from some unknown third party that X molested the child? Still not hearsay.

The "state-of-mind of the hearer [or reader]" principle of this section should not be confused with the state-of-mind principle of Part IV of this chapter, which deals with the state-of-mind of the *declarant*.

IV. OUT–OF–COURT STATEMENTS OR CONDUCT SHOWING THE DECLARANT'S STATE OF MIND OR BELIEF: F.R.E. 801(c)

Evidence of State of Belief for Its Own Sake

Evidence of the declarant's belief (even his express words stating his belief), offered to establish nothing beyond the belief, if the belief is relevant for itself alone, and not as indicating the fact believed, has frequently been admissible as non-hearsay even though it may seem to fit the definition of hearsay.

Suppose the government prosecutes Orange–O Co., a leading orange drink manufacturer, for promulgating the misleading impression that its product contains the juice of oranges. To prove that people generally are under the impression that Orange–O contains the juice of oranges, the government introduces the answers to questionnaires distributed in the population in which people said they believed Orange–O contains the juice of oranges. The problem would be the same if the government attempted to introduce, via testimony of those conducting the survey, the out-of-court oral answers given in an orally conducted survey.

Notice that the government is not trying to prove that the belief was correct—that Orange–O contains the juice of oranges. This would be against the government's interests in the litigation.

The government is merely attempting to prove by this evidence that persons (in the position of declarants, whom we call Ds) held such a belief. The accuracy of these Ds' perception of and assessment of the liquid is not relied upon by the offeror (government). In fact, the offeror is ultimately alleging that these Ds were mistaken. But the offeror *is* pressing for acceptance of the fact that these people, in these answers, were truly reporting, not a phenomenon in the outside world, but their own conscious belief. They may be lying, joking, or speaking carelessly about this belief, but hardly mistaken. It thus seems that the offeror's (government's) offered inference involves only one of the links (inferences) and its attendant sources of unreliability we spoke of earlier in the chapter: that is, it involves the inference of belief from outward manifestation (which outward manifestation is a statement in this case), attended by the possibility of insincerity (and perhaps misstatement); but it does not involve the inference that the belief correctly records external fact, which would be attended by the possibility of mistaken perception.

Thus, only some of the testimonial qualities that are ordinarily in question when a trier-of-fact is asked to accept reports of external fact made on or off the stand, are in question here with respect to the out-of-court declarant. Are there still enough testimonial qualities left in question to result in the barring of the evidence as hearsay because of the absence of the courtroom safe-guards?

How might it help to have the declarants on the stand? A bribe might be revealed. They might change their story because of greater care, fear, or consideration of the consequences to the parties. Suggestive or misleading questioning and susceptibility to it could be revealed, or prevented. It might be revealed that the particular persons questioned gained their impressions of Orange–O under atypical circumstances. Other misconduct in the survey might be revealed, such as the elimination of unfavorable answers or the screening of "questionees" beforehand in order to select only those who indicated they would give a favorable answer.

Is having the declarants on the stand the only way of protecting the opponent against these things? Are they within the traditional province of cross-examination? Are they the sort of thing for which cross-examination was designed? In answering these questions, consider the typical case of a witness on the stand reporting a fact like an auto accident or stabbing, for which cross-examination was designed and by analogy to which the notion arose that a declarant ought to be cross-examined, i.e., the notion underlying the hearsay rule.

Some decisions raising this survey issue have held that the evidence was not hearsay and was admissible. Even if the evidence clears the hearsay rule, the court will have to be satisfied, from the method of conducting the survey, etc., that the evidence is reliable enough to survive screening by the expert-testimony rules and the probative-prejudice balance represented by F.R.E. 403. Similar evidence has at times been rejected as hearsay. A policy ground for this would be that sincerity is in issue. Under F.R.E. 801(c), the test is whether the declarant's statement is offered "to prove the truth of the matter [stated]", which would seem to be the case here assuming the declarants stated "*I believe* Orange–O contains the juice of oranges". For the belief is then the matter stated and is also the matter sought to be proved. Unless the word "matter" in the Rule means "external matter" (like a car accident or a shooting), as opposed to an internal or mental matter, the conclusion this is hearsay is inescapable under the Rule. If so, the evidence would nevertheless fall within the state-of-mind exception and, perhaps, the catch-all. See chapters infra. Under the catch-all, reliability of how the survey was conducted would also be an issue.

There is some reason to define "matter" as "external matter" or "external fact", because then the situation covered by the hearsay rule would be most like a witness giving testimony in court, for which the courtroom safeguards were designed. Some other reasons are given in the next section. Courts vary on the definition of "matter" under the F.R.E.

Policy-wise, it should make no difference whether the out-of-court statement was "*I believe* Orange–O contains the juice of oranges" or "Orange–O contains the juice of oranges".[5] Both would be offered to show that the declarant believed it to contain the juice of oranges, not that it really did contain the juice of oranges. But technically, the former statement ("I believe . . .") is offered to prove the truth of the matter stated; whereas the latter is not. The matter stated in the former ("I believe . . .") is that the declarant held a certain belief. That is exactly what the government wants to prove—that the person held the belief she said she held. The matter stated in the second statement is simply that Orange–O contains the juice of oranges. The government is not trying to prove that Orange–O contains the juice of oranges. Thus, the latter statement, as distinguished from the former, is not of-

5. Assume throughout this discussion that "I believe" is not meant to connote doubt, just manner of speaking or precision.

fered to prove the truth of the matter stated, and is not hearsay.

Most statements on the stand in situations not involving hearsay are offered to prove the truth of the matter stated, e.g., an eye-witness on the stand in a murder case or auto accident case reports the relevant facts of a stabbing or crash. In hearsay cases it is generally only when the declaration is offered for the truth of the matter it states that questions of D's credibility arise, e.g., D has declared that X stabbed Y or went through a red light, in a murder or auto collision case; as opposed to D's declaration "yes" offered as constituting agreement in an oral contract case. Therefore, some definitions of hearsay (like F.R.E. 801(c)) state that we have hearsay whenever, and only when, the out-of-court declaration is offered for the truth of the matter declared. Adhering strictly to that definition in the present case, "*I believe* Orange–O contains the juice of oranges" would be hearsay, whereas "Orange–O contains the juice of oranges" would not be.

However, under a policy-oriented approach, it would seem that whichever statement was made, the issue of credibility is precisely the same and equally in need of or not in need of elucidation by the application of courtroom processes to the declarant. The result should not turn on the declarant's fortuitous selection of words. The declarant means the same thing, whichever formulation is chosen. Analysts who follow the "truth of the matter declared" definition just described and also liberally allow "implied declarations" would be in a quandary in the present case, because either of the two declarations ("I believe Orange–O contains the juice of oranges" and "Orange–O contains the juice of oranges") may be implied from the other. We would thus have an infinite circular regression. Such analysts would have to resort to something other than the "truth of the matter declared" definition and the doctrine of implied declarations, for a solution. The F.R.E. may well be in this bind.

Evidence of State of Belief for Its Own Sake: Intent, Knowledge, or Feelings

Under certain conditions, evidence of the state of mind or feelings of declarant will be received as non-hearsay or as an exception to the hearsay rule.

When a declarant (D) expresses a certain conscious state of mind (e.g., a conscious intent, belief, or knowledge) which that person holds contemporaneously with the expression, we can hardly suspect that D is mistaken about, misperceiving, or misremembering her own state of mind, because of her peculiar privity with it and its contemporaneity with the expression. She may, however, be insincere (lying or joking) about it, or misreporting it. There is perhaps some slight possibility that D is not aware of the true nature of her state of mind, but when it is a conscious state of mind this danger is minimal. It is fair to say that at least where the declarant expressly declares her present, conscious state of mind to be so-and-so, and this state of mind is offered for itself (assuming we have a case where such would be relevant) and not on a theory that it accurately reproduces an external fact, some of the fears responsible for the courtroom guarantees are removed. We have a rather reliable kind of evidence. The declarant is declaring or reporting an internal fact of consciousness, and the fact and the declaration are contemporaneous. There is not the same possibility of inaccuracy as where a witness on the stand (or a declarant off the stand) reports an external fact (in the real world) from which that person was removed in space (when observing it) and time (when reporting it), with all the attendant possibilities of misperception and failure of memory.

But if the state of mind is past rather than contemporaneous with the declaration, the opportunities for falsification and failure of memory are much greater and the special reliability is not present. Nor would it be present where the state of mind (e.g., belief) is contemporaneous with the declaration but offered to prove that it truly records (reproduces) some external fact. Thus in our original hypothetical (opening the chapter) involving Declarant's oral declaration "X shot Y", it adds nothing to the offeror's case to characterize Declarant's declaration as an expression of Declarant's *belief* that X shot Y, if the offeror is offering the belief in order to prove X shot Y. Nor would it change matters if Declarant had instead actually said "I believe X shot Y". (In this example, assume that it is made clear that "believe" is not used as an expression of doubt or lack of first-hand knowledge.) Though both forms of the statement are evidence of belief, the belief in both cases is offered as true. It is hearsay, whichever way it is phrased, so long as it is offered to establish X shot Y, which seems to be the only possible relevant purpose.

Courts vary as to whether evidence that meets the reliability criteria discussed above connected with statements of state-of-mind should be regarded as an exception to the hearsay rule, or not hearsay at all. Under the F.R.E. it depends on the interpretation of "matter" in Rule 801(c) as explained in the last section above. But there is also an exception for it under the F.R.E.

It is obvious that the principles espoused thus far in this section also apply to declarations of presently felt pain or lack of pain, or other feelings. Such declarations are relatively unobjectionable in terms of the concerns of this chapter if the conditions of concurrency with the declaration, relevance other than to infer external existing fact, etc., are met.

The principles of this section would be applicable to out-of-court manifestations of contemporaneous state of mind or feelings other than express declarations, such as conduct, and words not directly expressing a state of mind or feeling but perhaps doing so by implication. E.g., "You killed my brother," offered to show the child's dislike of her stepfather in a child custody battle.

Some applications of the above principles follow:

(1) "The Brakes Are Bad," Offered to Show (a) Faulty Brakes or (b) Notice. While taking a bus load of people on a scenic ride, D (declarant) says: "The brakes are bad. But don't worry." The bus has a collision and the company is sued for the negligence of its driver, D, the declarant. D's negligence is alleged to consist in the fact that D took a bus out, knowing the brakes to be bad, something a reasonable person would not have done. Assuming all appropriate rulings are requested and the law is followed, the plaintiff probably will be permitted to offer D's statement via occupants of the bus who overheard it; but only for purposes of establishing D's notice of the faulty brakes, not to establish that the brakes were in fact bad, which would have to be established by other evidence. In this hypothetical, we put aside the possibility D's statement might also come within exemptions from or exceptions to the hearsay rule for declarations against interest, admissions of a party or his agent, excited utterances, or present sense impressions. These could render the declaration admissible to prove the brakes were bad, as well as to show knowledge.

Assuming these other exemptions or exceptions are out of the picture, the jury will be instructed that, in deciding whether the brakes were bad, they are not to consider this evidence, but only such other evidence as may be adduced. The judge similarly will not consider this to be evidence on that issue, and will make peremptory rulings (directed verdicts, etc.) on that issue on the basis of whatever other evidence there is concerning it. Offering counsel will not be permitted to argue any but the permissible usage of the evidence. If there is no other evidence on the issue of the faultiness of the brakes or if such other evidence is obviously insufficient for the plaintiff to get to the jury, a verdict would have to be directed. One might well ask whether, at least where the evidence is before the tribunal on one issue, it ought not to be allowed whatever probativeness it rationally has on the other issue, at least with a judge.

If the issue of notice were not in the case, but only the issue of the soundness of the brakes, the evidence could not be received. In an appropriate case defendant company may offer to stipulate that if the brakes were bad, there was notice; or agree to liability if brake unsoundness is shown, without any showing of notice—all to avoid admissibility of this statement of the driver. In some circumstances, a court might hold the evidence inadmissible based on such an offer—in effect holding that the offer must be accepted. See discussion of *Old Chief*, supra, Chs. 3 & 4.

The reason for the ruling that the evidence is admissible to show notice is either (1) the statement of the driver is not offered to prove the truth of what he stated (that the brakes are bad) but rather to show his knowledge assuming the defectiveness of the brakes is shown another way; or (2) while the statement is the equivalent of the (implied) statement "I know the brakes are bad" (which *is* offered for the truth of what is stated in that implied statement, i.e., knowledge of bad brakes), that matter stated is his internal contemporaneous state of mind offered for itself and not as reflective of any other external fact. Reason (2) means the evidence is either not hearsay under the state-of-mind internal fact principle; or within the state-of-mind hearsay exception.

If the driver had made the statement after the accident, saying to someone out of court, "I knew the brakes were bad when I went out earlier," the statement would not come within the state-of-mind principle or hearsay exception, because it is a statement of past state-of-mind.

(2) "My Husband Is a Brute," Offered to Show (a) Husband's Character or (b) Wife's Attitude. Wealthy Mrs. Q says to her neighbor, "My husband John is a brute". The neighbor reports this on the stand for the defendant bus company in a suit by the husband (Mr. Q) against the bus company for the wrongful death of his wife (Mrs. Q) inflicted through negligently trapping her arm in the bus door and dragging her to her death. The bus company's reason for introducing such evidence is to reduce Mr. Q's damages—i.e., to show that Mr. Q could not have expected much of value from Mrs. Q had she lived. Let us assume the damages in a wrongful death action are loss of the survivor's monetary expectancy and support. The evidence is offered to show that, regardless of what may be the truth about John, Mrs. Q thought he was a brute, and probably would not be inclined to do more for him than she had to.

The statement is not hearsay because not offered to establish the truth of the matter stated, that John is indeed a brute, but rather to establish she *thought* John was a brute, whatever may really be the case; and that therefore she was not likely to give him generous amounts of money had she lived. As a matter of terminology, the statement is offered as circumstantial evidence of what she thought and might do.

If she had said (or the court under implied statement theory treats her statement as the equivalent of) "I think [or believe] my husband John is a brute", then this new statement *is* being offered to establish the truth of the proposition or matter or fact it states (that she indeed thinks or believes so-and-so), but since it is a fact of her internal mental state, it is within the state-of-mind principle and either is not hearsay or is within the exception for declarant's state-of-mind. Notice that the "truth of the matter stated [declared]" criterion may be met even though the matter stated [declared] and sought to be proved (what she thought) is only an intermediate proposition leading to an ultimate conclusion (her likely ungenerosity to him). This is an important point for all applications of the "truth of the matter stated by the declarant" concept in hearsay law: the matter stated (declared) by the declarant that is being offered as true, thus rendering the evidence hearsay, need not be some ultimate allegation in the case; it can merely be something that itself is of some further evidential significance. That is why the present authors prefer to use the phrase "truth of the matter stated" rather than "truth of the matter asserted", because "asserted" can be misunderstood to mean "asserted in the lawsuit", instead of what is really meant in the hearsay area, which is truth of the matter stated (asserted) *by the declarant*, not something stated (asserted) in the pleadings, charges, complaint or claims. "Asserted" seems to connote the latter meaning to students, which would be incorrect in this area.

Policy-wise, the statement (in whichever form: "I think ..." or "He is ...") is offered not to show the accuracy of Mrs. Q's belief (that John is indeed a brute), but to show that she held the belief, or felt a certain way toward John. Thus far, it fits the reliability criteria set out above concerning state-of-mind—that she is right on top of her current, declared state of mind and could hardly be mistaken.

But there is an additional link in the offered chain of inference: that because she had this belief, she probably would have acted in a certain way in the future. It would seem, however, that this is the kind of inference the jury customarily is deemed quite competent to assess and is not the special subject of the courtroom safeguards we have been discussing, at least insofar as they would be addressed to Mrs. Q and the need to have her on the stand.

Having her on the stand would, of course, enable the jury to more accurately guess what she might be expected to give him during life. Her feeling of hatred might have been fleeting and temporary, inspired by a very recent spat and evaporating again. She might not be the sort to carry these things out into action. She might be the kind of person who would have felt duty bound to give him considerable amounts of money, despite her feelings toward him. She might have been ashamed to have him go without luxuries and money. She might have been able to testify that what she said has no bearing on what she intends to do in the future. In speaking to her neighbor, she might have been attempting to create a certain impression, or speaking for a very limited purpose. She might be the sort of person who is given to overly extreme expressions or to making contradictory statements. She may have indeed contradicted herself on this matter many times. All this would be relevant to weight, if not admissibility, and would be elucidated more clearly if she were on the stand.

Nevertheless it would not be deemed indispensable to have her on the stand. We do not have inadmissible hearsay here. These considerations that we have said might be brought out were she on the stand, could be brought out other ways. Conceivably a judge might feel these considerations would bar the evidence under another concept, the probativity-and-counterweights balancing, such as F.R.E. 403, but not hearsay if the analysis is done properly.

Of course, it is extremely unrealistic to talk of putting her on the stand. She is dead. But if we felt there would be utility of the customary type in putting her on the stand, then hearsay logic would say we can't use her statement because we can't put her on the stand. The principle applies whether or not she is dead, e.g., a similar suit could be brought if she were injured.

A decision on similar facts to our "husband is a brute" hypothetical held that the evidence was admissible. The court would probably not have drawn a distinction based on whether or not she was dead and whether or not there was any other evidence concerning her proclivity to support her husband, although it is often said, in what is probably just dictum or philosophy addressed to generalities, that necessity is the reason why this kind of evidence surmounts the hearsay exclusion. Such necessity probably does not bear on the hearsay analysis, but on the balancing under rules like F.R.E. 403.

In an area like this, courts frequently treat the direct, express declaration of state-of-mind as hearsay (but within the exception for state-of-mind). A statement or conduct that only implies the state-of-mind, is frequently viewed as non-hearsay under some rubric like "circumstantial evidence of state-of-mind." Is this a sufficiently analytical approach for courts to take? Probably not. In addition, it should be noted, the balancing and weight problem can be more severe in the latter.

(3) The Molested Child's Description of the Premises, Offered (a) Not to Prove the Condition of the Premises, but (b) the Child's Knowledge of Them. Suppose a young child is taken to a man's house and sexually molested by him. The child cannot identify him, but at the police station she is able to recount the highly distinctive details of the furnishings of the house. At trial she can no longer even do this. At trial, her earlier description is introduced, and it is shown to tally spectacularly with the very distinctive furnishings of defendant's house (proved through other evidence, such as photos, etc.). Is her statement "There were green striped chairs, blue polka-dot curtains [etc.]" offered for its truth—i.e., to

establish that there were indeed green chairs and blue curtains there? (No.) But isn't her statement really or impliedly "The house where I was molested had green stiped chairs [etc.]" or "I was at a house of such-and-such description"? (Maybe.) Would this be being offered for its truth? (Yes, at least as to the latter.)

What if she was really (unbeknownst to the tribunal) recounting a place (defendant's place) she saw only on another occasion—say, in selling girl-scout cookies the week before—rather than the scene of the crime? Or suppose the details of the furnishings were learned from her mother or the police? Do you feel there are things that might be brought out if the statement could be subject to cross-examination? Are you uneasy enough about them to exclude the evidence?

In *Bridges v. State* (Wis.1945), this evidence was admitted on the theory that it was not offered for the truth of her statement but to "show her state-of-mind." In other words, that the traces in her mind indicated knowledge of information that likely came from being there, increasing the probability of the story of molestation by defendant (over what the probability would be if we had no evidence she was there). The problem whether the constitutional confrontation clause is violated by this evidence is not free from doubt, and some of the considerations you would want to think about in this connection are similar to those asked above, particularly those concerning the other possibilities about how she might have gotten the information and your comfort level with the fact that there will be no cross-examination. Frequently courts *sub silentio* allow the fact that the case involved child molestation to influence analysis, at least in a doubtful area.

Reputation

Testimony as to the reputation of a person usually is hearsay, especially when used to show that the person

possessed the quality reputed or acted in the way reputed. But there are some common uses of reputation that might not be regarded as hearsay, where only the mere existence of the reputation is sought to be proved. There are also some narrow exceptions to the hearsay rule for certain kinds of reputation.

If a witness (W) were to take the stand and testify "Q's reputation is such-and-such," the witness essentially would be saying that he has heard a number of Ds (declarants) on the street say either one or both of two things: "Q is a such-and-such" or "I have heard [from other Ds] that Q is a such-and-such". Let us see when such testimony by W (witness) would be hearsay.

Suppose B, the defendant in a libel action, attempts, via the above quoted testimony of W, to prove the truth of B's (defendant's) alleged defamatory statement that "Q is *reputed to be a thief*." B's purpose is to establish a defense of truth. In this example, assume the law of this jurisdiction is that if Q has the reputation, the defense of truth on the part of B is made out regardless of the falsity of the reputation itself. If W is saying, in effect, "I have heard a number of Ds say Q is a thief," the evidence would not seem to be hearsay, since it is immaterial whether the reputation (the out-of-court statements by the Ds that Q is a thief) is a correct portrayal of Q's actual nature or not. The issue is simply whether there *was* such a reputation (i.e., whether Ds said Q is a thief), not its or their accuracy (i.e., not whether Q is a thief). But does this rationale apply insofar as W is saying that W heard Ds say *they heard* Q is a thief? Now their accuracy is in issue: What if the Ds W heard are lying or mistaken about what *they* heard? This distinction is largely ignored in the cases.

Suppose that the alleged libel is "Q *is* a thief." (Not, as in the previous example, "Q is *reputed* to be a thief.") B (defendant) attempts, with W's testimony that Q has always had a reputation for thievery, to prove (for purposes of making out the defense of truth) that the allegedly libelous statement is true: that Q is indeed a thief. This is plainly hearsay. The out-of-court statements (the reputation) are clearly offered for their truth. It is hoped that the reputation will be credited—that the fact reputed (thievery) will be accepted as true. But see the hearsay exceptions for certain kinds of reputation, e.g., F.R.E. 803(19)–(21). Rule 803(21)(reputation as to character) *might* be held to apply to this situation.

Suppose that the same testimony is offered in the same case to prove *instead* that the libel did not significantly damage Q's already poor reputation. This would be offered to reduce damages. It would seem that exactly the same reasoning would apply as applied not in the last paragraph above, but the one before that: the accuracy of the reputation is not at all in issue—its mere nature and existence are. But again there is the possibility that W may also be reporting what the Ds said *they* heard, usually ignored by courts. The situation would be the same as respects Q's (plaintiffs) proof of *good* reputation on the same issue. The evidence is generally admitted, whichever party introduces it. There may be a cautionary instruction to the jury not to use the evidence on the issue of the truth of the charge that Q is a thief, for which purpose it would clearly be inadmissible hearsay, assuming no hearsay exception is held to apply.

Reputation introduced for purposes of the propensity (or character) reasoning discussed in Chapter 4 is hearsay, however viewed, because it is hoped that the reputation will be credited. Where it is admissible, a special exception to the hearsay rule is necessary (in addition to an exception to the character ban), and one has been created for it. See F.R.E. 803(21).

Briefly noted ✗

V. HEARSAY AND THE CONSTI- TUTION: THE CONFRONTA- TION CLAUSE

The Relationship Between Hearsay and the Confrontation Clause

Like the hearsay rule, the constitutional Confrontation Clause exerts constraints on the admissibility of statements made outside the trial, except that the Confrontation Clause applies only when the statement is introduced against the criminal defendant. The basic values behind the two rules are similar: the need for cross-examination and other courtroom safeguards. If the statement is to be successfully offered against a criminal defendant, both the jurisdiction's hearsay rule, and the constitutional Confrontation Clause, must be satisfied.

The Supreme Court recently changed its approach to constitutional confrontation. From 1980 to 2004 (under the so-called *Roberts* approach), the Court appeared willing to forego confrontation of the declarant wherever declarant's statement satisfied a traditional exception to or exemption from the hearsay rule, or even a new exception or exemption that seemed to assure a fair degree of trustworthiness on the particular facts. In contrast, now (under the new so-called *Crawford* approach) if the declarant does not testify, any hearsay statement of his that is deemed "testimonial" can normally only be admitted if he is unavailable and the defendant had a prior opportunity to cross-examine him.

The Sixth Amendment to the U.S. Constitution provides that a criminal accused shall have the right "to be confronted with the witnesses against him." Additionally, the Fifth and Fourteenth Amendments provide for "due process of law." The federal right of a federal criminal defendant to confrontation applies to state criminal proceedings as well, via the Fourteenth Amendment. "Due process" may incorporate some watered down notion of confrontation in civil cases as well, both state and federal, but it seldom comes up. State constitutions have somewhat similar provisions.

If we regard hearsay declarants as "witnesses" for constitutional purposes, then out-of-court statements of an absent declarant offered for their truth against a criminal defendant, pursuant to some hearsay exception, obviously pose a Confrontation Clause problem if the declarant is not on the stand: The defendant is not being "confronted with the witnesses against him".

The Supreme Court, however, has never gone this far. It has never banned all such hearsay in this fashion. Prior to 2004, the court did seem to regard all hearsay declarants as "witnesses" for constitutional purposes, but held that the right to confront witnesses of this type (declarants) was not needed if the trustworthiness of declarant's statement was reasonably assured because the statement came within a traditional "firmly rooted" hearsay exception or because of particular case-specific facts concerning the making of the statement. In such circumstances, the purpose of requiring confrontation (i.e., to provide reasonable assurances of trustworthiness) was deemed satisfied. This was an "instrumental" approach. It was concerned with the supposed underlying purpose of the Confrontation Clause. It could be contrasted with an "absolutist" position, that the procedure of confrontation is a mandatory end in itself regardless of benefits it may provide.

In *Crawford v. Washington* (S.Ct.2004), the Court changed to the present approach, a more "absolutist" one, normally banning as against accused, all statements of declarants who do not take the stand, offered for their truth, regardless of what hearsay exception or exemption they may come within and how reliable they may be, unless the declarant is unavailable and there was an earlier opportunity for cross-examination. But even this "absolute" approach to confrontation has some exceptions under *Crawford*: (1) Notwithstanding its evidentiary effect against defendant, if the statement is not "testimonial" (a concept having something to do with purpose), the declarant is not deemed a "witness" in the constitutional sense and confrontation is not required. (2) There is no right to confront the declarant if the defendant has forfeited the right by his or her conduct—for example, by killing the declarant to preclude declarant's testimony.

Though the link between the hearsay rule and the Confrontation Clause is now somewhat severed, the two still share some common philosophies and effects. They both frequently have the effect of screening out evidence that is unreliable. But that is not always the case. In some instances they exclude from evidence material that is reliable, even when better evidence cannot be obtained. And on occasion they permit evidence of little reliability, even when better evidence would seem to be at hand. Both these occurrences raise the risk that a falsity will be found. This happens because the two rules are concerned in part with what is moral, ethical, or fair, or unconditionally commanded by the constitution, which may in some instances diverge from what is conducive to accuracy.[6] Having the witness to the facts on the stand for confrontation and cross-examination (as both rules require) is to some extent an end in itself, aside from its effect on fact-finding accuracy. The law feels this notion must be enshrined, both to promote the popular satisfaction without which the legal system could not function, and because *Crawford's* historic analysis treats confron-

6. This is not wholly unknown in other evidentiary areas either, e.g., character evidence and privilege.

tation as a procedural right to cross-examination rather than as a substantive right to reliable evidence.[7]

Despite this partial disconnect from accuracy, statistically the hearsay rule and the confrontation requirement may have some beneficial effect on long term factual accuracy of the system generally, even if not in the specific case. They encourage lawyers and litigants over the long run to seek out more reliable evidence than second-hand evidence, even if accuracy in a particular case may be thwarted.[8]

The First Attempt at a Comprehensive Theory of the Confrontation Clause: "Unavailability," "Reliability," and "Firmly Rooted Exceptions": The *Roberts* Reliability Framework

Confrontation clause analysis has proven difficult for the Supreme Court, which has struggled and still struggles to articulate a cohesive theory of confrontation.

Ohio v. Roberts (S.Ct.1980) was the first attempt by the Court to design a relatively comprehensive framework for Confrontation Clause analysis. *Roberts* commanded that before a hearsay statement by a declarant who does not appear for trial could be admitted against a criminal defendant, there must be a showing (1) that the declarant is *unavailable* and (2) that there were indicia of *reliability* surrounding the statement. Reliability could be established either by (a) the presumption of trustworthiness that attends hearsay admitted pursuant to a "firmly

7. To the extent the concern is with appearing fair rather than with accuracy, there may be justification for limiting the concept discussed in previous sections, that conduct can be hearsay and require confrontation, to cases in which the conduct most obviously resembles testimony or accusation; and for applying the hearsay rule and the Confrontation Clause to cases of apparent accusation without confrontation even when accuracy is fairly well assured. This approach is consistent with the Court's reformulation of Confrontation Clause analysis.

8. Again, this is not entirely peculiar to this area of Evidence law.

rooted" hearsay exception or exemption (meaning a long-standing, traditionally recognized one),[9] or (b) by making an independent inquiry into the trustworthiness of the specific statement if the exception or exemption is not "firmly rooted".[10]

Later cases interpreting *Roberts* held that the firmly rooted hearsay exceptions for co-conspirators' statements, excited utterances, and statements for medical diagnosis and treatment did not require a showing of unavailability. See, e.g., *White v. Illinois* (S.Ct.1992). This was understood as signaling that unavailability was not constitutionally required of firmly rooted hearsay exceptions or exemptions, unless the specific exception or exemption was subject to an unavailability requirement.[11] In other words, a finding that a statement met a

9. Could a defendant challenge the presumption of trustworthiness? Probably not, unless perhaps there were very strong facts of unreliability peculiar to the particular case. *White v. Illinois* (S.Ct.1992) presumed statements to medical personnel are reliable even where the facts—a child identifying an abuser—did not fit the presumption because the child probably didn't understand that a false identification could hinder treatment (assuming such statements can *ever* be considered sufficiently related to the diagnosis or treatment under the exception).

10. For purposes of the Confrontation Clause, such hearsay was to be evaluated for trustworthiness (reliability) on the particular facts concerning the statement without regard to any independent corroboration, relying solely on the kind of statement and the circumstances of the making of the statement. Even though corroboration should have been excluded from consideration when the judge originally decided whether to admit the statement against the defendant, nevertheless, if the judge did admit the hearsay, and the defendant was convicted, appellate courts sometimes considered corroboration in their harmless error analysis.

11. *White* suggested that the unavailability originally required under *Roberts* is only required for the hearsay exceptions that traditionally already require unavailability (like those in F.R.E. 804) and perhaps any exception or exemption where the statement is part of an official proceeding or procured by police, since state overreaching is a special historical concern of the Confrontation Clause. The unavailability re-

firmly rooted hearsay exception like those in F.R.E. 803 or 804 appeared to mean that it also satisfied the Confrontation Clause.[12] This, of course, conflated confrontation and hearsay analysis. The definition of "firmly rooted" began to expand to include novel applications of traditional exceptions and then, further, to include some more recently created hearsay exceptions and exemptions.[13]

quirement (along with the particularized reliability requirement) might also have been imposed under the *Roberts/White* approach on statements coming in via new (i.e., not "firmly rooted") hearsay exceptions and exemptions, too, like F.R.E. 807 (the "catchall" exception), although this was not clear.

12. What hearsay exceptions were not "firmly rooted" so that reliability had to be assessed and unavailability might be required? Certainly the "catch-all" exception (F.R.E. 807 and state analogues). Newly minted special exceptions some jurisdictions created specifically for child hearsay were also in the same category. Declarations against penal interest made to law enforcement were also considered not firmly rooted.

13. *White* set the stage for the expansion of the definition of "firmly rooted." *Roberts* had appeared to rely on the long history of, and widespread nature of, the hearsay exception to justify affixing this label. *White*, on the other hand, found "firm rootedness" respecting the medical diagnosis or treatment exception to the hearsay rule, without any determination of how long there had been such an exception or whether the exception or the use made of it at this trial (a child identifying its abuser) were recent or widespread. Indeed, the medical diagnosis or treatment exception was of relatively recent origin. California still does not have a general equivalent of F.R.E. 803(4) (hearsay exception for statements made for purposes of medical diagnosis or treatment), and only adopted a medical exception for child abuse and neglect post-*White*. In general, statements of children that identify their abusers (as was involved in *White*) were only very recently brought under the exception—and only by a minority of jurisdictions—when *White* was decided. Other instances of expansions of established hearsay exceptions might include, for example, expert opinion admitted in a business record, a relatively new broadening of the traditional business records exception brought about by F.R.E. 803(6) and state analogues.

Crawford: Rejecting the *Roberts'* Reliability Framework for a "Testimonial" Approach

In *Crawford v. Washington* (S.Ct.2004), the Supreme Court undid 25 years of Confrontation Clause analysis, while giving little guidance about how to apply the new "testimonial" framework it substituted for *Roberts'* reliability test.

Crawford involved statements introduced at the defendant's trial as declarations against penal interest made by the defendant's wife (Sylvia) during police questioning while she was a potential suspect in the case. At trial, she was unavailable due to the invocation of marital privilege by her husband under state law, although she would arguably have been able to invoke the 5th Amendment on her own behalf. Her statements were admitted as reliable pursuant to *Roberts*. The U.S. Supreme Court reversed, after applying a historical analysis to re-define the content of the right to confrontation based on the right's contours in 1791. According to *Crawford*, the basic concern of the Confrontation Clause was to prevent the kind of abuses found in the trial of Sir Walter Raleigh, among others: principally the use of statements or affidavits garnered by the state ex parte.

The Court blasted *Roberts'* approach to confrontation as being "so unpredictable that it fails to provide meaningful protection from even core confrontation violations." *Crawford* said *Roberts* was both too broad (because it required the same analysis for all statements, regardless of whether they implicated the core concern of the Clause to prohibit ex parte garnered statements), and too narrow (because it permitted ex parte garnered statements that are reliable). Further, a "reliability" test begs the question, "how reliable?" The Court said:

> "Admitting statements deemed reliable by a judge is fundamentally at odds with the right of confrontation.

To be sure, the Clause's ultimate goal is to ensure reliability of evidence, but it is a procedural rather than a substantive guarantee. It commands, not that evidence be reliable, but that reliability be assessed in a particular manner: by testing in the crucible of cross-examination."

After *Crawford*, the threshold question is whether the hearsay is "testimonial". If so, it is only admissible if declarant takes the stand at trial for cross-examination, or is both unavailable and formerly subject to an opportunity for cross-examination on the statement.

The Court also recognized that the defendant could forfeit the right to confront through conduct aimed at procuring the unavailability of the declarant.[14] Similarly, the defendant's trial strategy can open the door to the testimonial statement, or its admission can be harmless error. If the witness testifies (as under, e.g., F.R.E. 801(d)(1)) *Crawford* notes that "when the declarant appears for cross-examination at trial, the Confrontation Clause places no constraints at all on the use of his prior testimonial statements" citing *California v. Green* (S.Ct. 1970). Presumably this applies regardless of whether the declarant at trial affirms, denies or does not recall making the statement or the material within it. This apparently continues the doctrine of *United States v. Owens* (S.Ct.1988) that sanctioned such a result.

The Court did not clearly define "testimonial", claiming that Sylvia Crawford's statement was testimonial under any of the definitions suggested in the various briefs in the case, some of which the Court recounts. Thus, conflicting decisions are commonplace depending on which definition mentioned in *Crawford* is adopted. The principal definitions of "testimonial statements" mentioned in *Crawford* are:

14. It is unclear whether the defendant must have the purpose of procuring unavailability, or whether the effect would be enough.

1) "Ex parte in-court testimony or its functional equivalent—that is, material such as affidavits, custodial examinations, prior testimony that the defendant was unable to cross-examine, or similar pretrial statements that declarants would reasonably expect to be used prosecutorially."

2) "Extrajudicial statements ... contained in formalized testimonial materials, such as affidavits, depositions, prior testimony, or confessions."

3) "Statements that were made under circumstances which would lead an objective witness reasonably to believe that the statement would be available for use at a later trial."

Crawford also made clear that:

"Involvement of government officers in the production of testimonial evidence presents the same risk, whether the officers are police or [as in historical times] justices of the peace. In sum, even if the Sixth Amendment is not solely concerned with testimonial hearsay, that is its primary object, and interrogations by law enforcement officers fall squarely within that class."

Further, *Crawford* indicated that a "recorded statement, knowingly given in response to structured police questioning [as in *Crawford* itself], qualifies under any conceivable definition" of testimonial, but that interrogation in more colloquial senses could also be embraced. In dicta, *Crawford* notes that plea allocutions, grand jury testimony, and prior trial testimony of declarants, if not cross-examinable by the defendant, are also encompassed; but business records and statements in furtherance of a conspiracy by their nature are not. *Crawford* also cryptically suggests that, as a matter of necessity, dying declarations are admissible, regardless of to whom they are made.[15]

15. These suggestions about particular hearsay exceptions and exemptions are anomalous and questionable, since the whole thrust of

Crawford left a number of unanswered questions: Would an excited 911 telephone call reporting an ongoing violent emergency be testimonial? When would on-the-scene statements to police be testimonial? Could statements to friends rather than police be testimonial? There were other questions, too.

Davis: Defining Emergencies in the Context of Excited Utterances Made to Law Enforcement

After two years of conflicting lower court decisions interpreting *Crawford*, the U.S. Supreme Court decided *Davis v. Washington* (S.Ct.2006). *Davis* consolidated two domestic violence cases (styled *Davis* and *Hammon* in the lower courts) involving excited utterances by the alleged victim, in which, as is common, the alleged victim did not testify. The Court upheld the admission of the statements made in the 911 call in *Davis* as non-testimonial because they were made in connection with an ongoing emergency, but reversed the conviction in *Hammon* because the statements there were made to police officers by the victim at the crime scene and were *not* taken to secure the situation but to gain evidence of a crime that was already over (defendant was in another room under police control). The decision cautioned that this bifurcation was not intended to govern all statements, let alone all statements given in response to police or police agents.

Like *Crawford, Davis* adopted an objective test, but one that may not be exactly the same as some implications of *Crawford*. *Davis* held:

"Statements are non-testimonial when made in the course of police interrogation under circumstances ob-

Crawford is that hearsay categories do not matter—that the inquiry will be a factual one to determine if the statement is "testimonial", regardless of what exception or exemption it may or may not come within.

jectively indicating that the primary purpose of the interrogation is to enable police assistance to meet an ongoing emergency. They are testimonial when the circumstances objectively indicate that there is no such ongoing emergency, and that the primary purpose of the interrogation is to establish or prove past events potentially relevant to later criminal prosecution."[16]

Davis emphasized that the 911 caller was talking in the present tense, and that the operator needed information to know what danger the officers would face in resolving the dispute. This was contrasted to the field investigation in *Hammon* where the victim denied any problem and was separated from the defendant (her husband) when she admitted her husband assaulted her. Thus, the 911 statements, in contrast to the field statements, were non-testimonial.

The Court also described the difference in the level of formality between the interrogation in *Crawford* and the 911 call in *Davis* as "striking." In *Crawford,* the declarant "calmly answered questions at a station house, with an officer-interrogator taping and taking notes," while in *Davis,* her "frantic answers were provided over the phone, in an environment that was not tranquil, or even safe." Thus, the 911 call, in contrast to Sylvia Crawford's statement, was not testimonial.

Even though there was greater formality in Sylvia Crawford's custodial interrogation than in *Hammon's* in-the-field questioning, *Davis* found that the threat of criminal prosecution for making a false statement to law enforcement officers was inherent in both situations and

16. While this passage seems to concentrate on the intention of the police officers, other parts of the opinion seem to concentrate on the knowledge or intention of the declarant with respect to whether the statement will be usable in a criminal case. The decision also seems to waffle somewhat between whether the standard is objective or subjective.

normally "imports sufficient formality" to render testimonial any statement given during an interrogation. Thus, statements given by a witness or victim at a crime scene as a result of "initial inquiries" are testimonial if they are "neither a cry for help nor the provision of information enabling officers immediately to end a threatening situation," but instead describe past events which may constitute a crime. The Court also suggested that statements made in the absence of any interrogation could also be testimonial.

Do *Crawford* and *Davis* imply that any statement to someone not working with or for law enforcement is necessarily non-testimonial? The Court seems to hold open the possibility that in certain circumstances, it could be testimonial. *Davis* noted that for purposes of the decision, the 911 operator would be treated as an agent of the police, without deciding whether and when a statement to a non-agent could be testimonial.

Is every 911 call non-testimonial under this formulation? Is every post-emergency statement to police testimonial? What are the factors to be considered? Two criteria that appear significant under *Davis,* are (1) is the defendant present or absent from the scene and (2) is the defendant under police control when the statements were made. Additional factors of some, but uncertain, significance may be (3) whether there was interrogation in some sense (although the Court suggests interrogation may not always be necessary), and (4) whether the recipient/questioner is associated with police or the government, and to what degree (although the Court declines to decide if this is always necessary). Certainly of some significance, is (5) the subjective or objective intention or knowledge of the questioner/recipient or declarant.

Do these cases imply that the only kind of emergency that will be considered to make a statement non-testimonial, is one involving a need to prevent the immediate violence and secure the immediate scene against violence? Would danger to property qualify? Or a health emergency of an injured victim? What about a need to prevent the killer, assaulter, or robber from doing it again in the vicinity, even if he has left the crime scene and is no longer a threat to that victim? There is little indication of an answer in these decisions.

Is the *Roberts* Framework Still Applicable to "Non-testimonial" Statements?

If the hearsay is not testimonial, *Crawford* left unsettled what if any confrontation test applies. *Davis* seems pretty clearly to reject any applicability of the Confrontation Clause to non-testimonial statements. The decision contains several passages indicating that the Confrontation Clause has nothing to say about non-testimonial statements, and concludes that the "testimonial" concept defines "not merely the 'core', but the perimeter" of the right to confrontation. As a result, non-testimonial hearsay would not be subject to any Confrontation Clause analysis.[17]

Yet, post-*Davis*, a few courts, state and federal, still apply the *Roberts* approach to non-testimonial hearsay. They argue that a significant holding that *Roberts* no longer has *any* vitality and that non-testimonial statements are completely unregulated by the Confrontation Clause, needs to have been stated more clearly by *Davis*. The reference in *Davis* is dicta, they say, since the non-testimonial 911 excited utterance held admissible in *Davis* would have satisfied *Roberts* analysis too. In other words, the result would have been the same, whether or not *Roberts* still applies to non-testimonial statements.

17. However, in an aggravated case, the admission of very unreliable non-testimonial hearsay might violate Due Process, a matter which is not dealt with by these cases.

Moreover, they argue, *Crawford* seemed to embrace the result in *Idaho v. Wright* (S.Ct.1990), which excluded (on confrontation grounds) unreliable hearsay of a child to a *private* doctor (which, it is assumed, would be deemed a non-testimonial statement under the new analysis), thereby implying that non-testimonial hearsay is subject to constitutional Confrontation Clause regulation. But, to the contrary, perhaps *Crawford* felt the statements in *Wright* were actually *testimonial* because made to a doctor selected by the police. See generally Raeder, *Remember the Ladies and Children Too: The Impact of Crawford on Domestic Violence and Child Abuse Cases,* 71 Brooklyn Law Review 311 (2005).

It is probably not a proper reading of the law after *Davis* to say that the *Roberts* line of cases still applies to non-testimonial hearsay statements. The fairest reading is that non-testimonial statements are unregulated by the federal Confrontation Clause.[18] But the states are free to provide more protection to the criminal defendant under their own constitutional confrontation clauses, and some therefore still apply confrontation-clause scrutiny— i.e. the *Roberts*-type analysis—to non-testimonial statements.

18. Thus Justice Alito says in *Whorton v. Bockting* (S.Ct. 2007; *Crawford* not retroactive) that *Crawford* eliminated Confrontation Clause protection concerning unreliable non-testimonial hearsay. This is a considerable restriction of the reach of the Confrontation Clause as compared with *Roberts*, which applied Confrontation Clause analysis to *all* hearsay statements used by the prosecution, not just testimonial ones. But the new approach probably makes exclusion more certain whenever the Confrontation Clause *does* apply (assuming that "testimonial" is a more definite term than "reliable" or "firmly rooted" under *Roberts*). A regime in which *Crawford* applies to testimonial and *Roberts* to non-testimonial statements would be quite favorable to the defense. But, as indicated above, under the most likely reading of *Crawford/Davis*, the *Roberts* scrutiny (indeed, *all* Confrontation Clause scrutiny) is removed from the prosecution's non-testimonial statements. This seems quite pro-prosecution, but remember that, in exchange, prosecutors can no longer justify testimonial statements as reliable or firmly-rooted as they could under *Roberts*.

As the federal definition of "testimonial" develops, the federal Confrontation Clause may apply to only a very small percentage of hearsay statements—those involving efforts by the state to obtain the statement where there is danger of governmental overreaching, an historical concern of the Clause. In that event, states may choose to have a more expansive definition of "testimonial" and/or continue to apply a *Roberts*-type analysis to non-testimonial statements, under their own confrontation clauses.

Some Implications of the Law After *Davis*

In his dissent to the reversal of Hammon's conviction, Justice Thomas called the *Davis* standard "unworkable." The primary purpose test articulated by *Davis* clearly requires a case-by-case analysis, rather than a more simply applied bright line approach, such as "all statements made to law enforcement are testimonial," or "all statements that are accusatory in nature are testimonial." Bright line tests like these would find many more statements to be testimonial than under the Court's present approach.

Is *Davis* the death of domestic violence prosecutions if there is no 911 call? Victims in such cases frequently refuse to or are unable to testify. They often feel they need the abuser to survive, or fear him, or have been injured or killed by him. He may or may not have conditioned violence on the victim testifying, but she may be deterred regardless. Some victims feel they deserved the violence, and may refuse to testify for that reason. They may have children, complicating the decision. They may love the abuser or believe his (typical) promises to reform.

Thus, it may become necessary for the prosecution to offer the victim's out-of-court statements. Even if these statements are testimonial (and some will not be) the doctrine of forfeiture may apply. It would seem to apply more frequently in these than in other cases, including organized crime. *Davis* noted that domestic violence prosecutions are "notoriously susceptible to intimidation or coercion of the victim to ensure that she does not testify at trial."

Controversy exists over whether forfeiture applies when the victim was murdered or otherwise rendered unavailable, but there is no evidence that the motivation of the defendant was to prevent her from appearing at trial. Since historically witness tampering has been the basis of forfeiture doctrine, lack of intent may prevent a finding of forfeiture, but this is presently unclear. See generally Raeder, *Domestic Violence Cases After Davis: Is the Glass Half Empty or Half Full*, XV BROOKLYN JOURNAL OF LAW AND POLICY (2007).

It is also unclear how the *Crawford* and *Davis* criteria will be applied to child abuse cases. The child's statement in such cases is often offered via a videotape made by law enforcement or child welfare agencies cooperating with law enforcement, pursuant to special statutory child videotape provisions. There have been a number of recent reversals under the Confrontation Clause of convictions because of the introduction of such child videotapes, where the child did not testify at trial. But these statutory provisions may not be unconstitutional on their face, since many are written to encompass videos of children who appear at trial.

Some prosecutors argue that because children do not understand how trials work, objectively they cannot utter testimonial statements. This argument has been rejected by a number of courts on the grounds that the standard is (or should be) that of an "objective adult observer" rather than someone in the shoes of a child.

Nevertheless, hearsay statements of children made to parents and doctors have usually survived claims that they are testimonial because the purpose was not to make or obtain evidence and the statements were not to government agents. But every case must be viewed on its facts, particularly those involving referrals to doctors by officers. Should the existence of mandatory reporting requirements concerning child abuse have any effect on this analysis?

If children's out-of-court statements are going to be deemed "testimonial" in a large number of cases, it will become very important to these prosecutions that the children testify on the stand. The issue of the child's competency (which generally is scrutinized only if the child takes the stand) will assume heightened importance. See generally, Raeder, *Comments on Child Abuse Litigation in a "Testimonial" World: The Intersection of Competency, Hearsay and Confrontation After Davis,* 82 INDIANA LAW JOURNAL (2007).

Beyond Hearsay: Other Implications of the Confrontation Clause

Constitutional confrontation requirements may have implications for trial practice in addition to those concerning the hearsay rule.

The constitutional confrontation requirement is not directed only at the hearsay situation, of course. Two other principal uses of the confrontation clause may be mentioned.

(1) *Trial Witness Format: The Coy and Craig Cases*

The Confrontation Clause obviously and primarily regulates the format under which witnesses testify at trial, requiring open display and cross examination.

As just one aspect of this, there are numerous cases constraining the extent to which the judge can leave a government witness' direct testimony standing against the criminal defendant where cross examination has been prevented or truncated because the witness has become ill, died, or pled privilege, since the direct examination. The courts seem to do a weighing and balancing in this situation. Does *Crawford* allow this? But there are other more important Confrontation Clause issues concerning trial format to examine.

Just what are the features of the trial format the clause normally requires for witnesses who appear? Can at least some, especially fragile, government trial witnesses testify against a criminal defendant through a live camera hook-up or shielded by some kind of screen, perhaps to relieve trauma?

In *Coy v. Iowa* (S.Ct.1988), the Court rejected the use of a one-way mirror or screen to separate the adult defendant in a child-sexual-abuse case from his alleged child victim during the victim's testimony (including the cross examination) at trial. This was held by the Supreme Court to violate the defendant's right to face-to-face confrontation, at least where no "particularized finding" was made that this victim actually needed protection. In the court below there had been merely a generalized assumption that children needed protection in this kind of case.

Under the one-way mirror or screen procedure employed at trial, which the Supreme Court declared to have been improper, the judge's, jury's and defendant's view of the witness was not blocked; but the witness could not see the defendant. Full cross-exam questioning by defendant's counsel, was allowed, with answers given under oath and subject to the penalty for perjury, as with any witness. All parties, all counsel, all jurors, the judge, and the witness, could hear everything.

Justice Scalia, for the Court, stated that constitutionally, the witness must be able to see the defendant because, though this may deter an honest story and could traumatize a child, it may also deter a false story. But, Scalia says, regardless of any effect on accuracy, the constitution commands a certain procedure, "confrontation", which Scalia says plainly includes that the alleged victim see the accuser. Thus the procedure here was deficient.

Justice Scalia's language suggested he might feel the same way even if there were specific proof that the particular child would be severely traumatized by testifying in open court while viewing the defendant, but that question was reserved.

Subsequently, in *Maryland v. Craig* (S.Ct.1990), Justice O'Connor, writing for the Court, retracted from the strong language of Justice Scalia in *Coy*. She had written a concurrence in *Coy* stating that she felt that a particularized showing of likely trauma would make a difference. This view carried the day in *Craig*, becoming the view of the Court.

In *Craig*, live closed-circuit television was used to bring the child-victim-witness' live testimony into the courtroom from an adjacent room. Again the only visual blockage was of the witness seeing the defendant, as in *Coy*. Again, full, live, real-time cross-examination was done by the defendant's counsel. All parties, all counsel, the witness, the judge, and the jury could hear all proceedings. The oath and perjury penalty were the same as with any witness. The procedure was the functional equivalent of *Coy*, except perhaps that in *Coy* the witness' face viewed by the jury may have been a little more dimmed, although this is not absolutely clear and no legal significance was attached to it in either case. It could contrariwise be argued that a live view of the witness by the jury, as in *Coy*, is better than a television view, as in *Craig*.

But this time, the Supreme Court allowed the procedure because the trial court had made a case specific finding of likely trauma to this particular child and therefore of necessity to protect her.

Thus, the Court allows this kind of sheltered testimony if there is a case specific finding of likely trauma, rather than the generalized assumption thereof of *Coy*. The trauma must result from facing the accused and not merely from testifying in open court. Cf. Crump, *Child Victim Testimony, Psychological Trauma, and the Confrontation Clause: What Can the Scientific Literature Tell Us?*, 8 ST. JOHN'S JOUR. OF LEGAL COMMENTARY 83 (1992); 18 U.S.C.A. § 3509.

Bottom line, *Craig* indicates that the constitutional preference for face-to-face testimony must sometimes give way (at least in part) to practical considerations and the necessities of the case, when required to foster an important public policy, if reliability of the testimony is otherwise fairly well assured. *Craig* obviously sees the right to confrontation here as subject to some kind of balancing, yet this may render it vulnerable to reanalysis in light of *Crawford's* admonition that "[b]y replacing categorical constitutional guarantees with open-ended balancing tests, we do violence to their [the Framer's] design." So far, *Craig's* balancing test has not been successfully challenged.

Under *Roberts,* it was fair to ask if it made sense to require a particularized showing of this kind of need before slightly trimming in-court confrontation, as in *Craig*, but not demanding any showing at all before admitting out-of-court hearsay under a firmly rooted hearsay exception. If you were defense counsel, would you rather cross-examine a witness behind a screen or on a live television hook-up, than be denied any opportunity at all for cross-examination of that witness because her words come in through a hearsay exception?

Should the law be concerned that the mere use of a screen or video hook-up *itself* implies guilt to the jury? This did not play a legal role in these two cases. As a defense lawyer, what, if any, measures might you take, to try to minimize this effect?

Would a statute providing for admission of a videotape of child testimony, made before trial, be governed by the *Craig* standard, or the constitutional standard applicable to hearsay exceptions? Does it make any difference? See, for such a statute, 18 U.S.C.A. § 3509. Of course a statute cannot trump the constitution.

Attempts to expand testimony via remote transmission to otherwise unavailable adult witnesses has met with some success, particularly in civil cases and where all parties consent. However, the Supreme Court refused to adopt a proposed amendment to Rule 26(b) of the Federal Rules of Criminal Procedure that would have authorized contemporaneous, two way video presentation of a witness at a different location in exceptional circumstances so long as the witness would be considered unavailable for purposes of F.R.E. 804(a)(4)-(5). Justice Scalia decried such "virtual confrontation" as ignoring the difference in the constitutional standards applied to live testimony with those applied to out-of-court statements, while Justice Breyer would have let the rule be adopted given its thoughtful consideration pursuant to the Rules Enabling Act process. It is likely that such video testimony will continue to be requested in individual cases, since the Court's refusal to expand the use of remote technology is not equivalent to finding that this practice violates the Confrontation Clause in a particular case. Post *Crawford,* is any of this safe from challenge?

(If both parties consent, of course, there would probably be no problem.)

(2) The Criminal Defendant's Right to Cross Examine Without Undue Restriction of the Questions

There is yet another aspect of trial practice the constitutional Confrontation Clause affects. The clause can curtail evidentiary rules or rulings that unduly restrict criminal defense efforts in cross examination to expose ulterior motivations, biases, or weaknesses in the testimony of government witnesses. Cf. pp. 458–59.

For example, the clause may constrain but not eliminate a judge's discretion under rules like F.R.E. 403 and 611 to limit cross examination on grounds of undue protraction, confusion, prejudice, redundancy, harassment, etc. *Delaware v. Van Arsdall* (S.Ct.1986) held it error (albeit harmless on the facts) to refuse to permit defense cross examination into the possibility of collusion between the prosecution and a government witness, where the prosecution may have dropped unrelated charges against the witness as part of a "deal" with the witness. The Court added, however, that trial judges can impose reasonable limits on cross-examination, to avoid "harassment, prejudice, confusion of the issues, [compromising] the witness' safety, or interrogation that is repetitive or only marginally relevant," among other things.

This constitutional constraint on the judge may trump other rules of exclusion, too. An earlier case, *Davis v. Alaska* (S.Ct.1974) held that the Confrontation Clause required the trial judge to allow cross examination revealing that a major government witness was on probation from a juvenile court adjudication, despite a confidentiality statute barring such a showing. Consider also *Pennsylvania v. Ritchie* (S.Ct.1987) which held that the defendant had a due process right, for potential impeachment of his daughter who was the complainant in his rape case, to have the trial judge inspect, *in camera,* confidential, qualifiedly privileged state child protective agency records concerning her. The plurality found no confrontation violation since this discovery was sought pretrial, leaving this issue unsettled.

In *Smith v. Illinois* (S.Ct.1968), the Confrontation Clause was held to require disclosure of the identity of the government witness being cross-examined, because identity can be key to veracity. *Smith* involved the right to cross-examine the principal government witness as to real name and address, which the trial judge had refused to permit. The Court noted that the identification of witnesses is fundamental because it may lead to possible impeachment and help evaluate testimony. Therefore, the duty to disclose can trump even informer privilege.

Evidentiary restrictions for the protection of victims of crime have also been challenged under the Confrontation Clause. In *Olden v. Kentucky* (S.Ct.1988) (per curiam) it was reversible error to prohibit defense counsel's cross-examination of the white female complainant in a rape case designed to reveal her long standing, extra-marital, interracial sexual relationship with the defendant's half brother. The defendant claimed consent, and argued that because he had been seen with the complainant, she fabricated the rape charge to avoid jeopardizing her relationship with her boyfriend (the defendant's half-brother). The trial court had precluded the cross-examination on grounds that showing her interracial sexual affair with her boyfriend might prejudice the jury against her. While this case did not involve a rape shield provision, the trial judge's ruling was similar thereto.

In contrast, *Michigan v. Lucas* (S.Ct.1991) held that defendant's evidence of his own past sexual relationship with his alleged rape victim, offered to show likely consent, could be precluded by the judge on grounds that the defense failed to give the 10–day advance notice of such evidence required by the state's "rape shield" statute.

VI. THE DUE PROCESS AND COMPULSORY PROCESS CLAUSES

Aside from the Confrontation Clause, the Due Process and Compulsory Process clauses of the Constitution may also compel that the criminal defendant be allowed to present reliable evidence even if its admission is otherwise barred by evidentiary rules or rulings, such as F.R.E. 403, 611, the hearsay rule, privilege, rape shield, etc. Here the evidence need not always necessarily be specifically tied to effectiveness of cross-examination or impeachment.

As is shown immediately above, the criminal defendant may be able to use the Constitution to trump exclusionary evidentiary rules or rulings which interfere (in a major or arbitrary way or without good reason) with the right to present defense evidence. The pertinent constitutional clauses are not only those relating to confrontation, which appear expressly in the Sixth Amendment of the United States Constitution. In addition the Sixth Amendment provides: "In criminal prosecutions, the accused shall enjoy the right . . . to have compulsory process for obtaining witnesses in his favor. . . ." The Fifth and Fourteenth Amendments establish the general notion of "Due Process of Law." In federal law this last notion by interpretation incorporates the other two and includes additional concepts. The incorporation makes the rights applicable in state cases. It arguably also extends at least some of the rights, although in extremely diluted form, to civil cases and to the prosecution in criminal cases.

The case cited most frequently by the criminal defense to force admission of otherwise inadmissible hearsay is *Chambers v. Mississippi* (S.Ct.1973). In *Chambers*, the combined application of Mississippi's rule against impeaching one's own witness and Mississippi's rejection of hearsay declarations against penal interest violated the defendant's Due Process right to a fair trial. A third party had confessed to the crime, but the defense was unable to effectively bring this before the jury owing to these restrictive evidentiary rules. *Chambers* has been interpreted narrowly to require defense evidence only if it is extremely trustworthy. See also *Washington v. Texas* (S.Ct.1967) which struck down, under the Compulsory Process Clause applicable to states under Due Process, a Texas statute rendering incompetent to testify for one another, persons charged or convicted as co-participants in the same crime. The court stresses the absurdity and arbitrary nature of the statute and that it blindly blocked a whole category of defense witnesses.

Although more a constitutional rule of criminal discovery than evidence, it might be well for the reader to recall at this point that the prosecutor is obliged by *Brady v. Maryland* (S.Ct.1963) to disclose to the defense in timely fashion any significant exculpatory evidence the prosecutor knows about that the defense does not.

For more on the constitutional right of a criminal defendant to present evidence in defense despite contrary rules of evidence, and its limits, see Chapter 4, under Rape Shield, and Chapter 5, under "Policies Underlying Privileges", supra, particularly the *Egelhoff* and *Imwinkelried* citations. There is emerging, as a combination of all these various constitutional clauses, a very limited "constitutional right to defend". But as perusal of the cross-references just mentioned will show, the *Egelhoff* case seems to cut back on it drastically. *Rock v. Arkansas* (S.Ct.1987) (criminal defendant has a constitutional right to tell her story of the incident despite jurisdiction's rule against hypnotically refreshed testimony) contrasted with *United States v. Scheffer* (S.Ct.1997) (criminal defendant's lie detector expert may constitutionally be excluded because of jurisdiction's rule against lie detectors) suggests that the right may be stronger when it is the criminal defendant himself who wishes to testify to the material that has been attempted to be blocked.

The Court may have somewhat revived the viability of right-to-defend claims by defendants in *Holmes v. South Carolina* (S.Ct.2006). *Holmes* held that exclusion of defense evidence of third-party guilt on the ground that as a matter of law, no such proffered evidence could raise a reasonable inference as to defendant's own innocence when there is scientific forensic evidence of defendant's guilt, denied the defendant a fair trial.

The Court sums up the previous cases as articulating a generalized constitutional right to introduce important defense evidence unless the rule excluding it is shown to be a narrowly tailored, proportionate, non-arbitrary measure to advance a significant state interest. The decision, in applying this standard, still indicates that most rules of evidence will be upheld and that only the most egregious and extraordinary instances will violate this right.

CHAPTER 9

HEARSAY RULE MODIFICATIONS FOR ADMISSIONS AND WITNESSES' PRIOR STATEMENTS

I. MAPPING THE HEARSAY ESCAPE VALVES AND THEIR UNDERLYING POLICIES

"Exemptions" and "Exceptions" From the Hearsay Rule: F.R.E. 801–804

The Rules governing hearsay in F.R.E. Article VIII can be broken down into three main parts. First, Rules 801–802 contain a general rule against hearsay, together with the general definition of hearsay. But secondly, Rule 801 also contains two "exemptions," or types of specially defined non-hearsay. These exemptions cover narrowly drawn, carefully circumscribed classes of evidence which, under the general definition, would otherwise be hearsay, but which are removed from the general definition if the special conditions prescribed are met. The exemptions cover certain prior statements of witnesses; and party admissions. Third, Rules 803, 804, and 807 contain two lists of "exceptions" to the hearsay rule and a general but circumscribed "catch-all" exception. "Exemptions" and "exceptions" produce the same result: the evidence is not barred by the hearsay rule.

F.R.E. 802 states the general rule that hearsay is excluded from evidence. This exclusion is implemented

460

by a general definition of hearsay. Rules 801(a)(1), (b), and (c) provide this general definition. They define as hearsay any in-court evidence of a statement "made other than by the declarant while testifying at the hearing" provided it is offered to prove the "truth of the matter asserted" in the statement (a definition substantially imported from the common law).

But an absolute prohibition of hearsay would be intolerable. The basic definition and general inadmissibility provided by Rules 801 and 802 would make it impractical to prove many kinds of propositions crucial to litigation, if there were no escape from these Rules. Basic hearsay includes many kinds of valuable and indeed necessary evidence, from bank statements to the opposing party's admissions.

The common law addressed this problem by creating a large number of escape valves or exceptions to the hearsay rule. The F.R.E. do the same, but the F.R.E. use two different mechanisms for the escape valves. One is that F.R.E. 803 and 804 create a number of "exceptions" that are parallel to the common law, with some changes, and Rule 807 provides a general but circumscribed residual exception not explicitly recognized in the common law. The other is that the F.R.E. provide certain escape valves right in Rule 801, in the definition of hearsay itself, in what sometimes are called "exemptions," or defined non-hearsay. As the F.R.E. defines them, these are not exceptions, although they look like exceptions and perform in the same way; literally, the exemptions are defined as non-hearsay.

Specifically, the exemptions are in F.R.E. 801(d). Rule 801(d) defines two types of out-of-court statements as non-hearsay, even though they otherwise would be within the basic definition: (1) Admissions of a party opponent (defined analogously to a parallel common law exception) and (2) certain prior statements of witnesses (a departure from the common law).

We say that admissions and witness statements, then, are given "exemptions" from the hearsay rule. What this means, briefly, is that a statement made by a party, when offered by an opposing party, is not excluded by the hearsay rule. At common law, the statement fits an exception for admissions; under the F.R.E., it is defined as non-hearsay. The exemption for witnesses' statements allows the substantive use of certain prior inconsistent statements, prior consistent statements, and prior identifications. For example, a witness may be allowed to testify not only that he recognizes the defendant now, but also that he identified him earlier in a lineup. The F.R.E. exemption for witness statements changes the common law.

In addition, the Rules provide two "laundry lists" of *exceptions*: those requiring unavailability of the declarant (Rule 804) and those not so requiring (Rule 803). This basically codifies the common-law pattern. Frequently an expansive version of the common-law exception is codified. In addition, Rule 807 provides an innovation: a general mechanism for judicial creation of new exceptions in a particular case for especially deserving evidence missed by the standard exceptions. The exceptions, including this innovation, will be treated in the next chapter.

"Exceptions" and "exemptions" amount to the same thing. If they are placed within the definitional rule (801), we call them "exemptions." If they are in separate rules (803, 804, 807), we call them "exceptions." The common law usually spoke only of "exceptions," which included some of what, because of placement in the Rules, we would now call "exemptions" (specifically, party admissions).

If a distinction has to be made between the exemptions and the exceptions, it could be said, without airtight precision, that the reason for the exemptions is that there is something in the adversary process at trial that makes it fair to admit them. The reason for the exceptions is that there was something in the circumstances attending the declaration that suggests reliability and there is some form of necessity for the evidence at the trial.

Policies Underlying Hearsay Exceptions: Necessity and Trustworthiness

The common-law system developed a series of exceptions to the hearsay rule that reflected, in a rough, generalized way, two considerations: (1) necessity and (2) trustworthiness.

The common-law exceptions to the hearsay rule are said to reflect two factors: special necessity for, and special trustworthiness of, the particular category of hearsay embraced by the exception. The judgment of trustworthiness and necessity was made by the law for a category of evidence, rather than by the judge on a case-specific basis.

Many of the common-law exceptions require that the declarant be presently unavailable to testify respecting the matter. This is said to constitute the necessity. In other words, while her live testimony is preferred and must be used (rather than her hearsay declaration) if she is available, the hearsay is better than no evidence at all being introduced from this source, if she is not. Other exceptions reflected other kinds of necessity, frequently that the hearsay, closer to the occurrence and prior to litigation motivation, was better evidence.

Concerning trustworthiness, each exception was a category of evidence described in terms of certain general features that must exist on the face of the statement or in the circumstances surrounding its making, that were supposed to incline the declarant to trustworthy reporting.

A few examples will suffice for now. The common law evolved an exception for dying declarations, which usually were statements of a victim identifying her murderer. The victim's unavailability furnished the necessity factor. Trustworthiness was said to flow from the victim's motivation against falsehood as she prepares to "meet her maker" and abandons hope of personal earthly gain, knowing her death is imminent. The common law also created an exception for certain business records. Trustworthiness could be inferred from business reliance, and the absence of detailed memory of any one individual who could reproduce the information created the necessity.

Under the common-law system (at least after its developmental phase), all the necessity and trustworthiness in the world in a particular case would not get the hearsay in if the evidence did not come within the narrow, literal terms of an exception. There were a few opinions to the contrary (mostly dictum in decisions supportable on more conventional grounds such as the availability of an established exception). Later, these minority expressions formed the basis for the "catch-all" or "residual" hearsay exception in the Federal Rules of Evidence.

But under the overwhelmingly prevailing common-law view, even if the hearsay was the only way to prove a vital fact, and its trustworthiness was beyond doubt, if it did not come within the literal terms of an exception, it was not admissible. Excluded hearsay was sometimes more reliable and needed than evidence which was received under an exception—or, for that matter, than admissible evidence that was not hearsay at all. The necessity and trustworthiness of an offered piece of hearsay was not, under this common-law system, even attempted to be measured as such in particular cases. The assumption, often unwarranted, was made that there is special trustworthiness and necessity if the hearsay comes within the terms of an exception, and not otherwise.

Policies Underlying the Exemptions: Fairness and Pragmatism

This necessity-and-trustworthiness reasoning expresses the common-law policies underlying hearsay exceptions. The exemptions, as distinguished from exceptions, also express these two factors, but they also are based on broader considerations.

Use of an admission of a party opponent can be justified, for example, simply on the ground that it usually is fair for a party's own statements to be used against that party. This fairness policy has several dimensions. First, a party arguably should be responsible for his own disingenuous or careless remarks. Second, and perhaps more importantly, if the admission needs to be qualified, explained, or retracted, the party who issued it usually is in the best position to supply this missing evidence. The hearsay concerns about such matters as the oath, demeanor, confrontation, and cross-examination do not have the same force when the declarant is the same party who now wishes to attack the evidence. Thus, it makes sense to define admissions so that they are not hearsay, as the F.R.E. do, rather than to call them exceptions. However, it should immediately be added that admissions also can often be supported on the usual grounds for exceptions, trustworthiness and necessity.

Certain prior statements of presently testifying witnesses also are exempted. Again, the policies may include trustworthiness and necessity but go beyond those factors. This exemption requires that the witness testify in the case, now, as a predicate to use of the prior statement. Consequently, the hearsay concerns for cross-examination, demeanor, oath and confrontation do not apply in the same way. And there is another reason why we label certain prior witness statements as non-hearsay: pragmatically, it often makes little sense to expect the jury to distinguish hearsay use (substantive use) from non-hearsay use (credibility use) of the prior statement, and from the substantive use of the present testimony. An instruction to consider the prior statement only on credibility, and not for substantive purposes, may be more confusing than useful.

The Relationship of Exemptions and Exceptions to Other Parts of the F.R.E.

Many rules must be considered together when approaching potential hearsay. Among the rules likely to be important in addition to those in Article VIII (Hearsay) is Rule 403 (balance of probativity against countervailing factors). Rule 703, permitting experts to base testimony on proper hearsay, and Rule 807, the so-called "catch-all" exception to the hearsay rule, are frequently available as "end runs" around the hearsay rule.

Even if potential hearsay evidence clears the hearsay rule because of an exemption, exception, or non-coverage in the definition, it does not automatically become admissible. It may still run afoul of other rules, including, among others, those relating to relevance (Rules 401–402), character (Rules 404, 405, 412–15), safety measures (Rule 407), settlement (Rule 408), insurance (Rule 411), privileges (Rule 501), opinion (Rules 701–702), personal knowledge (Rule 602), authentication (Rule 901), or the original documents rule (Rule 1002). While some of these rules may speak in terms only of applicability to witnesses rather than declarants, they are on numerous occasions applied to both.

Perhaps most importantly, the evidence may still run afoul of Rule 403 (the "great override"), which clearly is applicable. Rule 403 allows a judge to exclude otherwise admissible evidence on a largely discretionary balancing of probativity against prejudice, confusion, time consumption, misleadingness and the like. Rule 403, like most of the other rules mentioned, is a one-way street: it does not license *admission* of evidence that is otherwise inadmissible under some other rule, such as the hearsay rule, but it normally allows *exclusion* of evidence that is otherwise admissible pursuant to a hearsay exception or otherwise.

In addition to rules which may render inadmissible even evidence which would seem to be admissible under a hearsay exemption or exception, the reader should consider rules with the opposite effect. In other words, even if evidence is hearsay, and not within an obvious exemption or exception, the offeror may be able to find ways around the hearsay rule under other rules. This, however, is more difficult, because the hearsay prohibition is not a balancing rule, but ostensibly is absolute.

Nevertheless, there are two frequently overlooked provisions that may be regarded as at least a *kind* of "end run" around the hearsay prohibition under the Federal Rules of Evidence—"end runs" whose status was not at all clear under the common law. They are:

(1) Rule 703 (which appears in Article VII, the "Opinion and Expert Testimony" article of the Rules). This rule provides that an expert may give an opinion and base it on certain kinds of reliable hearsay (or other inadmissible evidence). See Chapter 7, supra. Such hearsay might include, for example, surveys, studies, books, polls, and a variety of second-hand statements. See, e.g., *United States v. Golden* (9th Cir.1976) (Rule 703 allows drug enforcement agent to testify to standard prices of narcot-

ics in various cities based on hearsay of other agents). It is not a complete end run because, even though the hearsay-based opinion may be held admissible, the hearsay basis itself, that underlies the opinion, may be suppressed, in the discretion of the judge; and even if it comes in, at least in theory it cannot be used for its truth, but merely to support the opinion. However, Rule 703 often enables the offeror to get the message to the jury, even when it contains hearsay.

(2) The Flexible, So–Called "Catch-all" Exception in Rule 807. This is the innovative "catch-all" or residual exception to the hearsay rule. Technically, this provision is not an "end-run" around the hearsay rule, because it is in the hearsay article of the rules, and is merely another exception. But because the provision was not part of the common law and is frequently overlooked, it makes sense to think of it as a separate principle.

The "catch-all" provides that a judge can make new exceptions to the hearsay rule for hearsay in the particular case under certain conditions designed to insure that the evidence is deserving and needed and that the other party has a fair opportunity to combat it. The evidence must be found to be especially trustworthy and necessary, and the party relying on the catch-all must give advance and somewhat detailed notice to the other side.

Might use of these two "end runs," or of any broad hearsay exemption or exception, violate the right to confrontation under the Constitution? Under what conditions? See discussion of this constitutional right supra in Chapter 8 under "V. Hearsay and the Constitution: The Confrontation Clause." The Constitution, of course, overrides any applications of the Rules that are deemed inconsistent with the Constitution.

II. THE EXEMPTION FOR CERTAIN PRIOR STATEMENTS OF PRESENTLY TESTIFYING WITNESSES

The two types of exemptions are designated (1) "Prior Statement by Witness" and (2) "Admission by Party–Opponent." In this Section II we cover only the former. Prior witness statements were hearsay under the common law if used substantively, but the F.R.E. create an exemption *for certain types of them*.

Rule 801(d)(1) covers statements made at an earlier time by witnesses who are now testifying. Evidence of such statements is made substantively admissible *under certain conditions*. If they do not meet the conditions, and are offered substantively, that is, for their truth, they are hearsay, under the general definition of hearsay in Rule 801(c): "a statement other than one made by the declarant *while testifying at the trial or hearing*, offered in evidence to prove the truth of the matter asserted." The language we have italicized embraces not only statements by persons other than the witness, but statements of the witness made previously.

This substantive admissibility is a change from the prevailing common law, under which they were admissible not substantively, but rather only on the issue of credibility, a non-hearsay use because then they are not offered "for the truth of the matter they assert". At common-law prior witness statements could only be introduced substantively if the facts warranted application of some other hearsay exception.

Inconsistent Statements "Under Oath" in "Prior Proceedings": F.R.E. 801(d)(1)(A) more liability involved

At common law, a prior inconsistent statement of a presently testifying witness could not be considered by the trier-of-fact for its truth (i.e., substantively, as distinguished from impeachment). Thus, if it was the only substantial evidence tending to establish an element of a claim or defense, the party with the burden of proof on that issue would lose because the judge could not submit the claim or defense to the jury. Adherence to that rule was not unbroken, however. See, e.g., Cal. Evid. Code 1235, 1236, 1238.

The F.R.E. eliminate (in certain safeguarded situations) the traditional ban on substantive use, without disturbing the traditionally permitted credibility use (which is not a hearsay matter at all, since the evidence is not offered for its truth). Rule 801(d)(1)(A) provides that if the statement is inconsistent with the witness' present testimony and was made at a prior "proceeding" under oath and subject to perjury penalties (for example a grand jury proceeding, whether or not in the same or even a similar case), the evidence is exempt from the hearsay rule, notwithstanding that there may not have been any opportunity to cross-examine at the earlier proceeding (as there usually will not have been at a grand jury proceeding).

The extent to which other types of government investigations (besides the grand jury) may be considered "proceedings" is still unsettled, particularly for statements to law enforcement officials. Of course they would also have to be under oath and subject to perjury penalties, to comply with the rule. Should the swearing of an affidavit before a notary be considered a "proceeding" that qualifies? Is the word "perjury" in the rule confined technically to the offense of perjury or can other "false swearing" penalties qualify? In *United States v. Castro–Ayon* (9th Cir.1976), an interrogation under oath by the Border Patrol qualified.

The Uniform Rules of Evidence version of Rule 801(d)(1) as it relates to prior inconsistent statements in *civil* cases does not require the statement to have been sworn nor to have been made at a proceeding nor to have been subject to perjury penalties. Thus statements made on the street or over the back fence can qualify. For criminal cases, the rule is identical to the Federal Rule. An earlier draft of the Federal Rule omitted these requirements as to both civil and criminal cases, which is, essentially, the California position.

If the statement does not qualify for substantive use, must jurors be told that the statement can only be used for impeachment? Judges appear not to have any sua sponte duty to give the jury such a limiting instruction, but normally must do so upon appropriate request. Judges usually let in such statements if there is a legitimate credibility purpose. In an aggravated case, the danger of misuse may tip the balance against this. An instruction, however, will normally be deemed a sufficient safeguard against misuse. The computation is a Rule 403 computation.

Can a person be convicted when the only evidence on an element of the offense is a substantively admissible prior inconsistent statement? It would seem that if the statement was made under oath and subject to perjury penalties in a proceeding, and the witness is currently presented on the stand, the statement might be sufficient to convict. But in some states, any inconsistency, however thoughtlessly made, anywhere, could be sufficient to supply a key element. (And see F.R.E. 801(d)(1)(C), below.)

Prior Consistent Statements: F.R.E. 801(d)(1)(B)

Rule 801(d)(1)(B) provides that if the prior statement is consistent with the witness' present testimony, it is exempt from the hearsay rule (and thus can be used "for its truth", i.e., substantively, not just on credibility), *but only if it tends to "rebut" an "express or implied charge"* of *"recent fabrication," "improper motive,"* or *"improper influence."* It need not have been made at an earlier proceeding nor been under oath nor subject to perjury penalties. What qualifies as the requisite charge of fabrication or improper motive or influence has generated substantial dispute. Isn't it arguable that such a charge is inevitably implied whenever the facts are contested? Courts have not seen it that way.

The reason for the "charge" requirement in the F.R.E. is that under traditional law, which did not allow the evidence to come in substantively, it could come in to support credibility but (because of courtroom economies) only when there had been an attack on credibility. Under most decisions, the attack had to be in the form of the kind of "charge" articulated here, and courts were cautious in permitting the rehabilitation.

Tome v. United States (S.Ct.1995) continued the cautious common-law tradition, holding that out-of-court consistent statements made *after* the alleged reason for fabrication or alleged improper influence or motive arose, were not admissible under Rule 801(d)(1)(B). Logically, only if made *before* such event would the statement tend to suggest that the event did not influence the story and thus tend to rebut the idea of fabrication, as required by the rule.

In *Tome*, the prosecution introduced seven statements of a child who was the alleged victim of sexual abuse at the hands of her father. The statements were made after a custody battle had been initiated by the mother, but before the mother's complaint to the authorities. This evidence was presented by articulate and credible witnesses, in contrast to the testimony of the child on the stand who gave one and two word answers implicating the father in response to leading questions on direct, and whose cross-examination yielded little more information. The father alleged the child was implicating him out of a desire to live with the mother. The seven prior consistent statements of the child, vividly describing the defendant's conduct in graphic terms, went well beyond the in-court testimony and painted a cohesive picture of the alleged abuse.

The Supreme Court indicated that the prior statements did not pre-date the alleged motive to fabricate (the motive to live with the mother) and thus could not qualify for admission under the rule (and perhaps not on credibility either, although that is not entirely clear; by virtue of F.R.E. 401–403 the common law doctrines of credibility use continue but there was some vagueness in some courts as to its exact parameters).

Perhaps the Supreme Court took too literal or narrow a view about exactly what motive to fabricate was being alleged. The child's motive to fabricate may well have been of a different kind or intensity once charges were filed with the authorities. Perhaps the mother's urgency increased at some point. The prior consistent statements maybe could be argued to have pre-dated *those* influences. This argument may be open in future cases.

The Court in *Tome* expressly left open whether any of the statements could be introduced via the catch-all or other hearsay exceptions. On remand, the lower court reversed the conviction because much of the hearsay was inadmissible on any theory. The catch-all was held not to apply for the same reason that prevented admission as prior consistent statements: the child arguably had a motive to fabricate in order to stay with her mother.

After *Tome*, the use of prior consistent statements is problematic to bolster child testimony. Many child abuse allegations are first voiced during the parent's separation, in some measure due to the fact that this is often the first time the child can complain without being under the immediate control of the alleged abuser.

Prior consistent statements of defendants would also appear to be suspect if made after the commission of the criminal act. In other words, once the act has occurred, isn't there always a motive to fabricate?

After *Tome*, the question remains whether prior consistent statements still can be introduced solely for credibility (witness rehabilitation), even if they do not meet the 801 definition.

Some jurisdictions like California also admit prior consistent statements which predate any prior inconsistent statements introduced by the opposing party, regardless of motive to fabricate. This can be the rule for either substantive or credibility use, or both. In California, it is both.

There is also a problem lurking in these provisions of the F.R.E. as to exactly what is a consistent or inconsistent statement. For one example, what about a situation where the witness earlier supplied information but his present posture is that he doesn't remember the facts, or doesn't know anything, and thus he does not report perceiving "inconsistent" facts? What if he explains away a seeming discrepancy? What if the witness is evasive? Can a statement be neither consistent nor inconsistent? The question, then, is, How inconsistent (or consistent) must a statement be to come under the provision for inconsistent (or consistent) statements? This issue is treated in the chapter on impeachment, where the courts are seen to be pragmatic rather than exclusionary on this point; but the same approach doesn't *necessarily* apply here. See *California v. Green* (S.Ct.1970) (inconsistent statement based on evasiveness and lack of memory); *United States v. DiCaro* (7th Cir.1985) (feigned amnesia treated as inconsistency).

Prior Statements of Identification: F.R.E. 801(d)(1)(C)

Even before the adoption of the F.R.E., some states had enacted (or judicially created) a hearsay exception for prior identifications of a person, made by present witnesses. Under Rule 801(d)(1)(C), such an identification statement is exempt from the hearsay rule (provided it is based on personal perception) regardless of whether it is consistent or inconsistent or made at an earlier proceeding or under oath or subject to perjury penalties or offered in response to any charge of influence, motive, or fabrication. Identification statements are confined under 801(d)(1) to identification of a person, as opposed to a thing. Presumably, the identification could be of any relevant person in a civil or criminal context and need not be any of the central actors. The rule includes, among others, identification statements made on the street, at the stationhouse, at a lineup, at a photographic array, or even at the crime scene itself. (Query: Is a *failure* to identify admissible?)

There is no requirement that the statement of identification must have been made soon after perceiving the individual, as there is, for example, in Section 1238 of the California Evidence Code (must be "fresh in memory"). Thus, there could be reliability (memory and influence) problems. Perhaps such a requirement could sometimes be imposed pursuant to Rule 403 which requires that probativity must be found not to be substantially outweighed by prejudice, time consumption, or confusion. See also constitutional discussion of how the statement was obtained, below.

Can a witness who witnesses another make an identification testify under this rule when the person who identified the defendant does not remember? Probably, so long as the identifier is here for cross examination. See "The Results of the Prior Statement Exemptions: Constitutional and Pragmatic Aspects", immediately infra.

Exactly what is and is not a "statement of identification of a person" (to use the words of the rule) presents problems, as statements conceivably within that phrase may range from naming by name a person through pointing at or describing an unknown person to furnishing weaker circumstantial information useful in finding the right person, such as identifying his car, giving his license plate number, recounting a facial feature, or referring to a person by job, position, or occupation, e.g., "the usher did X", "the person at the desk did Y", "the bank manager did Z", etc. But remember, the rule also requires that the statement be made "after perceiving the person." In the license or car example, the maker of the statement would have to have seen the person in the car, at the very least. What about a statement to police arriving at a scene, "She assaulted me." Is that a report of a crime, or a statement of identification? A similar problem occurs in child abuse cases, where complainant states that a known individual (e.g., stepfather, relative or family friend) committed a criminal act.

Is a composite drawing of a suspect created through interaction with a police officer or a computer a prior identification within the rule? Will it survive analysis under other rules, such as 403?

The Results of the Prior Statement Exemptions: Constitutional and Pragmatic Aspects

Constitutional Aspects

(1) *Method of Taking of Prior Statement: Right to Counsel and to Due Process.*

Throughout our discussion of the prior statements rule, we are of course assuming that applicable constitutional safeguards surrounding the obtaining of the prior statement have been complied with. For example, in the case of prior statements of witnesses against him, a criminal defendant may have the right to counsel, and to be free of unnecessarily suggestive or reliability-impair-ing circumstances under due process, at certain line-ups, show-ups, or other identifications conducted under government auspices, where the witness' statement identifying the defendant may have been obtained. Such constitutional cases spelling out this right as *United States v. Wade* (S.Ct.1967), *Gilbert v. California* (S.Ct.1967), *Stovall v. Denno* (S.Ct.1967), *Biggers v. Tennessee* (S.Ct. 1968), *Kirby v. Illinois* (S.Ct.1972), and their progeny, are not meant to be, and probably could not be, affected by the rule. Under appropriate circumstances a taint of this kind may render inadmissible not only the out-of-court identification, but a second, resultant, in-court identification as well. Congress has attempted in the Omnibus Crime Control Act of 1968 to overrule this constitutional doctrine insofar as it may prevent an eyewitness from making an in-court identification. See 18 U.S.C.A. § 3502. Is this legislation constitutional? Courts have attempted to construe the statute narrowly to avoid a conflict, but at least one trial court simply disregarded the statute to the extent it suggested an unconstitutional result, which of course is the correct view when constitution conflicts with statute.[1] On the status of constitutional safeguards at photographic spreads for criminal identification, see *United States v. Ash* (S.Ct.1973).

(2) At Trial: Confrontation.

Because by definition the witness must testify at trial to fall within the exemption, the admission of prior inconsistent, consistent, or identification statements under a provision like 801(d)(1) generally does not pose a confrontation clause problem. See, e.g., *California v. Green* (S.Ct.1970) (giving federal constitutional approval to the even broader California rule allowing inconsistent

---

1. A companion provision attempting to make admissible defendants' voluntary confessions despite failure of the government to give or comply with constitutionally required *Miranda* warnings finally bit the dust on this basis in *Dickerson v. United States* (S.Ct.2000).

statements, in a case where witness affirms making statement but reverses himself on substance; court reserves question if witness can't remember underlying facts—but see *Owens* immediately infra); *Nelson v. O'Neil* (S.Ct.1971) (still o.k. where witness denies making statement and substance of it and tells opposite story on stand).

Any doubts about this seem substantially laid to rest by *United States v. Owens* (S.Ct.1988). *Owens* held that a victim's out-of-court identification of his assaulter (offered under F.R.E. 801(d)(1)(C), identification statements) was admissible and proper under both the rule and the confrontation clause, where the victim testified at trial and was available for cross-examination even though he only remembered making the identification (which he, expressing trust in its truth, and a hearer testified to on direct exam), and had no present memory of who assaulted him (owing to later-onset amnesia from the assault). In other words, while he was physically available at trial, he was effectively insulated from many kinds of cross-examination probing. For though the questions could be asked, he would meet them with the answer "I can't remember." The Court found no difficulty in declaring the witness available for and subject to cross-examination, thus meeting the Rule 801(d)(1) and confrontation requirements. Does *Owens* control if the witness denies memory *both* of whether he made the former statement *and* of the facts recounted in it? One could argue that such a witness is not "subject to cross examination concerning the statement," in any effective sense, under the rule and the Constitution, when a lack of memory of this dimension greets every question. However, as the Court said in *Owens*, the witness's memory failure can be brought home to the jury; and as the Court further pointed out there, this in itself may be effective cross-examination that will satisfy the requirement. Anyway, *Owens* states that the opportunity to ask questions is what is guaranteed, not any particular result or answer. (Nor *any* answer?) Apparently, opportunity for *effective* or *successful* cross-examination is not required. However, see the alternative interpretation of the rule offered later in this section—i.e., that the witness may be required to *testify concerning the prior statement*, not just testify about anything and then be cross-examined on the prior statement. Has he here?

Pragmatic Aspects

The three-pronged hearsay exemption of 801(d)(1) means former statements of witnesses play a more important role at trials than may be realized. Consequently, it is extremely important for attorneys on both sides to seek diligently to obtain early statements from witnesses and to seek to find out what statements already exist in the hands of the opponent or otherwise. Both these points are especially applicable to grand jury statements.

Federal criminal discovery rules are not well suited to this premium on investigation, at least not for the defendant, since only limited discovery is available to him. The prosecution has fairly extensive investigative tools, not the least of which is the grand jury.

Primarily due to the inconsistent-statement branch of the rule (but also the other branches as well), grand jury statements, formerly usually usable only on credibility, now play a much broader role. This increases the importance of the grand jury. Whenever prosecutors believe that favorable witnesses might, with passage of time, turn coat because of fear of or relationship with the defendant (e.g., family, friend, colleague, or romantic interest), the rule provides great incentive to call the witness quickly before a grand jury. The government conceivably could build its entire case on such statements. At the very least, the statements can help the prosecution persuade the jury or survive a motion for directed acquittal.

Prosecutors have gained the most from the prior statements rule, since they have the burden of proof at trial, are in a position to convene and subpoena witnesses for the grand jury, and must often rely in prosecutions on perhaps criminally connected or timid witnesses who may turn (or be turned) against the prosecution between grand jury and trial, once the impact of their testimony becomes known and understood.

The premium on former statements should help convince a judge there is the strong special need the criminal defense is required to demonstrate under discovery law to get grand jury transcripts of witnesses. In federal court, witness statements can be withheld in criminal cases until after direct examination. See the "Jencks" Act, 18 U.S.C.A. § 3500; Fed. R. Crim. Pro. 26.2.

The new admissibility of grand jury statements goes beyond admissibility in the immediate case growing out of the particular grand jury proceeding. The grand jury testimony can be used in other cases as well, for example, a civil antitrust case. The original grand jury proceeding may, but need not have, involved antitrust. Similarly, the rule licenses the use of testimony given in one trial at a later trial, whether or not in the same case and regardless of whether the issues are totally unrelated or one was criminal and the other civil.

While this all may seem to present dangers that the motivation to be accurate and careful, and to explore, was less or directed at different issues in the first proceeding than in the second, the theory is that, unlike the former testimony exception to the hearsay rule (Rule 804(b)(1)), the declarant is presently on the stand, reducing the significance of these dangers.

Under all three branches of the prior statements rule (although probably most easily pictured under the identification branch), if the former statement was not broached on direct-examination of the witness who made it, may it be introduced later through extrinsic evidence at a time when the witness has left the stand? The rule places no limit on how or when the statement may be evidenced: the witness need not necessarily recount or acknowledge it; instead, it may be evidenced by extrinsic evidence, i.e., another witness who heard it, a document embodying it, or a recording. There is no express limitation as to when this may take place. Cf. Rule 613. The requirement remains, however, that the witness must be "subject to cross-examination concerning the statement." This may be done by calling the witness back to the stand.

There is a reading of the rule that would prevent what is discussed in the last paragraph. If we read "concerning the statement", in the rule language quoted, as also applying to some earlier parts of the same sentence in the rule, that is, to language saying the declarant must "testify", then the evidence would be inadmissible. For he did not "testify concerning the statement" although he was "subject to cross-examination concerning the statement."

III.   THE EXEMPTION FOR ADMISSIONS OF A PARTY OPPONENT, HER AGENT, OR HER CO–CONSPIRATOR

The Common Law: An Exemption or Exception

This is among the most important exceptions to or exemptions from the hearsay rule. Under the common-law system, continued under codes like the F.R.E., when a formal party (P) to the case (or P's agent or co-conspirator, under certain circumstances) has made a statement outside the trial, that statement, *if offered against P*, is regarded as either not hearsay (because exempt, as under modern codes), or as an exception to the hearsay rule (the common-law view). In either event the result is the same: the evidence is not subject to the hearsay objection. Availability of the declarant is immaterial under party admissions.

The declaration need not have been damaging (nor perceived as damaging) at the time made, so long as it is a piece of evidence that is damaging to the party's case at the trial. However, this factor could affect weight and, in an extreme case, admissibility under Rule 403 or similar rule or common-law concept. But as a practical matter accomplishing exclusion or significant weight reduction of an admission can be a very uphill battle.

It is easy to see the rationale for receiving into evidence against a party, admissions personally made by her. Lack of cross-examination is at the heart of the hearsay ban. How can a party ever effectively cross-examine herself? Or object to not being able to do so? The party can always disclaim or offer explanations for the statement (e.g., by testifying) once it is admitted. Less clear is the rationale for admitting against the party the so-called *vicarious* admissions made by an agent or co-conspirator of the party, also embraced by the admissions doctrine.

A considerable amount of opinion and even second-hand knowledge has usually been tolerated in these outside-the-trial statements, both at common law and under the codes, at least where the party rather than her agent or co-conspirator made the statement (and in some jurisdictions, even then). The rationale for this broad approach is either that P should have (would have) investigated carefully; or that we don't wish to lose entirely this valuable evidence which cannot really be rephrased to avoid the opinion or second-hand material, as a live witness's statement on the stand can. Based on this, the broad approach seems less justified for personal admissions not known when made to be damaging, and for vicarious admissions, but many courts apply it regardless.

Again, these factors could affect weight, and, in an aggravated case, admissibility under a rule or concept like F.R.E. 403 (although as indicated, admissions seem to be especially favored as evidence by both judges and juries).

Admissions and confessions need not be distinguished for our purposes. The former term is generally used where a damaging fact is admitted; the latter where there is a complete confession of guilt (criminal guilt, usually). Both are embraced by the rule under discussion. This exception or exemption should not be confused with that for "declarations against interest," which is more stringent in some respects, and less in others, and which is covered later in this book. Under "declarations against interest", the declarant need not be a party nor linked to a party by any agency or co-conspiracy principle. The exception is established if the declarant makes a declaration (known then by him to be damaging to his own interests) that is also relevant in some way to the later civil or criminal lawsuit in which it is offered, to which neither he nor any principal nor conspirator of his need be a party.

The Federal Rules: An Exemption From Hearsay for Admissions of Approximately the Common Law Dimensions—F.R.E. 801(d)(2)

F.R.E. 801(d)(2) exempts admissions of a party, a party's agent, or co-conspirator, from the hearsay rule, *if they are used against the party.*

Basically, the common law doctrine is continued by the Federal Rules of Evidence, with a few modifications, as will subsequently emerge. Let us examine each of the types of admission recognized by the rule.

Individual or Personal Party Admissions: Express and Implied (or Adoptive) Admissions: F.R.E. 801(d)(2)(A) and (B)—Essentially the Same as the Common Law Position

(a) Express Admissions

The simplest kind of admission is a statement uttered or written by an individual opposing party personally. Rule 801(d)(2)(A) provides an exemption from the hearsay rule for such statements.

"Admission of a party" means any statement that can be used against the party. It need not embrace more than a minor link in the chain of evidence against the party, and it need not have been against the party's interest when made. Indeed, it may have been beneficial and self-serving. For example, a puffed statement by the party valuing property for a loan can be used as an admission of its worth. Remember, all we mean when we say something is within the admissions doctrine is that it is receivable in evidence; it can be countered before the jury with other evidence, argument, or even the human experience of the jury; it is not "binding" or irrefutable; and will weigh whatever, if anything, the jury thinks it is worth, together with the other evidence in the case. But, practically speaking, juries usually find it quite credible.

The only legal admissibility requirement respecting damaging nature is that the statement is offered against (and is against) the party's case now, in some relevant way. In these respects, "admission," as used in the law of hearsay, does not mean "admission" as lay people use that term.

(b) Implied or Adoptive Admissions

Another, more complicated, kind of admission made by a party personally can be called an "adoptive" admission. Rule 801(d)(2)(B) essentially codifies the common-law concept that adoptive admissions are removed from the ban of the hearsay rule, by extending party admissions treatment to any "statement of which the party has manifested an adoption or belief in its truth."

Adoptive admissions may be illustrated by the following example. One person makes a statement damaging to another person (the party) who agrees with it, saying it is true. The second person is held to have adopted the words of the first. The principle would be the same if verbal expressions (or obvious actions like a nod) tantamount to agreement, rather than express agreement, are used by the second person. If the statement of the first person were offered itself as evidence of the facts it recounts, rather than as the basis for interpreting meaning into the assent of the second, it would normally be inadmissible hearsay. But it is the (implied) statement of the second that is being offered as the real evidence here, and that is a party admission, since we are assuming that, unlike the first person, the second person is a party and the statement relevantly hurts his case.

A less apparent, but still valid, example would be where the second person agrees, not verbally or by obvious conduct, but by less obvious conduct, perhaps by remaining silent where a reasonable person would contest the statement if it weren't true (usually the statement is an allegation or accusation). See generally, on adoption of another's statement by silence, *United States v. Hoosier* (6th Cir.1976) (defendant's silence in face of girl friend's recital of incriminating facts is an adoptive admission). Generally, an adoptive party admission is a statement of another in which the party has manifested belief.

In strict theory, an exemption from the hearsay rule probably does not need to be found in order to admit into evidence the kind of admission by conduct illustrated by the silence example above. At least under the Federal Rules of Evidence. This is because the silence probably is not hearsay in the first place. So no exemption (like the party admissions principle) is needed. Why is it not hearsay in the first place? Because the silence is probably not conduct intended by the actor as an assertion, even though it may manifest his belief in the truth of the statement (or such belief may be one reasonable inference), which is sufficient to make the silence relevant but not to make it hearsay. Under the F.R.E., conduct not intended by the "declarant" (here the silent party) to be an assertion (that is, to communicate a message to others) is not a "statement" for purposes of the hearsay rule, and thus is not hearsay. See Rule 801(a)(2). It is debatable whether this conduct would be found by the judge, in her power to determine such preliminary facts for evidentiary purposes under Rule 104(a), to be so intended. There will frequently be this ambiguity about conduct, and that is the problem with this "intention" test.

Nevertheless, the hearsay exemption for adoptive admissions under Rule 801(d)(2)(B) (statements in which the party has manifested belief) is broad enough to encompass this kind of conduct, silence in the face of accusation, if needed.

The common-law requirement that the circumstances surrounding an alleged adoptive admission be such that a jury could rationally find that a reasonable person in the putative adopter's shoes was signifying adoption, does not expressly appear in the rule, although it certainly is implied by the rule's requirement that the party have "manifested adoption or belief". In the adoption by silence example, the requirement translates into showing circumstances were such that a reasonable person would respond if the statement were untrue.

The "reasonable person" requirement is probably not a hearsay-related concept at all. Instead it is one of relevance or probativity balanced against prejudice, misleadingness, time consumption, etc., which would be imposed on the evidence whether the evidence is affected by the hearsay rule or not, by virtue of Rule 403 or perhaps Rule 104(b).

In the "admission by silence" context, the reasonable person requirement is often said to require that the statement responded to by silence must have been (1) a definite statement (2) of fact (3) understood by the silent person, (4) that affected him, (5) calling for a reply if untrue, (6) concerning a matter of which the silent person had knowledge, (7) in circumstances where he was able to answer. Another phraseology requires that it be "normal, natural, and possible to respond."

These are merely a particularized application of the requirement that any words or conduct offered as agreeing with or acquiescing in a stated fact or accusation, and therefore constituting an admission, must, in the circumstances, be fairly construable as indicating belief in the facts stated.

If the person expected to respond was preoccupied with giving first aid at a crash scene, or was himself dazed or injured, or was too far away to hear or be heard, these conditions of admissibility might not be met.

If the failure to respond to a potentially incriminating fact is in police presence, particularly if the standard warnings concerning the right to remain silent are given, a prudent person, though innocent, might remain silent and not deny the matter or not assert what he might otherwise be expected to assert. The silence might be inadmissible either because there is no reasonable inference of acquiescence to be drawn from it, or perhaps because it might impact a constitutional right.

Of course, admissibility of these, or any, implied admissions, does not mean that all these same factors cannot be argued to the extent they would affect weight before the jury. A jury might even be convinced that as a general matter, people do not respond, and the silence means nothing. A few jurisdictions take this view as a matter of law. But not the F.R.E.

Cf. *Doyle v. Ohio* (S.Ct.1976) (impermissible use of silence to police following *Miranda* warning; impeachment; constitutional decision); *United States v. Hale* (S.Ct.1975) (silence in police situation inadmissible as impeachment by prior inconsistent conduct; decision on ground of probativity under federal evidence law); *Jenkins v. Anderson* (S.Ct.1980) (semble; *Miranda* warning not involved; use of pre-arrest silence not unconstitutional if state evidence law wishes to permit it). These cases generally involved failure to come forward with a defense later asserted at trial rather than silence in response to a specific statement of fact. Silence in a police custodial situation should be distinguished from private discussion on both constitutional and evidentiary grounds, as suggested above.

An unanswered question is whether the reasonable person test is a preliminary fact falling under Rule 104(a) (for the judge to determine) or Rule 104(b) (for the jury to determine if the judge finds some substantial evidence). Rule 104(b) covers preliminary facts upon which relevance depends. Many preliminary facts will have an ambiguity as to whether they relate to relevance.

Adopting a Writing. Regarding silence in the face of an accusation or adverse statement, it should be noted that the problem can arise also in connection with writings sent but not responded to nor denied. Some special patterns or tendencies are discernible in the cases applying the reasonable person test in this context, and they have solidified into matters of law in some jurisdictions.

It is generally regarded to be of significance that the failure to respond was to a bill or statement of account or amount owing. Reasonable people are deemed inclined to respond to all false billings.

If the writing is not of that character, then the decisions seem to look to whether or not there has been a regular course of dealings between the parties. Reasonable persons normally do not respond to non-bill letters that are "bolts out of the blue".

If the evidence is held admissible, these factors may be pointed out to affect weight.

Other Implied Admissions. The same "manifest belief" provisions of the rule might also be construed to cover other kinds of implied admissions—conduct that a jury could find manifests belief in a damaging proposition but not necessarily a proposition directly presented at that moment by another person.

Thus, a jury might find implied admissions of fault or adverse fact in certain circumstances where parties make bribes (or bribe attempts) to witnesses; suppress or destroy evidence; flee; fail to adduce certain evidence that should be peculiarly available to them (this may have other evidential force, too); take safety measures after an injury; offer to compromise or settle a claim; assert privilege, etc., all depending on the facts.

Extrinsic policy factors might step in to bar some of these, even if there is no hearsay problem and high probativity (with low prejudice, misleadingness, and time consumption), in certain of these cases. See, e.g., Rules 407 (remedial, safety, or corrective measures), 408 (settlement and compromise), 409 (payment of medical expenses), and privilege assertion policies. Usually the hearsay problem can be overcome, either by the party admission exemption or by the conclusion that the conduct is not hearsay because not an intended "statement."

Adoptive and implied statements of the type discussed in these entire sections can also be conceived of where it is agents or co-conspirators of a party making the admission, pursuant to the sections below, and indeed in connection with other hearsay and with the other exemptions and exceptions generally.

Vicarious Admissions: (1) Admissions of Conventional Agents: F.R.E. 801(d)(2)(C) and (D)—Compared With Common Law

Let us turn now to another kind of admission in Rule 801(d)(2). That is, party admissions via others who have a formal relationship to the party. We call these "vicarious admissions". They break down into admissions via one's conventional agent, and admissions via one's co-conspirator. The latter is also a form of agency, though an unconventional one. But we will consider it as a separate concept from conventional agents. In the present section, we treat only admissions via a conventional agent.

Who is an agent for these purposes? The Federal Rules of Evidence have broadened the test.

Under the common law, an employee needed to be authorized (either expressly or impliedly) to *make* the statement before it could be used against the principal. Thus, the common law confined admissions to authorized "speaking agents" and authorized "writing agents".

The F.R.E., however, do not so confine the exemption, and the difference is significant. An agent's statement qualifies under the F.R.E. if it either satisfies the "authorized speaking or writing agent" theory (Rule 801(d)(2)(C)); or *relates to* something that is part of the agent's job (relates to something within the "scope of his employment" for the party) and is made while he is still employed (Rule 801(d)(2)(D)), even though he is not authorized to speak or write. In other words, the statement qualifies if either its *making,* or *what it tells,* was part of his job. This approach might admit statements of a janitor in a suit against a large corporation that employs him, if his statements, for example, admitted the janitor's failure to clean the floor in a slip-and-fall case.[2] The common-law test would not admit this, since he was not authorized, neither expressly nor impliedly, to speak or write about this matter. The difference between the two theories is in the thing that must be authorized: making the statement, versus the activity related in the statement.

(a) The Narrow Common Law View: Confinement to Authorized "Speaking" and "Writing" Agents

Under the common law view, which requires express or implied authorization to make the statement, a truck driver's admission that he was going too fast would not be usable against his company in a lawsuit growing out of the collision, but the company's claims agent's statement to the family of the injured person that the driver was going too fast, would. The authority granted to the driver is to "shut up and drive," that is, not to make statements. But the claims agent is expressly or impliedly empowered to talk settlement, including discussing the facts necessary to arrive at settlement.

(b) The Broader "Scope of Employment" View Under F.R.E. 801(d)(2)(D)

Under the test adopted by the F.R.E., both statements would be admissible against the company: the claims

2. We are assuming he was still employed and not fired, at the time he made his statement. This is a requirement under the kind of agent-statement added by the F.R.E., to safeguard against grudge statements and those with only a motive to deflect liability.

agent's because it is expressly or impliedly authorized to be made, Rule 801(d)(2)(C); and the driver's because it relates to something that is part of his job—driving—even though making a statement is not. Rule 801(d)(2)(D). Of course, driving too fast is not part of his job. This raises the question of how general the characterization of what he is talking about should be: driving or driving too fast. To avoid this problem, the rule uses the phrase "within the scope of his agency or employment," borrowing the phrase from tort and contract liability law and agency law. In those bodies of law, it has been resolved that doing an authorized act is "within the scope" even if done negligently or in a wrongful manner.

The effect of the new expansion (the (D) provision of the rule) is limited, however, by the requirement of current agency. Thus, if the driver no longer worked for the company at the time of making his statement, it could not be used against the company. This principle avoids the problem of grudge statements after a discharge that was perhaps motivated by his causing the injury and reduces the likelihood of improper inducements to continue employment.

(c) F.R.E. Abolition of Common Law Prohibition of In–House Admissions

The Rules appear also to abolish the common-law distinction between statements made by employees or agents to, on the one hand, their employer, principal, fellow employees, or company files; and, on the other hand, to outsiders. The so-called "in-house" statements could not qualify under the common law as admissions of the employer or principal (unless, under one view, they were final reports somehow adopted by the employer or principal). Both inside and outside statements now are governed by the same tests: those of Rules 801(d)(2)(C) and 801(d)(2)(D) in federal jurisdictions.

(d) Non–Inclusion of the Predecessor-in-Interest Principle in F.R.E. Admissions

The Rules fail to recognize one kind of agency recognized at common-law: the "predecessor-in-interest" or "privity admissions" principle, which held that if a previous titleholder of property made a statement that reflects on the property, the statement could be used against a subsequent titleholder of the same property, if the previous titleholder made the statement while he had title. In other words, the one titleholder is treated as the "agent" of the other, for party admissions purposes, though in reality he is not. The predecessor-in-interest concept has also been applied to other interests than property title. Although this principle, recognizing such agency for party admissions purposes, has not survived in the Federal Rules of Evidence, the "declarations against interest" exception to the hearsay rule (Rule 804(b)(3)) will frequently, though not always, admit such statements without the necessity of any "agency" theory of attribution. In particular circumstances where there are some special indicia of trustworthiness, the so-called catch-all exception may also apply.

(e) Broad Applications of F.R.E. Provisions

For the broad potential of the traditionally-rooted (C) provision of the rule (authorized speaking and writing agents), see *United States v. Iaconetti* (E.D.N.Y.1976) (government official makes company agent his own agent under Rule 801(d)(2)(C) for purposes of making statements, when government official solicits bribe from him and expects solicitation to be transferred to other company personnel).

A lawyer's opening statement to a jury can be considered an admission of the client in some circumstances. The lawyer is probably expressly or impliedly authorized to say what he says, unless he goes way out of bounds. Lawyers in negotiating sessions would be subject to similar analysis. Even out of bounds statements might qualify if they relate to the lawyer's authorized job. Privilege and Rule 408 would also have to be considered. What if the lawyer is representing the government? This is in some doubt, because courts split, concerning an analogous party-admissions question: whether statements by law enforcement officials can be introduced against the government in a prosecution. What might be the rationale preventing introduction? See *Lippay v. Christos* (3d Cir.1993).

(f) Former Pleadings as Possible Admissions

Former pleas and pleadings (pleas and pleadings in other cases, whether withdrawn or not; amended or superseded or withdrawn ones in the present case; etc.), and statements made in connection with them, are obvious candidates for attempts to find and use damaging admissions and impeaching statements inconsistent with the same party's present position. Thus, if the original complaint charged a now-dismissed defendant with causal negligence in terms that suggested it was the only causal negligence involved, the present defendant at trial may be able to offer that complaint as an admission of the plaintiff. Even though there now is an amended complaint, the earlier pleading was a statement by the plaintiff's agent, his lawyer.

Most jurisdictions provide some constraints on the use of some pleas or pleadings in this fashion. The constraints come from outside the hearsay rule and the party admission principle. They have their source in policy concerns (such as encouraging plea bargaining and settlement, and preserving unencumbered the freedom the law of pleading allows to make, withdraw, and alter pleas) and concerns about probativity and misleading the jury.

Thus, in various jurisdictions, admissibility may depend upon whether civil or criminal pleadings are involved, what the plea or admission sought to be used is, whether it was a "no contest" plea, whether the present proceedings are civil or criminal, whether the evidence is offered for substantive use, whether the pleading was withdrawn, or whether it was signed or sworn to (verified) by the party or just submitted by his lawyer.

F.R.E. 410 provides a limited "immunity" from use, in subsequent civil and criminal proceedings, of certain criminal pleas (i.e., "nolo contendere" pleas and withdrawn guilty pleas), statements to a judge in connection with entering any of the foregoing, and plea discussions with a government attorney. One issue which receives inconsistent treatment is the admissibility of small fines voluntarily paid for traffic infractions by motorists who are later sued civilly. Cf. *Hancock v. Dodson* (6th Cir. 1992).

Vicarious Admissions: (2) Co–Conspirator Statements: F.R.E. 801(d)(2)(E)—Compared With Common Law

Both at common law and under the F.R.E., a statement of a party's co-conspirator can be used against the party as a party admission under certain circumstances.

This hearsay exemption for co-conspirator statements is regarded by the government as an important weapon in combating drugs, terrorism, and white collar crime, but it applies beyond that. In theory it can be used by either side in any civil or criminal case, regardless of whether conspiracy is part of the formal charges or not, and in fact it is continually used in a wide variety of such cases.

The theory supporting the co-conspirator hearsay exemption (or exception, at common-law) is that when individuals join a conspiracy, they are irrebuttably deemed by the law to have authorized all co-conspirators to make statements on their behalf to advance the goals of the conspiracy, or at least they take the risk of such statements that are made for that purpose. In other words, this exemption has an agency basis, just as that for statements by ordinary employees.

Thus, there is some overlap between the co-conspirator provisions and the ordinary agent provisions. It has never satisfactorily been resolved as to what to do if the co-conspirator provision would exclude a statement of a co-conspirator but the ordinary agency provisions would admit it. Solutions range from admitting the statement on the theory the provisions are cumulative, to excluding because the co-conspirator route is exclusive for *criminal* agencies, partnerships, or employment situations, that is, any relationship that has an illegal character.

What qualifies as a co-conspirator statement? As under prevailing common-law, the statement must be made in the course of and in furtherance of a conspiracy, by a fellow conspirator. Generally, these requirements have been broadly interpreted. While "gossip" is typically excluded as not advancing the conspiracy, discussions to keep the conspirators informed of past events or to solicit co-operation of others or to gain access to commit the crime have been admitted. The fact that a conspirator is arrested does not necessarily terminate the conspiracy, although it may prevent statements made by the arrested conspirator to the police from being introduced under this exemption. After the crime conspired-about has been committed, particularly if a major number of the conspirators are caught, the conspiracy is usually deemed to be over, unless there is a continuing co-operative effort (conspiracy) to cover up.

States sometimes go even farther, abandoning some of these restrictive requirements, as did Georgia's co-conspirator rule, which survived a confrontation clause attack in *Dutton v. Evans* (S.Ct.1970), at least under confrontation law as it then was.

This hearsay exemption should not be confused with the theory that admits, against all conspirators, statements of any one of them that are part of advancing the conspiracy, on the separate grounds that the statements are actually part of the crime of conspiracy and are thus not offered for their truth or their credibility. The crime of conspiracy consists of an agreement and one or more overt acts by any conspirator to carry the aims of the conspiracy forward. If a conspiracy is charged, and the statement is offered as an overt act (e.g., a threat or extortion) or as the agreement which forms or defines the conspiracy, it is an operative fact (verbal act) and therefore not hearsay. The doctrines are often difficult to distinguish and have similar requirements, and courts frequently do not differentiate between them.

Bourjaily v. United States (S.Ct.1987) settled that under the F.R.E.'s hearsay exemption, Rule 801(d)(2)(E), the judge determines whether, on the facts of the particular case, the predicate requirements—that there must have been a conspiracy embracing the party and the declarant, and that the declaration must have been made during the course of and in furtherance of the conspiracy—are satisfied.

The Court in *Bourjaily* held that Rule 104(a) prescribes the procedure for all such preliminary determinations. As a result, inadmissible evidence including hearsay—indeed the very piece of hearsay that is itself in question—may be consulted in determining whether the prosecution has met its foundational burden by a preponderance of the evidence, the Court said. This "bootstrapping" feature of the F.R.E., which now apparently applies to all Rule 104(a) determinations, was a sharp break from prior law which required the foundation for the statement to be established by independent (though not necessarily admissible) evidence. Some courts had deemed sufficiency of the foundation to be a jury issue.

A few states such as California still give two bites at the apple: first, letting the judge initially decide if a juror could find sufficient foundation, and second, instructing jurors that they can disregard the statement if they find the foundation to be inadequate.

There had also been some confusion earlier, in various jurisdictions, including federal circuits, as to what was the degree of proof to judge or jury required by the burden, particularly where the case was also a conspiracy case. *Bourjaily*, as indicated, establishes the burden is to prove to the judge by a preponderance.

Bourjaily left open whether the alleged co-conspirator statement in question can itself *alone* be sufficient to establish its foundation. It is clear from the decision that it can be considered with other evidence in establishing the foundation. A subsequent modification of Rule 801(d)(2) prohibits it being sufficient. The amendment applies the same regime applicable to co-conspirator statements, to the foundation for all vicarious admissions under the Rules.

The rule of admissibility of co-conspirator statements is not confined to conspiracy cases nor even to criminal cases. Similarly, the alleged co-conspirator can be unindicted, as was the case in *United States v. Nixon* (S.Ct. 1974). The defense is not entitled to have the statement struck when in a criminal conspiracy case the conspiracy count is taken away from the jury due to the government's inability to present enough evidence of conspiracy for a jury to find guilt beyond a reasonable doubt. This result points out how differing standards of proof can apply in the same case; here, preponderance applies to the evidentiary foundation, while proof beyond a reasonable doubt is required for guilt.

Because the predicate evidence of conspiracy often is diffuse, circumstantial and lengthy, there has been controversy concerning how the judge should receive this foundation information. Although some courts require a hearing held out of the jury's presence, obtaining a reversal for procedural missteps is difficult. Judges are understandably reluctant to sit through elaborate pre-presentations of circumstantial evidence that will have to be repeated before the jury, which it will be if at least one of the main criminal charges is the same conspiracy, as is frequently the case.

Often, therefore, such statements are conditionally admitted, subject to later completion of the foundation in the normal course of the trial. This process results in the defense being required to renew its objection if the foundation is lacking at the conclusion of the prosecution's case-in-chief. However, because most conspirator statements are central to the issues being decided, if the judge later determines that the foundation is insufficient, any ensuing instruction to disregard may be unrealistic. Yet the only other alternative may be a mistrial, which often is an unsatisfactory result in terms of judicial economy in a lengthy multiparty action.

You might think that to be consistent with her finding insufficiency of the foundation, the judge would also have to dismiss the case for insufficient evidence. But remember, there may be other counts than the conspiracy count. Or the foundational insufficiency may have gone not to whether there was a conspiracy, but whether the declarant was a member, or made the statement during and in furtherance of it.

Admissions and Confessions of Alleged Criminals: Constitutional Considerations

The Constitution of the United States (as interpreted) mandates that no court in the land shall admit an "involuntary" confession against its maker in a criminal case. The "voluntariness" of a confession is to be determined from a "totality of the circumstances" in each case. The rule against involuntary confessions is often said to be concerned with (a) the unreliability of coerced confessions, (b) the fact that where some coercion can be shown, more probably took place, and (c) regulating and "civilizing" police practice. See *Arizona v. Fulminante* (S.Ct.1991).

Certain factors have now become largely self-sufficient reasons for exclusion regardless of what the totality of circumstances may indicate about voluntariness. Only one situation will be treated in detail here: that dealt with in the case of *Miranda v. Arizona* (S.Ct.1966). The decision in that case issued out of the Fifth (self-incrimination) and Sixth (right to counsel) amendments, which are also deemed implicit for these purposes, in the Fourteenth Amendment (due process applicable to state proceedings). The principle enunciated in *Miranda* has come to largely dominate the area of confessions. The *Miranda* decision has generated an enormous literature, which is critical as well as supportive.

Miranda mandates that statements made by an arrested person during custodial interrogation cannot be used against that individual unless certain conditions were met at the time. Before being questioned, the defendant must have been told that she need not say anything, that anything she says may be used against her, that she may consult with a lawyer before and during the questioning, and that the state will provide her with a lawyer if she cannot afford one. Only express voluntary waiver of these rights by the accused will suffice as waiver. And she may remain silent on the advice of, against the advice of, or without the advice of, a lawyer. Of course, a suspect might volunteer a statement without questioning in which case the rule is inapplicable. See *California v. Beheler* (S.Ct.1983). At what point there is an arrest or suspicion has focused sufficiently so that *Miranda* warnings must be given, can be difficult to determine. Statements obtained in violation of *Miranda* rights are inadmissible (except perhaps for impeachment), even if under evidentiary rules they would be admissible.

A number of opinions have clarified *Miranda*'s reach. For example, a public safety exception to *Miranda* was articulated in *New York v. Quarles* (S.Ct.1984). Concerning what constitutes interrogation, see *Rhode Island v. Innis* (S.Ct.1980) and *Illinois v. Perkins* (S.Ct.1990). On attempts to question without counsel in various circumstances, see *Edwards v. Arizona* (S.Ct.1981) and *Minnick v. Mississippi* (S.Ct.1990). On later *Miranda* warnings curing earlier defective ones, see *Oregon v. Elstad* (S.Ct. 1985). On whether failure to inform the suspect that his family has retained counsel will vitiate valid warnings, see *Moran v. Burbine* (S.Ct.1986).

A statement of an accused obtained in violation of *Miranda* sometimes can be used for impeachment when the defendant takes the stand and testifies contrary to it. See *Harris v. New York* (S.Ct.1971).

An attempt by Congress to overrule the inadmissibility doctrine of *Miranda* and to substitute therefore an exclusive test of voluntariness of the confession, was held to be unconstitutional in *Dickerson v. United States* (S.Ct. 2000).

In Chapter 8, Section V, we have discussed constitutional confrontation issues. If a custodial admission or confession of one criminal names or implicates another as well as himself, in the crime, the Confrontation Clause normally will prohibit admission against the non-maker if the maker cannot be cross-examined.[3]

3. The maker normally cannot be cross-examined because of the privilege against self-incrimination. The statement is, of course, admissible against the maker as a party admission. As a matter of evidence law under the modern codes, it would seem that this could also be a declaration against penal self-interest (another hearsay exception) as

And using it against the maker in a joint trial of both, even with jury instructions not to use it against the non-maker, may be considered constitutionally prejudicial to the non-maker, unless the implications against the non-maker can be sufficiently obscured, perhaps by redaction. See *Bruton v. United States* (S.Ct.1968). But cf. *Parker v. Randolph* (S.Ct.1979) for special circumstances. See also *Lee v. Illinois* (S.Ct.1986), *Cruz v. New York* (S.Ct.1987), *Richardson v. Marsh* (S.Ct.1987), and *Gray v. Maryland* (S.Ct.1998).

Additional constitutional restrictions on confessions may also come into play. For example *Kuhlmann v. Wilson* (S.Ct.1986), continues a line of cases which curtail the admission of incriminating statements made to jailhouse informants based on Sixth Amendment (right to counsel) claims.

well as a party admission, and thus should come in against both. But *Williamson v. United States* (S.Ct.1994) indicates that implicating another normally is not against self-interest (particularly in a custodial setting), at least as a matter of *federal* evidence law. At any rate, such a statement would be inadmissible against the non-maker under the Confrontation Clause.

CHAPTER 10

EXCEPTIONS TO THE HEARSAY RULE

I. POLICIES UNDERLYING HEARSAY EXCEPTIONS (SEE THE PRECEDING CHAPTER)

In the preceding chapter, we saw that hearsay exceptions usually have been based on two rationales: trustworthiness and necessity.

F.R.E. 803 and 804 generally list the same exceptions that the common law recognized, but they are expressed in the Rules in more liberal form, favoring admissibility. The rules also have a new, broad, innovative exception frequently referred to as the "catch-all" provision, even though it is closely circumscribed.

II. EXCEPTIONS FOR WHICH UNAVAILABILITY IS NOT REQUIRED: F.R.E. 803

As did the common law, the Federal Rules of Evidence divide the exceptions into two groups. The exceptions in Rule 804 require that the declarant be unavailable to testify in court, while those under Rule 803 do not. In general, the exceptions under the F.R.E. are broader than at common law.

Present Sense Impressions and Excited Utterances: F.R.E. 803(1) and (2)

(a) Excited Utterances—The More Traditional of the Two

At common law, excited utterances constituted a well-established exception. Out-of-court declarations about an exciting or startling occurrence made under stimulus of the excitement in a spontaneous fashion, before time for reflection and fabrication (i.e., the special "trustworthiness"), were admissible regardless of the availability of the declarant (the "necessity" being the supposed superiority to declarant's present testimony). This principle is codified under F.R.E. 803(2).

The declaration will normally state details of some catastrophe, collision, or accident, right on the scene or at some reasonable time thereafter while the stress of excitement is still upon the declarant. And though it is not formally required, the exciting occurrence usually will also be the very occurrence ultimately in controversy. F.R.E. 803(2) requires that the declaration relate to the startling occurrence because otherwise its bona fides would be suspect, but not that the occurrence be the subject of the case so long as the occurrence and the matter declared about it are relevant to the case in some way.

The excited utterances exception was formerly loosely referred to as the "res gestae" exception. The quoted term in liberal translation means "the facts of the occurrence itself".

That same term is also used for certain other exceptions which in loose speech are classified together with excited utterances as "spontaneous statements," e.g., declarations of present sense impression, dying declarations, or even declarations of state of mind, feelings, or sensations.

"Res gestae" can also mean out-of-court utterances which themselves have legal significance ("operative facts"), such as those constituting a contract or gift, or which are offered for some other similar purpose, that does not depend on the utterance's credibility or the truth of the matter stated in it. Such utterances are not hearsay in the first place.

"Res gestae" is not an independent principle or exception to the hearsay rule, and if evidence does not fit one of the recognized principles or exceptions removing the evidence from the hearsay ban, then the evidence will be inadmissible.

The term "res gestae" is not found in the F.R.E. or modern codes. The reader should always cite to the specific rule in question, rather than to "res gestae". You must address the particular problem with which you may be faced, in terms of specific requirements of the applicable rule, principle, exemption, or exception.

One may question whether an exciting occurrence fosters perceptual and reportorial accuracy, or tends to fluster. This will be grist for counsel in arguing weight to the jury. But as a matter of admissibility, at least under this hearsay exception, the law is satisfied when the reflective, deliberative, fabricative capacity is stilled. Care or lack of it seems to be regarded as of secondary importance. Would you say the prime danger of hearsay is dishonesty rather than mistake?

In most jurisdictions, so long as the excitement lasts, the declaration need not be contemporaneous with but can come after the occurrence. The length of time the excitement is deemed to last depends on such circumstances as how exciting the occurrence is and the declarant's involvement in it. The totality of the circumstances is considered by the judge in making the preliminary factual determination upon which admissibility hinges, that is, whether the statement was made while under the stress of excitement. See F.R.E. 104(a).

The factors the judge will consider, none alone being conclusive or determinative, are factors such as: the form, manner and wording of the declaration (e.g., was it narrative or exclamatory/ejaculatory; was it volunteered or in response to questions?), the timing (length of time between the occurrence and the declaration), the demeanor of the declarant at the time, traits of the individual declarant, the declarant's bystander versus victim status, how close the declarant was to the event, how much in danger, the kind of event, and other similar factors.

There are even a few cases where excitement has been held to last for days, or to have been re-kindled even later by another event such as a discussion or photograph concerning the original event. See *United States v. Napier* (9th Cir.1975), admitting an excited utterance identifying the assailant, where the exciting event was seeing assailant's picture in the paper, not the original assault.

On occasion, hearing a shocking conversation (e.g., a price-fixing conspiracy or agreement hatched between one's business colleagues) has been held to be an exciting event where the statement was made fairly soon after coming out of the meeting. One decision suggests that an extended period of unconsciousness in the hospital following an automobile collision can be disregarded as an "excitement cooling" period if the statement about the accident was made upon waking up under the illusion the accident had just happened.

Again, all these factors will be grist for arguments of weight if the evidence survives the admissibility determination.

Statements of adult rape victims are typically treated no differently than other types of victims in evaluating timing. However, some courts have extended the rationale for excited utterances to any uncalculated statements made by child victims of sexual abuse on the theory that children have no motive to falsify. Thus, statements made hours, days, and even months after the event have been permitted as excited utterances.

There are several reasons why prosecutors argue for admission as an excited utterance rather than relying on one of the recent state child hearsay exceptions or the catch-all, assuming the jurisdiction has such provisions. First, unlike other hearsay exceptions, which under caselaw may require a "competent" declarant, i.e., one who understands the need for truth, excited utterances rely on stress for their trustworthiness. Thus, the knotty question of whether a child understands the duty to tell the truth (or for that matter what it is to be truthful) need not be addressed. Second, confrontation clause analysis required trustworthiness of the statement for exceptions that are not firmly rooted. Since *White*, supra, Chapter 8, identified excited utterances as a firmly rooted hearsay exception, statements falling within it required no additional analysis to satisfy the Constitution. But this constitutional distinction based on firm-rootedness is probably no longer viable (at least under federal constitutional law), and little constitutional advantage is to be gained based on what hearsay exception is selected. See Chapter 8, Section V, supra.

There is generally no inflexible requirement under the Rule that the declarant be involved in the exciting occurrence, other than as a spectator, but this factor will have an influence on the degree of excitement and hence on the amount of time allowed between occurrence and utterance before the declaration will no longer be considered spontaneous and stimulated by the excitement of the occurrence. For example, if the declaration "X shot Y" was made by a bystander in the heat of that very occurrence, it would in all likelihood qualify, but *perhaps* not if made 24 hours later. The later statement *might* qualify if it were Y that made it (although the opponent could point out the lapse of time and consequent possibility of forgetfulness and fabrication to the jury as a matter of weight in closing argument).

Can declarant be an unknown stranger or must she be identified? There is no requirement of identity in the rule, but if there is doubt about whether the declarant had first-hand knowledge, generally required of witnesses and declarants (cf. F.R.E. 602), the court may require identity as a way to satisfy itself on that score. See *Bemis v. Edwards* (9th Cir.1995), holding that a 911 call by an unidentified person who simply reported the events was not within 803(1) or 803(2).

(b) Present Sense Impressions—A More Recent Expansion of Excited Utterances

The later common law expanded the excited utterances exception to include declarations of "present sense impression", that is, declarations recounting something the declarant was perceiving as she was perceiving it, even if she was not excited. Instead of the "guarantee" of trustworthiness provided by excitement, we have here the temporal requirement of simultaneity of perception and declaration. There would be no time to deliberate and fabricate or forget. As in excited utterances, the declaration could then reliably be offered to prove the fact perceived and declared, whether the declarant was available or not.

This relatively late-breaking common-law development was picked up and codified by the F.R.E. and its progeny, under Rule 803(1), which increased the common law's time period for the declaration to during the perception *or "immediately thereafter"*, a somewhat flexible notion but not as flexible as the permissible time under excited utterances.

Thus, under the F.R.E., hearsay is admissible if the declarant was actually excited (Rule 803(2)) or if the statement was made relatively simultaneously with the event or condition reported (Rule 803(1)). The expansion to present sense impressions opens up the door to many declarations that would have been barred under the excited utterances rule, because, although immediate, they were not excited. Arguably, for example, a contemporaneous diary or tape recorded entry might fall within the present sense impression rule. Of course, the excited utterance rule is still needed for declarations that are not immediate enough (but are excited). In some states, both rules are increasingly being used to admit statements by complainants in domestic violence cases when they refuse to testify at trial. See Friedman & McCormack, *Dial-In Testimony*, 150 U.Pa.L.Rev. 1171 (2002).

Nexus and Opinion Under Both:

A requirement found under most versions of the excited utterance rule is continued under the F.R.E.: The statement must "relate to" the exciting event or condition. "Relate to" is capable of varying interpretations, broad and narrow.

A similar (but narrower?) requirement is prescribed for present sense impressions: The statement must "describe or explain" the event or condition. The thought in both cases is that broader statements have suspect motivation. The statements are reasonably trustworthy so long as the declarant is sticking to what people would normally be focused on in these situations: the facts of the matter occupying their current attention.

Some states may require both excited utterances and present sense impressions to "describe" the event, a substantial but understandable stricture. Some require one or other or both to describe the "declarant's own conduct," a very narrow rule indeed. See, e.g., Cal. Evid. Code 1241.

This latter requirement would have rejected the very statements which spawned the present sense exception. In *Houston Oxygen Co. v. Davis* (Tex.Com.App.1942), a driver commented to her passenger about the car which passed them before the accident in question, that the people must have been drunk, and would be wrecked if they kept speeding.

Notice that in *Houston Oxygen* the declaration contains a kind of broad or even ultimate opinion, perhaps of a kind that might not have been tolerated in a statement made on the stand. See Chapter 7. While practice differs even under the modern codes, there is a tendency to more liberally receive opinions in these declarations, possibly even declarations under most hearsay exceptions, because to do otherwise results not merely in the rephrasing that takes place when the opinion rule is enforced for on-the-stand statements, but results in the total loss of the evidence.

Declarations of Declarant's Concurrent State of Mind and the Like: F.R.E. 803(3)

This exception to the hearsay rule embraces declarations by a declarant concerning her currently held state of mind or emotions, feelings, sensations, and the like (i.e., matters of internal consciousness), when offered for (and relevant for) themselves or as a basis for certain "forward-looking" inferences about subsequent intention or conduct, but generally not to establish past or presently existing external fact (as where declarant's belief or memory would be offered as truly reflecting some event of consequence to the lawsuit) except in certain cases involving wills.

The operative principles of this exception are stated supra, Chapter 8, in the sections relating to declarations of declarant's state of mind or belief, etc. As noted there, the selfsame principles mean either that the declarations are not hearsay, or they constitute a hearsay exception. The result is the same.

The special trustworthiness is said to inhere in the peculiar privity the declarant has with her own internal consciousness, and the contemporaneousness of the declaration and the thing (fact of internal consciousness) declared. The declarant would hardly be mistaken or forgetful about the thing declared (do you agree?), although she might still be insincere (lying or joking). Here, quite the opposite of the case under excited utterances above, the doctrine seems more concerned with insuring against mistake than against conscious deception. Perhaps insuring against one or the other produced an exception when our law was developing.

Unavailability of the declarant is not required except in some non-F.R.E. type jurisdictions in some of the forward-looking inference cases, below, particularly the more doubtful variety.

The assumed superiority of the hearsay (closer to the relevant time) over any present testimony of declarant (supposedly now infected with memory loss and litigation motivation) supplies the theoretical "necessity".

It is sometimes said that necessity also inheres in the fact that there are few reliable alternative ways to elucidate a relevant state of mind or emotion. But evidence is usually received under this "state of mind" exception regardless of the availability of alternative ways to prove the state of mind. And the state of mind or emotion itself is not always of critical importance in every case where the exception is applied. Sometimes it is of only circumstantial importance, and other circumstances are available. In some non-F.R.E. type jurisdictions, alternative proof may be considered in some of the more doubtful forward-looking inference cases, below.

Under this hearsay exception relevant hearsay expressing that the declarant is "angry," "sleepy," or "in pain" is commonly admitted. In a personal injury case, for example, the plaintiff may offer what sometimes is called (perhaps unjustly) moan-and-groan evidence, consisting of testimony of bystanders or those visiting him in the hospital, or working or living with him in the days, months, or years after the infliction of the injury, recounting the injured person's complaints. This, of course, is to maximize damages. The evidence is admissible unless barred by some other rule of evidence than the hearsay rule. Of course, weight of evidence is a separate question.

The declaration need not be made contemporaneously with the infliction of the injury producing the pain or feeling; it need only be contemporaneous with the pain or feeling itself. The more spontaneous the declaration is, of course, the more weight it will have.

Other hearsay commonly received through this exception might be declarations of intention voiced during execution of documents or wrongful acts, where the intention itself is legally significant. If the *declaration* rather than the *intention* is the legally significant thing, then, of course, we do not have hearsay in the first place, even aside from any state of mind principle, because the declaration is not offered for its truth. Also, in some of the examples embraced by the sentence opening this paragraph, the party admissions principle may also be applicable, depending on the facts.

Previous declarations of children concerning how they feel toward each parent, offered in custody disputes, also can fit this exception. So can declarations of why declarants withdrew business or patronage or left a job—for example because of certain misconduct of defendant proved another way—offered to show causation of damages. Mistaken beliefs of declarants as to the nature of a product sold to them can be offered to help prove the deceptive tendencies of the sales pitch or advertising. In rare cases a court will exclude because of too great a danger of a jury's misuse of this evidence to establish some fact other than the state of mind, which misuse might violate the hearsay rule.

Although They Are Declarations of Declarant's Current State of Mind, Declarations of Memory or Belief to Establish the Fact Remembered or Believed Are Not Permitted: Such "Backward–Looking" Inferences Are Prohibited

If the declarant's declared state of mind (belief) is relevant only because it reflects an external fact of the present or past, which fact itself is the thing of significance to the lawsuit (e.g., "I believe, or have the mental impression or picture of Mary stabbing John" offered in a prosecution of Mary for the stabbing)[1], then the state of mind exception is inapplicable. Any other view would result in a total destruction of the hearsay rule and its policies. A statement cast in the quoted form to prove the stabbing has all the same credibility problems as a direct declaration of the stabbing that does not contain the words relating to mental state. Any hearsay statement could be made admissible by the simple expedient of regarding it as cast in the quoted form. Underlying fact statements are not allowed to sneak in under the state-of-mind doctrine in this fashion.

1. The example works even if the thing remembered or believed is some fact of lesser significance to the lawsuit, as long as it is relevant, e.g., that Mary was at the location where the stabbing took place.

There is an exception to this principle for will contests. In the area of wills and estates litigation, statements like "I remember I made (or revoked) such-and-such will to John" are allowed on the part of the decedent or testator, even if they are declarations of a recollection of the underlying fact of making or revoking, offered to establish that fact. Indeed, the law does not require that there be any reference by the declarant to mental state at all. Thus, the words "I remember" do not have to be there. They are implied. Notice that the declaration must recount something concerning the declarant's *own* act with respect to his *own* will.

Statements of Intention Under the State of Mind Exception, Offered as Circumstantial Evidence of Declarant's Probable Subsequent Conduct: "Forward–Looking" Inferences Permitted

Here, the declaration is offered as circumstantial proof of probable conduct subsequent to the declaration, assuming such conduct is relevant to the case. Specifically, a statement of intention to do an act in the future can be offered to prove that the declarant probably carried out that intention by acting on it.

Thus, under the state-of-mind exception as it appears in both the common-law and the F.R.E., the following statements by a declarant, reported by a witness who heard them, would be admissible despite the hearsay rule: "I intend to kill you," offered to show both the intent and that the declarant probably did the killing, or "I'm going to Cripple Creek tomorrow," offered as circumstantial evidence to show that the declarant probably went.[2] *Mutual Life Ins. Co. of New York v. Hillmon*

2. This in turn might be relevant to the lawsuit, for example, as circumstantial evidence indicating the charred-beyond-recognition body found there was the body of the declarant (say for purposes of a lawsuit on an insurance policy), or to implicate another known to have been there, in the death of the declarant.

(S.Ct.1892). Under this principle, a declaration "I will deliver the deed only when paid" was permitted to help prove that possession of the deed without payment was fraudulently obtained.

In the intent to kill example, an intent declared by declarant on day one could be used to show that the killing by him on day two was intentional (rather than, say, an accidental discharge of the gun in the hands of the declarant), in addition to showing declarant actually did the deed (was the one in whose hands the gun discharged). Thus, two forward looking inferences from the expressed state of mind are involved and permitted: that the same state of mind existed on the next day, and that it was acted upon. Query, could a declaration of a later state of mind be used as circumstantial evidence that the person may have had the same state of mind earlier, so long as that is not what was stated? If it was stated, the requirement that the declaration and the state of mind declared be contemporaneous, would be violated.

Declarant's Declaration of His Own State of Mind Used to Prove Another Person's Probable Subsequent Conduct

What if the declaration is used to prove another person's probable conduct, other than the declarant's? Suppose a declarant said "I am going with Frank to Cripple Creek tomorrow." Should this out-of-court declaration, reported in court by an overhearer or otherwise evidenced in court, be admissible to prove not only that the declarant went, but also that Frank went? See *Hillmon*, supra, which answers "yes," in dictum; *People v. Alcalde* (Cal.1944), which seems to say "yes," but dissent by Judge Traynor says "no". The facts of *Alcalde* perhaps are distinguishable from our example because the statement in *Alcalde* was in the form "I'm going out with

Frank this evening," and was used to implicate Frank in the killing of the female declarant who made the statement. The implications about declarant and about Frank were inseverable. For the fascinating factual background of *Hillmon*, see MacCracken, *The Case of the Anonymous Corpse,* American Heritage 51 (June 1968).

Under the F.R.E., whether the "forward-looking inference" principle covers such third persons is left to interpretation. The U.S. House of Representatives legislative history of Rule 803(3) asserts that the state-of-mind rule is not to be used to show conduct of the other person mentioned by the declarant, notwithstanding the absence of anything definitive in the text of the rule and an ambiguous reference to *Hillmon* in the earlier Advisory Committee Note. The latter is ambiguous as to which branch of *Hillmon* they were expressly approving: reception of the declaration to prove the *declarant* went, or that the *other* went with him, or both?

The U.S. House statement referred to is a statement in a report of the committee responsible for the legislation in the House. The role of such a committee report of a single House of Congress in the interpretation of a rule is unclear. The Senate Committee Report, and the joint House and Senate Conference Committee Report which reconciled the two versions of the F.R.E. bill for final passage, make no such statement about the question we are discussing.

Subsequent cases contrary to the House Committee Report include *United States v. Moore* (2d Cir.1978), and its progeny, which permit statements so long as independent evidence corroborates the third party's conduct. For example, in the hypothetical just above, other evidence would be needed to link Frank to Cripple Creek. See also *United States v. Pheaster* (9th Cir.1976), a trial prior to the Rules that allowed it (perhaps without the qualification) but noted a variety of contrary views. Thus, the decisions are in some conflict, even under the F.R.E.

An argument can be made that the declaration ought not to come in to show subsequent conduct of the other person than the declarant. The declarant has no special access to *that* person's intention. If declarant learned of it, it was probably through a statement of that other person, adding yet another layer of unreliable hearsay. The rule seems to refer only to *declarant's* state of mind.

On the other hand, perhaps the inference sought to be drawn about the other person's (non-declarant's) conduct does not really depend upon an inference that the declarant knows something about that person's intention. If a declarant says he intends to go somewhere with Frank, he probably tried to get Frank to go with him, and that increases the possibility he was successful in that endeavor.

Shepard v. United States (S.Ct.1933) illustrates the metaphysical lengths to which the hearsay rule and its exceptions can go. The statement of the deceased that "Dr. Shepard has poisoned me" was admitted in the trial court under the "dying declaration" exception to the hearsay rule, in a prosecution against Dr. Shepard for killing the deceased. The Court of Appeals held that the declaration did not meet the requirements of a dying declaration, since there was no evidence of a consciousness of impending death, but that the admission of the evidence could now be sustained on the theory that the declaration showed a "state of mind" not bent on suicide in answer to the defense of suicide. The Supreme Court reversed, holding that (a) under the theory upon which the evidence was admitted, the jury was not and could not have been instructed that the statement was evidence of this state of mind only and not more directly evidence that Dr. Shepard poisoned deceased; (b) defendant could not be faulted for failing to ask for such an instruction when the theory of admission was dying declaration; and (c) even if the "state of mind" theory of admission is sound and had been the one adopted by the trial court and the jury had been instructed to confine its consideration of the evidence to that, "[D]iscrimination so subtle is a feat beyond the compass of ordinary minds. The reverberating clang of those accusatory words would drown all weaker sounds." (Per Cardozo, J.)

Statements for Medical Diagnosis and Treatment: F.R.E. 803(4)

If a declarant knowingly states something that may influence diagnosis or treatment to his physician whom he is consulting for a malady or for other health reasons, the law of hearsay assumes he is probably telling the physician the full truth on it. He would not want to risk improper diagnosis, treatment, medication, operation, or other medical procedures. The incentive to trustworthiness is the relationship the patient perceives between the accuracy of his declaration and the quality of the treatment. This incentive is sometimes referred to as declarant's "selfish treatment interest" or "selfish health interest".[3] The significant factor under the logic of this rationale would seem to be whether the patient *believed* the information to be relevant to treatment, not whether the physician thought it was, nor whether it actually was. "Reasonably believed" is the phrase frequently used in order to safeguard against incredible claims. Unavailability is not required. The theoretical "necessity" is the

3. It should be noted that this assumed incentive is in tension with the notion under the physician-patient privilege that patients need the privilege to encourage them to tell the full truth to their doctors. The student may have wondered how it is that patient statements to medical personnel under the present hearsay exception ever get into court, since the doctor-patient privilege would be raised as a bar. One answer is that one of the exceptions to privilege usually applies, especially the one that holds there is waiver of this privilege by a patient who starts a personal injury action.

superiority of this evidence to what would be said at trial, after forgetfulness and litigation motivation have set in.

Another questionable rationale sometimes mentioned is that the physician's expertise somehow enhances reliability.

Unless special circumstances are present, certain declarations ordinarily could not be considered reasonably pertinent to treatment. These would include identifying the person inflicting the wound; indicating fault ("I was hit when the Jones' car ran the red light"); specifying the geographic location of where the injury occurred, and the like, as opposed to describing the instrumentality inflicting the wound, how it occurred, etc.

The trustworthiness rationale seems to extend to any statements that are motivated by the desire to obtain optimal health care, including statements of both objective (outside, external) and subjective facts, both past and present, if reasonably believed pertinent to diagnosis or treatment.

But prior to the adoption of the F.R.E., several courts eliminated from coverage all but statements of present bodily symptoms, feelings, and conditions, thereby excluding histories given by patients to doctors. Unlike these earlier decisions, F.R.E. 803(4) provides expressly that if intended for and reasonably pertinent to diagnosis and treatment, the declaration may relate to medical history, to past or present symptoms, pain or sensation, and the inception, cause, or external source of them. Narratives and responses to questions are permissible.

In consequence of the logic of the common-law rationale, if the physician was visited solely for purposes of preparing a case for litigation and not for health reasons, nothing said to the doctor could qualify for *this* common-law exception.[4]

In contrast, if the drafting Advisory Committee's Note on F.R.E. 803(4) is to be followed, the declaration under the F.R.E. may be made to a doctor consulted solely for purposes of preparing the doctor to testify, say in the patient's personal injury lawsuit, though the doctor never was nor will be a treating doctor. But such a statement appears to be outside the "health motivation" trustworthiness rationale of the rule. Indeed, the incentive to the declarant seems just the opposite.

The reasoning advanced by the Advisory Committee Note is that the doctor could testify as an expert and give the statement as one of the reasons for his opinion, under the rules relating to experts, regardless of what this rule provided.[5] See Rule 703. This Advisory Note to 803(4) suggests that such consultation is embraced by the language of 803(4) that provides that the declaration can be for purposes of "diagnosis" as well as "treatment". The Note thus appears to expand the rule beyond health-motivated diagnosis and treatment.

The implications of this go well beyond merely allowing declarations that would come in anyway. First of all, there's the point made in the footnote, immediately supra. Secondly, dubbing this "diagnosis" and putting it

4. Remember, though, that it may fall within another hearsay exception, depending on the facts. For example, if it describes the patient's current physical or mental state it might fall under the last exception, above.

5. This is no longer true under Rule 703. An amendment in the year 2000 gives the judge discretion as to whether or not to allow an expert who is testifying to her opinion to also testify to otherwise inadmissible statements she relied on in forming her opinion, even though her reliance may be justifiable and the opinion admissible. If the judge does admit the statements, there is to be an instruction limiting their role with the jury to assisting the jury to evaluate the opinion.

within a hearsay exception means that even if the doctor does not testify—say he is just a litigation consulting doctor behind the scenes—the declaration can still come in, e.g. via a nurse, document, or other form of evidence. Thirdly, if the doctor does testify but hasn't relied on the declaration to form his opinion, under the logical extension of the Note's rationale, he can testify to the declaration anyway. Fourth, if he did rely on the declaration, it now comes in, not merely as his basis, but *for its truth*, and no limiting instruction will be given, which is quite different than under Rule 703. Fifth, the Note's calling this "diagnosis" suggests that declarations made to a doctor in order to secure required clearance for health or life insurance or for employment, are also "diagnosis" and encompassed by the hearsay exception, notwithstanding that there is quite a different and perhaps opposite incentive operating, than the health incentive to tell the whole truth.

Perhaps an argument can be made to limit the reach of the Note to the case it gives in justification: a testifying expert who relies on the declaration.

F.R.E. 803(4) speaks only in terms of the purpose and reasonable pertinency of the declaration to diagnosis and treatment and makes no mention of who may make or receive the declaration. The Rule thus implies that the declaration may be made to, or for transmittal to (e.g., where a family member is used as an intermediary) any medical personnel, not merely physicians (e.g. a nurse or even an orderly); need not necessarily be made by the patient (e.g., the spouse, unbidden, may furnish information related to the patient's treatment); and may be made not only by the patient or someone for him, but by the doctor or other medical personnel to the patient, or between doctors or medical personnel concerning the case of an absent patient. Conceivably two lay people could discuss the health of a third, and the conversation would be covered if the thought was one would seek advice about the third from medical personnel.

We seem to have come full circle: a common-law exception dealing with statements by patients to physicians has been rephrased to dispense with both the patient and the physician. Rule 403 might on occasion be used to keep out some of the more remote examples. And of course the jury might not weigh some of them very heavily.

Cf. *Watts v. Smith* (D.C.App.1967), a collision case, in which, in an emergency, on the accident scene, the injured, unconscious party's relative furnished medical information for him to ambulance personnel. The case actually invoked excited utterances rather than the present exception.

Courts have varied about how expansively to view the term "medical" diagnosis and treatment. The business of licensed M.D.s, psychiatrists and psychologists is usually encompassed, and sometimes even unlicensed ones. Less recognized healing arts have met with mixed results, as have statements to social and welfare workers. Much depends on the particular facts.

Rule 803(4) has become one of the most cited rules in child abuse cases, a result that could not have been predicted when the F.R.E. were enacted. Although the rule's rationale depends on the patient understanding that wrong information can lead to misdiagnosis, in child abuse cases most courts do not ask whether the child is old enough to understand the relationship between falsity and bad medical advice. Instead, they simply rely on the fact that the doctor thought it useful to ask for the information in question, a theory which has never been primary in justifying the exception. See generally, Mosteller, *Child Sexual Abuse and Statements for the Purpose of Medical Diagnosis or Treatment,* 67 N.C. L. Rev.

257 (1989). Ironically, California, which has no general equivalent to 803(4), recently enacted an exception that admits medical statements of child abuse victims to doctors. See Cal. Evid. Code 1253.

A number of states also permit the identity of the assailant to be admitted in child abuse cases under this exception, as well as the facts of the abuse. The identity is said to be reasonably pertinent to the psychological aspects of treatment because treatment will differ if the child is being abused by a close friend or relative. This is seen as differentiating such statements from those given by an accident victim that the defendant's car ran the red light and hit her. This logic might be argued to make every statement uttered to a psychiatrist or psychologist, by adults as well as children, useful for treatment, since patients' beliefs about what caused their psychological difficulties affect their treatment. Indeed, even physicians are in a sense also treating, among other aspects, the psychological aspects of even predominantly physical injuries like broken legs.

Courts vary about whether Rule 803(4) reaches statements to social workers that are made in a child abuse context.

Prosecutors prefer admitting statements of children under this exception because the doctor or nurse is typically well-spoken, forceful, and credible, in stark contrast to many child witnesses. Moreover, as the constitutional discussion in Chapter 8 shows, *White* permitted such statements under this exception to be admitted without any additional confrontation clause analysis, because it was a traditional exception. Thus, unlike resort to a child hearsay exception, or a catch-all exception, no constitutional scrutiny of trustworthiness was necessary. See Raeder, *White's Effect on the Right to Confront One's Accuser,* 7 Criminal Justice Magazine 2 (Winter, 1993). However, this constitutional distinction based on whether a hearsay exception is traditional or not, is probably no longer viable (at least under federal constitutional law), and little constitutional advantage is to be gained based on what hearsay exception is selected. See Chapter 8, Section V, supra.

Past Recollection Recorded: F.R.E. 803(5)

This exception allows evidence of a memorandum made earlier by the witness, who then had personal knowledge of the facts or events recorded, and can vouch for its accuracy, provided that the witness cannot fully testify from memory now, even after looking at the memorandum.

The prototypical example is the bystander who wrote the license number of the getaway car on a slip of paper. If the bystander now cannot recall the number completely from memory, the recorded recollection exception may enable him to read the number on the slip of paper to the jury.

This theory of admissibility, known as Past Recollection Recorded, which is a hearsay exception, should be distinguished from refreshing recollection, known as Present Memory Refreshed, in which a document may be used to stimulate the witness' current memory. The latter, Present Memory Refreshed, is not a hearsay exception, because the document's contents are not the evidence, but rather the refreshed memory. See Chapter 6, section XI.

Typically, refreshment of the witness's memory by showing him the document, will be attempted as a precursor to establishing the foundation for the hearsay exception, recorded recollection. But if the witness remains vague, the earlier written statement substitutes for the present testimony if it comes within the present exception to the hearsay rule. The reason for adducing the testimony in such a two-step fashion is that, to use the present hearsay exception, it must be established (1) that the witness can no longer be stimulated to remember the facts, even by consulting the document, but (2) can remember the written declaration, which she remembers making or signing or otherwise adopting, (3) when the matter was fresh in her memory, and (4) she expresses confidence the writing accorded with her perception and memory of the recorded facts then.

Rule 803(5) broadens the traditional exception to the hearsay rule. No longer need it be shown that the witness has completely forgotten the event. Inability to testify fully and accurately is all that is required. While it always seems odd that the witness can affirm that the statement reflects her original knowledge correctly when she has little memory of the underlying facts themselves, surrounding circumstances and features of the face of the document like her signature or handwriting, etc., can suggest to her trustworthiness. For example, accuracy can be presumed when people inventory their possessions or give statements to the police, unless contrary evidence is introduced. Nothing as marked as this is needed, however. The judge will usually accept the word of the witness that she remembers making it and that it was accurate then. Her word will also usually be accepted concerning her lack of memory and refreshment thereof by the document.

The writing must have been made or adopted at a time when the facts recorded were still fresh in mind. What of a witness statement that is transcribed, but not reviewed until after the loss of memory occurred? Some states such as California specifically provide for this situation. The F.R.E. may allow such statements so long as the transcriber testifies to the accuracy of the transcription.

There is a question whether a "memorandum or record" under F.R.E. 803(5), must be written or can include a sound recording of an oral declaration. A recording would seem to be a "record" without too much of a stretch. It is clear that transcribed dictation can qualify at least if approved or adopted by the witness while the facts were still fresh in her memory, even, it would seem, if the original dictation was not by the witness. It does not make sense to require such fresh-memory approval or adoption of a sound recording if it is the witness's voice.

Rule 803(5) provides that the document may not be received as an exhibit, unless the opponent desires. Its contents are to be given to the jury by reading it aloud. This is to avoid the emphasis that results, to the detriment of the other oral testimony in the case, when a jury looks at exhibits or takes them to the jury room during deliberations.

Business Records: F.R.E. 803(6) ("Records of Regularly Conducted Activity")

When someone (for example a salesperson, "S") records facts (such as a sale S has made) in a book of entry or elsewhere, if S is available and testifies to the requisite elements (though S no longer recalls the sale itself), the entry will be admissible to prove the sale under the recorded recollection exception to the hearsay rule (the last section immediately above). And there is authority that the record similarly qualifies if the salesperson reported the sale to another who made the entry and both are available and testify so that between them they satisfy those requirements.

But eventually, probably because of the increasing size and complexity of more contemporary businesses, requiring these witnesses (or even showing they were unavailable or difficult to get) came to be perceived as a cumbersome and often impossible ritual, unnecessary if the records and steps involved in their preparation and maintenance could be shown by general testimony as to a business's procedures, to have been done as a more-or-less *routine practice in the regular course of business* by persons with a *business duty* to perform the role they played who had no likely litigation motivation or other special *indicia of untrustworthiness*. If matters were recorded *relatively promptly* so there was little time to forget or fabricate, the document would be received as a business record. Slim reason was seen to confine the type of transaction considered reliably recorded to something as mundane as sales data. The italicized words were the requirements.

Trustworthiness was variously said to inhere in the systematic business nature of the process, its routineness and regularity, its habitual or automatic nature, a presumed familiarity of the relevant personnel with their task, the business duty of each participant, the risk to their employment if they are inaccurate, the dependence of the business and its profits on accuracy, the absence of litigation motivation, and the timeliness of the recordation. Different decisions emphasized different ones of these "guarantees."

But most agreed that business people rely on these documents, and it would be perverse to exclude records which are the most trustworthy proof that the transaction took place. This was the special "necessity".

Thus, the business records hearsay exception was born, after a somewhat tortuous history, as an amalgam of statutes and case law even before the advent of the Federal Rules of Evidence. The doctrine as stated above is basically the doctrine as now contained in the Federal Rules of Evidence, Rule 803(6).

Today what constitutes a "business" for these purposes is frequently construed broadly. In most jurisdictions it need not be a commercial or profit enterprise. Rule 803(6) liberalized the definition of "business" to include practically any organization, profit or non-profit. Included is every "business, institution, association, profession, occupation, and calling of every kind, whether or not conducted for profit."

A conceivably even broader approach—rejecting the term "business" altogether and making 803(6) cover "any regularly conducted activity" instead—was itself ultimately rejected in the drafting process (although that terminology accidentally found its way into the title of the rule, where it misleadingly remains).

The extent to which personal records such as diaries and checks fall within the rule is still debated. Do household accounts qualify? Records of a neighborly poker group? The rule does require that the "business" activity be "regularly conducted".

The definition of "business" is so broad that it will be difficult to find regular activities that do not qualify. If, for example, a social club is thought to be too small or disorganized to come within the rule, the objection that it is not a "business" activity would be better put as an objection that the club cannot satisfy the final substantive clause in the rule, applicable to all business records: the records are inadmissible if "the source of information or the method or circumstances of preparation indicate lack of trustworthiness."

This trustworthiness language is somewhat unusual. Except for a similar trustworthiness provision under government records (Rule 803(8), where, strangely, the provision is phrased slightly differently), most of the principal hearsay exemptions and exceptions in the Rules do not have a special provision concerning trustworthiness—trustworthiness is presumed. Rule 403 would normally be the method for arguing that special circumstances require exclusion.

Whose burden is it to show the (un)trustworthiness of the record? Generally, courts will assume trustworthiness, unless the opposite is demonstrated.

Examination of a few recurring problematic kinds of business records will illustrate some useful generic features and problems of the rule.

Accident Investigation Reports

A company may conduct an investigation into wrongdoing or accidents occurring in the course of its business, and may produce reports in connection with the investigation. If offered in litigation to prove the facts they recount, they present a potential hearsay problem, in addition to possible privilege (e.g., attorney-client) and other evidentiary problems (e.g., is this a safety measure after an injury?). There are a number of hearsay exemptions and exceptions to consider, for example, party admissions. We will focus here, however, on whether such reports are within the business records hearsay exception.

Palmer v. Hoffman (S.Ct.1943), is the classic case excluding an accident report of a railroad (offered in its own behalf) as a non-routine record, because a railroad's business was not litigation. It suggests a number of grounds for objecting that records should not be received as business records, and raises a number of questions.

(1) Litigation versus Business Purpose. Records prepared for legal purposes or with potential litigation in mind have often been considered not to be in the "regular course of business." A more discriminating view looks to see whether the particular information offered from such a "legal purpose" record was in or against the interest of the business whose document it was—which frequently means, Who is offering it against whom?

If a favorable business record that had a possible legal motive behind its preparation is offered, by the business that prepared it, in litigation to support the business's own position in the litigation, the information's trustworthiness is suspect. If, however, the record is unfavorable to the business that prepared it, and is offered by the opposite party, against the business, it may be more trustworthy.

This last is the approach taken under F.R.E. 803(6). The problem is seen as one under the "trustworthiness" clause—giving the court considerable flexibility on the facts of each case to determine whether the "method or circumstances of preparation" are "trustworthy"—rather than as a doctrine about what can constitute a business record.

Rule 803(8) relating to government reports has similar trustworthiness language but has been interpreted more frequently to allow such documents. For example *S.E.C. v. General Refractories Co.* (D.D.C.1975) held that the Securities and Exchange Commission could introduce its own investigative findings against the defendant.

(2) Non–Routine Nature. An accident investigation report is hardly a repetitive activity of a company, the way recording sales might be. It is a much more isolated occurrence. In this sense it is not "routine" or in the "regular" course of business.

And yet it arises out of the regular course of business, is connected to regular business purposes, and is not extraordinary. It may even have been done on standing company orders to investigate whenever there is an accident. Such reports may be common in the industry as a whole. In these senses, it might be regarded as "routine" or at least in the "regular" course of business.

Consequently the question may be asked, What exactly do business records rules and decisions mean when they use these phrases "routine" and "regular course of business"?

Among the many questions suggested by the above is, Do they mean "regular" or "routine" for this particular company? Or for, say, the airline industry as a whole? Viewed over how long a time period? With many different kinds of businesses and records, this can make a great deal of difference.

Letters and memos which appear to be on an isolated or individual matter frequently present problems along these lines.

There may also be a general versus specific problem, particularly concerning letters and memos. If one takes a general enough view about the subject matter of a particular letter or memo, almost any can be made to seem routine. What level of generality/specificity is appropriate?

F.R.E. 803(6) says *not* that the *making* of the record must be the thing that is the regular course of business, but that the record must be "kept[6] in the *course of* a regularly conducted business activity"—which suggests that all that need be in the regular course of business is the running of the airline, in an airline accident report case, provided that the report is connected with the business, which it would be.

However, another special provision was inserted by Congress, perhaps to confine the rule somewhat: " . . . and if it was the regular practice of that business activity to make the [document or report]." There is, however, even in this, still some ambiguity about what "regular" means (repetitive? or normal business connected?), and whether "that business activity" refers to this particular company or the airline industry as a whole.

6. "Kept" probably doesn't connote exclusively "stored", but rather "made, maintained, and stored", as in the phrase "record keeping".

F.R.E. 803(6) fudges most of the questions dealt with under (1) and (2) above. They are largely relegated to treatment under the "trustworthiness" clause of the rule which calls for a rather subjective judgment on the totality of the individual circumstances as to whether the "method or circumstances of preparation indicate lack of trustworthiness." This provides the court with some flexibility perhaps not previously afforded by the *Palmer v. Hoffman* doctrine as it came to be applied.

A medical report on a plaintiff in a personal injury case done by a doctor employed by the defendant's insurance company can be analyzed in almost identical fashion insofar as all of the legal points discussed above in connection with accident investigation reports are concerned. An additional difficulty may be ambiguity about whether this is really the doctor's "business", which may depend upon the facts of his employment. Note that the federal rule was broadened to include opinions and diagnoses.

Police Records as Business Records

Police records have been received as business records. The police department may be regarded as the business. They illustrate some generic problems concerning the business records rule across-the-board.

(1) The Weak Link Problem: The First Person in the Chain: Outsider–Supplied Information. It is no bar to admissibility under Rule 803(6) as it was under some previous decisions that there were many participants in the process of making and maintaining the business record, as, for example, where one person observes the fact to be established (e.g., makes the sale), reports it to another, who reports it to yet another, who commits it to a computer, whose readout is offered in evidence. So long as there is sufficient foundational evidence from which it might be inferred that each of these steps was done

pursuant to duty in the regular course of business, and was done relatively promptly, Rule 803(6) admits this evidence.

It is perfectly acceptable under the business records exception in *most* jurisdictions, including the F.R.E., that the person making the entry physically offered had no knowledge of the facts entered, that is, the facts the document is offered to establish in the litigation. However, someone having such first-hand knowledge and having the business duty to have and report it, must have reported the facts to the recorder at or near the time those facts transpired, and each must have been playing the role they were regularly assigned by the business.

If the first person in the chain, who has the first-hand knowledge of the fact sought to be established in the litigation by the document, is not part of the business, many cases would exclude the record.

The reason for exclusion is that the outsider is not attended by the "guarantees" of trustworthiness (business duty and regularity, etc.). He is thus a "weak link".

For a classic case presenting the "first person is weak link" problem, see *Johnson v. Lutz* (N.Y.1930), holding a citizen-bystander's statement contained in an offered police report inadmissible to prove the truth of the facts reported by the bystander.

In effect, what we have here is double hearsay, i.e., hearsay within hearsay, or multi-level hearsay. For we have two out-of-court declarants whose trustworthiness could be suspected: the citizen, in making a declaration to the police officer; and the police officer, in writing the report. As F.R.E. 805 states, unless we can find a hearsay exception or exemption for each of them, "guaranteeing" the statement of each, the evidence should be inadmissible.

The police officer's writing down what he heard is attended by his official duty and regularity (business records). But what of the citizen bystander? Unless her statement was an excited utterance, present sense impression, or other hearsay exception or exemption, or is not offered for its truth but rather, say, to impeach her current testimony by inconsistent statement, the evidence should be inadmissible.

But suppose the bystander is under a legal duty to report accurately? Some decisions feel that this would be a sufficient "guarantee" here even though it is not itself a hearsay exception. Others do not. Some, quite erroneously, seem to feel that no guarantee at all is needed concerning a person outside the business in this situation—that business records covers the entire chain so long as the outsider's statement relates to something that is a concern of the business.

A similar situation can be presented by a hospital record compiled in part from what is said by the patient, assuming that the patient's statement is not itself covered by any independent hearsay exception or exemption such as the ones for statements to medical personnel or party admissions.

The problem comes up with other businesses, as well: a customer reports a slippery floor to a store manager, who writes it down. A citizen reports receiving obscene or threatening letters to the Post Office, which promptly records it.

The conflict of authority was not settled by the wording of Rule 803(6). Language clarifying that persons not inside the business are not encompassed was accidently dropped by Congress. See Rule 803(6), Supreme Court Draft, 56 F.R.D. 183 (1972).

Courts interpreting 803(6) have usually adopted the better view, which is that the first person in the chain, like all the others, must be part of the business and acting pursuant to regular business duty, if this exception is the sole one relied upon. The "regular course" requirement or "trustworthiness of source" provision has been used to achieve this result.

A way around the restriction is sometimes available: The person who is outside the business may be deemed to be in a joint enterprise with the business and thus part of a common business, or may be part of another business that is so deemed (or that may qualify for a second business records exception).

In both the business records and government records rule, the "trustworthiness" requirement, addressed above, refers to trustworthiness "of source" as well as of "other circumstances." Perhaps this provision was intended to be the principal means of addressing the outside-source issue. If so, it is conceivable that some outside sources that are not attended by their own hearsay exception may none-the-less qualify as trustworthy in some circumstances—for example, where they are under a legal duty to report accurately. Another approach is to see whether the outsider information is verified by the business creating the report, though even here decisions are not uniform. But there are cases supporting each of these approaches.

The "weak link" problem discussed in this enumerated section comes up in two forms: (1) where the record identifies that the fact reported is from an outsider (i.e., literally or essentially states that "X said Y"), which technically is a hearsay recounting of hearsay; and (2) where the record simply states fact Y as being so, although it was only learned from X, which technically is hearsay containing non-first-hand knowledge. The first is a genuine hearsay-within-hearsay (Rule 805) problem. The second is a "lack of personal knowledge within hearsay" (Rule 602) problem. Nevertheless, the analysis should be roughly the same.

(2) Can Police Records Still be Treated as Business Records Now That We Have a Separate Government Records Rule In a Number of Jurisdictions? It may be that, under the F.R.E., and similar codes, the business records exception no longer should be used in the police records situation, since Rule 803(8), public or government records and reports, is more tailored to them. But most of the same problems pointed out above exist under Rule 803(8); and also exist under the business records exception as to all sorts of records other than police records.

Can certain kinds of police or government records which are expressly not licensed under Rule 803(8), arguably be a business record of the police or agency as a "business?" *United States v. Cain* (5th Cir.1980) found that in view of the congressional intention expressed in 803(8) to exclude law enforcement records offered against the criminal accused, 803(6) could not be used to admit them. *United States v. Oates* (2d Cir.1977) deemed any other interpretation to have confrontation problems. More recent Confrontation Clause jurisprudence may confirm this. See supra, Chapter 8, Section V.

Hospital Records

A number of jurisdictions have special statutory or rule provisions concerning hospital records as evidence. But in most, as under the F.R.E., hospital records offered as affirmative evidence (as opposed to offered as a basis for expert testimony—see Chapter 7) are tested under the business records rule. Hospital records are frequently offered in personal injury cases to prove a fact or facts stated in them. They present some problems illustrative of business records generally.

(1) Non–Profit Status. In a very few jurisdictions, something cannot qualify as a business if it is conducted as a charitable or not-for-profit organization. Many hospitals have such a status. As noted above, there is no such restriction on the definition of "business" in F.R.E. 803(6).

(2) Routine, Regular. Some decisions question whether a hospital's record was "routine" or a "regular entry." In the context of hospital records this would be a problem only in the case of entries of a non-repetitive, unusual nature, as opposed to entries of temperature, vital signs, etc. But usually the requirement is relaxed to permit any health matter. To the extent extraneous information not related to diagnosis or treatment is recorded, there may be a problem.

(3) Opinions, Inferences, Conclusions. Hospital records can also illustrate another generic problem concerning business records: to what extent is an opinion, inference, or conclusion (e.g., a diagnosis) in a report admissible, and under what circumstances? After all, the writer is not present for cross-examination. We may not even know who rendered the opinion or whether she is qualified.

The most frequent answer under the traditional system was that they were inadmissible under all conditions, but even before the adoption of the F.R.E., there were different views.

Unlike the holding of many common law decisions, and provisions like current Cal. Evid. Code 1271, which confine admissible business records to those that set forth only "acts, events, or conditions", F.R.E. 803(6) expressly provides that the record may also contain "opinions or diagnoses." That, of course, is not entirely the end of the matter. There are other provisions in the F.R.E. that could be used to bar particular opinions or diagnoses that seem ill founded, or are rendered by unidentified or unqualified persons. E.g., the "trustworthiness" language in the rule itself; and Rules 403 and 702. Unlike the situations studied in Chapter 7, where the expert opiner is on the stand to be tested, and is thus given considerable latitude, the opiner here is not present for qualification or exploration. Cf. *Ricciardi v. Children's Hospital Medical Center* (1st Cir.1987), which rejected a medical record where the person who wrote a note in the hospital record two days after the surgery in question could not identify whom he got the information from concerning the surgery.

Decisions concerning these records range from extreme suspicion of nearly all conclusions, opinions, and diagnoses; to allowing them almost without limitation. Some draw a distinction between the more reliable kind, such as a diagnosis of a broken bone, and the kind subject to greater debate, such as that an injury may develop into cancer. See *Loper v. Andrews* (Tex.1966).

In some states, where judges were inclined to disallow conclusions or findings in laboratory reports unless the person responsible for the tests testified, statutes have been enacted which admit laboratory reports without requiring the testimony of the person who conducted or supervised the test.

(4) The Weak Link Problem: The First Person in the Chain: Outsider–Supplied Information. We treated this problem above under police records. However, it is worth brief revisiting in the context of hospital records.

For example, *Watts v. Delaware Coach Co.* (Del.Super.1948), held that a patient's oral statement incorporated into an offered hospital record is admissible for the truth of the facts it relates if they are "germane to treatment." This was conceived of as a requirement of the business records exception to the hearsay rule, as a part of "scope of business," the hospital being the business.

But a better conceptual framework would be to recognize that we have double hearsay ("hearsay within hearsay") in this kind of case. For we have two out-of-court declarants: the report's writer and the patient. A hearsay exception for each is required. While the business records exception covers or guarantees the accuracy of the writer of the report and subsequent steps in the maintenance of the report, it does not extend to the patient's statement.

But another hearsay exception, with its own peculiar "guarantee" of accuracy, may apply to the patient. For example, the exception for statements to physicians. Yet the motive to accuracy under that exception only operates if patients perceive that their health rides on the statement, and thus there is a well-recognized requirement, under that exception, that the statement be germane to treatment. Hence, we arrive at the "germaneness" requirement of *Watts* in another, sounder way. It is possible, however, that the measure of "germaneness" might be different under the statements to physicians exception, focusing on apparent germaneness to the patient. In *Watts*, the patient's statement also appeared to be a party admission.

Computerized Records

The business records rule is ill adapted to handling modern automated and computerized record-keeping, notwithstanding that Rule 803(6) expressly says it encompasses any "memorandum, report, record, or data compilation in any form."

One problem is with the requirement that it must be the regular business practice of the business to make the particular memorandum, report, record or data compilation offered, and that the offered item must be an item that is kept in the course of the company's regularly conducted business activity.

Applied literally, this means a computer printout ordered up for the litigation cannot qualify, particularly if (as may be needed for the litigation) it does any sorting, compiling, summarizing, selecting, or ordering of information from a larger batch of information. Cf. *United States v. Blackburn* (7th Cir.1993), excluding computer printouts that were created at the request of the F.B.I. as not being kept in the regular course of business, but admitting them pursuant to the catch-all exception, which requires trustworthiness; *United States v. Sanders* (5th Cir.1984), permitting printouts generated in preparation for litigation as business records since the printout program did not do any special operations to the data, but spewed it out exactly as it had been routinely put in for the business.

Most jurisdictions have relaxed in non-computer cases the ancient requirement that the item offered must be the record of original entry (e.g., the original sales slip). They allow subsequent transfers and re-recordations within the company if that is the regular business practice, and permit such subsequent copies of the information to be introduced; but only if the copy introduced is actually made in the regular course of business, not if it is produced specially for the litigation. Some common law courts additionally required that the original have been destroyed as part of the regular course of business.

Another problem is with timing. F.R.E. 803(6) is typical. Literally read, it seems to require that the item offered at trial be made at or near the time of the transaction it is offered to prove. A printout of selected information months or years later for litigation, would appear not to comply with this. But see *Sanders*, immediately supra, recognizing that when the printout makes no change in the data that was routinely entered into the computer near the time of the transaction, and merely reproduces it, the timing requirement is satisfied. The proximity of the original data entry, rather than the printout, to the transaction is what is important and meant by the rule.

The rule is also susceptible of both a loose and a strict reading concerning just how much needs to be shown about the details of the company computer system, in order to demonstrate that the information is truly information from the "regular course" and "regular practice" of the business; that it is genuine, not falsified or altered; and that the "source of information or method or circumstances of preparation" do not "indicate lack of trustworthiness". The fact that a computer is involved may or may not be held to shift or increase the burden on this. See *United States v. Young Brothers, Inc.* (5th Cir.1984), finding no need for a computer programmer to testify that the software was adequate.

Any requirement of a detailed showing engenders concern from financial and other institutions where security of the system is a concern. On the other hand, computer stored or generated information is peculiarly susceptible to hard-to-detect alteration.

As can be expected, courts, including federal courts, are all over the map on these points, some taking too jaundiced a view of computer materials, and some too mesmerized by the supposed infallibility of computers. Ingenious arguments of grammar are advanced to get around some of the more literal requirements of the rule. Sometimes requirements are ignored or. stretched. Sometimes they are read too restrictively. Sometimes deserving printouts are excluded. Sometimes very suspicious ones are admitted. The more comfortable judges get with computers, the less elaborate the foundation required for standard programs. The courts are also confused as to what kind of discovery to allow so that a party can prepare to challenge proposed offers of computer materials. (Recent amendments to the Federal Rules of Civil Procedure provide some limited guidance in this regard.)

Clearly what is needed is a special evidentiary rule taking account of the special susceptibilities but also the special value of computer materials.

The Foundation for Business Records Generally, Aside From Special Computer Problems

That the document complies with all the requirements of the business records doctrine is usually proved by the testimony of someone from the business who is either in a supervisory capacity, or a custodian of the record. Sales personnel familiar with sales records could also do it, for a sales record. Or a records librarian. A bookkeeper of the company is another common witness in this regard. F.R.E. 803(6) simply says "the custodian or other qualified witness."

The witness testifies to the system or practices of the company, that comply with the rule. He further testifies that the document offered comes from the company and from that system or practice.

The witness may have just joined the company. He need not have been around when the record was made, nor have had anything to do with its preparation. He need not have any personal knowledge of the making of the particular offered record or the facts in it. All he needs to know is the company's system and practices, and have a basis to believe the record is from them.

In the case of relatively informal or small businesses, it is common for the foundation to be laid by almost anyone in the office. A person paying a bill can give sufficient testimony to lay the foundation for the cancelled invoice. A person sending, and filing a copy of, a letter may perform a similar function for the letter.

There is some authority for the proposition that the foundation can be laid by any circumstantial evidence that reasonably gives rise to at least a prima facie inference that the record was kept in the regular course of business, without anyone from the business appearing. For example, testimony of the offering attorney's own investigator that she went to the business—say, a bank—and was given the record by someone in authority from a records department file drawer, and the record on its face appears to be a regular account record. For a case admitting a business record on facts somewhat like this, see *United States v. Quong* (6th Cir.1962).

Both the business record rule and the authentication rule have been amended to permit the foundation for business records to be laid by certification, as can be done for certain public records, and for international business records pursuant to federal statute. See discussion of Rule 902(11) & (12) in Chapter 11.

Government Records and Reports: F.R.E. 803(8) ("Public Records and Reports")

F.R.E. 803(8) provides a far-reaching government records exception to the hearsay rule, not widely recognized under previous law.

With some relatively minor qualifications, it renders admissible (insofar as the hearsay rule is concerned) three classes of records or reports of governmental offices and agencies: (A) reports of the "office's or agency's activities," (B) "matters observed" and "reported" pursuant to "duty," and (C) "factual findings resulting from" an authorized "investigation." The letters here correspond to the lettered subsections of the rule.

The "activities of the agency" category (the (A) category) has been construed to include a Department of Commerce report of the Department's informal policy of inducing airplane manufacturers to give priority to defense orders, which was offered to explain delay of other orders in a contract action on those other orders. See *Eastern Air Lines, Inc. v. McDonnell Douglas Corp.* (5th Cir.1976).

The (B) category (matters observed and reported pursuant to duty) might include a building inspector's report of, say, leaking water in a building he inspected. The (C) category (factual finding pursuant to investigation) might include a report of the same housing agency, after investigation, that a particular housing project was operating under unsanitary conditions.

Difficulty is sometimes encountered in deciding which of these categories a document fits into. This can be important because each category has somewhat different qualifications or requirements. For example, in *United States v. Ruffin* (2d Cir.1978), an incriminating statement by a taxpayer, recounted by an IRS agent in a report, was excluded because it was a "matter observed" by the agency and was therefore subject to that category's "law enforcement" exclusion.

Since the categories can overlap, courts do not always pinpoint which category covers the particular record before them. See, e.g., *In the Matter of Oil Spill by the Amoco Cadiz Off the Coast of France* (7th Cir.1992), noting that some of the reports fit under both (A) and (B).

The rule can be utilized in a wide variety of cases, e.g., litigation by private claimants who wish to introduce agency findings (concerning, for instance, discrimination, or securities or antitrust violations) against companies in federal court. See, e.g., *Cohen v. I.I.T.* (7th Cir.1975), where a teacher was allowed to support a private claim of sex discrimination, by introducing an H.E.W. finding to that effect. Of course they can be used defensively, too.

Similar opportunities under the rule abound in other areas where public administrative regulation and private litigation remedies co-exist, such as product safety, workplace safety, environmental protection, deceptive practices, labor, food and drugs, or rate regulation.

Apparently even the investigative findings of an agency's own staff may be used by the agency itself in judicial proceedings against an individual or company. See Point (2) infra.

Government investigative reports into a particular accident, as is somewhat frequent in the airline and train area, are not automatically excluded here, as some rulings would do under business records. Sometimes, however, there are special privileges against use in these areas.

On the face of the rule, there is no mention of the word "regular" which could imply "routine," although the report usually must be done pursuant to duty or be authorized.

Let us examine some limitations.

(1) Law Enforcement Records and the Like in Criminal Cases

Unlike business records, the government records exception has certain specific exclusions apparently directed at protecting citizens from government in certain situations.

Subsection (B) of the rule (matters observed and reported pursuant to duty) expressly excludes, in criminal cases, observations by "police" and "law enforcement personnel." Just how broadly to interpret this law enforcement exclusion has been widely debated. For example, *United States v. Hansen* (7th Cir.1978), held reports of building inspectors about building code violations were not law enforcement records since the violations only carry a fine and are not convictions. The Uniform Rules, in a departure, specifically permit criminal *defendants* to introduce law enforcement records.

Subsection (C) of the rule (covering official "findings") in criminal cases can only be used "against the government."

Thus, the exclusion reads differently depending upon the subsection used. The former forbids use "in a criminal case," presumably irrespective of which side offers it. The latter forbids use only if it is offered against the criminal accused; not if offered by him. It also defines the prohibited document as any government record, not just law enforcement records.

Consequently, if a police document is offered by an accused, his rights may depend upon how the document is characterized.

The court in *United States v. Smith* (D.C.Cir.1975) neatly avoided the difficult problem of characterizing the particular documents involved as class (B) or class (C) documents, by finding the intention of both versions of the exclusion to be the same: a libertarian intention to prevent use of police records against the accused, not an intention to disable the accused from presenting defensive material, which might present constitutional problems.

A way around the exclusion of law enforcement records was spelled out in *United States v. Grady* (2d Cir.1976). *Grady* makes an unwritten exception to the exclusion: "routine lists" of matters observed by law enforcement personnel are admissible against the accused, apparently in contrast to more extensive or detailed recorded observations of particular criminal activity or material compiled in connection with the particular case. Thus, lists made by Northern Ireland's police of the serial numbers of weapons found in Northern Ireland were held admissible in a U.S. prosecution here to prove defendant had illegally exported some of them from the United States and made false entries about them in federal firearms records.

The non-adversarial nature of the record has since become an important factor in favor of admissibility of public records in many criminal cases. See *United States v. Brown* (11th Cir.1993), admitting a police department's receipt for a gun; *United States v. Orozco* (9th Cir.1979), admitting computer cards of license plates observed passing the border; *United States v. Quezada* (5th Cir.1985), admitting an INS form showing defendant was arrested and deported.

But see Chapter 8, Section V, on confrontation, for a possible constitutional objection. Will this doctrine permitting non-adversarial routine police records be imported into Confrontation Clause jurisprudence?

Several decisions hold that under both the business records rule and the government records rule, police records concerning the case could not be introduced by the prosecution against the defendant, although defendant might be able to introduce them. The rationale is that Congress disfavored use of law enforcement records against the accused in a criminal case by expressly mentioning such records used in such a way in the government records rule. This exclusion should thus be imported into the "trustworthiness" qualification in the business records rule as well. Some suggest that any other interpretation might violate the confrontation clause.

In contrast to these cases, in the case of *United States v. Scholle* (8th Cir.1977), a Drug Enforcement Administration record showing the composition of narcotics as customarily seized by the D.E.A. was allowed under 803(6), the business records rule, against defendant to show that his narcotics were distinctive enough to be identified, notwithstanding the exclusion in 803(8) from the government records rule. (Would such a business record now be barred by the Confrontation Clause?)

The cases may be distinguishable on grounds that the information in *Scholle* was not compiled in connection with the particular case. The others involved case-specific lab reports, incident reports, etc.

Cf. *United States v. Sokolow* (3d Cir.1996), affirming admission of the government's summary of unpaid insurance claims as business records where the author testified; *United States v. Hayes* (10th Cir.1988), affirming admission of I.R.S. computer data against a criminal defendant as a business record.

Some decisions forbid resort to *any* other hearsay exception for documents that fail 803(8).

In 1999, Uniform Rule 803(6) was amended to exclude any public record that is inadmissible under 803(8) from being introduced pursuant to 803(6).

Most courts appear to feel that a police report, even though excluded by 803(8), can be admitted pursuant to Rule 803(5) (past recollection recorded) as long as the reporting police officer testifies, which ordinarily is the case under that exception. See, e.g., *United States v. Picciandra* (1st Cir.1986); *United States v. Sawyer* (7th Cir.1979).

This particular result may not entirely flout Congressional intention behind the exclusion because, at heart, the exclusionary provision was probably motivated by a confrontation-type concern that is reduced if the officer testifies. However, by definition under past recollection recorded, the officer will have little memory to cross-examine. But the Supreme Court has held this does not make cross-examination fatally defective for confrontation purposes. See *United States v. Owens* (S.Ct.1988).

For this reason there would likely be no actual confrontation clause violation.

It should be noted that California does not have a law-enforcement exclusion to its official records exception, though the scope of both its business and official records exceptions are narrower than the federal definitions. See Cal. Evid. Code 1280. Is this constitutional?

(2) "Self–Serving" Use of Government Records in Other Contexts: Civil Cases

If the agency that prepared a report offers it in the agency's own behalf, is the record automatically self-serving and inadmissible, as a general matter? At least if the agency had litigation in mind when the document was prepared?

The concept that it might be, was developed under the business records exception to the hearsay rule. See business records, supra, discussion concerning accident investigations.

Both the business records rule (803(6)) and the government records rule (803(8)) are expressly inapplicable if the "circumstances ... indicate [the record's] lack of trustworthiness." This proviso could furnish the basis under the F.R.E. for skepticism toward such self-serving records.

Unfortunately, it is unclear under the government records rule as to whether the quoted language is meant to apply to all three classes of records embraced by the rule or just the last. The language is tacked on to the end of the sentence that in sequence describes all three, thus creating the ambiguity. See *Melville v. American Home Assur. Co.* (E.D.Pa.1977), which suggests that the trustworthiness requirement applies only to the last category, and that where there is a choice, a document should thus be classed as belonging to the last category. Rule 803(8) of the Uniform Rules of Evidence was modified to clarify that the trustworthiness requirement applies to each category of public records and reports.

Nevertheless, it could be argued that Rule 403 imposes a trustworthiness requirement on all the classes. See, e.g., *Distaff, Inc. v. Springfield Contracting Corp.* (4th Cir.1993).

Despite the beguiling nature of the proposition that the arguably "self-serving" documents we are addressing should be excluded, a number of decisions under the Rule do not appear eager to exclude on this basis.

For example, In *S.E.C. v. General Refractories* (D.D.C. 1975), investigative findings of the S.E.C. staff showing securities violations on the part of the defendant were held admissible in behalf of the S.E.C. against the defendant to help prove the violations.

The Uniform Rules of Evidence, by amendment, provide specifically in 803(8) that government documents offered in litigation on behalf of the agency preparing them, are inadmissible.

(3) The Meaning of "Factual Findings Resulting From an Investigation"

One of the classes of documents licensed under 803(8) is "factual findings" that "result from an investigation." Thus the findings must be of a "factual" sort and must issue from an "investigation." To some extent, there is a tension between "factual" and "findings".

This portion of the rule potentially renders admissible an enormous number of formerly inadmissible government reports of the most determinative nature. It is the most expansive of the three categories under the rule.

For more than ten years after the adoption of the Rules, the interpretation of this provision was in dispute because of its murky legislative history. For example, the

House Report on the rule urges a strict construction of the word "factual;" the Senate Report rejected such a view; while the original Advisory Committee Note to the rule speaks of "evaluative reports" as being permissible. In *Beech Aircraft Corp. v. Rainey* (S.Ct.1988), the Supreme Court finally held that even extremely broad opinions and conclusions were admissible as factual findings.

Rainey was a products liability suit in which the only issue in dispute was whether the crash had resulted from pilot error or equipment malfunction (termed a "rollback"). The trial court had admitted a Navy J.A.G. report that included the opinion of the writer on the cause of the accident. The statement was self-labelled "opinion", acknowledged extreme difficulty in determining cause with any certainty, but ventured that the "most probable cause ... was the pilot[s'] failure to maintain proper interval" but that there remained "a possibility that a 'rollback' did occur." The Supreme Court upheld the admission of this evidence.

The Court held that "findings of fact" included nearly any conclusions that could reasonably be inferred from the evidence. It reached this result in part because of the analytical difficulty of separating "fact" from "opinion" and drawing gradations between, some of which would be admissible and some not.

In a somewhat defensive manner, the Court noted that one of the rule's safeguards against unprincipled or overly broad use was its requirement barring the admission of statements not based on "investigations" of the facts. But the justices gave no indication of what would be sufficient in that regard.

Rainey also did not decide whether *legal* conclusions contained in an official report could be admitted.

Some states still refuse to allow police accident reports in civil cases, particularly if they seem to express determinative conclusions. This is accomplished by statute or interpretation of the state analogue of Rule 803(8). Similarly, some federal statutes may also prohibit conclusions. See, e.g., *In re Cleveland Tankers, Inc.* (6th Cir. 1995), excluding the conclusion section of a Coast Guard accident report.

However, by-and-large, post-*Rainey* cases have made conclusions in administrative reports "commonplace" in litigation.

(4) Government Records Containing Information Obtained From Someone Outside the Office or Agency

Public records may contain statements of other absent persons, or information received from such absent persons. These persons may be outside the agency, not attended by agency duty. Are they thereby rendered inadmissible? (Put aside those criminal situations where introduction would violate the Confrontation Clause. See Ch. 8, section V.)

This is best analyzed as hearsay contained within hearsay. We treated this as the "first-person, weak link, outsider information" problem under business records, supra.

The government records rule (803(8)) does not contain express language either way. Of course the "findings" branch of the rule (subsection (C)) must embrace information from outside the agency, in a sense. Such information is incorporated into the findings. But may the component information also be set forth and admitted into evidence? Would it help the trier-of-fact to evaluate the findings?

The subsection (B) branch requires that a matter introduced under subsection (B) must have been "observed" and "reported" pursuant to legal "duty," but does not specify (although it may be implied) that it has to be done by a person within the agency. Someone outside the government may have a "duty" under law to observe and report to the agency.

In both the business records and government records rule, the "trustworthiness" requirement, addressed above, refers to trustworthiness "of source" as well as of "other circumstances." Perhaps this provision was intended to be the principal means of addressing the outside-source issue. Perhaps the determination is to be made on an *ad hoc* basis on the facts and totality of circumstances in each case, a somewhat subjective concept.

The government records cases are in some disarray on the question dealt with here. Compare, on the one hand, *In re Matter of Amoco Cadiz,* supra, and *In re Air Disaster at Lockerbie, Scotland, on Dec. 21, 1988* (2d Cir.1994), the latter admitting records even though the bureaucrat who filled out the government forms incorporated information furnished by others, stating that the Rule was not limited to excusing the presence of a document's author, but was a multilevel exception; with, on the other hand, *Moss v. Ole South Real Estate* (5th Cir.1991), excluding the hearsay itself on which the factual findings were based, but allowing the findings. Cf. discussion of Rule 703, in Chapter 7, supra, which may be applicable here. At a minimum, simply filing a report with a public agency will not convert it into an official record. See, e.g., *Marsee v. U.S. Tobacco Co.* (10th Cir. 1989). Transcripts of statements of witnesses in government agency investigations or hearings, should not be admissible for their truth, unless otherwise admissible. See language in *Smith,* supra.

(5) *The Trustworthiness Proviso and Rule 403: Other Unreliability Issues*

Rainey suggests that the way to attack evaluative reports is to focus on any factors in the particular case indicating lack of reliability, since trustworthiness is the touchstone of the rule and provides its biggest safeguard against overly broad use.

In addition to the trustworthiness proviso, opponents of government records might on occasion successfully invoke F.R.E. 403 and Article VII. *Daubert* factors must be considered as well.

Article VII, even after *Rainey*, has certain requirements concerning opinions and qualifications of experts that may apply. It could be emphasized that rigorous application of the limits rather than the liberalizations of Article VII is in order since the "opiner" is not on the stand for testing, elucidation, clarification, and exploration; and yet is likely to be considered a "double God", being both an expert and a government person.

In speaking of the admissibility of so-called "evaluative" reports under the government records rule, the Advisory Committee Note, apparently having reference to the "trustworthiness" requirement, or Rule 403, states several factors relating to the agency that may influence later admissibility: "(1) [T]he timeliness of the investigation . . . ; (2) the special skill or experience of the official . . . ; (3) whether a hearing was held and the level at which conducted . . . ; (4) possible motivation problems. . . . Others no doubt could be added."

Taking up this cue, an opponent of a government record, whether or not "evaluative," might, in an appropriate case, point, either for admissibility or weight, to the record's overly broad, conclusory, or unsubstantiated nature; a misleadingly different legal or factual issue or a term used in a confusingly different sense; the lack of a thorough agency investigation; the lack of a thorough (or any) hearing there; the lack of an opportunity for thorough (or any) confrontation of evidence there; the *ex parte* nature of proceedings there; the undue authority likely to be attached to a government pronouncement; and the agency's interest.

For example, a number of governmental reports on Airline Computerized Reservation Systems were excluded as untrustworthy where they did not reflect the real concerns of the business world and were interim or inconclusive in nature. See *United Air Lines, Inc. v. Austin Travel Corp.* (2d Cir.1989). Similarly, in *Angelo v. Bacharach Instrument Co.* (3d Cir.1977), pursuant to Rule 403, a determination letter issued by the Equal Employment Opportunity Commission was refused admission, since the letter was issued following an *ex parte* investigation in which the Commission conducted no formal proceedings, the letter was too conclusory, dealing with the ultimate issue, and the issue was somewhat different than in the present proceeding: the finding in the letter was only that there was "reasonable cause to believe...."

But it will be an uphill fight. Public records now appear to be presumed trustworthy, which shifts the burden to the party attempting to exclude the report. See, e.g., *Baker v. Elcona Homes* (6th Cir.1978), admitting a factual finding despite the lack of a hearing, because of the timeliness of the investigation, the skill of the investigator, and the lack of bad motivational factors; *United States v. School Dist. of Ferndale* (6th Cir.1978), holding that lack at the agency hearing of subpoena power, discovery, and hearing examiner expertise, were all merely matters of weight that did not bar admission of an agency finding of discrimination on the part of the school board.

In *Montiel v. City of Los Angeles* (9th Cir.1993), the city argued to exclude the "Christopher Commission" report. The Christopher Commission, comprised of citizens, officials, and experts from many areas and walks of life, had been especially established by the government specifically to explore the causes of the Los Angeles Riot.

The riot was also the subject of the suit, which attempted to pin liability for it on the city. While the decision questions whether ad hoc reports are within 803(8), and recognizes the possibility of exclusion pursuant to Rule 403, it remanded the case due to the cursory denial of the motion requesting admission of the report.

(6) *Some General Observations About Public Records*

Corporations who are subject to government regulation are the most affected. The rule provides a source of adverse evidence for use in public and private court litigation against them. However, it can also be used *by* them where there has been a favorable agency finding. It can be used either in prosecuting a claim, or in presenting a defense.

Several of the state codes patterned after the Federal Rules have a notice requirement in Rule 803(8). For example, North Dakota provides for advance notice of expected use of the rule and of certain particulars, and for calling of the maker of the report by the adverse party, where fact-findings are sought to be introduced. Nebraska provides a notice requirement for the entire Rule 803(8). The rule itself is drawn broadly.

Query: Does the "trustworthiness" of "source" language in both the business records and government records rule license discovery of and depositions of sources that informed the government or business? See Rule 806 allowing impeachment of hearsay declarants. Would information flow be inhibited by such a practice? Are there public policy, privilege, and First Amendment arguments against it?

Absence of an Entry in a Record: F.R.E. 803(7) and (10)

Rules 803(7) (absence of business record or entry) and 803(10) (absence of government record or entry) provide a hearsay exception for the absence of an expected or regular document or entry in the business or government context, to prove non-occurrence or non-existence of a matter—in short, the reverse of the business records and government records rule, dealing with proof of occurrence or existence—provided roughly analogous safeguards are in place. This would be evidence that something (which if it did happen would be expected to result in a document or entry under the systems in place) did not in fact happen. Thus a work record that shows the days a worker was present, but that contains no entry for August 10, is evidence that the worker was absent on August 10.

The absence of official records can be significant in criminal cases. For example, registration of a firearm can make the difference between legal and illegal possession of a firearm. Compare *United States v. Hale* (8th Cir. 1992) with *United States v. Yakobov* (2d Cir.1983) regarding affidavits asserting that after a diligent search no registration application or license could be located.

In *Yakobov*, the court addressed the issue whether this "absence of law enforcement record" evidence offered under 803(10)—the mirror image of "presence of law enforcement record" evidence under 803(8)—should, by analogy be barred by the law enforcement exception to Rule 803(8). The court refused to apply the bar, noting there was no similar exception to 803(10). The court refused to extend to Rule 803(10) the principle that if a document was inadmissible under Rule 803(8), it could not be admitted as a business record under 803(6). See also *United States v. Cepeda Penes* (1st Cir.1978), which permitted evidence of the absence of a government [enforcement-type] record against an accused because 803(10) has no law enforcement exclusion as there is in 803(8), while recognizing that an enforcement-type government or business record, if present, could not be so used.

Miscellaneous Rule 803 Hearsay Exceptions

There are miscellaneous additional exceptions to the hearsay rule that also do not require unavailability, discussion of which is precluded by the economies of this short work. Only a few will be mentioned:

Ancient writings: F.R.E. 803(16). At common law, and under the F.R.E., there is a hearsay exception for recitals in ancient writings. At common law, and under the F.R.E., they are writings that would also meet the requirements of authentication by antiquity. At common law and currently in states like California, this means at least 30 years of age, freedom from suspicion in appearance and custody, and, in some places in the case of deeds, possession given under the instrument. Rule 803(16) cuts the time period for documents qualifying for the ancient-records hearsay exception from thirty to twenty years. The same is done for the authentication requirement under Rule 901(b)(8). The other requirements are similar to the common law. While facts that authenticate an ancient document may also render the document admissible to prove the truth of its recitals as an exception to the hearsay rule, the two matters are conceptually distinct.

Treatises and other publications: F.R.E. 803(17)–(18).

F.R.E. 803(17) (market quotations, tabulations, lists, directories, and other compilations generally used or relied upon by the public or occupations) and 803(18) (learned treatises and articles) establish kinds of publications that are accepted as substantive, affirmative evidence despite the hearsay rule. Thus, publications of the kind indicated in the parenthesis are not confined, as they were under many older decisions, to the issue of credibility, that is, to impeachment of experts who testify contrary to them.

Consequently, a qualifying treatise or article can be used as an unsworn expert, often with better credentials than an actual witness. On the use of a treatise to forestall a directed verdict against plaintiff in a medical malpractice action, see *Maggipinto v. Reichman* (3d Cir. 1979). Cf. *Hemingway v. Ochsner Clinic* (5th Cir.1979).

The new substantive use of treatises and articles under 803(18), however, is attended by many of the procedural strictures formerly attached to impeachment use. This is because a primary rationale for allowing substantive use was that it is difficult for a fact-finder to eschew substantive use when this evidence is admitted for impeachment purposes. See Chapter 7, supra, under impeachment of experts. To avoid undue jury emphasis, and the jury discovering for itself out-of-context, inapplicable passages not examined and subject to challenge in open court, the treatise or article may be read aloud to the jury but not received as an exhibit.

Some states, such as California, still do not permit substantive use (unless otherwise admissible). And impeachment use may be procedurally somewhat restricted: In some jurisdictions the treatise or article must have been referred to, considered, or relied upon in forming the expert's opinion.

F.R.E. 803(18) would be available not only in those circumstances, but also if the item is called to the attention of the expert in cross-examination—so long as it is a "reliable authority", which the rule makes a general prerequisite in any case for the new substantive use. Query whether this requirement could be avoided if the offering party wishes only to use the evidence as impeachment.

There are a number of ways under the rule that this "reliable authoritativeness" can be established—through the challenged expert witness herself, by independent expert testimony, or by judicial notice. See *Dawsey v. Olin Corp.* (5th Cir.1986), affirming exclusion where no witness testified to the report's reliability and the expert testified it was not authoritative.

If the cross-examiner wishes to use the treatise or article on an expert who will not vouch for its authority or reliability, the proponent can ask to introduce the treatise subject to her own witness later testifying to its reliability. To the extent the work is indisputably reliably authoritative, 803(18) lets the court take judicial notice thereof.

Reputation concerning certain matters: F.R.E. 803(19)– (21). These provisions cover reputation as to: personal and family history, boundaries and general history, and personal character. This last is a noteworthy provision that, among other things, enables operation of the "character" rules discussed in Chapter 4, supra, which allow reputational proof of character for certain substantive and credibility purposes.

Certain court judgments: F.R.E. 803(22) (judgment of previous conviction) and 803(23) (judgment as to personal, family, or general history, or boundaries). These rules provide hearsay exceptions for admitting as evidence the judgments of courts, including civil judgments and criminal convictions, in certain cases. They are admissible to prove any fact "essential to the judgment", although there are qualifications. Under Rule 803(22) relating to judgments of conviction, a judgment on a plea of nolo contendere may not be used, nor may a conviction of a crime punishable by one year imprisonment or less, nor may the prosecution offer judgments of conviction rendered against someone other than the current defendant except for impeachment.

On the basis of this last qualification, an attempt to use Rule 803(22) to establish the status of third parties as illegal aliens in the defendant's trial for transporting undocumented aliens was rejected in *United States v. Diaz* (5th Cir.1991).

The pendency of an appeal may be shown but is no bar to admissibility.

III.   EXCEPTIONS FOR WHICH UNAVAILABILITY IS REQUIRED: F.R.E. 804

Some hearsay exceptions always required a showing of unavailability of the declarant before you could use the hearsay exception to get his out-of-court hearsay statement in. The theory is that the declarant's testimony is better than the hearsay, but the hearsay is better than no evidence at all. In the five hearsay exceptions falling into this category (former testimony, dying declarations, declarations against interest, declarations of personal or family history, and forfeiture by wrongdoing), the declarant must be unavailable under one or other of the kinds of unavailability enumerated in the rule defining unavailability (Rule 804(a)), **AND** his hearsay statement must fit the definition of one or other of the five hearsay exceptions as enumerated and defined in the rule setting forth the hearsay exceptions themselves (Rule 804(b)). (Emphasis intended.)

The Definition of Unavailability: F.R.E. 804(a)

At common law, unavailability did not necessarily mean the same thing for all of the common law hearsay exceptions requiring it, or in all jurisdictions. Variously, unavailability could consist of: death, absence beyond the reach of the jurisdiction that was not procured by the party seeking to invoke the exception (sometimes reasonable diligence to procure presence was required), assertion of privilege, and mental incompetence of proper magnitude. The mere fact that the declarant now tells a different or contrary story would not constitute unavailability, neither then nor now.

"Unavailability" as defined in Rule 804(a), is a unified concept for all the hearsay exceptions requiring it. In general, there are more kinds of unavailability recognized than at common law.

Unavailability under the F.R.E. embraces situations where the declarant (1) *will not testify*, e.g., rightfully or wrongfully claiming privilege or lack of memory, (2) *cannot testify* (due to death, mental or physical infirmity, or genuine lack of memory), or (3) *cannot be gotten*, being un-locatable despite diligent efforts, or not responsive to process (such as a subpoena) or other reasonable means.

One open issue is whether children who are (allegedly) victims of abuse are unavailable if they might be traumatized by testifying. Note that the definition of unavailability in 18 U.S.C.A. § 3509, a recent enactment allowing children to testify in alternative ways (e.g., outside the courtroom) in certain cases, includes trauma from testifying. The general question can arise for potentially traumatized adults, too.

A declarant is not deemed unavailable if the proponent of his declaration has procured that person's absence.

To establish unavailability under our number (3) above (i.e., where the witness *cannot be gotten*), the attorney must have attempted unsuccessfully to subpoena him or to use other "reasonable means" to procure his presence or (in the case of three of the hearsay exceptions) some alternative form of his testimony such as a deposition. Therefore, the witness simply being beyond the reach of the court's process may not be sufficient, as it was under some previous law. Cf. Fed. R. Civ. Pro. 32 which is somewhat different on this score as discussed infra near the end of the section on the former testimony hearsay exception.

As suggested above, in order to be able to introduce a *dying declaration*, a *declaration against interest*, or a *declaration of family history*, the attorney must, if reasonable, have attempted to obtain the declarant's alternative form of testimony on the matter such as by deposition, if his attendance at trial cannot be procured pursuant to our number (3) just above. Such alternative form of testimony is preferred to the other hearsay. This "alternative testimony" provision is not applicable if the attorney is attempting to use the *former testimony* hearsay exception or the *forfeiture by wrongdoing* hearsay exception rather than the hearsay exceptions mentioned (dying declarations, declarations against interest, or declarations of family history). In the case of the former testimony hearsay exception, if due diligence has not obtained the witness himself, the hearsay exception can be used.[7] Further, if the unavailability asserted in order to allow the attorney to use a dying declaration, declaration against interest, or declaration of family history, is not the kind dealt with in our number (3) (under which declarant can't be found), then the "alternative testimony" provision is not applicable. In other words, if the unavailability consists of the witness being dead, ill, privileged, or otherwise refusing to testify, the attorney is free of the need to try to obtain alternative testimony.

Following are the hearsay exceptions requiring a showing of unavailability. (We omit declarations of family history, to save time.) In each, the unavailability of the declarant constitutes the special "necessity" for admitting the evidence. As in the case of most hearsay exceptions, the special "trustworthiness" of the evidence in

7. By definition this is the case with the forfeiture by wrongdoing hearsay exception.

each exception is supposedly insured by the particular circumstance connoted by the name of the exception (different for each exception). Again, as with most hearsay exceptions, these circumstances surround the making of the declaration or inhere in the nature of the declaration itself. They are circumstances that are assumed to motivate the declarant to provide trustworthy information. They are conceptually distinct from facts which would corroborate the story told in the declaration. Such corroboration normally does not result in a hearsay exception.

Former Testimony: F.R.E. 804(b)(1)

Imagine that a previous trial has ended in a hung jury. Before the re-trial, a witness has died. The former testimony exception ordinarily allows the witness's testimony at the first trial to be used as evidence in the re-trial, via a transcript, recording, or someone's oral testimony as to it, even though it is hearsay. Any pertinent cross-examination that took place at the first trial comes in too.

Within limits, the exception has been expanded to include cases that are not mere re-trials. The previous proceeding has to be judicial in nature, with the opportunity for an examination there that seems satisfactorily equivalent to the cross-examination that would take place now at the later proceeding if the testimony were first presented now. For there is not going to be any cross-examination of the declarant now. Depositions can qualify, too, as the former proceeding under this rule.

Exposure of the witness' demeanor to the present factfinder is, regrettably, usually unavoidably missing except where a videotape is used to report the earlier testimony. But ordinarily it is a cold transcript, sound recording, or, rarely, an oral report.

At common law this exception applied only if there was an identity or substantial identity of parties, issues (legal as well as factual), and stakes, as between the two proceedings. The purpose of the identity requirement was to ensure that the opportunity for cross-examination, including the motive or incentive to cross-examine, would be much the same, so that the previous opportunity could stand in the stead of the later; and to avoid unfairness in binding a party by another party's opportunity. The effort was to "guarantee" that both the witness's and the cross-examiner's attention at the earlier proceeding were focused on the same issues with the same degree of intensity and same degree of realization of importance, as would be the case currently. The material that is currently important in the testimony should have been at least equally important then.

If these matters of motivation and incentive are assured, it should not matter whether the opportunity to cross-examine was actually exercised at the earlier proceeding or not. Presumably the same strategic considerations leading to the decision not to cross-examine would apply in both cases.

Assuming there was no change in issues or stakes, if the earlier trial was A vs. B & C and the later A vs. C, the change in parties was probably not significant. (Some courts, however, were very strict about identity.) But if a new party was *added* (or *substituted*) in the second trial, it would be unfair to admit *against him* the earlier testimony, as he had no opportunity to cross-examine. However, this may not apply if the new party was a formal successor, e.g., administrator, executor or other representative, of the party against whom the evidence was originally introduced. But some courts regarded as significant *any* change in parties, whether the party against whom the evidence was offered or otherwise, and whether the change was to a successor or not.

Some progressive courts permitted use against even a wholly new party who was not a formal successor if there was a substantial identity of interests and issues as between him and the one in his shoes earlier. A few of these courts would allow this only if the fight was in fact fought hard the first time. For example, this condition might be satisfied if suit No. 1 was a loss of consortium action brought by a husband for injury to his wife, suit No. 2 was the wife's own personal injury action against the same defendant for the same occurrence, and the husband and wife had the same lawyer (this last condition being *perhaps* dispensable). Some authorities adopting this view required that the opportunity to cross-examine have been utilized the first time, at least in the absence of any tactical justification for not cross-examining. In other words, some things that wouldn't matter in the ordinary situation may have been held to make a difference in these extended situations.

Where the first trial was a prosecution for a crime and the second a civil suit based on the same crime, it is easy to see that one party has changed, and in addition, as respects the alleged criminal, the stakes were probably higher in the earlier (criminal) case, but her burden of persuasion was lower. Thus, for example, the second suit might be one in which an insurance company sued by plaintiff for a loss alleges that the loss came about through plaintiff's own criminal act, where the alleged criminal act was the subject of the earlier criminal proceeding charging the present plaintiff. Or the second might be a tort suit against the alleged criminal for the offense. Can testimony against her in the former case (criminal) as to the doing of the act in issue, be used against her in the later (civil) case, assuming the witness is then dead? Let us analyze this.

The party against whom the evidence is to be used has not changed from the one case to the other. *If* both the stakes and burdens on her were the same or less in the second (the civil) case as compared with the first, there

might be considerable agreement that the answer should
be "yes", the evidence can be used—although not complete unanimity since many courts were very strict in
their identity requirement. But notice that the answer is
less clear in the case posed, because the lower burden of
proof *on her* in the criminal case makes us hesitate to
conclude her and her lawyer's relevant incentives, motives, and contemplations were as strong in the first case
as the second. Indeed, we should be doubly hesitant,
because we do not know anything about her relative
stakes in the two cases. We assume her stake is greater
in the first (the criminal) case, but that is not necessarily
so. We need to know what the penalty and damages
exposures are in the two cases. Suppose a small fine was
involved in the first (the criminal) case, and millions of
dollars in the second (the civil) case. Admittedly, normally a criminal case involves greater stakes than a civil
case. Some cases have let evidence like this in; some have
kept it out.

Why is unavailability required by the common law and
the F.R.E. under this particularly trustworthy hearsay
exception, attended as it is by judicial safeguards; and
not under some other hearsay exceptions? After all, the
former testimony, by definition, was given under oath, in
a proceeding, and subject to cross-examination and to
perjury law. The evidence, however, is testimonial. That
is, it is given at an official proceeding. The hearsay rule,
owing to its historical roots in combatting governmental
oppression, has always been skeptical of testimony created by official or governmental processes for a charge or
controversy—i.e., adversarial formal testimonial material.

Is Former Testimony Changed Under F.R.E. 804(b)(1)?

Issues and Stakes. Rule 804(b)(1), codifying the exception for former testimony, does not expressly provide

that the present and former proceedings need be identical, or even similar, as to issues or stakes. It does not speak in terms of issues and stakes at all. But what is required is that the opportunity and motive to examine (challenge, develop the testimony) were similar as between the two proceedings. That may lead to some comparative scrutiny of issues or stakes, as a practical matter. But it is a more flexible approach.

Parties. There is no express requirement that *all* the parties be identical. Only the party against whom the evidence is now offered is focused upon.

That party must be identical when the hearsay is offered in a criminal case. (But see *United States v. Deeb* (11th Cir.1994), using the "catch-all" exception, infra, as an end run around this identity requirement. The court admitted against defendant, testimony from his co-conspirator's trial at which defendant was neither present nor represented.) Some courts, despite the words of the rule, do not apply this party-identity concept when the evidence is offered against the prosecution.

Where the hearsay is being offered in a civil case, it is sufficient if that party is either identical or the earlier party was his predecessor-in-interest. (Thus, in a civil case, the *Deeb* court, immediately supra, may not have had to resort to the catch-all, depending on how strictly predecessor-in-interest is construed.)

The "motive" requirement, above, may on occasion require a broader look at *all* the parties. But again, there is more flexibility than under the strictest common law cases.

Defining predecessor-in-interest has proved difficult. Several courts appear to read this language out of the rule, by interpreting it to require only a community of interest, which is very little different from the requirement that there be a similar motive to challenge or develop the testimony, which is a separate requirement in the rule. See, e.g., *Lloyd v. American Export Lines, Inc.* (3d Cir.1978), where the Coast Guard, which had held a hearing concerning a fight aboard a merchant ship, was found to be a predecessor-in-interest of an individual seaman injured in the fight, in his later personal injury lawsuit based on the incident. Similarly, the government bringing antitrust claims has been treated as the predecessor-in-interest of later private antitrust claimants suing on the same claim. But other cases disagree, requiring a formal successor relationship such as administrator, executor, trustee in bankruptcy, or successor corporation.

In states such as California that have no privity (predecessor-in-interest) requirement, testimony against the plaintiff about the bus speed given in a personal injury suit brought by one passenger against a bus company, could be introduced against a second passenger bringing a later lawsuit against the company for the same collision, assuming the other criteria (including similar opportunity and motive) have been met. The broad but not the narrow interpretation of predecessor-in-interest in the federal cases would probably produce a similar result.

Application of Rule to Grand Jury Statements. In the case of *United States v. Salerno* (S.Ct.1992), the Supreme Court addressed the question whether the defense in a criminal case can introduce, at trial, grand jury testimony against the government when the declarant is unavailable. Rule 804(b)(1) admits earlier testimony when the opposing party had opportunity and similar motive to develop it by cross, direct, or redirect examination. Thus the former testimony exception usually cannot be used to admit against the defendant at trial, grand jury statements, because of the institutional absence at the grand jury of any representation of defendant or any possibility of cross-examination by him.

In *Salerno*, however, the evidence was offered *by* the defense *against* the government. The government *had* an opportunity at the grand jury, to examine the witness, and could have challenged any testimony exculpatory of defendant the witness gave. The defense argued that if the government called a witness before the grand jury, the person's exculpatory testimony should be able to be introduced at trial by the defendant as a matter of "adversarial fairness," irrespective of the government's motive to examine the witness. The Court disagreed, finding that a specific showing of similar motive must be proven before the testimony is admissible, just as in any case. It would seem that in this situation, the government's motive at the grand jury to debunk any statements exculpatory of the defendant, would often be quite sufficient. The case makes a useful generic point about Rule 804(b)(1): the earlier opportunity to examine does not necessarily have to be technically a *cross*-examination, so long as it is in an appropriately similar challenging posture. The rule is phrased so that any kind of examination might qualify in proper circumstances.

Confrontation Clause. Former testimony survived a confrontation clause challenge in the U.S. Supreme Court case of *Ohio v. Roberts* (discussed in Section V, Chapter 8). The ruling would be the same under the newer "testimonial" approach to confrontation discussed in that section because the former testimony exception involves both unavailability and earlier cross examination. *Roberts* admitted against the criminal defendant, preliminary hearing testimony of an unavailable witness, now a common event in criminal cases (despite the arguably differing motive to cross-examine), if the victim or witness is now dead, ill, or otherwise unavailable. The unavailability frequently asserted is that the witness can no longer be located or is outside subpoena range and will not come despite efforts and legal maneuvers. A good faith attempt must be made to obtain the witness' presence not only as a matter of the rule in most jurisdictions, but also under confrontation law. Live testimony is preferred to this evidence, if it can be obtained. Unavailability of the declarant is required not only by the rule, but by the Supreme Court as a matter of constitutional confrontation law.[8]

Multiple Levels of Hearsay. Actually, introduction of former testimony involves multiple levels of hearsay. The transcript is typically excepted as an official record or business record of the court reporter. His certification also solves authentication and best evidence problems (see Chapter 11). The testimony itself falls within Rule 804(b)(1). In addition, if the witness at the first proceeding testified to any out-of-court statement, it too must fit within a valid exception, exemption or non-hearsay rationale. The lack of objection at the earlier trial will not prevent a valid hearsay objection from being timely asserted at the present proceeding. Objections that could have been obviated at the earlier proceeding, such as to the form of the question, are somewhat more problematic.

Uses of Former Testimony That do Not Implicate This Exception. A transcript of previous testimony also may be used in many ways which do not implicate the exception. For example, a statement could be an admission, or it could be used to refresh or impeach a witness. It also could be introduced as substantive evidence under the hearsay exemption for a witness' prior inconsistent or consistent statement or statement of identification; or under the hearsay exception for past recollection recorded.

In civil cases, Fed. R. Civ. P. Rule 32(a)(3) provides an additional choice of route for substantive admissibility of a particular variety of Former Testimony (i.e., a deposition in the same case). It is in effect an optional alterna-

8. The Court will also give constitutional scrutiny to the unavailability found by the lower court, to be sure it meets constitutional standards.

tive to F.R.E. 804(b)(1). It has a different, generally more liberal, definition of unavailability than Rule 804(a). E.g., mere proof of geographic location beyond the process reach of the particular court may be sufficient, without resort to any additional "reasonable" efforts such as attempts to induce attendance or resort to process of other jurisdictions. Also, under Rule 32, the court has discretion to admit the deposition if, due to exceptional circumstances, it is in the interests of justice to admit it, even if unavailability is not established. Thus, the proponent who is offering deposition testimony is sometimes better able to obtain its admission under Rule 32.

Statements Under Belief of Impending Death (Known as "Dying Declarations"): F.R.E. 804(b)(2)

At common law, this exception applied only in criminal homicide prosecutions (not necessarily only murder) where the declarant was alleged to be the victim, and on her deathbed made a statement implicating or exculpating the accused. At the time of making the statement, the declarant must have been in extremis (i.e., imminently about to die), must have known that she was, and must have abandoned hope of recovery. She must have perished from that very injury, which must be the one alleged to have been inflicted by the accused.

The trustworthiness theory is that one would not falsify before meeting her Maker and will have abandoned all hope of worldly gain. That the rationale is dubious is revealed by certain questions: What about atheists? Vengeful people? People who may hope to benefit their survivors? Do people really "change their spots" or do they get worse? No distinctions or allowances were made along these lines.

The necessity aspect of the rationale may seem obvious: the most important witness is dead. But nothing rode on whether there were indeed other witnesses. The confinement to homicide cases was justified on the grounds that homicide was where there was greatest need. But if the evidence is not considered good enough for other cases, can we really say there is a need for it in the most serious cases? Isn't there quite the opposite need: a need to screen *more* carefully evidence that may result in life imprisonment or the death penalty? Is there a need to get the wrong person?

At common law, a few jurisdictions expanded the dying declaration exception to apply in other than criminal homicide cases. In contrast, a few more skeptical jurisdictions permitted an instruction highlighting the potential shortcomings of such statements.

Despite its questionable basis, the concept of the exception has endured, and indeed expanded. F.R.E. 804(b)(2) widens the traditional rule, which applied only in homicide prosecutions, to include all civil cases, but in criminal actions it is still confined to homicide. This strange line seems to have even less rationale than the common law. Now, the most serious and the least serious cases are embraced. The in-between ones are not.

Further, under F.R.E. 804(b)(2), a declaration concerning the cause or circumstances of declarant's believed imminently impending death is admissible insofar as the hearsay rule is concerned even though death may not really be imminent and he may not really be dying. The Federal Rule, unlike the common law, recognizes other forms of unavailability than death: all of those recognized in 804(a), discussed above. Consequently the rule would apply in a civil trial based on an attempted murder or grievous assault, where the declarant survives, but is unavailable for some other reason. However, the declarant still must have *believed* that death was imminent at the time the declaration was made.

Under the Federal Rule, the injury or disease under whose impetus the declarant speaks, does not have to be the subject of the civil or criminal lawsuit, nor does the person inflicting it, if indeed there is any such person. So long as the dying declaration is relevant in some way and survives other rules of evidence, the declaration comes in. However it must be a declaration concerning the cause or circumstances of the believed impending death.

By enacting the dying declarations rule in basically its common-law shape, the Federal Rules of Evidence continue to have faith in its questionable rationale; continue to ignore that persons imminently about to die (or believing themselves to be) probably have enfeebled or flustered capacity to perceive, remember, and recount;[9] and continue the strange rule that the supposed guarantee of trustworthiness somehow ceases to operate in mid-sentence as soon as the sentence strays to matters other than the cause or circumstances of the death, without inquiry into the sort of matters they are. Apparently abolished is the odd notion that the guarantee ceases to operate if the dying declaration is offered in connection with another death—say, for example, in connection with a prosecution for the death of a companion killed by the same assailant at the same time as part of a common incident.

Declarations Against Interest: F.R.E. 804(b)(3)

By "against interest" we mean statements such as "the property is not mine" (a statement against proprietary interest), or "I have not paid yet; I still owe the money" (a statement against pecuniary interest) or, in some jurisdictions in some situations, "I obtained the money by removing it secretly from the drawer" (perhaps a statement against penal interest since it may implicate in crime; it may also be adverse to other

9. This, however, is a good argument going to weight.

interests). The ultimate test is a pragmatic one: The statement must be so much against interest that a reasonable person would not make it unless it were true. It is easy to see that statements of this kind are somewhat trustworthy.[10]

General Parameters of the Against–Interest Hearsay Exception Both at Common Law and Today

This distinct exception is best described by contrasting it with admissions of a party, with which it must not be confused. Except as noted under the Federal Rules heading below, the law here is generally the same under both the F.R.E. and the common law.

At common law, as today, a declaration against interest was a declaration by a declarant, who was not necessarily a party nor a person bearing any relation to a party, which was known by the declarant at the time of making of the statement to be against his pecuniary, proprietary, or (in some jurisdictions) penal interest, and which somehow became relevant in a lawsuit usually between other parties unrelated to himself. In other words, he is usually a "stranger" to the litigation, unlike the case of party admissions. He just happens to have known something useful to the litigation. He is, in a sense, an absent independent witness, in most cases.

This exception, unlike party admissions, requires (a) unavailability of the declarant, and (b) knowledge that

10. Students sometimes become confused and believe that any statement made under penalty of law is a "statement against interest." We do not mean, by the phrase "against interest" under the present exception, a statement which, if true, is harmless or beneficial to the declarant, but will be penalized (that is, will hurt her) if she is speaking an untruth—for example, a statement to a governmental authority which is punishable under law if false. There is no exception embracing such a statement. "Declarations against interest" means statements which *if true* are self-damaging, by virtue of the facts related.

the declaration is against his interest. Party admissions applies regardless of whether the statement was against interest when made, so long as it is against the party's interests now. Parties are not required to be unavailable under party admissions, but unavailability is a prerequisite for admission under declarations against interest. Unlike party admissions, the declarant need not be a party nor related to a party, and his statement can be used not only against him and those in some relationship with him, as in party admissions; but against others as well.

Why are the requirements, as just outlined, different for the two principles? Notice particularly the requirement that the statement be known to be against interest when made, which is the whole rationale of trustworthiness under the present hearsay exception. Party admissions is not based on that. It is based on adversary fairness, in the main. What is the "necessity" factor under the two rules, which we have said lies, with trustworthiness, behind escape valves to the hearsay rule? Under the present rule it is the unavailability of the declarant. Under party admissions, it is the presumed greater honesty at the time the admission was made.

The opinion and first-hand knowledge rules are frequently relaxed (insofar as the out-of-court declarant is concerned) for admissions of a party, but at least some courts refuse to do so for declarations against interest. Indeed, this difference may result in an adverse statement admitting legal fault which was previously made by the decedent not being admitted in a wrongful death action (where he is not technically a party), whereas had he lived and sued, the statement would have been admissible as a party admission.[11] Some states correct this

11. Let us explain this a bit more: His statement in our example contains opinion or second-hand information: a statement of legal fault.

specific anomaly by statute. See, e.g., Cal. Evid. Code 1227.

Of course, a particular out-of-court statement may come within both exceptions. This would seem to be the case where one of two codefendants has made an out-of-court confession or admission implicating both, and she is "unavailable" in the sense that she refuses to testify, asserting her privilege against self-incrimination. We would expect the incriminating statement to be admissible against both: against the one as her own admission, and against the other as a statement against the interests of the declarant.

But either because of a special (perhaps constitutional) criminal dispensation, or because the reference to the non-confessor is not itself against the interests of the confessor, or because at common-law, penal interest did not qualify under the exception, the incriminating statement traditionally has been considered inadmissible against the one who did not make it. In *Crawford v. Washington*, treated supra in Section V (Confrontation Clause) of Chapter 8, the U.S. Supreme Court made it clear that a statement incriminating both the declarant and the defendant made to authorities ordinarily could not constitutionally be admitted against the defendant by the state as a declaration against interest. The confessor in most jurisdictions generally could not be regarded as speaking as agent for the other co-defendant for purposes of the exception for party admissions[12], since the statement would usually be made after completion of and

Where he is not a party, his statement comes in, if at all, not as a party admission which may countenance opinion or second-hand information, but rather only as a declaration against interest or other hearsay exception, which may not.

12. That is, the co-conspirator exemption from the hearsay rule.

ordinarily not in furtherance of the joint crime, frequently to authorities.

Where the two are co-defendants, and the confessor will not take the stand, and the reference to the non-confessor cannot be deleted, *Bruton v. United States* (S.Ct.1968), and its progeny, require a severance of the trials or a forgoing of use of the confession, on confrontation clause grounds, because of the inefficacy of an instruction to the jury to use the evidence against only the confessor. For example, *Cruz v. New York* (S.Ct.1987) reversed a conviction where the non-testifying co-defendant's confession that incriminated the defendant was admitted, despite a limiting instruction and admission of the defendant's own confession.

Richardson v. Marsh (S.Ct.1987) held that admission of a non-testifying codefendant's confession did not violate the confrontation clause where the confession was redacted to eliminate statements directly inculpating the codefendant. In contrast, *Gray v. Maryland* (S.Ct.1998) reversed a conviction where the redaction was accomplished by substituting the word "deleted" for the codefendant's name.

Multi-faceted Statements. Many situations arise where the statement is both "against the declarant's interest" and "in the declarant's interest" to make, at one and the same time, in different respects, or in different parts of the statement.

One example might be the jointly implicating custodial confession of a co-defendant mentioned above. Does the motive to perhaps please the authorities, or curry or obtain a favor, or share blame, outweigh the against-interest aspect? In *Williamson v. United States* (S.Ct. 1994), the Court held, in interpreting F.R.E. 804(b)(3), that it usually does, as respects parts of the statement that implicate the other person, at least when the statement is made in an official custodial setting. *Crawford,* supra, now would render unconstitutional use of such a statement against the non-maker accused.

Another example might be where declarant's money is being held, say by a bank, and, in order to obtain her money being so held, the declarant complies with the bank's request and makes a statement damaging her spouse's claim for damages against the bank in another matter.

Sometimes severing the various parts of the statement can take care of the matter, but, as in at least the last case, that may be unsatisfactory.

In this situation, a determination must be made as to the preponderant motivation of the declarant and whether it acts as some substantial indicator of reliability.

Another kind of dual aspect statement that has often confused courts is illustrated by a statement "I owe ten thousand dollars." This statement is really two statements, one in the declarant's interest to make, and one against his interest to make: "I owe not less than, nor more than, ten thousand dollars." In such a case, we should look to see which implied statement is really being offered at the trial. This depends upon whether the evidence is being offered to establish that $10,000 was owed, or to rebut the contention that more than $10,000 was owed.

When is "Self–Serving" an Objection? The objection is often made to evidence of many different sorts, that the evidence is "self-serving." Some courts seem to be under the impression that any evidence involving self-serving statements, that is, statements it is in the stater's interest to make, is inadmissible. That is not so. It is only where the evidence must be against interest to be admissible, as in the case of hearsay admissible under the present exception, or perhaps under party admissions in a slightly different sense, that "self-serving" would be a valid objection. Similarly, evidence might be inadmissible in the rare case where the evidence, because of its self-serving nature, is so without value, or so likely to deceive the jury, that the probative-prejudice-time balance tips to exclude it. See also the discussion, supra this chapter, under business records and government records, where litigation-motivated documents offered by the party making them might be deemed to violate certain requirements of those rules, because they are "self-serving."

Special Aspects Under the Federal Rules of Evidence

At strict common law, only statements directly on their face against pecuniary or proprietary interest were included in this exception. See the dispute between the majority and the dissent in *Gichner v. Antonio Troiano Tile & Marble Co.* (D.C.Cir.1969). The Federal Rule adds penal interest and statements affecting civil claims or defenses (if not already covered by the other interests) and removes the requirement of "directly on its face." It need only be such a statement as, in combination with facts and circumstances, would tend to be against the interest to such an extent that a reasonable person would not make the statement if it were untrue.

Earlier drafts had expressly included another interest: statements exposing their maker to hatred, ridicule, or disgrace, to the requisite extent. This language is found in the law of California, Texas, and several other states. It has generated few decisions. It is not in the final Federal Rule. Under the F.R.E., if such statements are to qualify, they must be shown to be against one of the recognized interests (such as pecuniary interest) in the degree required by the rule generally, that is, in such a degree that a reasonable person would not make such a statement if he believed it untrue. Do you think deleting the special language from the draft precludes this argument?

Focus on Declarations Against Penal Interest Offered in Criminal Cases: Third Party Confessions

There is a class of statements against penal interest that deserves special attention: third-party confessions in criminal cases, offered to exculpate or inculpate (jointly incriminate) the accused. Of course, which of these two ways they are offered depends on what they say. The common law, for several reasons, refused to admit even those that exculpate. See *Donnelly v. United States* (S.Ct. 1913). On the technical level, this was said to be required because declarations against *penal* interest could not qualify under the hearsay exception, and they were only indirectly against pecuniary or proprietary interest.

(1) Third Party Confessions Exculpatory of the Criminal Defendant on Trial

With this particular variety of the evidence, common-law courts additionally feared what was sometimes called "death row shopping"—the wholesale obtaining of statements confessing to sole commission of crimes by inmates with nothing to lose from clearing their "friends" and perhaps something to gain in terms of promises of payment or care for their families—in short, deals that could not be proved. Contrary to the courts, commentators argued that all against-penal-interest statements should be treated on a par with other against-interest statements, that is, admitted into evidence if they are found to be truly and sufficiently against interest.

Application of this common law rule to prevent the exculpatory variety of this evidence can in certain circumstances violate due process, at least if it operates to deprive a criminal defendant of reliable, strongly corroborated evidence that he did not commit the crime. See *Chambers v. Mississippi* (S.Ct.1973) (multiple confessions by a third party, with circumstances corroborating the confessions).

The F.R.E. adopt a compromise: Confessions of third parties, offered to exculpate, are admissible if they meet the test of other against-interest statements *and* are clearly corroborated.

This provision has provoked controversy on an equal protection rationale. Why are exculpatory statements likely to be more problematic than inculpatory ones? Interestingly, the solution of some courts is to require corroboration for both types of declarations.

An amendment has been proposed but deferred that would retain corroboration for exculpatory statements, but adds a special trustworthiness requirement for inculpatory ones. The amendment awaits study as to whether the confrontation decisions of *Crawford* and *Davis* (supra, Ch. 8, section V) affect the need for or shape of the amendment.

(2) Inculpatory Ones

With respect to those statements that inculpate (jointly incriminate), an earlier draft of the F.R.E. tried to render them inadmissible. Under the final rule, they are treated like other statements against interest: they must be truly and on balance against interest in the requisite degree, a requirement that can pose special problems with these inculpatory statements: the motivation may not be entirely selfless. For example, a co-criminal or alleged co-criminal might make a jointly incriminating statement implicating the accused as well as himself, in order to share or alleviate his own guilt or blame, or to obtain prosecutorial or custodial favor of some kind, or in response to threats from that source, or for some other self-seeking reason.

Occasionally the self-serving part can be severed off and excluded (redacted), but typically this defeats its relevance. For example, if the declaration "Defendant and I robbed the bank" is redacted to get rid of the not-necessarily-against-self-interest part, the statement becomes "I robbed the bank", which may have little relevance in a trial of defendant. To give another example, if one deletes "The defendant robbed the bank," from a larger statement admitting that the declarant drove the getaway car, this latter statement may not be helpful to the prosecution in the defendant's trial unless other evidence links the declarant to the defendant.

Where the potentially self-serving part (the part implicating the defendant) was a minor part of the thrust of the declaration at the time, another alternative was to allow it in as ancillary to the against-interest part. But in *Williamson v. United States* (S.Ct.1994), the Supreme Court held as a matter of F.R.E. interpretation that each part of the declaration must be looked at separately to determine if it is against interest. Most references to defendant or that incriminate defendant in these declarations will fail this test. Most, but not all. For example, in the getaway car example above, if there is other evidence that defendant was seen in the car with declarant at some little distance from the bank ten minutes after the robbery, the declaration (minus the direct reference to defendant robbing the bank) might be admissible and quite probative against the defendant. See, e.g., *Ciccarelli v. Gichner Systems Group, Inc.* (M.D.Pa.1994).

New Supreme Court Confrontation Clause jurisprudence would normally render use of such statements against the non-maker unconstitutional if the statement was made in custody or to legally implicate the non-maker or under analogous "testimonial" circumstances. See *Crawford v. Washington*, supra, in Chapter 8, Section V.

Waiver by Misconduct: F.R.E. 804(b)(6)

A new hearsay exception was added to the list in 804(b) as the final exception. This is Rule 804(b)(6). Added in 1997, it is entitled "Forfeiture by Wrongdoing." It provides for admissibility, insofar as the hearsay rule is concerned, of any declaration, whether covered by another hearsay exception or not, "offered against a party that has engaged or acquiesced in wrongdoing that was intended to, and did, procure the unavailability of the declarant as a witness." The inclusion of this provision is aimed at preventing litigants from taking advantage of their own misconduct in procuring the unavailability of the declarant as a witness. It would be unfair to allow the party to raise a hearsay objection—basically an objection that the witness is not here testifying—to exclude the hearsay statements of witnesses who have been prevented from testifying by that party. This would include, among others, parties who have witnesses killed to prevent their testimony, as well as those who bribe or convince witnesses not to come.

Some difficult problems of proof are engendered concerning whether the party did it; whether the intention was to prevent testimony; and whether conversations with witnesses concerning the desirability or possibility of not testifying or of pleading privilege—perhaps conversations witnesses may have with lawyers for a party—are considered "wrongdoing". The possibility of little criminal trials within trials is presented. Rule 104(a)'s preponderance of the evidence standard applies for these preliminary fact determinations.

A number of cases had previously reached similar results to the new rule. Particularly in criminal cases, decisions had focused on waiver of constitutional confrontation clause rights through wrongdoing such as witness tampering. For example, *United States v. Rouco* (11th Cir.1985) found a waiver regarding an undercover agent who was later killed during an attempt to arrest the defendant. Cf. *State v. Jarzbek* (Conn.1987), where threats made during a crime prevented a child from testifying. Some state cases require that the foundation be established by clear and convincing evidence.

IV.   THE CATCH–ALL OR RESIDUAL HEARSAY EXCEPTION

F.R.E. 807 (the "catch-all") allows the judge to create new exceptions to the hearsay rule for particular evidence if certain conditions are met.

The "catch-all" exception in its current form may be summarized as follows: If special necessity for the evidence and special trustworthiness equivalent to the standard exceptions can be shown, the provision empowers the judge to create an ad hoc exception to admit a particular piece of hearsay evidence in a particular case, provided that adequate advance notice has been given, including particulars of both the statement and its declarant. Available alternative proof is to be considered in deciding necessity, and the evidence is to be compared with evidence admissible under other exceptions in deciding trustworthiness.

A few cases give the flavor of the rule. *Chestnut v. Ford Motor Co.* (4th Cir.1971) addresses the admissibility of a statement made while the declarant (driver) was in the hospital in the weeks following his car crash. The cause of the crash was the subject of this personal injury product liability litigation. Upon suddenly waking up briefly after the very lengthy accident coma, the declarant, the plaintiff, blurted out that the car lights had closed on the pitch-black road, thereby implicating the defendant auto manufacturer. The declarant was the only one who knew exactly what had happened. At the time of trial, the declarant had amnesia. The court compared the hearsay to an excited utterance or spontaneous statement, citing the catch-all, and suggesting this evidence might be within it.

On the necessity requirement, the rule and the cases ask, is there other equally good evidence reasonably available on the matter? *Workman v. Cleveland–Cliffs Iron Co.* (N.D.Ohio 1975) rejected a deceased declarant's statement as to what his supervisor had him do that led to the fatal accident, because it was not necessary in view of the fact that the supervisor and other eyewitnesses were available to testify.

On the notice requirement, courts vary between rigid and flexible interpretation, sometimes even within the same circuit. Compare *United States v. Iaconetti* (2d Cir.1976), holding that five days' notice given during trial satisfies the rule, even though the rule might be read to require pretrial notice, with *United States v. Ruffin* (2d Cir.1978) imposing a rigid pre-trial notice requirement. See also *United States v. Pelullo* (3d Cir. 1992), finding lack of notice was not harmless error. The Uniform Rules of Evidence have expressly adopted the view espoused in *Iaconetti* in their "catch-all" exception.

Some courts dispense with notice when it is impossible or impractical to get the information needed for the notice, rather than excluding the evidence. This is probably a misreading of the rule. See *United States v. Medico* (2d Cir.1977), where an unidentified member of a crowd outside a bank called out the license plate number of the bank-robbery get-away car, and the identity of that crowd member could not be ascertained despite diligent efforts. The court dispensed with the requirement of notification of the identity of this declarant, citing circumstances of extreme trustworthiness and the extra time to prepare to meet this evidence offered the opponent in the trial court.

Notice is an important requirement because it can go a long way toward blunting the policy objections associated with admitting hearsay—that the opponent of the hearsay never gets a chance to explore the declarant and his story through cross-examination. If there is an adequate discovery system, adequate funds for discovery, investigation, and witness production, and a provision like Rule 806 allowing impeachment of declarants, notice enables the opponent of the evidence to investigate and depose the declarant, show defects in his evidence, and even bring him forward to trial if necessary. However, the down side, at least for the opponent of the evidence, is that the cost of these measures and risk if declarant is unavailable falls on him instead of the proponent. A number of jurisdictions and the Uniform Rules make more use of notice provisions than the F.R.E. do.

Does the catch-all provide a needed safety valve for the F.R.E., and desirable flexibility to cover unanticipated but worthy evidence; or is it simply a way to admit what used to be called "rank hearsay?" One argument is that without a catch-all, the other exceptions would be stretched and subject to tortured interpretations to accommodate deserving hearsay. Unlike a common-law system, there are severe limits to how much words in a code like the F.R.E. can be stretched. In a common-law system, the words can be re-formulated periodically.

The Drafting of the Catch–All Exception: F.R.E. 807

Professor Rothstein pleads guilty to coining the misnomer "catch-all" now in common use for this provision.[13] The intention of the rule as finally drafted was most assuredly not to catch "all" or even "most." Although courts vary in their adherence to this intention, Congress clearly meant to leave the vast majority of "in the hall" or "over the back fence" statements inadmissible hearsay.

13. It was at the stage of the drafting when the rule was much broader than currently. Prof. Rothstein was a Congressional consultant on the drafting. The catch-all is also referred to as the residual or equivalency exception.

This restrictive intent is seen in the progress between the draft as it went to Congress, and as it came from Congress in its finally enacted, current form. The two sets of provisions are printed below, together with an even earlier draft, which we may call the pre-Supreme–Court draft. The three are presented in chronological order:

(1) The Pre–Supreme–Court Draft (March 1969). This language appeared as the opening phrase of both Rule 803 and Rule 804, in lieu of a final "catch-all" exception:

"A statement is not excluded by the hearsay rule if its nature and the special circumstances under which it was made offer [strong] assurances of accuracy [not likely to be enhanced by calling the declarant as a witness even though he is available] [and the declarant is unavailable as a witness]. By way of illustration only, and not by way of limitation, the following are examples of statements conforming with the requirements of this rule:" [Here followed the list of exceptions presently contained in Rules 803 and 804. The bracketed language above concerning availability-unavailability indicates the difference in the phrase as it was used in Rule 803 and Rule 804. In addition, "strong" appeared in 804.]

(2) The Draft That Went to Congress (Supreme–Court–Approved Draft, Nov. 1972). The above language, i.e., (1) immediately above, was deleted from the two rules; the illustrations became hearsay exceptions; and the last exception in each rule read as follows:

"[Also excepted from the hearsay rule are] statements not specifically covered by any of the foregoing exceptions but having comparable circumstantial guarantees of trustworthiness."

(3) The Congressionally Enacted (1975) Version adopts the approach of (2) above, but amends the language to read as follows:

"[Also excepted from the hearsay rule are] statements not specifically covered by any of the foregoing exceptions but having equivalent circumstantial guarantees of trustworthiness, if the court determines that (A) the statement is offered as evidence of a material fact; (B) the statement is more probative on the point for which it is offered than any other evidence which the proponent can procure through reasonable efforts; and (C) the general purposes of these rules and the interests of justice will best be served by admission of the statement into evidence. However, a statement may not be admitted under this exception unless the proponent of it makes known to the adverse party sufficiently in advance of the trial or hearing to provide the adverse party with a fair opportunity to prepare to meet it, his intention to offer the statement and the particulars of it, including the name and address of the declarant."

This version has now been moved from its enacted position in Rules 803(24) and 804(b)(5), where it appeared in identical form, to a new single location, current Rule 807.

While many of the qualifiers added in this last quoted version are non-specific and vague, it is clear that Congress meant by them to limit the reach of the "catch-all."

As each of the drafts was put forward, it was met by cries of distress from the conventional bench and bar, and from politicians who did not wish to cede too much power to the judiciary. Although some such anciently exercised judicial power to create new exceptions to the hearsay rule must be responsible for the accumulation of exceptions we call the traditional exceptions, and a few modern decisions have recognized such a power prior to the Federal Rules, apparently a broad unconfined power of this kind is unacceptable to many members of the modern bench, bar, and Congress.

One objection raised was the unpredictability of such a power, and the consequent difficulty in planning, advising on, and estimating the expenses and risks of, litigation. Indeed, even under the current limited version of the power, there are widely divergent interpretations of its reach.

The Catch–All as Interpreted

Professor Raeder undertook a detailed study of the catch-all, which found that more than half of all hearsay offered under the catch-all was being admitted. See Raeder, *A Response to Professor Swift: The Hearsay Rule At Work: Has It Been Abolished De Facto by Judicial Discretion?* 76 Minn.L.Rev. 507 (1992); *Confronting the Catch–Alls*, 6 Criminal Justice Magazine 30 (Summer, 1991); and *The Effect of the Catch–Alls on Criminal Defendants: Little Red Riding Hood Meets the Hearsay Wolf and Is Devoured*, 25 Loyola L.A. L. Rev. 925 (1992). Prosecutors were the most prolific as well as the most successful users of the catch-all, and criminal defendants the least successful, although some of this may change in view of the U.S. Supreme Court's new view of the Confrontation Clause under *Crawford* and *Davis,* that restricts use against criminal defendants, of most outside-of-trial statements made to government agents or before government organs or are otherwise deemed "testimonial". See supra, Chapter 8, Section V.

Many courts apply a special analysis for catch-all statements in order to satisfy the trustworthiness requirement of the rule. They measure trustworthiness by the immediate circumstances at the time the statement was made, and the nature of the statement itself, rather than looking at corroboration of the statement. This is because the rule itself requires "circumstantial guarantees of trustworthiness" that are "equivalent" to those required by the hearsay exceptions in Rules 803 and 804. It is also because the U.S. Supreme Court, in *Idaho v. Wright* (S.Ct.1990), seemed to embrace such a view.

Can declarations that seem to be expressly excluded from a particular hearsay exception or exemption be brought within the catch-all? For example, consider grand jury statements, or prior statements of present witnesses, that do not meet the requirements of 801(d)(1) or 804(b)(1), or dying declarations or excited utterances that do not relate to the occurrence itself. Presumably, such a "near-miss" was not intended to be excluded from the catch-all if some additional unanticipated circumstance of trustworthiness can be pointed to. A similar problem arises with vicarious admissions that do not meet the test of agency such as so called "privity admissions".

Attempts to narrow the reach of the catch-all, in keeping with the legislative intent of restricting it to exceptional circumstance, have not fared well in the courts. Judge Becker's opinion that the catch-all should not apply to "near misses," i.e., hearsay that just fell short of recognized exceptions, *Zenith Radio Corp. v. Matsushita Elec. Indus. Co.* (E.D.Pa.1980), was rejected because it "puts the federal evidence rules back into the straightjacket from which the residual exceptions were intended to free them." *In re Japanese Electronic Products Antitrust Litigation* (3d Cir.1983).

The catch-all has been used most frequently for the introduction of the following categories of statements:

(1) *Child hearsay.* See, e.g., *Wright, supra*; *United States v. Ellis* (1st Cir.1991), admitting a social worker's testimony of a child's statements concerning play with anatomically correct dolls.

(2) *Grand jury testimony.* See, e.g., *United States v. Fernandez* (11th Cir.1989), finding no per se exclusion of grand jury testimony under the residual exception.

(3) *Quasi business and official records which fail to satisfy 803(6) and (8).* See, e.g., *United States v. Nivica* (1st Cir.1989) (Mexican bank records); *United States v. Elkins* (11th Cir.1989) (a letter by the purported head of Libyan military authorizing purchase of jet aircraft).

(4) *Statements made to law enforcement officials that are prior consistent or inconsistent statements of trial witnesses not fitting the Rule 801 definitions.* See, e.g. *United States v. Marshall* (7th Cir.1988) (inconsistent); *United States v. Obayagbona* (E.D.N.Y.1985) (consistent).

(5) *Statements to law enforcement officials by declarants not present at trial.* Such declarants have ranged from accomplices, to spouses, to victims, to truly disinterested individuals. See, e.g., *United States v. Roberts* (8th Cir.1988), admitting a statement incriminating the defendant although given by his sister at a time when she had an incentive to lie to the police.

Some (but not all) of the evidence found in these categories would now be barred by the U.S. Supreme Court's new Confrontation Clause jurisprudence. It depends very much on the factual circumstances. See Chapter 8, Section V, supra.

Hearsay Exceptions Outside the Current F.R.E.: Child Hearsay and Other Exceptions

The most common hearsay exception not found in the F.R.E. is the exception for child hearsay.[14] Child hearsay exceptions in the states vary greatly, ranging from those which simply require trustworthiness, to those which have detailed requirements, often difficult to meet. Some mandate that the child be available to testify, while

14. See Uniform R. 807 ('86 rev. in which Prof. Rothstein participated and '99 rev. in which Prof. Raeder participated); and A.B.A. Rept. supra in Preface to this book. Some of the provisions of these sources were precursors of state provisions and of 18 U.S.C.A. § 3509 concerning alternative and protective formats for child testimony.

others apply only if the child is unavailable. Under the F.R.E. and state codes patterned after the F.R.E., child hearsay which does not fit other exceptions (whether narrowly or flexibly construed), can only be admitted pursuant to the catch-all. Courts will often permit child hearsay under the catch-all even if the child is a witness. The necessity is typically based on the child's inarticulate or contradictory testimony at trial.

A number of states are experimenting with more novel hearsay exceptions. California has been particularly active in this regard with specific exceptions for victim's statements describing physical injury or threats thereof, statements of elder or dependent adult victims of abuse, and sworn statements regarding gang-related crimes, as well as several child hearsay exceptions. In part, this may be a function of California's not having a general catch-all.

Of course, like statements under any hearsay exception, to the extent that the particular circumstances may render particular statements under these new exceptions "testimonial" pursuant to the U.S. Supreme Court's new Confrontation Clause jurisprudence, they will be in constitutional jeopardy if the statement is to be used against the criminal defendant and declarant does not take the stand or (in the case of a declarant deemed unavailable) has not been cross-examinable at some earlier time. See supra, Chapter 8, Section V.

V.   FINAL THOUGHTS ABOUT HEARSAY

Multiple Hearsay and Impeachment: F.R.E. 805–806

Scattered throughout the chapters discussing hearsay have been a number of references to multiple layers of hearsay, variously called hearsay-within-hearsay, double hearsay, triple hearsay, etc. Whenever more than one out-of-court declarant is involved, hearsay analysis must focus on each, finding a legitimate exception, exemption or non-hearsay rationale for each statement. So long as each is admissible, it makes no difference how many statements are part of the declaration in question (F.R.E. 805). Of course, the more layers involved, the less likely that the jury will find the evidence highly probative. And F.R.E. 403 may step in at some point.

Another issue raised in passing has been the impeachment of hearsay declarants whose declaration comes in via an exception to or exemption from the hearsay rule. F.R.E. 806 permits such impeachment to the same extent as allowed against a witness. Requirements attending impeachment rules that may be impossible to execute in this context, are altered expressly or impliedly to fit the context. Thus, for example, declarant's inconsistent statements may be introduced without affording him an opportunity to deny or explain them.

To the extent the out-of-court declarant is also made an in-court witness (by either the offering side or the opponent), the availability of impeachment is self-evident. In this situation, Rule 806 provides that the declarant may be examined on the declaration by the opponent of the declaration, as if under cross-examination, even if that is the party who called the witness to the stand.

However, remember, impeachment under 806 is not limited to declarants who become witnesses, but is appropriate for all out-of-court declarants. Declarant's truthfulness may be attacked or supported as if he had testified.

CHAPTER 11

AUTHENTICATION, EXHIBITS, AND THE BEST EVIDENCE (ORIGINAL WRITING) RULE

I. AUTHENTICATION OF DOCUMENTS AND REAL EVIDENCE

Authentication by Indications That the Item Is What Its Proponent Claims: F.R.E. 901

Documents and "real" evidence (tangible objects) must be "authenticated" by evidence sufficient for a jury to find that they are what their proponents claim, except for a small group of documents viewed as "self-authenticating."

In general, wherever the probative value of a piece of evidence depends upon some fact, at least enough evidence of that fact to warrant a trier-of-fact to find that fact, is prerequisite to admissibility. This general principle is embodied in F.R.E. 104(b) and is called "relevancy conditioned on fact." Its specific application to writings and objects is called "authentication" (or "identification", a term we will not use in this connection) and it generally is governed by F.R.E. 901. Authentication, therefore, can be viewed as a special case of relevancy conditioned on fact.[1]

Thus, where the relevance of a document depends upon its issuance by a certain person or source, the law

1. But see, for a critique as to whether this almost universal view is indeed technically correct, Rothstein, *Intellectual Coherence in an Evidence Code*, 28 Loy. L.A. L. Rev. 1259 (1995).

has evolved rules concerning what will be a satisfactory quantum of evidence of that authorship. This is the subject of *authentication of a writing*.

It has its obvious parallels concerning objects—for example, where a lawyer offers in evidence a weapon (purporting to be the weapon used in a crime), a photograph, movie film, videotape, or sound recording (all purporting to reproduce something relevant), a blood or other specimen (purporting to come from a certain person or thing), or a scientific test result (purporting to have been conducted on a certain person or thing). In each case there is a purported or claimed connection to a person, thing, or occurrence, which makes the evidence relevant.

In these cases, there must be certain minimum assurances that the evidence is what it purports to be and what its proponent claims—i.e., that the evidence is what it is offered as being, and is what its value depends upon. In other words, the claimed connection must be *authenticated*. Even if the jury could be relied upon to spot evidence not meeting this standard, it would be a waste of time to receive it.

The quantum of proof required under both the common law and the F.R.E. seems to be more than the amount that would warrant a reasonable person in the affairs of daily life to assume authenticity. This approach is probably justifiable because falsification is more likely in connection with trials. Compare F.R.E. 901(a) (requiring evidence "sufficient to support a finding") with F.R.E. 901(b) (giving examples of predicates that are considered sufficient under that standard). The latter examples all seem to be more than just a bare minimum "sufficient to support a finding" if we have only daily life and not litigation in mind.

For example, in the ordinary affairs of daily life, someone receiving a letter bearing a purported signature of a
person might reasonably assume that the person named
in the signature signed it. In the courtroom, however, it
is not sufficient evidence of signing by X that a signature
purporting to be X's appears on the document, without
some minimal additional proof of the authenticity of the
signature. This proof may take the form of testimony by
the signatory, one who witnessed the signing, a handwriting expert comparing a proven exemplar, or anyone
having some minimal acquaintance with the person's
signature. Other proof is also acceptable, including circumstantial evidence such as peculiar penmanship characteristics, peculiar knowledge on the part of the writer,
display of a proven handwriting sample to the jurors for
their own comparison with the questioned signature,
certain government certificates of authenticity, or proper
business custody, as well as stipulation or admission.

Authentication in Special Situations: Circumstan-
tial Evidence, Chain of Custody, Voices, and
Self–Authentication

Authentication is not confined to the specific predicates in Rule 901(b), which are illustrative only. Any
method that minimally suffices to support a finding will
do. The showing may consist of circumstantial inferences. For example, authenticity has been found where a
letter on its face directly responds to another letter sent
to the purported signatory or where the writer or others
in a position to know acted in some fashion indicating
authenticity, as, e.g., engaging in prolonged business
relations apparently based on the document. Extreme
age (traditionally over 30 years, but 20 under F.R.E.
901(b)(8)) has been held to authenticate documents, if
there are other factors such as regularity on the document's face, proper custody, and (in some places under
some circumstances) possession taken under the docu-

ment. The theory is that it is unlikely that a fraud was laid so many years ago to bear fruit so many years later.

Authentication does not generally require that the persons in the "chain of custody" of the document be produced. However, showing a relatively secure chain of custody may be useful as a tactical matter or even as a matter of admissibility where there is evidence of alteration or substitution.

Showing a relatively preservation-conducive chain of custody is most often required for items whose condition is subject to spontaneous change or tampering, such as biodegradable samples or controlled substances.

As to authentication concerning who made statements heard by a witness over the telephone, it is not enough that the voice identified itself by name. It may be enough, however, if the voice was, in addition, recognized by the witness or if the telephone number called by the witness was that of the person and there was no other person by that name at that number. See F.R.E. 901 (b)(5) and (6).

Authentication by comparison to an exemplar requires an authentic exemplar. While some states, like California, consider authenticity of the exemplar to be an issue decided by the judge, the F.R.E. treats it no differently than other authentication matters. Thus, the judge simply determines whether a reasonable juror could find the exemplar to be authentic.

Authentication is required of documents whether they are offered as legal instruments themselves having legal consequences (as, e.g., a contract, deed, or will), or as evidence of (recital of) facts that are in issue. The latter, of course, would also require a hearsay exception or exemption. It is also important to realize that a document that has satisfied the authentication requirement is only rebuttably presumed authentic. In addition, even an authentic document may violate, and be attacked under, other evidence rules. Typically, when one considers the admissibility of a document, one must address authentication, best evidence, hearsay, and in criminal cases the right to confront witnesses. Other rules may also be applicable, such as Rule 403, or those relating to privileges, offers of compromise, insurance, character, safety measures, etc. Almost any rule of evidence may apply in a given case.

A small group of documents have been held to be self-authenticating on their faces, which means that a rebuttable presumption of authenticity arises from their mere appearance. F.R.E. 902 is one of the most expansive provisions in this regard, listing as self-authenticating certain seal-bearing and certain not-seal-bearing official domestic and foreign public documents and publications. Also listed are newspapers; periodicals; trade inscriptions, signs, tags, and labels; acknowledged (notarized) documents; commercial paper and related documents; and items specifically so provided by statute. It is implied that certain seals and certificates themselves also qualify. Self-authentication of all these categories means the documents will be accepted as issuing from the sources they purport to issue from, not that they speak the truth on other matters.[2]

In all these instances, it will usually be sufficient that the document *appears* to be one of these enumerated kinds of document.

Rule 902(11) (domestic business records) and (12) (foreign business records) were added in the year 2000, to permit a certificate to substitute for a live witness in laying the foundation required by Rule 803(6) for admission of a business record under the business record exception to the hearsay rule. These certification rules allow the record's custodian or other qualified person to

2. The latter is the subject of the hearsay rule.

certify in writing, rather than appearing to testify, that the record (1) was made, at or near the time of the occurrence of the matters set forth in the record, by or from information transmitted by, a person with knowledge of those matters; (2) was kept in the course of the regularly conducted business activity; and (3) was made by the regularly conducted business activity as a regular practice. This is normally all that is required to lay the foundation for admission as a business record under the hearsay exception. In addition, advance written notice of intention to use the certification provision is required, and the record must be made available for advance inspection, to afford the opponent a full opportunity to test the adequacy of the foundation. Might there be a Confrontation Clause problem with such certificates in certain circumstances?

Satisfying the authentication requirement as described in this chapter does not mean a trier-of-fact *must* find the signature or document genuine—only that it may. Usually showings of inauthenticity once this foundation has been laid, are matters of weight for the trier-of-fact to consider. Only rarely will they defeat the foundation for admissibility.

II. THE ORIGINAL WRITING OR BEST EVIDENCE RULE

The Basic Rule: F.R.E. 1001–02

To prove the contents of a writing, the law generally requires the original document, where available, rather than secondary evidence. The rule applies only when the content of the writing is at issue, not when the writing recounts facts that are sought to be proved by other evidence of them independent of the writing. Contents are in issue when the document is offered as a legally operative writing, as in the case of a deed, will, or contract; or when the document is offered as a recounting of, that is, evidence of, other

legally operative events, as where the document is offered as an exception to the hearsay rule.

The "Best Evidence Rule," alternatively known as the "Original Documents" or "Original Writings" Rule, is a rule narrowly confined to writings or items such as sound or video recordings, photographs, or computer printouts, that can be analogized to writings. Basically, it requires the best available form of evidence of a writing. There is no general requirement of the best form of evidence of anything else in the rest of Evidence law.

The rule is this. Whether offered as operative legal instruments (deeds, wills, contracts), or as proof of facts related in their contents (via an exemption from or exception to the hearsay rule), writings may be proved only by introduction of the original, unless the original has become unavailable without serious fault (bad faith) on the part of the offering party.

The doctrine originated at a time when civil discovery was minimal, and it therefore ensured that the writing itself would be present in court to "speak for itself."

If there is such unavailability without serious fault, secondary evidence of the contents will be admissible. In this situation, some jurisdictions are indifferent as to the form of secondary evidence, so long as it is reliable and otherwise admissible. See F.R.E. 1004. Others, like California, require the *best available* form of secondary evidence, and only if a better form is unavailable will a less desirable form be permitted. Under this view, a copy is generally regarded as preferable to oral testimony recounting the contents. Some copies are regarded as better than others. The order of preference is usually certified copies, photostats, carbons, and hand-written facsimiles.

But under the common law, some copies were regarded as worthy of being considered originals. Copies actually signed (with an original, not copied, signature) come within this category and are often called "duplicate originals" (not to be confused with the term "duplicate" used in the F.R.E., discussed below). Business transactions often involve signatures put to many copies along with the original, resulting in "duplicate originals," all of which would be treated as originals by evidence law. The F.R.E. continue this, and expand it as follows.

Duplicates: The "Matrix" Provision—F.R.E. 1003

A number of common law courts eventually accorded nearly the same treatment as that for originals to carbon copies that are not duplicate signed originals, and a growing body of law (principally statutory) began according similar treatment to photostatic copies, at least where they are kept in the ordinary course of business. Officially certified copies of official documents are also often so treated. This is to avoid loss, destruction, wear, or alteration of the original.

Under F.R.E. 1001(4) and 1003, carbons and photostatic copies, whether bearing an original signature or not, and whether kept in the ordinary course of business or not, are accepted in the same manner as originals, unless as respects the ones without an original signature, a genuine issue of authenticity of the original is raised or it would otherwise be unfair, on the facts of the particular case.

These non-original-signature ones are called "duplicates," defined as writings "produced from the same impression," or from "the same matrix," or by photography or similar means. The photocopier is a fixture of modern life, and people rely on the duplicates it produces as readily as they would on originals. Unless there is an issue of authenticity or unfairness, so do the F.R.E. Thus, ordinarily, a party who has both an original and a

Xerox or other "duplicate" may introduce either, at her option.

"Originals" in the case of photos are the negative and any print; and, in the case of computer materials, any accurate screen showing or printout. Rule 1001(3).

The Narrowness of the Original Writing Rule: Only When the "Content" of the Writing Is What Is to Be Proved

The best evidence rule is not a general rule requiring the best available evidence of all facts sought to be proved in lawsuits. Instead, it is a narrow rule, that only applies when the contents of a writing are in issue.[3]

Consequently, it does not apply when a writing is mere evidence of something else and that "something else" is sought to be proved independently of the writing, e.g., through an eyewitness.

For example, if an eyewitness to an occurrence tells her story once in a writing, and subsequently tells it again thereafter orally—then even though we have readily available the earlier and the later accounts, the best evidence rule (putting aside hearsay questions for the moment) is not violated by introducing the later oral statement (which might or might not be the eyewitness' current testimony on the stand).

The later statement is not "evidence of the contents of the [earlier] writing" but is an account from perception and memory, and thus the best evidence rule would not exclude the later oral statement even though the earlier written one is available.

So, too, where a witness tells a story at an informal interview, and someone overhears it, as well as a transcript being taken. Assume we want to prove at trial what was said at the interview and both the transcript

3. Or certain things analogous to writings.

and the overhearer are available. The best evidence rule is not at issue, and either the transcript or the overhearer may be used; they are both independent evidence *of what was said at the interview.* The overhearer is not testifying to what the transcript said, and therefore the testimony is not secondary evidence of the contents of a writing. Note, there may or may not be a hearsay problem.

Thus, we re-emphasize: testimony about an occurrence (e.g., an automobile collision) by one with first-hand knowledge is not regarded as "secondary evidence of a writing" even where the facts of the occurrence are also related in writing, whether by the witness or someone else, even though the writing came earlier than the testimony. Hence, such testimony is beyond the reach of the best evidence rule. It is otherwise if the testimony in this same case were that the writing states such-and-such, assuming we get around the hearsay rule.

On a more basic point, it is worth repeating that there is no general rule that only the best available evidence of a fact sought to be proved is admissible—no universal best evidence rule. Indeed, "the best evidence rule" requires only the best of available alternative proofs of the contents of a writing. This doctrine is best viewed as an exclusionary rule, forbidding evidence other than the writing. Most other facts may be proved by the best evidence available to the party, or by the worst, or anything in between, at the party's option, so long as the other rules of evidence are complied with. To make this crystal clear, the tendency is growing to refer to the best evidence rule as the "original documents rule" and to drop the phrase "best evidence." See F.R.E. Article X and the Advisory Committee's Notes thereto.

Some Exceptions to the Best Evidence Rule

A common provision is that the best evidence rule does not apply when the writing, recording, or photograph is not closely related to a controlling issue. Thus it is commonly said that writings introduced to prove a "collateral matter" (not necessarily used in the same sense as under impeachment), that is, to prove something not critical to the main issues in the case, are not subject to the best evidence rule. See F.R.E. 1004(4).

To prevent wear-and-tear and loss of certain public records, properly certified copies thereof are usually accepted on a par with originals. See F.R.E. 1005.

The requirement of the original is similarly relaxed to freely permit proof of contents by the admission of an opponent. F.R.E. 1007. And the requirement is relaxed where an opponent in possession of the original has failed to produce it upon request. F.R.E. 1004(3).

Summaries, charts, or calculations, are allowed if necessary for otherwise admissible complex, voluminous writings, recordings, or photos, which cannot conveniently be examined in court, assuming the originals or duplicates of these underlying materials are made conveniently available to opponents for copying and examining. See F.R.E. 1006. This would include not only charts or written or computerized summaries, but also summaries by means of oral testimony by an expert. Other rules of evidence must also always be satisfied, too, of course.

III. THE PAROL EVIDENCE RULE

Evidence of prior oral statements (known as "parol evidence") is inadmissible to vary, contradict, or add to the terms of certain written instruments, subject to some exceptions. The parol evidence rule is actually part of the substantive law of contracts, deeds, and wills rather than evidence.

Certain oral and written expressions are given legally binding effect in a fashion that cannot be described as evidentiary. Contracts, deeds, and wills are examples.

These are basically different from oral or written expressions offered to prove the facts they recount, where it is those facts themselves, and not the expression, that have the legal consequences, such as where a statement detailing an automobile collision is offered in a personal injury case pursuant to an exception to or exemption from the hearsay rule.

In the case of contracts, deeds, and wills, there will often be an earlier and a later expression, and a question may arise whether and to what extent the later supersedes the earlier, not only as to matters expressly inconsistent between the two, but as to matters that can logically coexist and matters covered by the earlier one but not mentioned in the later one.

This would seem to be a problem of substantive contract law (or will or deed law), to be decided by the jury on the basis of the intent of the parties. But at least in theory that is not the way it is handled, for certain policy reasons, when the *earlier expression is oral* and the later is written. The judge (not the jury) first decides (usually without the aid of the earlier expression) whether the "parol evidence" rule applies, or its exceptions.

The parol evidence rule is that "parol evidence [i.e., evidence of *prior* or *contemporaneous* oral expressions] is *inadmissible in evidence* to vary, contradict, or add to the terms of a written instrument." There are a number of exceptions and qualifications, of differing scope and number in different jurisdictions. E.g., the rule may be inapplicable if the writing is incomplete, or only a partial memorandum, or not a full integration of the terms; or if the oral expression is a separate or collateral agreement; or if the writing is ambiguous. Additional exceptions may apply concerning matters that go to the "basic validity" of the undertaking, or specific performance.

IV. THE MANNER OF INTRODUCING
EXHIBITS

How Exhibits Are Treated

"Exhibit" is a term that refers to tangible items of evidence, as opposed to testimony. They must comply with the rules of evidence, just as any other evidence must, and certain additional mechanical steps (such as marking) are also required for clarity of presentation in the record.

An exhibit can be a document, chart, photograph, x-ray film, motion picture, videotape, sound recording, specimen, model, weapon, drugs, or other thing. It may be merely an explanatory aid such as a chart, blackboard drawing, or computer animation/simulation, putting together facts otherwise in evidence (or sometimes facts not actually introduced but perhaps made available outside of trial that might be admissible but may be complex). Or it could be something that is evidence itself, in a more direct sense, such as a writing offered as evidence of the truth of the statements therein, a written contract offered in a suit upon the contract, the murder weapon offered in a homicide prosecution, a piece of clothing offered to aid identification, the narcotics seized in a drug bust, or the exhibiting of a child to establish paternity by resemblance (viewed with suspicion by many courts). Or it could be documents used to impeach or to refresh recollection. The terms "demonstrative," "real," "tangible," or "autoptic" are often applied to some of these kinds of items.

Exhibits are, of course, subject to all the ordinary rules of evidence. They may also be subject to additional requirements, such as authentication and/or best evidence. And they may be required to undergo a "marking" process to keep track of them in the record.

In regard to authentication, a police officer may have to relate how he seized the gun now offered in evidence from the defendant, tagged it with the officer's initials, placed it in an evidence locker, and retrieved it for court. On occasion, more than one witness will be necessary to prove such a relatively secure sequence, called a "chain of custody", for an item.

This requirement is common with drugs, which have been seized by an officer, sealed in some type of container, and sent to the laboratory where the drugs were analyzed and then resealed. Whether a break in a secure chain, i.e., a possibility of unauthorized access, is substantial enough to defeat admissibility or goes merely to weight, is a topic of much debate, depending in large measure on the likelihood of something untoward happening. An airtight chain is not required—merely some reasonable assurance that the chance of tampering, change, substitution, or contamination, accidental or intentional, is not great.

Authentication in this fashion of items, as distinct from documents, is sometimes called "identification", a term we will not use in this respect.

In the case of explanatory aids, and photographs, videotapes, and motion pictures purporting to depict a scene or event in issue, the most frequently invoked principle of evidence is the one embodied in F.R.E. 403, the probative-prejudice-misleadingness-time-consumption rule of judicial discretion. The question under that principle as applied here is usually whether the item *fairly* represents or depicts the thing it purports to represent or depict, and whether it is needed. The item will be scrutinized for any important misleading characteristics.

Complicated, voluminous documents and like materials may be put into evidence through a summary or chart, but the underlying documents and materials must themselves be admissible (usually under 803(6)), and, if not actually introduced into evidence, must be made available beforehand to the opposing side. See F.R.E. 1006, which provides an exception to the best evidence rule for this kind of thing. Pursuant to Rule 403, the summary or chart must be a fair and accurate representation and not misleading. F.R.E. Article VII, and the *Daubert* factors, may set some parameters if an expert is required to prepare and present the representation, since he or she would essentially be giving an opinion. Computer animations/simulations of litigated events can come within these principles. Courts sometimes allow these kinds of evidence even if the underlying material is inadmissible and/or not made available. What principle might justify this?

The Procedure for Exhibits, From Marking, to Conveyance to the Jury

Exhibits ordinarily also require some additional mechanical steps. They normally must be "marked." Unless the attorneys and court officials have done it in advance of the hearing, just prior to referring to an exhibit for the first time at trial, the offering attorney requests aloud the court reporter or other official provided therefor, to "mark [the item] as '[Plaintiff's] Exhibit No. [1] for Identification'." This legend is then actually affixed to the exhibit, and thereafter the exhibit can be referred to by that name ("Plaintiff's Exhibit No. 1") without confusion and in a fashion that will be clear in the written transcript of the words spoken at the trial. (Cases are reviewed on the written record.)

If the attorney later wishes to "introduce the exhibit into evidence" after laying whatever legal predicate is necessary, and if the exhibit is held admissible, counsel then, again by simple request spoken aloud, "offers in evidence Plaintiff's Exhibit No. 1," and if it is admitted by the judge, it becomes Plaintiff's Exhibit No. 1 in evidence, no longer merely for identification, before the jury. The court reporter will enter a notation either on an exhibit list or on the exhibit itself that says that it is in evidence, not merely marked for identification. In the alternative, in some courts the judge's ruling itself appearing on the record is sufficient. A wise attorney will try to assure the ruling appears in the record in any event, so no misunderstanding arises later. In a multi-exhibit case, it is also wise to keep a running list of all exhibits to be used at trial, with two separate columns opposite each, one column to check off when the exhibit is marked for identification, and the other to check off when the exhibit is introduced into evidence.

Too often attorneys realize only at the end of the case that they have fatally forgotten to introduce into evidence a critical document which has only been marked for identification. The consequences of "introducing an exhibit into evidence" are that for purposes of instructions to the jury, for purposes of meeting or defeating burdens of proof (both the production burden and persuasion burden, including directed verdicts and findings, i.e., for purposes of deliberations of the judge and jury), and for purposes of arguments, the exhibit is deemed to be in evidence and usable in the case. It becomes a part of the record for purposes of judicial review, and the jurors usually may take it with them when they retire to consider the case, at least (in some courts) if they request. Some courts make a separate determination on whether exhibits may be taken to the jury room.

In a number of jurisdictions, exhibits may not be offered during cross-examination, subject to some discretion on the judge's part. In some, such introduction by defendant during the plaintiff's or prosecutor's case may result in a forfeiture of defendant's right to move for a directed verdict at the close of that case.

Generally, before an exhibit is admitted in evidence (and this is especially true of a writing), opposing counsel must have an opportunity to examine it. Many courts will not permit a document that has been admitted into evidence to be used in the case unless it has been read to the jury. It is good practice to read it or otherwise convey it to the jury immediately upon admission. The reading may be done by the witness, if one having something to do with the document is on the stand, as is usually the case, or by the attorney. The judge may also allow the document to be circulated to the jury at that time. The document may be a transcript of another proceeding or a deposition, which is a common form of impeachment or establishing facts via an exception to or exemption from the hearsay rule. If so, an alternative and dramatically effective method of reading it aloud is to have the attorney read the questions and the witness read the answers. Even though the witness and attorney may not be the same ones that are in the transcript, this role-playing can be effective.

After a case is closed, exhibits normally remain part of the record. Methods are available for securing their return to the parties.

It is often desirable to get the marking for identification and even the question of the admissibility (a quite distinct question) of exhibits taken care of in sessions prior to the trial. Marking, rulings, and stipulations can be requested then as well as at the trial. Stipulations or rulings as to authenticity or best evidence have nothing to do with whether the evidence is acceptable under other rules. In cases subject to Federal Rule of Civil Procedure 26(a)(3), any anticipatable objections to documents, exhibits or deposition testimony must be timely raised before trial or they will be waived unless excused by the court for good cause.

Closely allied to the subject of tangible evidence is the subject of jury views: in certain situations the court in its discretion may be receptive to the suggestion that it is appropriate for a jury to go to view particular premises that cannot be satisfactorily described in, brought to, or reproduced in, the courtroom. The same is also possible in a non-jury trial, where the suggestion may be more convenient.

"Views" are typically treated as evidence. In some jurisdictions unauthorized views are presumed to be prejudicial because of the inability of counsel to "confront" such evidence.

Examples of Foundations for Exhibits and of Objections

The steps for introducing an exhibit, then, begin with having it marked. The attorney then proceeds to have it identified, and the foundation for its admissibility laid, by the witness. It must be tendered to opposing counsel. The attorney then formally offers the exhibit. Opposing counsel may object; if so, the proponent must be ready to justify admittance. If not objected to, or if the objection is overruled, the judge will order the exhibit "admitted" or "received." The proponent must obtain a clear ruling and an affirmative record of its reception, following which it usually is read, or shown, or interpreted, or passed, to the jurors. The following is an example:

Q. (By counsel): What happened next, if anything?

A. (By witness): I received a letter from the defendant.

Q. Ms. Reporter, will you please mark this written instrument—appearing to be a letter to Ms. Jane Brown from Mr. Fred Smith dated April 4, 2007— "Plaintiff's Exhibit No. 1," for identification? [The

[Court reporter marks it, often with a tag or sticker, or sometimes by writing on it.]

Q.   (To witness): Ms. Brown, I show you what has been marked as Plaintiffs Exhibit No. 1 for identification, and I ask you whether or not it is the letter to which you have referred. Is it?

A.   Yes, it is.

Q.   How do you recognize it?

A.   I recognize Mr. Smith's signature. I had seen it many times before then.

Q.   Your honor, I offer Plaintiffs Exhibit No. 1, being the letter spoken of by Ms. Brown, in evidence. I have tendered it to opposing counsel for examination.

The Court: Since there is no objection, it is admitted. [The court reporter makes a notation to this effect, in addition to the judge's ruling on the record.]

Q.   Now, Ms. Brown, while the bailiff passes a copy of Plaintiff's Exhibit No. 1 to the jury, let me refer you to the first paragraph. . . .

The opposing counsel may object to the exhibit at or before the offer. If the grounds are sensitive, counsel may include an optional preface to the objection: "May we approach the bench, your Honor?" The objection is stated simply: "I object to Plaintiff's Exhibit No. 1 for the reason that [here follow specific reasons]." In the alternative, counsel may request that the court reserve ruling (e.g., "until we have had an opportunity to cross-examine Ms. Brown respecting it"), or that the court allow early cross-examination at this point, known as "voir dire," directed at admissibility, either in or out of the jury's hearing. Or counsel may object to part of the exhibit: "I object that only the second paragraph of the exhibit is admissible, for the reason that . . ., and I therefore move that other portions of the exhibit be covered or excised."

Laying the foundation for (authenticating) a photograph or videotape usually involves merely producing a witness to say that the scene depicted is known to the witness and is accurately portrayed. The witness need not be the photographer, just someone with personal knowledge of the scene. No chain of custody need be shown. In some jurisdictions or in some circumstances the testimony may have to be that it accurately portrays the scene as it was at the relevant time. Sometimes this will be an issue of admissibility only if raised by the opponent and there seems to be a danger of misleading. Sometimes it would not be an issue of admissibility at all, but only weight.

Authenticating a voice recording as a recording of a certain conversation in some jurisdictions can be done in an analogous fashion to that described for photographs. Anyone who heard the conversation testifies to accuracy. But some jurisdictions are more suspicious in this situation and may require testimony of the recording equipment operator, a showing of the system, and/or a tight chain of custody.

The Rule of Completeness: F.R.E. 106

F.R.E. 106 codifies the common-law "Rule of Completeness:" If a party offers a document or part of a document, and another document or part is necessary to give a fair picture or avoid misleading the trier, or to put the matter into proper context, the party may be required to introduce *at that same time* the needed additional material.

In an appropriate case the rule might require admittance not just of another portion of a letter, for example; but perhaps a whole chain of letters and replies in a file, or even material from another file.

It is not entirely clear what is to be done if the additional material is inadmissible under some other rule of evidence, such as privilege or hearsay. Decisions differ, and distinctions are drawable based on different rules of evidence and different fact situations. The purpose of the additional material may be for context, which may not be a prohibited purpose under the other rule of evidence. Also, under the completeness rule, the judge requires the original offering party to put the additional material in, possibly waiving objection; if that party refuses, the judge may refuse the original offer.

The rule applies to writings and recorded statements. It does not apply to events, conversations, or oral evidence that is not written or recorded. Some judges, however, have applied analogous principles to evidence not strictly within the rule, pursuant to an inherent power such as that codified in F.R.E. 611 or 403, supplemented by the exhortation to fairness in F.R.E. 102, which states the lofty goals of the F.R.E.

* * *

There you have it. The course in Evidence. You are not ready to try a case yet, but you are closer. We hope you enjoyed it. We did.

*

APPENDIX

FEDERAL RULES OF EVIDENCE FOR UNITED STATES COURTS

Table of Rules

ARTICLE I. GENERAL PROVISIONS

Rule
101. Scope.
102. Purpose and Construction.
103. Rulings on Evidence.
  (a) Effect of Erroneous Ruling.
  (b) Record of Offer and Ruling.
  (c) Hearing of Jury.
  (d) Plain Error.
104. Preliminary Questions.
  (a) Questions of Admissibility Generally.
  (b) Relevancy Conditioned on Fact.
  (c) Hearing of Jury.
  (d) Testimony by Accused.
  (e) Weight and Credibility.
105. Limited Admissibility.
106. Remainder of or Related Writings or Recorded Statements.

ARTICLE II. JUDICIAL NOTICE

201. Judicial Notice of Adjudicative Facts.
  (a) Scope of Rule.
  (b) Kinds of Facts.
  (c) When Discretionary.
  (d) When Mandatory.
  (e) Opportunity to Be Heard.
  (f) Time of Taking Notice.
  (g) Instructing Jury.

ARTICLE III. PRESUMPTIONS
IN CIVIL ACTIONS AND
PROCEEDINGS

Rule
301. Presumptions in General in Civil Actions and Proceedings.
302. Applicability of State Law in Civil Actions and Proceedings.

ARTICLE IV.   RELEVANCY AND ITS LIMITS

401. Definition of "Relevant Evidence."
402. Relevant Evidence Generally Admissible;   Irrelevant Evidence Inadmissible.
403. Exclusion of Relevant Evidence on Grounds of Prejudice, Confusion, or Waste of Time.
404. Character Evidence Not Admissible to Prove Conduct;   Exceptions;   Other Crimes.
      (a)   Character Evidence Generally.
      (b)   Other Crimes, Wrongs, or Acts.
405. Methods of Proving Character.
      (a)   Reputation or Opinion.
      (b)   Specific Instances of Conduct.
406. Habit;   Routine Practice.
407. Subsequent Remedial Measures.
408. Compromise and Offers to Compromise.
409. Payment of Medical and Similar Expenses.
410. Inadmissibility of Pleas, Plea Discussions, and Related Statements.
411. Liability Insurance.
412. Sex Offense Cases;   Relevance of Alleged Victim's Past Sexual Behavior or Alleged Sexual Predisposition.
      (a)   Evidence Generally Inadmissible.
      (b)   Exceptions.
      (c)   Procedure to Determine Admissibility.
413. Evidence of Similar Crimes in Sexual Assault Cases.
414. Evidence of Similar Crimes in Child Molestation Cases.
415. Evidence of Similar Acts in Civil Cases Concerning Sexual Assault or Child Molestation.

ARTICLE V.   PRIVILEGES

501. General Rule.

ARTICLE VI.   WITNESSES

601. General Rule of Competency.
602. Lack of Personal Knowledge.
603. Oath or Affirmation.
604. Interpreters.
605. Competency of Judge as Witness.
606. Competency of Juror as Witness.
      (a)   At the Trial.

Rule
      (b)   Inquiry Into Validity of Verdict or Indictment.
607.   Who May Impeach.
608.   Evidence of Character and Conduct of Witness.
      (a)   Opinion and Reputation Evidence of Character.
      (b)   Specific Instances of Conduct.
609.   Impeachment by Evidence of Conviction of Crime.
      (a)   General Rule.
      (b)   Time Limit.
      (c)   Effect of Pardon, Annulment, or Certificate of Rehabilitation.
      (d)   Juvenile Adjudications.
      (e)   Pendency of Appeal.
610.   Religious Beliefs or Opinions.
611.   Mode and Order of Interrogation and Presentation.
      (a)   Control by Court.
      (b)   Scope of Cross-Examination.
      (c)   Leading Questions.
612.   Writing Used to Refresh Memory.
613.   Prior Statements of Witnesses.
      (a)   Examining Witness Concerning Prior Statement.
      (b)   Extrinsic Evidence of Prior Inconsistent Statement of Witness.
614.   Calling and Interrogation of Witnesses by Court.
      (a)   Calling by Court.
      (b)   Interrogation by Court.
      (c)   Objections.
615.   Exclusion of Witnesses.

ARTICLE VII.   OPINIONS AND EXPERT TESTIMONY

701.   Opinion Testimony by Lay Witnesses.
702.   Testimony by Experts.
703.   Bases of Opinion Testimony by Experts.
704.   Opinion on Ultimate Issue.
705.   Disclosure of Facts or Data Underlying Expert Opinion.
706.   Court Appointed Experts.
      (a)   Appointment.
      (b)   Compensation.
      (c)   Disclosure of Appointment.
      (d)   Parties' Experts of Own Selection.

ARTICLE VIII.   HEARSAY

801.   Definitions.
      (a)   Statement.
      (b)   Declarant.
      (c)   Hearsay.
      (d)   Statements Which Are Not Hearsay.

Rule
802. Hearsay Rule.
803. Hearsay Exceptions; Availability of Declarant Immaterial.
    (1) Present Sense Impression.
    (2) Excited Utterance.
    (3) Then Existing Mental, Emotional, or Physical Condition.
    (4) Statements for Purposes of Medical Diagnosis or Treatment.
    (5) Recorded Recollection.
    (6) Records of Regularly Conducted Activity.
    (7) Absence of Entry in Records Kept in Accordance With the Provisions of Paragraph (6).
    (8) Public Records and Reports.
    (9) Records of Vital Statistics.
    (10) Absence of Public Record or Entry.
    (11) Records of Religious Organizations.
    (12) Marriage, Baptismal, and Similar Certificates.
    (13) Family Records.
    (14) Records of Documents Affecting an Interest in Property.
    (15) Statements in Documents Affecting an Interest in Property.
    (16) Statements in Ancient Documents.
    (17) Market Reports, Commercial Publications.
    (18) Learned Treatises.
    (19) Reputation Concerning Personal or Family History.
    (20) Reputation Concerning Boundaries or General History.
    (21) Reputation as to Character.
    (22) Judgment of Previous Conviction.
    (23) Judgment as to Personal, Family, or General History, or Boundaries.
804. Hearsay Exceptions; Declarant Unavailable.
    (a) Definition of Unavailability.
    (b) Hearsay Exceptions.
805. Hearsay Within Hearsay.
806. Attacking and Supporting Credibility of Declarant.
807. Residual Exception.

ARTICLE IX. AUTHENTICATION
AND IDENTIFICATION

901. Requirement of Authentication or Identification.
    (a) General Provision.
    (b) Illustrations.
902. Self-Authentication.
903. Subscribing Witness' Testimony Unnecessary.

ARTICLE X. CONTENTS OF WRITINGS,
RECORDINGS, AND PHOTOGRAPHS

1001. Definitions.

Rule
1002. Requirement of Original.
1003. Admissibility of Duplicates.
1004. Admissibility of Other Evidence of Contents.
1005. Public Records.
1006. Summaries.
1007. Testimony or Written Admission of Party.
1008. Functions of Court and Jury.

ARTICLE XI.   MISCELLANEOUS RULES

1101. Applicability of Rules.
    (a)   Courts and Judges.
    (b)   Proceedings Generally.
    (c)   Rule of Privilege.
    (d)   Rules Inapplicable.
    (e)   Rules Applicable in Part.
1102. Amendments.
1103. Title.

ARTICLE I.   GENERAL PROVISIONS

Rule 101.   Scope

These rules govern proceedings in the courts of the United States and before the United States bankruptcy judges and United States magistrate judges, to the extent and with the exceptions stated in rule 1101.

Rule 102.   Purpose and Construction

These rules shall be construed to secure fairness in administration, elimination of unjustifiable expense and delay, and promotion of growth and development of the law of evidence to the end that the truth may be ascertained and proceedings justly determined.

Rule 103.   Rulings on Evidence

(a) Effect of erroneous ruling.   Error may not be predicated upon a ruling which admits or excludes evidence unless a substantial right of the party is affected, and

(1) Objection. In case the ruling is one admitting evidence, a timely objection or motion to strike appears of record, stating the specific ground of objection, if the specific ground was not apparent from the context; or

(2) Offer of proof. In case the ruling is one excluding evidence, the substance of the evidence was made known to the court by offer or was apparent from the context within which questions were asked.

Once the court makes a definitive ruling on the record admitting or excluding evidence, either at or before trial, a party need not renew an objection or offer of proof to preserve a claim of error for appeal.

(b) Record of offer and ruling. The court may add any other or further statement which shows the character of the evidence, the form in which it was offered, the objection made, and the ruling thereon. It may direct the making of an offer in question and answer form.

(c) Hearing of jury. In jury cases, proceedings shall be conducted, to the extent practicable, so as to prevent inadmissible evidence from being suggested to the jury by any means, such as making statements or offers of proof or asking questions in the hearing of the jury.

(d) Plain error. Nothing in this rule precludes taking notice of plain errors affecting substantial rights although they were not brought to the attention of the court.

Rule 104. Preliminary Questions

(a) Questions of admissibility generally. Preliminary questions concerning the qualification of a person to be a witness, the existence of a privilege, or the admissibility of evidence shall be determined by the court, subject to the provisions of subdivision (b). In making its determination it is not bound by the rules of evidence except those with respect to privileges.

(b) Relevancy conditioned on fact. When the relevancy of evidence depends upon the fulfillment of a condition of fact, the court shall admit it upon, or subject to, the introduction of evidence sufficient to support a finding of the fulfillment of the condition.

(c) Hearing of jury. Hearings on the admissibility of confessions shall in all cases be conducted out of the hearing of the jury. Hearings on other preliminary matters shall be so conducted when the interests of justice require, or when an accused is a witness and so requests.

(d) Testimony by accused. The accused does not, by testifying upon a preliminary matter, become subject to cross-examination as to other issues in the case.

(e) Weight and credibility. This rule does not limit the right of a party to introduce before the jury evidence relevant to weight or credibility.

Rule 105.   Limited Admissibility

When evidence which is admissible as to one party or for one purpose but not admissible as to another party or for another purpose is admitted, the court, upon request, shall restrict the evidence to its proper scope and instruct the jury accordingly.

Rule 106.   Remainder of or Related Writings or Recorded Statements

When a writing or recorded statement or part thereof is introduced by a party, an adverse party may require the introduction at that time of any other part or any other writing or recorded statement which ought in fairness to be considered contemporaneously with it.

ARTICLE II.   JUDICIAL NOTICE

Rule 201.   Judicial Notice of Adjudicative Facts

(a) Scope of rule.   This rule governs only judicial notice of adjudicative facts.

(b) Kinds of facts.   A judicially noticed fact must be one not subject to reasonable dispute in that it is either (1) generally known within the territorial jurisdiction of the trial court or (2) capable of accurate and ready determination by resort to sources whose accuracy cannot reasonably be questioned.

(c) When discretionary.   A court may take judicial notice, whether requested or not.

(d) When mandatory.   A court shall take judicial notice if requested by a party and supplied with the necessary information.

(e) Opportunity to be heard.   A party is entitled upon timely request to an opportunity to be heard as to the propriety of taking judicial notice and the tenor of the matter noticed.   In the absence of prior notification, the request may be made after judicial notice has been taken.

(f) Time of taking notice.   Judicial notice may be taken at any stage of the proceeding.

(g) Instructing jury.   In a civil action or proceeding, the court shall instruct the jury to accept as conclusive any fact judicially noticed.   In a criminal case, the court shall instruct the jury that it may, but is not required to, accept as conclusive any fact judicially noticed.

ARTICLE III.   PRESUMPTIONS IN CIVIL ACTIONS AND PROCEEDINGS

Rule 301.   Presumptions in General in Civil Actions and Proceedings

In all civil actions and proceedings not otherwise provided for by Act of Congress or by these rules, a presumption imposes on the party against whom it is directed the burden of going forward with evidence to rebut or meet the presumption, but does not shift to such party the burden of proof in the sense of the risk of nonpersuasion, which remains throughout the trial upon the party on whom it was originally cast.

Rule 302.   Applicability of State Law in Civil Actions and Proceedings

In civil actions and proceedings, the effect of a presumption respecting a fact which is an element of a claim or defense as to which State law supplies the rule of decision is determined in accordance with State law.

ARTICLE IV.   RELEVANCY AND ITS LIMITS

Rule 401.   Definition of "Relevant Evidence"

"Relevant evidence" means evidence having any tendency to make the existence of any fact that is of consequence to the determination of the action more probable or less probable than it would be without the evidence.

Rule 402.   Relevant Evidence Generally Admissible; Irrelevant Evidence Inadmissible

All relevant evidence is admissible, except as otherwise provided by the Constitution of the United States, by Act of Congress, by these rules, or by other rules prescribed by the Supreme Court pursuant to statutory authority. Evidence which is not relevant is not admissible.

Rule 403. Exclusion of Relevant Evidence on Grounds of Prejudice, Confusion, or Waste of Time

Although relevant, evidence may be excluded if its probative value is substantially outweighed by the danger of unfair prejudice, confusion of the issues, or misleading the jury, or by considerations of undue delay, waste of time, or needless presentation of cumulative evidence.

Rule 404. Character Evidence Not Admissible to Prove Conduct; Exceptions; Other Crimes

(a) Character evidence generally. Evidence of a person's character or a trait of character is not admissible for the purpose of proving action in conformity therewith on a particular occasion, except:

(1) Character of accused. In a criminal case, evidence of a pertinent trait of character offered by an accused, or by the prosecution to rebut the same, or if evidence of a trait of character of the alleged victim of the crime is offered by an accused and admitted under Rule 404(a)(2), evidence of the same trait of character of the accused offered by the prosecution;

(2) Character of alleged victim. In a criminal case, and subject to the limitations imposed by Rule 412, evidence of a pertinent trait of character of the alleged victim of the crime offered by an accused, or by the prosecution to rebut the same, or evidence of a character trait of peacefulness of the alleged victim offered by the prosecution in a homicide case to rebut evidence that the alleged victim was the first aggressor;

(3) Character of witness. Evidence of the character of a witness, as provided in Rules 607, 608, and 609.

(b) Other crimes, wrongs, or acts. Evidence of other crimes, wrongs, or acts is not admissible to prove the character of a person in order to show action in conformity therewith. It may, however, be admissible for other purposes, such as proof of motive, opportunity, intent, preparation, plan, knowledge, identity, or absence of mistake or accident, provided that upon request by the accused, the prosecution in a criminal case shall provide reasonable notice in advance of trial, or during trial if the court excuses pretrial notice on good cause shown, of the general nature of any such evidence it intends to introduce at trial.

Rule 405. Methods of Proving Character

(a) Reputation or opinion. In all cases in which evidence of character or a trait of character of a person is admissible, proof may be made by testimony as to reputation or by testimony in the form of an opinion. On cross-examination, inquiry is allowable into relevant specific instances of conduct.

(b) Specific instances of conduct. In cases in which character or a trait of character of a person is an essential element of a charge, claim, or defense, proof may also be made of specific instances of that person's conduct.

Rule 406. Habit; Routine Practice

Evidence of the habit of a person or of the routine practice of an organization, whether corroborated or not and regardless of the presence of eyewitnesses, is relevant to prove that the conduct of the person or organization on a particular occasion was in conformity with the habit or routine practice.

Rule 407. Subsequent Remedial Measures

When, after an injury or harm allegedly caused by an event, measures are taken that, if taken previously, would have made the injury or harm less likely to occur, evidence of the subsequent measures is not admissible to prove negligence, culpable conduct, a defect in a product, a defect in a product's design, or a need for a warning or instruction. This rule does not require the exclusion of evidence of subsequent measures when offered for another purpose, such as proving ownership, control, or feasibility of precautionary measures, if controverted, or impeachment.

Rule 408. Compromise and Offers to Compromise

(a) Prohibited uses. Evidence of the following is not admissible on behalf of any party, when offered to prove liability for, invalidity of, or amount of a claim that was disputed as to validity or amount, or to impeach through a prior inconsistent statement or contradiction:

(1) furnishing or offering or promising to furnish—or accepting or offering or promising to accept—a valuable consideration in compromising or attempting to compromise the claim; and

(2) conduct or statements made in compromise negotiations regarding the claim, except when offered in a criminal case and the negotiations related to a claim by a public office or agency in the exercise of regulatory, investigative, or enforcement authority.

(b) Permitted uses. This rule does not require exclusion if the evidence is offered for purposes not prohibited by subdivision (a). Examples of permissible purposes include proving a witness's bias or prejudice; negating a contention of undue delay; and proving an effort to obstruct a criminal investigation or prosecution.

Rule 409. Payment of Medical and Similar Expenses

Evidence of furnishing or offering or promising to pay medical, hospital, or similar expenses occasioned by an injury is not admissible to prove liability for the injury.

Rule 410. Inadmissibility of Pleas, Plea Discussions, and Related Statements

Except as otherwise provided in this rule, evidence of the following is not, in any civil or criminal proceeding, admissible against the defendant who made the plea or was a participant in the plea discussions:

(1) a plea of guilty which was later withdrawn;

(2) a plea of nolo contendere;

(3) any statement made in the course of any proceedings under Rule 11 of the Federal Rules of Criminal Procedure or comparable state procedure regarding either of the foregoing pleas; or

(4) any statement made in the course of plea discussions with an attorney for the prosecuting authority which do not result in a plea of guilty or which result in a plea of guilty later withdrawn.

However, such a statement is admissible (i) in any proceeding wherein another statement made in the course of the same plea or plea discussions has been introduced and the statement ought in fairness be considered contemporaneously with it, or (ii) in a criminal proceeding for perjury or false statement if the statement was made by the defendant under oath, on the record and in the presence of counsel.

Rule 411. Liability Insurance

Evidence that a person was or was not insured against liability is not admissible upon the issue whether the person acted negligently or otherwise wrongfully. This rule does not require the exclusion of evidence of insurance against liability when offered for another purpose, such as proof of agency, ownership, or control, or bias or prejudice of a witness.

Rule 412. Sex Offense Cases; Relevance of Alleged Victim's Past Sexual Behavior or Alleged Sexual Predisposition

(a) Evidence generally inadmissible. The following evidence is not admissible in any civil or criminal proceeding involving alleged sexual misconduct except as provided in subdivisions (b) and (c):

(1) Evidence offered to prove that any alleged victim engaged in other sexual behavior.

(2) Evidence offered to prove any alleged victim's sexual predisposition.

(b) Exceptions.

(1) In a criminal case, the following evidence is admissible, if otherwise admissible under these rules:

(A) evidence of specific instances of sexual behavior by the alleged victim offered to prove that a person other than the accused was the source of semen, injury or other physical evidence;

(B) evidence of specific instances of sexual behavior by the alleged victim with respect to the person accused of the sexual misconduct offered by the accused to prove consent or by the prosecution; and

(C) evidence the exclusion of which would violate the constitutional rights of the defendant.

(2) In a civil case, evidence offered to prove the sexual behavior or sexual predisposition of any alleged victim is admissible if it is otherwise admissible under these rules and its probative value substantially outweighs the danger of harm to any victim and of unfair prejudice to any party. Evidence of an alleged victim's reputation is admissible only if it has been placed in controversy by the alleged victim.

(c) Procedure to determine admissibility.

(1) A party intending to offer evidence under subdivision (b) must:

(A) file a written motion at least 14 days before trial specifically describing the evidence and stating the purpose for which it is offered unless the court, for good cause requires a different time for filing or permits filing during trial; and

(B) serve the motion on all parties and notify the alleged victim or, when appropriate, the alleged victim's guardian or representative.

(2) Before admitting evidence under this rule the court must conduct a hearing in camera and afford the victim and parties a right to attend and be heard. The motion, related papers, and the record of the hearing must be sealed and remain under seal unless the court orders otherwise.

Rule 413. Evidence of Similar Crimes in Sexual Assault Cases

(a) In a criminal case in which the defendant is accused of an offense of sexual assault, evidence of the defendant's commission of another offense or offenses of sexual assault is admissible, and may be considered for its bearing on any matter to which it is relevant.

(b) In a case in which the Government intends to offer evidence under this rule, the attorney for the Government shall disclose the evidence to the defendant, including statements of witnesses or a summary of the substance of any testimony that is expected to be offered, at least fifteen days before the scheduled date of trial or at such later time as the court may allow for good cause.

(c) This rule shall not be construed to limit the admission or consideration of evidence under any other rule.

(d) For purposes of this rule and Rule 415, "offense of sexual assault" means a crime under Federal law or the law of a State (as defined in section 513 of title 18, United States Code) that involved—

(1) any conduct proscribed by chapter 109A of title 18, United States Code;

(2) contact, without consent, between any part of the defendant's body or an object and the genitals or anus of another person;

(3) contact, without consent, between the genitals or anus of the defendant and any part of another person's body;

(4) deriving sexual pleasure or gratification from the infliction of death, bodily injury, or physical pain on another person; or

(5) an attempt or conspiracy to engage in conduct described in paragraphs (1)–(4).

Rule 414. Evidence of Similar Crimes in Child Molestation Cases

(a) In a criminal case in which the defendant is accused of an offense of child molestation, evidence of the defendant's commission of another offense or offenses of child molestation is admissible, and may be considered for its bearing on any matter to which it is relevant.

(b) In a case in which the Government intends to offer evidence under this rule, the attorney for the Government shall disclose the evidence to the defendant, including statements of witnesses or a summary of the substance of any testimony that is expected to be offered, at least fifteen days before the scheduled date of trial or at such later time as the court may allow for good cause.

(c) This rule shall not be construed to limit the admission or consideration of evidence under any other rule.

(d) For purposes of this rule and Rule 415, "child" means a person below the age of fourteen, and "offense of child molestation" means a crime under Federal law or the law of a State (as defined in section 513 of title 18, United States Code) that involved—

(1) any conduct proscribed by chapter 109A of title 18, United States Code, that was committed in relation to a child;

(2) any conduct proscribed by chapter 110 of title 18, United States Code;

(3) contact between any part of the defendant's body or an object and the genitals or anus of a child;

(4) contact between the genitals or anus of the defendant and any part of the body of a child;

(5) deriving sexual pleasure or gratification from the infliction of death, bodily injury, or physical pain on a child; or

(6) an attempt or conspiracy to engage in conduct described in paragraphs (1)–(5).

Rule 415. Evidence of Similar Acts in Civil Cases Concerning Sexual Assault or Child Molestation

(a) In a civil case in which a claim for damages or other relief is predicated on a party's alleged commission of conduct constituting an offense of sexual assault or child molestation, evidence of that party's commission of another offense or offenses of sexual assault or child molestation is admissible and may be considered as provided in Rule 413 and Rule 414 of these rules.

(b) A party who intends to offer evidence under this Rule shall disclose the evidence to the party against whom it will be offered, including statements of witnesses or a summary of the substance of any testimony that is expected to be offered, at least fifteen days before the scheduled date of trial or at such later time as the court may allow for good cause.

(c) This rule shall not be construed to limit the admission or consideration of evidence under any other rule.

ARTICLE V.   PRIVILEGES

Rule 501.   General Rule

Except as otherwise required by the Constitution of the United States or provided by Act of Congress or in rules prescribed by the Supreme Court pursuant to statutory authority, the privilege of a witness, person, government, State, or political subdivision thereof shall be governed by the principles of the common law as they may be interpreted by the courts of the United States in the light of reason and experience. However, in civil actions and proceedings, with respect to an element of a claim or defense as to which State law supplies the rule of decision, the privilege of a witness, person, government, State, or political subdivision thereof shall be determined in accordance with State law.

ARTICLE VI.   WITNESSES

Rule 601.   General Rule of Competency

Every person is competent to be a witness except as otherwise provided in these rules. However, in civil actions and proceedings, with respect to an element of a claim or defense as to which State law supplies the rule of decision, the competency of a witness shall be determined in accordance with State law.

Rule 602.   Lack of Personal Knowledge

A witness may not testify to a matter unless evidence is introduced sufficient to support a finding that the witness has personal knowledge of the matter. Evidence to prove personal knowledge may, but need not, consist of the witness' own testimony. This rule is subject to the provisions of rule 703, relating to opinion testimony by expert witnesses.

Rule 603. Oath or Affirmation

Before testifying, every witness shall be required to declare that the witness will testify truthfully, by oath or affirmation administered in a form calculated to awaken the witness' conscience and impress the witness' mind with the duty to do so.

Rule 604. Interpreters

An interpreter is subject to the provisions of these rules relating to qualification as an expert and the administration of an oath or affirmation to make a true translation.

Rule 605. Competency of Judge as Witness

The judge presiding at the trial may not testify in that trial as a witness. No objection need be made in order to preserve the point.

Rule 606. Competency of Juror as Witness

(a) At the trial. A member of the jury may not testify as a witness before that jury in the trial of the case in which the juror is sitting. If the juror is called so to testify, the opposing party shall be afforded an opportunity to object out of the presence of the jury.

(b) Inquiry into validity of verdict or indictment. Upon an inquiry into the validity of a verdict or indictment, a juror may not testify as to any matter or statement occurring during the course of the jury's deliberations or to the effect of anything upon that or any other juror's mind or emotions as influencing the juror to assent to or dissent from the verdict or indictment or concerning the juror's mental processes in connection therewith. But a juror may testify about (1) whether extraneous prejudicial information was improperly brought to the jury's attention, (2) whether any outside influence was improperly brought to bear upon any juror, or (3) whether there was a mistake in entering the verdict onto the verdict form. A juror's affidavit or evidence of any statement by the juror may not be received on a matter about which the juror would be precluded from testifying.

Rule 607. Who May Impeach

The credibility of a witness may be attacked by any party, including the party calling the witness.

Rule 608. Evidence of Character and Conduct of Witness

(a) Opinion and reputation evidence of character. The credibility of a witness may be attacked or supported by evidence in the form of opinion or reputation, but subject to these limitations: (1) the evidence may refer only to character for truthfulness or untruthfulness, and (2) evidence of truthful character is admissible only after the character of the witness for truthfulness has been attacked by opinion or reputation evidence or otherwise.

(b) Specific instances of conduct. Specific instances of the conduct of a witness, for the purpose of attacking or supporting the witness' character for truthfulness, other than conviction of crime as provided in rule 609, may not be proved by extrinsic evidence. They may, however, in the discretion of the court, if probative of truthfulness or untruthfulness, be inquired into on cross-examination of the witness (1) concerning the witness' character for truthfulness or untruthfulness, or (2) concerning the character for truthfulness or untruthfulness of another witness as to which character the witness being cross-examined has testified.

The giving of testimony, whether by an accused or by any other witness, does not operate as a waiver of the accused's or the witness' privilege against self-incrimination when examined with respect to matters that relate only to character for truthfulness.

Rule 609. Impeachment by Evidence of Conviction of Crime

(a) **General rule.** For the purpose of attacking the character for truthfulness of a witness,

(1) evidence that a witness other than an accused has been convicted of a crime shall be admitted, subject to Rule 403, if the crime was punishable by death or imprisonment in excess of one year under the law under which the witness was convicted, and evidence that an accused has been convicted of such a crime shall be admitted if the court determines that the probative value of admitting this evidence outweighs its prejudicial effect to the accused; and

(2) evidence that any witness has been convicted of a crime shall be admitted regardless of the punishment, if it readily can be determined that establishing the elements of the crime required proof or admission of an act of dishonesty or false statement by the witness.

(b) **Time limit.** Evidence of a conviction under this rule is not admissible if a period of more than ten years has elapsed since the date of the conviction or of the release of the witness from the confinement imposed for that conviction, whichever is the later date, unless the court determines, in the interests of justice, that the probative value of the conviction supported by specific facts and circumstances substantially outweighs its prejudicial effect. However, evidence of a conviction more than 10 years old as calculated herein, is not admissible unless the proponent gives to the adverse party sufficient advance written notice of intent to use such evidence to provide the adverse party with a fair opportunity to contest the use of such evidence.

(c) Effect of pardon, annulment, or certificate of rehabilitation. Evidence of a conviction is not admissible under this rule if (1) the conviction has been the subject of a pardon, annulment, certificate of rehabilitation, or other equivalent procedure based on a finding of the rehabilitation of the person convicted, and that person has not been convicted of a subsequent crime that was punishable by death or imprisonment in excess of one year, or (2) the conviction has been the subject of a pardon, annulment, or other equivalent procedure based on a finding of innocence.

(d) Juvenile adjudications. Evidence of juvenile adjudications is generally not admissible under this rule. The court may, however, in a criminal case allow evidence of a juvenile adjudication of a witness other than the accused if conviction of the offense would be admissible to attack the credibility of an adult and the court is satisfied that admission in evidence is necessary for a fair determination of the issue of guilt or innocence.

(e) Pendency of appeal. The pendency of an appeal therefrom does not render evidence of a conviction inadmissible. Evidence of the pendency of an appeal is admissible.

Rule 610. Religious Beliefs or Opinions

Evidence of the beliefs or opinions of a witness on matters of religion is not admissible for the purpose of showing that by reason of their nature the witness' credibility is impaired or enhanced.

Rule 611. Mode and Order of Interrogation and Presentation

(a) Control by court. The court shall exercise reasonable control over the mode and order of interrogating witnesses and presenting evidence so as to (1) make the interrogation and presentation effective for the ascertainment of the truth, (2) avoid needless consumption of time, and (3) protect witnesses from harassment or undue embarrassment.

(b) Scope of cross-examination. Cross-examination should be limited to the subject matter of the direct examination and matters affecting the credibility of the witness. The court may, in the exercise of discretion, permit inquiry into additional matters as if on direct examination.

(c) Leading questions. Leading questions should not be used on the direct examination of a witness except as may be necessary to develop the witness' testimony. Ordinarily leading questions should be permitted on cross-examination. When a party calls a hostile witness, an adverse party, or a witness identified with an adverse party, interrogation may be by leading questions.

Rule 612. Writing Used to Refresh Memory

Except as otherwise provided in criminal proceedings by section 3500 of title 18, United States Code, if a witness uses a writing to refresh memory for the purpose of testifying, either—

(1) while testifying, or

(2) before testifying, if the court in its discretion determines it is necessary in the interests of justice,

an adverse party is entitled to have the writing produced at the hearing, to inspect it, to cross-examine the witness thereon, and to introduce in evidence those portions which relate to the testimony of the witness. If it is claimed that the writing contains matters not related to the subject matter of the testimony the court shall examine the writing in camera, excise any portions not so related, and order delivery of the remainder to the party entitled thereto. Any portion withheld over objections shall be preserved and made available to the appellate court in the event of an appeal. If a writing is not produced or delivered pursuant to order under this rule, the court shall make any order justice requires, except that in criminal cases when the prosecution elects not to comply, the order shall be one striking the testimony or, if the court in its discretion determines that the interests of justice so require, declaring a mistrial.

Rule 613.   Prior Statements of Witnesses

(a) Examining witness concerning prior statement. In examining a witness concerning a prior statement made by the witness, whether written or not, the statement need not be shown nor its contents disclosed to the witness at that time, but on request the same shall be shown or disclosed to opposing counsel.

(b) Extrinsic evidence of prior inconsistent statement of witness. Extrinsic evidence of a prior inconsistent statement by a witness is not admissible unless the witness is afforded an opportunity to explain or deny the same and the opposite party is afforded an opportunity to interrogate the witness thereon, or the interests of justice otherwise require.   This provision does not apply to admissions of a party-opponent as defined in rule 801(d)(2).

Rule 614.   Calling and Interrogation of Witnesses by Court

(a) Calling by court. The court may, on its own motion or at the suggestion of a party, call witnesses, and all parties are entitled to cross-examine witnesses thus called.

(b) Interrogation by court. The court may interrogate witnesses, whether called by itself or by a party.

(c) Objections.   Objections to the calling of witnesses by the court or to interrogation by it may be made at the time or at the next available opportunity when the jury is not present.

Rule 615.   Exclusion of Witnesses

At the request of a party the court shall order witnesses excluded so that they cannot hear the testimony of other witnesses, and it may make the order of its own motion.   This rule does not authorize exclusion of (1) a party who is a natural person, or (2) an officer or employee of a party which is not a natural person designated as its representative by its attorney, or (3) a person whose presence is shown by a party to be essential to the presentation of the party's cause, or (4) a person authorized by statute to be present.

ARTICLE VII.   OPINIONS AND EXPERT TESTIMONY

Rule 701.   Opinion Testimony by Lay Witnesses

If the witness is not testifying as an expert, the witness' testimony in the form of opinions or inferences is limited to those opinions or inferences which are (a) rationally based on the perception of the witness, and (b) helpful to a clear understanding of the witness' testimony or the determination of a fact in issue, and (c) not based on scientific, technical, or other specialized knowledge within the scope of Rule 702.

Rule 702.   Testimony by Experts

If scientific, technical, or other specialized knowledge will assist the trier of fact to understand the evidence or to determine a fact in issue, a witness qualified as an expert by knowledge, skill, experience, training, or education, may testify thereto in the form of an opinion or otherwise, if (1) the testimony is based upon sufficient facts or data, (2) the testimony is the product of reliable principles and methods, and (3) the witness has applied the principles and methods reliably to the facts of the case.

Rule 703. Bases of Opinion Testimony by Experts

The facts or data in the particular case upon which an expert bases an opinion or inference may be those perceived by or made known to the expert at or before the hearing. If of a type reasonably relied upon by experts in the particular field in forming opinions or inferences upon the subject, the facts or data need not be admissible in evidence in order for the opinion or inference to be admitted. Facts or data that are otherwise inadmissible shall not be disclosed to the jury by the proponent of the opinion or inference unless the court determines that their probative value in assisting the jury to evaluate the expert's opinion substantially outweighs their prejudicial effect.

Rule 704. Opinion on Ultimate Issue

(a) Except as provided in subdivision (b), testimony in the form of an opinion or inference otherwise admissible is not objectionable because it embraces an ultimate issue to be decided by the trier of fact.

(b) No expert witness testifying with respect to the mental state or condition of a defendant in a criminal case may state an opinion or inference as to whether the defendant did or did not have the mental state or condition constituting an element of the crime charged or of a defense thereto. Such ultimate issues are matters for the trier of fact alone.

Rule 705. Disclosure of Facts or Data Underlying Expert Opinion

The expert may testify in terms of opinion or inference and give reasons therefor without first testifying to the underlying facts or data, unless the court requires otherwise. The expert may in any event be required to disclose the underlying facts or data on cross-examination.

Rule 706. Court Appointed Experts

(a) **Appointment.** The court may on its own motion or on the motion of any party enter an order to show cause why expert witnesses should not be appointed, and may request the parties to submit nominations. The court may appoint any expert witnesses agreed upon by the parties, and may appoint expert witnesses of its own selection. An expert witness shall not be appointed by the court unless the witness consents to act. A witness so appointed shall be informed of the witness' duties by the court in writing, a copy of which shall be filed with the clerk, or at a conference in which the parties shall have opportunity to participate. A witness so appointed shall advise the parties of the witness' findings, if any; the witness' deposition may be taken by any party; and the witness may be called to testify by the court or any party. The witness shall be subject to cross-examination by each party, including a party calling the witness.

(b) **Compensation.** Expert witnesses so appointed are entitled to reasonable compensation in whatever sum the court may allow. The compensation thus fixed is payable from funds which may be provided by law in criminal cases and civil actions and proceedings involving just compensation under the fifth amendment. In other civil actions and proceedings the compensation shall be paid by the parties in such proportion and at such time as the court directs, and thereafter charged in like manner as other costs.

(c) **Disclosure of appointment.** In the exercise of its discretion, the court may authorize disclosure to the jury of the fact that the court appointed the expert witness.

(d) Parties' experts of own selection. Nothing in this rule limits the parties in calling expert witnesses of their own selection.

ARTICLE VIII.   HEARSAY

Rule 801.   Definitions

The following definitions apply under this article:

(a) Statement. A "statement" is (1) an oral or written assertion or (2) nonverbal conduct of a person, if it is intended by the person as an assertion.

(b) Declarant. A "declarant" is a person who makes a statement.

(c) Hearsay. "Hearsay" is a statement, other than one made by the declarant while testifying at the trial or hearing, offered in evidence to prove the truth of the matter asserted.

(d) Statements which are not hearsay. A statement is not hearsay if—

(1) Prior statement by witness. The declarant testifies at the trial or hearing and is subject to cross-examination concerning the statement, and the statement is (A) inconsistent with the declarant's testimony, and was given under oath subject to the penalty of perjury at a trial, hearing, or other proceeding, or in a deposition, or (B) consistent with the declarant's testimony and is offered to rebut an express or implied charge against the declarant of recent fabrication or improper influence or motive, or (C) one of identification of a person made after perceiving the person; or

(2) Admission by party-opponent. The statement is offered against a party and is (A) the party's own statement, in either an individual or a representative capacity or (B) a statement of which the party has manifested an adoption or belief in its truth, or (C) a statement by a person authorized by the party to make a statement concerning the subject, or (D) a statement by the party's agent or servant concerning a matter within the scope of the agency or employment, made during the existence of the relationship, or (E) a statement by a coconspirator of a party during the course and in furtherance of the conspiracy. The contents of the statement shall be considered but are not alone sufficient to establish the declarant's authority under subdivision (C), the agency or employment relationship and scope thereof under subdivision (D), or the existence of the conspiracy and the participation therein of the declarant and the party against whom the statement is offered under subdivision (E).

Rule 802. Hearsay Rule

Hearsay is not admissible except as provided by these rules or by other rules prescribed by the Supreme Court pursuant to statutory authority or by Act of Congress.

Rule 803. Hearsay Exceptions; Availability of Declarant Immaterial

The following are not excluded by the hearsay rule, even though the declarant is available as a witness:

(1) Present sense impression. A statement describing or explaining an event or condition made while the declarant was perceiving the event or condition, or immediately thereafter.

(2) Excited utterance. A statement relating to a startling event or condition made while the declarant was under the stress of excitement caused by the event or condition.

(3) Then existing mental, emotional, or physical condition. A statement of the declarant's then existing state of mind, emotion, sensation, or physical condition (such as intent, plan, motive, design, mental feeling, pain, and bodily health), but not including a statement of memory or belief to prove the fact remembered or believed unless it relates to the execution, revocation, identification, or terms of declarant's will.

(4) Statements for purposes of medical diagnosis or treatment. Statements made for purposes of medical diagnosis or treatment and describing medical history, or past or present symptoms, pain, or sensations, or the inception or general character of the cause or external source thereof insofar as reasonably pertinent to diagnosis or treatment.

(5) Recorded recollection. A memorandum or record concerning a matter about which a witness once had knowledge but now has insufficient recollection to enable the witness to testify fully and accurately, shown to have been made or adopted by the witness when the matter was fresh in the witness' memory and to reflect that knowledge correctly. If admitted, the memorandum or record may be read into evidence but may not itself be received as an exhibit unless offered by an adverse party.

(6) Records of regularly conducted activity. A memorandum, report, record, or data compilation, in any form, of acts, events, conditions, opinions, or diagnoses, made at or near the time by, or from information transmitted by, a person with knowledge, if kept in the course of a regularly conducted business activity, and if it was the regular practice of that business activity to make the memorandum, report, record, or data compilation, all as shown by the testimony of the custodian or other qualified witness, or by certification that complies with Rule 902(11), Rule 902(12), or a statute permitting certification, unless the source of information or the method or circumstances of preparation indicate lack of trustworthiness. The term "business" as used in this paragraph includes business, institution, association, profession, occupation, and calling of every kind, whether or not conducted for profit.

(7) Absence of entry in records kept in accordance with the provisions of paragraph (6). Evidence that a matter is not included in the memoranda, reports, records, or data compilations, in any form, kept in accordance with the provisions of paragraph (6), to prove the nonoccurrence or nonexistence of the matter, if the matter was of a kind of which a memorandum, report, record, or data compilation was regularly made and preserved, unless the sources of information or other circumstances indicate lack of trustworthiness.

(8) Public records and reports. Records, reports, statements, or data compilations, in any form, of public offices or agencies, setting forth (A) the activities of the office or agency, or (B) matters observed pursuant to duty imposed by law as to which matters there was a duty to report, excluding, however, in criminal cases matters observed by police officers and other law enforcement personnel, or (C) in civil actions and proceedings and against the Government in criminal cases, factual findings resulting from an investigation made pursuant to authority granted by law, unless the sources of information or other circumstances indicate lack of trustworthiness.

(9) Records of vital statistics. Records or data compilations, in any form, of births, fetal deaths, deaths, or marriages, if the report thereof was made to a public office pursuant to requirements of law.

(10) Absence of public record or entry. To prove the absence of a record, report, statement, or data compilation, in any form, or the nonoccurrence or nonexistence of a matter of which a record, report, statement, or data compilation, in any form, was regularly made and preserved by a public office or agency, evidence in the form of a certification in accordance with rule 902, or testimony, that diligent search failed to disclose the record, report, statement, or data compilation, or entry.

(11) Records of religious organizations. Statements of births, marriages, divorces, deaths, legitimacy, ancestry, relationship by blood or marriage, or other similar facts of personal or family history, contained in a regularly kept record of a religious organization.

(12) Marriage, baptismal, and similar certificates. Statements of fact contained in a certificate that the maker performed a marriage or other ceremony or administered a sacrament, made by a clergyman, public official, or other person authorized by the rules or practices of a religious organization or by law to perform the act certified, and purporting to have been issued at the time of the act or within a reasonable time thereafter.

(13) Family records. Statements of fact concerning personal or family history contained in family Bibles, genealogies, charts, engravings on rings, inscriptions on family portraits, engravings on urns, crypts, or tombstones, or the like.

(14) Records of documents affecting an interest in property. The record of a document purporting to establish or affect an interest in property, as proof of the content of the original recorded document and its execution and delivery by each person by whom it purports to have been executed, if the record is a record of a public office and an applicable statute authorizes the recording of documents of that kind in that office.

(15) Statements in documents affecting an interest in property. A statement contained in a document purporting to establish or affect an interest in property if the matter stated was relevant to the purpose of the document, unless dealings with the property since the document was made have been inconsistent with the truth of the statement or the purport of the document.

(16) Statements in ancient documents. Statements in a document in existence twenty years or more the authenticity of which is established.

(17) Market reports, commercial publications. Market quotations, tabulations, lists, directories, or other published compilations, generally used and relied upon by the public or by persons in particular occupations.

(18) Learned treatises. To the extent called to the attention of an expert witness upon cross-examination or relied upon by the expert witness in direct examination, statements contained in published treatises, periodicals, or pamphlets on a subject of history, medicine, or other science or art, established as a reliable authority by the testimony or admission of the witness or by other expert testimony or by judicial notice. If admitted, the statements may be read into evidence but may not be received as exhibits.

(19) Reputation concerning personal or family history. Reputation among members of a person's family by blood, adoption, or marriage, or among a person's associates, or in the community, concerning a person's birth, adoption, marriage, divorce, death, legitimacy, relationship by blood, adoption, or marriage, ancestry, or other similar fact of his personal or family history.

(20) Reputation concerning boundaries or general history. Reputation in a community, arising before the controversy, as to boundaries of or customs affecting lands in the community, and reputation as to events of general history important to the community or State or nation in which located.

(21) Reputation as to character. Reputation of a person's character among associates or in the community.

(22) Judgment of previous conviction. Evidence of a final judgment, entered after a trial or upon a plea of guilty (but not upon a plea of nolo contendere), adjudging a person guilty of a crime punishable by death or imprisonment in excess of one year, to prove any fact essential to sustain the judgment, but not including, when offered by the Government in a criminal prosecution for purposes other than impeachment, judgments against persons other than the accused. The pendency of an appeal may be shown but does not affect admissibility.

(23) Judgment as to personal, family, or general history, or boundaries. Judgments as proof of matters of personal, family or general history, or boundaries, essential to the judgment, if the same would be provable by evidence of reputation.

(24) [Transferred to Rule 807]

Rule 804. Hearsay Exceptions; Declarant Unavailable

(a) Definition of unavailability. "Unavailability as a witness" includes situations in which the declarant—

(1) is exempted by ruling of the court on the ground of privilege from testifying concerning the subject matter of the declarant's statement; or

(2) persists in refusing to testify concerning the subject matter of the declarant's statement despite an order of the court to do so; or

(3) testifies to a lack of memory of the subject matter of the declarant's statement; or

(4) is unable to be present or to testify at the hearing because of death or then existing physical or mental illness or infirmity; or

(5) is absent from the hearing and the proponent of statement has been unable to procure the declarant's attendance (or in the case of a hearsay exception under subdivision (b)(2), (3), or (4), the declarant's attendance or testimony) by process or other reasonable means.

A declarant is not unavailable as a witness if exemption, refusal, claim of lack of memory, inability, or absence is due to the procurement or wrongdoing of the proponent of a statement for the purpose of preventing the witness from attending or testifying.

(b) Hearsay exceptions. The following are not excluded by the hearsay rule if the declarant is unavailable as a witness:

(1) Former testimony. Testimony given as a witness at another hearing of the same or a different proceeding, or in a deposition taken in compliance with law in the course of the same or another proceeding, if the party against whom the testimony is now offered, or, in a civil action or proceeding, a predecessor in interest, had an opportunity and similar motive to develop the testimony by direct, cross, or redirect examination.

(2) Statement under belief of impending death. In a prosecution for homicide or in a civil action or proceeding, a statement made by a declarant while believing that the declarant's death was imminent, concerning the cause or circumstances of what the declarant believed to be impending death.

(3) Statement against interest. A statement which was at the time of its making so far contrary to the declarant's pecuniary or proprietary interest, or so far tended to subject the declarant to civil or criminal liability, or to render invalid a claim by the declarant against another, that a reasonable person in the declarant's position would not have made the statement unless believing it to be true. A statement tending to expose the declarant to criminal liability and offered to exculpate the accused is not admissible unless corroborating circumstances clearly indicate the trustworthiness of the statement.

(4) Statement of personal or family history. (A) A statement concerning the declarant's own birth, adoption, marriage, divorce, legitimacy, relationship by blood, adoption, or marriage, ancestry, or other similar fact of personal or family history, even though declarant had no means of acquiring personal knowledge of the matter stated; or (B) a statement concerning the foregoing matters, and death also, of another person, if the declarant was related to the other by blood, adoption, or marriage or was so intimately associated with the other's family as to be likely to have accurate information concerning the matter declared.

(5) [Transferred to Rule 807]

(6) Forfeiture by wrongdoing. A statement offered against a party that has engaged or acquiesced in wrongdoing that was intended to, and did, procure the unavailability of the declarant as a witness.

Rule 805. Hearsay Within Hearsay

Hearsay included within hearsay is not excluded under the hearsay rule if each part of the combined statements conforms with an exception to the hearsay rule provided in these rules.

Rule 806. Attacking and Supporting Credibility of Declarant

When a hearsay statement, or a statement defined in Rule 801(d)(2)(C), (D), or (E), has been admitted in evidence, the credibility of the declarant may be attacked, and if attacked may be supported, by any evidence which would be admissible for those purposes if declarant had testified as a witness. Evidence of a statement or conduct by the declarant at any time, inconsistent with the declarant's hearsay statement, is not subject to any requirement that the declarant may have been afforded an opportunity to deny or explain. If the party against whom a hearsay statement has been admitted calls the declarant as a witness, the party is entitled to examine the declarant on the statement as if under cross-examination.

Rule 807. Residual Exception

A statement not specifically covered by Rule 803 or 804 but having equivalent circumstantial guarantees of trustworthiness, is not excluded by the hearsay rule, if the court determines that (A) the statement is offered as evidence of a material fact; (B) the statement is more probative on the point for which it is offered than any other evidence which the proponent can procure through reasonable efforts; and (C) the general purposes of these rules and the interests of justice will best be served by admission of the statement into evidence. However, a statement may not be admitted under this exception unless the proponent of it makes known to the adverse party sufficiently in advance of the trial or hearing to provide the adverse party with a fair opportunity to prepare to meet it, the proponent's intention to offer the statement and the particulars of it, including the name and address of the declarant.

ARTICLE IX.   AUTHENTICATION AND IDENTIFICATION

Rule 901.   Requirement of Authentication or Identification

(a) General provision. The requirement of authentication or identification as a condition precedent to admissibility is satisfied by evidence sufficient to support a finding that the matter in question is what its proponent claims.

(b) Illustrations. By way of illustration only, and not by way of limitation, the following are examples of authentication or identification conforming with the requirements of this rule:

(1) Testimony of witness with knowledge. Testimony that a matter is what it is claimed to be.

(2) Nonexpert opinion on handwriting. Nonexpert opinion as to the genuineness of handwriting, based upon familiarity not acquired for purposes of the litigation.

(3) Comparison by trier or expert witness. Comparison by the trier of fact or by expert witnesses with specimens which have been authenticated.

(4) Distinctive characteristics and the like. Appearance, contents, substance, internal patterns, or other distinctive characteristics, taken in conjunction with circumstances.

(5) Voice identification. Identification of a voice, whether heard firsthand or through mechanical or electronic transmission or recording, by opinion based upon hearing the voice at any time under circumstances connecting it with the alleged speaker.

(6) Telephone conversations. Telephone conversations, by evidence that a call was made to the number assigned at the time by the telephone company to a particular person or business, if (A) in the case of a person, circumstances, including self-identification, show the person answering to be the one called, or (B) in the case of a business, the call was made to a place of business and the conversation related to business reasonably transacted over the telephone.

(7) Public records or reports.   Evidence that a writing authorized by law to be recorded or filed and in fact recorded or filed in a public office, or a purported public record, report, statement, or data compilation, in any form, is from the public office where items of this nature are kept.

(8) Ancient documents or data compilation.   Evidence that a document or data compilation, in any form, (A) is in such condition as to create no suspicion concerning its authenticity, (B) was in a place where it, if authentic, would likely be, and (C) has been in existence 20 years or more at the time it is offered.

(9) Process or system.   Evidence describing a process or system used to produce a result and showing that the process or system produces an accurate result.

(10) Methods provided by statute or rule.   Any method of authentication or identification provided by Act of Congress or by other rules prescribed by the Supreme Court pursuant to statutory authority.

Rule 902.   Self–Authentication

Extrinsic evidence of authenticity as a condition precedent to admissibility is not required with respect to the following:

(1) Domestic public documents under seal.   A document bearing a seal purporting to be that of the United States, or of any State, district, Commonwealth, territory, or insular possession thereof, or the Panama Canal Zone, or the Trust Territory of the Pacific Islands, or of a political subdivision, department, officer, or agency thereof, and a signature purporting to be an attestation or execution.

(2) Domestic public documents not under seal.   A document purporting to bear the signature in the official capacity of an officer or employee of any entity included in paragraph (1) hereof, having no seal, if a public officer having a seal and having official duties in the district or political subdivision of the officer or employee certifies under seal that the signer has the official capacity and that the signature is genuine.

(3) Foreign public documents. A document purporting to be executed or attested in an official capacity by a person authorized by the laws of a foreign country to make the execution or attestation, and accompanied by a final certification as to the genuineness of the signature and official position (A) of the executing or attesting person, or (B) of any foreign official whose certificate of genuineness of signature and official position relates to the execution or attestation or is in a chain of certificates of genuineness of signature and official position relating to the execution or attestation. A final certification may be made by a secretary of embassy or legation, consul general, consul, vice consul, or consular agent of the United States, or a diplomatic or consular official of the foreign country assigned or accredited to the United States. If reasonable opportunity has been given to all parties to investigate the authenticity and accuracy of official documents, the court may, for good cause shown, order that they be treated as presumptively authentic without final certification or permit them to be evidenced by an attested summary with or without final certification.

(4) Certified copies of public records. A copy of an official record or report or entry therein, or of a document authorized by law to be recorded or filed and actually recorded or filed in a public office, including data compilations in any form, certified as correct by the custodian or other person authorized to make the certification, by certificate complying with paragraph (1), (2), or (3) of this rule or complying with any Act of Congress or rule prescribed by the Supreme Court pursuant to statutory authority.

(5) Official publications. Books, pamphlets, or other publications purporting to be issued by public authority.

(6) Newspapers and periodicals. Printed materials purporting to be newspapers or periodicals.

(7) Trade inscriptions and the like. Inscriptions, signs, tags, or labels purporting to have been affixed in the course of business and indicating ownership, control, or origin.

(8) Acknowledged documents. Documents accompanied by a certificate of acknowledgment executed in the manner provided by law by a notary public or other officer authorized by law to take acknowledgments.

(9) Commercial paper and related documents. Commercial paper, signatures thereon, and documents relating thereto to the extent provided by general commercial law.

(10) Presumptions under Acts of Congress. Any signature, document, or other matter declared by Act of Congress to be presumptively or prima facie genuine or authentic.

(11) Certified domestic records of regularly conducted activity. The original or a duplicate of a domestic record of regularly conducted activity that would be admissible under Rule 803(6) if accompanied by a written declaration of its custodian or other qualified person, in a manner complying with any Act of Congress or rule prescribed by the Supreme Court pursuant to statutory authority, certifying that the record—

(A) was made at or near the time of the occurrence of the matters set forth by, or from information transmitted by, a person with knowledge of those matters;

(B) was kept in the course of the regularly conducted activity; and

(C) was made by the regularly conducted activity as a regular practice.

A party intending to offer a record into evidence under this paragraph must provide written notice of that intention to all adverse parties, and must make the record and declaration available for inspection sufficiently in advance of their offer into evidence to provide an adverse party with a fair opportunity to challenge them.

(12) Certified foreign records of regularly conducted activity. In a civil case, the original or a duplicate of a foreign record of regularly conducted activity that would be admissible under Rule 803(6) if accompanied by a written declaration by its custodian or other qualified person certifying that the record—

(A) was made at or near the time of the occurrence of the matters set forth by, or from information transmitted by, a person with knowledge of those matters;

(B) was kept in the course of the regularly conducted activity; and

(C) was made by the regularly conducted activity as a regular practice.

The declaration must be signed in a manner that, if falsely made, would subject the maker to criminal penalty under the laws of the country where the declaration is signed. A party intending to offer a record into evidence under this paragraph must provide written notice of that intention to all adverse parties, and must make the record and declaration available for inspection sufficiently in advance of their offer into evidence to provide an adverse party with a fair opportunity to challenge them.

Rule 903. Subscribing Witness' Testimony Unnecessary

The testimony of a subscribing witness is not necessary to authenticate a writing unless required by the laws of the jurisdiction whose laws govern the validity of the writing.

ARTICLE X. CONTENTS OF WRITINGS, RECORDINGS, AND PHOTOGRAPHS

Rule 1001. Definitions

For purposes of this article the following definitions are applicable:

(1) Writings and recordings. "Writings" and "recordings" consist of letters, words, or numbers, or their equivalent, set down by handwriting, typewriting, printing, photostating, photographing, magnetic impulse, mechanical or electronic recording, or other form of data compilation.

(2) Photographs. "Photographs" include still photographs, X-ray films, video tapes, and motion pictures.

(3) Original. An "original" of a writing or recording is the writing or recording itself or any counterpart intended to have the same effect by a person executing or issuing it. An "original" of a photograph includes the negative or any print therefrom. If data are stored in a computer or similar device, any printout or other output readable by sight, shown to reflect the data accurately, is an "original".

(4) Duplicate. A "duplicate" is a counterpart produced by the same impression as the original, or from the same matrix, or by means of photography, including enlargements and miniatures, or by mechanical or electronic re-recording, or by chemical reproduction, or by other equivalent technique which accurately reproduces the original.

Rule 1002. Requirement of Original

To prove the content of a writing, recording, or photograph, the original writing, recording, or photograph is required, except as otherwise provided in these rules or by Act of Congress.

Rule 1003. Admissibility of Duplicates

A duplicate is admissible to the same extent as an original unless (1) a genuine question is raised as to the authenticity of the original or (2) in the circumstances it would be unfair to admit the duplicate in lieu of the original.

Rule 1004. Admissibility of Other Evidence of Contents

The original is not required, and other evidence of the contents of a writing, recording, or photograph is admissible if—

(1) Originals lost or destroyed. All originals are lost or have been destroyed, unless the proponent lost or destroyed them in bad faith; or

(2) Original not obtainable. No original can be obtained by any available judicial process or procedure; or

(3) Original in possession of opponent. At a time when an original was under the control of the party against whom offered, that party was put on notice, by the pleadings or otherwise, that the contents would be a subject of proof at the hearing, and that party does not produce the original at the hearing; or

(4) Collateral matters. The writing, recording, or photograph is not closely related to a controlling issue.

Rule 1005. Public Records

The contents of an official record, or of a document authorized to be recorded or filed and actually recorded or filed, including data compilations in any form, if otherwise admissible, may be proved by copy, certified as correct in accordance with rule 902 or testified to be correct by a witness who has compared it with the original. If a copy which complies with the foregoing cannot be obtained by the exercise of reasonable diligence, then other evidence of the contents may be given.

Rule 1006. Summaries

The contents of voluminous writings, recordings, or photographs which cannot conveniently be examined in court may be presented in the form of a chart, summary, or calculation. The originals, or duplicates, shall be made available for examination or copying, or both, by other parties at reasonable time and place. The court may order that they be produced in court.

Rule 1007. Testimony or Written Admission of Party

Contents of writings, recordings, or photographs may be proved by the testimony or deposition of the party against whom offered or by that party's written admission, without accounting for the nonproduction of the original.

Rule 1008. Functions of Court and Jury

When the admissibility of other evidence of contents of writings, recordings, or photographs under these rules depends upon the fulfillment of a condition of fact, the question whether the condition has been fulfilled is ordinarily for the court to determine in accordance with the provisions of rule 104. However, when an issue is raised (a) whether the asserted writing ever existed, or (b) whether another writing, recording, or photograph produced at the trial is the original, or (c) whether other evidence of contents correctly reflects the contents, the issue is for the trier of fact to determine as in the case of other issues of fact.

ARTICLE XI. MISCELLANEOUS RULES

Rule 1101. Applicability of Rules

(a) Courts and judges. These rules apply to the United States district courts, the District Court of Guam, the District Court of the Virgin Islands, the District Court for the Northern Mariana Islands, the United States courts of appeals, the United States Claims Court, and to United States bankruptcy judges and United States magistrate judges, in the actions, cases, and proceedings and to the extent hereinafter set forth. The terms "judge" and "court" in these rules include United States bankruptcy judges and United States magistrate judges.

(b) Proceedings generally. These rules apply generally to civil actions and proceedings, including admiralty and maritime cases, to criminal cases and proceedings, to contempt proceedings except those in which the court may act summarily, and to proceedings and cases under title 11, United States Code.

(c) Rule of privilege. The rule with respect to privileges applies at all stages of all actions, cases, and proceedings.

(d) Rules inapplicable. The rules (other than with respect to privileges) do not apply in the following situations:

(1) Preliminary questions of fact. The determination of questions of fact preliminary to admissibility of evidence when the issue is to be determined by the court under rule 104.

(2) Grand jury. Proceedings before grand juries.

(3) Miscellaneous proceedings. Proceedings for extradition or rendition; preliminary examinations in criminal cases; sentencing, or granting or revoking probation; issuance of warrants for arrest, criminal summonses, and search warrants; and proceedings with respect to release on bail or otherwise.

(e) Rules applicable in part. In the following proceedings these rules apply to the extent that matters of evidence are not provided for in the statutes which govern procedure therein or in other rules prescribed by the Supreme Court pursuant to statutory authority: the trial of minor and petty offenses by United States magistrates; review of agency actions when the facts are subject to trial de novo under section 706(2)(F) of title 5, United States Code; review of orders of the Secretary of Agriculture under section 2 of the Act entitled "An Act to authorize association of producers of agricultural products" approved February 18, 1922 (7 U.S.C. 292), and under sections 6 and 7(c) of the Perishable Agricultural Commodities Act, 1930 (7 U.S.C. 499f, 499g(c)); naturalization and revocation of naturalization under sections 310–318 of the Immigration and Nationality Act (8 U.S.C. 1421–1429); prize proceedings in admiralty under sections 7651–7681 of title 10, United States Code; review of orders of the Secretary of the Interior under section 2 of the Act entitled "An Act authorizing associations of producers of aquatic products" approved June 25, 1934 (15 U.S.C. 522); review of orders of petroleum control boards under section 5 of the Act entitled "An Act to regulate interstate and foreign commerce in petroleum and its products by prohibiting the shipment in such commerce of petroleum and its products produced in violation of State law, and for other purposes", approved February 22, 1935 (15 U.S.C. 715d); actions for fines, penalties, or forfeitures under part V of title IV of the Tariff Act of 1930 (19 U.S.C. 1581–1624), or under the Anti-Smuggling Act (19 U.S.C. 1701–1711); criminal libel for condemnation, exclusion of imports, or other proceedings under the Federal Food, Drug, and Cosmetic Act (21 U.S.C. 301–392); disputes between seamen under sections 4079, 4080, and 4081 of the Revised Statutes (22 U.S.C. 256–258); habeas corpus under sections 2241–2254 of title 28, United States Code; motions to vacate, set aside or correct sentence under section 2255 of title 28, United States Code; actions for penalties for refusal to transport destitute seamen under section 4578 of the Revised Statutes (46 U.S.C. 679); actions against the United States under the Act entitled "An Act authorizing suits against the United States in admiralty for damage caused by and salvage service rendered to public vessels belonging to the United States, and for other purposes", approved March 3, 1925 (46 U.S.C. 781–790), as implemented by section 7730 of title 10, United States Code.

Rule 1102. Amendments

Amendments to the Federal Rules of Evidence may be made as provided in section 2072 of title 28 of the United States Code.

Rule 1103. Title

These rules may be known and cited as the Federal Rules of Evidence.

†